Charles Spurgeon, 1854

the LOST SERMONS *of*

C. H. SPURGEON

the LOST SERMONS *of*
C. H. SPURGEON

His Earliest Outlines and Sermons Between 1851 and 1854

Vol. 7

Volume Editors JASON G. DUESING · GEOFFREY CHANG · PHILLIP ORT

B&H ACADEMIC

NASHVILLE, TENNESSEE

The Lost Sermons of C. H. Spurgeon, Volume 7
Copyright © 2022 by Jason G. Duesing and Spurgeon's College
Published by B&H Academic
Nashville, Tennessee

Standard Edition ISBN: 978-1-0877-3374-6
Collector's Edition ISBN: 978-1-0877-3376-0

Dewey Decimal Classification: 252
Subject Heading: SPURGEON, CHARLES H. / SERMONS / CHRISTIAN LIFE—SERMONS

Special thanks to Spurgeon's College, spurgeons.ac.uk

Unless otherwise indicated, Scripture quotations are taken from the King James Version.

Scripture quotations marked NIV are taken from the Holy Bible, New International Version®, NIV® Copyright ©1973, 1978, 1984, 2011 by Biblica, Inc.® Used by permission. All rights reserved worldwide.

Scripture quotations marked NKJV are taken from the New King James Version®. Copyright © 1982 by Thomas Nelson. Used by permission. All rights reserved.

The web addresses referenced in this book were live and correct at the time of the book's publication but may be subject to change.

As in previous volumes of this series, Spurgeon's punctuation has at times been modified in the transcriptions for readability, though the project team has carefully sought not to change his meaning. Where grammar or misspellings have been corrected in the transcripts, or occasional content clarifications have been necessary, they are noted with brackets to clearly distinguish from his originals.

The marbled paper for the cover of the collector's edition was created by Lesley Patterson-Marx, lesleypattersonmarx.com

Printed in China

1 2 3 4 5 6 7 8 9 10 RRD 27 26 25 24 23 22

DEDICATION

To C. H. Spurgeon, who had hoped
to publish these sermons in his lifetime.
We rejoice that what was lost is now found.

CONTENTS

CONTENTS

CONTENTS

CONTENTS

FOREWORD

I consider it an incredible honour to write the foreword to Volume 7 of *The Lost Sermons of C. H. Spurgeon*, the largest volume of this important series. When I took up my role as the principal of Spurgeon's College at the start of September 2017, I became the thirteenth person to hold the position, and I was aware not only of this project but also of its significance.

The argument for the *Lost Sermons* project was compelling. The original notebooks, which the series brings to life, are stored as part of the college's heritage collection from the life and ministry of its founder. It is no secret that Charles wanted to see them published, and this volume covers the transition period from his ministry in Waterbeach to the beginning of his ever-growing ministry in London (1853–1854). The *Lost Sermons* series has become and will continue to be a rich treasure-store for pastors and scholars alike. While there is no doubt as to the historical importance of this project, its enduring spiritual relevance to servants of the living, sovereign Lord in the contemporary world of the twenty-first century is its uncompromising focus on the Scriptures and the whole counsel of God that they proclaim.

In his Gospel, Luke recorded the wonderful story of the two disciples on the road to Emmaus (24:13–35). In this well-known and well-loved story, the eyes of the disciples "were opened and they recognized him," the resurrected Lord Jesus (v. 31 NIV). After he "disappeared from their sight," they asked each other, "Were not our hearts burning within us while he talked with us on the road and opened the Scriptures to us?" (v. 32 NIV). I do not think there is a preacher alive who has not spoken on this beautiful concept: when the Scriptures are opened, believers can feel as though their hearts have been warmed (metaphorically, set on fire) through the exposition of the living and eternal truth of God's Word.

Something deep and profound is contained in this principle. As I looked through the various sermon outlines and headings contained within Volume 7, I was struck—quite forcefully—by the breadth and scope of the young Spurgeon's preaching. The apostle Peter stated in 1 Pet 2:1–3: "Rid yourselves of all malice and all deceit, hypocrisy, envy, and slander of every kind. Like newborn babies, crave pure spiritual milk, so that by it you may grow up in your salvation, now that you have tasted that the Lord is good" (NIV). Paul, writing to the church in Corinth, reminded the believers, "I gave you milk, not solid food, for you were not yet ready for it. Indeed, you are still not ready" (1 Cor 3:2 NIV).

The Scriptures that the risen Lord Jesus opened to the two men on the road to Emmaus would of course have been from what we refer to as the Old Testament, or the Hebrew Bible. It is striking to note how often Charles preached from various parts of the Old Testament: the Law, History, Poetry, Wisdom, and the Prophets. When young Charles added the breadth of texts from the New Testament, what a magnificent, life-enriching banquet was served to the people of God! There was milk for those young in their faith and "solid food" for those longer on the road in their Christian pilgrim journey—a Spirit-motivated, balanced diet for those of whom Charles had pastoral charge. I wonder how many hearts were set on fire by the Prince of Preachers as he opened the Bible from Genesis to Revelation throughout his life and ministry.

For those of us today who understand that the Scriptures are the living, eternal truth of God, the challenge is that our social context is very different from that of the nineteenth century. God's truth, revealed in Christ and contained in the Scriptures, is external to the individual and is therefore considered oppressive by some, in that it can deny the "truth" of a person's inner experience. Pilate's retort, "What is truth?" to the Lord Jesus's statement that he "was born and came into the world . . . to testify to the truth" and that "everyone on the side of truth listens to me" (John 18:37–38 NIV), is alive within an intellectual structure that pervades almost every aspect of modern life in the Anglosphere. The atheist philosopher Friedrich Nietzsche railed against Christianity because it was based on what he considered to be a transcendent moral code. From his perspective, this was harmful to human realization.

There are many today within certain expressions of Christianity who view much of the Old Testament and parts of the New Testament as embarrassing, troubling, or in some cases, deeply problematic. Marcionism is alive and flourishing. While few people would claim that they are followers of Marcion of Sinope, the principle of creating one's own, edited version of the Bible is a phenomenon within the "church" that sociologists have observed and commented on. Secular sociologist Steve Bruce, in his latest book, *British Gods*, observes that large parts of the modern church have rejected hell but kept heaven and present the Christian faith as therapy.[1] Christian Smith and Melinda Lundquist Denton, in their book *Soul Searching: the Religious and Spiritual Lives of American Teenagers*, use the term "Moralistic Therapeutic Deism" (MTD), which for them describes the emerging Christian adult's sensibility and identity. In the authors' view, MTDs are nice, responsible individuals whose faith makes them feel good and secure, and whose Christianity is lived on the surface.[2]

The United Kingdom is perhaps twenty to thirty years further down the road to being a post-Christian country than is the United States. In *British Gods*, Bruce argues that since the 1851 Census of Religious Worship, "the typical Briton has gone from churchgoing Christian, to nominal Christian, to non-Christian who nonetheless thinks religion (in the abstract at least) is a good thing, to being someone who supposes that religion does more harm than good."[3] The current demand for "safe places" even within Christian settings often means that anything external that is inconsistent with an individual's internal "truth" will be viewed as oppressive and therefore harmful, even having the characteristic of violence.

While it is premature to talk about the church in the West facing a form of persecution, the signs are nevertheless troubling. Yet I am convinced that the Scriptures (the Old and New Testaments), when opened and explained, have that unique characteristic that can set hearts ablaze because the redeemed heart of the Christian believer is encountering eternal truth.

Charles Haddon Spurgeon was often ridiculed and mocked in the popular press of his day. His principled stand in the Downgrade Controversy involved a profound personal cost. Still, in both the life-sized bronze statue of him that I walk past every day outside our campus chapel, and in the various oil paintings of the more mature and renowned servant of God inside the college's main building, I am reminded that from the beginning of his ministry until the very end, Charles preached the whole counsel of God from every book in the Bible so that his hearers would encounter the risen, exalted Lord Jesus Christ and find life eternal through faith in Jesus's name. *The Lost Sermons of C. H. Spurgeon*, and in particular the ones in Volume 7, are a testimony to Charles's desire to preach truth to believers and non-believers because

---

1   Steve Bruce, *British Gods: Religion in Modern Britain* (Oxford, UK: Oxford University Press, 2020).

2   Christian Smith and Melinda Lundquist Denton, *Soul Searching: the Religious and Spiritual Lives of American Teenagers* (New York: Oxford University Press, 2005).

3   Bruce, *British Gods*, 270.

his Lord had set him apart to bring living waters from God's well of salvation. The rich treasure-store contained in this volume for the believer who wants to enrich their own soul and those of others, is a wonderful and precious gift that I pray may endure for many generations.

PHILIP J. MCCORMACK
Spurgeon's College
London, United Kingdom
2021

EDITORS' PREFACE

In 1903, when Charles Spurgeon's sons decided to offer his 12,000-volume pastoral and theological library for sale, they could find no takers in England. With the rise of Modernism, his books—which reflected the theology of the Puritans—were now seen as antiquated. For almost two years the library sat idle, and the family gave away large portions of it to the Baptist Union, the Pastors' College, and other pastors and friends. When E. Y. Mullins, president of The Southern Baptist Theological Seminary in Louisville, Kentucky, expressed interest in the library, historian Champlin Burrage, who was an expert in Puritan thought and literature, wrote to him, saying that the library

> consisted largely of old Puritan commentaries, etc, which evidently today are almost worthless. Spurgeon evidently was no scholar, and I fear he did not buy books that are worth much today . . . save your money for better uses. Others agree with me in this opinion of the value of Spurgeon's library.[1]

But in 1905, the Missouri Baptists learned that Spurgeon's library could be purchased. This matter was raised in the Missouri Baptist General Association in October, and the messengers subscribed the purchase price within ten minutes.[2] Their offer was promptly presented and accepted by the family.

By January 1906, the books arrived in Missouri and were stored at William Jewell College, the theological seminary of Missouri Baptists in that day. Though only about half of the original 12,000 volumes remained, the collection contained the most important parts of Charles's pastoral library: works of theology, biblical commentary, hymnody, pastoral ecclesiology, homiletics, practical ministry, history, and more. The

---

1   Champlin Burrage, "Letter from Burrage to Mullins," January 3, 1906, The Southern Baptist Theological Seminary Archives.

2   For a history of the relocation of Spurgeon's library from his home to William Jewell College before its acquisition by Midwestern Baptist Theological Seminary, see Adrian Lamkin, "The Spurgeon Library of William Jewell College: A Hidden Treasure among Baptists in America," *Baptist History and Heritage* 19, no. 4 (October 1984): 39–44.

school created a Victorian reading room modeled after Charles's study, and for 100 years, these books were accessible to scholars and visitors alike. Then, in 2006, the library was sold once again, this time to Midwestern Baptist Theological Seminary in Kansas City, Missouri.

Under the leadership of Jason K. Allen, The Spurgeon Library was established in 2015. Housing nearly 6,000 volumes of Charles's pastoral library, along with numerous other books, artifacts, and letters, this center exists to uphold the life and legacy of C. H. Spurgeon for the church. Though his ministry and theology were once considered irrelevant by his successors, we believe that for those who hold fast to Christian orthodoxy, Charles Spurgeon remains a model of faithfulness.

Why Spurgeon?

Charles Spurgeon is a figure of titanic proportions, and the more one knows about his life, the more incredible it becomes. Carl F. H. Henry was right to call him "one of evangelical Christianity's immortals."[3] While God used Charles to accomplish much—founding sixty-six parachurch ministries,[4] spreading the gospel through the translation of his sermons into nearly forty languages,[5] and planting fifty-three new Baptist churches in twenty years[6]—it was not his accomplishments which made him immortal; rather, it was the white-hot intensity with which he championed the best of evangelical virtue.

Evangelistic Fervor

Charles was an aggressively loving and earnest evangelist who considered it a "joy worth worlds to win souls."[7] He believed the gospel pulpit ought not to be a "refrigerator"

---

3   Carl F. H. Henry, quoted in Lewis Drummond, *Spurgeon: Prince of Preachers*, 3rd ed. (Grand Rapids: Kregel, 1992), 11.

4   C. H. Spurgeon, ed., *Sword and Trowel; A Record of Combat with Sin & Labour for the Lord*, 37 vols. (London: Passmore & Alabaster, 1865–1902), July 1884:373. Hereafter, *ST*. See also Marianne Farningham, *Spurgeon: The People's Preacher* (London: Walter Scott, n.d.), 251–52.

5   C. H. Spurgeon, *C. H. Spurgeon's Autobiography. Compiled from His Diary, Letters, and Records, by His Wife, and Private Secretary*, 4 vols. (London: Passmore & Alabaster, 1897–1900), 4:291. Hereafter, *Autobiography*.

6   *ST* Annual Report of the Pastors' College 1877–8, 1878:240–63.

7   C. H. Spurgeon, *The Metropolitan Tabernacle Pulpit: Sermons Preached and Revised by C. H. Spurgeon*, vols. 7–63 (London: Passmore & Alabaster, 1861–1917; Pasadena, TX: Pilgrim Publications, 1970–2006), 15:27. Citations refer to the Pilgrim edition. Hereafter, *MTP*.

but rather a "furnace."[8] In fact, he famously admonished his students, saying, "We do not go snow-balling on Sundays, we go fire-balling; we ought to hurl grenades into the enemy's ranks."[9]

However, Charles also knew that "we win by love."[10] When he exhorted his own congregation to personal evangelism, he instructed them to "ask God to give you a tender heart and a sympathizing soul," because "a hard heart can never win a soul."[11] Genuine love for the lost was the "*sine qua non* of success."[12]

While Charles is remembered for his evangelistic courage and zeal, it is right to remember his humble beginnings. As a new convert, this sixteen-year-old boy from Essex cut his teeth by distributing tracts and "telling, in humble language, the things of the Kingdom of God."[13] He started small, admitting that "I might have done nothing for Christ if I had not been encouraged by finding myself able to do a little."[14] He encouraged all accordingly, saying, "Timidity often prevents our usefulness in [personal evangelism], but we must not give way to it. . . . We must school and train ourselves to deal personally with the unconverted."[15]

Personal Holiness

Not only was Charles a beacon of evangelistic zeal; he also lived a life of uncompromised consecration and devotion to the Lord Jesus Christ. At the present time, the steady cascade of deconstructions and apostasy has shaken the faith of many. And yet, as always, hindsight proves to be 20/20. Consider these words from the newly converted Charles:

> In that day when I surrendered myself to my Saviour, I gave Him my body, my soul, my spirit; I gave Him all I had, and all I shall have for time and for eternity. I gave Him all my talents, my powers, my faculties, my eyes,

8   *ST* February 1880:58.

9   C. H. Spurgeon, *The Soul-Winner; or, How to Lead Sinners to the Saviour* (New York: Fleming H. Revell, 1895), 69.

10   *MTP* 15:30.

11   *MTP* 15:30–31.

12   *MTP* 15:31, italics in the original.

13   *Autobiography* 1:180.

14   *Autobiography* 1:180.

15   *MTP* 15:34.

my ears, my limbs, my emotions, my judgment, my whole manhood, and all that could come of it.[16]

Even though Charles would have to wade through seas of controversy, never once was he plagued by scandal. He believed that genuine, holy living was essential to gospel ministry and advancement, and he remarked like a father that "I have no greater love than this, that my children walk in the truth."[17] For those who are weary of the failures of modern men and women, remember to look back to the "cloud of witnesses" who have finished well (Hebrews 11).

Christian Philanthropy

Charles also exemplified the Christian virtue that David Bebbington has termed "activism"—the passionate belief that the gospel must be expressed in action.[18] Charles not only preached the gospel, but he built a free seminary to train working-class ministers. Similarly, he not only preached about caring for the widow and the orphan, but he built two orphanages and seventeen almshouses for widows.

Charles was compelled to service by gracious gratitude for what Christ had done. His reflections on the victorious suffering of Christ once provoked him to exclaim: "Brother, sister, what art thou doing for Jesus? I charge thee by the nail-prints of his hands, unless thou be a liar unto him, labour for him!"[19] He further charged his congregation to "lay not down thy harness, but work on as long as thou shalt live," and be ready to "live in his service, and die in his service!"[20]

When Charles later reflected on the twenty-fifth anniversary of his ministry, he cautioned his congregation by noting, "The middle passage becomes difficult, then, because things grow ordinary and common-place which aforetime were striking and

---

16   *Autobiography* 1:180.

17   *MTP* 15:35.

18   See Phillip Ort, Timothy Gatewood, and Ed Romine, "Charles Spurgeon: The Quintessential Evangelical," in *Midwestern Journal of Theology* 18, no. 1 (Spring 2019): 104–25.

19   *MTP* 19:132.

20   *MTP* 19:132.

remarkable."[21] Fearing the "pride of achievement," he warned, "We shall do no more when we imagine that we have done enough."[22]

Theological Integrity

Additionally, Charles knew that making a decision for truth entailed a "corresponding protest against error,"[23] and protest he did. Over the course of his thirty-eight-year ministry in London, Charles engaged in several controversies, the final one being the Downgrade Controversy, which erupted in 1887.[24] This controversy proved to be his fiercest fight as higher-critical methodologies from continental Europe wreaked havoc on English congregations and denominations. Spurgeon poignantly documented this decline:

> A new religion has been initiated, which is no more Christianity than chalk is cheese. . . . The Atonement is scouted, the inspiration of Scripture is derided, the Holy Spirit is degraded into an influence, the punishment of sin is turned into fiction, and the resurrection into a myth.[25]

Charles was bold and tenacious in denouncing "modern thought" as any attack on the authority, inerrancy, or sufficiency of God's Word and thereby an assault on "the life of our religion."[26] Although the controversy would lead to his withdrawal from[27] and subsequent censure by[28] the Baptist Union, Charles knew that the battle for the Bible was "the Thermopylae of Christendom,"[29] and so he resolved:

21 C. H. Spurgeon, *Memorial Volume: Sermons and Addresses Delivered in the Metropolitan Tabernacle, Newington, in Connection with the Presentation of a Testimonial to Pastor C. H. Spurgeon, to Commemorate the Completion of the Twenty-Fifth Year of His Pastorate* (London: Passmore & Alabaster, 1879), 8.

22 *Memorial Volume*, 9.

23 *ST* September 1887:465.

24 *ST* August 1887:397.

25 *ST* August 1887:399.

26 *ST* June 1888:259.

27 *ST* November 1887:558–60.

28 *ST* February 1888:81.

29 *ST* May 1888:205. Here "Thermopylae" refers to the last stand of King Leonidas and his Spartan warriors, who sacrificed their lives at the Battle of Thermopylae (480 BC) to prevent the Persian king Xerxes's land invasion of Greece.

If for a while the evangelicals are doomed to go down, let them die fighting, and in the full assurance that their gospel will have a resurrection when the inventions of "modern thought"' shall be burned up with fire unquenchable.[30]

A Common Man

However, for all these attainments, Charles's humility as a common man—a mere "dying man" among "dying men"[31]—crowns his ministry. When the country-born nineteen-year-old moved to London in April 1854, he found himself on the *south side* of the river. The Southwark borough that was home to the New Park Street Chapel enjoyed "the infamous distinction of a pre-eminently evil reputation" and a "meanness which proceeds from extreme poverty and decay."[32] To complicate matters, when Charles arrived at New Park Street, the dwindling congregation could not pay him a regular salary. Rather, he was paid by a fluctuating and meager seat rent.[33] Furthermore, Charles's ministry would commence under the Broad Street Cholera Outbreak of 1854. In his autobiography he recounted:

> When I had scarcely been in London twelve months, the neighborhood in which I labored was visited by Asiatic cholera, and my congregation suffered from its inroads. Family after family summoned me to the bedside of the smitten, and almost every day I was called to visit the grave.[34]

While many ministers hid from the deadly disease, Charles charted a different course:

> All day, and sometimes all night long, I went about from house to house and saw men and women dying, and, oh, how glad they were to see my face! When many were afraid to enter their houses lest they should catch the

---

30   *ST* August 1887:400.

31   Richard Baxter, *The Poetical Fragments of Richard Baxter* (London: printed for William Pickering, 1821, The Spurgeon Library), 35.

32   Helen Douglas-Irvine, *History of London* (New York: James Pott, 1912), 364.

33   *Autobiography* 2:123. Here, "seat rent" refers to the common Victorian practice of renting pews or seats for congregants. While the Church Building Act of 1818 legitimated the practice as a means of fundraising, limited "free seats" were generally provided for the poor. John Charles Bennett, "The English Anglican Practice of Pew-Renting, 1800–1960," PhD diss., University of Birmingham, 2011, 1.

34   *Autobiography* 1:371.

deadly disease, we who had no fear about such things found ourselves most gladly listened to when we spoke of Christ and of things Divine.[35]

Yet Charles refused to be deterred by these challenges. He was content that God had placed him in a rough neighborhood, with a poor congregation, in the middle of a cholera outbreak. And although he would endure mocking and scorn for serving a low-class congregation, he believed that "God has owned me to the most degraded and off-cast; let others serve their class: these are mine, and to them I must keep."[36] And so, a world-famous preacher who, by conservative estimates, made 50 million dollars from book sales alone, was content to spend himself shepherding the least of these.

A Final Word

Charles once declared, "I would fling my shadow through eternal ages if I could."[37] Indeed, his shadow has come to us through his legacy. Carl Henry was right to call him an "immortal"; Charles's enduring influence will be found in his exemplification of evangelical virtue. In this regard, Charles was like one of David's mighty men: his labors for the Lord defy imitation, but the sacred convictions he cherished invite it.

The Lost Sermons has been a nearly decade-long project by The Spurgeon Library, inviting Christians to consider Charles's life and ministry once again. In publishing this final volume of his earliest sermons, accompanied by many stories of his life and ministry, our goal is to continue to highlight the example of the Prince of Preachers for the encouragement and strengthening of the church. But even as you take in these sermons, dear reader, please remember: don't get stuck looking *to* Spurgeon; rather, look *through* Spurgeon to Jesus Christ.

GEOFFREY CHANG
JASON G. DUESING
PHILLIP ORT
Volume Editors
May 1, 2021

---

35   *Autobiography* 1:371.
36   *Autobiography* 2:52.
37   W. A. Fullerton, *C. H. Spurgeon: A Biography* (London: Williams and Norgate, 1920), 181.

PROJECT RESEARCH TEAM

General Editor

Jason G. Duesing

Volume Editors

Geoff Chang
Jason G. Duesing
Phillip Ort

Project Coordinator

Phillip Ort

Spurgeon Library
Research Assistants

Aaron Day
Timothy Gatewood
Ronni Kurtz
Quinn Mosier
Ed Romine
Adam Sanders
Devin Schlote
Garrett Skrbina

With Special Thanks to

Jason K. Allen, President, Midwestern Baptist Theological Seminary
The Spurgeon Library

Midwestern Baptist Theological Seminary
Kansas City, Missouri

Spurgeon's College
London, England

ABBREVIATIONS

ARM	*An All-Round Ministry: Addresses to Minsters and Students.* London: Passmore & Alabaster, 1900. Reprint: Pasadena, TX: Pilgrim, 1983.
Autobiography	*C. H. Spurgeon's Autobiography. Compiled from His Diary, Letters, and Records, by His Wife, and His Private Secretary.* 4 vols. London: Passmore & Alabaster, 1899–1900. The Spurgeon Library.
Lectures	*Lectures to My Students: A Selection from Addresses Delivered to the Students of the Pastors' College, Metropolitan Tabernacle.* London: Passmore & Alabaster, 1893. The Spurgeon Library.
LS	*The Lost Sermons of C. H. Spurgeon.* 7 vols. Nashville, TN: B&H Academic, 2016–2022.
MTP	*The Metropolitan Tabernacle Pulpit: Sermons Preached and Revised by C. H. Spurgeon.* Vols. 7–63. London: Passmore & Alabaster, 1861–1917. Reprint: Pasadena, TX: Pilgrim Publications, 1970–2006.
Notebook	*Spurgeon Sermon Outline Notebooks.* 11 vols. Heritage Room, Spurgeon's College, London. K1/5, U1.02.
NPSP	*The New Park Street Pulpit: Containing Sermons Preached and Revised by the Rev. C. H. Spurgeon, Minister of the Chapel.* 6 vols. London: Passmore & Alabaster, 1855–1860. Reprint: Pasadena, TX: Pilgrim Publications, 1970–2006.
ST	*The Sword and the Trowel; A Record of Combat with Sin & Labour for the Lord.* 37 vols. London: Passmore & Alabaster, 1865–1902. The Spurgeon Library.

INTRODUCTION

Charles Haddon Spurgeon (1834–1892), perhaps the greatest preacher of the nineteenth century, once counseled his students regarding sermon preparation:

> Your pulpit preparations are your first business, and if you neglect these, you will bring no credit upon yourself or your office. Bees are making honey from morning till night, and we should be always gathering stores for our people. I have no belief in that ministry which ignores laborious preparation.[1]

This counsel was not given in the context of a leisurely ministry, but by a servant of the Lord who regularly preached eight times a week, and sometimes as much as twelve or thirteen times a week.[2]

How did Charles ever find the time to work on these sermons? During the week, his days were filled with editing sermons, proofing articles, chairing church meetings, teaching his students, meeting with members and inquirers, and much more.[3] Saturday evenings, however, were particularly devoted to preparing for the Sunday sermon. At 6 o'clock, he would say to his guests, "Now, dear friends, I must bid you 'Good-bye,' and turn you out of this study; you know what a number of chickens I have to scratch for, and I want to give them a good meal tomorrow."[4] Often, his work would go late into the night.

---

1   *Lectures* 1:98.
2   *Autobiography* 2:81.
3   *Autobiography* 4:63–91.
4   *Autobiography* 4:64.

His Saturday evenings were an important aspect of his "pulpit preparations." But in another sense, Charles's preparations never stopped. Whether he was riding on the railway to his next preaching appointment, strolling in his garden, or writing correspondence, he was always on the lookout for sermon material. "Watch for subjects as you go about the city or the country. Always keep your eyes and ears open, and you will hear and see angels. The world is full of sermons—catch them on the wing."[5]

For Charles, sermon preparation was not just an activity, it was a way of life. His sermons, then, are not the result of a scholar sequestered in his study; they are the product of a preacher steeped in the Scriptures and engaged in the church and the world. Amid all the activities that filled his days, Charles's sermons reflect his thoughts and meditations as he faced the challenges of life from week to week. Now, with the completion of *The Lost Sermons of C. H. Spurgeon*, a new window into his life and thought has been opened.

In the first volume of the *Lost Sermons*, we encounter Charles as a young Christian in the spring of 1851, learning to preach as a part of the lay preacher's association at St. Andrew's Baptist Church in Cambridge. Sermon by sermon, we trace his development as he goes from village to village, drawing from influences such as John Gill and Charles Simeon. By October 1851, Charles would be called as pastor of the Baptist chapel in the village of Waterbeach. The next five volumes of sermons reveal young Charles growing not only as a preacher but as a pastor. Writing to his father, who was pressuring him to leave Waterbeach and pursue a college education, Charles declared, "I have many opportunities of improvement now; all I want is more time. . . . I have plenty of practice; and do we not learn to preach by preaching?"[6]

For more than two years, Charles faithfully labored as the bi-vocational pastor of Waterbeach Chapel, working in Cambridge as a tutor during the week and continuing his itinerant preaching ministry in the evenings and on the weekend. Now, in the seventh and final volume of the *Lost Sermons,* we pick up in the latter half of 1853. These sermons tell the story of the young preacher's transition from ministering in a small, agricultural community to pastoring in the heart of the British Empire.

5   *Lectures* 1:98–99.
6   *Autobiography* 1:244.

"A Perfect Furor": Spurgeon in London

In late November 1853, Charles received an invitation to preach at London's New Park Street Chapel. One of the deacons, having learned about the young pastor from a friend, was encouraged to invite Charles to supply the pulpit.

This historic congregation had previously been pastored by notable figures such as Benjamin Keach, John Gill, and John Rippon, and had played a leading role among Baptist churches in England. But in recent decades, due to an unwise relocation and frequent pastoral transitions, the congregation had begun to decline.[7] Their most recent pastor had a short ministry of just two years and had left the previous June. Now, the once-large congregation of more than a thousand attendees had dwindled to just a few dozen people. Writing to the London Baptist Association on December 14, 1853, presiding deacon James Low shared, "We regret that, during the past year, we have made no additions to our numbers in consequence of our being without a Pastor, and that we have nothing particular to communicate to the Association. . . . Brethren, pray for us."[8]

On the Sunday after Low's letter—December 18, 1853—nineteen-year-old Charles Spurgeon ascended the pulpit to preach.[9] Barely a hundred people were in that cavernous room capable of seating 1,200. But on that cold morning, the congregation heard a kind of preaching they had never heard before:

> . . . reminding you that there is no change in [God's] power, justice, knowledge, oath, threatening, or decree, I will confine myself to the fact that His love to us knows no variation. How often it is called unchangeable, everlasting love.
>
> He loves me now as much as He did when first He inscribed my name in His eternal book of election. He has not repented of His choice. He has not blotted one out; there are no erasures in that book. All who are written are safe.

---

7 Under the leadership of John Rippon, the congregation moved from Carter Lane to an out-of-the-way location on New Park Street in Southwark, London. "New Park Street is a low-lying sort of lane close to the bank of the River Thames, near the enormous breweries of Messrs. Barclay and Perkins, the vinegar factories of Mr. Potts, and several large boiler works. The nearest way to it from the City was over Southwark Bridge, with a toll to pay. No cabs could be had within about half-a-mile of the place, and the region was dim, dirty, and destitute, and frequently flooded by the river at high tides. . . . That God, in infinite mercy, forbade the extinction of the church, is no mitigation of the shortsightedness which thrust a respectable community of Christians into an out-of-the-way position, far more suitable for a tallow-melter's business than for a meeting-house." *Autobiography* 1:315.

8 *Autobiography* 1:340.

9 For the sermons Spurgeon preached that day, see *Autobiography* 1:321–37.

Nor does He love me less now than when He gave that grand proof of love,
His son Jesus; even now, He loves me with the same intensity as when He
poured out the vials of justice on His darling to save rebel worms.[10]

The congregation was thrilled with what they heard. When the service ended,
they pressed the deacons to invite this young man back to preach. One of the deacons
remarked that if the people wanted him to return, they should go home and invite
their neighbors, lest Charles be discouraged at their small size. And so, the people did.
By that evening, attendance had doubled.[11]

The deacons did invite Charles back to preach. The original arrangement was
for him to preach three more times the following January, but before the end of the
month, the congregation passed a unanimous resolution inviting him to supply the
pulpit for six months. More than pulpit supply, this served as a trial period during
which the entire church evaluated Charles as their potential new pastor.

In the coming weeks, this once-dwindling congregation began to experience
a revival under his preaching: "The place was filled, the prayer-meetings were full
of power, and the work of conversion was going on."[12] So, on April 19, 1854, the
congregation at the New Park Street Chapel in London voted almost unanimously to
call nineteen-year-old Charles Spurgeon to be their pastor. The next Sunday, Charles
would preach his final sermon at Waterbeach Chapel, and by the following week, he
would take up the Park Street pastorate.

Soon after his arrival, the city of London was stirred with the news of the boy-
preacher from the Fens (that is, the Fenlands, a coastal plain in eastern England). The
roads and bridges leading to Charles's chapel were blocked by traffic each Sunday.
Before long, the congregation outgrew their space and needed to expand. During
construction, Charles rented large venues such as Exeter Hall and the Surrey Gardens
Music Hall to accommodate the growing crowds, but hundreds of people were still
being turned away. A year after his arrival, one newspaper reported:

---

10   *Autobiography* 1:325.

11   "Somebody asked me how I got my congregation. I never got it at all. I did not think it my business
to do so, but only to preach the gospel. Why, my congregation got my congregation. I had eighty,
or scarcely a hundred, when I preached first. The next time I had two hundred—every one who
had heard me was saying to his neighbor, 'You must go and hear this young man.' Next meeting we
had four hundred, and in six weeks[,] eight hundred. That was the way in which my people got my
congregation." C. H. Spurgeon, *Speeches: At Home and Abroad* (London: Passmore & Alabaster, 1878),
65–66.

12   *Autobiography* 1:351.

He has created a perfect *furor* in the religious world. Every Sunday, crowds throng to Exeter Hall—where for some weeks past he has been preaching during the enlargement of his own chapel,—as to some great dramatic entertainment. The huge hall is crowded to overflowing, morning and evening, with an excited auditory, whose good fortune in obtaining admission is often envied by the hundreds outside who throng the closed doors.[13]

No sooner was the building expansion finished than the congregation once again outgrew their space. The challenge of space vexed Charles. As pastor, he lamented how the membership had grown to exceed the added seating of the New Park Street Chapel. This meant that if the congregation were to observe the Lord's Supper in their building, hundreds of members would not be able to participate.

With so many being converted, Charles feared that he could not responsibly bring them into church membership and care for them properly. The only options he could think of were either to build a larger building or to quit the pastorate altogether and become a traveling evangelist.[14] Unsurprisingly, his congregation would not let him quit. Rather, they would approve the construction of a magnificent new building, seating well over 5,000. The Metropolitan Tabernacle would be finished in the spring of 1861, seven years after Charles's arrival, ushering in a new era of organization and expansion in his ministry.

The Significance of *The Lost Sermons*

It is easy to recount the story of Charles Spurgeon's arrival in London as a kind of Elijah story. In 1 Kings 17, Elijah comes on the scene suddenly with virtually no background information and then goes on to play a pivotal role in Israel's history. Likewise, many in Charles's day wondered at this young preacher's origins. One paper described him as "a comet that has suddenly shot across the religious atmosphere."[15] But there was one group that was not at all surprised at Charles's success, namely, his congregation at Waterbeach. When Charles received the invitation to supply the pulpit in London, one of his deacons "shook his head, and remarked that . . . he always knew that his

---

13   *Autobiography* 2:55. italics in the original.
14   *Autobiography* 2:313.
15   *Autobiography* 2:55

minister would be run away with by some large church or other."[16] Upon Charles's return, his congregation "wept bitterly at the sight of [him]," knowing it was only a matter of time before his departure.[17]

Before *The Lost Sermons*, the revival that took place in London in the first seven years of Charles's ministry was something of a mystery. How was this teenage preacher able to preach such powerful and eloquent sermons without a college education? But with the publication of the seven volumes of *The Lost Sermons*, the veil has been pulled aside, revealing the formative years of his ministry before London. Charles Spurgeon was not a comet that came out of nowhere. His star was already burning brightly in Waterbeach. During his pastorate there from 1851 to 1854, "it pleased God to turn the whole place upside down. In a short time, the little thatched chapel was crammed, the biggest vagabonds of the village were weeping floods of tears, and those who had been the curse of the parish became its blessing."[18] And as this volume reveals, the sermons that Charles preached in London were first preached in Waterbeach. In other words, revival came to Waterbeach before it ever came to London.

But even his ministry in the Waterbeach years should not be imagined as an overnight success. Before Charles was known as the Prince of Preachers, he first had to learn how to preach. Up to this point, *The Lost Sermons* have revealed an earnest young preacher steeped in Puritan theology and maturing in his ability to handle the Scriptures and communicate God's Word effectively. Undoubtedly, Charles's congregation at times sat through sermons where they didn't always track with him. The young preacher's own sense of weakness and dependence on God are revealed in the prayers scribbled at the conclusion of many of his sermons. Nonetheless, each sermon was preparing Charles for his future ministry.

Volume 7 of *The Lost Sermons* contains messages that Charles preached from the summer of 1853 to the fall of 1854. They encompass the final year of his pastorate in Waterbeach and the first year of his pastorate in London. These sermons link to *The New Park Street Pulpit* series, which begins in January 1855. Together with *The Metropolitan Tabernacle Pulpit*, these three collections form an unbroken chain of forty years' worth of sermons from the greatest preacher of the nineteenth century.

16   *Autobiography* 1:317.
17   *Autobiography* 1:342.
18   *Autobiography* 1:228.

The Lost Sermons of C. H. Spurgeon—399 sermons—February 1851 to Autumn 1854

The New Park Street Pulpit—347 sermons—January 1855[19] to November 1860

The Metropolitan Tabernacle Pulpit—3,216 sermons—December 1860 to January 1892[20]

Sources and Method of *The Lost Sermons*

The publication of volume 7 of *The Lost Sermons of C. H. Spurgeon* marks a further transition in the project. The introduction to volume 1 of *The Lost Sermons* projected the series to run a total of twelve volumes, one for each sermon notebook housed in the Heritage Room Archives at Spurgeon's College in London.[21] However, since Notebooks 10–12 contain non-sermonic material, the Project Research Team refined the total scope to Notebooks 1–9. Within that space, the entirety of Charles's earliest unpublished sermons, totaling almost 400, appear.[22]

Volumes 1–6 of *The Lost Sermons* sought to provide "a critical work that can be accessed by academics and laity alike," with copious footnotes providing references to primary and secondary sources, definitions of unfamiliar terms, explanations of cultural references, connections between other sermons preached by Charles, and relevant biblical passages.[23] Each of those volumes focused on one sermon notebook. Volume 7 finishes the project by publishing the final three sermon notebooks, numbers 7–9, in one volume. Due to size constraints, this volume provides a one-page introduction for each sermon rather than lengthy critical footnotes. The content of these introductions varies, but they provide historical context, theological analysis, and sermon comparisons in order to aid and interest the reader. Facsimiles and transcriptions of each sermon are still provided, though adjustments have been made to reduce the page count. Also, as before, Charles's punctuation has at times been modified in the transcriptions for readability, though the project team has carefully sought not to change his meaning.

---

19 *The Metropolitan Tabernacle Pulpit* contains three sermons that were preached in 1854: "The Saints Heritage and Watchword," preached November 6 (*MTP* 50:529–40), "The Birth of Christ," preached December 24 (*MTP* 40:601–12), and "A Visit to Bethlehem," also preached December 24 (*MTP* 50:613–24).

20 Many of Charles's sermons were published posthumously. The final *MTP* (Vol. 63) was published in 1917. The Spurgeon Library at Midwestern Baptist Theological Seminary is currently working to make all of Spurgeon's sermons from the sixty-three volumes of the *New Park Street Pulpit* and the *Metropolitan Tabernacle Pulpit* available on spurgeon.org, along with his monthly magazine, *The Sword and the Trowel*, and many other publications.

21 *LS* 1:22.

22 What remains for a future project is the analysis and presentation of Notebooks 10–12.

23 See "Sources and Method" in *LS* 1:29–33.

Where grammar or misspellings have been corrected in the transcripts, or occasional content clarifications have been necessary, they are noted with brackets to clearly distinguish from his originals. As with the previous volumes, our hope is that this volume will be of interest to all audiences.

Here is a representation of the contents of the sermon notebooks housed in the Heritage Room Archives at Spurgeon's College in London that form the substance of *The Lost Sermons of C. H. Spurgeon* project:

Notebook 1: 90 total pages
(81 pages of sermon text, 4 blank pages, and 5 miscellaneous pages)

Notebook 2: 140 total pages
(135 pages of sermon text, 2 blank pages, and 3 miscellaneous pages)

Notebook 3: 140 total pages
(135 pages of sermon text, 2 blank pages, and 3 miscellaneous pages)

Notebook 4: 123 total pages
(114 pages of sermon text, 7 blank pages, and 2 miscellaneous pages)

Notebook 5: 123 total pages
(115 pages of sermon text, 5 blank pages, and 3 miscellaneous pages)

Notebook 6: 128 total pages
(120 pages of sermon text, 6 blank pages, and 2 miscellaneous pages)

Notebook 7: 125 total pages
(113 pages of sermon text, 11 blank pages, and 1 miscellaneous page)

Notebook 8: 178 total pages
(167 pages of sermon text and 11 blank pages)

Notebook 9: 164 total pages
(147 pages of sermon text and 17 blank pages)

With the publication of volume 7, Charles Spurgeon's long-unfulfilled intention is now finally complete. As Susannah Spurgeon shared in her husband's *Autobiography*:

> Mr. Spurgeon had himself intended, long ago, to publish a selection from [his first outlines]; in the Preface to *The New Park Street Pulpit* for 1857, he announced that he hoped shortly to issue a volume of his earliest Sermons, while Pastor at Waterbeach, but this was prevented by the pressure of his rapidly-increasing work.[24]

As *The Lost Sermons of C. H. Spurgeon* finally see their publication, we join Susannah in her assessment that these earliest sermons "are valuable, not only because of their intrinsic merits, but also as the first products of the mind and heart which afterwards yielded so many discourses to the Church and the world, for the glory of God and the good of men."[25]

JASON G. DUESING
General Editor; Volume Editor

GEOFFREY CHANG
Volume Editor

PHILLIP ORT
Project Coordinator; Volume Editor

---

24   *Autobiography* 1:213.
25   *Autobiography* 1:213.

THE SERMONS

NOTEBOOK 7 (SERMONS 323–349)

"THE GENERAL JUDGMENT"

Editor's Summary

The first sermon for Notebook 7 was preached sometime in 1853 during a Sunday morning gathering for worship (see introduction of Sermon 328, "The Faultless People"), most likely at Waterbeach Chapel. Like other Sunday morning sermons in previous notebooks, the outline for this sermon is longer and more detailed, reflecting additional time spent in study and preparation during the week.

It appears that Charles preached from Rom 14:10 one other time in his ministry, "The Judgment Seat of God" (*MTP* 27, Sermon 1601). In comparing the two sermons, we see Charles's development as a preacher. The later sermon is easier to follow, emphasizing three memorable points: the judgment will be (1) universal, (2) personal, and (3) divine. There, Charles followed Paul's argument in the surrounding context more closely. In this earlier sermon, Charles uses Romans 14 as a starting point to teach systematically on the doctrine of judgment. His enthusiasm as a young theologian is evident in his willingness to delve into more difficult questions (or "enquiries") in relation to final judgment, such as:

- In what sense will the apostles and saints judge the world?
- Will the sins of good men be published to the world?
- How will bad men be judged? Will they be judged for refusing to accept Christ?
- How long will the judgment take?
- How will Christ be seen by all the people of the world at his return?

These questions may reflect Charles's pastoral care for his people, who could have raised them in the course of conversations. But like many of his previous sermons, such questions also reflect Charles's study of John Gill, as the sermon structure closely follows Gill's subheadings and theological insights. John Gill, *Body of Doctrinal Divinity* (London: printed for the author, 1769), 2:1049–64.

Charles's sermon mirrors Gill's work until the last subpoint, where Charles moves to the need for "Preparation" in response to this doctrine. For Charles, the point of preaching on judgment was not theological speculation but to call people to repentance and faith in Christ. As he concludes here, "Seek divine aid, Christ's righteousness, and atonement." Or as he wrote in his later sermon:

> God declares that every man shall bow before him, and confess his authority; but what word of exhortation stands before that oath of his? I wish I could make it flash out at this moment in letters of light right round the building—"Look unto me, and be ye saved, all the ends of the earth: for I am God, and there is none else." That mercy-message stands side by side with the judgment prophecy. Come, then, dear hearts, you that are guilty, come and bow before your God ere he ascends the throne of judgment. *MTP* 27:316.

323

THE GENERAL JUDGMENT

Romans 14:10

"Why dost thou judge thy brother? or why dost thou set at nought thy
brother? for we shall all stand before the judgment-seat of Christ."

There are two judgments passed on men. The first takes place when the soul leaves the body, when it is judged and its eternal state settled upon evidence of the sins the soul committed. But the judgment that is now to occupy our attention is that which takes place after the resurrection, when body and soul are tried and condemned for their mutual crimes.

I. I WILL ATTEMPT TO GIVE A FEW REASONS FOR BELIEVING THAT THERE WILL BE A JUDGMENT.

II. OFFER A FEW REMARKS AS TO THE JUDGE.

III. ENQUIRE WHO WILL BE JUDGED.

IV. EXAMINE THE RULE OF JUDGMENT.

V. MAKE SOME REMARKS AS TO TIME, PLACE, AND DUE PREPARATION FOR IT.

I. <u>REASONS FOR BELIEVING IN A FUTURE JUDGMENT.</u>

1. Because all nations have in their religion some trace of it.
2. Man's own conscience admits it.
3. The justice of God requires it.
4. Certain temporal judgments substantiate it.

But 5. Revelation is the great source of information with regard to it. Enoch, Abraham, Job, Moses, Hannah, David, and Solomon all affirm it while it is often the burden of New Testament gospels and epistles.

II. A FEW REMARKS AS TO THE JUDGE.

1. It will be God, though only the [S]on will sit openly. Man could not remember all the actions etc., if even one, much less so many. Man again could not discern in some cases between the good and evil. Man might be unjust. Man has not the power necessary for a work so vast.

2. It will be Christ. That honour may be put on him. That he may delight his saints and terrify his enemies. That there may be a visible judge, the God[-] man will occupy the throne. And that men may not complain of harshness.

Enq. The apostles and saints are said to judge the world. In what sense[?] They will sit by the side of the judge and express their approbation.

III. ENQUIRE WHO WILL BE JUDGED.

Angels who have fallen and men both good and bad.

1. <u>Good men</u> will be judged: for their own satisfaction.

                                        for the world's convincing.

                                        for Jesus' Glory.

They will be judged first: for they rise first.

                                        for they are most honourable.

Enq. Will their sins be published to the world? If they are it will not confound them but extol free grace. But we rather think that as they are all forgiven they will not be mentioned any more for ever.

2. <u>Bad men</u> will be judged according to their works. All of them, however high and lofty as well as the mean and poor. Their acts, words, deeds will be read aloud.

Enq. Will they be condemned for not accepting Christ? Yes, decidedly so. Nothing but their own sin prevented them from being saved. What a vast number, yet more shall be omitted. How will they all see the judge? Ah we know not. But that they all will see him we firmly believe. And quick and dead shall be there.

IV. EXAMINE THE RULE OF JUDGMENT.

1. Conscience itself will be able clearly to decide.
2. God's omniscience will clear all doubts.
3. The Book of Providence will testify against them.
4. The Law and word of God.
5. As to the saved the book of life.

V. MAKE SOME REMARKS AS TO TIME, PLACE, AND PREPARATION.

<u>Time</u>. At the last day, but when, no one knows. The day will probably last many years. God took seven days to make a world; he will not condemn it hastily.

<u>Place</u>. Not in any valley for none is large enough. But (I think) on the wide earth, Jesus, like the sun, will shine on the world so that all may see. At least on one side, and it may be by some peculiar power exercised on the atmosphere he may be seen all over the earth at once.

<u>Preparation</u>. Let it be speedy for he may come at any time. Let it be real and in order that it may be so. Let it be divine. Seek divine aid, Christ's righteousness, and atonement.

And may the Lord remember us, in that day.

Amen through Jesus.

596.

"PARTAKING OTHER MEN'S SINS"

Editor's Summary

Reflecting on his early days of preaching, Charles once described the process of looking for a sermon text thus:

> I confess that I frequently sit hour after hour praying and waiting for a subject, and that this is the main part of my study; much hard labor have I spent in manipulating; topics, ruminating upon points of doctrine, making skeletons out of verses, and then burying every bone of them in the catacombs of oblivion, drifting on and on over leagues of broken water, till I see the red lights, and make sail direct to the desired haven. I believe that, almost any Saturday in my life, I prepare enough outlines of sermons, if I felt at liberty to preach them, to last me for a month, but I no more dare to use them than an honest mariner would run to shore a cargo of contraband goods. *Lectures* 1:88.

Here, perhaps, is one of those buried skeletons.

Seeing that Charles's main point and sermon divisions correspond fairly closely to Henry Sacheverell's famous sermon "The Communication of Sin," it is possible that Charles was influenced by it. See Henry Sacheverell, *The Communication of Sin: A Sermon Preach'd at the Assizes Held at Derby, August 15th, 1709* (London: printed for Henry Clements at the Half-Moon in St. Paul's Church-Yard, 1709). As we saw in the previous sermon, Charles did not hesitate to draw from other sources as he prepared his sermons.

Why was this sermon left unfinished? Perhaps Charles no longer "felt at liberty to preach [it]" and left it alone. However, the fact that he also left additional blank pages for himself suggests that he may have initially intended to come back and finish it. Another possible explanation is that Charles simply ran out of time. Because the sermon lacks a number at the end to mark a preaching occasion, it appears that he never attempted to preach it in this unfinished state.

Many years later, Charles would preach on 1 Tim 5:22, "Accomplices in Sin" (*MTP* 53, Sermon 3055). That sermon would have a very different structure, so he likely didn't draw from this sermon outline. However, his main idea remained the same:

> Why should we seek to avoid being partakers of other men's sins? This will be a sufficient answer—Because we have more than enough sins of our own, and cannot also carry other people's. *MTP* 53:428.

PARTAKING OTHER MEN'S SINS

1 Timothy 5:22

"Lay hands suddenly on no man, neither be partaker of other men's sins: keep thyself pure."

Sin is a most loathsome and abominable thing. It came into the world from hell and owes much of its present power to the powers of the pit. We have all enough of it without getting any more from others. The text therefore startles us and we exclaim, "Can it be possible that in addition to my own sins I may be a partaker in the sins of others[?] There are six ways I will mention whereby we may be partakers in other man's sins.

1. ASSISTANCE IN IT.

2. APPROBATION OF IT.

3. EXAMPLE.

4. ENTICEMENT TO IT.

5. COMMAND TO DO IT.

6. CARELESSNESS OF OUR DUTIES.

1. ASSISTANCE IN IT.

In all good actions he that assist[s] is esteemed worthy of a share of honour, so [too] the abettor of evil must partake in the sin. In the case of Saul who took care of the clothes. Solomon who built altars for his wives.

2. APPROBATION OF IT.

[This page is followed by two blank pages in Charles's notebook.]

"HOW TO MEET EVIL TIDINGS"

Editor's Summary

Since Charles only allocated a single page for this sermon—which he neither finished nor even began to compose—it's possible that he initially intended to pair it with the previous sermon, one for the Sabbath morning and one for the afternoon. The morning sermon would then have been a warning against partaking in others' sins, and the afternoon sermon would have been a call to courage in the face of evil.

If this was his intention, then it would explain why, having abandoned the morning sermon, Charles also left the afternoon sermon unfinished.

HOW TO MEET EVIL TIDINGS

Psalm 112:7

*"He shall not be afraid of evil tidings: his heart is fixed, trusting in the L*ORD.*"*

[Blank]

"PLUNGING IN THE DITCH"

Editor's Summary

In four steps, this sermon traces the experience of conviction leading up to conversion in the life of a sinner: (1) the Spirit's gracious conviction of sin, (2) the sinner's efforts to cleanse himself, (3) God's sovereign frustration of the sinner's efforts, and (4) the sinner turning to Christ. While these notes do not reveal any personal illustrations, every point of this sermon corresponded to Charles's own experience. For example, the second point describes how sinners "[seek] cleansing at the wrong place" in response to the Spirit's conviction. In his autobiography, Charles admitted.

> I am bold to say that, if a man be destitute of the grace of God, his works are only works of slavery; he feels forced to do them. I know, before I came into the liberty of the children of God, if I went to God's house, I went because I thought I must do it; if I prayed, it was because I feared some misfortune would happen in the day if I did not; if I ever thanked God for a mercy, it was because I thought I should not get another if I were not thankful; if I performed a righteous deed, it was with the hope that very likely God would reward me at last, and I should be winning a crown in Heaven. *Autobiography* 1:84.

Interestingly, these notes lack a number at the end to mark a preaching occasion, so it is unclear if Charles ever preached this sermon. However, he did preach the Job 9 text again in 1886: "Washed to Greater Foulness" (*MTP* 32, Sermon 1908). That sermon shares the same structure and many of the same insights as this earlier one, so it's possible that Charles returned to this original outline thirty-plus years later.

Charles didn't expect every Christian's experience of conversion to be exactly the same, but he did believe that every conversion must include some conviction of sin before receiving the gospel. Therefore, Charles did not shy away from preaching powerfully about sin: "Every man is full of sin but only a few feel it." Or, as he stated in his later sermon:

> Let me put the truth before you as plainly as I can by speaking of your body in order to describe your soul. You probably imagine that your physical constitution is sound and healthy. I grant you all you ask on that score; yet you are but flesh and blood, like the rest of our mortal race, and therefore you are exposed to every disease which waylays your fellow creatures. Even so, your deceitful heart is capable of as desperate crimes as the vilest of sinners ever committed. The evil propensity lurks within, it needs only the contagion of society, or the temptation of Satan to bring it out. Does not this alarm you? It ought to do so. *MTP* 32:364.

Having shown sinners their sin, Charles's ultimate goal was to point them to Christ, the Fountain of all mercy, and to teach them to "[hope] alone in divine grace."

PLUNGING IN THE DITCH

Job 9:30–31

*"If I wash myself with snow water and make my hands never so clean; yet shalt
thou plunge me in the ditch, and mine own clothes shall abhor me."*

It is pleasing in the wilderness to find the track of men and to see the footsteps of
the flock [revive] our spirits. When we can sit in God's house and hear our own
experience related it is very pleasant. For this reason perhaps, older ministers are
generally more sweet in discourses to God's people, but it is not certain that [their
discourses] are more useful. May it please the Holy Spirit to guide me, so that you
may be able to see the track and ascertain whether you are in it.

I. THE GRACIOUS SOUL HAS A SENSE OF SIN.

II. IT OFTEN SEEKS CLEANSING AT THE WRONG PLACE.

III. IF IT DOES SO, GOD PLUNGES IT IN THE DITCH.

IV. BUT AT LAST HE GOES TO THE FOUNTAIN.

I. THE GRACIOUS SOUL HAS A SENSE OF SIN.

Every man is full of sin but only a few feel it.

This arises { from the very nature of the disease.
from a want of due consideration.
from ignorance of the evil of sin.

But when the great Spirit comes he shows man his sin by divers means,

{ by the ministry of the word and other means.
by exciting serious thought.
by constant and energetic strivings.

In some this endures for a long time; in others short. Some by it are overwhelmed with distress, others not so much so, but in all somewhat.

This is good { for it makes man value mercy.
it makes him hate sin afterwards.
it thus ensures perseverance in holiness.
it makes a man patient in trouble.

II. IT OFTEN SEEKS CLEANSING AT THE WRONG PLACE.

I do not know whether all do so but I did, and I know many of God's children have done so.

These attempts are { generally very earnest.
often very arduous.
sometimes persevering.
sometimes deceptive.

The reasons why they do so are { pride unsubdued.
ignorance of the truth.
the suggestions of Satan.

It seems natural men should be anxious to heal the disease which makes them smart, but how foolish to apply an ointment which makes it worse.

III. IF SO, GOD PLUNGES IT IN THE DITCH.

He will not suffer his children thus to perish.

1. God awakens conscience.
2. He allows them to fall.
3. Divine light increases.

And by each of these the poor soul sinks deeper in the mire until he abhors his own clothes. The natural tendency of this is to drive to despair and this is only prevented by secret influence put within. Experience alone can explain this.

IV. BUT AT LAST HE GOES TO THE FOUNTAIN.

Where he ought to have gone before and now he goes—
trembling lest he be not received.

humbly confessing his guilt.
hoping alone in divine grace.
joyfully embracing the cross.
cheerfully bearing reproach.

God is honoured and man is saved.

Sermon No. 327

"PRAISE YE THE LORD"

Editor's Summary

Based on Psalm 148:1, Charles's 600th preaching occasion was a unique meditation on the singing and service of God's people both in heaven and on earth, with the majority of its focus dedicated to the singing of God's people in Scripture and throughout church history. This sermon was preached at Waterbeach. *Autobiography* 1:277, 281–84.

Charles loved the congregational singing of the church. In 1866, he published a hymnal entitled *Our Own Hymn-Book* for use at the Metropolitan Tabernacle. One of its distinctive features was that it included songs from many Christian traditions, reflecting Charles's broad knowledge of Christian hymnody.

> The area of our researches has been as wide as the bounds of existing religious literature, American and British, Protestant and Romish, ancient and modern. Whatever may be thought of our taste we have used it without prejudice; and a good hymn has not been rejected because of the character of its author, or the heresies of the church in whose hymnal it first occurred; so long as the language and the spirit commended the hymn to our heart we included it, and believe that we have enriched our collection thereby. C. H. Spurgeon, *Our Own Hymn-Book. A Collection of Psalms and Hymns for Public, Social, and Private Worship* (London: Passmore & Alabaster, Paternoster Buildings, 1885, The Spurgeon Library), vi–vii. Hereafter, *Our Own Hymn-Book*.

Interestingly, the older Spurgeon who published the hymnal would willingly draw from both "Protestant and Romish" literature, but here in his younger days, we see Charles referring to the Roman Catholic hymn *Te Deum* as an "abomination to [God]." So, in this 1853 sermon, Charles focuses on the rich tradition of Protestant

33

hymnody and on writers such as Isaac Watts, John Wesley, Philip Doddridge, John Newton, William Cowper, and Augustus Toplady, among many others.

Charles's love of hymns began at an early age, when his grandmother promised him a penny for each hymn he memorized. Charles learned them so fast that his grandmother had to reduce the price to a halfpenny, and then again to a farthing! In later years he would remark, "No matter on what topic I am preaching, I can even now, in the middle of any sermon, quote some verse of a hymn in harmony with the subject." *Autobiography* 1:43–44.

He demonstrates this ability in this sermon. While Charles does not make a direct gospel appeal, the hymn quotes reveal his preference for songs that focus on Jesus Christ and his saving work. Each quote might have served as a prompt for the entire verse (which Charles likely could recite from memory) as a way of telling his hearers about what Christ had done to save them. However, the sermon does not end with singing but with a call to practical service.

More than modeling a love for hymns, Charles sought to model for his people a life of active service to Christ. To Charles, this meant being a minister and a preacher of God's Word. In whatever sphere God had placed Charles's congregants individually, their pastor challenged them to serve with "acts of charity, liberality, and holy labour for souls." In the conclusion of this sermon, Charles exhorts his listeners, "Let us then begin song and service below that soon we may continue our worship on high with a sweeter song and nobler service."

PRAISE YE THE LORD

Psalm 148:1

"Praise ye the LORD. Praise ye the LORD from the heavens: praise him in the heights."

Having once and again exhorted you to the most excellent work of praising God, it may seem unnecessary to mention it again. Yet it is most probable that some of you have neglected the duty and if you have not, you will find your soul still prepared to hear more on the subject that you may rise to higher flights and more animated strains. There are two places where we can praise God – In Heaven and on earth. There are two great ways of ~~serving~~ praising God – By Song and by service.

I. ON EARTH WE HAVE TWO WAYS OF SERVING GOD. BY SONG AND BY SERVICE.

By Song, Almost all great events have been celebrated in song and poets have been busy, using their utmost ability to sing the same. The oldest book next to the Bible sings of the ten years' siege of Troy. Virgil, the almost equal of the mighty Homer, sang "Arms and the man." The Taking of Jerusalem, the discovery of India, battles, wars, births, and even the sinking of ships have founds poets to celebrate them.

In early times the wily priests called in music and poetry into their false worship. Whether Jupiter or Baal, Baachus or Molock, Venus or Thammuz, Dagon or Neptune, hymns and paeans were chanted in their praise making valleys and mountains ring with "Io Triumphé" or "Evoe Bacchus, Evoe Bacchus."

Nor has true religion, [the] offspring of heaven who draws her life blood from the cross, refused to employ poetry in worship of the great Jehovah who says, "I am, and there is none else." In our days the poet of the sanctuary puts into our mouths his simple yet harmonious strains [which] sometimes we sing:

"Behold the glories of the Lamb" or
"What equal honours shall we bring."

Or in lowlier notes we join our cheerful songs, or solemnly grand, sing "Keep silence all created things." Our friends opposite, the Wesleyans, have the warm and fervent strains of Wesley:

"Hark the herald angels sing"
"Jesus, lover of my soul"
"Oh, for a heart to praise my God."

Then we have Doddridge: "Jesus I love thy charming name"
                          "Grace tis a charming sound."

Sometimes, "all hail the power of Jesus name" rises loftily to a noble tune. Then the once African blasphemer [John Newton], converted in the storm while standing at the helm by a text his mother taught him, sings sweetly:

"How sweet the name of Jesus sounds"
"Sweeter sounds than music knows"
"When any turn from Zion's ways."

Or his companion, amiable, tender, loving Cowper sings:

"There is a fountain filled with blood"
"God moves in a mysterious way."

Toplady, strong in faith, sings: "A debtor to mercy alone"
                                   "Jesus immutably the same"
                                   "Rock of ages."

But why enumerate when we all have a large store of sacred poetry, dear to us even from childhood treasured in our memories. If we go back to the times of the second reformation we find the Covenanters in Scotland and the old conventiclers of England under such men as Baxter, Bunyan, Cameron, etc., etc., ever fond of hymning God's praises.

In the first reformations Luther's hymns and ballads did more than his massive tomes and "Give to the winds thy fears" will be sung where his other works were never seen.

Look on yon Alpine steeps and but here and there a cottage is seen; but wait awhile and you shall hear from her then unconquor'd sons the songs of praise to the God of the truth. These shall reach heaven while the Te Deum and Chant of the [V]ales are an abomination to him. In apostolic times the prison of Philippi heard the voice of Paul and ~~silence~~ Silas mingled in praise. Peter advises us to sing, and our Lord on some occasions did the same himself. Mary and Elizabeth sing praises.

Go to the age of the prophets and their whole books are songs.

"In that day shall a new song"
"To every one that thirsteth."

Retreat still further till the golden age of psalmody. <u>Solomon</u> and David especially are full of it.

"Oh, come let us sing unto the Lord"
"Bless the Lord Oh my soul"
"Make a joyful noise etc."

And who can forget the song of Deborah, or Moses[?] Who does not believe that long [ere] that time, the sons of God in their meetings at [the] throne sing praises[?] Yea, I believe with Milton that in Eden's garden sublimer songs were heard than we fallen beings can think of.

"These are thy glorious works"

Perhaps the 148th Psalm and this of Milton's are the two most sublime pieces of poetry in existence. Let us then sing unto the Lord.

<u>By Service</u>, we may praise God as much as by song. Our common duties should be done in such a spirit that they may become spiritual worship. Then the temple worship of the Lord's house on Sabbath and week-day. Then acts of charity, liberality, and holy labour for souls, say the tract distributor, S. S. teacher, minister, deacon. Above all the missionary risking all for his master's

honour and service. In some way let us serve our God. Let us be like the woman who broke the alabaster box of precious ointment, loving much since much is forgiven.

II. IN HEAVEN, THE SAME TWO MODES OF PRAISING GOD ARE EMPLOYED.

<u>By Song</u>. Archangels and their hosts praise him now as they have ever done. We read that these sons of God shouted for joy on Creation[']s morning and they have ever done so, especially when a prodigal returns. The saints now mingle their notes and sing what angels cannot sing: the sufferings of Immanuel for them. How sweet their voices, how matchless their tunes, how glorious the noise. How magnificent the concert when all the ransomed throng at once shall sing to him who loved them and washed them in his blood.

By Service. Even in the garden Adam had to till the ground, nor in heaven are idlers found; they are employed. Some are ministering spirits, some attendant angels, some are studying the perfections of Deity, and others are framing music to his praise. They have, doubtless, far more to do with us than we wot of. God who makes all his creatures work, work together in harmony, and work for good, will not leave his noblest creatures unemployed.

Let us then begin <u>song</u> and <u>service</u> below that soon we may continue our worship on high with a sweeter <u>song</u> and nobler <u>service</u>.

600.

"THE FAULTLESS PEOPLE"

Editor's Summary

This sermon is significant for at least two reasons. First, it reveals Spurgeon's growing maturity as the pastor of Waterbeach Chapel. Having preached the previous week on God's judgment "with all its grand and terrible accompaniments" (see Sermon 323, "The General Judgment"), Charles now wanted to comfort his people with a sermon on the result of God's judgment and their future joy.

As one who preached week after week to the same congregation, he sought to communicate "the whole counsel of God" (Acts 20:27 NKJV), both in its warnings and its promises. But this sermon on heaven had plenty of practical application for the church on earth. Charles called the church to love one another. He urged them to serve one another and the lost. He longed with them for a greater love for God. And having experienced the loss of many dear church members, Charles pointed his people to the hope of glory.

The contrast between this sermon and Charles's first sermon at Waterbeach, "Salvation from Sin" (*LS* 1:230–34), is striking. The first one was rich in doctrine but light on personal application. Here, more than 550 sermons later, Charles's preaching continues to be robustly theological but also sweetened with pastoral affection and experience. Thus it is no wonder that when he received an invitation to preach in London later that fall, one of his deacons "shook his head very gravely" and remarked that "he always knew that his minister would be run away with by some large church or other." *Autobiography* 1:317. This relates to the second reason for the significance of this sermon.

The next time Charles preached "The Faultless People" was on December 18, 1853, the evening sermon during his first pulpit supply at the New Park Street Chapel in London. When he had arrived at this church, the building seemed foreboding and Londoners seemed to Charles as "flinty-hearted barbarians." But as he entrusted himself to God, "he had a happy Sabbath in the pulpit, and spent the interval with warm-hearted friends." *Autobiography* 1:319.

Many years later, preaching again on Rev 14:5, Charles recalled:

That text brings back to my recollection the second sermon I preached to this church, one Sabbath evening, when we were but few. . . . I had great joy, as a youth, in expatiating upon the perfect blessing of being altogether "without spot, or wrinkle, or any such thing." *MTP* 39:427.

He would preach this sermon again on a future occasion, and it was eventually published in *The Baptist Messenger*. (A full transcript of that sermon can be found in *Autobiography* 1:326–37.) It largely follows the outline here, though one difference stands out. Charles concluded his later sermon not with a meditation on our future glory but with a call to trust in Christ—a characteristic feature of his later preaching:

Oh! trust Him, trust Him, TRUST Him, TRUST HIM! He is a good Christ, and a great Christ. Ah, great sinner! trust thou to His blood and righteousness; and thou, even thou, the filthiest, the vilest, the off-cast, the undeserving, the ill-deserving, and hell-deserving sinner, even thou shalt yet wear a blood-washed robe, spotless and white; even thou shalt sing the perfect song, and be perfect thyself, for thou shalt be "without fault before the throne of God." *Autobiography* 1:337.

THE FAULTLESS PEOPLE
Revelation 14:5

"In their mouth was found no guile: for they are without fault before the throne of God."

Last Sabbath we considered the general judgment with all its grand and terrible accompaniments. We will now muse awhile in sweet meditation on the acquitted people, found faultless among the wicked. We only mentioned their trial and suggested the question as to whether their sins would be read aloud. We observed that whether published or not, they would be superlatively happy with either course. Here we have the result of their trial. See Jude 24, Eph. V.27, Col. I.22, and a verse in Sol. Song. "Thou art all fair etc." – these are parrallel places.

I.   THEIR ~~STATE~~ CHARACTER. *"without fault"*

II. THE PERSONS. *"they"*

III. THE POSITION. *"before the throne"*

I.   <u>THE CHARACTER</u> *"without fault"*

Our character now is just the opposite. We are full of faults and failings of one kind or other. 'Tis a consummation devoutly to be wished, to be set free from sin and fault.

I. <u>As a body</u>, one great church, they are free from fault. There are said to be three great evils to be lamented in the church now: Schism, Covetousness, and Indevotion. I think that it is but too true that these are our great blots, but thanks to the cleansing stream these shall be washed away.

I think our great fault is want of love.

<u>Want of love to our Brethren</u> which causes Schism so that sects and parties are more cared for than our common Christianity, which causes members of the same church to be distant and cool to one another, makes strife, quenches the hallowed flame of piety. This is not known in heaven; they love perfectly, and with regard to this are without spot.

<u>Want of love to souls</u> is another sad fault. It makes us idle, lukewarm, covetous, hardhearted. When it is removed we are zealous, ardent, anxious. The faultless congregation [is] full of love to souls. When an heir of glory is begotten, they sing aloud unto their God and doubtless view with intense interest every work of Jesus for man.

<u>Want of love to our God</u>. This is I believe the root of the two former wants. We do not love Jesus in any degree proportionate to his deserts, his love to us etc., etc. Nor does the Father receive due gratitude for our election, justification, and creation. Nor is the Holy Ghost praised aright for calling, quickening, and sanctifying us. This is a foul blot which we ought to wet with our tears. But in heaven it is not known, for there they love God with all their heart. They love his will, his worship, his courts, [and] his presence.

2. <u>As individuals</u> they are faultless.

<u>Free from the faults we can see in ourselves</u>. With all the dimness of our moral vision, conscience still sees, yea it cannot avoid seeing sin in us. There are the sins of youth, habits firmly rooted by practise for years, angry passions, irregular desires, pride, sloth, with a whole train of sins too numerous to mention, all seemingly unconquerable, all heinous. But we shall have none of these soon if in heaven, and the saints there are free from all those faults we see in ourselves.

<u>Free from the faults men see in us</u>. Our enemies especially can see with the lynx eye and have the unhappy power of multiplying and magnifying faults. We have all failings which are unknown to us and it seems natural to the best of men to err, but in heaven they are without fault even from their enemies. Satan, the lost, and [the] hosts of hell cannot lay anything to their charge. They are fully absolved and law cannot touch them.

<u>Free from the faults God sees in us</u>. His eyes behold our secret parts, they try the reins and the heart. Some things in nature men cannot see because, or have not seen,

> Because they are ignorant of their existence.
> Because of their minuteness.
> Because of their distance.
> Because of their subtle nature.

So in the matter of sin.

> Some sins are sins of ignorance; these we cannot see being unaware of their sinfulness.
> Some sins are in our opinion small, though not really so; these we see not.
> Some sins do not seem to affect us, our age, or our country, but the evil is remote and therefore we often do not perceive it.
> Some sins are like electricity, galvanism etc., very subtle. So in fact are all sins but some escape us.

Now all these sins the Great all-seeing eye discerns in us, but in them none, whatever they [say,] are faultless. Thrice happy character.

II. <u>THE PERSONS</u> . . . . . . *"they"*

These faultless persons who are they? Are they anchorites, hermits, prophets, martyrs, or who are they[?] We will give a list[:] There is Abel saved by his blood, who cries not for vengeance. Noah not now intoxicated. Enoch walking still with God. Abraham not now denying his wife. Jacob not crafty. Joseph who would not consent to sin. Moses truly meek. Joshua, Caleb, Eli cleansed of his one great fault, and Samuel. David once adulterer with Bathsheba, and Solomon the uxorious monarch. Jehoshaphat not assisting Ahab, and Hezekiah free from the vanity he once indulged. Manasseh taken from the dungeon. Jonah now loving the service of his master. Jeremiah, Malachi, and the blessed three, the sweet triumvirate Peter, James, John. And Mary, and Mary Magdalene, and Stephen, and Lydia, and Paul. And the Fathers now truly seeing their father. And Pascal, Luther, Calvin, Knox, Baxter, Bunyan, Fuller, and Williams. Carey and Knibb But why enumerate[?] There are my friends, members of our church:

> our mild sister Day.
> our young sister Burling.
> our beloved sister Charles.
> and the venerable Morris.

These all had their faults, we could see some of them; but they have none now.

> <u>All pardoned</u> sinners will be faultless.
> <u>All justified</u> sinners will be faultless.
> <u>All sanctified</u> sinners will be faultless.

A pardoned man cannot be touched in earthly courts by an officer of justice. But though free from punishment, the stain is still on his character. But whom God pardons he pardons so that not even the guilt remains. The sin itself passes away. A justified sinner wearing Jesus Christ's own garments is as spotless as the Saviour himself. He wears the same righteousness and shines therein. Faith puts this on. A sanctified sinner is more holy than one who had never sinned, for that would be nature's work. Sanctification is divine. Friends, we must try and search out some of these marks in ourselves and if we find them we may confidently believe that we shall be of the faultless congregation.

III. <u>THE POSITION</u> *"before the throne"*

Even before that throne they appear faultless. Some men will be <u>driven from</u> the throne in anger but not so the righteous. We too often live at a <u>distance from</u> the throne but there we shall ever dwell before it. God sits <u>on</u> the throne, there we cannot be. Jesus sits <u>on the righthand</u> and we must not seek as James and John to sit there. Moses went <u>behind</u> the throne and saw the train of Jehovah, his hinder garments. We often lie like slaves <u>beneath</u> the throne, but there we shall dwell <u>before the throne</u>. Ever beholding him so far as the spirit of man is capable of the vision. Ever receiving his smile, his protection, his overflowing love. This is heaven, this is glory. When? when? shall I enjoy it[?] To dwell before the throne, free from fault . . . this we should pray for, pant after, and live prepared for.

> Oh my Father aid me for Jesus' sake.
> <u>Amen</u>.

603. 674

"THE PROMISE NOW FULFILLING"

Editor's Summary

In this short sermon outline on Isa 49:11–12 (a text that he did not preach again), Charles focuses on how Scripture prophecy was being fulfilled in his day.

He was always careful in his approach to prophetic passages. Preaching in 1874, Charles declared:

> Some hearers are crazy after the mysteries of the future. Well, there are two or three brethren in London who are always trumpeting and vialing. Go and hear them if you want it, I have something else to do. I confess I am not sent to decipher the Apocalyptic symbols, my errand is humbler but equally useful, I am sent to bring souls to Jesus Christ. *MTP* 21:91.

(Here Spurgeon was not using the word "vialing" in its literal sense. He appeared to be making a metaphorical allusion to the trumpets and bowls of Revelation. Any explanation of his usage would be too long.)

As in other times throughout church history, there were preachers who sought to provide specific events and timelines to biblical prophecies. Charles, on the other hand, remained fixed on the primary message of Scripture, namely, salvation in Jesus. This does not mean, however, that he shied away from preaching prophecy. Nor did he fail to view current events through the lens of redemptive history. Rather, as this sermon demonstrates, Charles saw Isa 49:11–12 being fulfilled as the gospel was taken to the ends of the earth through the mission movement that began with William Carey.

Charles also mentions the missionary work in China. Coincidentally, he would likely have preached this sermon around the time that Hudson Taylor left England on his first voyage to China in the fall of 1853. Taylor would give the rest of his life to spreading the gospel in China.

Writing in 1869, Charles commended Taylor's work:

No mission now existing has so fully our confidence and good wishes as the work of Mr. Hudson Taylor in China. It is conducted on those principles of faith in God which most dearly commend themselves to our innermost soul. The man at the head is "a vessel fit for the Master's use." His methods of procedure command our veneration—by which we mean more than our judgment or our admiration; and the success attending the whole is such as cheers our heart and reveals the divine seal upon the entire enterprise. *ST* January 1869:32.

In later years, Charles would be a big supporter of Taylor's ministry—giving and receiving funds, sending out workers from his church, having Taylor speak at his church, providing updates through *The Sword and the Trowel*, and more. But Charles's support of missions would not be limited to China. Workers, funds, sermons, and correspondence went out from the Metropolitan Tabernacle throughout the British Empire to the ends of the earth.

As Charles explains in this sermon, God's providential rule does not mean that Christians are to be passive. Rather, even as God's Word promises that "all men shall bow before him" and "this is now hurrying on to an accomplishment," God's people are to "watch, work, and wait" in faith.

THE PROMISE NOW FULFILLING

Isaiah 49:11—12

"I will make all my mountains a way, and my highways shall be exalted. Behold, these shall come from afar: and, lo, these from the north and from the west; and these from the land of Sinim."

Some promises are fulfilled, some wait their future fulfillment, some are now fulfilling.

I. DIFFICULTIES OVERCOME.

As Napoleon and Hannibal crossed mountains, so will our Leader. Many mountains now oppose. Rome, Heathenism, persecutions, etc., but these are removing now.

II. THE ROAD LAID OPEN.

As causeways and railroads are exalted, so will God make a highway for his own purposes. The gospel will be known everywhere. This is fulfilling.

III. NATIONS CONVERTED.

All men shall bow before him. Even this is now hurrying on to an accomplishment. See China, the land of Linen and hopeful signs in other lands.

Let us watch, work, and wait.

607.

"THE MIND OF CHRIST"

Editor's Summary

Scholars have observed that Charles's preaching consistently pointed his hearers to faith in the cross of Christ, a feature that is seen again and again in these early sermons. But the East Anglican influence of hyper-Calvinism and Antinomianism in Charles's day also meant that he had to preach the commands of Scripture, such as here in Phil 2:5. *Autobiography* 1:258. Drawing from a text that he did preach again, this sermon focuses on Jesus Christ as the ultimate example for Christian morality.

Charles highlights three aspects of Christ's example: his human relationships, his service, and his sufferings. Why does Charles emphasize these in a sermon that is focused on the imperative of Phil 2:5? It appears that he is following the rest of the passage in his outline, namely, that Christ "was made in the likeness of men," "took upon him the form of a servant," and "became obedient unto death, even the death of the cross" (vv. 7–8). This illustrates something else that is important to note: as creative and gifted a preacher as Charles was, he usually stuck to the text in his preaching, drawing his points, insights, and applications from meditating on the wider context.

Surprisingly, the sermon outline does not contain a call to repentance and faith in Christ (though such a call may have been given extemporaneously). Rather, this sermon is addressed to Christians, urging them to follow the example of their Captain. Though Charles expected that there would be non-Christians or nominal Christians in his audience, he spoke to his congregation as brothers and sisters, "professed servants of the most high God," and the "little band of God's elect." As such, they were exhorted to live out the mind of Christ.

Charles's conclusion summarizes his theology of works: "May the good Spirit guide us in this way, this perfect way, this pure way. And thus by the blood of Jesus may we have power (privilege) to become the sons of God." In saying that his hearers had the power to become the sons of God, Charles didn't mean that obedience earned their adoption. This is only possible "by the blood of Jesus." Rather, it is in following Christ's example that Christians live out their sonship and prove that his Spirit dwells in them.

Preaching in 1876, Charles proclaimed:

> You cannot be Christ's servant if you are not willing to follow him, cross and all. What do you crave? A crown? Then it must be a crown of thorns if you are to be like him. Do you want to be lifted up? So you shall, but it will be upon a cross. In following Christ, you must be prepared to suffer persecution, loss, and, if need be, even death itself. Will you have Christ as your Lord and Master on these terms? If not, you cannot have him at all. *MTP* 50:124–25.

THE MIND OF CHRIST
Philippians 2:5

"Let this mind be in you, which was also in Christ Jesus:"

This was addressed by Paul to the Christians at Philippi, and indeed to all believers throughout the world. Dear Brethren, as the professed servants of the most high God, many solemn duties devolve upon us; it is no light thing to be a King's son. Our mode of profession by Immersion in the flood is solemn, the renewal of our vow at the table of the Lord is solemn, our destiny, our faith, our expectations, all are most solemn. Hear then ye little band of God's elect. Your captain speaks and says, "Let your mind be as mine."

False religions cannot advise their adherents to follow their leader. Vile as Greece and Rome were, they would have been far worse if the same mind had been in all their citizens as was in their gods—say Jupiter, Venus, or Bacchus. The Brahmin who shows the triple godhead of Brahma, Krishna, and Siva, with their necks surrounded by human skulls, their hands full of murderous weapons, mangled bodies around them, surely he dare not advise the Hindoos to possess the mind of such gods or surely earth would be drowned in blood. Mahomet, lustful and cruel, well is it all his followers are not of his mind. Or, should the Mormon imitate Joseph Smith, he must be a liar, a seducer, a bigamist, yea, [a] polygamist. Or if the pope be set up for an example; some popes have been vile enough, and the present one is not a man much to be imitated. But the Christian minister can address his hearers and with confidence say, "Let the same mind be in you which was in Christ Jesus."

I. IN THE RELATIONSHIPS WE SUSTAIN.

II. IN THE SERVICES WE PERFORM.

III. IN THE SUFFERINGS WE ENDURE.

I. IN THE RELATIONSHIPS WE SUSTAIN.

Christ sustained many of the relationships of life, though there were some which of course he did not sustain, such as natural parent, natural husband or wife, and others.

But very many he did sustain:

<u>As a son</u>. He entered this world, born of the royal family of David, but of a branch of it forgotten, poor and despised. A manger formed the domain of the King. How many a time the youthful Jesus waited on his Father, or brought some little token of love to his mother, we cannot tell, but we have a specimen fact beautifully illustrative of the tenor of his life—the journey to Jerusalem and his being subject to them up to 30 years of age. In after life, at first view we seem to imagine he slighted his mother, but the expressions are eastern and are not in the least disrespectful. On the contrary, at the wedding supper, and even on the cross how kind and loving to the most blessed of women. Young disciples, yea older disciples, ever practise holy respect and love to your parents.

<u>As a master</u>. Though infinitely superior to his servants, they were as friends to him. When he reproved, how gently, and yet if better, how firmly he performed the office. However, the mastership was merged in his teaching.

<u>As a teacher</u>. How simple were his teachings to the ignorant, how patient his endurance of the tardy progress of his disciples, how irreproachable in his converse.

<u>As a friend</u>. How firm in his attachment, even to the cowards who fled from him in his agonies. How sympathizing his bosom, how tender his feelings, how uniform and constant. He is now the friend that sticketh closer than

<u>A Brother</u>. This too he is, and kind indeed.

<u>As a Father</u>. Spiritually, he is a model Father in patience, love, care, and mildness.

<u>As a Husband</u>. He loved the Church and gave himself for it. Let husbands imitate him. As far as possible let us follow him in these.

<u>As a **Servant**</u> to his Father, he wore the humble garb and performed the menial duties of a servant and was obedient unto death.

<u>As a **Subject**</u> of the Roman empire he paid the tribute money.

<u>As a **Preacher**</u>. How faithful, how arduous his labours, how fervent, how loving. Even kings might reap advantage if they would imitate him <u>as a Prince</u>, and senators might learn of him who will be <u>ruler and judge</u> of all Mankind. But surely we in our stations can find something in Jesus to imitate, and by God's help let us resolutely enter upon it.

II. IN THE SERVICES WE PERFORM.

By this I mean the services which we render to God and his great cause of religion. We must if truly Christians engage in some holy and pious work, and in its performance we must imitate his spirit. Let us have[:]

1. <u>A humble mind</u>. Some men boast of their doings—this spoils them and they fail of their reward. But Jesus sought not publicity: "see thou tell no man," "he hid himself." He despised no service: "washed the saints' feet," "talked with an adulteress on the well," made fishermen his companions, [and] yielded to an ignominious crucifixion. Let us too be humble in our service.

2. <u>A loving mind</u>. His empire is love, and by love it was established. Some of us have not love enough. We are too rough, but Jesus spoke in a loving tone to all, save to hypocritical Pharisees, and then his anger was holy love to sincerity and to their souls. Majestic sweetness sat enthroned upon his lofty brow, and though more marred than any man's, yet still a light of love played o'er it and revealed his kindness.

3. <u>An active mind</u>. [Forever] intent on his Father's business, from Dan to Beersheba he went about doing good. Many wearing miles, many toilsome days, many arduous labours fell to the share of our captain. Let us too be no longer sluggish, but awake our powers to run the heavenly race.

4. <u>A persevering mind</u>. Not turned back by Satan's temptations, his bad reception ~~fro~~ at the hands of his fellow townsmen, the scoff, the jeer, slander, threat etc., but he held on resolutely. He was not as some who run well for a time and then leave the great road they pretended to love, but [as a] brave hearted one, he went on, on, on.

5. <u>A self-denying mind</u>. Some will obey as far as it is pleasant so to do, but the true son of heaven will not flinch at self-denials. Jesus bore a cross from the manger to Calvary. His life was one of cross-bearing, but he despised the shame out of his great love for us. Let us learn to deny ourselves.

6. <u>A devout mind</u>. This is absolutely necessary to render our labours useful and acceptable. Jesus was eminently devout. His public career was opened by a uniquely protracted season of devotion. Cold mountains and chilly midnight saw him bend in fervent supplication. Often did he [offer spontaneous] petitions. In the garden and on the cross he prayed. Surely this is far more necessary for us than for one so pure, one in nature a God. Let us then strive to be devout.

III. <u>IN THE SUFFERINGS WE ENDURE</u>.

Our life is a mixture of doing and bearing. To bear God's will is oftener more of a labour than to do his will. Jesus is an example to us here also. He had, as we have, sufferings bodily and mental, springing from natural and religious causes. In enduring these he is a model. He had[:]

1. <u>A submissive mind</u>. He never tried to shun his Father's rod, nor even the sword which fell heavily on him as our Shepherd. How beautiful a picture is a submissive man or woman. How foolish is the opposite conduct.

2. <u>A patient mind</u>. He entered upon his sufferings submissively and bore them more than manfully—it was like a God. No murmur ever came from his lip and it is not said he shed tears for himself though he did for others.

3. <u>A forgiving mind</u> to his persecutors. Let me especially urge this upon those who have to endure scorn and reproach: be not provoked but endure calmly, and ever return the fire of persecution by one of fervent love.

Thus have I tried to shew you Jesus, the mirror of perfection. Do not look and go away to forget, but labour to be followers of God as dear children. May the good Spirit guide us in this <u>way</u>, this perfect way, this pure way, and thus by the blood of Jesus may we have <u>power</u> (privilege) to become the sons of God. Lord Bless us.

<u>Amen, Amen.</u>

604. 609.

"EZEKIEL'S WHEELS"

Editor's Summary

Charles preached on this text at one other time during his ministry: "God's Providence" (*MTP* 54, Sermon 3114). Though we do not have a date for that sermon, we know it was preached before 1861 at the New Park Street Chapel, just a few years after this occasion at Waterbeach. Charles probably used these notes to prepare for the later sermon, based on how it followed the same outline and referenced many of the same points. For this earlier sermon, he likely drew from *Matthew Henry's Commentary* on Ezek 1:15–21. Many of his points here overlap with Henry.

A couple of things stand out about this message. First, it reveals a robust angelology. Charles begins by reviewing a sermon on Ezek 1:5 that he had probably preached more than a year earlier, "The Cherubim" (*LS* 5, Sermon 233). In reminding his listeners of the glories and perfections of the angelic beings, he seems to have mirrored Henry's point that Ezekiel begins with a vision of God's heavenly power in the cherubim and then moves to a vision of God's earthly reign in the wheels of providence. But Charles's angelology really comes out in point 2. Here, we see his belief that angels are heavily involved in God's dealings with this world. He states that angels are "our guardians," a point he would unpack in his later sermon:

> Every Christian has a guardian angel, who flies about him, and holds the shield of God over his brow, keeps his foot lest he should dash it against a stone, guards him, controls him, manages him, injects thoughts into his mind, restrains his evil desire and is the minister and servant of the Holy Ghost, to keep him from sin, and lead him to righteousness. Whether I am right or wrong, I leave you to judge; but perhaps I have more angelology in me than most people have. *MTP* 54:496.

Clearly, Charles strongly believed in the supernatural world. But he did not allow this belief to lead to vain speculation or a wrong passivity. Rather, he used it to encourage obedience and perseverance in faith.

Second, this sermon reveals Charles's robust view of the sovereignty of God. Amid the revolving circumstances of providence, God's love is the "one point which does not move," like "the centre of the axle." Knowing this, the Christian can find great encouragement in the assurance that "there's not a sparrow or a worm but's found in [God's] decrees."

As Charles stated in his later sermon:

> I believe that every particle of dust that dances in the sunbeam does not move an atom more or less than God wishes—that every particle of spray that dashes against the steamboat has its orbit as well as the sun in the heavens—that the chaff from the hand of the winnower is steered as surely as the stars in their courses—that the chirping of an aphis over a rosebud is as much fixed as the march of the devastating pestilence, and the fall of sere [withered] leaves from the poplar is as fully ordained as the tumbling of an avalanche. He who believes in God must believe this truth. *MTP* 54:502.

Therefore, it is the Christian's duty to "trust . . . at all times." Even when God's rod is heavy upon our lives, we are called to "kiss the rod" and pray that "his will be done."

331

EZEKIEL'S WHEELS
Ezekiel 1:15–21

"Now as I beheld the living creatures, behold one wheel upon the earth by the living creatures, with his four faces. The appearance of the wheels and their work was like unto the colour of a beryl: and they four had one likeness: and their appearance and their work was as it were a wheel in the middle of a wheel. When they went, they went upon their four sides: and they turned not when they went. As for their rings, they were so high that they were dreadful; and their rings were full of eyes round about them four. And when the living creatures went, the wheels went by them: and when the living creatures were lifted up from the earth, the wheels were lifted up. Whithersoever the spirit was to go, they went, thither was their spirit to go; and the wheels were lifted up over against them: for the spirit of the living creature was in the wheels.

When those went, these went; and when those stood, these stood; and when those were lifted up from the earth, the wheels were lifted up over against them: for the spirit of the living creature was in the wheels."

On a past occasion we gave attention to the living creatures. It will be of service to us to refresh our memory with the account of them. Four evidently living creatures appeared before the prophet. They were like a man, but superior as to the possession of four faces and four wings. Their solid feet were straight and so round that they were able to ~~turn~~ move in any direction without turning. They were glorious in brightness. Their hands under their wings, onward flight, four faces, rapid motion, upward wings, and depend[e]nce on the Spirit have all a meaning worthy of a brief explanation. We now must turn our eyes to the wheels:

I. PROVIDENCE COMPARED TO A WHEEL.

This comparison was admired among the classics for we are told of a certain king who, when led in triumph preserved a serene countenance and, looking on the chariot wheel, remarked that such was human life.

57

1. Providence often changes the positions of [people]; sometimes they are exalted, at another time depressed. Let these on high remember that time may bring them down, and let the depressed reflect that a time of exaltation may arise.

2. Yet Providence like a wheel has one point which does not move, which is the centre of the axle. God's love. This is the pivot on which all terrestrial things move, the great centre around which they revolve.

3. When we look at it, as a wheel revolving with inconceivable rapidity, we forget the spokes and see nothing but one mighty orb matchless in symmetry.

II. PROVIDENCE CONNECTED WITH ANGELIC AGENCY.

Angels have more to do with providence than we imagine. In extraordinary cases they have been the agents, visibly, of its operations, but ordinarily they are also intimately connected with God's doings. Upon good men they exercise an influence, they are our guardians, they sometimes doubtless suggest thoughts, they ascend and descend from us to God. Upon bad men they may, perhaps, be the means of restraining their wrath and turning their minds in the required direction. If it be not so, yet they follow the wheels, beholding their wonders, and the same spirit of unswerving obedience is visible in both. God's decreed will is done on earth even as it is in heaven.

III. PROVIDENCE UNIVERSAL.

The four faces looked towards the four quarters of the earth and thus shewed their universal agency. Just as the eyes of a picture seem to be turned upon us from whatever quarter we look at it, so does providence ever regard each of us. If I am banished and wander on trackless oceans, or roam in boundless deserts, even there is providence. Mungo Park and the moss. All creatures come beneath its eye, but above all it works for the elect's sake. There's not a sparrow or a worm but's found in his decrees. The whale which swallowed Jonah and the worm which smote the gourd were under the same all[-]ruling power. Providence is by the cradle and the coffin, the bridal and the grave. The prison, the cottage, the lazar house [hospital for lepers], the palace. God is there. In battles, plagues, earthquakes, revolutions, and all great convulsions there is as manifest an overruling of God as in the calm, still, silent motion of the moon. Rejoice then, beloved; the eye is upon thee, and never can'st thou be removed from its inspection.

IV. <u>PROVIDENCE, UNIFORM AND CONSTANT.</u>

It is said to be in one likeness and to be but one wheel, and true though startling, is it that Providence is one. It seems to be entirely at variance with itself, but it is not really so; it is one. The history of Joseph shows how apparently adverse events are still only parts of a grand organism for some one end. We shall see at last when the pieces of the puzzle are put together, when the wheels of the machinery are all put in their places, that all things are working together and that Providence is one.

Sweet or bitter, storm or calm, wealth or poverty, all are from one hand, for one design, from the same motive, viz, love. There is consistency and uniformity.

Providence is one.

V. <u>PROVIDENCE LIKE THE SEA.</u>

The colour is beryl, sea green, and sometimes blue. Now this is a pleasing figure somewhat like the wheel, but more sublime.

1. The sea is ever in motion. So by night or by day the great process of providence is going on; unobserved or regarded, it never stays its activity.

2. The sea has many changes. Storms and tempests, currents, waves, floods, ebbs and flows, etc., so has providence a variety of motions.

3. The sea obeys not man. It wetted the feet of Canute, it washed away the treasures of John, it broke the bridge of Xer[x]es. Navies may ride it, but it tosses them like a feather on its bosom. The land is man's slave, but the sea is free. So providence owns not man's power; God disposes. Man cannot order his own steps.

4. Yet the sea is ruled by God. He bids it roar or bids its clamour cease. He makes its tides return at regular intervals and not a drop moves save as law commands it.

5. The sea is not to be measured or fathomed; it is too vast, too profound. So is the wonderful providence of God.

Such is providence, an ocean.

VI. <u>PROVIDENCE IS INTRICATE</u>. *"Wheel within a wheel"*

Gabriel asks not the reason why, nor God the reason gives. Yet man stands and challenges one thing after another as if his Maker ought to do nothing without telling him the reason. It appears intricate but it is not therefore faulty, but rather, it is still wheel within a wheel. One wheel acting on and moving another, and all the wheels moving by mutual occasion. We must not expect to know all; it ever has been intricate. Yet sometimes we may see instances of providence. Yea every day. But when it is not so, let us remember that Providence is usually intricate.

VII. <u>PROVIDENCE IS ALWAYS CORRECT.</u>

Man's works often need alteration. God's never do. Man often has to turn aside, to amend errors in practise, or to adopt a better plan. The Eternal, on the contrary, turns not, but moves in one undeviating course. His Spirit is the soul of all providence, and therefore it is well directed.

VIII. <u>PROVIDENCE IS AMAZING.</u>

Who can look at it without wonder[!] The Andes, those snow-clad mountains, cause a thrill of reverence and awe to pass o'er us. But what is their sublimity to that of Providence[?] We may suppose an ant looking at the mountains and we can scarce imagine how dreadful such a mass would appear. So these rings are so high that they are dreadful. If we look at the extent, wonderful intricacy, yet marvellous consistency and consummate wisdom of providence, we must exclaim, "Oh, the heights and depths." Even the man who feels that it works for <u>his</u> good must see that it is <u>dreadful</u>.

IX. <u>PROVIDENCE IS FULL OF WISDOM.</u>

It is full of eyes, it is no blind fate or fortune, no inevitable necessity destitute of design, but it is full of wisdom. The eyes regard all creatures that live, and every conceivable circumstance of every one. [Providence] does not allow one thing to injure another; it sees all things aright and guides the sands of life so that their orbits do not interfere with each other. No man can detect an oversight, flaw, or mistake. [God's] ways are perfect, just, and wise. God has an eye for me, for you.

> Trust, believer, at all times.
> Admire, believer, thy God's wisdom.
> Kiss the rod, believer; his will be done.

Help oh Great one.

610.

"TAKING GOD'S NAME IN VAIN"

Editor's Summary

This sermon on Exod 20:7 (a text that Charles would not preach again) contains a snapshot of his understanding of the use of the law in the Christian life. As noted previously, Charles was deeply aware of the prevalence of Antinomianism throughout his region. Citing various reasons, its adherents denied any need for Christians to keep the law. Charles considered such teaching "dangerous to society" and instructed his congregation to avoid the Antinomian "as an infidel."

But there were also other errors to avoid. Where Antinomianism nullified the law, legalism declared that "the law of works is the way of salvation, or at least a part of the way." Charles himself apparently struggled with legalism. Before his conversion, he confessed that he "had been waiting to do fifty things," until a preacher in a Methodist chapel called him to simply look to Christ and be saved. *Autobiography* 1:106.

Though Charles was forever grateful for the ministry of that Methodist chapel, he did not join that congregation, due in large part to their view on perfectionism. These people, often Wesleyans, believed it was possible for a Christian to reach a state where he or she was no longer sinning. Charles encountered such people during his ministry at Waterbeach.

One man, who said he was perfect, called upon me once, and asked me to go and see him, for I should receive valuable instruction from him if I did. I said, "I have no doubt it would be so; but I should not like to go to your house, I think I should hardly be able to get into one of your rooms." "How is that?" he inquired. "Well," I replied, "I suppose that your house would be so full of angels that there would be no room for me." He did not like that remark. *Autobiography* 1:262.

What, then, is a proper understanding of the law in the Christian life? In his explanation here regarding the third commandment, Charles highlights the threefold use of the law. The law exists to show regenerated believers how to live. This is the third use of the law. They are to avoid perjury, irreverent use of God's name, profane language and songs, irreverent use of Scripture, and more. Such commands are "a rule of life" for the Christian.

The second use of the law pertains to its role in society. In many cases, the law continues to be a guide for the ordering of human society. Here, Charles observes how swearing, which was once considered honorable, was being recognized "in most circles [as] a low and vulgar thing." Likewise, human courts recognize the sinfulness of perjury and "call God to witness the truth or a lie."

Most importantly, however, Charles highlights the first use of the law, "which is to reveal sin to us. To make the rebel tremble and fly for mercy to the Most High." Having explained the nature of the prohibition, its sinfulness, and its penalty, Charles concludes by calling all guilty sinners to "seek mercy at the foot of the cross" and by reminding believers "that such we were until sovereign grace claimed us."

TAKING GOD'S NAME IN VAIN

Exodus 20:7

*"Thou shalt not take the name of the Lord thy God in vain; for the
Lord will not hold him guiltless that taketh his name in vain."*

There has been great mistake with regard to the law of God. On the one hand the
Pharisee and legalist declare that the law of works is the way of salvation, or at least
a part of the way. This [is] an exceedingly erroneous opinion but the contrary is
even worse. When the Antinomian says that men are not bound to keep the law,
some asylum should be found for a man so dangerous to society.

The legalist does not lead men plainly into sin, but the Antinomian teaches
immorality by wholesale and is as much to be avoided as an infidel. Some good men
do not like to hear much of the law and even go the length of crying it down. How
unlike Paul, who said the law is holy and just and good, but I am carnal, sold under
sin. I charitably hope that some Christians do not know what they are talking
about when they talk of the Abrogation of the Law and call a man a legalist who
urges its commands on man's conscience. For man to say with one breath, "I am a
sinner," and in the next to say [that] the law is not binding on him, is only to show
his ridiculous folly. For how can he sin if there is no law[?] Some again will even say
that what is sin in other men is no sin in them, and yet if brother Wesley comes in
and talks about perfection—poor man—he is told he knows nothing aright, for sin
is in every man. Ah! what absurdities some men believe.

The true use of the law to believers is as a rule of life, and at the risk of being called
a legalist I will endeavor as God helpeth me to speak of your rule of life. But there is
another use of the law which is to reveal sin to us. To make the rebel tremble and fly
for mercy to the Most High. Oh that this purpose might be answered in some souls.

I. I WILL ENDEAVOR.

I. TO EXPLAIN THE NATURE AND EXTENT OF THE PROHIBITION.

II. TO SHEW ITS SINFULNESS.

III. TO MARK ITS PENALTY.

I. TO EXPLAIN THE NATURE OF THE PROHIBITION.

It is exceedingly broad like every other command of the great lawgiver, and takes in a great variety of sins besides the act of using the name of God profanely. Indeed a man might never do this and yet might be guilty of a breach of this command. But clearly:

1. All perjury is forbidden by this command. What can be much worse than to call God to witness the truth of a lie, yet some have dared to do it and God has most righteously resented the insult by some tremendous judgment. No crime should be more detested than this.

2. All use of God's name in an irreverent manner. Some men put in God's name at the end of almost every sentence, and even Christians are too apt to use his name too freely in common conversation as "God bless ye," quickly said and little thought of. Willful profanity is often, like perjury, punished by awful judgments and is an immense crime.

3. All use of profane language, even when the name of God is not mentioned. Cursing and swearing are forbidden, and those common words which some good men use very near approaching to the nature of an oath ought to be avoided. This too has been punished.

4. All idle and irreverent use of Scripture. For instance, quoting it in jokes and in relating anecdotes. Such as the one of Sydney Smith about "except these bonds," "is thy servant a dog." All railings at the Word, treating it with contempt, etc.

5. I may here condemn all songs of a loose, indecent, or profane character. Not however wishing to stop singing, but song-singing. This is one reason why I dare not enter a theatre or dancing room, because there is pretty certain to be some profanity. Who is there among us innocent of this sin[?] Let us all bow down and acknowledge it.

II. TO SHOW ITS SINFULNESS.

It is, in my opinion, a mistake to say that all sins are alike in God's sight. I must, for conscience tells me so, I must think that some sins are more heinous than others. Though alike in nature, yet not in degree. Though none are small, so we may say there are no small elephants, yet one elephant may be larger than another. Well, I think this sin is one of the greatest of those forbidden in the [D]ecalogue.

1. It is a personal insult to God. Other sins do but touch his dominion but this is aimed at the king himself. It is high treason against his government. It shows that such a soul is hardened in sin and is the culminating point of impiety. To plead drunkenness as an excuse is pleading one sin in excuse of another. Every thing a man does when drunk he ought to be punished double for instead of less. Profanity is high treason and open rebellion.

2. It is not attended with any honour, profit, or pleasure, and therefore temptation cannot be pleaded as an excuse. It was once honourable in society to swear, but that dissolute age is now feeling its full desert in the place of torment. Now it is esteemed in most circles a low and vulgar thing to swear, and nothing lends much more to lower a man's character than this profane habit.

    It never was, nor ever can be profitable, as Rowland Hill said "I will swear when I can see the use of it." So might we say, for some sins are apparently profitable, but blasphemy is foolish because unprofitable. Surely it is not pleasurable. I should be at a loss to tell where the pleasure of this sin can be found. I even believe it to be a source of pain, for surely at certain seasons the blasphemer must feel terrified at his own oaths, and his imagination will conjure up things of terror, the ghosts of his profanity.

3. It is a sin which the most stultified conscience must condemn—the common light of natural reason teaching us better. The poor heathen were reverent to their idol gods, and shall the enlightened child of civilized Britain curse the great Jehovah[?] It is a sin so heinous that it must have been a heavy part of the load of punishment borne by the Redeemer. O that men were wise to embrace his atonement.

III. TO MARK ITS PENALTY.

1. There is a sentence pronounced upon it unlike any other command.

2. It seems to hint that although no sin will go unpunished, this one above all others will be marked.

3. It seems to insinuate, I think, even more immediate punishment than is pronounced on other sins because some are apt to extenuate this because it does not seem to injure our neighbours.

Now, dear friends, if guilty break it off; otherwise you cannot be guiltless. Seek mercy at the foot of the cross. And let those of us who are believers remember that such we were until sovereign grace reclaimed us.

Help me Oh my Master.

611.

"KEEPING THE ORDINANCES"

Editor's Summary

Given Charles's success and growing reputation as a preacher beyond his own pulpit, it would be easy for modern readers to forget that his ministry was rooted in a local church. Yet he pastored locally throughout his ministry, not only in Waterbeach but in London. This sermon on 1 Cor 11:2 (a text he would not preach again) provides a glimpse into his churchmanship.

It appears that this sermon was preached in the context of a baptismal service. Speaking to the baptism "candidates," Charles begins by highlighting the trait that should be characteristic of Baptists, namely, that they "strive to keep the ordinances." What does keeping the ordinances look like?

First, it means congregational participation. Charles believed that the ministry of the church was not to be restricted to the officers of the church but rested ultimately on the congregation. Therefore, congregations should uphold a regenerate membership through a process of "admission and excommunication." Though churches had a pastor and "deacons" (he would not implement elders until 1859, during his pastorate in London), Charles understood that ordinances were to be guarded by every member of the church. "Each individual member is a trustee of the ordinances and [is] bound to regard himself as such." Christians could do this by joining the church and rightly participating in her ordinances, "obey[ing] in all things your Master's behests." Additionally, the congregation should protest any attempt by some future pastor or church authority to alter the church's teaching on these ordinances.

The second feature of Charles's ecclesiology was a strict adherence to God's Word in the worship of the church. Within the Reformed tradition to which he belonged, this is known as the Regulative Principle, which states that the church should only practice in their worship what Scripture mandates either by explicit command or example. We see this conviction in the third point of this sermon, as Charles criticizes "Popery," baptismal regeneration, Puseyism, and infant baptism as "alteration[s]" and additions to what God delivered in his Word. Charles even criticizes those who would baptize by sprinkling because "it is not going into the water, it is not burial." Any practices outside of Scripture's commands were man-made inventions that must be rejected.

In closing, Charles commends the baptismal candidates for keeping the ordinances by coming forward to be baptized and joining the church. However, this is only the first step. From this point forward, they are called, along with the members of the church, "to remember your charge and keep it firmly."

Preaching decades later, in 1882, Charles forthrightly declared:

WE have no respect whatever for the ordinances of men in religion. Anything that is only invented by churches, or councils, is nothing whatever to us. We know of two ordinances instituted by the Lord Jesus Christ—the baptism of believers and the Lord's supper; and we utterly abhor and reject all pretended sacraments of every kind. *MTP* 45:421.

KEEPING THE ORDINANCES

1 Corinthians 11:2

*"Now I praise you, brethren, that ye remember me in all things,
and keep the ordinances, as I delivered them to you."*

Some good people seem to imagine that a man cannot be faithful unless he finds fault with everybody, but Paul here gives the Corinthians praise, and doubtless every body of Christians has some traits deserving of commendation.

The Primitive Methodist is full of zeal.

The Wesleyan loves to invite sinners to Jesus.

The Churchman is reverent in God's house, etc., etc.

The Baptist strives to keep the ordinances.

I. THE ORDINANCES.

These are distinct from the doctrinal, or practical, or experimental part of religion. They are, so to speak, the dress of our religion, the ceremonial part of it. There are:

The Ordinances of God's House – Public worship, the ministry, singing, public prayer.

The Ordinance[s] of the Church – Admission and excommunication, deacons, brotherhood, etc.

The Ordinances of Christ – Baptism and the Lord's supper. I call them by this name for they have a closer relation to Christ than the others. The [F]irst is the emblem of the agonies, burial, and resurrection of the Saviour. The Second [is] the memorial, yet more evidently, of his flesh and blood. His sacr[i]fice and atonement.

Let us remark:

> How simple and free from pomp or show.
> How sublimely beautiful.
> How profitable for our souls.

II. THE TRUSTEES.

Paul delivered the ordinances into the hands of the church and thus constituted it the guardian of the ordinances. Not the government, not the lordly order of bishops, not the ministry, but each individual member is a trustee of the ordinances and [is] bound to regard himself as such. Away with apostolic succession, a good man is a successor of the apostles if like them he is diligent in good works and labours of love.

How gloriously have our ancestors kept this trust; in caves and mountains they concealed the treasure. In the fastnesses of Switzerland, in the dungeons of England. Remember Anne Askewe, the Baptist Martyrs, etc. Remember S^t. Bartholomew, Smithfield, and remember too that you, each of you as Christian men, are now the successors of these men and the trustees of the ordinances delivered unto you. May God give unto you their noble spirit.

III. THE CHARGE.

"To keep them as delivered." Not to suffer any increase in number, no additional ceremonies to be fashioned. Not to allow an alteration in the persons receiving, or the mode of exercising. Let me remark:

1. That Popery is not keeping the ordinances as they were delivered, but contrariwise the murdering and mangling of them all.
2. Baptismal Regeneration and all its accompanying Puseyism is not thus keeping them. It is a prostitution of them.
3. Infant Baptism is a violation of this rule, for everywhere we find believers baptized and nowhere infants.
4. Sprinkling is not keeping the ordinances; it is not going into the water, it is not burial, it is a mere remnant of Popery.
5. Neglect of any ordinance by good men is not keeping this rule. Oh, my dear friends, why do you delay to join the Church and obey in all things your Master's behests[?]

1. To the Candidates. Well done that ye thus keep the ordinances, live worthy of them.
2. To Christians still holding back. Come now, remember your charge and keep it firmly.
3. To worldlings. Behold these Christians and seek like them to be converted, [and] like them afterwards to be baptized.

637.

Sermon No. 334

"THE THREE MERCIES"

Editor's Summary

Preaching on Exod 19:4, a text he would not preach from again, Charles spiritualizes this statement about God's deliverance of Israel from Egypt as a picture of God's rescue of Christians from their sin. This kind of spiritualizing was a common practice for Charles. It enabled him to point hearers to God's saving work in Christ while preaching the Old Testament.

Many years later, Charles would deliver a lecture to his pastoral students titled "On Spiritualizing" (*Lectures* 1:102–16). Scholars have observed that Charles didn't always abide by his own instructions. Yet it's clear from that lecture that he sought to be disciplined in his biblical interpretation. This sermon provides a few good examples of that discipline.

First, Charles acknowledges the primary context of Exod 19:4. As he would later instruct his students,

> The first sense of the passage must never be drowned in the outflow of your imagination; it must be distinctly declared and allowed to hold the first rank. . . . The Bible is not a compilation of clever allegories or instructive poetical traditions; it teaches literal facts and reveals tremendous realities: let your full persuasion of this truth be manifest to all who attend your ministry. *Lectures* 1:108.

We see this modeled when he carefully notes that the passage is the word of the prophet to God's people after the Lord's defeat of the Egyptians. Only after making that clear does Charles transition to spiritualizing: "We too have Egyptians."

Second, he makes full use of biblical metaphors. He told his students, "When you have exhausted all the Old Testament types, you have left to you an heirloom of a

75

thousand metaphors." One example here is in his picture of God's salvation as carrying Israel on eagles' wings. Charles sees something of God's strength, loftiness, safety, and love, and he applies these concepts to the salvation of the believer through the gospel.

Beyond metaphors, however, Charles perceived the historical books of the Bible "as a whole to be arranged with a view to symbolical teaching." *Lectures* 1:109. In other words, so many of the events, characters, ceremonies, and places of the Old Testament are filled with New Testament meaning. Summarizing the story of Exodus and Numbers, he taught his students:

> An elect people by the blood of the Lamb are saved from Egypt. This is Exodus. . . . Then in the wilderness of this world, as pilgrims from Egypt, the house of bondage, to the promised land beyond Jordan, the trials of the journey are learnt, from that land of wonders and man's wisdom to the land flowing with milk and honey. This is the book of Numbers. *Lectures* 1:109.

For Charles, these were not mere historical events. Rather, through them, God was teaching and picturing how he would one day save his people from sin and death. Therefore, along with Israel, Christians can look forward to the day when God brings them home "into everlasting glory."

THE THREE MERCIES

Exodus 19:4

*"Ye have seen what I did unto the Egyptians, and how I bare
you on eagles' wings, and brought you unto myself."*

It was often the custom of the prophets to make appeals to God's people as to his faithfulness. Doubtless if each one were asked there would be an unanimous reply from the ten thousand thousand tongues, "Not one good thing hath failed."

I. THE VICTORY. *"what I did to the Egyptians."*

Long and bitter was the contest, but the Lord conquered. We too have Egyptians.

Sins, from which we have been now set free, yet they harass our march—but soon they shall die.

Doubters, Election, Vocation, Perseverance, etc. Doubters these worry us but their doom is at hand.

II. THE CARRIAGE. *"eagles wings."*

Eagle fabled to have only one young one.

Strong wing,	that can never fail to sustain us.
Lofty wing,	carrying us beyond this world.
Safe wing,	none can harm if he bears.
Loving wing,	the eagle is tender and exposes its own body to save its young.

III. <u>THE HOME.</u> *"brought you to myself."*

This is home indeed, all else is foreign land. We are brought home:

By conversion, Jesus becomes our salvation.
By recovery when we have backslidden.
By death and entrance into everlasting glory.

Bless us Oh Holy One.

615.

"JESUS CHRIST THE SAME ETC."

Editor's Summary

Charles preached on this text at least three more times in his ministry: "The Immutability of Christ" (*NPSP* 4, Sermon 170); "Jesus Christ Immutable" (*MTP* 15, Sermon 848); and "The Unchangeable Christ" (*MTP* 40, Sermon 2358). The first and last of these sermons show little influence from this early Waterbeach sermon. However, the middle sermon, "Jesus Christ Immutable," contains quite a bit of overlap with this sermon, sharing a similar outline and introduction, and similar points. "Jesus Christ Immutable" was preached at the Metropolitan Tabernacle on January 3, 1869, nearly fifteen years later. As such, it provides an interesting case study for analyzing how Charles's preaching developed over that period of time.

A few observations can be made. First, Charles grew more disciplined with his use of scriptural references. In this earlier sermon, "Jesus Christ the Same Etc.," he spends a significant portion of his first point providing a lengthy inventory of the various names of Christ found in the Old and New Testaments. In the later sermon, he would go straight to his main point: expounding on the meaning of the name of Jesus Christ. Charles still drew from a wide range of Scripture passages to explain that name, but as a preacher, he became willing to cut out extraneous material in order to remain focused on the main point of that section.

Second, the later sermon would evidence Charles's ongoing study and increasing understanding of Scripture. While "Jesus Christ Immutable" starts with the sermon structure and points seen here, Charles went on to bring new insights, illustrations, and applications into it—for example, sharing about his study of Mr. Henry Craik, a Hebrew scholar from Bristol, who explained that the name Jesus "comes from a root signifying amplitude, spaciousness, and then it comes to mean setting at large, setting free, delivering, and so comes to its common use among us, namely, that of Savior." *MTP* 15:4. All of this indicates a preacher who was continuing to learn and always on the hunt for new insights and treasures to share with his people.

Finally, we see Charles's growth as a preacher in his development of application. Both sermons certainly feature applicable material throughout, but a common feature of these Waterbeach sermons is the brief points of application that conclude each sermon. They're almost an afterthought. However, in the later sermon, he would combine the second and third points outlined here and create a new third point for considering "our Lord's evident claims" as a result of his unchanging character:

> If our Lord be "the same yesterday, and today, and for ever," then, according to the connection of our text, he is to be followed to the end. . . . The next evident claim of Christ upon us is that we should be steadfast in the faith. . . . If Jesus Christ be thus immutable, he has an evident claim to our most solemn worship. Immutability can be the attribute of none but God. . . . He claims also of us next, that we should trust him. If he be always the same, here is a rock that cannot be moved; build on it. . . . And, lastly, if he be always the same, rejoice in him, and rejoice always. *MTP* 15:11–12.

JESUS CHRIST THE SAME ETC.

Hebrews 13:8

"Jesus Christ the same yesterday, and to-day, and for ever."

It is said of Louis XIV that he once said, "I had rather hear the repetitions of Bourdalone than the novelties of another." Truly there are some things that have the charm [today] and lose it tomorrow, and but a very few that are always charming. Jesus' name needs no novelty to recommend it to you. Its mere repetition is delightful to the ear.

But to our text:

I.   THE TITLE. *"Jesus Christ."*

II. THE ATTRIBUTE. *"the same."*

III. THE DURATION. *"yesterday, today, and forever."*

I.   <u>THE TITLE.</u> *"Jesus Christ."*

This is not his only name, he has many others.

> <u>**Seed of the Woman**</u>, was the first one given to him. <u>**Angel**</u>, he is styled, since he is the Messenger of the Covenant of Grace. <u>**Shiloh**</u>, was the name Jacob gave him. The peaceable one, the Saviour. <u>**Me[l]chizedek**</u> too is his name and office. <u>**The Prophet**</u>, like unto Moses in fidelity, wisdom, justice, and honour. <u>**The Redeemer**</u>, was Job's favourite mode of speaking of him <u>**The Holy One**</u> he is called by David and Daniel. <u>**The Anointed**</u>. Hannah, David, and Daniel sang of. Isaiah, the evangelical prophet, heaped title upon title and

81

in sublime tones calls him the "<u>**wonderful**</u>, <u>**the counsellor**</u>, <u>**Immanuel**</u>, <u>**the Mighty God**</u>, <u>**the Lord our Righteousness**</u>, <u>**the Branch**</u>, <u>**Mighty to save**</u>, <u>**the Shepherd**</u>, <u>**the Breaker**</u>." Zechariah calls him as Isaiah had done, <u>the stone</u>. And Malachi closes by calling him the <u>**Sun of Righteousness**</u>. *Solomon called him **Wisdom**, John Baptist opens the new economy by "behold the <u>**Lamb of God**</u>" etc. John the Evangelist delights in the name "<u>**Word of God**</u>," and wondrous are his titles in the apocalypse. Mary called him **Rabboni**, the young man "**good Master**," [h]is foes called him **Nazarene**, **Beelzebub**, but the name whereby he is most commonly known is:

Jesus Christ.

Jesus – A name meaning Saviour. Just as Joshua led the people into the promised land, so will our Joshua. This is the name given at the annunciation, and again at his birth in the manger. The Shepherds heard the song "unto you is born this day a Jesus which is Christ the Lord." This is the name the blind man called him by, and oh sweet thought, this name was nailed over his head at his crucifixion. This name the angels used when they said "ye seek Jesus," and again, "this same Jesus who has gone up etc." Pause soul, and sound this name in thine ears again. Let its full toned harmony enchant thee. Jesus. How sweet the name of Jesus sounds. Surely this is the name I will call him by in heaven, and 'tis the name the angelic hosts sing of.

Christ – This is a royal title, a kingly and triumphal name. He is Christ to each of us, for we hope we have anointed him by faith with the oil of our love. Peter called him Christ many times. He was Christ here, but he will be more visibly Christ when the great coronation day comes. Till then, let us say and feel "for me to live is Christ," let us glory in the cross of Christ, let us have him for our Christ. Oh my Christ Jesus, I would I loved thee more than I can love.

II. <u>**THE ATTRIBUTE**</u>. *"the same."*

Being "very God of very God," he is most certainly immutable, let us remark: <u>In Nature</u>, <u>Office</u>, <u>in Doctrine</u>.

<u>In Nature</u>. He is the same. He has the same Power and wisdom as ever. The same tenderness of mind, the same love to his people, the same feeling for them.

In Office. He was set apart from all eternity as our Salvation, he has now finished the work, but he still carries on the same scheme. He has not swerved from his purpose, or laid down the great labour he once undertook.

In Doctrine. What he once taught is truth now. There is no new Gospel, nor is the old one altered. If any man preach any other, let him be accursed. Some want a new Bradshaw to leaven every mouth, but no, the same one must be used still. He is wholly the same in these points, there is not so much as the shadow of a turn in him. He is "<u>the same</u>."

III. <u>THE DURATION</u>. *"Yesterday, today, and forever."*

Let us take the three terms in 3 senses:

<u>In the widest sense, it means</u>
Yesterday, before time began in election and covenant.
Today, in time, in incarnation, redemption etc.
For ever, in eternity, in glory. . . . . . . he is the same.

<u>In a more limited sense</u>.
Yesterday to our forefather, Adam, Abraham, Noah, David, the apostles etc.
Today in our age and time.
For ever, to our descendants in future time.
　　He is and ever will be the same.

<u>In the most limited sense</u>
Yesterday in my past experience.
Today in my present exigencies.
Tomorrow in future trials.
　　I shall ever find him the same.

Let us learn:

1. To value this world at a little since it passeth away.
2. To esteem Christ most highly since he is ever our friend.

　　　　Oh Jesus help thine unworthy <u>one</u>.

617. 621.

"THE MEANS AND THE BLESSINGS"

Editor's Summary

It appears that Charles intended to write a sermon on Prov 21:31—a text he would not preach again—but like "Partaking Other Men's Sins" and "How to Meet Evil Tidings" (Sermons 324 and 325), he was not able to finish it. However, unlike those sermons, Charles did preach "The Means and the Blessings" at least once, as unfinished as it was. At the bottom of the page is Charles's notation that this was his 618th sermon. Given the lack of notes, this sermon was apparently preached extemporaneously.

In *Lectures to My Students*, Charles taught on the usefulness of extemporaneous speaking. A pastor never knows when he "may be called upon to preach at a moment's notice." In those situations, the skill of impromptu speech will be "as precious as the gold of Ophir." *Lectures* 1:156. Having preached his very first sermon extemporaneously, Charles understood this well. Later on in his ministry, he would intentionally look for ways to cultivate this skill.

Ever since I have been in London, in order to get into the habit of speaking extemporaneously, I have never studied or prepared anything for the Monday evening prayer-meeting. I have all along selected that occasion as the opportunity for off-hand exhortation; but you will observe that I do not on such occasions select difficult expository topics, or abstruse themes, but restrict myself to simple, homely talk, about the elements of our faith. When standing up on such occasions, one's mind makes a review, and inquires, "What subject has already taken up my thought during the day? What have I met with in my reading during the past week? What is most laid upon my heart at this hour? What is suggested by the hymns or the prayers?" It is of no use to rise before an assembly, and hope to be inspired upon subjects of which you know nothing; if you are so unwise, the result will be that as you know nothing you will probably say it, and the people will not be edified. But I do not see why a man cannot speak extemporaneously upon a subject which he fully understands. Any tradesman, well versed in his line of business, could explain it to you without needing to retire for meditation; and surely we ought to be equally as familiar with the first principles of our holy faith; we ought not to feel at a loss when called upon to, speak upon topics which constitute the daily bread of our souls. *Lectures* 1:158–59.

Whether the absence of notes here was intentional or accidental, Charles likely approached this as a challenge and an opportunity for growth rather than viewing it as a misfortune.

THE MEANS AND THE BLESSING

Proverbs 21:31

"The horse is prepared against the day of battle: but safety is of the Lord."

[Blank]

[Blank]

618.

"FULL ASSURANCE"

Editor's Summary

In his autobiography, Charles recounted his pastoral care for a member of his church in Waterbeach who struggled with assurance of salvation:

> Among my early hearers at Waterbeach was one good old woman whom I called "Mrs. Much-afraid." I feel quite sure she has been many years in Heaven, but she was always fearing that she should never enter the gates of glory. She was very regular in her attendance at the house of God, and was a wonderfully good listener. She used to drink in the gospel; but, nevertheless, she was always doubting, and fearing, and trembling about her own spiritual condition. *Autobiography* 1:239.

We do not know if "Mrs. Much-afraid" ever heard this sermon, but it was very much with congregants like her in mind that Charles preached this sermon on full assurance. Though he lists 1 Tim 1:12 as the sermon text (a passage he would not preach on again), he gives little time to expositing it. Rather, he uses it as an introduction for a sermon on the topic of full assurance—what it is, what are its advantages, and how to attain it.

Charles's teaching on this subject is marked by careful pastoral work. In his first point, he clearly instructs the Antinomians in his congregation that full assurance does not lead to laziness or pride. Instead, "the truly assured man will be diligent" and humbly trust in Christ's righteousness. At the same time, for those in the congregation who were like "Mrs. Much-afraid," Charles teaches that assurance "is not absolutely necessary for salvation." In spite of a person's many fears and doubts, such experiences do not bring about the destruction of their souls. To the rest of his congregation, Charles charges them to "not condemn those who are weak in the faith," but instead to "foster the tender plant." In clearing up these various misunderstandings, their pastor sought to speak both to the presumptuous and the fearful, and he called his congregation to love one another in spite of their different experiences.

Having cleared those errors, Charles does not leave his people passively waiting for God to give them assurance. Rather, in the rest of the sermon, he motivates them with the blessings of assurance and urges them to pursue assurance of salvation through the proper means of grace, exercising their faith through obedience, meditation, and prayer. These activities in themselves do not produce assurance, but they do foster faith in Christ, the Source of all assurance. This is the secret to assurance: not confidence in our works, but in Christ.

Writing many years later, Charles confessed:

At this moment I possess a comfortable and clear assurance that I have eternal life; but my ground of confidence today is exactly what it was when first I came to Christ. I have no confidence in my confidence, I place no reliance upon my own assurance. My assurance lies in the fact that "Christ Jesus came into the world to save sinners," and that "Whosoever believeth in him hath everlasting life": I do believe in him, and therefore I know I have eternal life. Brethren, do not stir beyond that, keep to your first faith. However far you go in other directions, stand fast in your undivided faith in Jesus. *MTP* 30:408.

FULL ASSURANCE

1 Timothy 1:12

*"I thank Christ Jesus our Lord, who hath enabled me, for that
he counted me faithful, putting me into the ministry."*

This passage is a real gem. The words of generals and princes have been much esteemed and often repeated. Nelson's "England expects etc." Wellington's "Would to God night or Blücher were come." Caesar's "Veni, vidi, vici." Leonidas' "come and take them etc., etc." But these are dim of lustre and lack the rich setting in gold which this verse has. A poor despised man trusting in one yet more despised than himself and boasting that he felt no doubt of his safety.

But now to the subject of full assurance, which it seems Paul enjoyed, and John, for he said "We know that we etc." It has been enjoyed in modern times and in all times. See Toplady's Hymn "a debtor etc.," and Watts' "When I can read my title clear." Doubtless too some of us have had seasons when we were full of faith giving glory to God.

I shall endeavour to speak of it:

I.   SHOWING ITS NATURE.

II. [SHOWING] ITS ADVANTAGES.

III. THE MEANS OF ITS ATTAINMENT.

I.   <u>SOME REMARKS ON THE NATURE OF ASSURANCE.</u>

And here I must endeavour to move away first of all some objections that are made to it, owing to wrong conceptions of it.

1. <u>It will not lead to sloth</u>. Some, it is true, who boast of being assured are negligent of the means, but true assurance never leads a man to this. False presumption does, but the truly assured man will be diligent. The security of the prize wings our feet to win it.

2. <u>It will not lead to pride</u>. Presumption makes men glory in their being elect etc., but true assurance so makes us lie flat on the promise that we have a constraint put upon us to give all glory to the Master. Doubts are often [a] very proud thing. When we doubt our worthiness that is pride in its very essence, for we ought never to have but one worthiness in our eye, and that the righteousness of Christ.

3. <u>It is not absolutely necessary for salvation</u>. It is nowhere said "He that is assured shall be saved," but only "He that believeth." As the old Puritans used to say, "~~faith~~ assurance is necessary to the well-being of Christian life but not to its being." A man may be a child of God and yet have doubts. We must not condemn those who are weak in faith.

4. <u>It is not always the same</u>. Some graces, being absolutely necessary to Christian existence, never can be lost. But assurance, though a highly ornamental and useful part of the Christian body, is not a vital organ and may be diminished and even totally removed, though with much injury to the soul, yet without its absolute destruction.

5. <u>It is nowhere condemned in God's word but always commended</u>. There is no premium offered to unbelief but the encouragement is to faith. Where a could we have looked for so long a list of heroes in faith if assurance had not been theirs[?] The more faith the more glory to God.

II. <u>THE ADVANTAGES OF ASSURANCE.</u>

1. <u>In duty</u>. It serves to give us zeal, love, and courage. It is like the live coal on the lip of Isaiah. In preaching, in prayer, in any labour, how it nerves us, how it acts like generous wine invigorating the whole frame.

2. <u>In trial</u>. Temporal afflictions become only feathers when assurance is present. Bereavment and sickness are sweetened. Loss of property is little regarded. Persecution is borne joyfully, yea, and the loss of all things only seems the loss of so much dross.

3. <u>In temptation</u>. The lion's howl is not a terror. Lust, corruption, evil desire, and Satanic suggestions may all be put to flight by the simple word "I know etc."

4. <u>In death</u>. It is the rod and staff, guiding and supporting. It treads on the dragon's head. It giveth joyful victory and exalts our Jesus. Doubts being removed, the cold flood does not affright.

III. <u>THE MEANS OF ITS ATTAINMENT.</u>

Every Christian has a right to it, and every Christian may attain it. It is not exclusively the privilege of advanced believers for even babes in grace have possessed it. Some earlier than others. Some have much to impede them in their endeavours to reach so blissful a consummation, but we repeat our belief that it is in the reach of all true Christians and ought not to be so rare a grace as it is at present.

1. Exercise of faith already possessed, for the use of the arm will strengthen it.
2. Strict obedience to all our Father's will, for any sin harboured will breed doubts.
3. Progress in grace. This shall we know if we follow on to know.
4. Much meditation, study of the Bible, and abundance of earnest prayer.
5. While our Father adds the gift of his Holy Spirit to render the word effectual.

How well would it be if all our Church enjoyed this so that we were all fully ready to fight the Lord's battles. But as some are weak, let us foster the tender plant and never put one drop of water on those who show some symptoms of stronger faith than others.

Oh Lord give it to me and to the hearers. Amen.

<u>for J.C. sake</u>.

624.

"THE SENTENCE OF THE WICKED"

Editor's Summary

Charles regularly preached on eschatology and the eternal state during his time at Waterbeach. He opens this sermon with a brief reminder of other such sermons. In "The Dawn of Latter-Day Glory" (*LS* 6:350–83), Charles described the glories of the coming Millennium. "The Great Conflagration" (*LS* 5:46–57) was another memorable message on the end of the world that the congregation would have likely remembered.

In the weeks and months preceding this sermon, Charles preached at least three other eschatological messages: "The General Judgment," "Praise Ye the Lord," and "The Faultless People" (Sermons 323, 327, 328). These left a deep impression on his hearers and were used by God to bring about a revival among the people of Waterbeach. Many years later, a church member, Ebenezer Smith, would record the effect of one of these sermons.

On another occasion he could not sleep on Saturday night, and early in the morning ere the light had dawned he awoke me. The perspiration was streaming from his forehead, he told me he had seen a vision of Hell. He described the last things, the Judgment, the wailing, the torments and the shriek of the lost, until I grew frightened. The next morning he preached his marvelous sermon on the Final Conflagration, one of the most awful sermons that was ever heard from a Christian pulpit. Men and women swayed in agony. It was a mental torture unknown in our churches to-day. It seemed as though he shook his audience over the Pit, until the smoke of God's wrath filled their eyes and made them weep, and entered their throats until they gasped for mercy. It was not done for effect. The power lay in the fact that it was real to the preacher. He had lived through a nightmare of a terrible experience and it was being used to a holy purpose. He was deeply in earnest and men knew it. He never preached a religion he had simply learned, but a truth that had been cut into his soul by a deep and rich experience. Ebenezer Smith, *Two Centuries of Grace: Being a Brief History of the Baptist Church, Waterbeach: An Address at the Centenary Meeting* (Cambridge, UK: Cambridge University Press, 1903), 15–16.

At least two things are striking about Smith's comments. First and foremost, Charles preached about judgment and hell not "for effect." Neither did he treat these as theoretical or academic subjects. Rather, judgment and hell were weighty, eternal realities that Charles felt deep in his soul, impressed indelibly, even supernaturally, by a terrifying vision. This enabled him not only to preach with vividness but to plead with urgency for the salvation of sinners ("Flee sinner Flee. Behold the Lamb who taketh away sin"). Far from driving people away, Charles's preaching awakened his hearers to God's judgment and their need of a Savior.

Second, Smith's description of Charles shaking his audience "over the Pit, until the smoke of God's wrath filled their eyes" is particularly striking, and is reminiscent of Jonathan Edwards's famous sermon, "Sinners in the Hands of an Angry God." This sermon, "The Sentence of the Wicked," may well have had a similar effect on Charles's congregation. This would not be the last time he would preach on hell. Charles would carry this "deep and rich experience" into the pulpit for the rest of his life.

THE SENTENCE OF THE WICKED

Matthew 25:41

"Then shall he say also unto them on the left hand, Depart from me, ye cursed, into everlasting fire, prepared for the devil and his angels."

We have had, I trust, several very profitable discourses on the great things of futurity. We looked at the coming Millen[n]ium, the conflagration of the Universe, the acquittal of the righteous, and their song of victory. We have now one more subject which it would be highly improper to omit and that is the damnation of the wicked. Oh may God make the subject of much use for arousing the slumbering, dead sinner.

I. I WILL MENTION THE NAMES GIVEN TO THIS TORMENT IN SCRIPTURE.

II. I WILL MENTION WHEREIN IT CONSISTS.

III. ENQUIRE AS TO DEGREES.

IV. LOOK AT ITS DURATION.

I. THE NAMES IT IS CALLED BY IN SCRIPTURE.

Hell is the usual term and how dreadful when we read it is prepared for Satan. Fire, this being the most excruciating instrument of torture, and to be burnt being unbearable. Hell is compared to such a fire. Sometimes Brimstone is put with it, being one of the most combustible of all bodies and being highly offensive whilst in fusion. "Tophet," from a valley where children used to be sacr[i]ficed to Moloch. Afterwards [it was] the sewer and kennel of Jerusalem where bodies were left to rot. <u>A prison</u>. Where spirits are confined, strong, well secured, comfortless. No liberty, no happiness, no release. <u>Darkness</u>, outer darkness. Without a single gleam of hope, or spark of glimmering day. <u>The Bottomless pit</u>, a chasm unfathomable, an abyss from whose dreary mouth we may well shrink back appalled. <u>The Second death</u>. Death is awful in its terrors, dreadful in its pains, terrible in its stern realities. Oh the second death. It is the death of deaths. <u>The worm</u> that never dies. To be eaten of worms, worm eaten, putrid, eaten alive, gnawed by reptiles, crawled over by aspies [snakes]. <u>Tearing in pieces</u> is another terrible figure. Just as lions rend men in pieces, as the Elephant crushes or the wheel breaks the bones. So sinner shalt thou be broken in the torments of hell.

II. WHEREIN THE TORMENT CONSISTS.

Of this of course we know but little. But it will certainly consist of punishment of loss and punishment of sense.

> <u>Punishment of loss</u>. The loss of God, of Christ, of the society of angels, of the communion of saints, of the crown of life, of heaven, this is one very great item in the punishment of lost souls.

> <u>Punishment of sense</u>. Which will consist of two parts, viz, torment of body and agony of soul.

>> The <u>body</u>, having shared in the sin, must share in the penalty. If it be asked how flesh can endure fire without destruction we answer that the children in the furnace [Shadrach, Meshach, and Abednego] furnish an illustration. The asbestos may be put into the fire but it cannot be destroyed, and why not the new body of sinners[?] Who knows but that there may be a kind of fire which will torment but not destroy. The body will be racked in all its members as they were the gates of sin. So shall they be channels of retribution. Eyes, ears, hands, feet, nose.

>> <u>The soul</u> in all its faculties shall suck in damnation. Conscience, memory, judgment, desire, prospective powers, etc.

>> Oh wretched state of dark despair.

III. ENQUIRE AS TO DEGREES.

Scripture says but little as to degrees of glory or degrees of punishment; doubtless much is left to our judgment. <u>We must think that sinners will differ in hell even as saints in heaven</u>. Such great sinners as false prophets, impostors, or popes should have an exemplary punishment. T. Paine, Voltaire, Hume, Gibbon, Owen, and men of the Nero, Commodus and Bonner stamp with atrocious murderers will be made capable of more torment. <u>But every vessel will be full</u>. All will have a full portion of burning wrath. There will be no cause to congratulate ourselves on the smallness of our pain if we ever come there. We shall have more than enough to do to bear our share. Oh may God avert such horrid doom from us all.

IV. AS TO ITS DURATION.

1. As the soul is immortal so will hell be eternal.
2. Sin unatoned for will never be burned out, but the debt will still remain.
3. As there is no hope, so there can be no end of it, for then the end would cause hope.
4. As heaven is eternal so must hell be.

Flee Sinner Flee. Behold the Lamb who taketh away sin.

Help. Help. Help

625

"JOY IN HEAVEN OVER PENITENTS"

Editor's Summary

As far as we know, this is the next sermon that Charles preached after "The Sentence of the Wicked." (We have no record of his 626th preaching occasion.) The short manuscript likely indicates that this was the sermon he composed for that Sunday's afternoon service. Given the heaviness of the morning message, Charles probably provided this sermon as a refreshing contrast, meditating on heaven's joy over the repentant. The congregation that had trembled over the pit of hell earlier that day would now be reminded that repentance "is God's work" and that the angels "rejoice . . . know, sympathize. They believe final perseverance."

The first point appears to be the longest one. We find traces of the morning sermon here, as he defends the preciousness of the soul "because of its capability for awful pain." However, his main point is the soul's value. Some of Charles's listeners might have concluded that God's judgment on the wicked means that, in the eyes of the Almighty, human souls are dispensable or worthless. Their pastor corrects that thinking, pointing to heaven's joy as proof that every sinner is eternal and of infinite value to God.

This conviction marked Charles's ministry at Waterbeach from the beginning. Writing about his first convert and the value of a soul, Charles recalled:

It was Richard Knill, that blessed missionary of the cross to whom I am personally so deeply indebted, who said that, if there were only one unconverted person in the whole world, and if that person lived in the wilds of Siberia, and if every Christian minister and every private believer in the world had to make a pilgrimage to that spot before that soul were brought to Christ, the labor would be well expended if that one soul were so saved. This is putting the truth in a striking way, but in a way in which everyone who realizes the value of immortal souls, will heartily concur.

When I began to preach in the little thatched chapel at Waterbeach, my first concern was, Would God save any souls through me? They called me a ragged-headed boy, and I think I was just that; I know I wore a jacket. After I had preached for some little time, I thought, "This gospel has saved me, but then somebody else preached it; will it save anybody else now that I preach it?" . . .

How my heart leaped for joy when I heard tidings of my first convert! I could never be satisfied with a full congregation, and the kind expressions of friends. I longed to hear that hearts had been broken, that tears had been seen streaming from the eyes of penitents. How I did rejoice, as one that findeth great spoil, one Sunday afternoon, when my good deacon said to me, "God has set His seal on your ministry in this place, sir." Oh, if anybody had said to me, "Someone has left you twenty thousand pounds," I should not have given a snap of my fingers for it, compared with the joy which I felt when I was told that God had saved a soul through my ministry! . . . I felt like the boy who has earned his first guinea, or like a diver who has been down to the depths of the sea, and brought up a rare pearl. *Autobiography* 1:232.

JOY IN HEAVEN OVER PENITENTS

Luke 15:10

"Likewise I say unto you, There is joy in the presence of the angels of God over one sinner that repenteth."

This exquisitely beautiful chapter is indeed milk for babes and is full of rich comfort for the broken spirit. Here we see:

I.   THE VALUE OF A SOUL.

"One sinner" is the expression used. Now we rejoice over converted nations but forget the value of a single soul.

1. Precious because of its eternity.
2. Precious because of its capability for happiness.
3. Precious because of its capability of awful pain.
4. Precious from the harm one sinner may do.
5. Precious from the good one sinner may do.

"One sinner"—let us muse on the value.

II. THE BEAUTY OF PENITENCE.

Angels rejoice not over palaces, victories etc.
But repentance: Is God's work
                          It is the mark of great things

III. THE SYMPATHY OF ANGELS.

They rejoice, they therefore know, sympathize. They believe final perseverance. They are our guards, we never need fear ghosts or apparitions. They are often ministers of comfort to the saints.

Oh how rightly they judge when they sing over a new born soul.

627. 628. 633. 635.

"REJOICING IN PERSECUTIONS"

Editor's Summary

As a student of the English Reformation, Charles knew well the stories of martyrs who were burned at the stake under Queen Mary. John Foxe's *Actes and Monuments* (more popularly known as *Foxe's Book of Martyrs*) was one of Charles's favorite books. Even though the stories recounted in its pages had taken place decades before, they still reminded Charles of his second-class status as a Nonconformist, a non-Anglican.

Charles's family faced certain civil restrictions because of their faith. Both his father and his grandfather were Nonconformist pastors. His grandfather had succeeded an Independent minister who was ejected in 1662 for his refusal to abide by the Book of Common Prayer. Charles himself lived in Cambridge and yet could not study at the local university because he was a Baptist.

His youth also provoked the scorn of other preachers. After Charles preached at one meeting, a minister remarked publicly how "it was a pity that boys did not adopt the scriptural practice of tarrying at Jericho till their beards were grown before they tried to instruct their seniors." *Autobiography* 1:298. On another occasion, an aged minister, upon seeing Charles for the first time, lamented with disgust at "boys going up and down the country preaching before their mother's milk is well out of their mouths." G. H. Pike, *Charles Haddon Spurgeon, Preacher, Author, Philanthropist* (Toronto: S. R. Briggs, 1886), 48. Yet in all these things, Charles understood that hatred and reproach are the Christian's lot. Far from seeking revenge or shrinking in fear, the Christian is called to rejoice in persecution.

Charles sought to model this for his people, assuring them in this sermon that "when I have been much ill spoken of I can witness to the faithfulness of God that I have had so much more the grace that I could really 'leap for joy' and counted calumny and scorn to be sweet music." These early experiences of opposition served to prepare the young pastor for far greater persecution to come.

Recorded in his *Autobiography* is a poem entitled "The Noble Army of Martyrs" that Charles composed before leaving for London. The first two stanzas read,

> Rouse thee, Music! Rouse thee, Song!
> Noble themes await thee long.
> not the warrior's thund'ring car,
> not the battle heard afar,
> not the garment rolled in blood,
> not the river's redden'd flood;
> Subjects more sublime I sing,
> Soar thee, then, on highest wing!
>
> Sing the white-robed hosts on high,
> Who in splendor suns outvie;
> Sing of them, the martyr'd band,
> With the palm-branch in their hand:
> Fairest of the sons of light,
> Midst the bright ones doubly bright.
> *Autobiography* 1:300.

REJOICING IN PERSECUTIONS

Luke 6:22–23

"Blessed are ye, when men shall hate you, and when they shall separate you from their company, and shall reproach you, and cast out your name as evil, for the Son of man's sake. Rejoice ye in that day, and leap for joy: for, behold, your reward is great in heaven: for in the like manner did their fathers unto the prophets."

In nature there is a wonderful supply of means for the removal of inconvenience and the cure of ills. Is it cold? There is the fire. Are we heated? There is the cooling brook.

Does the sun beat upon us? Yonder is the spreading beech. In trackless ocean the compass marks my way. In darkness the flint affords the seed of flame, in storms my house is [unscathed] by the means of the wondrous rod. But there are some diseases nature knows no cure for. Some exigencies in which we must be left to grapple alone. Who can withstand the cholera, consumption, paralysis, or others of the mighties in the hosts of death[?] Nature has not a supply for all needs.

But revelation has, Christianity most surely has, a balm for every wound, a cure for every ill. Here is one of the peculiar ills of Christians and the great remedy for it. Yea, such a remedy that it maketh the disease very desirable and causes the blueness of the wound to work our health.

I.   PERSECUTION THE CHRISTIAN'S LOT.

II. JOY AT IT HIS CONSTANT DUTY.

III. FUTURE GLORY HIS GREAT REWARD.

I. <u>PERSECUTION THE CHRISTIAN'S LOT</u>.

If a man asks me for a decided proof of the doctrine of human depravity I would turn my finger at once to that dark spot in earth's history. Spot did I say[?] Rather that black cloud called Persecution. It commenced as early as the great division when one was accepted and [. .] unto the other there was no respect.

Abel's blood still cries from the ground and since that first martyrdom the enemy has never ceased to plague the seed of the Lord, and many a torrent of blood has gushed. See Noah, Lot, Jacob, Joseph, Moses, the Israelites, David, Elijah, the prophets, Daniel, the three, even until John's beheading. Then comes our Master, his apostles, the saints in pagan times, the Albigenses, the Reformed Church, dissenters, and our own denomination.

Fox[e]'s book of Martyrs might well be continued even until the present hour. There is no sin which Jesus will be more likely to punish (speaking after me) than that of willfully persecuting his members, tormenting his own spiritual body. It is a sin against the common rights of man. It is now a sin against our country. It is downright war with heaven. It grows by degrees.

1. <u>They hate us</u>. Some because our religion hurts their craft, others because it thwarts their desires, and others because it is a protest against their sin. Some too are of a domineering spirit and hate us because our doctrines are productive of liberty and are the great levellers of caste and pride. O sad that men should hate God's servants; is it so with any of my hearers or have you passed from death unto life and therefore love the brethren[?]

2. <u>They separate us from their company</u>. As soon as a man became a follower of Jesus he was put out of the synagogue. On Bartholomew's day the Nonconforming Ministers were expelled [from] their pulpits and now how much there is of the separating spirit. We are called schismatics, but those are the sinners who cut us off and so make a schism. Oh, how glad will they be of our company one day.

3. <u>They reproach us</u>. The faults we commit have no mantle of love put over them but are magnified into crimes: and we, be [we] ever so faultless, are not secure for hoarse envy will croak lies if truth fail her. All eminent men have been slandered. David, Jesus, Paul, Luther, Whitefield, yea all who enter

the lion's den and beard him manfully. This is a trial, but oh what it is really when compared with tortures others endure.

4. <u>They cast out our name as evil</u>. Their hatred goes so far that the very name becomes a thing loathsome and obnoxious. We are tabooed, but our name is written on high, and even on earth it may one day be famous. Beyond this they cannot now go with us, here the proud waves are staid.

II. JOY UNDER PERSECUTION IS THE CHRISTIAN'S DUTY.

Some will say, "Is this possible?" We reply, "most certainly it is." Otherwise our Saviour would not have commanded it. True, nature cannot of itself love slander, persecution, etc., but grace can do all things. It is omnipotent. See how strongly it is put: "rejoice ye in that day and leap for joy." Ancient Christians used to rush in crowds to the judgment seats and courted martyrdom as a glory. When Leonidas the father of Origen was put to death, Origen, being only 17, desired to share the honour with him, but his mother, not wishing to lose both in one day, hid all his clothes, where upon he wrote to his father, "Take heed, turn not for our sake."

Laurence the deacon, being after other tortures, at last put on a gridiron with a slow fire under it, [and] when one side had been roasted called out joyously to the emperor

> "This side is broil'd sufficient to be food
> For all who wish it to be done and good."

And when he had been turned and roasted similarly on the other side, he said with great serenity "I am roasted enough and only want serving up" and so died. And in our own land, in more modern times, remember Rowland Taylor of Hadley, how cheerily he addressed his family when he knew that the hour was hastening and how he jokingly told the sheriff that he had been deceived himself and had deceived many in Hadleigh. And when they rejoiced, he explained that he had expected to have been buried in Hadley churchyard, but now would be disappointed and the worms would lose their expected feast on his stout body.

Robert Glover of Coventry was for some time after his condemnation in great darkness, feeling much the absence of God's presence, but as his martyrdom approached he exclaimed "he is come, he is come" and died in extacy. So then, [since] it is possible to rejoice in the great waterfloods, surely much more in the smaller streams. When I have been much ill spoken of, I can witness to the faithfulness of God that I have had so much the more grace that I could really "leap for joy" and have counted calumny and scorn to be sweet music.

1. <u>Rejoice because you are yourselves honoured</u>. To be a sufferer for Christ is a weight of honour under the weight of which an angel might stagger. Oh to die for Jesus. To wear the crown of martyrdom, this is bliss indeed. If we suffer any persecution let us think ourselves much honoured to be counted meet to follow in a humble manner "the noble army of martyrs." Men will give much for honour. Here is true honour before God and his holy angels. We laugh at our foes for they are lacing our coats for us when persecuting.

2. <u>Rejoice because Christ is honoured</u>. If you endure well you will advance his cause. The devil is a fool still, for he has not learned to leave off persecuting though 5000 years [of] experience must have taught him his folly. How you will honour your master. We of all others ought to honour Christ by patient endurance for all our service is stained, rather beautified, with the blood of martyrs. Our very Bible yet blushes with the blood of Tyndale. Our ministry is descended from a murdered race. The deep waters of our holy Baptism are dyed with blood, our sweet Pilgrims Progress has the smell of Bedford gaol upon it, our church-book tells of men who also suffered for righteousness' sake. All this is honourable to the grace that sustains and overrules. Let us leap for joy at being able to furnish gems for our Redeemer's crown. Many have been converted by beholding the constancy of Xn sufferers—but one more reason for present joy remains which is:

III. FUTURE GLORY IS THE GREAT REWARD.

Though we merit no reward yet we shall have it of grace. . . . . . . Martyrs and others who suffer for Christ will shine brightest among the stars in heaven. The veteran adorned with scars stands highest in the ranks. Ah, little do our foes imagine that by their lies and calumnies they are wreathing fresh garlands of amarynth to bind our brows for ever. If similar characters shall find each other and make friendships in heaven, how blest will it be to be companions with the soldiers of the cross who nobly dared to die. Wait but a moment and the reward cometh.

1. Is there a persecutor here, a calumniator[?] I forgive thee so far as I am personally concerned but I bid thee beware how thou touchest the apple of the eye of the Almighty.

2. Is there one here not persecuted[?] Well I am not glad for thee. Search and See if thou art in the way everlasting. Ask thyself whether thou art right with God or no, and oh I beseech thee, prepare for death.

3. To you who are persecuted. Bear it patiently, yea joyfully look at you[r] starry crown. Be sure of thine own religion and then come fair or come foul, come calm or come storm.

630.

Bless me Oh Father
　For Jesus' sake.

Amen

"THE TESTIMONIES OUR HERITAGE"

Editor's Summary

Charles preached on this text at least one other time in his career, "The Believer's Heritage of Joy" (*MTP* 41, Sermon 2415). That sermon—delivered on a Sunday evening, May 22, 1887—shares a similar four-point outline as this earlier sermon, though he reworded the points and changed the content. Thus it's possible that Charles used "The Testimonies Our Heritage" as a starting point for the sermon that he preached more than thirty years later.

Charles clearly loved the Bible. These early sermons reveal a deep and broad knowledge of both the Old and New Testaments. However, he understood that the world stood opposed to the Bible. As a pastor, part of his job was to guard against any who would undermine the Christian's confidence in God's Word. In this sermon, Charles reminds his congregation of the great price that was paid by those who made the Scriptures available: "For it Wickliffe laboured and Tyndale burned. Our sires held it with iron grasp and resolutely resisted those who would rob them and their children of the treasure."

In the coming years, Charles would witness a worldly attack on Scripture, not through violence but through unbelief. In his 1887 sermon on Ps 119:111, he would lament at the growing number of those who denied the Word of God.

There are persons, I am told—deists—who believe in God, but who do not believe in the Word of God. They believe, then, in a God who has never spoken, a silent God, a God who has, at any rate, never spoken to his noblest creatures most capable of understanding his mind. To them, God is one who remains locked up forever in exclusiveness, except so far as his works may reveal him. *MTP* 41:253–54.

These words were spoken just before the Downgrade Controversy, where Charles would take a stand for the truthfulness of the Bible.

Amid defending the Bible, Charles was also committed to proclaiming the Bible. He believed that from beginning to end, the Bible contained one central message: the gospel of Jesus Christ. This is what Charles sought to proclaim in every sermon. In the later sermon, he would declare, "The greatest testimony of God in all the world is Jesus Christ. He is God's testimony embodied. . . . He is God's testimony concerning divine love, for God so loved us that he gave his Son to die for us." *MTP* 41:255.

Though Charles would not be martyred for his stand in the Downgrade Controversy, this fight would nonetheless bring him deep sorrow. And yet he understood what was at stake in this fight for the Bible. As he says in this sermon:

> In this world, the pardon of our sin, restoration to our lost position, love of Christ, the promises, adoption, and the hope of final perseverance.
>
> In the next, deliverance from the dread anger of God, acquit[t]al at his bar, the enjoyment of heaven, the concert of the choirs of glory, eternal extasy of joy.

341

THE TESTIMONIES OUR HERITAGE

Psalm 119:111

"Thy testimonies have I taken as an heritage for ever; for they are the rejoicing of my heart."

It is a solemn thing to talk with God. It is a solemn thing to mention our feelings before the dread [S]upreme. Happy [is] the man who can lay his hand upon his heart, bend his knee, and lifting his eye to heaven say, "Thy testimonies have I taken as an heritage for ever, for they are the rejoicing of my heart."

I.   THE HERITAGE – *"Thy testimonies"*

II. THE APPROPRIATION – *"have I taken"*

III. THE LEASE – *"for ever"*

IV. THE JOY – *"for they are the rejoicing of heart"*

I.   <u>THE HERITAGE</u>.

A Christian has no property of his own accumulation. His labour is, until grace renews him, all unprofitable, and when converted, still his best industry, he will confess, deserves not a farthing. It is an heritage, not an earned property.

<u>The Bible</u> to read for ourselves without note or comment. This a precious heirloom; for it Wickliffe laboured and Tyndale burned. Our sires held it with iron grasp and resolutely resisted those who would rob them and their children of the treasure. Good Adam Thompson cared not to lose his all so that the bible for tenpence might fulfil the promise of Tyndale, that the boy with team and

115

the plow should soon know scripture as well as the lordly prelates. Let us esteem the Word of God.

The Contents of the Bible which are vast indeed. **In this world**, the pardon of our sin, restoration to our lost position, love of Christ, the promises, adoption, and the hope of final perseverance. **In the next**, deliverance from the dread anger of God, acquit[t]al at his bar, the enjoyment of heaven, the concert of the choirs of glory, eternal extasy of joy. This is our heritage.

A heritage is certain. The result of our own efforts we may never see, but what was left before we were born we may be as sure of as earthly things can be. But in a more superlative sense, the great things of our heritage are an entail. They must come to every adopted child; no chancery can rob him of it, no unrighteous heir can defraud us of the claim founded on the equity of God.

A heritage is the result of another's labour. The son receives only what his predecessors have earned. Each shilling has their sweat on it. Some one toiled for it and so our heritage cost our Saviour cries and groans.

A heritage supposes relationship. This is a question of the self enquiry for each of us. Am I related to the Father of Lights[?] Do I love him? Am I like him? Can I trust him? Am I regenerate and adopted? Well, if I have not a foot of land to call my own and no estates to inherit, yet here is a broad heritage worthy of a king's son.

II. THE APPROPRIATION. *"have I taken"*

What is commonly called the taking of it up. Now the Christian will not take up his heritage until he enters the mansions of the blest—but in one sense he does take it up, even here.

1. He eats the fruit. The grapes of Eschol he is enabled to enjoy even in the wilderness. If I can pluck from the tree as much as I like, then surely it is mine. Joy, peace, etc. are the produce.
2. He expels the Canaanite. He takes it by force of arms; each fresh victory gives him a better title to the heritage, or at least brings him nearer the actual possession.
3. He holds the title deed by which the actual inheritance is rendered Secure.

Now comes another self examining question: have I taken these testimonies to be my heritage[?] Can I honestly think so[?]

1. Then I shall sit loose by the world.
2. I shall feel a solid satisfaction.
3. I shall enjoy a quiet expectation.

Is this your choice? Have you chosen the good part[?]

III. THE LEASE. *"for ever"*

Some property leaves the owner after a certain number of years, some flies away just when it will, but ours is forever.

1. <u>This is the wish of the Christian</u>. He does not want to turn back. He [would] rather die than return to his old ways.

2. <u>This is the promise of God</u>. Signed with the heart's blood of Jesus, the promise cannot fail us. He abideth faithful and strong, consolation is one of his gifts to his sons.

Oh muse my soul on this "for ever!" The same Christ whose name is thy music now will be the same in yon bright world. No time, no age, no change, for ever!! This is an enduring substance. Friend are you willing to have Christ forever[?] Temporary Christians are useless. We want enduring substances if we are to be heirs of an enduring habitation in eternity.

IV. THE JOY. *"they are the rejoicing of my heart"*

He who finds no joy in religion, has no religion. <u>Religion is calculated to give joy</u>, solid confidence, peace with God, [c]ommunion with the Spirit, whispers of mercy, smilings of divine love, and strong promises all combining make Religion happy. <u>Religion is calculated to give glorious joy</u>. Its joy is lasting. Its pleasures real. Its delights spiritual. They leave no sting, cause no remorse, never cloy on the appetite, [and] forsake not in distress.

Have I found religion to be the rejoicing of my heart? Do I follow it because I love it? or because of custom, my fear, my situation in society etc.? Do I delight in the Bible[?]

Friends here is Room for great searching of heart. You may if right bask in a sunshine of joy. Live much on, and in your inheritance, bear with patience your troubles, looking to the heritage you will soon enter.

    May thy blessing be upon me
        Oh my Father.

631

Sermon No. 342

"IN THE DAY OF ADVERSITY CONSIDER"

Editor's Summary

Referring to the renowned preacher William Jay, Charles noted in his autobiography, "While I was living at Cambridge, I once heard Mr. Jay, of Bath, preach. . . . I remember with what dignity he preached, and yet how simply." *Autobiography* 1:208.

Charles's appreciation of Jay began early in his ministry and is evident in his collection of Jay's *Works* and *Sermons*, which are held today in The Spurgeon Library at Midwestern Baptist Theological Seminary in Kansas City, Missouri. This particular sermon is attributed to Jay and can be found in his *Works*. William Jay, *The Works of William Jay Collected and Revised by Himself*. Vol. 6 (London: C. A. Bartlett, 1842–1843, The Spurgeon Library), 189–223. Jay's original lecture only contained two points, which correspond closely to the first two points of Charles's sermon. Charles then took Jay's concluding exhortations and call to Christ and used them for his third and fourth points.

Though Charles drew heavily from Jay for this message on adversity, he would soon be able to preach out of his own experiences, encountering many difficulties in the coming years that would shape his ministry and deepen his dependence on God. "The greatest ordeal of [his] life" took place less than four years after this sermon, on October 19, 1856 at the Surrey Gardens Music Hall. *Autobiography* 2:201. Having outgrown the New Park Street Chapel and Exeter Hall, Charles's congregation had voted to secure the Royal Surrcy Gardens—which seated up to 12,000—for Sunday evening worship. This was a controversial decision because the building had previously been devoted to worldly amusements. Yet there was no other place that could hold the crowds that were coming.

However, the events of that night took a tragic turn. During the service there suddenly came multiple cries of "Fire!" "The galleries are giving way!" "The place is falling!" This resulted in a massive stampede, and many in the crowd were trampled. Seven people died that night, while many more were seriously injured. In the coming days, Charles was mercilessly attacked in the press, and he sank into a severe depression, unable to work or write or preach. The trauma of this catastrophe stayed with Charles for the rest of this life. People wondered if he would ever recover.

What was it that brought Charles out of his depression? On his first Sunday back in the pulpit two weeks later, Charles shared "the single reflection" which "had such a power of comfort on my depressed spirit," based on Phil 2:9–11:

> Amidst much tumult and divers rushings to and fro of troublous thoughts our souls have returned to the darling object of our desires, and we have found it no small consolation after all to say, "It matters not what shall become of us: God hath highly exalted him, and given him a name which is above every name: That at the name of Jesus every knee should bow." *NPSP* 2:378.

In this earlier sermon, Charles reminds his congregation that God uses adversity for correction and instruction, and comforts them with the message that "you are not to bear [troubles] alone. Jesus is by you." Surely these words were truer than he knew. But in the Surrey Gardens catastrophe, he learned something else: not only the presence of Christ amid suffering but the exaltation of Christ above all adversity. Indeed, trouble would prove to be a painful but "blessed school."

342

Jay

IN THE DAY OF ADVERSITY CONSIDER

Ecclesiastes 7:14

"In the day of prosperity be joyful, but in the day of adversity consider: God also hath set the one over against the other, to the end that man should find nothing after him."

There is not a man who has not either by sickness in his own person, bereavement, or temporal distress had a day of adversity. As every day has some peculiar duty belonging to it, so we find this day has the duty of Consideration. Consideration begins early in our Christian experience and is at all times very useful for our spiritual growth.

I. <u>LET US CONSIDER THE REASON OF A CHRISTIAN'S ADVERSITY.</u>

    1. Correction. What son is there whom his Father chasteneth not.
    2. Prevention. To keep us from some evil. Better than a cure.
    3. Probation. Trial, that God may be honoured.
    4. Instruction. Trouble is a blessed school.
    5. Usefulness. In comfort, warning, guiding others.

II. <u>LET US CONSIDER THE RELIEF A CHRISTIAN MAY ENJOY.</u>

    1. His sorrows are not <u>peculiar</u>, others endure the same.
    2. Not <u>casual,</u> providence sends them all.
    3. Not <u>penal</u>. Not the sword but only the rod.
    4. Not <u>unalloyed</u>. They might be worse.

5. <u>You are not to bear them alone</u>. Jesus is by you.
6. <u>Not to last always</u>. But for a moment and then gone.

III. <u>LET US CONSIDER OUR OWN CHARACTER</u>.

1. Am I now repining[?] This is wrong.
2. Am I now unconverted in adversity[?] It says consider.
3. Am I broken in Spirit and longing to be saved[?] Then:

IV. <u>LET US CONSIDER CHRIST[']S CHARACTER</u>.

He invites, he is sincere, he never spurns. I shall be welcome to his arms. He will never forsake, he will be with me all through life and with me in death.

Will you go with the man[?]
 Lord bless us.

634. 636. 641

"CHRISTIAN CITIZENSHIP"

Editor's Summary

Ever since finding a copy of Bunyan's *The Pilgrim's Progress* in his grandfather's attic, Charles admired the famous allegorist. Bunyan's stories awakened within Charles a vision of the Christian life as a lifelong journey and war, individually and corporately. It's no surprise, then, that we find Charles seeking to awaken a similar vision in his people through the use of allegory. Many years later, however, he would caution his students about this practice: "Mr. Bunyan is the chief, and head, and lord of all allegorists, and is not to be followed by us into the deep places of typical and symbolical utterance. He was a swimmer, we are but mere waders, and must not go beyond our depth." *Lectures* 1:114.

As a young preacher, Charles was himself learning to use allegory to present the Bible's teaching (see also "Joining a Church," *LS* 6, Sermon 322). Using Eph 2:19 as the text for this baptismal sermon (one he would not preach again), Charles meditates on the citizenship of the Christian in the church and, at the same time, provides a unique glimpse into his own ecclesiology.

He envisions the church as a city with two parts: "[t]he Lower City and the Upper City." The Upper City, the New Jerusalem, is perfect, forever secure, and the dwelling place of divine love. The Lower City is the local church on earth, and though built on a good foundation, is inhabited by strangers and foreigners ("aliens") as well as godly citizens. It is "subject to some grief and pain," and marked by sin and conflict. Charles's distinction here is not between the universal and local church but between the church triumphant and the church militant.

These cities are separated by the river of death, but they still make up one city. The only way into the Upper City is through the Lower City. Charles admonishes his hearers, "We are none of us yet in the Upper City, let us search and see if we have come in by the gate into the Lower One." Upon entering the Lower City by the narrow gate, the new believer will come upon "a fountain in which the [baptismal] candidate is to be plunged." Baptism is the initiatory rite that testifies of every Christian's "love to the Redeemer" and shows the world their citizenship. In other words, the Christian life takes place inside the church. It is as citizens of the City that Christians are called to appropriate their privileges and fulfill their duties of service to one another and to their Lord. Nevertheless, the point of the church is not only to build up her citizens but to attract those who are in the world. The life of the church is her own witness.

On the day he preached this sermon, Charles stated, "I have chosen a subject which I trust will be useful to [the baptismal candidates] in showing them the dignity to which they are now admitted, to members in causing them to rejoice more and more, and to you ye unconverted ones in making your hearts long to come with us." Concluding the service with a celebration of the Lord's Supper, Charles makes one more appeal to the outsider:

> Now we are about to sit down at a New Jerusalem table, spread in common for all believers. Let us come as citizens and may God grant unto us to rejoice in the dignity conferred upon us.
>
> Would that some of you would also come, for yet there is room and none are excluded who come by the gate.

CHRISTIAN CITIZENSHIP

Ephesians 2:19

*"Now therefore ye are no more strangers and foreigners, but fellow
citizens with the saints, and of the household of God."*

This morning we were privileged to see some of the followers of our Lord put on
his name by holy Baptism. We hope in a little while, at the close of the service, to
receive them into Church fellowship and sit down with them at the supper of the
Lord. I have chosen a subject which I trust will be useful to them in showing them
the dignity to which they are now admitted, to members in causing them to rejoice
more and more, and to you ye unconverted ones in making your hearts long to come
with us. We will not tarry long remembering what we were, truly we were strangers
and foreigners. Either open enemies to the church of God or else aliens living with
them, mingling in their assemblies but not really of them, not enjoying the freedom
of the City, but now we are fellow citizens of Zion.

I. CITIZENSHIP IMPLIES A CITY.

We too have a city beautiful for situation, the joy of the whole earth. Zion the
beloved city of David. Salem the city of peace, or Jerusalem the city of holy
peace. New Jerusalem, since it has a new covenant, has new regulations, [and] is
newly erected from a new pattern. It is not an earthly city.

It is built on Mountains. Jerusalem stood in the midst of the hills, so also doth
our city. Some cities stand on such steep places that they are impregnable; so
is this. Kings and armies have assaulted it from the time of Pharaoh to the
present, yet has it remained unscathed. An Mount Predestination, Mount
Calvary, Mount Adoption, Mount Covenant are some of the names of the
mountains.

<u>It has strong Bulwarks</u>. Let us mark her towers and count her bastions. She has walls and bulwarks so that she is doubly secured. There is one castle called <u>Omnipotence</u> out of which such great guns are fired that every thing is carried before them. In this castle you may see Moses' Rod, [Samson]'s bone, Jael's nail, Shamgar's oxgoad, David's sling, etc., all which did miracles on the behalf of the city.

<u>Omniscience</u> is another strong tower. <u>Immutability</u> again is a mighty bulwark, but perhaps the most beautiful castle is the one called <u>Love</u>. Divine love, infinite and eternal. Truth too bids defiance to the lies of hell. On each castle waves the bloodstained banner with the city arms, the Cross.

<u>It has only one Gate</u>. The outer city has but one gate, sometimes called the gate of tears. It has two pillars called faith and repentance. This Gate is narrow and no burden either of sin or our works can by any means come in thereat. **It has two parts.** The Lower City and the Upper City. There is a narrow river which divides the two over which there is no bridge.

The Lower City is built of solid stone and has good foundations, but it is not built of such polished stones as the upper city, which is of pure white marble. This outer city sometimes has aliens in it who have no right to be there. [They have] come over the wall. The inhabitants are holy but not perfectly so. They are subject to some grief and pain. Sometimes they disagree and persons living in one street find fault with those in another, but upon the whole it is very, very much better in order and happiness than any city upon earth beside, though it is surpassed by the Upper city. All the true sons of this lower city, when they cross the river, are welcome to **the Upper City**, which indeed passeth my power to describe. Its walls are of alabaster studded with precious stones. By reason of the vast quantity of gold in it, it sparkleth like the sun. Mortal eye cannot behold it, its inhabitants are never sick. They are without spot or blemish. God is there. Music sometimes is heard across the river. This city has four gates, and into it every hour there comes a great crowd. Abel was the first to enter it, and since then myriads have crossed the flood and entered its gates. We are none of us yet in the Upper City. Let us search and see if we have come in by the gate into the Lower One.

II. CITIZENSHIP IMPLIES ADMISSION TO THE FREEDOM OF THE CITY.

Some are born free of certain cities but none are by birth freemen of this, for we are all by nature heirs of wrath. When the freedom of a city is given, there are rites to be performed—such as passing through a brook at Alnwick etc. The Secret Benefit Societies have their initiation and there is a secret initiation into this city which none but the freeman knows: white stone a token of old.

All I can tell you is that he has to go through the narrow gate I mentioned. But that passage through the gate of tears is terrible beyond degree, but it is the only way. You may come over the wall but it will not avail. After going through the gate there is a fountain in which the candidate is to be plunged; the fountain is filled with blood drawn from Immanuel's veins, and it is wondrous to behold how white and how beautiful [the candidates] appear when they come from the washing. Then follows the robing, when our nakedness is put away and a glorious wedding garment makes us like princes. This is the toga of heaven.

Now my hearers, the all-important question is have you been thus initiated, have I passed through this indispensable preparative for true citizenship[?] There is too a public recognition of this initiation to be made to the world by immersion in water, in imitation of the death, burial, and resurrection of Jesus. [Thus] it is the [bound] duty of all Christian men to execute in testimony of their love to the Redeemer. Once truly free of this city, it lasts for ever, and nothing more will be required for entrance into the Upper City save the passage of the river Jordan.

You my friends who have this day been baptized. Be careful that the secret initiation be right lest you be counted but as intruding aliens and not as true[-] born citizens.

III. CITIZENSHIP IMPLIES PECULIAR PRIVILEGES.

In ancient Rome a citizen might not be beaten before conviction; he had the right of appeal to Caesar, a share in the distribution of spoils, a vote etc., etc. So now corporate bodies have their charters. We will [for] a moment or two look at Zion's Charter.

1. The first article in it is Rom. VIII. 1 and 33.34. Freedom from condemnation. Is not this a precious grant to Zion's citizens[?]

2. The second article you may read in I Cor. II. 7 to end. That is the Illumination of the Spirit, the indwelling of the Holy Ghost. All believers enjoy this. This is the earnest of the inheritance.

3. The third is near the text, it is the communion of the saints. See 14th verse.

4. The fourth is the verse immediately before my text. It is access to God at all times by his son Jesus Christ. In prayer we may enter within the veil.

5. The fifth is perpetual safety, for this the great King of the place has promised and is able to ~~perform~~ afford.

6. Acceptance at last in the day when he shall make up his jewels, which is the crown of all.

A short summary of privileges is contained in these words: Justification, Access to the throne, Communion with Saints, Illumination, Adoption, Providence, Adoption.

IV. CITIZENSHIP IMPLIES PECULIAR DUTY.

1. Service in war on behalf of our good city, earnestly contending for the faith.
2. Obedience to the governor, the Prince Immanuel who is our sovereign liege Lord.
   Baptism
   Lord's Supper
   Good Works
3. Love to all the saints and doing all we can to serve them.
4. Desire and labour after the souls of others that more citizens may be admitted to our Zion. This we must practise much.

Now we are about to sit down at a New Jerusalem table, spread in common for all believers: let us come as citizens and may God grant unto us to rejoice in the dignity conferred upon us. Would that some of you would also come, for yet there is room and none are excluded who come by the gate.

Help me oh Lord.

638

Sermon No. 344

"THE MIDNIGHT CRY"

Editor's Summary

In the nineteenth century, infant mortality was as high as 25 percent and life expectancy as low as forty-two years. When Charles was converted, he began looking for ways to serve the church, and right away he encountered the reality of death. One of his earliest ministries was visiting the sick. He recounted one of those visits, how "those creaking stairs trembled beneath my weight, . . . that bottomless chair afforded me uneasy rest, and . . . the heat and effluvia of that sick room drove my companion away." *Autobiography* 1:181. On another occasion, Charles visited a youth from his Sunday school class who lay dying. "I saw him, and talked to him, and tried to point him to the Savior, and heard at last the death-rattle in his throat; and as I went downstairs, I thought everybody a fool for doing anything except preparing to die." *Autobiography* 1:184. Perhaps it was this experience that led young Charles to give a Sunday school address on death, "the dreadful sword hanging by a single hair above the head of the ungodly," on June 2, 1850. *Autobiography* 1:141.

This ministry to the dying and bereaved would continue during his pastorate at Waterbeach. The *Lost Sermons* record at least two funeral messages: "Consider Your Ways" (*LS* 5, Sermon 261) and "Fear Not I Am with Thee" (*LS* 6, Sermon 302). They reveal a pastor who walked with his flock through the valley of the shadow of death and who understood his responsibility to prepare his congregation for death.

This sermon on Matt 25:6 (a text he would not preach again) was preached for that reason. After one of his visits to a deathbed, Charles remarked how much he was affected by the reality of death, and yet how easily its realities were forgotten; "in an hour or so, all things took their usual shape, and I began to think that I was not dying after all, and I could go away and be as unconcerned as before." *Autobiography* 1:184.

Knowing the human propensity to live in denial, Charles sought to ready his people by awakening them to the reality of death.

This topic would be a recurring theme in his ministry, and Charles would often seize opportunities for this reminder. On one occasion in 1878, a member of his church was overcome by fits during a prayer meeting. The congregation was disturbed by the man's cries as he was carried out of the building for treatment. Charles, however, sought to restore order to the meeting by reflecting on what had taken place: "When we are engaged in prayer, or in any other form of worship, interruptions may occur, especially in large assemblies. We cannot expect all nature to be hushed because we are bowing the knee. . . . Rather let us learn a lesson from a painful incident." Having opened his extemporaneous address by reminding his people of the gift of health and the need to care for the sick around them, he concluded the prayer meeting with this solemn exhortation:

> This interruption speaks to us with a still deeper and more solemn tone. Our friend is not dead, but might readily enough have been so. That cry says to me — "Prepare to meet thy God." We are liable to death at any moment and ought always to be ready for it: I mean not only ready because we are washed in the blood of the Lamb, but because we have set our house in order and are prepared to depart. . . . Could we now, dear friends, at this moment resign our breath, and without further preparation enter upon the eternal world? *ST* August 1878:403–4.

THE MIDNIGHT CRY

Matthew 25:6

"At midnight there was a cry made, Behold, the bridegroom cometh; go ye out to meet him."

The coming of the bridegroom may be understood in two senses: the second coming of Christ in Judgment, or his coming in death to every creature under heaven. As to the first, the coming of the Son of Man in the clouds of heaven will be in power and great glory. It will be usher'd in with divers portents, death-struggles as it were of dying earth. All nature will ring with the cry of his coming, and with a shout shall he descend. With the blast of trumpet and terrible thunder the dead and the living shall stand before him. All shall see him whom they have pierced. Hark the shout, "Behold he cometh."

But I shall in this discourse apply it wholly to death coming to us as individuals.

There is an hour coming when each of us, whatever our present character, shall hear this summons. "He cometh." Moreover, when it is heard there is no alternative save obedience. Go we must. The strong man must bow, and the mighty man must be humbled. Wisdom and knowledge, grandeur, riches, benevolence and religion avail us not. There is no discharge in this war. Since then this is inevitable, let us bid the present uncertainties farewell and gaze on future realities. Whether you listen to me or no, whether you retire to laugh or to pray, this is a fact which you may disregard but cannot escape, viz. that the hour is coming when the cry of my text will be heard at your door and be spoken not to your child or parent, but to you, and surely it will not take one thorn out of your death pillow to remember that you heard tonight to scoff and retired to forget.

I. WE SHALL MEDITATE ON THIS SUMMONS WITH RESPECT TO THE ENTIRE RACE.

1. It is intensely solemn. At midnight the cry was heard. Now midnight is a solemn time. When the moon and her attendant stars walks through the silent sky and all is hushed, how solemn all seems. On sea, on the mountain top, in the forest, in your own room, and even in the empty street, there is a something solemn. We wonder not that the ignorant believe that the sheeted dead do at midnight visit this, our earth, for indeed it is a solemn hour. The villain fears to lie on his bed by night alone. Many a hardened wretch trembles in lonely midnight. "By night the atheist half believes a God." We do not wonder that many good men have chosen the shades of midnight as their oratory. This example, sanctified by our Master, was one which David sometimes indulged in, "at midnight will I arise." Whit[e]field used to retire to an aged tree in an avenue at Oxford and there commune with God. And we do not know but perhaps Nicodemus did the same. Night then is a solemn hour. I add my testimony.

At midnight then the cry is heard to show us the solemnity of death. Death is intensely solemn, more so than night. Revelry may disturb the silence of night, but surely death is too awful thus to be generally broken in upon. True, there are some brute minds who contemn death—the soldier furious in battle, the hardened pirate, or the suicide—but to men in the mass, death is a solemn thing. There are probably none here who will dissent from this. Death is solemn. Be it the death of a Wellington, a Napoleon, or of a pauper, death is a solemn thing to witness, corpses are cold things which cool the blood of gaiety. And if solemn to witness how much more to endure.

Flesh tread softly 'tis the couch of an immortal, no noise is there save the sob of the almost widow and the sigh of the well nigh orphan. The watch alone prates on, the lapse of time. A cold clammy sweat is on his brow, they wipe it off, they put the pillow that he may be more erect and now comes the death-struggle. All alone he must grapple the tyrant; the pulse fails, a groan and yet another. The eye is glassy, the hand is motionless, the heart beats not, the breath is gone. He is dead. Do you turn away? Look here once more. Is it not solemn work to die[?]

Be it the deathbed of a sinner, or a saint of Israel, or of Esau, of Samuel or of Nabal, of David or of Herod, of John or of Demas 'tis at all times and to all a solemn thing to die. The hour is solemn. We hear of no mirth or jest from the virgins then. No, there is then but one wish, "Let me die the death of the righteous." Oh ye young, ye gay, ye proud, ye must die and find it solemn work to do so.

Prepare to meet thy God.

2. <u>It is generally unexpected.</u> Even when disease has been cutting the root, the tree falls unexpectedly. The pale cheek of consumption wears a hectic flush promising health. Ah, cruel mockery. Death nips the promise. Like some cliff worn at the base by a foaming torrent, we wonder that it has not fallen, yet wonder when it does.

   Now this parable of the midnight cry sets out this idea—they were alsleep and suddenly they are startled by the piercing cry, "He comes. He comes." Who would have thought it[?] Death often gives no rap but bursts the door. You say, "Why is not notice given that you may prepare in time?" We reply, "It is given, prepare now." "But why are we not seriously informed of the day and the hour?" Why because you would be worse than now. You would trifle till the last hour. But now uncertainty is your monitor, it bids you <u>now</u> prepare. Few like Hezekiah know the length of their days. Do not wish to know but flee at once. And if there be one consumptive young woman or one young man whose frame is weak, I say beware. **He cometh.**

3. <u>It usually sets men preparing.</u> All the virgins arose and trimmed their lamps. The foolish as well as the wise. But ah, too late for one. The true Xn will have nothing to do but to commit his soul to God and fall asleep, but others have far more to do. The convict wished to prepare when the day of execution is coming. The sinner at sea begins to pray and you yourselves when sick have done the same, but in almost every instance too late.

   You mention the instance of the thief [on the cross] but I remind you of his companion. The pains and dying strifes of that hour are enough to fill one's hands without the trouble of fruitless prayers or agonizing groans. <u>Prepare now for he comes.</u> To all it is solemn and unexpected and puts them upon Preparation.

II. WE SHALL REFLECT ON THIS SUMMONS WITH RESPECT TO THE WICKED.

Its effect on their mind may be expressed in one word, **Terror**. ~~It~~ If the inhabitants of Pompeii were aroused at midnight and warned that streams of lava were rushing down from Vesuvius what would [their] consternation be, especially if in the solemn hour of night[?] When we are aroused by fire or startled by the thief we feel terror, and thus will the wicked when they wake as from a dream. "In hell he lift[s] up his eyes."

When an ungodly man does but dream of hell, his mind is terribly excited like the man Bunyan describes. Dreams do make his blood chill within him. What then must the reality be[?] Go to the bedside of Voltaire, D'Alembert, or Payne, or to some you know of. Some indeed die like brutes as to their carelessness but hell wakes them. Soon thou too shalt quiver oh despiser. Beware lest the fiat has gone forth. Ghosts of sins, demons of imagination, all the dark sayings of ministers and threatenings of Scripture will haunt your bedside and terror shall indeed seize hold upon you.

56 Hymn. II Book. Watts.
2 Hymn. II Book. Watts.

III. WE WILL NOW MEDITATE ON THE SUMMONS AS IT REGARDS THE RIGHTEOUS.

1. It may come when they are sleepy. A Christian is never wholly unprepared to die, but he may be in an undesirable state for a Christian. If I might choose, I would die in a pulpit. Who would wish to die angry[?] A Christian man may be very worldly just before death, his lamp may want trimming. Let us take heed that we be found watching. If asked to attend the theatre, the ball, or the tavern let us ask ourselves how we should like to die there.

"Such is that awful that tremendous day,
Its coming who can tell, for as a thief
Unheard, unseen it steals through night's dark shades,
Perhaps as here I sit,
And rudely carol these incondite lays,
Soon may the hand be stretch'd and dumb the mouth

That lisps the faltering strain, Oh may it ne'er
Intrude upon an ill-spent hour, but find
Me wrapt in meditation high hymning,
My Great Creator, etc." by Dr. Glynn.

2. It will be joyful. It is the bridegroom not the judge. The friend not the avenger. Sometimes the joy develops itself in a calm repose like David, "although my house," or Jacob, or Moses, or Stephen. At other times it is extacy, "singing aloud." But at all times the midnight cry is acceptable and the dying bed of a saint resembles much the Ode of Pope, "<u>Vital spark of etc</u>." Your question now is "am I a wise or a foolish virgin[?]" Be decided.

The Lord bless me and you
Amen

644. 646.

"THE BELOVED"

Editor's Summary

Drawing from a text he would not preach from again, Charles offered up this sermon to reach hearts more than minds.

The Song of Solomon, as Charles read it, was a love song that can be comprehended by the "Beloved," those who love God. Therefore, Charles understood the text as being about Christ. Christ approaches believers swiftly like the gazelle, a Redeemer coming over the hills to deliver us. Yet he is also, like the gazelle, concealed behind a wall, which Charles interprets as the wall of sin that must be removed. Finally, though concealed, Christ looks on his beloved as "the fond lover," to see what we are doing and what we need. Charles concludes the sermon by pointing to faith in Christ as that which manifests him to the believer.

While not the most exacting exegesis and interpretation of Charles's preaching ministry, this sermon does point to biblical truth and reminders of the ways that sin can hinder the believer's walk with Christ. As Spurgeon would later remark:

Have we not told you ten thousand times over that whosoever will may take the water of life freely? If there be any barrier it is not with God, it is not with Christ, it is with your own sinful heart. You are welcome to the Savior now, and if you trust him now he is yours for ever. *MTP* 17:534.

THE BELOVED
Song of Solomon 2:9

"My beloved is like a roe or a young hart: behold, he standeth behind our wall,
he looketh forth at the windows, shewing himself through the lattice."

The Bible contains a revelation intended not so much to inform the head
as to touch the heart. The remembrance of this will keep us from many
misapprehensions with regard to it. The Book in which our text stands is put into
its due position by this suggestion. A letter meant to excite love or to express it
would be worded very differently from one only intended to convey information.
This book is a love song and none can understand it but those who are in love with
"<u>my Beloved</u>," "<u>the altogether lovely</u>."

I. <u>CHRIST'S APPROACH TO US</u>. *"like a roe"*

1. When he came to be <u>Redeemer</u>, he was at an immense distance from us, by
    dignity, by nature. But he came swiftly, o'erleaping hills, and became like us.

2. When he came as <u>Pardoner</u> in our own personal experience, we sighed and
    groaned but he came in haste and delivered us.

3. When he comes as <u>Our Relief</u>.in trial, in deep affliction, to support and
    deliver, he comes with all the speed love can give. Ah, how slowly do we move
    towards him, how sluggish. Mountains affright us, and oh what mountains
    we sometimes heap up of sin, but he comes over them. Has he approached to
    you of late, or do you mourn his absence[?]Perhaps he <u>is</u> nigh only. He is not
    seen. Which leads us to

II. CHRIST'S CONCEALMENT FROM US. *"he standeth"*

Of course this is the world of concealment when compared with the next. One wall or another is the hiding place of deity. Once it was the veil, then Jesus' humanity; now [that] these are rent there is a wall still. <u>Our wall</u>, says the text, because we built it by our sins, our unbelief, our forgetfulness. Ah, it may be it is some idol which is a wall, and it must be pulled down. He hideth behind <u>our</u> wall.

III. CHRIST'S OBSERVATION OF US. *"he looketh etc."*

When we cannot see him he can see us. He looketh out of love and concern for our souls.

1. He looketh to see how our graces flourish.
2. He looketh to see what is our need.
3. He looketh to see when to [remove] ⎫ trouble.
          or lay on ⎭
4. He looketh to see what we are doing for him.

Surely he often feels

    1. <u>Grief</u> at our deficiencies and wanderings.
    2. <u>Astonishment</u> at our repeated follies,
and seldom 3. <u>Joy</u> at our progress and growth.

Yet with all our faults he looks again and again as the fond lover on his beloved.

IV. CHRIST'S MANIFESTATION TO US. *"he showeth etc."*

Sometimes faith sees him as the Saviour of its spirit. "<u>Behold</u>" as if to express rapture.

1. Dimly, through the lattice.
2. Instrumentally, by the use of means.
3. Personally, he showeth not his works or words but himself.

    Oh may [he] be seen and beloved by us all.

649.

"THE CONSOLATION OF ISRAEL"

Editor's Summary

Charles preached on this text once more, "Simeon" (*MTP* 11, Sermon 659), and also treated it as a part of two other sermons: "Simeon's Swan Song" (*MTP* 39, Sermon 2293) and "Christ Seen as God's Salvation" (*MTP* 55, Sermon 3177).

In this one, Charles presents a wonderful biography of Simeon the priest, followed by doctrinal application. Though what is known of Simeon is brief, he was someone Charles held in high esteem for his faith in waiting for the Messiah.

Charles discusses what it meant for Simeon to wait. Simeon waited while many rejected Jesus. Now all of creation waits just as Simeon did. His wait represents the Christian's yearning for the second coming of Christ and the "advent of the Consolation of Israel."

Reflecting on that description of the Messiah, Charles explains that only Jesus could bring such consolation both then and now. For those suffering in persecution, Jesus is consolation. For those bearing up under the ordinary troubles of life, Jesus is their consolation too. Such comfort comes through the gospel, which contains consoling doctrines and consoling promises.

The doctrines of election and justification by faith bring solace to the believer unlike any others. They are "wells of honeyed water for mourners." Similarly, the promises of perseverance, peace, and joy bring consolation "sweet to the needy soul." Even more, the Holy Spirit brings Christ, our final consolation.

As Charles would preach:

The grand truth of the union of the saints with Christ, if it be once understood, what a means of peace it is! He that believeth in Christ is one with him, a member of his body, of his flesh, and of his bones, one with Christ by eternal and indissoluble union, even as the Father is one with the Son. If this be known, together with the doctrine of the covenant, the attribute of immutability, the eternal purpose, and the marriage union between Christ and his elect, deep peace must be enjoyed, like the calm of heaven, like the bliss of immortality. *MTP* 23:156.

THE CONSOLATION
OF ISRAEL

Luke 2:25

"Behold, there was a man in Jerusalem, whose name was Simeon; and the same man was just and devout, waiting for the consolation of Israel: and the Holy Ghost was upon him."

Some men leave a large biography behind them containing deeds good and evil. Others leave only blots and blemishes, and a few only those things which are lovely and excellent. As specimens of the three classes, take Johnson, [Blank], and of the last Simeon. Short as is his history known to us, yet how completely though briefly is his character depicted. <u>A just man</u>, a compendium of all the virtues due to our fellows. As a merchant honest, as a master fair, as a ruler upright, as a servant faithful, as a citizen unblemished in character. A just man would keep all the 6 commands of the second table. But he was <u>a devout man</u> too, one who served God as well as Caesar. Justice is the external, the body of virtue—devotion is the internal, the soul of it. He was not a Pharisee in outwardly observing what inwardly he loathed. He was devout, not formal. He fasted and went to the temple, but not to be seen of men. He was really devout.

And being devout he did what every pious Jew was then doing: he waited for the coming of the Messiah. He knew that the seventy weeks were fulfilled.

I.   <u>THE EXPECTATION</u>. *"Waiting etc."*

Simeon was an old man and perhaps had already passed the natural boundary of mortal life, God having revealed to him that until Messiah came he should not die. The old man, fully prepared, was ever in the holy posture of a waiting servant. Not waiting for decay but for that sight which through the windows of his creaking tabernacle he hoped to see. This posture of expectation was

143

common to all the saints of the Old Testament. From the day when Eve hailed the birth of Cain as that of <u>the man</u>, the Lord; all through that long, long avenue of years till the angel-song to the shepherds, saints looked for him. That Hebrew who offered his son said, "God will provide a Lamb." He who had once a stone for his pillow looked with his dying eyes to the coming of Shiloh. The mighty law-giver, the greatest man under the Israelite theocracy, believed in the advent of a prophet like to himself. He who well earned the name of Israel's sweet Psalmist talked in songs of "My Lord." He who spoke more of Christ than other prophets saw him with no clouded gaze. But time would fail me to trace the unbroken line of expecting worthies whose epitaph Paul has written in terse language, "these all died in faith."

The Messiah at last appears, and what was once a virtue becomes a sin. The Jewish race reject him and still remain in the posture of their forefathers, "<u>waiting</u>." Ah how vain. "<u>Lo here and lo there</u>" they listened to. Barcochab and a hundred other pretenders sprung up and deceived them. They are scattered over the face of all the earth, yet unwearied by disappointment they still await the coming of him who is to restore the Kingdom to Israel. Oh Poor wanderer, here he is, wait no longer.

There is however a sense in which we may still wait for the advent of the Consolation of Israel. We may expect his second coming. We may earnestly long and wait for his love-visits, and sinners may in earnest prayer yet wait his approach in mercy. The whole creation is now in the same posture as Simeon, waiting for the moment of deliverance from sin and final restoration to its pristine loveliness and order. Let us too as servants be waiting for our Lord. Let us not sleep as do others.

II. <u>THE FULLFILMENT</u>. *"the consolation of Israel"*

Simeon expected to see a Messiah, <u>he did so</u>; but [moreover] expected one worthy of the glorious title here mentioned, and we are sure that in this too he was not disappointed. The Messiah has been the "Consolation" of his people. Let men dispute the truth of our religion, there is one fact they dare not deny, viz, that our religion does give consolation.

See the sons of God in <u>Persecution</u> from Abel till now. Observe how calmly they meet death. A small remnant hidden perhaps in caves as in Jezebel's days have still held fast the truth. See Daniel and the three Holy Children. Observe Stephen and all the apostles. Paul in prison etc., and come down to our times and the same thing is fact. Men die calmly under tortures too horrid to be mentioned. They have a consolation overcoming pain and agony. See them in the <u>ordinary troubles</u> of life. Losses, crosses, bereavement or sickness, how resigned, how peaceful if compared with the ungodly. Facts are needless as illustrations, for every Christian household presents a specimen. Every day confirms the fact that religion brings consolation.

Turn aside to the Believer's <u>deathbed</u> if you wish to see a great sight. Here is the best of enthusiasm, here vapours cool, solids only remain. By the side of such men as Halyburton, or Janeway, or Knox, or Payson, we learn that there is consolation in Israel. <u>Halyburton</u> as a sign of his joy, when speechless, lifted up his hands and clapped them. <u>Janeway</u> cried, "Oh that I could now express the thousandth part of the sweetness which I now find in Christ! You little think what a Christ is worth upon a deathbed. Oh the glory, the unspeakable glory I now behold. My heart is full, my heart is full . . . . You would not have the heart to detain me could you see what I see." <u>Knox</u> said, "the day is now come, which I have so often and intensely longed for, in which I shall be dissolved and be with Christ." And <u>Payson's</u> death was too seraphic for description.

Truly there is consolation for Israel.

III. <u>THE EXPLANATION.</u>

The fact that Israel is consoled is undoubted. Now comes the enquiry, <u>how is it</u>? This we propose to explain as God enables us. The Gospel contains and affords:

<u>Consolatory doctrines</u>. So far as the gospel description of man is concerned it certainly cannot comfort much. It represents him as ruined and helpless. But take the doctrines in which Christ appears and then you gain floods of consolation. <u>Election</u> droppeth honey if we feel that we are elect of God. Then what care we for distress, persecution or trouble[?] <u>The doctrine of the covenant</u> made on our behalf by the Trinity ensuring the safety of the elect. <u>Justification by Faith</u>, that [keystone] of all gospel truth, is so needful for consolation that one is apt to doubt if there can be any [were] this not believed. . . . All those doctrines which concern the nature and attributes of

God, all those that deal with either the manhood or Godhead of our Redeemer, and all which declare the might of the Spirit are wells of honeyed water for mourners. Now what are gospel doctrines but Christ portrayed on paper, his heart made legible[?] Here in <u>doctrines</u> is a vein of consolation.

<u>Consolatory Promises</u> are scattered all over the sacred page thick as stars in the firmament. Those which promise <u>Final Perseverance</u> are choice grapes of Eschol. Where can comfort be if this be untrue[?] Some promise <u>Peace</u>, <u>Joy</u>, Comfort, Support, and each in his season becomes sweet to the needy soul. There is one star of the first magnitude, viz. the Promise of Heaven which is consolation refined. Distilled Comfort. Essential oil of consolation. Next to this is a promise now beginning to be fulfilled, namely that of the second coming of Christ and the universal spread of his kingdom. The toiling labourer sows in hope that soon will be realized.

But neither of these console us without the <u>consolatory influences of the Holy Spirit</u> which render the doctrine and the promise all they are intended to be. What a calm it spreads over us which we cannot trace to any manifest agency. Like the wind seen only in its effects. It is only to those who are under the power of the great Spirit who really enter with delight into the hidden places of consolation hidden in our Lord Jesus Christ.

Christian why hang thy head, why wear the weeds of woe[?] Cheer up brother, he is <u>thy</u> consolation. Worldling, consolation is what thy wealth cannot buy, nor thy rioting afford. Trade then in this article with him who alone can give it thee, My Master, the Consolation of Israel.

Help, Oh Father.
Through thy Son

652

"DISTRACTIONS IN WORSHIP"

Editor's Summary

Charles preached on this text twice more during his career: "Abram and the Ravenous Birds" (*MTP* 7, Sermon 420) and "Driving Away the Vultures from the Sacrifice" (*MTP* 33, Sermon 1993). In this message, he endeavored to show that even in passages of Scripture that appear unremarkable at first, there is opportunity for instruction.

For this text, Charles upholds Abraham's devotion to God in the mundane activities of life and points to him as someone Christians should imitate. The patriarch remained faithful even though alone, and sincere even though he had every reason to falter. He maintained a simple devotion without pomp and followed God's directions for the sacrifice.

Charles also notes how Abraham responded when his worship of God was interrupted. Birds of prey came along unwanted, which Charles uses to draw comparisons to the Christian's battle with distracting thoughts, pride, the fear of man, envy, and unbelief. These "birds" of interruption swiftly come, but like Abraham, the believer must respond.

Again presenting Abraham's conduct as an example to follow, Charles shows how this forefather of the faith observed the birds, assessed the danger they brought, and then acted to drive them away from his presence, finally persevering. The Christian must respond in kind to any interruption in their worship and devotion to God.

Charles would one day remind fellow believers, "There will also come the long sieges of temptation, and many a man has fallen by little and little; but if the law of his God is in his heart, he will be proof against even them." *MTP* 52:416.

DISTRACTIONS IN WORSHIP
Genesis 15:11

"When the fowls came down upon the carcases, Abram drove them away."

It has been well said by Mrs. H. B. Stowe that the Bible is a book which gains rather than loses by slow spelling. It certainly gains by careful inspection, while many other books become less bright when under scrutiny. Sometimes in the chapter of history there is some gem we little thought of finding.

Let us make another remark, that Scripture gives us such real history that the naturalness of it strikes at [once]. There is none of the unlikelihood of romance about it; one feels surprised at its homeliness, yet let us remember that these little touches of real life are not meant alone to strike us with the vivid feeling of reality, but they have also another purpose to serve—they are for our instruction. Let us see by the mighty one's help, if we cannot in this short episode find some profitable thoughts.

I. ABRAHAM'S ENGAGEMENTS.

He was not in business, but retired to do homage to his God. Only one thing was his object and that one thing devotion.

1. It was <u>singular</u> devotion, for we do not know that in all the earth there was another engaged in the same way. Idolaters there were in crowds, but only one worshipper of Jehovah. How hard to follow Christ all alone yet we must do so, as he did. Melchizedek and Lot.

2. It was <u>earnest</u> devotion. There was nothing to tempt him to hypocrisy, for he was a solitary worshipper. He showed his heartiness by ready compliance

with the command. Well will it be, if we are all found sincere to-day in God's house offering heart service.

3. It was <u>simple</u> devotion. No groined arches roofed this temple. No stained windows cast a coloured light along a marble aisle. No rubric or liturgy. No genuflexions, robes, forms, pomp or splendor. The green sod, the twinkling stars, the rustic altar, the simple prayer, a man and God. Away, Away with the foolish trash pride brings.

4. It was <u>Scriptural</u> devotion; as there was nothing added of man's device, so there was nothing omitted of God's ordaining. As a sacr[i]fice was necessary for a sinner to come to God with, he brought one, and as God had ordained what that sacr[i]fice should be, he accepted the same with joy, not seeking any other. So let us never dare come without an offering and let us remember one is appointed, even the sacr[i]fice of the agonies and death of Jesus of Nazareth.

5. It was <u>necessary</u> devotion. Some things are optional, as eating or fasting etc., but true devotion is absolutely necessary. The embodiment of it may be optional but the spirit is absolutely requisite and a man cannot be a Christian without it. The most eminent need it, and they who use it most will be most eminent. Let us imitate Abraham.

II. ABRAHAM'S INTERRUPTIONS

Even in his solemn worship he was disturbed. Certain Carnivorous Birds fell upon the carcass as their prey. Now this was altogether an unavoidable interruption. He did not bring the birds there and therefore it was not his fault. Let us when interrupted always enquire if they are of this kind.

1. <u>Distracting thoughts</u>. These will come when least required. If much in business or in anxiety then in they creep, and if we are at leisure then they like gaudy flies come vainly in and out of our hearts. If these be allowed true devotion is gone.

2. <u>Pride</u>. Pride of dress sometimes operates, pride of rank comes in, love of form and pompous ritual. Love of learning and polish in the minister. Too good an opinion of ourselves and slight thoughts of sin. Pride spoils the service of either minister, deacon, S. S. Teacher, or private Member. It spoilt the Pharisee...... Pride of Science spoils the devotion of many wise ones.

3. <u>Fear of Man</u>. This is a sad rioter on our devotion, sometimes indeed swallowing all. If we pray or preach under this influence, farewell to any sort of devotion.

4. <u>Envy</u>. When you envy one minister because he is more popular than your own, you spoil your service. If you envy brother <u>So and So</u> his gift in prayer, or the office he holds, or his superior wealth, then farewell anything approaching to true devotion.

5. <u>Unbelief and Lukewarmness</u>. A pair of greedy lazy vultures are a sad annoyance. Languor in prayer, want of fervour and intense earnestness combined with small reliance on the promise cut the traces of piety. Surely Brethren some of these birds torment you or I am much mistaken. Birds they are and swiftly come.

III. ABRAHAM'S CONDUCT.

Let us regard his conduct that we may as far as possible imitate him.

1. <u>He observed the birds</u>. Some men never reflect as to whether they are devout or not. They are there. There's the sacr[i]fice, and whether birds eat it or no they care not. Like the door they turn in and out and that is all. The first step to reform is to see the evil. You see Abram looking at one moment at the sacrif[i]ce and then at the birds.

2. <u>He disliked their presence</u>. He did not say, "Well it is so but I like it to be so." No, "away birds from me, I do not want you." Some know they sleep but are not sorry for it. They are aware it is wrong to be at the altar and have the heart away but they do not lay it to heart.

3. <u>He did his best to prevent their coming</u>. Some say they are sorry but do not try to alter. Make it a matter of prayer. Put up [a spontaneous] petition. Weep over it. Shout at the birds. Throw texts at them. Drive them away.

4. <u>He persevered in it</u>. Again and again they returned but just as often there was Abram. All day long in the frosty night and then in the burning sun, even until evening, he continued at his holy employment. Let us do so too.

Lord help.

<u>Amen</u>.

653

Sermon No. 348

"CONCEALMENT THE GLORY OF GOD"

Editor's Summary

Charles preached on this text one other time, "God's Glory in Hiding Sin" (*MTP* 49, Sermon 2838), more than two decades later, in 1877.

In the sermon here, he explores the doctrine of God and the mysteries both past and present that are not easily discerned by finite humanity. While some people think much has been "solved" about the universe, Charles notes that the wise realize that much more remains hidden. No matter how far humanity progresses, there are limits to what can be known and understood.

While he does not expound much in this manuscript about the mystery of the Trinity, he would later say:

> The mysterious doctrine of the Trinity, and the equally mysterious and sublime doctrine of eternal generation are best let alone by feeble minds. I do not think there are half-a-dozen men alive who ought to meddle with the last. . . . The Sonship of our Lord is a great and marvellous mystery, to be meekly and reverently received, but never to be disputed about, except by those gigantic minds which belong to the past rather than the present. We might like to see two Titanic Puritans enter the field of controversy—two such men, for instance, as Dr. John Owen and Charnock—one might travel a thousand miles to see them grapple one of these lofty subjects; but when the little men of these days meddle with them, it saddens the humble-minded, and affords enlightenment to none. *MTP* 9:234.

151

In discussing the present, Charles acknowledges that God clearly still conceals much from human understanding. Even more so with regard to the future. Very little has been revealed about what is to come.

Later on, he would elaborate with these words:

> If you knew the future, it might make you idle, but it ought to make you diligent; if you knew the future, it might make you vain, but it should make you humble; if you knew the future, it might make you despondent, but it should make you trust. At any rate, knowing nothing at all about it, obey the voice of the Holy Ghost, who saith, "Commit thy way unto the Lord: trust also in him and he shall bring it to pass: and he shall bring forth thy righteousness as the light, and thy judgment as the noon-day." *MTP* 25:128.

However, Charles saw benefit in what is concealed, explaining that for God to withhold knowledge humbles us, spares us from misery, and keeps us from wasting time pondering that which we are not meant to know—all of which prompted a spirit of thankfulness in Charles's heart.

CONCEALMENT THE GLORY OF GOD

Proverbs 25:2

"It is the glory of God to conceal a thing: but the honour of a king is to search out a matter."

How infinitely is man inferior to his [M]aker. Though his Maker's masterpiece on earth, yet how far beneath his Maker is he. If we consider his moral attributes, or those of power, self-existence, eternity etc., we feel that there is an infinite difference. In Knowledge also this may be noted. He is omniscient, we are ignorant.

I.   CONCEALMENT . . . WHAT IS CONCEALED?

The ignorant man thinks every thing plain, the wise man sees concealment every where. Upon the very <u>face of nature</u> is written the word concealment. We scarce know really the reason of anything. The names we give to the laws and powers of nature are but covers for our ignorance. True, we every day advance in knowledge, but when most advanced we are but in the elements of earth's philosophy.

There are paths man cannot tread, caverns he cannot enter, heights he cannot climb, and depths unfathomable. There is not one of us but what has about us something we cannot understand—the mariner sees the needle tremble to the pole he knoweth not how, the astronomer beholds a fiery meteor cleave the skies [and] he wonders whence it came, the farmer sees blight and mildew devour his corn and disease seize on a most precious root, [yet] he is ignorant of the cause. The day has its mysteries, its winds, its storms and hurricanes, and night the hour of wonder astonishes us with its Northern lights, its comets, and other wondrous sights. Lift your eyes on high, turn them around or beneath; we are in a cloud, and as Job said we know nothing.

153

Coming out of nature's darkness into the light of gospel <u>revelation</u>, here too, much is concealed. Thanks be to God, nothing essential to our happiness is hidden but much that would gratify our curiosity. Even revelation is very much an obvelation.

<u>Of the past</u>. How much is concealed of the past. The existence and preexistence of three Persons in the Trinity is told us. We read of the bringing forth of the Son and the procession of the Spirit, but how we know not; it is a mystery our minds cannot grasp. The decrees of God as to Salvation and Rejection though abundantly revealed, and heartily to be believed, but much about them is dark. Why God made all his creatures fallible? How sin came first? Why some are chosen more than others? How decrees consist with free agency? How the decree of an evil thing is consistent with God's holiness and a thousand more questions, the proper answer to all of which is, "It is the glory of God to conceal a thing." Coming down from the creation, how many things in history we should like to ask. All the sciences would beg for information but here again we find, "It is the glory of God to conceal a thing."

Then following on to the era of our Lord, we want to know what is emphatically <u>the</u> mystery, God manifest in the flesh! Was he in heaven and on earth at once, then how could he combine deity and humanity[?] Where was he when the tomb contained his body? Where were the souls of those whom he restored to life? How was it that men were possessed of devils? [And] a crowd of questions the answer to which is the text and that alone. But not only is the past concealed.

<u>The present</u> is clouded too. We are in a fog, and the space immediately around appears to be light but is it so? No. Is not the present position of the world a puzzle[?] Is not Providence a depth? Are not the wheels high? If you are an unconverted man, how dark all is to you. This is your own fault, but even if a Christian, how little do you know of yourself. You do not know how it is the Spirit operates upon you. You do not know how it is you are preserved. Your contending natures, the reason of your troubles, etc., all these make you wonder and you can only say "It is the glory of God to conceal a thing."

<u>The Future</u>. This is the great unknown. The present and past men will pretend to know but here [their] strained eyes refuse to give them Knowledge. Every step of it is a black impenetrable cloud. Scarce is the next hour known to us. The astrologer, the soothsayer, and wizard are as blind as others. Revelation

tells us a little, and but a little. It tells us there is a judgment, but when, no man knoweth. A heaven, but what it is or where, tongue cannot say. Death is the bourne [from] whence no traveler returns. The reign of Christ, millennial glories, heaven's employment, hell's torments, and all Futurity lies under a v[e]il most thick. We will not long to see, for it is the glory of God to conceal a thing! But it is also for our profit.

II. CONCEALMENT, ITS BENEFITS.

We may be sure it is for our profit. God does not do it merely as a man for mystery sake, but he has a design. None of his acts are hidden because they are evil as man's are, nor because he fears man would thwart his purposes. But he has some profit designed by it.

Let us remark that certainly more knowledge of concealed things would not benefit us. What would be the good of our knowing how the Holy Spirit operates, or how he proceeded from the Father and the Son, etc., etc., etc [?] [But] more knowledge gives not more humility. But more than this we propound the proposition that this concealment is good for us.

1. The laborious discovery of hidden truth, and even the attempt to discover it, is useful to our faculties. It helps to develop our powers. Children must have harder lessons by degrees and learning these prepares them to grapple with greater difficulties.

2. This labour has another effect, it tends to humble us. If we had nothing to learn we should be more arrogant than now.

   We should scorn to be second even to the Most High. Lord, I thank thee for necessary ignorance, though I repent of that which is unnecessary.

3. Much now done would be left undone if the future were known. The son who would die early would be uneducated, the house unbuilt, the mission left, the colony unfilled, the rich man about to sink unserved, the dying untended; we should be all self and all else undone.

4. Much misery would be caused by a knowledge of the future. We should be all Jeremiahs. If our lot was to be good, our present pleasures would be untasted. We should be sighing for the future good. If unhappy, then we should not enjoy the present through dread of the future. Either way misery

is before us. But now hope gilds all. The lamb licks the butcher's hand. We live with "sufficient for the day is the evil thereof."

5. Heaven is sweeter in prospect through our little knowledge here. My knowing in part makes me long to know even as I am know[n]. There all knots shalls be untied, difficulties unravelled, doubts resolved, truth made manifest, and now:

III. CONCEALMENT, THE REFLECTIONS IT SUGGESTS.

1. How foolish to forestall troubles by anticipating them. They are concealed, let them be. God will manage them.
2. How foolish of us to be proud of our knowledge when we know so little.
3. How unwise to spend our time on subjects purposely made obscure.
4. How thankful we should be that all we need know, we may know.

Here is a lesson fof comfort, humility, wisdom, and thankfulness.

Open mine eyes Oh Lord.

660.

"CHRIST THE REVELATION OF GOD"

Editor's Summary

Charles did not preach specifically on this text again but did address it as a part of these messages: "The Believer's Present Rest" (*MTP* 55, Sermon 3169); "Christ Made Sin" (*MTP* 56, Sermon 3203); "'Our Light Affliction'" (*MTP* 57, Sermon 3244); and "Why the Gospel Is Hidden" (*MTP* 58, Sermon 3288).

Charles begins here with a reflection on a question that is common to humanity: Who is God? Societies throughout history have attempted to answer this, but the truth is, humanity remains blind and cannot answer the question unless God reveals himself. As Charles notes, God is not obligated to do so; nevertheless, because God desired to save those he has chosen, he *has* revealed himself.

He does so first through general revelation, though he is not seen to the degree that the sinner will find rest. The law of the Old Testament reveals God in part, but not the full mystery of his mercy and plan to redeem. Only in Christ is God made known to the degree that the sinner can see him. In Christ, humanity catches sight of God himself: God's wisdom, God's holiness, God's justice, God's truth, and God's love.

Spurgeon would later proclaim:

There is an infinite majesty about every line of Scripture, but especially about that part of Scripture in which the Lord reveals himself and his glorious plan of saving grace, in the person of his dear Son Jesus Christ. The cross of Christ hath a great claim upon you. Hear what Jesus preaches from the tree. He says, "Incline your ear, and come unto me: hear, and your soul shall live." *MTP* 34:150.

CHRIST THE REVELATION OF GOD

2 Corinthians 4:16

*"For which cause we faint not; but though our outward man
perish, yet the inward man is renewed day by day."*

One of the most natural questions arising in the mind of man is "what is God?" We see him in his works as existing. "[W]hat and who is he?" The child asks it, and in our times we can give a proper reply, but in other times how different. The ancient heathen attempted to solve the question and various were the results of their blind search. God is great and glorious said some, therefore the sun is God. He is strong and powerful therefore the crocodile or the elephant must be God. He is terrible therefore the tiger, or lion, or other monster must be God. He is eternal then the snake, or ancient then he lives in an oak.

Some taking a higher range thought God to be a being like themselves, and as they knew well enough they could not themselves manage an universe, so they thought God could not—so they divided it and set [gods] over various provinces of nature. These gods their poets described as always disputing about dominion, fighting, lying, stealing, and the male and female gods ever unfaithful to the marriage vows. Some of them more debauched than men and in more bestial forms, and as the people are never better than their gods, so they were all sunken into sins not fit to be mentioned. Earth was Sodom on a large scale. Sodom degenerated. True, a few choice spirits rose a little above the common herd, but ah how soon they fell or were cut off by their neighbours, and what was the acmé these choice ones reached[?] Why this: that there was a God, but they knew no more. In one sentence the sum of their philosophy was on the Athenian altar, "to the unknown God."

158

The world by wisdom knew not God. God is not obliged to reveal himself, nor will he to gratify vain man's idle curiosity. But he has a nobler purpose, he has from all eternity determined to save an elect people. Now this cannot be done unless they are brought to know him. God therefore reveals himself.

<u>In creation</u> he is revealed, will that suffice[?] Can the mourner find any comfort here? If this will effect the purpose, then God will not make a superfluous revelation. It will not. Fly the wide world o'er, fly to yonder planets, and yet on. Here is no rest for the sole of the sinner's foot.

<u>In law</u> will this answer the purpose[?] Will Sinai avail? No, the law drops no honey from its lip. The wrath-denouncing trumpet gives its blast and mercy flees. Hope dies. Away sinner, away.

<u>In Christ</u> in the fulness of time God is revealed and gloriously revealed to the sinner. Let us turn aside and see the great sight:

1. Here is the <u>essential godhead</u>. Scripture very expressly declares Christ to be God. His reading men's thoughts, healing the sick, raising the dead, creating the food, stilling the sea, ruling demons etc., all declare him God.

2. Here is the <u>wisdom of God</u>. The devising of a plan of [life] from death, pardon through vengeance, grace through wrath, and a thousand other paradoxes. To remake man, to renew his nature, to restore him safely were works of wisdom shining in Christ. Believer bring thy difficulties to the wise one.

3. Here is the <u>Holiness of God</u>. A life without a spot or blemish, a heart free from corrupt desires or imaginings. Invulnerable by all the fiery darts of temptation, unturned from rectitude by any trial. Like the sun unswerving. Christian here is thy righteousness.

4. Here is the <u>Justice</u> of God. It had been seen before in the sacr[i]fice, in judgment in Satan's expulsion from heaven. It would have been seen in the final damnation of all. But Calvary lets it shine out with singular, unrivalled splendor. When Brutus put his sons to death a wondering world beheld his inflexible firmness. So here men and angels saw the Justice of God on Calvary.

5. Here was the <u>truth of God</u>. A god without truth would be no God. Our God is the "only true" God. He had promised a Saviour to Adam and the echo

of those words spoken in Eden quivered in the air for 4000 years, so that prophets and kings waited for its fulfilment. It came at last Christ, the truth of God proved and manifested to all. And now beloved, will you doubt your covenant God[?] Will he not fulfil the small promises[?]

6. Here was the <u>love of God</u>. This was indeed the preeminent glory of the Redeemer, that he reflected and embodied the love of God. He was not the cause of God's love but the channel of it. "Herein is love" as if he had hunted everywhere and now "eureka." Oh believer, surely the Holy one will give thee eyes to see this attribute shining like the sun in mid-heavens. Trust it.

Truly Christ is the impress of his father, like the wax and the seal.
Oh, Jesus give me to behold thee and to unfold thee. Look Sinner, Saint.

661

[This page is followed by two blank pages in Charles's notebook.]

Rom. XIV. 10   The General judgment.   323

There are two judgments passed on men the first takes
place when the soul leaves the body when it is judged
& its eternal state settled. upon evidence of the sins
the soul committed — but the judgment that
is now to occupy our attention is that which takes
place after the resurrection, when body & soul are
tried and condemned for their mutual crimes.

I. I will attempt to give a few reasons for believing
        that there will be a judgment. —
II. Offer a few remarks as to the judge.
III. Enquire who will be judged.
IV. Examine the rule of judgment.
V. Make some remarks as to time, place & due
        preparation for it.

I. Reasons for believing in a future judgment.
    1. Because all nations have in their religion some trace of it.
    2. Man's own conscience admits it.
    3. The justice of God requires it.
    4. Certain temporal judgments substantiate it
Part 5. Revelation is the great source of information
        with regard to it.
Enoch, Abraham, Job, Moses, Hannah, David & Solomon
    all affirm it while it is often the burden of
        New Testament gospels & epistles.

II. A few remarks as to the judge.
    1. It will be God. — though only the son will sit
openly.   Man could not remember, all the actions
&c of even one, much less so many. Man again
could not discern in some cases between the good
& evil. Man might be unjust — Man has

not the power necessary for a work so vast.
    2. It will be Christ.   That honour may be put
on him.   That he may delight his saints &
terrify his enemies.   That there may be a
visible judge - the God man will occupy the throne.
And that men may not complain of harshness.
    Eng.   The apostles, & saints - are said to judge the
world — in what sense.   They will sit by the side
of the judge & express their approbation.

III. Enquire who will be judged.
    Angels who have fallen & men both good & bad.
    1. Good men will be judged for their own satisfaction
                                                            for the world's convincing
                                                            for Jesus Glory
        They will be judged first. — for they rise first
                                                            for they are most honourable
Eng. will their sins be published to the world?
    If they are it will not confound them but extol free grace
    But we rather think that as they are all forgiven
they will not be mentioned any more for ever.
    2. Bad men — will be judged according to their works.
all of them however high & lofty as well as the mean & poor.
their acts, words, deeds will be read aloud.
Eng. will they be condemned for not accepting Christ!
    Yes. decidedly so, nothing but their own sin
prevented them from being saved
    what a vast number — yet none shall be omitted.
How will they all see the judge? Ah we know not.
    But that they all will see him we firmly
believe.   And quick & dead shall be there.

IV. <u>Examine the rule of judgment</u> —
1. Conscience itself will be able clearly to decide.
2. God's omniscience will clear all doubts
3. The Book of Providence will testify against them
4. The Law & word of God.
5. As to the saved the book of life

V. <u>Make some remarks as to time, place, & preparation</u> —
time. — at the last day, but when no one
Knows. — The day will probably last many
years. God took seven days to make a world
he will not condemn it hastily. —
place. — not in any valley for none is large enough,
But (I think) on the wide earth. Jesus like
the sun will shine on the world so that all
may see. at least on one side & it may be by some
peculiar power exercised on the atmosphere
he may be seen all over the earth at once.
preparation. — Let it be speedy for he may come
at any time. — Let it be real & in order that
it may be so let it be divine. Seek divine
aid. Christ's righteousness & atonement.
And may the Lord remember us.
in that day. Amen through Jesus.

596.

324.   1. Tim 22.   Partaking other men's sins.
Sin is a most loathesome & abominable thing.
It came into the world from hell & owes much
of its present power to the powers of the pit
We have all enough of it without getting
any more from others — the text therefore
startles us and we exclaim 'Can it be possible
that in addition to my own sins I may be a
partaker in the sins of others.
There are six ways I will mention whereby we
may be partakers in other men's sins.
1. Assistance.   in it
2. Approbation.   of it
3. Example.
4. Enticement.   to it
5. Command.   to do it.
6. Carelessness of our duties.

1. Assistance in it.
In all good actions he that assist is esteemed
worthy of a share of honour, so the abettor of
evil must partake in the sin.
In the case of Saul who took care of the clothes.
Solomon who built altars for his wives.

2. Approbation of it.

325.
Ps. 112. 7.   How to meet evil tidings.

Job. IX. 30. 31.   Plunging in the ditch.   326.

It is pleasing in the wilderness to find the track of men
and to see the footsteps of the flock revives our Spirits.
When we can sit in God's house & hear our own
experience related it is very pleasant. For this
reason perhaps older ministers are generally more
sweet in the discourses to God's people — but it is not
certain that they are more useful.   May it please
the holy Spirit to guide me, so that you may be
able to see the track & ascertain whether you see in it.

I.   The Gracious soul has a sense of sin.
II. It often seeks cleansing at the wrong place.
III. If it does so, God plunges it in the ditch.
IV. But at last he goes to the fountain.

I. The gracious soul has a sense of sin.
Every man is full of sin but only a few feel it
This arises . { from the very nature of the disease.
             { from a want of due consideration
             { from ignorance of the evil of sin.
But when the great Spirit comes he shows
man his sin by divers means,
        { by the ministry of the word & other means
        { by exciting serious thought.
        { by constant & energetic strivings
In some this endures for a long time in others short
Some by it are overwhelmed with distress,
others not so much so, but in all somewhat.
this is good. { for it makes man value mercy.
              { it makes him hate sin afterwards.
              { it thus ensures perseverance in holiness
              { it makes a man patient in trouble

II. It often seeks cleansing at the wrong place.
I do not know whether all do so but I did & I
know many of God's children have done so.
These attempts are { generally very earnest.
                   { often very arduous.
                   { sometimes persevering.
                   { sometimes deceptive

The reasons why they do so { pride unsubdued
                       are { ignorance of the truth
                           { the suggestions of Satan
It seems natural men should be anxious to heal
the disease which makes them smart, but how
foolish to apply an ointment which makes it worse.

III. If so God plunges it in the ditch.
He will not suffer his children thus to perish.
        1. God awakens conscience.
        2. He allows them to fall.
        3. Divine light increases
& by each of these the poor soul sinks deeper in
the mire until he abhors his own clothes.
   The natural tendency of this is to drive to despair.
and this is only prevented by secret influence
but within.   Experience alone can explain this
IV. But at last he goes to the fountain.
   Where he ought to have gone before & now he
goes -   trembling lest he be not received.
                humbly confessing his guilt.
                hoping alone in divine grace.
                joyfully embracing the cross.
                cheerfully bearing reproach.
God is honoured & man is saved. —

Ps. 148. 1   Praise ye the Lord.   327

Having once and again exhorted you to the most
excellent work of praising God – it may seem
unnecessary to mention it again. Yet it is
most probable that some of you have neglected
the duty & if you have not you will find
your soul still prepared to hear more on the
subject that you may rise to higher flights
and more animated strains.

These are two places where we can
praise God – In Heaven & on earth.

There are two great ways of ~~serving~~
praising God – By Song & by service.

I. On Earth we have two ways of serving
God. By Song & by service

By Song. Almost all great events have
been celebrated in song & poets have been
busy, using their utmost ability to sing
the same. The oldest book next to the
Bible sings of the ten years siege of Troy.
Virgil the almost equal of the mighty Homer
sang "Arms & the man." The Taking of Jerusalem
the discovery of India, battles, wars, births
& even the sinking of ships have founds
poets to celebrate them.

In early times the wily priests called in
music & poetry into their false worship.

Whether Jupiter or Baal, Bacchus or Molock,
Venus or Thammuz, Dagon or Neptune
hymns & paeans were chanted in their praise
making valleys & mountains ring with
Io Triumphe' or Evoe Bacchus, Evoe Bacchus

Nor has true religion offspring of heaven
who draws her life-blood from the crop, refused
to employ poetry in the worship of the
great Jehovah who says I am, & there is none else.

In our days the poet of the sanctuary puts
into our mouths his simple yet harmonious
strains sometimes we sing.

Behold the glories of the Lamb   or
what equal honours shall we bring –
or in lowlier notes we join our cheerful songs.
or solemnly grand sing Keep silence all created things –
our friends opposite the Wesleyans have the warm
& fervent strains of Wesley.

Hark the herald angels sing
Jesus lover of my soul
Oh for a heart to praise my God.
Then we have Doddridge. Jesus I love thy charming name
Grace tis a charming sound
Sometimes "all hail the power of Jesus name rises
loftily to a noble tune
Then the once African blasphemer converted in
the storm while standing at the helm by

a text his mother taught him sing sweetly

 How sweet the name of Jesus sounds
  Sweeter sound than music knows,
 When any turn from Lion's ways,

or his companion, amiable, tender, loving Cowper
sing

 There is a fountain fill'd with blood.
  God moves in a mysterious way,

Toplady strong in faith sing "A debtor to mercy alone.
  Jesus immutably the same
   Rock of ages.

But why enumerate when we all have a large
store of sacred poetry, dear to us even from childhood
treasured in our memories. If we go
back to the times of the second reformation
we find the Covenanters in Scotland & the
old conventiclers of England under such men
as Baxter Bunyan, Cameron, &c &c ever fond
of hymning God's praises.

In the first reformation Luther's hymns &
ballads did more than his massive tomes
& "Give to the winds thy fears" will be sung
where his other works were never seen

Look on yon Alpine steeps & but here & there
a cottage is seen but wait awhile & you shall
hear from her then unconquer'd sons the songs
of praise to the God of the truth. These shall
reach heaven while the Te Deum & chant
of the vales are an abomination to him.

In apostolic times the prison of Phillipi heard
the voice of Paul & silence mingled in praise
Peter advises us to sing & our Lord on some
occasions did the same himself. —
Mary & Elizabeth sing praises. —

Go to the age of the prophets & their whole
books are songs. In that day shall a new song.
  He every one that thirsteth

Retreat still further till the golden age
of psalmody Solomon & David especially
are full of it.
  Oh come let us sing unto the Lord
  Bless the Lord oh my soul
  Make a joyful noise &c

And who can forget the song of Deborah,
or Moses — who does not believe
that long e'er that time the sons of God
in their meetings at throne sung praises

Yea, I believe with Milton that in
Eden's garden sublimer songs were heard than
we fallen beings can think of
 ". These are thy glorious works"

Perhaps the 148th Psalm & this of Milton's
are the two most sublime pieces of
poetry in existence. Let us then
  sing unto the Lord

By _Service_, we may praise God as much as by song,
our common duties should be done in such
a spirit that they may become spiritual worship.

Then the temple worship of the Lord's house
on Sabbath and week-day.

Then acts of charity, liberality & holy
labour for souls. Say the tract-distributor,
SS teacher – minister – deacon.
above all the missionary risking all
for his master's honour & service.

In some way let us serve our God.
Let us be like the woman who broke
the alabaster box of precious ointment
loving much, since much is forgiven.

II. In Heaven the same two modes
of praising God are employed.

By _Song_. Archangels & their hosts praise him
now as they have ever done. We read that
these sons of God shouted for joy on Creation's
morning & they have ever done so, especially
when a prodigal returns, The saints now
mingle their notes & sing what angels
cannot sing the sufferings of Immanuel
for them. How sweet their voices, how
matchless their tunes, how glorious the noise

How magnificent the concert when all the
ransomed throng at once shall sing to
him who loved them & washed them in his blood.

By _Service_. Even in the garden Adam had
to till the ground, nor in heaven are
idlers found, they are employed. Some
are ministering spirits, some attendant
angels, some are studying the perfections
of Deity & other are framing music to his
praise. They have, doubtless, far more
to do with us than we wot of. God who
makes all his creatures work, work
together in harmony. & work for good,
will not leave his noblest creatures
unemployed.——

Let us then begin _song_ & _service_ below
that soon we may continue our
worship on high with a sweeter
song & nobler _service_.

600.

Rev. XIV. 5.   The faultless people   328

Last Sabbath we considered the general judgment
with all its grand & terrible accompaniments — we
will now muse awhile in sweet meditation
on the acquitted people, found faultless among
the wicked.   We only mentioned their trial
& suggested the question as to whether their
sins would be read aloud — we observed
that whether published or not — they would
be superlatively happy with either course.
     Here we have the result of their trial.
See Jude. 24. Eph. V. 27. Col. 1. 22. & a verse in
Sol. Song. "Thou art all fair &c — these are parallel places.
I.   Their state character. "without fault"
II. The persons.   "they"
III. The position. "before the throne"

I.   The Character "without fault"
     our character now is just the opposite, we are
full of faults and failings of one kind or other.
Tis a consummation devoutly to be wished,
to be set free from sin & fault.
1. As a body — one great church, they are free
from fault.   There are said to be three
great evils to be lamented in the church now.
     Schism. Covetousness & Indevotion.
I think that it is but too true that these
are our great blots — but thanks to the
cleansing stream these shall be washed away.

I think our great fault is want of love
want of love to our Brethren — which causes Schism
so that sects and parties are more cared for
than our common Christianity — which causes
members of the same church to be distant
& cool to one another, makes strife, quenches
the hallowed flame of piety — this is not
known in heaven. they love perfectly & with
regard to this are without spot.
want of love to souls is another sad fault
it makes us idle, lukewarm, covetous,
hardhearted — when it is removed we are
zealous, ardent, anxious — the faultless
congregation are full of love to souls.
when an heir of glory is begotten they, sing
aloud unto their God & doubtless view
with intense interest every work of Jesus for me
want of love to our God — this is I believe
the root of the two former wants — we
do not love Jesus in any degree proportionate
to his deserts. his love to us &c &c. nor does the
Father receive due gratitude for our election
justification & creation — nor is the Holy Ghost
praised aright for calling, quickening & sanctifying us.
     This is a foul blot which we ought to
wet with our tears — But in heaven it
is not known for these they love God.
with all their heart. They love his will,
his worship, his courts. his presence.

2. **As individuals** - they are faultless.

Free from the faults we can see in ourselves. With all the dimness of our moral vision - conscience still sees - yea it cannot avoid seeing sin in us.

There are the sins of youth, habits firmly rooted by practise for years, angry passions, irregular desires, pride, sloth, with a whole train of sins too numerous to mention all seemingly unconquerable. all heinous.

But we shall have none of these soon if in heaven — & the saints there are free from all those faults we see in ourselves.

Free from the faults men see in us — our enemies especially can see with the lynx eye - & have the unhappy power of multiplying & magnifying faults — We have all failings which are unknown to us & it seems natural to the best of men to err - but in heaven they are without fault even from their enemies.

Satan, the lost & hosts of hell cannot lay anything to their charge - they are fully absolved — & law cannot touch them.

Free from the faults God sees in us - His eyes behold our secret parts, they try the reins & the heart. Some things in nature men cannot see because, or have not seen

Because they are ignorant of their existence.

Because of their minuteness.

Because of their distance.

Because of their subtle nature

So in the matter of sin —

Some sins are sins of ignorance these we cannot see being unaware of their sinfulness

Some sins are in our opinion small though not really so these we see not.

Some sins do not seem to affect us, our age or our country but the evil is remote & therefore we often do not perceive it.

Some sins are like electricity, galvanism &c very subtle - & in fact are all sins but some escape us.

Now all these sins the great all-seeing eye discerns in us — but in them none whatever they are faultless.

Thrice happy character. —

II. **The persons** ..... "they".

These faultless persons - who are they? Are they anchorites, hermits, prophets. martyrs or who are they.

We will give a list.

There is Abel saved by his blood who cries not for vengeance. Noah not now intoxicated. Enoch walking still with God.

Abraham not now denying his wife. Jacob not crafty. Joseph who would not consent to sin.

Moses truly meek. Joshua, Caleb. Eli cleansed of his one great fault & Samuel. David once adulterer with Bathsheba & Solomon the uxorious monarch.

Jehoshaphat not assisting Ahab & Hezekiah free
from the vanity he once indulged. Manasseh
taken from the dungeon. Jonah now loving
the service of his master. Jeremiah, Malachi
& the blessed three, the sweet triumvirate
Peter, James & John — & Mary & Mary
Magdalene & Stephen & Lydia & Paul.
And the Fathers now truly seeing their father.
And Pascal — Luther, Calvin, Knox,
Baxter, Bunyan, Fuller & Williams
Carey & Knibb — But why enumerate
these are my friends — members of our
church — our mild sister Day.
    our young sister Burling
    our beloved sister Chas.les
    & the venerable Morris
These all had their faults, we could
see some of them but they have none now
All pardoned sinners will be faultless.
All justified sinners will be faultless.
All sanctified sinners will be faultless.

a pardoned man cannot be touched in earthly
courts by an officer of justice — but though
free from punishment, the stain is still
on his character — but whom God
pardons he pardons so that not even
the guilt remains. The sin itself
passes away —

A justified sinner wearing Jesus Christs own
garments is as spotless as the Saviour
himself — he wears the same righteousness
& shines therein — faith puts this on.
A sanctified sinner is more holy than
one who had never sinned for that would
be natures work - Sanctification is divine.
    Friends we must try & search out some
of these marks in ourselves & if we find
them we may confidently believe that
we shall be of the faultless congregation.
III. The position " before the throne"
Even before that throne they appear faultless.
Some men will be driven from the throne in
anger but not so the righteous.
we too often live at a distance from the throne
but there we shall ever dwell before it.
God sits on the throne, there we cannot be,
Jesus sits on the righthand & we must not
seek a James & John to sit there
Moses went behind the throne & saw the
train of Jehovah, his hinder garments.
we often lie like slaves beneath the throne
but there we shall dwell before the throne
Ever beholding him so far as the

spirit of man is capable of the vision.
Ever receiving his smile, his protection, his
overflowing love. This is heaven, this is
glory — when? when? shall I enjoy it.

To dwell before the throne, free from
fault --- this we should pray for,
pant after & live prepared for.

It my Father aid me for Jesus sake
603. 674   Amen

Is. XL. IX. 11.12. The promise now fulfilling. 329

Some promises are fulfilled, some wait their future
fulfilment, some are now fulfilling.

I. Difficulties overcome. As Napoleon & Hannibal
crofsed mountains so will our Leader. Many
mountains now oppose. Rome, Heathenism,
persecutions &c but these are removing now

II. The road laid open. As causeways &
railroads are exalted so will God make
a highway for his own purposes. The
gospel will be Known everywhere, this is fulfill.

III, Nations converted. All men shall bow
before him, even this is now hurrying on to
an accomplishment. See China, the land
of Sinim & hopeful signs in other lands

Let us watch, work & wait —
607.

330   Phil. II. 5. The mind of Christ.

This was addrefsed by Paul to the Christians
at Phillippi & indeed to all believers throughout
the world. Dear Brethren, as the
profefsed servants of the most high God many
solemn duties devolve upon us; it is no
light thing to be a King's son. Our
mode of profefsion by Immersion in the flood
is solemn, the renewal of our vow at the
table of the Lord is solemn, our destiny
our faith, our expectation all are
most solemn. Hear then ye little
band of God's elect. Your captain speaks
& says "Let your mind be as mine".

False religions cannot advise their
adherents to follow their leader.

Vile as Greece & Rome were — they would
have been far worse if the same mind
had been in all their citizens as was in
their gods — say Jupiter. Venus or Bacchus.

The Brahmin who shows the triple
godhead of Brahma, Vishnu, & Siva - with their
necks surrounded by human skulls,
their hands full of murderous weapons,

As a son. he entered this world, born of the
royal family of David, but of a branch of it
forgotten, poor and despised. A manger formed
the cradle of the King. — How many a
time the youthful Jesus waited on his Father,
& brought some little tokens of love to his mother.
we cannot tell but we have a specimen
fact beautifully illustrative of the tenor
of his life - the journey to Jerusalem &
his being subject to them up to 30 years
of age. In after life at first it never we
seem to imagine he slighted his mother
but the experiences are eastern & are not in
the least disrespectful - on the contrary
at the wedding. supper, & even on the cross
how kind & loving to the most blessed of women
Young disciples, ye older dis-ciples never
practise any disrespect & love to your parents.
As a master. though infinitely superior
to his servants they were as friends to him.
When he reproved how gently & yet if better
how firmly he performed the office.
However the mastership was merged in his teach-
As a teacher. How simple these his
teachings to the ignorant how patient
his endurance of the tardy progress of

mangled bodies around them; surely he dare
not advise the shedding to profess the mind
of such gods or purely earth would be drowned. Though
all his followers are not of his mind,
Mahomet. lustful & cruel - well is it
& should the Mormon imitate Joseph
Smith, he must be a liar, a seducer, a
bigamist. yea polygamist - some prophes
be set up for an example; some prophes
have been vile enough & the predecessor
is not a man much to be imitated.
But the christian minister can
address his hearers & with confidence say
Let the same mind be in you which was
in Christ Jesus ?

I. In the relationships we sustain.
II. In the services we perform.
III. In the sufferings we endure.

I. In the relationships we sustain.
Christ sustained many of the relationships
which though these were some which of
life. though he did not sustain - such as natural powers,
natural husband or wife & others. —
But very many he did sustain.

his dis-ciples, how irreproachable in his converse.
As a friend . How firm in his attachment even
to the cowards who fled from him in his agonies.
How sympathizing his bosom, how tender
his feelings, how uniform & constant .
He is now the friend that sticketh closer than
a Brother .. this too he is & kind indeed.
as a Father - spiritually, he is a model
Father in patience, love, care & mildness.
as a Husband - he loved the Church &
gave himself for it . Let husbands imitate him
as far as possible let us follow him in these.
as a Servant to his Father, he wore the
humble garb & performed the menial duties
of a servant & was obedient unto death .
as a Subject of the Roman empire he paid
the tribute money .
as a preacher . how faithful, how arduous
his labours, how fervent, how loving,
Even kings might reap advantage if they
would imitate him as a Prince , & senators
might learn of him who will be ruler
& Judge of all Mankind - but surely
we in our stations can find something
in Jesus to imitate . & by God's help
let us resolutely enter upon it .

II . In the services we perform .
By this I mean the services which we render
to God & his great cause, of religion
we must if truly Christians engage in some
holy & pious work and in its performance
we must imitate his spirit . Let us have.
1 . A humble mind . Some men boast of their
doings - this spoils them & they fail of their
reward - But Jesus sought not publicity.
"See thou tell no man" "he hid himself"
He despised no service . "washed the saints
feet", "talked with an adultress on the well"
made fishermen his companions, yielded
to an ignominious crucifixion .
Let us too be humble in our service.
2. A loving mind . His empire is love &
by love it was established. Some of us
have not love enough . we are too rough
but Jesus spoke in a loving tone to all, save
to hypo-critical Pharisees & then his anger
was holy love to sincerity & to their souls.
Majestic sweetness sat enthroned upon
his lofty brow & though more marred than
any man's yet still a light of love
played o'er it & revealed his kindness.

3. <u>An active mind</u>. for ever intent on his Father's business, from Dan to Beersheba he went about doing good. Many weary miles, many toilsome days, many arduous labours fell to the share of our captain.

Let us too be no longer sluggish, but awake our powers to run the heavenly race.

4. <u>A persevering mind</u>. not turned back by Satan's temptations, his bad reception at the hands of his fellow townsmen, the scoff, the jeer, slander, threat &c - but he held on resolutely. He was not as some who run well for a time and then leave the great road they pretended to love but, brave hearted one, he went on, on, on.

5. <u>A self-denying mind</u>. Some will obey as far as it is pleasant so to do. but the true son of heaven will not flinch at self denials. Jesus bore a cross from the manger to Calvary. His life was one of cross-bearing, but he despised the shame out of his great love for us.

Let us learn to deny ourselves.

6. <u>A devout mind</u> - this is absolutely necessary to render our labours useful & acceptable. Jesus was eminently devout. His public career was opened by a singularly protracted season of devotion. Cold mountains & chilly midnight saw him bend in fervent supplication. Often did he ejaculate petitions. In the garden & on the cross he prayed.

Surely this is far more necessary for us than for one so pure, one in nature a God let us then strive to be devout.

III. <u>In the sufferings we endure</u>.

Our life is a mixture of doing and bearing. To bear God's will is oftener more of a labour than to do his will. Jesus is an example to us here also.

He had, as we have, sufferings bodily & mental, springing from natural & religious causes. In enduring these he is a model. He had.

1. <u>A submissive mind</u>. He never tried to shun his Father's rod, nor even the sword which fell heavily on him as our Shepherd. How beautiful a picture is a submissive man or woman. How foolish is the opposite conduct.

2. <u>A patient mind</u>. He entered upon his sufferings submissively & bore them more than manfully - it was like a God.

331   Ezek. I. 15–21   Ezekiel's wheels.

On a past occasion we gave attention to the living creatures. It will be of service to us to refresh our memory with the account of them.

Four evidently living creatures appeared before the prophet. They were like a man, but superior as to the possession of four faces & four wings. Their solid feet were straight & so round that they were able to move in any direction without turning. They were glorious in brightness. Their hands under their wings, onward flight, four faces, rapid motion, upward wings & dependance on the Spirit have all a meaning worthy of a brief explanation.

We now turn our eyes to the wheels.

I. Providence compared to a wheel.

This comparison was admired among the classics for we are told of a certain king who, when led in triumph preserved a serene countenance & looking on the chariot wheel remarked that such was human life.

1. Providence often changes the positions of, sometimes they are exalted, at another time depressed. Let those on high remember that time may bring them down & let the depressed reflect that a time of exaltation may arise.

No murmur ever came from his lip & it is not said he shed tears for himself though he did for others

3. A forgiving mind. to his persecutors. Let me especially urge this upon those who have to endure scorn and reproach be not provoked but endure calmly, & ever return the fire of persecution by one of fervent love.

Thus have I tried to shew you Jesus the mirror of perfection. Do not look and go away to forget but labour to be followers of God as dear children.

May the good Spirit guide us in this way, this perfect way, this pure way. & thus by the blood of Jesus may we have power (privilege) to become the sons of God — Lord Bless us.

Amen. Amen

604. 609.

2. Yet Providence like a wheel has one point which does not move, which is the centre of the axle. God's love. This is the pivot on which all terrestrial things move, the great centre around which they revolve.

3. When we look at it, as a wheel revolving with inconceivable rapidity, we forget the spokes & see nothing but one mighty orb matchless in symmetry.

II. Providence connected with angelic agency.

Angels have more to do with providence than we imagine. In extraordinary cases they have been the agents, visibly, of its operations. but ordinarily they are also intimately connected with God's doings.

Upon good men they exercise an influence, they are our guardians, they sometimes doubtless suggest thoughts, they ascend & descend from us to God.

Upon bad men they may, perhaps, be the means of restraining their wrath, & turning their minds in the required direction. If it be not so, yet they follow the wheels beholding their wonders. & the same spirit of unswerving obedience is visible in both. God's decreed will is done on earth even as it is in heaven.

III. Providence universal.

The four faces looked towards the four quarters of the earth & thus shewed their universal agency. Just as the eyes of a picture seem to be turned upon us from whatever quarter we look at it, so does providence ever regard each of us.

If I am banished & wander on trackless oceans or roam in boundless deserts even there is providence. Mungo Park & the moss. All creatures come beneath its eye but above all it works for the elect's sake. There's not a sparrow or a worm but's found in his decrees. The whale which swallowed Jonah & the worm which smote the gourd were under the same all ruling power. Providence is by the cradle & the coffin, the bridal & the grave. The prison, the cottage, the lazar house, the palace. God is there. In battles, plagues, earthquakes, revolutions & all great convulsions there is as manifest an over ruling of God as in the calm, still, silent motion of the moon.

Rejoice then, beloved, the eye is upon thee, & never can'st thou be removed from its inspection.

IV. Providence uniform & constant.

It is said to be in one likeness & to be but one wheel, & true, though startling, is it that Providence is one. It seems to be entirely at variance with itself but it is not really so, it is one. The history of Joseph shows how apparently adverse events are still only parts of a grand organism for some one end. We shall see at last when the pieces of the puzzle are put together, when the wheels of the machinery are all put in their places, that all things are working together & that Providence is one, Sweet or bitter, storm or calm, wealth or poverty, all are from one hand, for one design, from the same motive, viz. love. There is consistency & uniformity. Providence is one.

V. Providence like the Sea.

The colour is beryl, sea green & sometimes blue. Now this is a pleasing figure somewhat like the wheel, but more sublime. 1. The sea is ever in motion. So by night or by day the great process of providence is going on, unobserved or regarded, it never stays its activity.

2. The sea has many changes. Storms & tempests, currents, waves, floods, ebbs & flows &c so has providence a variety of motions. 3. The sea obeys not man. It wetted the feet of Canute, it washed away the treasures of John, it broke the bridge of Xerxes. Navies may ride it but it tosses them like a feather on its bosom. The land is man's slave, but the sea is free. So providence owns not man's power, God disposes. Man cannot order his own steps. 4. Yet the sea is ruled by God. He bids it roar or bids its clamour cease. He makes it tides return at regular intervals & not a drop moves save as law commands it. 5. The sea is not to be measured or fathomed, it is too vast, too profound so is the wonderful providence of God. Such is providence an ocean.

VI. Providence is intricate

Wheel within a wheel. Gabriel asks not the reason why nor God the reason gives. Yet man stands & challenges one thing after another as if his Maker ought to do nothing without telling him the reason.

It appears intricate but it is not therefore faulty, but rather it is still wheel within a wheel. One wheel acting on & moving another, & all the wheels moving by mutual coercion.

We must not expect to know all it ever has been intricate. Yet sometimes we may see instances of providence. In every day. but when it is not so let us remember that Providence is usually intricate

VII. Providence is always correct.

Man's works often need alteration. God's never do. Man often has to turn aside to amend errors in practise, or to adopt a better plan. The Eternal on the contrary turns not but moves in one undeviating course. His Spirit is the Soul of all providence & therefore it is well directed.

VIII. Providence is amazing.

Who can look at it without wonder. The Andes, those snow-clad mountains cause a thrill of reverence & awe to pass o'er us but what is their sublimity to that of Providence. We may suppose an ant looking at the mountain

and we can scarce imagine how dreadful such a mass would appear. so these rings are so high that they are dreadful.

If we look at the extent, wonderful intricac, yet marvellous consistency. & consummate wisdom of providence, we must exclaim oh the heights and depths. Even the man who feels that it works for _his_ good must see that it is dreadful.

IX Providence is full of wisdom.

It is full of eyes; it is no blind fate or fortune, no inevitable necessity destitute of design but it is full of wisdom. The eyes regard all creatures that live & every conceivable circumstance of every one.

It does not allow one thing to injure another it sees all things aright & guides the sands of life so that their orbits do not interfere with each other

No man can detect an oversight, flaw or mistake; his ways are perfect, just and wise. God has an eye for me, for you.

Trust, believer, at all times
Admire, believer, thy God's wisdom.
Kiss the rod believer, his will be done.
Help oh great one.

610.

Ex. XX. 7. Taking God's name in vain. 332

There has been great mistake with regard to the law of God. On the one hand the Pharisee & legalist declare that the law of works is the way of salvation or at least a part of the way. This an exceedingly erroneous opinion but the contrary is even worse. When the Antinomian says that men are not bound to keep the law, some asylum should be found for a man so dangerous to society.

The legalist does not lead men plainly into sin but the Antinomian teaches immorality by wholesale & is as much to be avoided as an infidel. Some good men do not like to hear much of the law & even go the length of crying it down. How unlike Paul who said the law is holy & just & good but I am carnal sold under sin. I charitably hope that some Christians do not know what they are talking about when they talk of the Abrogation of the Law & call a man a legalist who urges its commands on mans conscience. For man to say with one breath I am a sinner, & in the next to say the law is not binding on him, is only to show his ridiculous folly.

For how can he sin if there is no law. Some again will even say that what is

sin in other men is no sin in them, & yet if brother Wesley comes in and talks about perfection — poor man — he is told he knows nothing aright, for sin is in everyman.

Ah! what absurdities some men believe. The true use of the law to believers is as a rule of life & at the risk of being called a legalist I will endeavour as God helpeth me to speak of your rule of life. But there is another use of the law which is to reveal sin to us. To make the rebel tremble & fly for mercy to the Most High. Oh that this purpose might be answered in some souls.

F. I will endeavour :
I. To explain the nature & extent of the prohibition
II. To shew its sinfulness.
III. To mark its penalty.

I. To explain the nature of the prohibition. It is exceeding broad like every other command of the great lawgiver & takes in a great variety of sins besides the act of using the name of God profanely. Indeed a man might never do this and yet might be guilty of a breach of this command. But clearly.

1. All perjury is forbidden by this command.
What can be much worse than to call God to witness the truth of a lie, yet some have dared to do it & God has most righteously resented the insult by some tremendous judgment. No crime should be more detested than this.

2. All use of God's name in an irreverent manner.
Some men put in God's name at the end of almost every sentence and even Christians are too apt to use his name too freely in common conversation as "God bless ye" quickly said & little thought of. Wilful profanity is often like perjury punished by awful judgments & is an immense crime

3. All use of profane language even when the name of God is not mentioned. Cursing & swearing are forbidden & those common words which some good men use very near approaching to the nature of an oath ought to be avoided. This too has been punished.

4. All idle & irreverent use of Scripture.
For instance quoting it in jokes & in relating anecdotes. Such as the one of Sydney Smith about "except these bonds" "is thy servant a dog". All railing at the word, treating it with contempt &c —

5. I may here condemn all songs of a loose indecent or profane character. Not however wishing to stop singing but song-singing. —

This is one reason why I dare not enter a theatre or dancing room because there is pretty certain to be some profanity. Who is there among us innocent of this sin. Let us all bow down & acknowledge it.

II. To shew its sinfulness.
It is, in my opinion, a mistake to say that all sins are alike in God's sight. I must, for conscience tells me so, I must think that some sins are more heinous than others. Though alike in nature yet not in degree.
Though none are small, so we may say there are no small elephants yet one elephant may be larger than another. Well I think this sin is one of the greatest of those forbidden in the decalogue.

1. It is a personal insult to God. Other sins do but touch his dominion but this is aimed at the king himself. It is high treason against his government. It shows that such a soul is hardened in sin & is the culminating point of impiety. To plead drunkenness as an excuse, is pleading one sin in excuse of another. Every thing a man does when drunk he ought to be punished double for, instead of less.
Profanity is high treason & open rebellion.

2. It is not attended with any honour, profit,
or pleasure and therefore temptation cannot
be pleaded as an excuse.
It was once honourable in society to swear but
that dissolute age is now feeling its full desert
in the place of torment; now it is esteemed
in most circles a low and vulgar thing
to swear & nothing tends much more to lower
a man's character than this profane habit.

It never was, nor ever can be profitable, as
Rowland Hill said "I will swear when I can
see the use of it" so might we say. For
some sins are apparently profitable but
blasphemy is foolish because unprofitable.

Surely it is not pleasurable. I should be
at a loss to tell where the pleasure of this
sin can be found. I even believe it to
be a source of pain, for surely at certain
seasons the blasphemer must feel terrified
at his own oaths & his imagination will
conjure up things of terror, the ghosts of
his profanity.—
3. It is a sin which the most stultified
conscience must condemn — the common
light of natural reason teaching us better.
The poor heathen were reverent to their
idol gods — & shall the enlightened child

of civilized Britain curse the great Jehovah.
It is a sin so heinous that it must have
been a heavy part of the load of punishment
borne by the Redeemer. O that men were
wise to embrace his atonement.
III. To mark its penalty.
1. There is a sentence pronounced upon
it unlike any other command.
2. It seems to hint that although no
sin will go unpunished — this one above
all others will be marked.
3. It seems to insinuate I think even
more immediate punishment than
is pronounced on other sins — because
some are apt to extenuate this because
it does not seem to injure our neighbour.

Now, dear friends, if guilty break it
off otherwise you cannot be guiltless,
seek mercy at the foot of the cross. —
And let those of us who are believers
remember that such we were until
sovereign grace reclaimed us.

Help me O My Master.

611.

I Cor. XI. 2. Keeping the ordinances.   333

Some good people seem to imagine that a man cannot be faithful unless he finds fault with everybody, but Paul here gives the Corinthians praise & doubtless every body of Christians has some traits deserving of commendation.

The Primitive Methodist is full of zeal.
The Wesleyan loves to invite sinners to Jesus.
The Churchman is reverent in Gods house.
&c &c. ——
The Baptist strives to keep the ordinances.

I. The Ordinances.
these are distinct from the doctrinal or practical or experimental part of religion they are so to speak the dress of our religion, the ceremonial part of it. there are.

The Ordinances of Gods House, public worship, the ministry, singing, public prayer.

The Ordinance of the Church — admission & excommunication, deacons, brotherhood &c

The ordinances of Christ — Baptism & the Lord's supper. I call them by this name, for they have a closer relation to Christ than the others. The first is the emblem of the agonies, burial & resurrection of the Saviour — The Second the memorial yet more evidently of his flesh & blood. His sacrafice and atonement.

Let us remark
How simple & free from pomp or show.
How sublimely beautiful
How profitable for our souls.

II. The Trustees.
Paul delivered the ordinances into the hands of the church & thus constituted it the guardian of the ordinance.   Not the government, not the lordly order of bishops, not the minister but each individual member is a trustee of the ordinances & bound to regard himself as such.   Away with apostolic succession, a good man is a successor of the apostles if like them he is diligent in good works & labours of love.

How gloriously have our ancestors kept this trust, in caves & mountains they concealed the treasure. In the fastnesses of Switzerland, in the dungeons of England.

Remember Anne Askews, the Baptist Martyrs—&c.—   Remember St Bartholomew Smithfield.— & remember too that you each of you as Christian men are now the successors of these men & the trustees of the ordinances delivered unto you.

May God give unto you their noble spirit

334. Ex. XIX. 4. The Three Mercies.

It was often the custom of the prophets to make appeals to Gods' people as to his faithfulness. Doubtless if each one were asked there would be an unanimous reply from the ten thousand thousand tongues. Not one good thing hath failed.

I. The Victory. "what I did to the Egyptians." Long & bitter was the contest, but the Lord conquered. We too have Egyptians. Sins, from which we have been now set free, yet they harass our march - but soon they shall die. Doubters, Election. Vocation. Perseverance &c Doubters these worry us but their doom is at hand.

II. The Carriage. "eagles wings. Eagle fabled to have only one young one. Strong wing, that can never fail to sustain us. Soft wing, carrying us beyond this world. Safe wing. none can harm if he bears. Loving wing, the eagle is tender & exposes its own body to save its young

III. The Home "brought you to myself." This is home indeed, all else is foreign land. We are brought home. By Conversion — Jesus becomes our salvation By recovery when we have backslidden By death & entrance into everlasting glory. Bless us Ol Hol one.

615.

III. The Charge.

"To keep them as delivered" Not to suffer any increase in number, no additional ceremonies to be fashioned. Not to allow an alteration in the persons receiving, or the mode of exercising. Let me remark.

1. That Popery is not Keeping the ordinances as they were delivered but contrariwise the murdering & mangling of them all.

2. Baptismal Regeneration & all its accompanying Puseyism is not thus Keeping them, it is a prostitution of them.

3. Infant Baptism is a violation of this rule for everywhere we find believers baptized & no where infants.

4. Sprinkling is not keeping the ordinance. it is not going into the water, it is not burial, it is a mere remnant of Popery.

5. Neglect of any ordinance by good men is not Keeping this rule. Oh, my dear friends, why do you delay to join the Church and obey in all things your Master's behests.

1. To the Candidates - well done that ye thus keep the ordinances, live worthy of them.

2. To Christians still holding back. Come now remember your charge & keep it firmly.

3. To worldlings. Behold these Christians & seek like them to be converted, like them afterwards to be baptized.

637.

Heb. XIII. 8. Jesus Christ the same &c. 335

It is said of Louis XIV that he once said "I had rather hear the repetitions of Bourdaloue than the novelties of another." Truly there are some things that have the charm to day & lose it to morrow & but a very few that are always charming. Jesus' name needs no novelty to recommend it to you, its mere repetition is delightful to the ear.

But to our text.

I. The Title. "Jesus Christ."

II. The Attribute. "the same"

III. The Duration. "yesterday, to day & forever".

I. The Title. "Jesus Christ."

This is not his only name, he has many others. Seed of the Woman, was the first one given to him. Angel, he is styled since he is the Messenger of the Covenant of Grace. Shiloh, was the name Jacob gave him, the peaceable one. the Saviour. Melchizedek too is his name & office. The Prophet-like unto Moses. in fidelity wisdom. justice & honour. The Redeemer, was Job's favourite mode of speaking of him. The Holy one he is called by David & Daniel

The Anointed. Hannah, David, & Daniel sang of Isaiah, the evangelical prophet. heaped title upon title & in sublime tones calls him the "wonderful, the counsellor," the Mighty God, the Lord our Righteousness, the Branch, Mighty to save, the Shepherd, the Breaker Zechariah calls him as Isaiah had done the stone, & Malachi closes by calling him the Sun of Righteousness.

* Solomon called him wisdom, John Baptist opens the new economy by behold the Lamb of God &c. John the Evangelist delights in the name "Word of God & wondrous are his titles in the apocalypse. Mary called him Rabboni, the young man "good Master", His foes called him Nazarene, Beelzebub but the name whereby he is most commonly known is

Jesus Christ.

Jesus — a name meaning Saviour just as Joshua led the people into the promised land so will our Joshua. This is the name given at the annunciation & again at his birth in the manger. The Shepherds heard the song "unto you

II. The Attribute. "the same"

Being "very God of very God", he is most certainly immutable. Let us remark.

In Nature. Office, in Doctrine.

In Nature. He is the same. He had the same Power & wisdom as ever. He is the same love to his people. The same feeling for them. He was yet apart from all eternity as our Salvation. He has now finished the work, but he still carries on the same scheme. He has not reversed from his purpose, or laid down the great labour he once undertook;

In Doctrine. What he once taught is truth now. There is no new Gospel. Nor is the old one altered. You may preach any other, let him be accursed. Some want a new Broadchurch to leaven every mouth but no the same we must he read still.

He is wholly the same in these points; there is not so much as the shadow of a turn in him.

He is "the same"

---

is born this day a Saviour which is Christ the Lord." This is the name the blind man called him by. & the sweet thought this name was nailed over his head at his Crucifixion. This name the angels used when they said "Ye seek Jesus" & again "this same Jesus who has gone up &c." — . Pause & dwell & found this name in thine ear again, let its full toned harmony enchant thee, faded. How sweet - the name of Jesus sounds surely this is the name I will call him by in heaven. 'tis the name the angelic hosts sing of.

Christ — this is a royal title, a Kingly & triumphal name. He is Christ to each of us. We have anointed him by faith with the oil of our love. Peter called him Christ many times. He was Christ here but he will be more so when the great coronation day come — He is Christ, let us pay for me to live is Christ, let us love him for even Christ Jesus. I would I loved thee more than I can love.

III. The Duration. Yesterday, today & forever.
    Let us take the three terms in 3 senses.
In the widest sense. it means.
    Yesterday, before time began in election & covenant
    Today, in time, in incarnation, redemption &c
    Forever, in eternity, in glory —— He is the same
In a more limited sense
    Yesterday to our forefather, Adam, Abraham
        Noah, David, the apostles &c —
    Today in our age & time
    For ever, to our descendants in future time
        He is & ever will be the same.
In the most limited sense
    Yesterday, in my past experience
    Today in my present-exigencies
    Tomorrow in future trials
        I shall ever find him the same.
Let us learn.
    1. To value this world at a little
        since it passeth away.
    2. To esteem Christ most highly
        since he is ever our friend —
            Lord Jesu help thine unworthy
                    one

617. 621.

337 I Tim. I.12. Full Assurance

This passage is a real gem. The words of
generals & princes have been much esteemed
& often repeated. Nelsons "England expects &c"
Wellington. "would to God night or Blucher were come"
Cæsars, veni, vidi, vici. Leonidas "come & take them"
&c. &c. But these are dim of lustre
& lack the rich setting in gold which this
verse has. A poor despised man trusting
in one yet more despised than himself
& boasting that he felt no doubt of his safety.

But now to the subject of full assurance
which it seems Paul enjoyed & John for
he said "We know that we &c"__ It has
been enjoyed in modern times & in all
times. See Toplady's Hymn 'a debtor &c_
& Watts, "When I can read my title clear",
Doubtless too some of us have had seasons
when we were full of faith giving glory to God..

I shall endeavour to speak of it

I. Showing its nature
II.   its advantages
III   the means of its attainment-

I Some remarks on the nature of assurance.
& here I must endeavour to move away
first of all some objections that are made to
it owing to wrong conceptions of it.

1. It will not lead to sloth. Some it is true
who boast of being assured are negligent of the
means but true assurance never leads a
man to this. False presumption does
but the truly assured man will be diligent.
  The security of the prize wings our feet
to win it.

2. It will not lead to pride. Presumption
makes men glory in their being elect &c but
true assurance so makes us lie flat on the
promise that we have a constraint put
upon us to give all glory to the Master.
Doubts are often very proud thing. When
we doubt our worthiness that is pride
in its very essence - for we ought never
to have but one worthiness in our eye
& that the righteousness of Christ.

3. It is not absolutely necessary for salvation
  It is nowhere said He that is assured shall be
saved but only He that believeth. assured
  As the old Puritans used to say 'faith is
necessary to the wellbeing of Christian life
but not to its being. A man may be
a child of God & yet have doubts. We must
not condemn those who are weak in faith.

4. It is not always the same
Some graces being absolutely necessary to
Christian existence never can be lost, but
assurance though a highly ornamental &
useful part of the Christian body, is not
a vital organ & may be diminished &
even totally removed, though with much
injury to the soul yet without its absolute
destruction.

5. It is nowhere condemned in God's word
but always commended.
There is no premium offered to unbelief
but the encouragement is to faith. Where
could we have looked for so long a
list of heroes in faith if assurance had
not been theirs. The more faith the
more glory to God.

II The advantages of assurance.

1 In duty. It serves to give us zeal, love
& courage. It is like the live coal on the
lip of Isaiah. In preaching, in prayer,
in any labour how it nerves us, how
it acts like generous wine invigorating
the whole frame.

2. In trial. Temporal afflictions become
only feathers when assurance is present

Bereavement & sickness are sweetened, Loss of property is little regarded – Persecution is borne joyfully, yea & the loss of all things only seems the loss of so much dross.

3. In temptation. The lion's howl is not a terror. Lust, corruption, evil desire & Satanic suggestions may all be put to flight by the simple word "I Know &c".

4. In death. It is the rod & staff guiding & supporting. It treads on the dragon's head, It giveth joyful victory & exalts our Jesus, Doubts being removed the cold flood does not affright.

III. The means of its attainment.

Every Christian has a right to it & every Christian may attain it it. It is not exclusively the privilege of advanced believers for even babes in grace have possessed it. Some earlier than others. Some have much to impede them in their endeavours to reach so blissful a consummation, but we repeat our belief that it is in the reach of all true Christians & ought not to be so rare a grace as it is at present.

1. Exercise of faith already possessed, for the use of the arm will strengthen it.

2. Strict obedience to all our Father's will, for any sin harboured will breed doubts.

3. Progress in grace. This shall we know if we follow on to know

4. Much meditation, study of the Bible and abundance of earnest prayer.

5. While our Father adds the gift of his Holy Spirit to render the word effectual.

How well would it be if all our Church enjoyed this so that we were all fully ready to fight the Lord's battles. But as some are weak let us foster the tender plant & never put one drop of water on those who show some symptoms of stronger faith than others

Oh Lord give it to me & to the hearers. Amen for J. C. sake

624.

Matt XXV. 41. The Sentence of the wicked. 338

We have had I trust several very profitable discourses on the great thing of futurity.
We looked at the coming Millenium, the conflagration of the Universe, the acquital of the righteous & their song of victory, we have now one more subject which it would be highly improper to omit & that is the damnation of the wicked.
Oh may God make the subject of much use for arousing the slumbering, dead Sinner.

I. I will mention the names given to the torment in Scripture.
II. I will mention wherein it consists.
III. Enquire as to degrees.
IV. Look at its duration.

I. The Names it is called by in Scripture.
Hell is the usual term & how dreadful when we read it is prepared for Satan.
Fire, this being the most excruciating instrument of torture & to be burnt being unbearable. hell is compared to such a fire. Sometimes Brimstone is put with it being one of the most combustible of all bodies & being highly offensive

whilst in fusion.
"Tophet" from a valley where children used to be Sacraficed to Moloch, afterwards the sewer & kennel of Jerusalem where bodies were left to rot.
A prison. where Spirits are confined strong, well secured, comfortless. no liberty, no happiness, no release
Darkness, outer darkness, without a single gleam of hope, or spark of glimmering day
The Bottomless pit, a chasm unfathomable an abyss from whose dreary mouth we may well shrink back appalled.
The Second death. Death is awful in its terrors, dreadful in its pains, terrible in its stern realities. Oh the Second death
It is the death of deaths.
The worm that never dies. To be eaten of worms, wormeaten, putrid, eaten alive, gnawed by reptiles, crawled over by aspics
Tearing in pieces is another terrible figure. Just as lions rend men in pieces. as the Elephant crushes or the wheel breaks the bones. So Sinner shalt thou be broken in the torments of hell.

II. Wherein the torment consists.

Of this of course we know but little. But it will certainly consist of punishment of loss, & punishment of sense.

punishment of ~~loss~~ — The loss of God, of Christ, of the society of angels, of the communion of saints, of the crown of life, of heaven, this is one very great item in the punishment of lost souls.

punishment of sense. Which will consist of two parts, viz, torment of body & agony of soul.

The body having shared in the sin must share in the penalty. If it be asked how flesh can endure fire without destruction we answer that the children in the furnace furnish an illustration.

The asbestos may be put into the fire but it cannot be destroyed & why not the new body of ~~sinners~~. Who knows but that there may be a kind of fire which will torment — but not destroy.

The body will be racked in all its members as they were the gates of sin so shall they be channels of retribution. Eyes, ears, hands, feet, nose,

The soul in all its faculties shall suck in damnation. Conscience, memory, judgment, desire, prospective powers &c.

Oh wretched state of dark despair.

III. Enquire as to degrees.

Scripture says but little as to degrees of glory or degrees of punishment, doubtless much is left to our judgment.

We must think that sinners will differ in hell even as saints in heaven.

Such great sinners as false prophets impostors or popes should have an exemplary punishment. T. Paine, Voltaire, Hume, Gibbon, Owen, & men of the Nero, Commodus & Bonner stamp with atrocious murderers will be made capable of more torment.

But every vessel will be full. All will have a full portion of burning wrath. There will be no cause to congratulate ourselves on the smallness of our pain if we ever come there. We shall have more than enough to do to bear our share. Oh may God avert such horrid doom from us all.

339 Luke XV. 10   Joy in heaven over penitents.
This exquisitely beautiful chapter is indeed
milk for babes & is full of rich comfort for
the broken in spirit. Here we see.
I. The value of a soul.
"one sinner" is the expression used, now we
rejoice over converted nations but forget
the value of a single soul. —
1. Precious because of its eternity
2. Precious because of its capability for happiness
3. Precious because of its capability of awful pain.
4. Precious from the harm one sinner may do.
5. Precious from the good one sinner may do.
"one sinner" — let us muse on the value.
II. The beauty of penitence.
angels rejoice not over palaces, victories &c
But repentance   Is God's work
It is the mark of great things
III. The sympathy of angels.
They rejoice — they therefore know — sympathize
they believe final perseverance. They
are our guards, we never need fear
ghosts or apparitions — they are often
ministers of comfort to the saints.
Oh how rightly they judge when they sing
over a new born soul   627. 628. 633 635

IV. As to its duration.
1. As the soul is immortal so will hell be eternal
2. Sin unatoned for will never be burned
out, but the debt will still remain
3. As there is no hope, so there can be no
end of it for then the end would cause hope
4. As heaven is eternal so must hell be.
Flee Sinner Flee. Behold the
Lamb who taketh away sin
Help. Help. Help

625

Luke VI. 22. 23. Rejoicing in Persecution   340.

In nature there is a wonderful supply of
means for the removal of inconveniences &
the cure of ills .   Is it cold? There is the fire.
Are we heated? There is the cooling brook,
Does the sun beat upon us? Yonder is the
spreading beech .   In trackless ocean the
compass marks my way ; in darkness the
flint affords the seed of flame , in storms
my house is scatheless by the means of the
wondrous rod ...   But there are some
diseases nature knows no cure for, some
exigencies in which we must be left
to grapple alone .   Who can withstand
the cholera, consumption, paralysis ,
or others of the mighties in the hosts of
death .   Nature has not a supply for all need.

But revelation has, Christianity most
surely has, a balm for every wound
a cure for every ill .   Here is one of
the peculiar ills of Christians & the
great remedy for it . Yea such a
remedy that it maketh the disease
very desirable & causes the blueness of
the wound to work our health .

I. Persecution the Christian's lot .
II. Joy at it his constant duty .
III. Future glory his great reward

I. Persecution the Christian's lot .
If a man asks me for a decided proof
of the doctrine of human depravity I
would turn my finger at once to that
dark spot in earth's history, — spot
did I say — rather that black cloud
     called Persecution .
It commenced as early as the great
division when one was accepted & the
unto the other there was no respect.
Abel's blood still cries from the ground
& since that first martyrdom the
enemy has never ceased to plague the
seed of the Lord & many a torrent of
blood has gushed .   See Noah, Lot
Jacob, Joseph, Moses, the Israelites, David,
Elijah, the prophets, Daniel, the three,
even until John's beheading . Then
comes our Master, his apostles, the
saints in pagan times , the Albigenses,
the Reformed Church , dissenters,

3. They *reproach* ed us. The faults we commit
have no mantle of love held over them; but
are magnified into crimes; and we be ever
so faultless we are not secure for slanderers every
[?]. We escape lies of truth fail her. All
[God's] even have been slandered. Heard
Jesus, Paul, Luther, Whitefield yea all with
[leader] the Lord Jesus and heard him mournfully.
This is a trial but oh what is it really
when compared with tortures others endure.

4. They cast out our name as evil. Their hatred
goes so far that the very name becomes a
thing loathsome & obnoxious. We are
tabooed — but our name is written on high,
& even on earth it may one day be famous.

Beyond this they cannot now go
with us, here the proud waves are stayed.

<u>II</u>. Joy under Persecution is the Christian duty
Some will say "Is this possible?" We reply
"most certainly it is." Otherwise our Saviour
would not have commanded it.
There, nature cannot of itself love slander
persecution &c but grace can do all
things. It is omnipotent. See how
strongly it is put "rejoice ye in that day
& leap for joy." Ancient Christians

and our own denomination).
Fox! book of Martyrs might well be
reprinted even until the present hour.
There is no sin which Jesus will be more
likely to punish speedily than that of
wilfully persecuting his neediest. Tormenting
his own spiritual body. It is a sin against
the common rights of man. It is now a sin
against our country. It is downright war
with heaven. — If proved by degrees.

1. They hated us. Some because our religion
hurts their craft; others because it thwarts
their desires & others because it is a protest
against their sin. Some too are of a domineering
spirit and hate us because our doctrines are
destructive of liberty and are the great levellers
of caste and pride. O sad that men should
hate God's servants, is it so with any of my
hearers or have you passed from death
unto life & therefore love the brethren.

2. They separated us from their company. As
soon as a man became a follower of Jesus
he was put out of the synagogue — but
Bartholomew's day. The Nonconforming Ministers
were expelled their pulpits & now how much
these is of it. The separating spirit. We are
called schismatics but those are the sinners
who cut us off & to make a schism.
Oh how glad will they be of our company one day.

used to rush in crowds to the judgment
seats and courted martyrdom as a glory.
When Leonidas the father of Origen was put
to death, Origen being only 17 desired to share the
honour with him but his mother not
wishing to loose both in one day hid
all his clothes, whereupon he wrote to his
father. "Take heed, turn not for our sake."
Laurence the deacon being, after other
tortures at last put on a gridiron with a
slow fire under it, when one side had
been roasted called out joyously to the emperor
"This side is broil'd sufficient to be food
"For all who wish it to be done & good."
& when he had been turned & roasted
similarly on the other side he said with
great serenity "I am roasted enough and only
want serving up" and so died,
And in our own land in more modern
times remember Rowland Taylor of Hadley
how cheerily he addressed his family when
he knew that the hour was hastening
and how he jokingly told the sheriff that
he had been deceived himself & had deceived
many in Hadleigh & when they rejoiced,
he explained that he had expected to have
been buried in Hadley churchyard but
now would be disappointed & the worms
would lose their expected past on his stout body.

Robert Glover of Coventry was for some time
after his condemnation in great darkness
feeling much the absence of God's presence
but as his martyrdom approached he
exclaimed 'he is come, he is come' & died
in extacy.
So then it is possible to rejoice in
the great waterfloods surely much more
in the smaller streams. When I have
been much ill spoken of I can witness
to the faithfulness of God that I have had
so much the more grace that I could really
"leap for joy" & have counted calumny
and scorn to be sweet music.
1. Rejoice because you are yourselves honoured.
To be a sufferer for Christ is a weight of
honour under the weight of which an
angel might stagger, oh to die for Jesus.
To wear the crown of martyrdom this is
bliss indeed. If we suffer any persecution
let us think ourselves much honoured
to be counted meet to follow in a
humble manner "the noble army of martyrs"
Men will give much for honour, here
is true honour before God & his holy
angels. We laugh at our foes for they
are lacing our coats for us when persecuting

2. Rejoice because <u>Christ is honoured</u>. If you endure well you will advance his cause. The devil is a fool still for he has not learned to leave off persecuting though 5800 years experience must have taught him his folly. How you will honour your master. We of all others ought to honour Christ by patient endurance for all our service is stained rather beautified with the blood of martyrs. Our very Bible yet blushes with the blood of Tyndale. Our ministry is descended from a murdered race. The deep waters of our holy Baptism are dyed with blood, our sweet Pilgrims Progress has the smell of Bedford goal upon it, our church-book tells of men who also suffered for righteousness sake. All this is honourable to the grace that sustains & overrules. Let us leap for joy at being able to furnish gems for our Redeemers crown.

Many have been converted by beholding the constancy of Xn sufferers — but one more reason for present joy remains which is.

<u>III. Future glory is the great reward.</u>

Though we merit no reward yet we shall have it of grace —— Martyrs & others who suffer for Christ will shine brightest among the stars in heaven. The veteran adorned with scars stands highest in the ranks. Ah little do our foes imagine that by their lies and calumnies they are wreathing fresh garlands of amarynth to bind our brows for ever. If similar characters shall find each other & make friendships in heaven how blest will it be to be companions with the soldiers of the cross who nobly dared to die wait but a moment & the reward cometh

1. Is there a persecutor here, a calumniator I forgive thee so far as I am personally concerned but I bid thee beware how thou touchest the apple of the eye of the Almighty

2. Is there one here not persecuted. Well I am not glad for thee. Search & see if thou art in the way everlasting. Ask thyself whether thou art right with God or no and th I beseech thee prepare for death.

3. To you who are persecuted. bear it patiently, yea joyfully, look at you starry crown; be sure of thine own religion & then come fair or come foul, come calm or come storm.

630.

Bless me Oh Father For Jesus sake.

<u>Amen</u>

Ps. CXIX. III   The testimonies our heritage.   341

It is a solemn thing to talk with God. It is a solemn thing to mention our feelings before the dread supreme. Happy the man man who can lay his hand upon his heart, bend his knee & lifting his eye to heaven say "Thy testimonies have I taken as an heritage for ever, for they are the rejoicing of my heart." — — — — —

I. The Heritage. — "Thy testimonies" —
II. The Appropriation "have I taken" —
III. The Lease — "for ever"
IV. The Joy - "for they are the rejoicing of my heart."

I. The Heritage.

A Christian has no property of his own accumulation. His labour is until grace renews him all unprofitable & when converted, still his best industry, he will confess, deserves not a farthing.

It is an heritage, not an earned property. The Bible to read for ourselves without note or comment. This a precious heirloom for it Wickliffe laboured & Tyndale burned our sires held it with iron grasp and resolutely resisted those who would rob

them and their children of the treasure. Good Adam Thompson cared not to lose his all so that the bible for tenpence might fulfil the promise of Tyndale that the boy with team and the plow should soon know scripture as well as the lordly prelates.   Let us esteem the word of God.

The Contents of the Bible which are vast indeed In this world the pardon of our sin, restoration to our lost position, love of Christ, the promises, adoption & the hope of final perseverance. In the next, deliverance from the dread anger of God, acquital at his bar, the enjoyment of heaven, the concert of the choirs of glory, eternal ecstasy of joy.

This is our heritage.
A heritage is certain, the result of our own efforts we may never see, but what was left before we were born we may be as sure of as earthly things can be. but in a more superlative sense the great things of our heritage are an entail.

They must come to every adopted child, no chancery can rob him of it no unrighteous heir can defraud us of the claim founded on the equity of God.

inheritance is rendered secure.

Now comes another self-examining
question have I taken these testimonies to be
my heritage. Can I honestly think to

1. How I shall sit loose by the world.
2. I shall feel a solid satisfaction.
3. I shall enjoy a quiet expectation.

& this your choice, I have you chosen the good part

III <u>The Sense</u>   "... for ever."

Some prophets leaved the owner after a
certain number of years, some fled away
just when it will; but ours is forever.

1. This is the wish of the Christian, he does
not want to turn back. He had rather
die than return to his old ways.
2. This is the promise of God. Signed with
the hearts blood of Jesus, the promise cannot
fail us, he abideth faithful & strong
consolation is one of his gifts to his own.

He made my soul ow this "for ever"!
the same Christ whose name is they made
now will be the same in you bright world,
in time, no age, no change, for ever!!
this is an enduring substance. Friend are you
willing to have Christ for ever — temporary
Christians are useless — we want enduring
inheritances if we are to be heirs of an enduring
habitation in eternity

a heritage is the result of another's labour, the
how received only what his predecessors have
earned; each shilling had their sweat on
it, done one toiled for it to do our heritage
cost our Saviour cries and groans.
a heritage supposed relationship. This is
— question of self enquiry for each of us's?
Am I related to the Father of Lights! @ So I
love him. Am I like him. How can I trust
him? Am I regenerate & adopted!
Well if I have not a foot of land — to
call my own, no one entitled to inherit, yet —
here is a broad heritage worthy of a King. An-
take it up even here.

II <u>The Appropriation</u> "have I taken of it
what is commonly called the taking of it
up. Now the Christian will not take up
his heritage until he calls the mansions
of the blest — but in one sense he does
take it up even here.

1. He eats the fruit. the grapes of Eshcol he is entitled
to enjoy now in the wilderness. If I can pluck
from the tree as much as I like them surely
it is mine. [?] peace & he are the assurance
2. He rejoices the Canaanite. He takes it by force
of arms, can't fresh victory gives him a
better little to the heritage as at last brings
him nearer the actual possession —
3. He holds the titledeed by which the actual

342. Eccl VII.14   In the day of Adversity consider.   7²

There is not a man who has not either by sickness in his own person, bereavement, or temporal distress had a day of adversity. As every day has some peculiar duty belonging to it so we find this day has the duty of Consideration. Consideration begins early in our Christian experience & is at all times very useful for our Spiritual growth.

I. Let us consider the Reason of a Christian's adversity
1. Correction. What son is there whom his Father chasteneth not.
2. Prevention. to keep us from some evil. Better than a cure
3. Probation. Trial. that God may be honoured.
4. Instruction. Trouble is a blessed School.
5. Usefulness. In comfort. warning. guiding others.

II. Let us consider the Relief a Christian may enjoy
1. His sorrows are not peculiar others endure the same
2. Not casual. providence sends them all
3. Not penal. not the Sword but only the rod.
4. not unalloyed. They might be worse.
5. you are not to bear them alone. Jesus is by you.
6. not to last always. But for a moment & then gone.

III. Let us consider our own Character
1. Am I now repining. this is wrong.
2. Am I now unconverted in adversity - it says consider
3. Am I broken in Spirit & longing to be saved, then

IV. Let us consider Christs Character.
He invites, he is sincere, he never spurns
I shall be welcome to his arms, he will never forsake. he will be with me all through life and with me in death.
Will you go with the man.
        Lord bless us

634. 636. 641

IV. The Joy.   "they are the rejoicing of my heart"

He who finds no joy in religion, has no religion
Religion is calculated to give joy, solid confidence, peace with 3rd Communion with the Spirit, whispers of mercy, smilings of divine love, & strong promises all combining make Religion happy
Religion is calculated to give glorious joy. Its joy is lasting. Its pleasures real, Its delights spiritual
They leave no sting, cause no remorse, never cloy on the appetite, forsake not in distress.

Have I found religion to be the rejoicing of my heart? Do I follow it because I love it? or because of custom, my fear, my situation in society &c? do I delight in the Bible

Friends here is Room for great searching of heart You may if right-bask in a sunshine of joy. Live much on & in your inheritance, bear with patience your troubles looking to the heritage you will soon enter.
        May thy blessing be upon me
                Oh my Father.

631

Eph. II. 19 Christian Citizenship   343

This morning we were privileged to see some of the followers of our Lord put on his name by holy Baptism — we hope in a little while, at the close of the service, to receive them into Church fellowship and sit down with them at the supper of the Lord. I have chosen a subject which I trust will be useful to them in showing them the dignity to which they are now admitted, to members in causing them to rejoice more & more, & to you ye unconverted ones in making your hearts long to come with us. We will not tarry long remembering what we were, truly, we were strangers & foreigners. Either open enemies to the church of God or else aliens living with them, mingling in their assemblies but not really of them, not enjoying the freedom of the city, but now we are fellow citizens of Zion.

I. Citizenship implies a City.

We too have a city, beautiful for situation the joy of the whole earth. Zion the beloved city of David. Salem the city of peace or Jerusalem the city of holy peace. New Jerusalem since it has a new covenant, has new regulations, is newly erected from a new pattern. It is not an earthly city

It is built on Mountains. Jerusalem stood in the midst of hills, so also doth our city. Some cities stand on such steep places that they are impregnable so is this. Kings and armies have assaulted it from the time of Pharoah to the present yet has it remained unscathed.

Mount Predestination. Mount Calvary, Mount Adoption, Mount Covenant. are some of the names of the mountains.

It has strong Bulwarks. Let us mark her towers and count her bastions. She has walls and bulwarks so that she is doubly secured. There is one castle called Omnipotence out of which such great guns are fired that every thing is carried before them. In this castle you may see Moses Rod, Sampsons bone, Jael's nail, Shamgar's oxgoad, David's sling &c all which did miracles on the behalf of the city. Omniscience is another strong tower Immutability again is a mighty bulwark but perhaps the most beautiful castle is the one called Love divine love, infinite & eternal Truth too bids defiance to the lies of hell. On each castle waves the blood stained banner with the city arms, the Cross. It has only one Gate. The outer city has but one gate, sometimes called the gate of tears. It has two pillars called faith & repentance. This Gate is narrow

This city has four gates and into it every hour there comes a great crowd. Abel was the first to enter it and since then myriads have crossed the flood & entered its gates.

We are none of us yet in the Upper City let us search & see if we have come in by the gate into the Lower One.

II. Citizenship implies admission to the freedom of the city.

Some are born free of certain cities but none are by birth freemen of this for we are all by nature heirs of wrath. When the freedom of a city is given there are rites to be performed — such as passing through a brook at Alnwick &c. The Secret Benefit Societies have their initiation and there is a secret initiation into this city which none [white stone a token of old] but the freeman knows. All I can tell you is that he has to go through the narrow gate I mentioned. But that passage through the gate of tears is terrible beyond degree, but it is the only way. You may come over the wall but it will not avail.

After going through the gate there is a fountain in which the candidate is to be plunged, the fountain is filled

and no burden either of sin or our own works can by any means come in thereat.

It has two parts. The Lower City & the Upper City there is a narrow river which divides the two over which there is no bridge.

The Lower City is built of solid stones & has good foundations but it is not built of such polished stones as the upper city which is of pure white marble. This outer city sometimes has aliens in it who have no right to be there [come over the ...]. The inhabitants are holy but not perfectly so. They are subject to some grief and pain. Sometimes they disagree & persons living in one street find fault with those in another, but upon the whole it is very very much better in order & happiness than any city upon earth beside though it is surpassed by the Upper city. All the true sons of this lower city when they cross the river are welcome to the Upper City. which indeed passeth my power to describe. Its walls are of alabaster studded with precious stones by reason of the vast quantity of gold in it it sparkleth like the sun. Mortal eye cannot behold it, its in- -habitants are never sick. They are without spot or blemish. God is there. Music sometimes is heard across the river.

III. Citizenship implies peculiar privileges.

In ancient Rome a citizen might not be beaten before conviction, he had the right of appeal to Cæsar, a share in the distribn of spoils, a vote &c. &c. So now corporate bodies have their charters. We will a moment or two look at Lions Charter.

1. The first article in it is Rom. VIII 1 & 33.34 Freedom from condemnation. Is not this a precious grant to Lion's citizens.

2. The second article you may read in 1 Cor. II 7—to end. That is the Illumination of the Spirit, the indwelling of the Holy Ghost — all believers enjoy this. This is the earnest of the inheritance.

3. The third is near the text, it is the Communion of saints. see 14 verse.

4. The fourth is the verse immediately before my text. it is access to God at all times by his Son Jesus Christ. In prayer we may enter within the veil.

5. The fifth is perpetual safety for this the great King of the place has promised and is able to ~~perform~~ afford

6. Acceptance at last in the day when he shall make up his jewels, which is the crown of all.

with blood drawn from Immanuel's veins and it is wondrous to behold how white & how beautiful they appear when they come from the washing. Then follows the robing when our nakedness is put away & a glorious wedding garment makes us like princes. This is the toga of heaven.

Now my hearers, the all-important question is have you been thus initiated, have I passed through this indispensable preparative for true citizenship.

There is too a public recognition of this initiation to be made to the world by immersion in water, in imitation of the death, burial & resurrection of Jesus. This it is the bounden duty of all christian men to execute in testimony of their love to the Redeemer.

Once truly free of this city it lasts for ever, and nothing more will be required for entrance into the Upper City save the passage of the river Jordan.

You my friends who have this day been baptized. Be careful that the secret initiation be right lest you be counted but as intruding aliens and not as true born citizens.

A short summary of privileges is contained in these words Justification, Access to the throne, Communion with Saints, Illumination, Adoption, Providence, Adoption.

IV Citizenship implies peculiar duty.

1. Service in war on behalf of our good city earnestly contending for the faith.

2. Obedience to the governor, the Prince Immanuel who is our sovereign liege Lord. [Baptism, Lords supper, good works]

3. Love to all the saints and doing all we can to serve them

4. Desire & labour after the souls of others that more citizens may be admitted to our Zion. This we must practise much.

Now we are about to sit down at a New Jerusalem table spread in common for all believers: let us come as citizens and may God grant unto us to rejoice in the dignity conferred upon us.

Would that some of you would also come for yet there is room & none are excluded who come by the gate

Help me oh Lord.

638

344. Matt XXV. 6 The Midnight Cry.

The coming of the bridegroom may be understood in two senses — the second coming of Christ in Judgment — or his coming in death to every creature under heaven.

As to the first, the coming of the Son of Man on the clouds of heaven will be in power and great glory. It will be usher'd in with divers portents, deathstruggles as it were of dying earth. All nature will ring with the cry of his coming & with a shout shall he descend, with the blast of trumpet and terrible thunder — the dead & the living shall stand before him, all shall see him whom they have pierced.

Hark the shout "Behold he cometh."

but I shall in this discourse apply it wholly to death coming to us as individuals.

There is an hour coming when each of us, whatever our present character shall hear this summons. "He cometh"

Moreover when it is heard there is no alternative save obedience. Go we must. The strong man must bow & the mighty man must be humbled. Wisdom & Knowledge, grandeur, riches,

benevolence & religion avail us not. There is
no discharge in this war. Since then this is
inevitable let us bid the present uncertainties
farewell & gaze on future realities. Whether
you listen to me or no, whether you retire
to laugh or to pray, this is a fact which you
may disregard but cannot escape, viz. that
the hour is coming when the cry of my text
will be heard at your door and be spoken
not to your child or parent but to you
and surely it will not take one thorn out
of your death pillow to remember that you
heard tonight to scoff & retired to forget.

I. We shall meditate on this summons with
respect to the entire race.

1. It is intensely solemn. At midnight the
cry was heard. Now midnight is a solemn
time. When the moon & her attendant
stars walks through the silent sky & all
is hushed, how solemn all seems. On
sea, on the mountain top, in the forest,
in your own room & even in the empty
street there is a something solemn.

We wonder not that the ignorant believe
that the sheeted dead do at midnight
visit this our earth, for indeed it is a
solemn hour. The villain fears to lie
on his bed by night alone. Many a
hardened wretch trembles in lonely
midnight. "By night the atheist half
believes a God."

We do not wonder
that many good men have chosen the
shades of midnight as their oratory. This
example sanctified by our Master, was
one which David sometimes indulged in.
"at midnight will I arise." Whitfield
used to retire to an aged tree in an avenue
at Oxford & there commune with God & we
do not know but perhaps Nicodemus
did the same. Night then is a
solemn hour. I add my testimony.

At midnight then the cry is heard
to show us the solemnity of death.
Death is intensely solemn, more so
than night. Revelry may disturb the
silence of night but surely death is too
awful thus to be generally broken in
upon. True there are some brute
minds who contemn death, the soldier
furious in battle, the hardened pirate
or the suicide — but to men in the mass
death is a solemn thing. There are
probably none here who will dissent
from this. Death is solemn. Be it the
death of a Wellington, a Napoleon or
of a pauper death is a solemn thing
to witness, corpses are cold things

which cool the blood of gaiety. And if solemn to witness how much more to endure.

Hush tread softly 'tis the couch of an immortal, no noise is there save the sob of the almost widow & the sigh of the well nigh orphan. The watch alone prates on, the lapse of time. A cold clammy sweat is on his brow, they wipe it off, they put the pillow that he may be more erect & now comes the death struggle, all alone he must grapple the tyrant, the pulse fails, a groan & yet another, the eye is glassy, the hand is motionless, the heart beats not, the breath is gone, He is dead. Do you turn away? Look here once more Is it not solemn work to die.

Be it the deathbed of a sinner or a saint of Israel or of Esau, of Samuel or of Nabal, of David or of Herod, of John or of Demas 'tis at all times & to all a solemn thing to die. The hour is solemn.

We hear of no mirth or jest from the virgins then. No there is then but one wish Let me die the death of the righteous. Oh ye young, ye gay, ye proud, ye must die & find it solemn work to do so Prepare to meet thy God.

<u>2.</u> It is generally unexpected. Even when disease has been cutting the root the tree falls un-expectedly. The pale cheek of consumption wears a hectic flush promising health. Ah cruel mockery. Death nips the promise.

Like some cliff worn at the base by a foaming torrent, we wonder that it has not fallen yet wonder when it does.

Now this parable of the midnight cry sets out this idea — they were asleep & suddenly they are startled by the piercing cry, he comes, he comes.

Who would have thought it. Death often gives no rap but bursts the door. You say "why is not notice given that you may prepare in time?" we reply "it is given, prepare now". But why are we not seriously informed of the day & the hour?" Why because you would be worse than now. You would trifle till the last hour. But now uncertainty is your monitor, it bids you now prepare. Few like Hezekiah know the length of their days. Do not wish to know but flee at once. And if there be one consumptive young woman or one young man whose frame is weak I say beware. <u>He cometh.</u>

3. It usually sets men preparing. All the virgins arose & trimmed their lamps. The foolish as well as the wise. But ah too late for one. The true Xn will have nothing to do but to commit his soul to God & fall asleep but others have far more to do.

The convict wished to prepare when the day of execution is coming, The sinner at sea begins to pray & you yourselves when sick have done the same but in almost every instance too late.
You mention the instance of the thief but I remind you of his companion. The pains and dying stripes of that hour are enough to fill ones hands without the trouble of fruitless prayers or agonizing groans.
Prepare now for he comes.
To all it is solemn & unexpected & puts them upon Preparation

II. We shall reflect on this summons with respect to the wicked.
Its effect on their mind may be expressed in one word Terror. If the inhabitants of Pompeii were aroused at midnight and warned that streams of lava were rushing down from Vesuvius what would their consternation be, especially if in the solemn hour of night. When we are aroused by fire,

or startled by the thief we feel terror & thus will the wicked when they wake as from a dream. "In hell he lift up his eyes."
When an ungodly man does but dream of hell his mind is terribly excited like the man Bunyan describes dreams do make his blood chill within him,
What then must the reality be. Go to the bedside of Voltaire, D'Alembert or Payne. or to some you know of. Some indeed die like brutes as to their carelessness but hell wakes them. Soon thou too shalt quiver oh despiser. Beware lest the fiat has gone forth. — Ghosts of sins demons of the imagination, all the dark sayings of ministers & threatenings of Scripture will haunt your bedside & terror shall indeed seize hold upon you.
56 Hymn. II Book. Watts.
9. Hymn. II Book. Watts.

III. We will now meditate on the summons as it regards the righteous.
1. It may come when they are sleepy.
A Christian is never wholly unprepared to die but he may be in an undesirable state for a Christian. If I might choose I would die in a pulpit. Who would wish to die angry. A Christian man

345   S. Song. II. 9. The Beloved.   See. 360.

The Bible contains a revelation intended not
so much to inform the head as to touch the
heart. The remembrance of this will keep us
from many misapprehensions with regard to
it.   The Book in which our text stands
is put into its due position by this suggestion.
A letter meant to excite love or to express
it would be worded very differently from
one only intended to convey information.
This book is a love song and none can
understand it but those who are in love with
"my Beloved", "the altogether lovely".

I. Christ's approach to us. "like a roe".
1. When he came to be Redeemer. he was at an
immense distance from us, by dignity, by nature
but he came swiftly. o'erleaping hills & became like us.
2. When he came as Pardoner in our own
personal experience. we sighed and groaned
but he came in haste & delivered us
3. When he comes as our Relief in trial, in
deep affliction, to support & deliver he comes
with all the speed love can give.
Ah how slowly do we move towards
him, how sluggish, Mountains affright
us & oh what mountains we sometimes
heap up of sin but he comes over them
Has he approached to you of late or
do you mourn his absence. Perhaps he is nigh only.

may be very worldly just before death, his
lamp may want trimming. Let us take
heed that we be found watching. If
asked to attend the theatre, the ball, or the
tavern let us ask ourselves how we should
like to die there
"Such is that awful that tremendous day
"Its coming who can tell, for as a thief
"Unheard, unseen it steals through nights dark shade
Perhaps as here I sit
And rudely carol these incondite lays
Soon may the hand be stretch'd & dumb the mouth
That lisps the faltering strain, Oh may it n'eer
Intrude upon an ill-spent hour, but find
Me wrapt in meditation high hymning
my Great Creator. &c by Dr Glynn —
2. It will be joyful. It is the bridegroom
not the judge. The friend not the avenger.
Sometimes the joy developes itself in a
calm repose like David "although my house"
or Jacob, or Moses, or Stephen.
At other times it is extacy "singing aloud"
but at all times the midnight cry is
acceptable & the dying bed of a saint resembles
much the ode of Pope. "Vital spark of &c"
Your question now is am I a wise or
a foolish virgin. be decided
The Lord bless me & you
Amen
644. 646.

346   Luke. II. 25. The Consolation of Israel

Some men leave a large biography behind them containing deeds good & evil. Others have only blots and blemishes & a few only those things which are lovely & excellent.

As specimens of the three classes take Johnson,   & of the last Simeon.

Short as is his history known to us, yet how completely though briefly is his character depicted.   A just man, a compendium of all the virtues due to our fellows. As a merchant honest, as a master fair as a ruler upright, as a servant faithful as a citizen unblemished in character

A just man would keep all the   to commands of the second table.

But he was a devout man too, one who served God as well as Caesar - justice is the external, the body of virtue — devotion is the internal, the soul of it. He was not a Pharisee, outwardly observing what inwardly he loathed. he was devout, not formal he fasted & went to the temple but not to be seen of men. He was really devout.

And being devout he did what every pious Jew was then doing, he waited for the coming of the Messiah. He knew that the seventy weeks were fulfilled

---

he is not seen. Which leads us to

II. Christ's concealment from us. "he standeth

Of course this is the world of concealment when compared with the next. One wall or another is the hiding place of deity, once it was the vail — then Jesus' humanity, now these are rent there is a wall still our wall says the text because we built it by our sins, our unbelief, our forgetfulness Ah it may be it is some idol which is a wall & it must be pulled down. He hideth behind our wall.

III. Christ's observation of us "he looketh

When we cannot see him he can see us. He looketh out of love & concern for our souls.
1. He looketh to see how our graces flourish.
2. He looketh to see what is our need.
3. He looketh to see when to remove & trouble
4. He looketh to see what we are doing for him. (or lay on)

Surely he often feels.
1. Grief at our deficiencies & wanderings.
2. Astonishment, at our repeated follies
& seldom 3 Joy at our progress & growth.

Yet with all our faults he looks again & again as the fond lover on his beloved.

IV. Christ's manifestation to us. "he sheweth &c

Sometimes faith sees him as the Saviour of its spirit. "behold" as if to express rapture.
1. Dimly. through the lattice,
2. Instrumentally. by the use of means,
3. Personally. he sheweth not his works or words but himself.

Oh may be seen & beloved by us all.

649.

I. The expectation. "Waiting &c"

Simeon was an old man & perhaps had already passed the natural boundary of mortal life, God having revealed to him that until Messiah came he should not die. The old man fully prepared was ever in the holy posture of a waiting servant. Not waiting for decay but for that sight which through the windows of his creaking tabernacle he hoped to see. ———— This posture of expectation was common to all the saints of the Old Testament. From the day when Eve hailed the birth of Cain as that of the man, the Lord; all through that long, long avenue of years till the angel-song to the shepherds, saints looked for him. That Hebrew who offered his son said, God will provide a Lamb. He who had once a stone for his pillow looked with his dying eyes to the coming of Shiloh. The mighty lawgiver, the greatest man under the Israelite theocracy believed in the advent of a prophet like to himself. He who well earned the name of Israel's sweet Psalmist talked in songs of "my Lord". He who spake more of Christ than other prophets saw him with no clouded gaze. But time would fail me to trace the unbroken line of expecting worthies whose epitaph Paul has written in terse language "these all died in faith". ———— The Messiah at last appears and what was once a virtue becomes a sin. The Jewish race reject him & still remain in the posture of their forefathers' "waiting" Ah how vain. "Lo here & lo there" they listened to. Bar cochab & a hundred other pretenders sprung up and deceived them they are scattered over the face of all the earth, yet unwearied by disappointment they still await the coming of him who is to restore the Kingdom to Israel, the Poor wanderer here he is, wait no longer. ———— There is however a sense in which we may still wait for the advent of the Consolation of Israel, — we may expect his second coming — we may earnestly long & wait for his love-visits and sinners may in earnest prayer yet wait his approach in mercy. ———— The whole creation is now in the same posture as Simeon, waiting for the moment of deliverance from sin and final restoration to its pristine loveliness & order. Let us too as servants be waiting for our Lord. Let us not sleep as do others.

II. **The Fulfilment** — "the consolation of Israel"

Simeon expected to see a Messiah, he did so;
but moreover expected one worthy of the glorious
title here mentioned & we are sure that in
this too he was not disappointed. The
Messiah has been the "Consolation" of his people.

Let men dispute the truth of our religion
there is one fact they dare not deny, viz,
that our religion does give consolation —

— See the sons of God in Persecution
from Abel till now; observe how calmly
they meet death. A small remnant hidden
perhaps in caves as in Jezebel's days have
still held fast the truth. See Daniel & the
three Holy Children — observe Stephen & all
the apostles. Paul in prison &c & come
down to our times and the same thing
is fact. Men die calmly under tortures
too horrid to be mentioned. They have a
consolation overcoming pain & agony.

— See them in the ordinary troubles
of life. Losses, crosses, bereavement or
sickness how resigned, how peaceful;
compared with the ungodly. Facts are
needless as illustrations for every Christian
household presents a specimen. Every
day confirms the fact that religion brings consolation

— Turn aside to the Believers deathbed
if you wish to see a great sight. Here is
the test of enthusiasm, here vapours cool
solids only remain. By the side of such

men as Halyburton, or Janeway, or Knox or
Payson we learn that there is consolation in
Israel. Halyburton as a sign of his joy,
when speechless lifted up his hands and clapped
them. Janeway cried "Oh that I could now
express the thousandth part of the sweetness
which I now find in Christ"! You little think
what a Christ is worth upon a deathbed,
oh the glory, the unspeakable glory I now behold.
My heart is full, my heart is full.....
You would not have the heart to detain me
could you see what I see." Knox said
"the day is now come, which I have so often
and intensely longed for, in which I shall be
dissolved & be with Christ". — & Payson's death
was too seraphic for description.

Truly there is consolation for Israel.

III. **The Explanation.**

The Fact that Israel is consoled is undoubted
now comes the enquiry how is it? This
we propose to explain as God enables us.

The Gospel contains & affords
Consolatory doctrines. So far as the gospel
description of man is concerned it certainly
cannot comfort much. It represents him
as ruined & helpless. But take the
doctrines in which Christ appears &
then you gain floods of consolation.

Election droppeth honey if we feel that
we are elect of God. Then what care

we for distress, persecution or trouble.

The doctrine of the covenant made on our behalf by the Trinity ensuring the safety of the elect.

Justification by Faith that key stone of all gospel truth is so needful for consolation that one is apt to doubt if there can be any where this not believed..... All those doctrines which concern the nature and attributes of God, all those that deal with either the manhood or Godhead of our Redeemer & all which declare the might of the Spirit are wells of honied water for mourners.

Now what are gospel doctrines but Christ pourtrayed on paper, his heart made legible

Here in doctrines is a vein of consolation

Consolatory Promises are scattered all over the sacred page thick as stars in the firmament. Those which promise Final Perseverance are choice grapes of Eschol. Where can comfort be if this be untrue, Some Promise Peace, Joy, Comfort, Support and each in his season becomes sweet to the needy soul. There is one Star of the first magnitude. viz the Promise of Heaven which is consolation refined, Distilled Comfort, Essential oil of consolation next to this is a promise now beginning to be fulfilled, namely that of the second coming of Christ and the universal spread of his Kingdom. The toiling labourer sows in hope that soon will be realized

But neither of these console us without the Consolatory influences of the Holy Spirit which render the doctrine and the promise all they are intended to be. What a calm it spreads over us which we cannot trace to any manifest agency. Like the wind seen only in its effects. It is only to those who are under the power of the great Spirit who really enter with delight into the hidden places of consolation hidden in our Lord Jesus Christ.

— Christian why hang thy head, why wear the weeds of woe. Cheer up broken he is thy consolation —

— Worldling, consolation is what thy wealth cannot buy, nor thy rioting afford — Trade then in this article with him who alone can give it thee, My Master, the Consolation of Israel!

Help. th Father.
Through th Son

652

347]   Gen. XV..11.   Distractions in worship   347

It had been well said by Mrs H.B. Stowe that the Bible is a book which gains rather than loses by slow spelling. It certainly gains by careful inspection; while many other books lose brightness when under scrutiny, whereas there is sometimes in the commonest passage some gem we little thought of finding.

— Let us make another remark that the Scriptures gives us such real history that the natural nerve of it strikes at one. There is none of the unlikelihood of romance about it; one feels surprised at its home-liness; yet let us remember that these little touches of real life are not meant alone to strike us with the vivid feeling of reality; but they have also another purpose to serve — they are for our instruction. Let us see by the mighty ones' help, if we cannot in this short episode find some profitable thoughts.

I. Abraham's Engagements.

He was not in this life, but retired to do homage to his God. Truly one thing was his object and that one thing devotion.

1. It was singular devotion, for we do not know that in all the earth these worshippers engaged in the same way, but only one worshipper of Jehovah. How hard to follow Christ all alone, yet we must do so, as he did & not with violet & not [...]

2. It was earnest devotion. There was nothing to tempt him to hypocrisy; for he was a solitary worshipper. He showed his heart-zeal by ready compliance with the command. Well will it be, if we are all found thus to-day in God's house offering heart-devotion.

3. It was simple devotion. No vaulted arch roofed his temple. No stained windows cast a coloured light along a marble aisle. No rubric or liturgy. No genuflexions, the robed forms, pomp, or splendor. The green sward, the twinkling stars, the rustic altar, the simple prayer, a man & God. Away, away with the foolish trash pride brings.

4. It was Scriptural devotion, as there was nothing added of man's device, so there was nothing omitted of God's ordaining. As a sacrifice was necessary for a sinner to come to God with, the one he brought out, and as God had ordained what that sacrifice should be, he accepted the same with it, not seeking any other. So let us never dare come without an offering & let us remember one is appointed even the sacrifice of the agonies & death of Jesus of Nazareth.

5. It was necessary devotion. Some things are spiritual as eating or fasting &c but these

devotion is absolutely necessary. The embodiment
of it may be optional but the spirit is absolutely
requisite and a man cannot be a Christian
without it. The most eminent need it, &
they who use it most will be most eminent,
Let us imitate Abraham.

II. **Abraham's interruptions**

Even in his solemn worship he was disturbed.
Certain Carnivorous Birds fell upon the
carcase as their prey. Now this was altogether
an unavoidable interruption. He did not
bring the birds there and therefore it was
not his fault. Let us when interrupted
always enquire if they are of this kind.

1. Distracting thoughts. These will come
when least required. If much in business
or in anxiety then in they creep & if we
are at leisure then they like gaudy flies
come vainly in & out of our hearts.
If these be allowed true devotion is gone,

2. Pride. Pride of dress sometimes operates,
pride of rank comes in, love of form &
pompous ritual. Love of learning & polish
in the minister. Too good an opinion
of ourselves & slight thoughts of sin.
Pride spoils the service of either minister,
deacon, S.S. Teacher, or private Member.
It spoilt the Pharisee — Pride of Science
spoils the devotion of many wise ones.

3. Fear of Man. This is a sad rioter on our
devotion, sometimes indeed swallowing all.
If we pray or preach under this influence
farewell to any sort of devotion.

4. Envy. When you envy one minister because
he is more popular than your own, you spoil
your service. If you envy brother So & So his
gift in prayer, or the office he holds,
or his superior wealth then farewell
anything approaching to true devotion.

5. Unbelief & Lukewarmness a pair of
greedy lazy vultures are a sad annoyance.
Languor in prayer, want of fervour & intense
earnestness combined with small reliance
on the promise cut the traces of piety. —
Surely Brethren some of these birds
torment you or I am much mistaken.
Birds they are & swiftly come —

III. **Abraham's conduct.**

Let us regard his conduct that we may
as far as possible imitate him.

1. He observed the birds. Some men never
reflect as to whether they are devout or not.
They are there. There's the sacrafice & whether
birds eat it or no they care not. Like
the door they turn in and out & that is all.
The first step to reform is to see the
evil. You see Abram looking at one
moment at the sacrafice & then at the birds

348 Prov. XXV. 2. Concealment the glory of God.

How infinitely is man inferior to his maker
Though his Maker's masterpiece on earth, yet
how far beneath his Maker is he. If we
consider his moral attributes or those of power,
selfexistence, eternity &c we feel that there is
an infinite difference — In Knowledge also
this may be noted. He is omniscient, we are
ignorant.

I. Concealment — what is concealed?

The ignorant man thinks every thing plain
the wise man sees concealment every where.

Upon the very face of nature is written
the word concealment. We scarce know
really the reason of anything, The names
we give to the laws & powers of nature
are but covers for our ignorance.

True we every day advance in Knowledge
but when most advanced we are but
in the elements of earth's philosophy.

There are paths man cannot tread, caverns
he cannot enter, heights he cannot climb
& depths unfathomable. There is not one
of us but what has about us something
we cannot understand — the mariner
sees the needle tremble to the pole he knows
not how, the astronomer beholds a fiery

2. He disliked their presence. He did not say
well it is so but I like it to be so. No
away birds from me I do not want you,
Some know they sleep but are not sorry
for it — They are aware it is wrong to be
at the altar & have the heart away but
they do not lay it to heart.

3. He did his best to prevent their coming
Some say they are sorry but do not try
to alter. Make it a matter of prayer,
Put up an ejaculatory petition, Weep
over it. Shout at the birds. Throw texts
at them - Drive them away.

4. He persevered in it. Again & again
they returned but just as often there was
Abram. All day long in the frosty
night and then in the burning sun
even until evening he continued at his
holy employment. Let us do so too.

Lord help. Amen

653

and a thousand more questions the prophet
answer to all of which is — "It is the glory of
God to conceal a thing"#—

Coming down from this creation how many
things in his history we should like to ask;
All the sciences reveal by information;
but here again we find "It is the glory of
God to conceal a thing"!

Then following on to that era of our Lord
we want to know what is emphatically
the mystery, God manifest in the flesh!
'Twas he in heaven + on earth at once; then
how could he combine deity + humanity.
Where was he when the words contained
his body? Where were the souls of those
whom he restored to life? How was it
that men were possessed of devils? + &c
&c of questions the answer to which
is the teach + that alone. But not
only is the past concealed —

The Present is clouded too. We are in a
fog, and the space immediately around
appears to be light but is it so? No.
Is not the present world a puzzle. Is not Providence a
depth? Are not the wheels high?
If you are an unconverted man how
dark all is to you, but even if a Christian how little
do you know of yourself. You do not

---

meteors cleave the skies; he wonders whence
it came; the farmer feels blight + mildew
destroy his clew + disease seize on a
most precious root; he is ignorant of the
cause.

The day had its mysteries; its
winds, its storms + hurricanes; + night the
hour of wonders astonishes us with its
lights, its comets, + other wondrous
sights. Lift your eyes on high, turn them
around or beneath; we are in a cloud +
as job said we know nothing.

Coming out of nature's darkness into
the light of gospel revelation; here too,
much is concealed. Thanks be to God
nothing essential to our happiness is hidden
but much that would gratify our curiosity.
Even revelation is very much an obvelation.

Of the Past — How much is concealed
of the Past —

The existence + preexistence
of three Persons in the Trinity is told us.
The mode of the bringing forth of the Son +
the procession of the Spirit, but however know
not — it is a mystery, our minds cannot grasp.
The decrees of God as to Salvation + Rejection
though almost fully revealed, it hath to be
believed but much about them is dark.
Why did God made all his creatures fallible?
How did man come first? Why some are chosen
more than others? How did creed consist
with free agency? How the decree of God
to permit evil thing is consistent with God's holiness

know how it is the Spirit operates upon you
You do not know how it is you are preserved
your contending natures, the reason of your
troubles &c all these make you wonder &
you can only say "It is the glory of God to conceal a thing"
The Future. This is the great unknown
the present & past men will pretend to know
but here there strained eyes refuse to give
them knowledge. Every step of it is a
black impenetrable cloud. Scarce is the
next hour known to us. The astrologer, the
soothsayer & wizard are as blind as
others. Revelation tells us a little & but
a little. It tells us there is a judgment
but when no man knoweth. A heaven
but what it is or where tongue cannot say.
Death is the bourne whence no traveller returns.
The reign of Christ, millenial glories,
heavens employment, hell's torments & all
Futurity lies under a vail most thick.
We will not long to see. for it is the
glory of God to conceal a thing!
But it is also for our profit.

II. Concealment — its benefits.
We may be sure it is for our profit. God
does not do it merely as man for mystery
sake. but he has a design,
None of his acts are hidden because
they are evil as man's are, nor because
he fears man would thwart his purposes
But he has some profit designed by it.

Let us remark that certainly more knowledge
of concealed things would not benefit us.
What would be the good of our knowing how
the Holy Spirit operates or how he proceeded
from the Father & the Son &c &c &c.
  more knowledge gives not more humility.
But more than this we propound the
proposition that this concealment is good for us.

1. The laborious discovery of hidden truth &
even the attempt to discover it is useful
to our faculties. It helps to develope our
powers. Children must have harder
lessons by degrees & learning these prepares
them to grapple with greater difficulties.

2. This labour has another effect, it tends
to humble us. If we had nothing to learn
we should be more arrogant than now
we should scorn to be second even to the
most High. Lord I thank thee for necessary
ignorance, though I repent of that which is unnecessary.

3. Much now done would be left undone
if the future were known. The son who
would die early would be uneducated
the house unbuilt, the mission left,
the colony unfilled, the rich man about
to sink unserved, the dying untended,
we should be all self. & all else undone.

4. Much misery would be caused by a
knowledge of the future. We should be
all Jeremiahs. If our lot was to be

349   2 Cor. IV. 16.   Christ the Revelation of God.

One of the most natural questions arising in the mind of man is "what is God?" we see him in his works as existing. "what & who is he? The child asks it & in our times we can give a proper reply but in other times how different. The ancient heathen attempted to solve the question & various were the results of their blind search. God is great & glorious said some therefore the sun is God. He is strong & powerful therefore the crocodile or the elephant must be God. He is terrible therefore the tiger or lion or other monster must be God. He is eternal then the snake or ancient then he lives in an oak

Some taking a higher range thought God to be a being like themselves & as they knew well enough they could not themselves manage a universe so they thought God could not — so they divided it & set gods over various provinces of nature. These gods their poets described as always disputing about dominion fighting lying, stealing & the male & female gods ever unfaithful to the marriage vows, Some of them more debauched than men & in more bestial forms & as the people are never better than their gods so they were all sunk

good our present pleasures would be untasted we should be sighing for the future good, if unhappy then we should not enjoy the present through dread of the future. Either way misery is before us! But now hope gilds all. The lamb licks the butcher's hand! We live with "sufficient for the day is the evil thereof". —

5. Heaven is sweeter in prospect through our little knowledge here. My knowing in part makes me long to know even as I am known. There all knots shall be untied, difficulties unravelled, doubts resolved, truth made manifest, & now

<u>III.</u> Concealment.   the reflections it suggests.

1. How foolish to forestall troubles by anticipating them. they are concealed let them be. God will manage them

2. How foolish of us to be proud of our knowledge when we know so little.

3. How unwise to spend our time on subjects purposely made obscure.

4. How thankful we should be that all we need know, we may know.

Here is a lesson for comfort, humility, wisdom, & thankfulness.

Open mine eyes Oh Lord.

660.

into sins not fit to be mentioned. Earth was
Sodom on a large scale, Sodom degenerated.
True a few choice spirits rose a little above
the common herd, but ah how soon they fell
or were cut off by their neighbours & what was
the acmé these choice ones reached, why
this that there was a God, but they knew no
more, in one sentence the sum of their
philosophy was on the Athenian altar, "to the
unknown God"
The world by wisdom knew not God.
God is not obliged to reveal himself, nor will
he to gratify vain man's idle curiosity.
But he has a nobler purpose, he has from
all eternity determined to save an elect people.
Now this cannot be done unless they
are brought to know him.
God therefore reveals himself—
In creation he is revealed will that
suffice— Can the mourner find any
comfort here? If this will effect the
purpose then God will not make a
superfluous revelation. It will not.
Fly the wide world o'er, fly to yonder
planets & yet on — here is no rest for
the sole of the sinners foot.
In law will this answer the purpose
Will Sinai avail? No the law drops no
honey from its lip, the wrath-denouncing
trumpet gives its blast & mercy flees. Hope
dies. Away sinner away.—

In Christ in the fulness of time God is revealed
and gloriously revealed to the sinner. let us
turn aside and see the great sight.
1. Here is the essential godhead. Scripture
very expressly declares Christ to be God.
His reading men's thoughts, healing the sick,
raising the dead, creating food, stilling the
sea, ruling demons &c all declare him God.
2. Here is the wisdom of God. The devising
of a plan of live from death, pardon through
vengeance, grace through wrath & a thousand
other paradoxes. To remake man, to renew
his nature, to restore him safely were works
of wisdom shining in Christ.
Believer bring thy difficulties to the wise one.
3. Here is the Holiness of God. A life
without a spot or blemish, a heart free
from corrupt desires or imagining.
Invulnerable by all the fiery darts of
temptation, unturned from rectitude by
any trial. Like the sun unswerving.
Christian here is thy righteousness.
4. Here is the justice of God. It had
been seen before in the sacrifice, in judgment
in Satans expulsion from heaven, it
would have been seen in the final
damnation of all. But Calvary lets it
shine out with singular, unrivalled

Splendor. When Brutus put his sons to death
a wondering world beheld his inflexible
firmness, so here men & angels saw the
justice of God on Calvary.
5. Here was the truth of God. A god
without truth would be no God. Our God
is the "only true" God. He had promised
a Saviour to Adam & the echo of those
words spoken in Eden quivered in the
air for 4000 years, so that prophets &
Kings waited for its fulfilment. It came
at last Christ, the truth of God proved
and manifested to all. And now
beloved will you doubt your covenant God
will he not fulfil the small promises.
6. Here was the love of God. This was
indeed the preeminent glory of the Redeemer
that he reflected & embodied the love of God.
He was not the cause of God's love but the
Channel of it. "Herein is love" as if he
had hunted everywhere & now "eureka"
 Oh believer surely the Holy one will give
thee eyes to see this attribute shining like
the sun in mid heavens. trust it.
 Truly Christ is the impress of his father, like
the wax & the seal.
 Oh Jesus give me to behold
thee & to unfold thee. Look Sinner, Saint.
661

THE SERMONS

NOTEBOOK 8 (SERMONS 351–379)

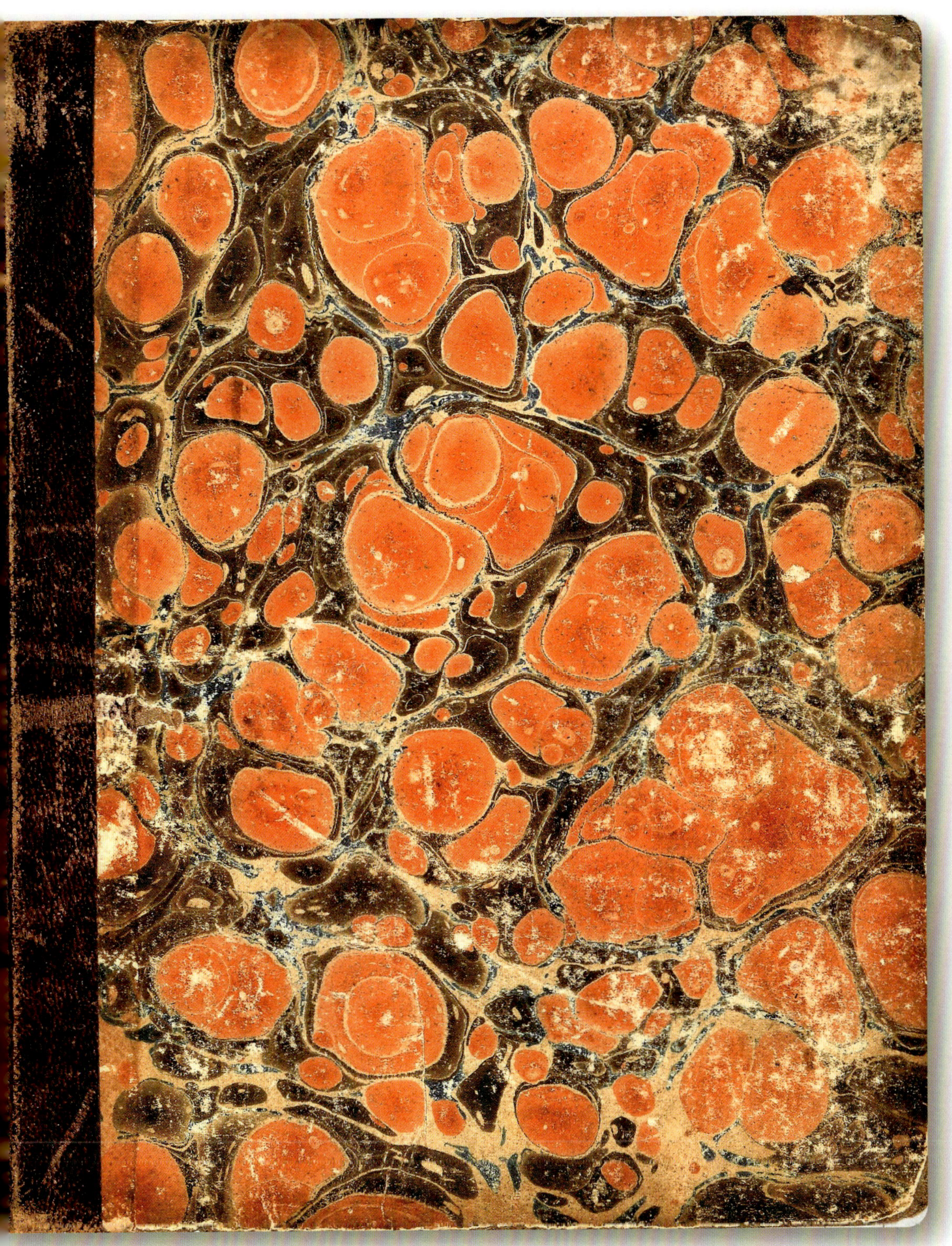

"THE FATHER OF LIGHT"

Editor's Summary

On Saturday evening December 17, 1853, Charles Spurgeon found himself in a cramped boarding house in London. Due to his growing reputation, he had been invited by the historic New Park Street Chapel to preach the following morning. This would be his first time preaching in the metropolis.

His fellow lodgers were amused to see this country boy with his "huge black satin stock" and "blue handkerchief with white spots." They were even more tickled to learn that he had been invited to preach and they gladly regaled the lad with stories of the great divines and their unmatched oratory and meticulous preparation. As he prepared for bed, Charles wondered if he was out of his depth. Recounting that long night, he wrote,

> That Saturday evening in a London boarding-house was about the most depressing agency which could have been brought to bear upon my spirit. On the narrow bed I tossed in solitary misery, and found no pity. . . . I had no friend in all that city full of human beings, but felt myself to be among strangers and foreigners, and hoped to be helped through the scrape into which I had been brought. *Autobiography* 1:318.

The next morning, Charles made the long walk to Southwark, winding though lanes and alleys and praying for God's help. Arriving at the New Park Street Chapel, he was awestruck at its size, which to him suggested "an audience wealthy and critical, and far removed from the humble folk to whom my ministry had been sweetness and light." *Autobiography* 1:319. Yet as he stepped into the building, Charles found a small congregation of less than a hundred people gathered inside this cavernous space. And unlike the previous night's lodgers, they received him warmly.

And so, on that day, nineteen-year-old Charles Spurgeon mounted the pulpit of the New Park Street Chapel for the very first time, preaching for the 673rd time and using the notes of his 351st sermon, "The Father of Light." The congregation that day heard the kind of preaching they had not heard in a long time—preaching that extolled the majesty of God and yet was understandable; that thundered the reality of sin and yet held forth the grace of the gospel. The people were thrilled. Many rushed home to invite their neighbors back that evening (see Sermon 328, "The Faultless People"), and attendance doubled. Reflecting on that experience, Charles recounted, "The Lord helped me very graciously, I had a happy Sabbath in the pulpit, and spent the interval with warm-hearted friends; and when, at night, I trudged back to the Queen Square narrow lodging, I was not alone." *Autobiography* 1:319.

For the next thirty-eight years, Charles would occupy this pulpit and preach thousands of sermons reaching millions of people. All those sermons would tell the same message of the love of God in Christ that Charles preached on his first Sunday there.

He loves me now as much as He did when first He inscribed my name in His eternal book of election. He has not repented of His choice. He has not blotted one out; there are no erasures in that book. All who are written are safe.

Nor does He love me less now than when He gave that grand proof of love, His son Jesus; even now, He loves me with the same intensity as when He poured out the vials of justice on His darling to save rebel worms.

THE FATHER OF LIGHT

James 1:17

"Every good gift and every perfect gift is from above, and cometh down from the Father of lights, with whom is no variableness, neither shadow of turning."

Some sciences and objects of study are to us inexhaustible. We might ever find fresh matter for instruction, wonder, and research. If we dive with the geologist and bring up skeletons of extinct monsters, signs of great convulsions, old and new formations, or if we soar aloft and with the astronomer measure heaven and count the stars, we should ever be lost in the new discoveries we should make. The same may be said of all the natural sciences. Whatever the subject, it does not seem possible that man should say, "I have nothing to learn, I am master of it all."

But should it one day happen that our race should so progress, and become so increased in power as to leave nothing unknown, should nature be stript of all her mystery—the heavens, the sea, the earth, all perfectly understood—there will yet remain one subject upon which the sons of men may meditate, dispute, and labour, but it shall still be unknown. That subject is God, of whom with humble reverence I am now to speak. May it please the great Spirit of Wisdom to enlarge our minds and guide our hearts into an understanding of the portion of truth concerning Him made manifest in the text. We have here:

I.   A MAJESTIC FIGURE.

II. A GLORIOUS ATTRIBUTE.

III. A GRATEFUL ACKNOWLEDGEMENT.

I. A MAJESTIC FIGURE.

God is here called "The Father of Lights," comparing him to the sun. It is most true that this lower world is the reflection of the upper. In it, once, the face of God might be seen as on some glassy lake; but sin has ruffled it, and the portrait is broken and presented only in pieces. Yet there are the pieces, the wrecks of the picture; we will not throw them aside. Let us lift up our eyes on high and behold the only object worthy to be called an emblem of Deity. We think we can see several ideas couched in the figure:

1. <u>Independence, or Self-Existence</u>. God is the only self-existent being; the sun is not really so, but he is far more independent than any other object we know of.

    All else of nature is borrowed. Vegetables draw their nourishment from the soil, animals from them or from one another, man from all—he is the greatest beggar in the universe. The moon lights her nightly orb at the sun's lamp. The planets trim theirs from his storehouse. Mother Earth is dependent on the sun; and despite the pride of her children, what is she but a tiny globule dancing in the rays of that majestic orb? The sun gives but takes not, bestows on all, receives from none, leans on none, but lives alone, in its own solemn loneliness.

    Such is God, the **I Am**, who sits on no borrowed throne, begs no leave to be. All things are of Him, and by Him. He needs them not; where they all annihilated, it would not injure Him. He could exist and has existed alone. He has all in Himself. On Him all things lean; He leans on none.

    But we can scarce speak of Him:

    > "Who, light Himself, in uncreated light,
    > Invested deep dwells awfully retired,
    > From mortal eye or angel's purer ken.
    > Whose single smile has from the first of time
    > Fill'd overflowing all the lamps of heaven
    > That beam for ever through the boundless sky;
    > But should He hide His face, oh astonish'd sun
    > And all th' extinguish'd stars, would loosening reel
    > Wide from their spheres, and Chaos come again."

2. <u>Sublimity</u> is another idea suggested by the figure. The sun is one of the most magnificent of created existences. When he ~~it~~ shows ~~it~~himself, the moon and stars conceal their blushing faces. Seen in any part of his course, he is a grand object. When first he tinges the sky, when he sits in mid heaven, or retires in splendor, grandeur is one of his attributes. He is too bright for our eyes to gaze upon ~~see~~, although we are at such a vast ~~an infinite~~ distance from him.

So is God. Who shall describe Him? His servants are all glorious, the starry floor of His throne is glorious. What must He be Himself?

"Imagination's utmost stretch in wonder dies away."

Well may angels veil their faces, for even their eyes could not endure His brightness. No man can see Him. His train was all Moses saw. Borrow the eagle's eye and wing, soar out on until the glory overcomes you and you fall reeling to earth again. Do it again and again and you will see that this is all man can see of Him, viz., that He cannot be seen. Clouds and darkness are round about Him, for He may truly have it said of Him.

"Dark with excessive light Thy skirts appear."

3. <u>Power</u>, again, seems a prominent idea. The sun is as a giant coming out of his chamber, and like a strong man he rejoices to run a race. He drags the whole immense system along in his mighty course, nor dare any oppose him. Were it possible, how mightily would he still move on!

So is our God in His power. No one knowest His might; it is like Himself, infinite. He speaketh and his Word is power. He willeth and his will is omnipotence. Who can thwart His purposes? Shall nature? No. The hills melted like wax, etc. They skipped like rams. The floods divide. Fire singes not. Beasts are tamed. He lifteth his fingers, the flood arises. He droppeth it, the waters assuage. In vain could mountains, torrents, starts, and elements war with Him.

Who can conquer in battle with Him! Shall man? No, He counteth them as the drop of the bucket. He sitteth in Heaven and hath them in derision. Shall devils in hell withstand him? No! Once have they fallen from the battlements of Heaven and in vain is their loudest roar. Satan is chained, and led as a conquer'd monarch in victory. He is God's slave and unwillingly doth His will. Oh beloved, what a God is here! Put this thought under thy pillow, and when troubles rise, calmly sleep on, for His power protecteth.

4. But – <u>Beneficence</u> seems even more the leading idea. ~~The Sun is the great philanthropist.~~ He is necessary to our being. No light, no heat, no life, no rain, nothing without him. He is necessary to our well-being. The sun is indeed a great philanthropist; he visits every land, freely he gives, and gives to all. The prisoner he visits in his cell, the peasant in his cottage, freely and largely he bestows. Curse him or bless him, he is the same; he does not refuse his light even to the felon!

Such is God, the good, the greatly good. Should He remove His face, Heaven would not be Heaven. All the universe would be a valley of bones, a perfect charnel house. Oh how good is He! He confines not His mercies to a race. The Hottentot, etc., are welcome. The evil receive His grace and lose their former nature. He gives to sinners, and to the unthankful; and if men were not by nature blind, they would see by His light for the defect is in them, and not in Him.

Yon sun has shone on my cradle, it will beam on my deathbed, and cast a gleam into my grave. So doth God, the Beneficent. He gilds our path with sunshine; [E]arth were a gloomy vault without Him. With Him, it is light and joyous, the porch of a more joyous state.

II. A GLORIOUS ATTRIBUTE.

The apostle [James], having thus introduced the figure, finding that it did not bear the full resemblance of the invisible God, seems constrained to amend it by a remark that, unlike the sun, our Father had no turning or variableness.

The sun has [a] <u>parallax</u>; he rises at a different time each day, he sets at different hours. He moves into different parts of the heavens. He is clouded, eclipsed, and even suffers a diminution of light from some mysterious decrease of the lumineferous light which surrounds him. He has [a] <u>tropic</u> or turn. Now he turns his chariot to the south, until at the solstice God bids him reverse his rein, and he visits us once more.

But God is ~~here~~ superior to all figures. He is immutable. The sun changes, mountains crumbles, the ocean shall dry, the stars shall wither from the vault of night; but He, and He alone, remains the same. Were we to enter into a full discourse on the subject of immutability, our time, even if multiplied by a high number, would fail us. But, reminding you that there is no change in His power, justice, knowledge, oath, threatening, or decree, I will confine myself to the fact that His love to us knows no variation. How often it is called <u>unchangeable</u>, everlasting love.

He loves me now as much as He did when first He inscribed my name in His eternal book of election. He has not repented of His choice. He has not blotted one out; there are no erasures in that book. All who are written are safe.

Nor does He love me less now than when He gave that grand proof of love, His son Jesus; even now, He loves me with the same intensity as when He poured out the vials of justice on His darling to save rebel worms. We have all had times which we considered times of special love, when His candle shone round about us and we basked in His smile; but let us not suppose that He really loved us more then than now. Oh no! He then discovered His love in a way pleasing to flesh and blood.

But trials are equally proofs of His love. In fight, in the Valley of Humiliation, in the Valley of the Shadow of Death, in Vanity Fair, He will be the same, and love us neither more nor less than when we sing with seraphic voices the songs of Heaven. Death, sometimes, in the prospect, is very trying to flesh and blood; but if this truth of God's unchanging love were well remembered, it would not be such a trial, for we should know that He who helps Jacob to gather up his feet, David to say "Although, etc.," and Stephen to fall asleep, will be the same to you who trust in Him. Throughout eternity, there shall be no jars, not a breath of strife, but the same uninterrupted, blessed unity, shall prevail for ever. Thanks be unto Him for loving us.

III. <u>A GRATEFUL ACKNOWLEDGEMENT</u>.

The apostle, having introduced God as the Father of lights, and qualified the figure, now proceeds to ascribe all good gifts to Him alone.

If it seemed perfectly natural that at the rising of the natural sun, nature should welcome it with song, is it not even more so that, at the name of the greater Father of Lights, we should lift up a song? Now what is said here is what Angels can sing in Heaven; it is what Adam could have hymned in Paradise; it is what every Christian feels heartily <u>willing</u> to confess. Ever since the Fall, this verse has had an emphasis of meaning, since in us, by nature, there dwells no good thing, and our fall forfeited every right to any favour. So that our—

<u>Natural Gifts</u>, as beauty, eloquence, health, life, happiness, come from Him equally with our <u>graces</u>. We have nothing which we have not received. Earth, one day, shall make this song thrill through infinity; Heaven shall join the chorus; the region of chaos and old night shall shout aloud, and even hell's unwilling voice shall growl out an acknowledgement of the fact, that "<u>Every good gift and every perfect gift is from above and cometh down from the Father of lights, with whom is no variableness neither shadow of a turning</u>." I have succeeded, if with me you can say at the contemplation of Jehovah,

> "Glory be unto the Father, and to the
> Son and to the Holy Ghost, as it
> was in the beginning, is now, and
> ever shall be, world without end.
>   <u>Amen</u>."

668. 673

Sermon No. 352

"THE TWO BIRDS"

Editor's Summary

In this unfinished sermon from Lev 14:4–7 (a passage he would not preach from again), Charles provides a typological interpretation of the two birds offered in the ceremonial cleansing of a leper. In that offering, one bird was killed and the other was released. Charles saw a type of Christ in the bird that was sacrificed, and a type of the sinner in the bird that was set free.

It's impossible to know why Charles left the second point unfinished. However, since he still preached the sermon, marking his 669th preaching occasion, it appears he felt comfortable offering the second point extemporaneously. The two blank pages indicate that he intended to finish the sermon at a later time but never got around to it.

One of the more interesting features of "The Two Birds" is the introduction. Charles lived during a time when the expansion of the British Empire and the rise of modern travel opened up new lands for exploration. Opportunities arose for the study of other religions, leading to new works of comparative religions. In later years, Charles would have the opportunity to review such works in *The Sword and the Trowel*. He tended to be wary of them because he saw how these works undermined the uniqueness of the Christian faith; they argued that people all over the world are searching for God and that "all religions [are] essentially divine." *ST* March 1883:145; *ST* June 1890:292. In this they reflected the spirit of the age, which advocated for a universal tolerance that was "more ferocious than bigotry itself." *ST* June 1890:292.

At the same time, Charles recognized that Christians could provide scholarly studies of other religions from an orthodox perspective, which could be helpful in defending the Christian faith. One such work was George Rawlison's *The Religions of the Ancient World*, which affirmed that "there is one revelation, and that other religions

235

are the result of the depravity of man's nature." *ST* May 1883:240. Similarly, Charles appreciated James Wells's *Christ and the Heroes of Heathendom*, which defended the superiority of Christ over all other religious teachers: "Those who talk of our divine Lord as one among many teachers may here learn how far the best of those many are removed from him." *ST* November 1886:595.

It would be many more years before Charles would engage in these debates. But even in this early sermon, we see that he is aware of the religious scholarship of his day and encourages his people to apply the same kind of interest toward the study of the Jewish Old Testament. Ultimately, however, Charles believed that a true understanding of the Jewish religion could not be had apart from faith in Christ. He states here, "We . . . as Christians feel a deep interest in all the affairs of the peculiar nation since we believe that they and their rites were but types of our own more clear and glorious religion."

THE TWO BIRDS

Leviticus ~~15~~ 14:4—7

"Then shall the priest command to take for him that is to be cleansed two birds alive and clean, and cedar wood, and scarlet, and hyssop: and the priest shall command that one of the birds be killed in an earthen vessel over running water: As for the living bird, he shall take it, and the cedar wood, and the scarlet, and the hyssop, and shall dip them and the living bird in the blood of the bird that was killed over the running water: and he shall sprinkle upon him that is to be cleansed from the leprosy seven times, and shall pronounce him clean, and shall let the living bird loose into the open field."

It has been said "who that knows the worth of prayer but wishes to be often there?" and so it may be said of the Bible "who that knows its worth but wishes to be often reading it?" If we consider its variety it stands unrivalled, for it contains deep metaphysics, learned discourse on predestination, and other mysterious subjects, simple sermons, lengthened history, parables, fables, poetry, etc., etc. Amongst its varied contents there stands one subject worth of study viz the religion of that wonderful nation now called Jews.

Volumes have been written discussing the superstitions and ceremonies of Mexicans, Mahometans, etc. Why should not the Jewish religion be quite as worthy of study? Why? Men will not reply and yet neglect it, and we reply, it is the perversity of the human heart, which neglects it simply because it is revealed. If it had not been, it would have been an object of profound research.

We however, as Christians, feel a deep interest in all the affairs of the peculiar nation since we believe that they and their rites were but types of our own more clear and glorious religion. Here is the ceremony performed upon a leper after his healing. It was meet that such a mercy should not pass unnoticed. It seems right to record our thanks, for which reason I most heartily approve of thanksgivings after childbirth.

Let us draw nigh with reverence and let us not be offended if all that is visible be two little sparrows. The insignificance of the rite makes it a better sign of true obedience since it is all the more humbling to our pride. But let us look and we see:

I. CHRIST TYPIFIED IN THE BIRD WHICH DIED.

There are two birds, one of which must die. Christ or his people must die; the one or the other. Christ dies for them.

1. Death was necessary. God said death should be the forfeit of sin, and so it must be, and in order that it might be certified that it was really death. It was done publicly. So was Jesus publicly executed. Crowds saw him die. Soldiers left his legs unbroken. He was buried.

    It was done by shedding blood. Blood is a vital thing and its shedding [is], in ordinary if of man, a crime. Murder was punished. Things strangled were denied for food, and [blood] was a sacred thing. Yet was Jesus' shed, for without it there could be no remission. His head, back, feet, hands, and side ran [with] blood, his dying crimson made him a robe. He died a bloody sacrifice.

2. The Blood was shed in an earthen vessel. Why? Unless it was that Jesus must become like one of us ere he could die, or if he could die, it would not avail unless he died in human flesh.

    God had said man must die, and every syllable must be kept. Therefore, a bird is chosen of the same nature as the other, and to make it more vivid, an earthen vessel is required. A Body hast thou prepared me. We do not sufficiently notice the condescension of Christ in becoming incarnate, for it was great indeed. For a spirit to be trammeled with matter, confined in his motion etc., must be extremely disagreeable, yet this he did and became like unto us.

3. The running stream is suggestive of the spread of gospel blessings: for some drops would fall into the brook. Pass on to the river and so by the ocean to every shore. Like Wickliffe's ashes borne away by Severn to all parts: so has the power of Jesus' blood been felt amid frozen ice or torrid heats. It has spread and will [spread].

Perhaps too it suggests the fact that like a stream Christ ever runs, is inexhaustible, and undiminishable, constant and free. Wood, scarlet, and hyssop all played their part in the crucifixion and mark Jesus as the appointed victim.

II. THE SINNER.

[The rest of this page is blank in Charles's notebook.]

[Blank]

669

"THOU ART THE MAN"

Editor's Summary

Since his arrival at Waterbeach, Charles's preaching preparation had typically followed a pattern. He prepared new sermons during the week and preached them on Sundays at his church. For preaching engagements outside of his church, he usually used a previous message. Thus, his notebooks provide a generally chronological record of Charles's sermons. However, Notebook 8 marks a deviation: instead of preaching through his sermons in order, he apparently began writing them ahead of time, knowing they would be preached at a later date.

We see indication of it here. "Thou Art the Man" is his 681st preaching occasion. Yet the previous sermon was denoted as his 669th preaching occasion, meaning that Charles delivered at least twelve other sermons before this one, even though "Thou Art the Man" is the next outline in the notebook. Among those twelve are the two that he preached in London (Sermon 328, "The Faultless People," and Sermon 351, "The Father of Light") and two others that will come later in this notebook (Sermon 354, "The Branch," and Sermon 359, "Christ in You").

Another observation is that additional preaching occasions are missing. While Charles left an occasion unrecorded here and there in previous notebooks, we have at least fifteen preaching occasions missing between the start of Notebook 8 and Sermon 355 ("Christ Destroying the Works of the Devil"), which is the last preaching occasion recorded.

As for the sermon here—centered on 2 Sam 12:7, a text he would not preach from again—Charles presents the prophet Nathan as a model for ministers and argues for "the necessity of direct preaching." This would have been an unusual message to deliver to his Waterbeach congregation. Rather, it would have been more appropriate for a gathering of teachers and ministers. Charles included one such event in his autobiography:

> In the year 1853, I was asked to give an address at the annual meeting of the Cambridge Sunday School Union, in the Guildhall of that town. There were two other ministers to speak, both of them much older than myself; and, as a natural consequence, I was called upon first. I do not now recollect anything that I said on that occasion, but I have no doubt that I spoke in my usual straightforward fashion. I do not think there was anything in my remarks to cause the other speakers to turn upon me so savagely as they did when it came to their turn to address the large gathering. *Autobiography* 1:298.

After his talk, Charles was rebuked by an older minister for trying to "instruct [his] seniors." *Autobiography* 1:298. The young preacher was able to respond to the charge wisely, and in God's providence, he made an impression on Mr. George Gould of Loughton, who was in attendance. Gould would go on to tell his friend Thomas Olney at the New Park Street Chapel about Charles, and the rest is history.

Could it be that this sermon was the one given on that day? It's impossible to be sure. According to the preaching occasion record, this one was delivered after his first sermons in London, which would rule it out. Though given Charles's description of the sermon and the various oddities in his preaching "log," it's possible that "Thou Art the Man" was that sermon and one of the missing preaching occasions before London. Either way, Sermon 353 reveals a new development in Charles's ministry. He was not only preaching frequently, but he felt the freedom to encourage and instruct others in their preaching.

THOU ART THE MAN

2 Samuel 12:7

*"And Nathan said to David, Thou art the man. Thus saith the L*ORD *God of Israel,
I anointed thee king over Israel, and I delivered thee out of the hand of Saul."*

If we want heroes we must look for them amongst the great cloud of witnesses. It must be admitted that it requires more real courage coolly to perform an action than in the heat of passion or excitement to venture upon it. The one is mere animal excitement, an all but involuntary act, the first is the result of true bravery, based on solid conviction and sincere love of right.

I call Noah a hero, for amid the taunts of an ungodly world he continued his 120 years labours. I call Elijah a hero who ventured his all on his God when the bullock was consumed. I call the glorious three a triumvirate of heroes "be it known unto thee oh King we will not worship thy Gods etc." I defy the annals of history to bring forth a more noble mind tha[n] Daniel's, who prayed not fearing the wrath of ~~Babal~~ Persia's King.

Thus might I lead out a vast host of mighties who feared not the frown of any and courted the smiles of none. But I chose at once to introduce one of no mean ardor of whom it is said

"And Nathan said unto David, Thou art the man."

David had sinned awfully, but being an heir of mercy, God will not let him finally perish. Nathan shall be sent to warn him, but what prudence it required—and courage too. A parable is put into Nathan's mouth, he utters it; any other man could have done that. But see, the king does not see that it is meant for him, [so] now here is the act requiring boldness, to drive the arrow home.

Nathan does it. We picture the scene, how with solemn countenance he extends his arm, points his finger, and firmly says "Thou art the man."

It brings to my mind Knox and Queen Mary. But the case teaches us how necessary it is that every sermon should be accompanied with a direct application.

I. PERSONAL APPLICATION OF HIS SUBJECT THE MINISTER'S DUTY.

Our good old ancestors always wound up their sermons with an application. No matter if there had been sixty heads there would come at the end, as regular as clockwork, the improvement, or application; and I trust though we are not in habit of concluding with a formal "application," yet it is ever our aim to send the truth home to the heart. I shall attempt:

1. To show the necessity of direct preaching.

From analogy. The gospel is intended not to gratify the taste but to save the soul, to remedy a personal evil. Now in such a case how should we naturally act[?]

— Look at the house in flames. A man is asleep, how do we act? Shall we talk of the effect of a combination of gases to produce combustion and inform him that burning is a painful death[?] No, we cry out, "Fire, Fire, Man you are in danger, your house is burning."

— The physician who talks of death, alteratives, opiates, sudorifics, quinine etc. may talk on. We want the man who will say plainly, "there, that is your disease, and that your medicine."

— The soldier at the head of his troop will not descant on the origin of nations, the quality of steel, but will cry aloud, "On comrades, on. Conquer or die."

— Why then is the minister to deal in generalities when far more important matters are concerned[?] If your house be burnt and your body consumed, we remind you of a more awful conflagrations and more dreadful flames. So in each case.

From the nature of the thing. What is it that we preach[?] Is it a pleasing, enchanting theme to all? If so, then directness may be dispensed with, for men are ever ready to grasp that which gratifies their pride. But is it so? Quite the reverse. We preach a doctrine quite unpalatable to man. We tell him he is lost and depraved. We tell him God has it in his power to damn him and that if God saves him it will not be because he deserves it but because he will have mercy on whom he will have mercy. We tell [man] he cannot merit anything but must be saved by the death of Jesus.

This is the truth which so excited the enmity of the men of Nazareth that they tried to cast our Lord headlong. It has been opposed with unceasing rancor even to the death of its adherents. The carnal mind is at enmity to it and since it will not wound itself, the only way for us to do it ourselves [is] as the instruments of God. To show them not only what is truth but that, hate it as they may, it is truth which concerns them. "Thou art the man."

From Fact. The greatest success has always followed the preaching, the character of which has been directness. Take the case before us. Take Peter's sermon, or if you had rather, look at uninspired men. Look at Baxter who seemed to single each one out even as if there were none but that one hearing.

Whitefield was noted for this. If he preached on "thou God seest me," it was felt by all to be "thou God seest me." Every eye was on the preacher and as he unfolded his subject, the adulterer, thief, drunkard, etc. trembled to think of the eye which saw them. Before he had finished it would seem as if a trumpet were heard in the air. "Can any hide in secret that I cannot see him[?]"

The same may be said of Rowland Hill. "He speaks to me," would be the sentiment of every soul. My own experience and yours doubtless will corroborate the evidence, for it is only when we see our own interest in the subject that we can really profit by it. "Thou art the man" must tip every shaft from our bow.

2. To show the nature of direct preaching.

    1. It is not mentioning names or personality. This is much to be condemned, for it never does any good or in extreme cases. Our Savior did it, but then, he was omniscient. He might say, "ye generation of vipers," or "Son thy

sins are forgiven." We are uninspired and must know our position too well to pretend to wield the thunder bolts of Jove.

Occasions may, however, possibly occur when even personality is allowable, such as Bourdalone before Louis, when opening his eyes he said "thou art the man," or Latimer to Henry, or Knox to Mary; but few know how to do it, 99 out of a hundred miss their aim.

<u>It is imitating Christ</u>. Let us look at his ministry. His sermon at Nazareth, Luke IV. 25, was a bold declaration of divine sovereignty and [boldly] applied though the effect was his expulsion. Parable of the Vineyard, Matt. XXI. 45. The Scribes perceived that he spoke of them. How? No [n]ames were mentioned. The woman of Samaria, the rich young man, the persons who charged the woman with adultery. Now this is the way, happy is the man who understands the blessed art.

3. <u>To show the reason why we have so little of it</u>.

<u>Mistaken notions</u> of the office of the ministry. Some think it is to instruct only and therefore are argumentative, historical, and explanatory. Others think it is to interest, to refine, etc. These give us essays beautiful as marble statues, or if not quite as cold. Some good men as Porteus have had some error or other, or perhaps were too delicate, afraid of blood and broken bones.

<u>Want of piety</u>. Those who have little concern for their own souls cannot be expected to have much for others. He who does not prize religion above gold will not care for others and therefore will not deal with them as one in earnest straight home into their consciences. Give us more piety and then more directness.

<u>Want of courage</u>. Some are deficient in this qualification, but if cowardice be indulged it becomes a sin. See Jonah. If evil seems to threaten one if I speak the truth, I must remember that there are far worse [evils] impending if I do not. I must speak. I am not able to refuse on peril of wrath. Why should we fear[?] Let us speak truth and the aegis of Jehovah will cover us.

II. PERSONAL APPLICATION OF THE SUBJECT THE HEARER'S DUTY

<u>The Gospel is sent to men as individuals</u>. Every thing in it is personal, it is valueless if not applied. Christ himself avails not if he be not heartily received within. No one doctrine can edify or bless if not appropriated. If you would be saved you must seek for salvation as a single individual.

<u>You will be judged as individuals</u>. Men will not be judged by dozens or scores, not by towns or countries, but as single persons. You are responsible for yourselves. No proxies before the judgment seat: say what you will, <u>you</u> <u>must</u> appear.

<u>Men will be damned as individuals</u>. Each one shall have a hell to bear alone. "Depart" shall be sounded in the ear of each, cursed will be the name for every one. No getting through heaven's gate in a crowd. Why then so foolish as not to apply the truth to yourself[?] You will want to do so when you come to die.

Sinner, it is your own concern not mine. Let me entreat thee, bethink thyself a little. God says Man is lost, "Thou art the man." God says man cannot restore himself, "Thou art the man." God says their heart is evil, "Thou art the man." He says Jesus died to save. Perhaps "thou art the man." Who can tell, you may be an elect one? Let me see. Dost thou repent, "Thou art the man"[?] Art thou desirous of Christ, dost thou now cry to him, "Thou art the man"[?] Saints are safe, "Thou art the man." Heaven is for believers, "Thou art the man."

But do you sit hardened, then prepare for judgment for "Thou art the man"[?] Hell gapes, "thou art the man." God laughs at thy calamity, "thou art the man." I hear a shriek, I see a damned soul, "thou art the man.["]

Oh God give me thy might

<u>Amen. Amen</u>

681

"THE BRANCH"

Editor's Summary

This sermon was preached in December of 1853 in the days leading up to Christmas. In Ezekiel 17, God rebukes the exiled king of Judah for refusing to be planted in Babylon and looking to Egypt for deliverance. God then vows that He will judge Judah, and will plant his own tree to bear fruit and provide shelter.

Charles would preach on Ezek 17:24 on a future occasion, "Divine Destruction and Protection" (*MTP* 62, Sermon 3494), where he would focus on God's sovereign judgment of the proud and his exaltation of the poor: "Let the trees be silent before the Lord, for he cometh to judge them, and he judgeth them with much jealousy." *MTP* 62:15. "The Branch," however, takes a Christological focus, which is fitting given the time of year. Relying largely on Gill's commentary on this text, Charles interprets Ezekiel's prophecy as following the redemptive work of Christ, from his divine nature to his incarnation, crucifixion, and glorification. John Gill, *An Exposition of the Books of the Prophets of the Old Testament* (London: printed for the author, 1758, The Spurgeon Library), 2:82–83.

The incarnation was a source of wonder for Charles no matter the time of year. We see glimpses of his wonder here in this sermon. Holding to Nicene Christology, Charles affirms the full divinity of Christ: "He was far above principality etc., equal with God, coeternal with him, one with him." Yet in the incarnation, the Lord Jesus "was cut off from the glories and worship of the higher realms and tabernacled among men." For Charles, the glory of the incarnation is found in the union of true divinity and true humanity. "[Jesus] was just the person required, glory veiled in humility. Bone of our bone, and yet Lord over all, blessed for ever."

Preaching on another text, Charles would expand on these contrasting themes:

He was the Creator, and we see him here on earth as a creature; the Creator, who made heaven and earth, without whom was not anything made that was made, and yet he lieth in the virgin's womb; he is born; and he is cradled where the horned oxen feed. The Creator is also a creature. The Son of God is the Son of man. Strange combination! Could condescension go farther than for the Infinite to be joined to the infant, and the Omnipotent to the feebleness of a new-born babe? *MTP* 38:530.

But Charles did not attempt to explain the hypostatic union in these sermons. Rather, the manger prepared the way for the cross: "As he had to do with fallen man he was required to come as a humble person. . . . [In his] death, and burial he was a humble person." The proper response to Christ's incarnation is not to try to solve these theological mysteries, but rather to marvel: "Oh what a painful cutting off was this. Admire the love."

To all who would receive Christ by faith, no matter their nationality, rank, character, or age, they will find him to be a fruitful tree with strong branches of election, atonement, justification, calling, and perseverance—each loaded with fruits of "faith, hope, love, joy, confidence, support, etc." But Charles's vision extends beyond the salvation of the individual to the triumph of Christ over the universe. This was his grounds for certainty: not merely has God spoken, but God will most certainly work for his glory. As he preaches here:

We may be sure that the ultimate end of God's actions is his own glory. So will salvation work honour him. . . .

Triumph awaits the banners of the cross. In a few more years Hallelujahs will rend the heavens and the crown come to him whose right it is.

THE BRANCH

Ezekiel 17:22—24

*"Thus saith the Lord G*OD*; I will also take of the highest branch of the high cedar, and will set it; I will crop off from the top of his young twigs a tender one, and will plant it upon an high mountain and eminent: In the mountain of the height of Israel will I plant it: and it shall bring forth boughs, and bear fruit, and be a goodly cedar: and under it shall dwell all fowl of every wing; in the shadow of the branches thereof shall they dwell. And all the trees of the field shall know that I the L*ORD *have brought down the high tree, have exalted the low tree, have dried up the green tree, and have made the dry tree to flourish: I the L*ORD *have spoken and have done it."*

Short and weighty sayings always mark a noble mind, or at least Noble men have often employed them. As Caesar's *Veni, Vidi, Vici* etc.   but where are such sublimely sententious phrases as in Scripture[?] [Jesus] said "let there be light and there was light," "Lazarus come forth," "It is finished," and the one before us, "I the Lord have spoken and done it." None other could say so but he. His word is the same as deed, and both are infallibly connected. Let us see the great work:

I.   THE CHOICE

God having resolved to do a glorious work, namely salvation, selects some one to have the lead, management, and labor of it. This person, our Lord Jesus, is here described:

I.   <u>As a glorious person.</u>

<u>In his divinity.</u> He is truly the highest branch of the high cedar. He was far above principality etc., equal with God, coeternal with him, one with him.

<u>In his humanity.</u> He was as to his descent of the tribe of Judah, the house of David, of a royal race although a Carpenter's Son. He had all the air of a king about him. The features of David were manifest in his face. He was fairer

than the sons of men. Being also begotten of the Holy Ghost he was truly a glorious personage, and so fit for a glorious business. But as he had to do with fallen man he was required to come

As a humble person. A tender plant, a mere twig, despised and contemned. In his birth, education, estate, reputation, character, food, lodging, death, and burial, he was a humble person. He was just the person required, glory veiled in humility. Bone of our bone and yet Lord over all, blessed for ever.

II. THE PLANTING

God having chosen the Branch next cuts it off, and here is:

Christ's descent from heaven. He was cut off from the glories and worship of the higher realms and tabernacled among men.

Christ's death. He was cut off from the land of the living. Oh what a painful cutting off was this. Admire the love.

Christ's glory in his Church. Is set forth by his being planted on a mountain for stability, visibility, and loftiness. The church is indeed a mountain, and on this the branch is planted. In the affections of the bloodbought and bloodwashed throng. He died as the wheat that he might not be alone.

Three times [the tree] is repeated, perhaps to show that the three persons [the Trinity] are all concerned. Here is the tree of life planted in the midst of the Church.

III. THE FRUIT

Christ is no barren plant, though the mountain of the church is naturally strong ground. Christ brings forth boughs and fruit. The boughs are the great doctrines of grace, the great truths of our holy religion. As we seldom hear them mentioned, a catalogue of them may be interesting.

Election, personal, free, unconditional, eternal.
Atonement, sufficient, efficacious, infallible.
Justification.

Effectual Calling by the Holy Ghost's irresistible power.
Perseverance, certain, unfrustra[ta]ble.

These are great arms from the root, Jesus Christ, and are loaded with fruit. These fruits are the graces of Christians, their comfort and support. These are faith, love, hope, joy, confidence, support etc. Precious fruit, I will live on thee for ever.

IV. THE DWELLERS

All will not dwell there, but some of all sorts will.

<u>All countries</u>. Cold or hot. Savage or civilized, East or West, Black or White.

<u>All ranks</u>. Some kings, nobles and lords; tradesman, farmer, sailor, soldier, beggar, the Soudra and Pariah.

<u>All characters</u>, if believers, the zealous, hot, bold, fiery; the calm, deliberate, loving, gentile, serious, gay. Old greyheaded sinners saved, and those called early in life.

<u>All ages</u>, the babe, the youth, the man, the grey head, the old and decrepit. Some of all sorts are under his boughs.

V. THE GLORY

We may be sure that the ultimate end of God's actions is his own glory. So will salvation work honour him.

High trees shall be levelled, green ones withered. Triumph awaits the banners of the cross. In a few more years Hallelujahs will rend the heavens and the crown come to him whose right it is. Even so. Amen.

See here, believer, the plant of renown; make thy boast in the Lord, and triumph in thy God.

680

"CHRIST DESTROYING THE WORKS OF THE DEVIL"

Editor's Summary

Christmas Day of 1853 fell on a Sunday. Preaching in Waterbeach on 1 John 3:8—a text he would preach from at least one other time (see *MTP* 29:361–72)—Charles delivered a sermon on how Christ came to destroy sin, hell, and death. This was not a typical Christmas message on the incarnation. In this, we see something of Charles's nuanced relationship with the holiday.

As an heir of the Puritans, Charles rejected any historical or spiritual significance to December 25. On Christmas Eve in 1871, he reminded his congregants, "Certainly we do not believe in the present ecclesiastical arrangement called Christmas. . . . We find no Scriptural warrant whatever for observing any day as the birthday of the Savior; and, consequently, its observance is a superstition, because not of divine authority." *MTP* 17:697. At the same time, Charles understood the difficulties that his working-class congregation faced. Like him, many of them had moved from the country to the big city and rarely had opportunity to see their families. He was grateful for any holiday that brought families together and provided workers with a few days of rest. Preaching on Christmas Sunday in 1856, he declared,

> For my part, I wish there were twenty Christmas days in the year. It is seldom that young men can meet with their friends; it is rarely they can all be united as happy families; and though I have no respect to the religious observance of the day, yet I love it as a family institution, as one of England's brightest days, the great Sabbath of the year, when the plough rests in its furrow, when the din of business is hushed, when the mechanic and the working man go out to refresh themselves upon the green sward of the glad earth. *NPSP* 3:18.

However, on December 25, 1853, the mood at Waterbeach Chapel was somber. When Charles had received the invitation to preach at the New Park Street Chapel in late November, one of the deacons "shook his head, and remarked that . . . he always knew that his minister would be run away with by some large church or other, but that he was a little surprised that the Londoners should have heard of [him] quite so soon." *Autobiography* 1:317. Now, with Charles having preached in London the previous Sunday, many in the Waterbeach congregation shared their deacon's fears. Their pastor had agreed to fill the pulpit in London again on January 1, so it is possible that he gave the congregation this news sometime that day. Afterward, he wrote to his father about their response: "My people are very sad; some wept bitterly at the sight of me." *Autobiography* 1:342. Yet amid these events, Charles "made no allusion to the subject in the pulpit." Rather, as always, he was committed to preaching God's Word, and on this Christmas morning, he declared the stirring truth of *Christus Victor*. In spite of all their fears and uncertainties, the Waterbeach congregation could rejoice that Christ their Savior came to ruin Satan's efforts and triumph over him. "Christian[,] join the anthem this morning with all thy soul. '[Christ] hath destroyed the works of the devil.'"

CHRIST DESTROYING THE WORKS OF THE DEVIL

1 John 3:8

"He that committeth sin is of the devil; for the devil sinneth from the beginning. For this purpose the Son of God was manifested, that he might destroy the works of the devil."

This is the day (Xmas 1853) when we feel constrained to think of the birth of Jesus. Our neighbours do so, and little as we, the sons of the Puritans, are accustomed to regard days and weeks, yet it does not seem to us sinful or improper to remember the incarnation of our Lord today.

No act of Deity is more worthy of the attention of the universe than that rightly called, the manifesting of the Son of God. Even Creation, the sight of which made the morning stars sing together and the sons of God shout for joy, did not so much awake the admiration of celestials as the scene of God veiling himself in humanity.

If we rightly consider it we shall feel the same emotions. It is very right to read the book of nature, to see a present God in all and make this earth the helper of our devotion. But it is wrong to extol too much the study of nature, for to wise men it will not have so much [attraction] as the study of the mystery "God manifest in the flesh."

I will not bear you to Bethlehem and detain you with a view of the babe and his mother. I will not even lead out your mind to admire the love and the condescension of the wondrous act, although here would be a string of topics profitable to us. But rather, I will keep to the text and consider the purpose of this "manifestation."

The purpose mentioned in the text is but one link in a chain of purposes uniting the sinner saved and God glorified. "To destroy the works of the devil." Now we must understand all this in a certain sense, viz., for his people, for truly some of our race will feel eternally the "works of Satan," and for them these works are not destroyed. But for believers, Jesus came from his high glories to destroy Satan's works.

And what are the works of our great enemy[?] Come see, believer, the ruin of his labours and sing upon the desolations of his empire. His works are like himself: abominable, evil, and only evil. Thanks be to God for their destruction.

I.   SIN.   Three Works of Satan

II. DEATH.   Destroyed by the Son of God.

III. HELL.

I. <u>SIN</u>.

Is the work of Satan; there was no moral evil until he conceived it. He led astray the sons of the morning. He made war in heaven. He in the likeness of a serpent dropped the seed of sin into our mother's ear, from which has sprung a fearful harvest extensive as our earth. He laid the first black stone of the horrid palace which is now his dwelling, the chambers of sin.

But sin is destroyed by Jesus. It is driven from its haunts and as the result of the victory we see or shall see:

> 1. A rescued man.
> 2. A rescued world.

> 1. <u>A rescued man</u>. Man is full of sin. It is in him by nature and oh how deeply by practice. He is fallen as to every shadow of good and utterly gone astray. [He is] under the dominion of sin and so [is] captive to the devil. But Christ came to destroy sin for every believer and does actually accomplish the design.
>
> **His work for us.** His agonies and death bought for us pardon, justification, and acceptance with God. Our sins are put to death by his death. They were crucified on his cross and there expired. The devil by sin made me guilty, but Christ by his righteousness makes me innocent. I am in God's

sight as if I had never sinned. My sins are now annihilated, gone, never to return.

Pardoned soul thou mayest fling the gauntlet at the world and say "Who is he that condemneth[?]"

Sinner great as thy sin is, be not in despair; for this purpose was he manifested, to take away sin, and thine shall be taken away entirely the moment thou believest.

His work in us, which he works by the Holy Spirit in our hearts, is also most necessary to complete the destruction of sin, for even after pardon there still remains sin within us. Evil dispositions, desires, lusts are there but they must not reign there any longer. A stronger than he is come, and the strong man armed must keep the house no longer.

Conversion bursts the door—it is the beginning of the great sanctifying process. And what a beginning it is, worthy of a God. It is a completer reversion of the whole man. It is as if a river should reverse its course. The stormy sea becomes calm as a lake, and rock and adamant like melted wax. Sin is dethroned, and though it lurks in dens and caves its death knell is rung. It is a condemned outlaw. By the mighty work of the almighty Spirit, it groweth weaker and weaker until in glory the man becomes "without fault before the throne of God."

Thus is the work of Satan demolished in two great ways by Christ, and we see lost man, perfect as at first.

2. <u>A rescued world</u>. Man fell and the whole race fell in a mass. Let us look on the fallen world, made so by the craft of the devil. One is sickened at the first cursory view: we see armies marching to shed each other's blood, deluded crowds bowing down to blocks, cruel to one another, filthy, bestial. Let us a moment stay and review the sins of the world:

<u>Idolatry</u>, in its myriad forms, cruel, obscene, degrading, sickening, one of the masterpieces of the devil—but it shall be destroyed, yea it totters now. Bel boweth down and Nebo stoopeth, soon shall the gods be cast to moles and bats and this blindness be removed.

<u>War</u>, which is murder on a large scale, shall one day cease. Vultures and wolves have been gorged with the flesh of men. But hell's blood[-]red

flag shall be rent. The sword which is forged there shall be made a [ploughshare] and peace shall prevail.

Slavery, that plague spot on the fair hand of America, that curse of curses, shall be destroyed and the clank of the chain heard no more.

Oppression of every kind shall cease, no tyrant shall be found on earth.

Robbery, dishonesty, lying, anger, and bigotry all shall die. Nor shall . . .

Antichrist be spared. Great Babel shall fall, see, she reeleth to and fro, her hour hasteth when she shall sit in the ground. The queen shall be made naked and her flesh shall be burned.

Then comes a renovated earth; for this purpose is the Son of God manifested that he may destroy the works of the devil.

Shout, oh heavens, for the Lord hath done it.

> "Sin is vanquish'd sin is slain
> Christ hath broken the tyrants chain
> Dash'd the idols from their seat
> Made them dust beneath his feet
> Hush'd the shout and stayed the fight
> Clear'd away the shades of night.
> Shout the vict'ry once again
> Sin is vanquish'ed, sin is slain."

II. DEATH.

The second work of Satan is death. Adam and Eve would have lived on till now if they had not sinned. But sin has changed all nature. Now the skeleton form of death marches o'er the land and devours thousands at a meal. The world is a huge hospital, earth a grand cemetery for our race, its dust was much of it once alive. It is an Aceldama, or else a valley of dry bones.

But death itself shall find a death. Death is destroyed.

By the rich support given to the saints. Death ceases to be a punishment, in fact it is far more a blessing than a curse. Its triumphant shout drowns its feeble cry of pain. It is the gate of endless joy. Christian, death is destroyed.

<u>By the resurrection</u>. Death loses his prey, the body is released from his iron grasp. The old tyrant sat in a palace of skulls and bones, but it fled from him; bone came to its bone and lived.

Oh that resurrection morn, how will death weep to see its victims live. He shall disgorge his prey. His pall shall be rent into shreds, his coffin shall burst asunder, his grave rifled.

<u>By Immortality</u>. Death and Life have run a race and Death has won it hitherto. But Immortality is brought to light by the gospel, and the bright discovery has chased away the spectres of the grave, lit up the vault with joy, and broken the scythe of the mower.

III. <u>HELL</u>.

The chef'd'auvre of Satan is hell, and this is not destroyed for the unbeliever, but for the saint it is. Its numbers would have been infinitely greater if the elect had not been redeemed, but by Christ Hell has been despoiled and much depopulated. Its dungeons in which the saints should have been immured have been blasted with almighty thunder, the racks and fetters broken, its fires quenched so far as the elect are concerned. Satan is not king of hell, or rather soon he will not be. He will be chained himself and become like one of the rest.

Now let us, like as the Roman looked on the ruins of Carthage with pride, look on these ruins with joy. Fallen towers, broken chains, opened dungeons, battlements battered down. Hallelujah. Jesus is our hero, see he comes. Sing, oh ye angels, he comes, and at his chariot wheel drags three monsters: Sin, Death, and Hell. All hail, all hail. King of Kings, thou hast bruised the dragon and overcome his brood. See he smites off the head of each and holds their horrid heads aloft. The universe bends down in admiration, then claps its hands and sings aloud, "Glory, and praise, and power, and majesty, and dominion, and honour, and might unto thee, oh Son of God."

Christian, join the anthem this morning with all thy soul.

<u>"He hath destroyed the works of the devil."</u>

689

Sermon No. 356

"THE WORDS OF THE WISE"

Editor's Summary

This sermon marks a transition in Charles's notebooks. All the sermons after this point no longer contain a number for the preaching occasion. We can be confident that he preached some of these sermons (see, for example, Sermon 365, "Jesus Saves from Sin"; Sermon 367, "The Ministers"; and Sermon 385, "Paul's Commission"), so it's unclear why he stopped tracking them. One possible explanation is that Charles was simply too busy working as a tutor and preaching back and forth between London and Waterbeach. However, he had been busy with itinerant ministry and tutoring for several years already. Another explanation is that, as he gained experience, he no longer felt the need to number his sermons.

The last recorded preaching occasion was the previous sermon, which he delivered on the last Sunday of 1853. This likely means that the remaining forty-five untracked sermons were being delivered throughout the winter, spring, and summer of 1854. The earliest one we have recorded in the *Metropolitan Tabernacle Pulpit* is from November 5, 1854 (*MTP* 50, Sermon 2908). The remaining sermons in Notebooks 8 and 9 form a bridge from Charles's first sermons to his published sermons in the *New Park Street* and *Metropolitan Tabernacle Pulpit* series.

In this message on Eccl 12:11, a text he would not preach from again, Charles was again influenced by Gill in comparing God's Word to goads and nails. John Gill, *An Exposition of the Old Testament* (London: printed for the author, 1765, The Spurgeon Library), 4:585–86. As a preacher, Charles was confident in the confronting power of the Bible "to convince of sin," "to urge in duty," and "to defeat enemies." God's Word was not always to be a "soothing syrup"; it must also be "a goading word." Charles would at times find his hearers offended by his preaching, especially as he combatted

263

false teaching and the sins of his day. Yet this offense was not a failure, but evidence of Scripture's power.

The other function of the Word of God was to fasten God's people "to one another," "to the truth," and "to Christ." As a pastor, Charles understood that church unity could not be found in traditions, or denominational activities, or personal preferences. Rather, it must be found in the truth of God's Word. Against all those who worked for greater ecumenism at the expense of Scripture, Charles would declare, "I hope that, some day, we shall all bring our views to the test of the Sacred Scriptures. Then shall we have one Church, 'one Lord, one faith, one baptism.'" *MTP 46:105.*

To be sure, Charles was not opposed to church unity. He did not hesitate to partner with Baptists and Christians from other denominations, so long as they held to the Bible. It was as they held to the Scriptures that they were united to one another: "The more we study our Bibles the more we shall love each other. The words of men separate, many sermons are uncharitable, many conversations are schismatical, but the Bible is a binding book, and when its own words are used, and the creature lowered, then we shall see Unity."

THE WORDS OF THE WISE

Ecclesiastes 12:11

*"The words of the wise are as goads, and as nails fastened by the
masters of assemblies, which are given from one shepherd."*

We have no hesitation in referring these words to the "words of the wise" contained in the Scriptures. The words of other wise men are excellent and worthy of remembrance but the infallible words of inspired men are more to be reverenced.

Here we may remark how many more of these words are we possessed of than Solomon was. He was wise, but he that is least in the kingdom of heaven is greater than he, i.e. possesses more light, more of "the words of the wise." Here we have them collected in one volume, and not deficient in copies as in Josiah's time. Here we have:

I.   TWO FIGURES SETTING FORTH THE NATURE AND EFFECTS OF THE WORD.

II. TWO OFFICES IN RELATION TO THE GOING FORTH OF THE WORD.

I.   <u>TWO FIGURES SETTING FORTH THE NATURE AND EFFECTS OF THE WORD.</u>

Solomon was a wise man and put his knowledge of nature into use in his writings and preaching. There is scarce an object in nature which he does not make tributary to [God]—from the ant, spider, and coney, up to the eagle, horse, and lion. From this he rose on the way to the cesarim heberaea. Everything in pastoral household or city life he mentions in due place, and in our text he went to the herdsman and the carpenter and borrowed ideas from the goad and nails.

The words of the wise are as goads.

A goad was an instrument used for goading on, quickening the pace of cattle by pricking them.

To convince of sin. Men need something to arouse them, to make them feel, to penetrate into their hearts. Now the word of the Lord is sharper than any two edged sword. Heb. 4.12. It pricked the Jews to the heart. Acts II. 37. It is a sharp oxgoad penetrating the hide and leather covering of the sinner, his prejudice, his hardness, his contempt.

See it in Colonel Gardiner, Newton, Bunyan, and all sinners saved.

To urge in duty. Even the heirs of heaven need urging on to their portion. They are apt to pitch their tents, to be slothful, to sleep, to lag behind. Our God has many ways of urging us on by providential trials etc., but the sweetest method is by the goad of his word used by the ministry.

Every wise minister will use a little of the goad and every wise hearer will feel that he needs it. God's ministers are not always to be mixing soothing syrups and sedatives; they must also make the word a goading word, let their hearers be ever so much displeased. May God make it a goad to you and me.

To defeat enemies. When the ancient Israelites had neither sword nor spear they sharpened their oxgoads, and like Shamgar, did wonders therewith. So we also, leaving the sword and spear of logic and learning to Goliaths and Nimrods, go out with a weapon not carnal but mighty for the pulling down of [strongholds].

We attack infidelity in its Protean forms and rout it, we turn our weapons against Antichrist and the rocks on her hills, we overturn idolatry. Our missionaries land on an island with this oxgoad in their hands; war ceases, old superstitions flee, and the land is won. No empire can hold out, no enemy can conquer. It is destined to conquer. The oxgoad shall be the sceptre.

The words of the wise are as nails.

<u>Fastened</u>. Fastening themselves, the words of God go deep and take firm hold on us. Have we not found it so? Has not some warning text haunted us day by day? Has not some comforting one been with us we knew not why? Many texts have remained for years and have not been rusted out but were of use.

<u>Fastening</u>. Nails are used to fasten things together, and the words of the wise:

1. Do fasten us <u>to one another</u>. For when any disagreement would occur, in comes a promise as a quietus and binds us again into one body. The more we study our Bibles the more we shall love each other. The words of men separate, many sermons are uncharitable, many conversations are schismatical, but the Bible is a binding book, and when its own words are used and the creature lowered, then we shall see Unity.

2. They fasten us <u>to the truth</u>. Some are ever wavering, not knowing anything rightly, ever changing, carried away by every wind of doctrine. But the words of the wise fasten us so that we know what we believe. We may read controversial works and be unsettled, but reading the Bible will never unsettle any one, but [rather] confirm us in the faith. Here is solid ground for the sole of our foot. All doubts may be slain by these nails in the same way that Jael served Sisera.

3. The[y] fasten us <u>to Christ</u>. When we might altogether forsake him, some warning nails us to him. When faith would fail and let go its hold on the Beloved, then comes a text and binds a silken cord around him and us.

   When Satan drags us away the nail holds us still. It will not lose its hold. It has pierced our heart and his heart, and nailed them eternally together, and they cannot be rent asunder any more.

   Let us see if we have had any of these nails driven into us. Has the goad touched us[?] If so, here we can corroborate the evidence of the Preacher by our own experience.

Goads and nails fastened.

II. TWO OFFICES IN RELATION TO THE GOING FORTH OF THE WORD.

1. <u>The Masters of Assemblies</u>. No assembly can well be kept in order without a leader or master of assemblies. Such were the high priests, the prophets, and afterwards the Sajans or rulers of the Synagogues.

With us [it is] the minister who reads, expounds, offers prayer and preaches the word. The masters of assemblies should be God-sent, God-taught, and God-loving men. May God give us many such. Now the business of these men is to fasten the wise words:

<u>By simplicity of speech</u>. Explaining all dark passages, clearing up difficulties, and taking care not to make it hard by using learned language. Let it be the gospel *in dishabille*, it is "most adorn'd when unadorn'd the most."

<u>By illustration</u>. This is a mighty means of fastening truth. All the prophets used it and our Saviour was very copious in it. No <u>dry</u> discourses, but lively and interesting.

<u>By earnestness</u>. What a man does not feel himself he cannot well make others feel. We want warmth, we want love to souls and burning desire for their salvation, and then the nails would fasten.

<u>By the Spirit</u>. Our fastening will not avail if the great Spirit does not also come to our aid. But he can so deeply enfix it that the devil's irons can never wrench it out again.

Come friends, have you ever had the nail thus fastened? Has it penetrated and lodged in your memory, judgment, conscience, and heart?

2. <u>The one Shepherd</u>. There are many masters of assemblies but only one Shepherd. This is the common name of our Lord Jesus Christ and a very precious name. How sweetly doth it utter his nature and depict his worth. Shepherd. There is but one. Ministers are only sheep with bells on to lead the others. He is the great Bishop of Souls. Now it says that he gives the words. The masters of assemblies only fasten them. He <u>gives</u> them the nails.

Inspiration is the great work of the Spirit sent by our Lord. Every word of the Bible is inspired, not one letter (as originally given) can be confuted. It is from Jehovah as much as Creation itself.

Suggestion. God gives his ministers texts by suggesting them to their minds. He does not inspire us but he leads our minds to subjects.

Assistance. When he aids, the text seems to break itself up, divisions and thoughts grow up. We speak, our tongue runs on, thoughts flow apace, matter comes, and we rejoice to feel a happy liberty.

Now let us:
  Thank him for his words
        for a master of assemblies
  but more for the one Shepherd.

"UNPARALLELED SORROW"

Editor's Summary

This short sermon outline on Lam 2:12, a passage Charles would not preach from again, is a meditation on our suffering and Christ's suffering. In it, Charles takes Jeremiah's moving description of the weeping of his people under God's judgment as a type of the weeping and suffering of Christ.

Because of the brevity of this message, it's possible that it was written in the hours before a Sabbath afternoon or evening service. It also appears that Charles initially meant to preach on wrong and right complaints within the church, as seen in his introduction. Instead, he ended up writing two points that contrast the Christian's complaints versus Christ's complaints. Perhaps his haste in constructing this sermon contributed to the lack of clarity there.

Nevertheless, in "Unparalleled Sorrow" we have a brief window into Charles's pastoral care for his people during times of suffering. His first point is devoted to correcting all the wrong ways Christians are tempted to think about their suffering. Much of his teaching here is consistent with what he would teach in the future. For example, here he condemns complaining as "very wrong and foolish … false, … sinful." On another occasion, he would put it this way: "Whatever happens to you, there is nothing can happen to you worse than your being impatient, for of all troubles in the world that one can be troubled with, an impatient spirit is about the worst. O that ye would endeavor to conquer impatience." *MTP* 17:693.

Another point he makes here is that our afflictions are deserved. He would preach the same idea in a future sermon:

In your affliction humble yourself by confessing that you deserve all that you are suffering. Is it poverty? — then, dear child of God, own that you deserve poverty because of your love of the world. Is it physical pain? Then own how every erring member deserves to smart. It is a great thing to have wrung out of us the confession that our chastisement is less than our deservings, and that the Lord is not dealing with us after our sins, nor rewarding us according to our iniquities. *MTP* 29:426.

Charles would have denied that anyone can ever definitively interpret God's providence by connecting specific sins to specific sufferings. *NPSP* 3:379–80. At the same time, he believed that every affliction comes from the hand of God. Because of the reality of sin, suffering is part of God's curse on humanity, which all people deserve. Therefore, the Christian's response to suffering should not be to complain but to humble oneself before the Almighty.

The only exception to this merited suffering, of course, is Jesus. Here was one who never sinned, who did not deserve pain or grief, and yet "his death was unparalleled in sorrow." So why did he suffer? He did it not for himself, but "for others, his enemies." In other words, for all those who are tempted to complain in their affliction, "fly to him," the One who willingly suffered in their place in order to save them.

What we see here is that Charles's pastoral response to suffering was first and foremost theological. This is not to say that he was unfeeling or unsympathetic toward his people's pain. Certainly, these truths needed to be communicated patiently and tenderly to those who were in the midst of trials and hardships. But ultimately, Charles understood that equipping people with theological truth to counteract the temptation toward discouragement and complaining that comes during difficult times.

UNPARALLELED SORROW
Lamentations 2:12

"They say to their mothers, Where is corn and wine? when they swooned as the wounded in the streets of the city, when their soul was poured out into their mothers' bosom."

Jeremiah has well been called the weeping prophet. He is eloquent. The Eloquence of woe he had, which is the most moving of all.

There are innumerable touches of most unrivalled beauty. He wept o'er his beloved country, his temple, and his nation. Oh had we right feelings, we should weep over the church and over our fellow members. No troubles are really greater than church troubles.

Here is the church['s] complain[t]. We shall note:

I.   THE COMPLAINT IN THE WRONG MOUTH.

II. THE COMPLAINT IN THE RIGHT MOUTH.

I.   THE COMPLAINT IN THE WRONG MOUTH.

When a believer takes it to himself and wants all the world to behold his sorrow and consider it as unique, solitary, and unparalleled.

1. I will condemn the cry.
2. I will hush the cry.
3. I will supplant the cry.

1. I will condemn the cry. It is very wrong and foolish. It is false, it is sinful.

It arises from ignorance. Visit widows, asylums, unions, jails, dungeons, [and] hospitals, and they will tell you that you are not alone. It arises from impatience. It is proud nature kicking against its Maker.

2. <u>I will hush the cry</u>.

    You deserve it, therefore be still.
    Your God does it, resist not.
    Your benefit is designed by it.
    Your heaven will be brightened by it.

3. <u>I will supplant the cry</u>.

Consider how much better you are treated than some. You are a child of God, a reclaimed prodigal, a ransomed slave—therefore be glad, say:

    Was ever mercy so great
    As that bestow'd on me[?]

II. THE COMPLAINT IN THE RIGHT MOUTH.

Jesus could say it most truly, and if we look at him we shall profit by it.

His <u>life</u> was singularly painful. It was a life of Poverty, Persecution, Hatred, Ingratitude, Misrepresentation, Almost Loneliness. Besides his <u>sympathy</u> for others and his keen feelings at the <u>sight of sin</u> and a dreary <u>certainty of painful death</u> in the end.

    But his <u>death</u> was unparalleled in sorrow.
    He deserved it not in the least.
    He had no friend. Betrayed and forsaken.
    No one ever had more ignominy.
    God forsook him.
    Sin lay on him.

    But the wonder lies here.

It was for others, his enemies. Is it nothing to you, my hearers, did he not die for you[?] If he did not, then weep over your ruin for you are inevitably lost. But if he did, then fly to him, clasp his knees, and be his servant for ever.

    Oh God bless me or I am undone. <u>Amen</u>

"THE KING'S PASSAGE OF KIDRON"

Editor's Summary

Charles preached on this text at least one other time in his ministry, "The King Passing over Kedron" (*MTP* 60, Sermon 3431). It's difficult to know whether or not he developed the later sermon—written nearly fifteen years hence in 1869—from this earlier one, but the two outlines do show some overlapping content. Structurally, this message has two points, while the 1869 sermon has three. However, the first two points of both sermons follow the same basic themes.

When Charles did add a third point, he transitioned from the suffering of kings and the suffering of Christ to our personal experience of suffering: "III. A word or two to ourselves concerning our passing the brook Kedron." *MTP* 60:533. Assuming that he indeed drew from this sermon, then his third point is likely an expansion of the conclusion here: "Know assuredly that we must go over Kidron. There is no other road to heaven, but fear not, [the King] will help thee."

Like the previous sermon (Sermon 357, "Unparalleled Sorrow"), this one also deals with the topic of suffering. What's different, though, is that Charles takes a much more pastoral approach. In his later sermon, he would focus on David in order to remind and encourage his people that even the greatest men suffer.

In him there was no guile; he hated deception, and he loved his God with all his heart; and yet, for all that, he must needs pass over the brook Kedron. Hated by his subjects, despised by his darling child, with all the robes of royalty put aside, bare-footed and with sackcloth on his head, Jerusalem's best and greatest king makes his way into the wilderness. *MTP* 60:530.

In other words, suffering is not an unusual, and Christians should not be caught off guard. As they come to expect suffering and persecution, God's people can learn "contentment with our lot" and "thankfulness for any temporary release from trouble."

An even greater comfort, however, is that God has not abandoned them; Christ is with them in their suffering. In "Unparalleled Sorrow," Charles focused on Christ's innocence and the fact that his suffering was in the place of his people. Here, Charles presents Christ not only as our substitute but as the one who accompanies us in our suffering. He has "first gone over Kidron," but also, "he goes over with us: our troubles, sorrows and griefs. He bore all as our companion, yea he is our companion now, every black stream we cross." Far from begrudging our tears, our King is a compassionate companion who understands our sorrows. And because he too has passed over that brook, we can be confident that we will cross it as well. We will make it on the road to heaven, because he will help us.

> Be encouraged then, ye feeble bands of trembling Christians, encouraged in all your sufferings and griefs for Christ's sake, for as he yet rose from the dead and led captivity captive, even so shall the feeblest of his followers. *MTP* 60:533.

THE KING'S PASSAGE OF KIDRON

2 Samuel 15:23

"And all the country wept with a loud voice, and all the people passed over: the king also himself passed over the brook Kidron, and all the people passed over, toward the way of the wilderness."

There are many spots in the world of no great note geographically considered, but of immense interest as connected with actions of men.

The pass of Thermopylae, the rock of Plymouth, the village of Elstow, the church at Kidderminster. So in Palestine we have many a shrine: Bethlehem, Jerusalem, Gethsemane, and amongst a long list, the little brook Kidron.

I. KINGS HAVE TROUBLES.

We sometimes murmur because we have brook Kidrons to cross. It is some slight consolation that others have to cross it too. Rank does not exempt from trouble.

Reason proves it, for we can all see that wealth and power have to do with body, not with mind. Sceptres have no sway over pain and crowned heads are often aching heads.

History proves it. Sacred history accords a large amount of trial to kings. Saul, David, Hezekiah, Josiah, etc. Our own country tells us of many such case[s]. William I, Henry I, II, Ed. II, Rich. II etc., etc. Albert.

Now from this let us learn·
    Contentment with our lot.
    Resignation to trial.

Thankfulness for any temporary release from trouble.

II. <u>THE KING OF KINGS HAD TROUBLES.</u>

He crossed the brook K[i]dron on that gloomy night. One brook he went over <u>for</u> us. The brook of our sins. Kidron, the Black Brook, was the common sewer of the temple, all the filth ran there. All our sins have run into one stream and he has waded through the black tide. Let us muse awhile on Gethsemane. One brook he goes over <u>with</u> us: our troubles, sorrows, and griefs. He bore all as our companion, yea he is our companion now, every black stream we cross. Having suffered he has:

<u>Atonement</u> – he has gone over Kidron.
<u>Compassion</u> – he has gone over Kidron.
<u>Leadership</u> – he first has gone over Kidron.

Know assuredly that we must go over Kidron. There is no other road to heaven, but fear not, he will help thee.

Amen, oh King.

Sermon No. 359

"CHRIST IN YOU"

Editor's Summary

According to his record of preaching occasions, it appears that Charles preached this sermon at least three times in the week leading up to Christmas of 1853 (cf. Sermon 355, "Christ Destroying the Works of the Devil"). It would have been a fitting message for that time of year, as it provides a wonderful meditation on the person and work of Christ.

Thirty years later, Charles would preach on this text again: "Christ in You" (*MTP* 29, Sermon 1720) The structure and content of the later sermon mirrors this one, suggesting perhaps that Charles drew from it. Comparing these two sermons, it's striking to see how Charles's admiration of Christ is a consistent feature of his preaching. Here, he remarks, "One feels tempted at the name [of Christ] to run off in a strain of rhapsody in admiration" of the Lord's attributes. The descriptive phrases in the outline—"his creating wisdom," "Christ incarnate," "Christ the bleeding Redeemer"—are a prompt for the preacher to expound on the glories of Christ. In the later sermon, he marveled,

> Think of it! The Infinite an infant, the Ancient of days a child, the Ever Blessed a man of sorrows and acquainted with grief! The idea is original, astounding, divine. Oh, that this blending of the two natures should ever have taken place! Brethren, the heart of the gospel throbs in the truth. *MTP* 29:267.

In proclaiming Christ, the goal of Charles's preaching was for his hearers to find their joy in the Savior. "Do we know the music of the name of our beloved? Do we feel that his glorious name is our strength?" This resolve never wavered, as seen in Arnold Dallimore's biography of Spurgeon, where he tells the following story. Though the source is not provided, this account does reflect something of the impact of Charles's preaching in his day.

During the 1880s a group of American ministers visited England, prompted especially by a desire to hear some of the celebrated preachers of that land. On a Sunday morning they attended the City Temple where Dr. Joseph Parker was the pastor. Some two thousand people filled the building, and Parker's forceful personality dominated the service. His voice was commanding, his language descriptive, his imagination lively, and his manner animated. The sermon was scriptural, the congregation hung upon his words, and the Americans came away saying, "What a wonderful preacher is Joseph Parker!"

That evening they went to hear Spurgeon at the Metropolitan Tabernacle. The building was much larger than the City Temple, and the congregation was more than twice the size. Spurgeon's voice was much more expressive and moving and his oratory noticeably superior. But they soon forgot all about the great building, the immense congregation, and the magnificent voice. They even overlooked their intention to compare the various features of the two preachers, and when the service was over they found themselves saying, "What a wonderful Savior is Jesus Christ!" Arnold Dallimore, *Spurgeon: A New Biography* (Chicago: Moody Press, 1984), 216.

CHRIST IN YOU
Colossians 1:27

"To whom God would make known what is the riches of the glory of this mystery among the Gentiles; which is Christ in you, the hope of glory:"

A religion without mystery would be no religion at all. The mysteries of Popery, Mormonism, and Puseyism are mysteries well calculated to exalt and enrich their ringleaders, and requiring much faith on the behalf of their votaries.

They are mysteries of faith, or rather lies. Our mystery is a mystery of experience and is here put in few words, that although unknown by the natural, uninitiated man, the spiritual may discern the secret of the Lord.

I. CHRIST.

One feels tempted at the name to run off in a strain of rhapsody in admiration of his native glory, his creating wisdom, his wondrous titles, or his many crowns. But the Christ with whom our secret deals is Christ in humiliation, Christ incarnate, Christ the obedient Servant, Christ the bleeding Redeemer, then the rising conqueror, the constant intercessor, the Captain, the joy of our souls. Do we know the music of the name of our beloved? Do we feel that his glorious name is our strength? Then we must likely know the rest of the mystery.

II. CHRIST IN YOU.

Christ crucified will save none of us unless he becomes Christ *in* us. This is the Holy Spirit's work.

Christ <u>in</u> us is a comprehensive expression. It means, Christ <u>desired</u>. How earnestly does the penitent desire Christ and long for him more than they that watch for the morning. Do you?

Christ <u>believed</u> in, the first act of the new man in coming out of darkness is faith in Jesus. It succeeds <u>desire</u> which is groping in the dark. Do we cast ourselves wholly on the merits of his agonies and death[?] If so we know the mystery and may go on to . . .

<u>Christ beloved</u>. Love follows faith, it never precedes it. It is an embracing and pressing to the heart. It must be real, hearty, supreme, not effervescent but abiding. Have you this?

<u>Christ rejoiced</u> in follows and ever is the fruit of desire, faith, and love. This is Christ in you indeed when we can rejoice in trouble, yea in the article of death. Come let us see whether we understand this mystery. Christ <u>in</u> us.

III. <u>CHRIST IN YOU, THE HOPE OF GLORY</u>.

This is the finishing letter of the mystery, viz. to have a hope of glory. All men have a hope, but only a few have a hope of glory. But of that few, how very few have a <u>good</u> hope of glory. Let us see if our hope is good. If it is Christ in us which gives us hope, then it is right and good. Does our hope purify us[?] Does it abide in fiery trials[?] Dare you examine it[?] Is it built on the rock[?] If so, go on joyfully all the days of thy life for now thou knowest more than the wise men and the Ancients.

You know a mystery their philosophy knows not.

678. 686. 679

"THE BELOVED IN VARIOUS POSTURES"

Editor's Summary

Though Charles would go on to preach many sermons from the Song of Solomon, it appears he did not preach from this particular verse again. However, this sermon is a rewrite of one he delivered in the fall of 1853 (see Sermon 345, "The Beloved"), which perhaps explains why Charles also marked the sermon that follows, "Angels Charged with Folly," as his 360th.

This later sermon shares the same structure and much of the same content as "The Beloved" but shows greater refinement and clarity, reflecting something of Charles's development as a preacher even over a few months' time.

Like the Puritans before him, Charles interpreted the Song of Solomon as a love song between Christ and the church. Yet he wasn't afraid to press the imagery further, applying the love of Christ not only to the church but to the individual Christian. Preaching on another verse in the Song in 1880, he opened with this declaration: "We shall not enter into any profitless discussion this morning. We take it for granted that the Song of Solomon is a sacred marriage song between Christ and his church, and that it is the Lord Jesus who is here speaking of his church, and indeed of each individual member." *MTP* 26:133. Such a view of the Song promoted a warm, intimate understanding of the Christian's relationship with Christ.

For Charles, one of the ways this intimate relationship was expressed is in the Lord's Supper. He deemed it the "golden lattice" through which the Christian could see Christ "in part." Of course, Charles denied any Roman Catholic understanding of Christ's physical presence in the elements of the bread and the cup. Rather, in line with Calvin and against a bare memorialist view, Charles believed "in the real presence of Christ which is spiritual, and yet certain." Charles Haddon Spurgeon, *Till He Come: Communion Meditations and Addresses* (London: Passmore & Alabaster, 1896), 17. By calling it a spiritual presence, Charles was not diminishing the reality of Christ's presence; he was suggesting that, for the Christian, "the true and real presence of Jesus with his people" is grasped by faith. This understanding of Christ's presence in the Supper can be seen in one of the hymns he wrote:

> Amidst us our Beloved stands,
> And bids us view His pierced hands;
> Points to His wounded feet and sides,
> Blest emblems of the Crucified.
>
> What food luxurious loads the board,
> When at His table sits the Lord!
> The wine how rich, the bread how sweet,
> When Jesus deigns the guests to meet!
> *Our Own Hymn-Book*, 573.

Charles did not deny that communion with Christ could take place in all of life. As he says here, "Remember beloved he is looking at us now, at our Church, at our closet, at our life, at our heart." Nevertheless, Charles also understood that in the Lord's Supper, Christ can "especially" be seen by those who receive him by faith.

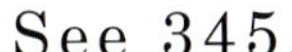

360

See 345.

THE BELOVED IN VARIOUS POSTURES

Song of Solomon 2:9

"My beloved is like a roe or a young hart: behold, he standeth behind our wall,
he looketh forth at the windows, shewing himself through the lattice."

Similitudes and allegories are beautifully adapted to fasten truth on our poor memories. Bunyan's Pilgrim makes us understand more of spiritual life than all other human works put together, and this Song tells us much of the love which subsists between Christ and his church in a manner likely to be remembered. It is to my well[-]beloved, touching my well[-]beloved.

I. CHRIST IN HIS APPROACHES.

He is like a roe or young hart, swift, overleaping all difficulties, and comely in his motions. So was Jesus.

When he came to earth. It was no unwilling descent but it was done with joyful alacrity.

When he went to die. No man took his life, he laid it down of himself and cheerfully gave up the ghost.

When he comes to the penitent. He rejoices to come, he is charmed at the sight of tears.

When he comes to the afflicted. No sooner do they call than he answers. Swiftly he comes to wipe our sorrows dry. He is never tardy, but before we call he often answers.

II. CHRIST IN CONCEALMENT.

He concealed his glory when on earth, or [else] it would have caused a conflagration and death to mortals. Often he conceals himself from his people, and the effect of that is searching, sorrow, repentance, and groaning out after him. This is the reason why he is gone. Because we treated him with coldness, loved another too much, harbored sin, or neglected duty.

Remember, if we have not the presence of the Lord Jesus Christ, it is our own fault he hides behind our wall. The wall we built ourselves, he has built none. Let us knock it down, whatever it may be.

III. CHRIST OBSERVING.

Though we cannot see him, he can see us. He ever looks through the windows. Sometimes he looks:

with grief to see our barrenness and death.

with care and anxiety lest one little plant should die outright, or one spark be quenched.

with love. Lovers love to see each other; so does our Saviour delight to behold us.

with joy when we do well, but ah how seldom is that. Remember beloved, he is looking at us now—at our church, at our closet, at our life, at our heart.

IV. CHRIST MANIFESTING HIMSELF.

Sometimes we see him, he is not wholly hidden. But we see in part, it is not plainly and clearly but only through the lattices.

We see by means, which are lattices. Prayer, Praise, the services of his house and especially the Lord's Supper are golden lattices.

Mark [how] he shews himself. We do not find him out by learning and research, but he is his own discoverer. He shows himself—not his works or words alone, but himself.

Question and application.

Sermon No. 360a

"ANGELS CHARGED WITH FOLLY"

Editor's Summary

One feature that consistently characterized Charles's sermons was his exalted view of God. From his very first message at the New Park Street Chapel (see Sermon 351, "The Father of Light") to this one, we observe Charles returning to this theme repeatedly.

In this thirteen-page sermon manuscript on a passage he would not preach from again, Charles exults in God as the all-powerful and all-wise Ruler of the universe. "Here then [is] the position of all God's servants, in that he asks no aid from them, does not trust his empire to them, asks no council, and communicates no secrets. Let us learn to humble ourselves before the mighty God of Jacob." One way that the young preacher illustrates the mightiness of God is by a comparison. Though the unfallen angels would terrify God's people with their power and knowledge, these heavenly beings are as helpless and ignorant as infants when compared to God. "Now if angels are so low, where shall we lie[?] What are we worms of the earth to be charged with[?]"

Charles's teaching on the omnipotence of God has a practical end here as well. His goal is to confront the pride of man. "Pride is natural to man. Every character and station has its peculiar pride, for pride has a thousand forms. . . . And as pride adapts itself to every rank, so does it append itself to every thing. . . . This pride assumes [a] thousand shapes."

These weren't the words of a bystander, but of one who himself struggled with pride. In the spring of 1850, before the success, the fame, the crowds, the book sales and speaking engagements, sixteen-year-old Charles wrote in his diary, "Oh, may I be kept humble! Pride dwells in my heart." . . . "Oh, to be humble, and to be always at the feet of Jesus!" . . . "Pride is yet my darling sin, I cannot shake it off." *Autobiography*

287

1:144–46. Even at that early point in his Christian life, Charles was sensitive to the reality of pride in his heart, sometimes feeling tempted to look down on the complacency of others and exalt his own devotion.

By 1854, Charles had known surprising success as a preacher. He had seen tremendous fruit in his preaching at Waterbeach and the surrounding villages, and now he had been invited to fill the pulpit at the New Park Street Chapel in London. Later that spring, he would be called as their minister, and the temptation of pride would only grow. In a letter written in March of 1855, Charles confessed to a friend,

> Somewhere in *nubinus* there lies a vast mass of *nebulae* made of advice given to me by friends, — most of it about humility. Now, my Master is the only one who can humble me. My pride is so infernal that there is not a man on earth who can hold it in, and all their silly attempts are futile; but then my Master can do it, and He will. Sometimes, I get such a view of my own insignificance that I call myself all the fools in the world for even letting pride pass my door without frowning at him. *Autobiography* 2:100.

Charles's strategy for fighting pride centered not on human effort or advice, but on a proper view of his Master. Only then did he see himself rightly. This was the lesson he was learning, and one that he sought to teach his people, urging them, "Let great thoughts of God give us low thoughts of ourselves. Let us seek to lie low at the feet of mercy."

ANGELS CHARGED WITH FOLLY

Job 4:17–19

"Shall mortal man be more just than God? shall a man be more pure than his maker? Behold, he put no trust in his servants; and his angels he charged with folly: how much less in them that dwell in houses of clay, whose foundation is in the dust, which are crushed before the moth?"

Pride is natural to man. Every character and station has its peculiar pride, for pride has a thousand forms. It enters the cottage, the peasant sitting at his door sits as much a monarch as Caesar. The milkmaid tosses her head as proudly as the belle at court. He who digs the dark mine, or sweeps the crossing, or cleans my boots has a pride in him. And as pride adapts itself to every rank, so does it append itself to every thing.

There is the pride of dress, the pride of wealth, the pomp of power, the parade of learning, and oh wonder [of] all men, there is the pride of religion. This pride assumes [a] thousand shapes. With the Catholic or Mormonite it is the pride of good works and among ourselves it is too often the same. Righteous self is the hardest foe we have to contend with. Justifying ourselves before God.

Eliphaz had once been convinced of the folly of this vice and labours to convince Job of it. We however will not look upon the words as those of Eliphaz but as they really are, the words of a being from the world of spirits whom Eliphaz saw. There is much talk at the present moment about spiritual manifestations. Now, instead of caring about these modern wonders, let us listen to the words of a well authenticated apparition and learn therefrom our own littleness.

Some have imagined as the rich man did that spirits would be fit messengers to proclaim the will of heaven. But how thankful we ought to be that men are our ministers and not spirits, for into what a state of dread was this good man thrown. We should not like to feel so terrified in God's house. May God grant however that the echo of the sentences of this terrible being may have a humbling effect on us. Three considerations to humble us:

I. THE POSITION OF ALL GOD'S SERVANTS.

II. THE POSITION OF ANGELS.

III. OUR OWN POSITION.

I trust that these three considerations may act as batteries against pride and utterly abase its loftiness; for this purpose I invoke divine assistance.

And now let us reflect on:

I. THE POSITION OF ALL GOD'S SERVANTS.

And at the mention of the word servants, what a train of ideas arise. For all things are the servants of God. The sun is but his footman, the ~~queen~~ moon a menial linkbearer of the darkness. Those wondrous orbs which roll in majestic circles, those erratic fires which burst upon us and then retreat, those lightnings which cleave the skies and the thunders which alarm the nations are but a portion of the brilliant retinue of servants who waith the behests of the omnipotent. Riding on the wings of the wind in his cloudy chariot he makes the clouds as the dust of his feet. All things obey him, animate as well as inanimate.

There is behemoth who drinks a river at a draught and leviathan who makes the deep boil like a pot, but Eliphaz here refers only to intelligent beings who are the servants of God in a higher sense. But here too we find an innumerable host comprising the glorious hierarchy of angels with their various ranks of principalities, powers, and dominions. Next follow the countless armies of the redeemed, triumphing in a blood-bought victory, and afterwards the multitudes on earth, ever faithful to their King.

In this one family we discern stars of the first magnitude. The undying Enoch. The faithful Abraham, the wrestling Israel, the meek Moses, the beloved Samuel, the seraphic David, perfect Job, bold Elijah, lamenting Jeremiah now rejoicing, etc. together with New Testament Saints and their worthy successors.

The heroes of the Alps, the confessors of Smithfield, the puritans, and the long squadrons of noble minds who yield not to the foe.

But of all these it must be said
<u>He put no trust in his servants.</u>

This is not said of his servants on earth alone but of those in heaven too. Truly we can see why he should put no trust in us for we cannot trust ourselves, so changing are we. So frail, so light, that every wind blows us about as it listeth, but of all his saints it is said "He put no trust in them."

1. <u>He does not expect or require any assistance from them.</u>

We talk of putting trust in men or princes and of putting trust in God, and we mean by that, expecting aid from them. But God has need of none of his servants. He does not want them as pillars to his throne. Like the world, he has nothing to hang on. His own all-sufficience bears the weight of his own glories up.

Turkey puts trust in England and France to uphold its power, but God rests on none. All the kings of the earth lean on their nobles, or their wealth, or their armies, but God is the only Potentate. When he bares his arm for war he does not depend on legions of angels but he treads the wine press alone.

He could do as well without us as with us. True, in his providence and grace he uses his servants as instruments, but they are nothing more—he could work without them. In Conversion, Saul. In Deliverance, Egypt. In Conquest, Gideon. In salvation, all alone. In fact he puts no reliance on our power as auxiliary to his own.

2. <u>He does not entrust any part of his dominions to their government.</u>

The heathen supposed that one God could not superintend all the universe, therefore their Zeus, or Jove, was represented as allotting different portions of his dominions to vicegerent Gods. Neptune shook his trident over the sea. Eolus ruled the winds. Flora was queen of flowers, Pluto [king] of hell etc.—but our God has no lords to whom he has entrusted principalities and regencies. But he governs himself.

Earthly monarchs entrust their states to ministers and judges, but he holds all authority and office in his own hands. Worms and angels, sparrows and planets, the hairs of our head and the stars of heaven, are all under one lord.

God has not left me or entrusted my soul to Gabriel. Truly angels minister unto us but we are not entrusted to their guidance, nor is even a fly. He overrules <u>all</u> mortal things. In him is all dignity vested. The shields of the earth are his. To him sceptres and crowns belong. We are all <u>directly</u> responsible to him and to him only. Let us not seek after power in the church, for God does not intend us to be masters.

3. <u>He puts no trust in their wisdom, he asks no counsel at their hands.</u>

There are three who hold council in heaven, and only three, and those three are one, the one God. But God never asks the advice of his servants:

In creation who instructed him[?] Is. XL. 12
In salvation, who devised the plan, who aided him in carrying it out[?]
In providence, who tells him how to act? None.

Not [even] Gabriel ever ventures to intrude his advice. He has no cabinet ministers, no privy council. What would the united wisdom, prudence, and sagacity of all intelligences amount to if compared with him[?]

Were we all Solomons, our learned lore would sound in his ear as the prattle of children. Our most prudent schemes would fail. He puts no trust in his servants. Let this humble us. Let us think less of our own wisdom and more of <u>his</u>. Let us rejoice that infinite wisdom is engaged for us, and no inferior powers, for God would not trust the salvation of his tiniest child in the hands of the wisest Sanhedrin of angels.

4. <u>He does not entrust his ~~power~~ secret decrees to them nor make them his confidantes.</u>

He has purposes which he reveals by the mouth of his servants the prophets.

He has secret purposes which neither mortal nor immortal knows of. The purposes of redemption were unknown to angels for they desired to look into those things. Most men make some one their confidante and entrust their secrets to a friend. But God's own bosom is the archive of his predestination. The day of Judgment is unknown, it may come to day or tomorrow. Of that day and hour knoweth no man, nor the angels of God.

Why should we seek foresight[?] Why desire to pry into the future[?] It is concealed. Let us learn humble deference and cast away impudent inquisitive curiosity. It is well for us that our own salvation is not entrusted to us. It is one of the decrees, but we are neither entrusted with the knowledge nor the fulfilling of the decrees of Jehovah. Newton's dream of the ring well sets out this idea. No man knows whose name is in the Lamb's book except by evidence, and the getting of the elect to glory is not entrusted to God's servants.

Here then [is] the position of all God's servants, in that he asks no aid from them, does not trust his empire to them, asks no council, and communicates no secrets. Let us learn to humble ourselves before the mighty God of Jacob. But here comes another thought.

II. THE POSITION OF ANGELS.

The wonderful apparition, having delivered itself of one sentence, pronounces another which at the first sound startles us exceedingly. As if not enough to trample on the pride of all the servants of God, angels themselves are made to bend.

He charged his angels with folly. Now we are so often speaking of angels as gloriously pure and without spot, and the word folly is so frequently applied to sin that we stand astonished to find seraphic hosts charged with folly.

The word folly is applied in scripture to the grossest crimes: Shechem's rape of Dinah. Gen. XXXIV. 7. Deut. XXII. 21. Achan's theft. Joshua. VII. 15. The violation of the concubine. Judg. XX. 6. In Psal. 85. 8. Folly means sin. And in 2 Tim. 3.9. Jannes and Jambres have their revolt described as folly. Now if folly in this place means the same as in every other, then we would have you notice the tense of the verb: he "charged," past; not "chargeth," present. If folly here implies sin, then this refers to the fallen angels, and should teach us a lesson not to rely on our own power and free will, for left to themselves even angels fell. Let us take heed that we rely on that mighty arm which held up and still holds up the elect angels, then are we safe.

But we think the "folly" here meant is not a sinful folly. For although all sin is folly, all folly is not sin. True it is that to sin in any way shows folly, or want of wisdom, but every want of wisdom does not show sin. Suppose that without learning Chinese I should go and preach the gospel to them in English: there would be no sin, but much folly.

Suppose I should venture alone on a rough sea, without any knowledge of oars: it would not be sin if I went to save a drowning sailor, but it would be folly. Now we think this is the folly intended in this place. We generally impute folly to children and, now and then in some conspicuous instances, to mistaken men. Now in this sense folly is used here:

In children there is a want of experience. Angels, though long lived now, are but as babes in God's sight; only yesterday and there were none. They are only creatures of the last moment, ephemeral insects in his eyes, though to us they seem so ancient.

In children there is a want of knowledge. So angels know little of the past and but little or nothing of the future. They are far wiser than we are, but in comparison with Him they know nothing.

In children there is a want of prudence. Angels must be very sagacious and wise but they are foolish when compared with that Mind which is God. They cannot see results and plan events in wisdom as he can. They are charged with folly.

In children there is little lofty thought. Children do not think of empires, of astronomy, or geology, but of trifles, of mere trifles. And though angels are lofty intelligences vastly superior to us, yet in the sight of the Lord of Hosts they are but children. Their thoughts are not his thought[s], as heaven is high etc.

In angels and children there is a want of strength to stand.

Now if angels are so low, where shall we lie[?] What are we worms of the earth to be charged with[?] But here comes the third:

III. OUR OWN POSITION.

This is as humiliating as anything, let us look at our:

<u>House</u>. Our body, it is not of ivory but of clay. Eastern houses made of clay can easily be broken into. They are not beautiful houses of ivory, not lasting mansions of marble, but clay.

Materialism is far from exalting, even when it ~~is~~ assumes forms the most glorious that can be conceived; but here is a materialism to which I am bound, which unites me with clay. Not with pearls and gold but with dust and earth and mud. Then let me be humble.

<u>Its foundation</u>. It rests on earth. I borrow my existence from its surface. If bread, the food whereupon is supplied, fails me, I die. My heavenly dependence is on a firm rock: but all my earthly hopes and dependences are based on dust. ~~I am mutable, changing, frail.~~

<u>Its frailty</u>. I am crushed before the moth. A tiny insect may cause my death. Or sooner than a moth, or like one, may I be crushed, ~~or like one, as easily as I put it between my fingers can~~ I [may] be taken out of this life. Let me then forego all pride.

My friends here are the three great inducements to humility. Let us allow them their proper weight. Let great thoughts of God give us low thoughts of ourselves. Let us seek to lie low at the feet of mercy. Humility exalts Christ and exalts us. Humility has all the promises, pride has none.

Henceforth bend thy knee in reverence more profound and tremble lest thou, a worm, should even seem to usurp divinity or justify thyself in his sight. Let the publican's prayer be ours ever, and may we rejoice to feel ourselves less than the least of all saints.

Father aid me by thy Spirit
through <u>the Son's</u> merit.

"LITTLE FLOCK"

Editor's Summary

It appears Charles left this sermon unfinished, but the reason for this is not clear. His outline shows that he was preparing to write a two-point sermon, one point for each verse of the passage. He would preach from Luke 12:32, "Little, but Lovely" (*MTP 63*, Sermon 3549), at a later time, though that sermon appears to be unrelated.

In expounding on Christ's command to "seek ye the kingdom of God," Charles imagines this advice being given "as a mother would give her son on leaving his home." This was not merely a quaint illustration but a personal one. Charles held a high view of the role of mothers in the spiritual formation of their children because he himself had been raised in a godly household. Writing many years later, he shared, "I am sure that, in my early youth, no teaching ever made such an impression upon my mind as the instruction of my mother; neither can I conceive that, to any child, there can be one who will have such influence over the young heart as the mother who has so tenderly cared for her offspring." *Autobiography* 1:68. He would go on to write the following tribute:

> Certainly, I have not the powers of speech with which to set forth my valuation of the choice blessing which the Lord bestowed on me in making me the son of one who prayed for me, and prayed with me. How can I ever forget her tearful eye when she warned me to escape from the wrath to come? I thought her lips right eloquent; others might not think so, but they certainly were eloquent to me. How can I ever forget when she bowed her knee, and with her arms about my neck, prayed, "Oh, that my son might live before Thee!" *Autobiography* 1:69.

Alongside the idea of a mother exhorting her son, Charles communicates his belief that the best time to pursue God is at a young age—with both a private decision and a public profession of faith that would be manifested in the decision to be baptized and join a church. His biblical stance was this: when it comes to the kingdom of God, "Seek it, to be a member of it."

Throughout the years, Charles would adopt a fatherly posture as he counseled young boys and girls to follow his example upon their conversion:

> When I was a boy of fifteen, I believed in the Lord Jesus, was baptized, and joined the Church of Christ; and nothing upon earth would please me more than to hear of other boys having been led to do the same. I have never been sorry for what I did then; no, not even once . . . The day I gave myself up to the Lord Jesus, to be His servant, was the very best day of my life; then I began to be safe and to be happy; then I found out the secret of living, and had a worthy object for my life's exertions, and an unfailing comfort for life's troubles. Because I would wish every boy, who reads these lines, to have a bright eye, a light tread, a joyful heart, and overflowing spirits, I therefore plead with him to consider whether he will not follow my example, for I speak from experience, and know what I say. *Autobiography* 1:149.

We do not know whether Charles ever preached this sermon. But we know his ministry would go on to encourage many young people to seek Christ's kingdom "earliest" and "chiefly."

LITTLE FLOCK

Luke 12:31–32

"But rather seek ye the kingdom of God; and all these things shall be added unto you. Fear not, little flock; for it is your Father's good pleasure to give you the kingdom."

Right well has it been said that like the stars on high, and the sun and moon, the words of God were written for all time and not for our forefathers only. And as we find the same light suits us, so will the same promises if we are in the same condition. I have taken two verses that there may be something for all. The first verse has in it:

I. GOOD ADVICE.

II. GOOD PROMISE.

I. <u>GOOD ADVICE.</u>

Such as a mother would give her son on leaving his home.

Some things we may not seek at all.
Some things we may seek in measure.
One thing we should seek chiefly:
    First. That is, earliest.
    First. That is, chiefly.

In taking a situation, in removing, in settling, in emigrating, in all, seek first the kingdom of God.

    Seek it, to be a member of it.
    Seek it, to spread its dominions.

May the God who sought you, set you seeking his kingdom more and more.

[This page is followed by two blank pages in Charles's notebook.]

"AARON'S ROD"

Editor's Summary

In this sermon on Num 17:8, a text he would not preach from again, Charles argues that true religion, like Aaron's rod, ought to produce a certain kind of fruit, giving evidence of God's approval. Charles possibly delivered this shorter message in a Sabbath afternoon or evening service, which would have allowed for more extemporaneous delivery.

Given that "Aaron's Rod" was preached during Charles's transition to London, there are a couple of features worth mentioning. First, he speaks against the nominal Christianity of his day: "All men in Great Britain call themselves Christians but they are not all so." Having spent a few weeks in London by this point, it's likely that the young preacher encountered people "who swear profanely," "who profane the Sabbath," who are "all high doctrine and no practice men," and so on. This was different from the Antinomianism of Waterbeach. This was a nominalism that professed a refined and respectable Christianity and took pride in national identity, yet produced no harvest. Charles considered such unfruitful professions of Christianity "dead and dry."

The other interesting feature of this sermon is his charge to the congregation to "test ministers." There were many ministers in England, but how many of them bore the fruit of God's approval? For Charles, this fruit included having an ability to teach ("talents"), sound doctrine, and congregational approval ("acceptance"). Even more, it meant a congregation stirred by the ministry of the Word ("Congregation affected. Some tears, some zeal, more prayer, many inquiries, hopeful signs."). And perhaps most confirming, it meant souls being saved: "Some few at least to God with full purpose of heart."

When he first began his ministry in Waterbeach, Charles longed to hear that someone had been converted under his preaching. He describes his joy when that day finally came:

> How my heart leaped for joy when I heard tidings of my first convert! . . . If anybody had said to me, "Someone has left you twenty thousand pounds," I should not have given a snap of my fingers for it, compared with the joy which I felt when I was told that God had saved a soul through my ministry! *Autobiography* 1:232.

Many more souls would be saved under Charles's ministry, but he never got over the joy of his very first convert. "She was the first seal to my ministry, and a very precious one." *Autobiography* 1:233.

Because of his passion to equip true ministers, Charles would go on to establish the Pastors' College. And the leading question he would ask any applicant was about their fruit: "We sought for earnest preachers, not for readers of sermons, or makers of philosophical essays. 'Have you won souls for Jesus?' was and is our leading enquiry of all applicants. 'If so, come thou with us, and we will do thee good.'" *Autobiography* 2:149.

Charles thoroughly believed this should be an ongoing mark in the work of a minister. Even as his students preached in various missions around town, their longing should be to see people converted. "If our preaching never saves a soul, and is not likely to do so," he said, "should we not better glorify God as peasants, or as tradesmen?" *ARM*, 175. Or as Charles himself prayed, "Oh how I long to bear fruit. God grant it by [Christ] Jesus. Amen."

AARON'S ROD

Numbers 17:8

"And it came to pass, that on the morrow Moses went into the tabernacle of witness; and, behold, the rod of Aaron for the house of Levi was budded, and brought forth buds, and bloomed blossoms, and yielded almonds."

On so important a matter as the priesthood Moses is commanded to make an appeal to God. This by no means sanctions the use of lots, ordeals, pricking for texts, etc., for none of these are commanded, nor are they for such important ends.

There are some things so deceptive and beyond our knowledge that we often wish we could make an appeal to God and receive a verbal answer: this is however a foolish wish, for the mode God told the Israelites of, we may use as well as they.

That is, see what rod doth blossom.

I. LET US TEST VARIOUS RELIGIOUS.

There are such a number that if we stand to analyze and examine we shall be dead ere we decide. Here however is an easy mode of decision. Which of them produces good fruit.

Infidelity. See its harvest reaped in the Reign of Terror. B[ud]dhism, Brahmanism, etc., produce cruelty, murder, infanticide, degradation. Catholicism with lust in [the] priest and vice in [the] people. Look at Mormonism.

But it is Protestantism, true and real, not spurious like Puseyism, which bringeth forth fruit. Turn your eye to England, Scotland, America, [and] Australia and see there the liberty and holiness.

II. LET US TEST CHARACTERS.

All men in Great Britain call themselves Christians but they are not all so, some are dead and dry enough.

1. We cast out all persons obnoxious to civil law.
2. All dishonest, defrauding men.
3. All loose, lascivious characters.
4. All who swear profanely.
5. All who profane the Sabbath.
6. All [who] neglect the Bible.
7. All prayerless persons.
8. All lovers of this world, covetous etc.
9. All who will not forgive.
10. All high doctrine and no practice men.
11. All self righteous persons.

One alone remains. The true, living soul.

III. LET US TEST MINISTERS.

All men are not called to this work. How can we tell whether they are or no[?]

1. <u>They bud</u>. They have talents, they preach true doctrines, they have acceptance.
2. <u>They blossom</u>. Congregation affected. Some tears, some zeal, more prayer, many inquiries, hopeful signs.
3. <u>They bear fruit</u>. Souls are saved. Some few at least turn to God with full purpose of heart.

Oh how I long to bear fruit.

God grant it by Xt Jesus.

<u>A</u>men

"THE PERPETUAL FIRE"

Editor's Summary

This sermon and Sermon 365 ("Jesus Saves from Sin") are the last two that Charles preached as the pastor of Waterbeach Chapel. He had been their pastor since October of 1851. Under his ministry, the church and even the village of Waterbeach had been transformed. "He began to preach there, and it pleased God to turn the whole place upside down." *Autobiography* 1:228. But on April 19, 1854, after a few months of having Charles as their pulpit supply, the congregation of the New Park Street Chapel in London voted nearly unanimously to call him as their pastor. These two sermons were likely preached at Waterbeach on the following Sunday.

Charles did not relish the idea of leaving his "little Garden of Eden." But he felt it was necessary for two main reasons. First, his agricultural congregation in Waterbeach could not adequately provide for him financially. Writing to a deacon at New Park Street, Charles confided, "I must soon be severed from them by necessity, for they do not raise sufficient to maintain me. . . . Had they done so, I should have turned a deaf ear to any request to leave them, at least for the present." *Autobiography* 1:348. Though the congregation did their best to provide for their pastor, he had to serve bi-vocationally, working as a tutor during the week, which prevented him from devoting himself fully to the ministry. Second, he saw God's providential hand in this turn of events. For a teenage country pastor who had never been to college to be called to a historic Baptist church in London, Charles had no explanation for this other than a sovereign move of God, and he submitted to it with fear and trembling.

I sought not to come to you, for I was the minister of an obscure but affectionate people; I never solicited advancement. The first note of invitation from your deacons came quite unlooked-for, and I trembled at the idea of preaching in London. I could not understand how it had come about, and even now I am filled with astonishment at the wondrous Providence. *Autobiography* 1:352.

So, having received the call from London and knowing he would accept it, Charles entered the pulpit on Sunday morning, April 23, 1854, and delivered this farewell sermon to his beloved people. Preaching from Lev 6:13, a passage he would not preach from again, Charles encourages his people that the perpetual fire of the gospel can never be put out. He charges them one last time to cultivate that fire in the church, in the home, and in their hearts. Next, he speaks specifically about his departure. His edits in the second point are particularly heavy, indicating perhaps that he wrestled with what he should say. Here was a loving pastor pointing his grieving people to a future hope. Though he was leaving, they could be confident that God would not leave them.

[As a] promise. God will never leave us without his presence, without a minister. See in past times in the history of the church He has raised up a successor, for the meeker men have been of forceful witness at the proper time. And though the fire has after burned dim, it has never been quite extinguished. So with yourselves, trust then for the future. And as to the future, we believe that the fire light shall yet burn brightly.

By the Rev. C. H. Spurgeon

THE PERPETUAL FIRE
Leviticus 6:13

"The fire shall ever be burning upon the altar; it shall never go out."

The Fire shall ever be burning upon the altar: it shall never go out. Altars are the first religious structures we read of. The date [and] the origin [are] in the most remote antiquity. It is probable that Cain and Abel offered their oblations upon altars.

The first distinct mention of an altar is in Gen 8.20 where it is recorded that Noah builded an altar unto the Lord. All along through the patriarchal period continual notice is taken of altars. Abraham never halted in his wandering without building an altar. Doubtless Isaac, of whom we know little, did the same, and on several occasions Jacob anointed stones, set up pillars, and erected altars.

When the Mosaic period arrived[,] a more complete revelation of the One God was given. In order that the unity of the people might be ensured, a place was selected where all sacrifices should be usually offered, viz., the tabernacle, the altars of the Lord of Hosts.

Amongst other altars in the sanctuary was one which was called the altar of incense, the fire upon which it is said was originally kindled by fire from heaven and was never suffered to die out until the Babylonian Captivity and perhaps not even then. This was the fire which was used for burning all the sacrifices, although no blood ever stained the altar itself save on the day of atonement. It was an incense altar not a sacrificial one. All other fire, saving this, was "strange fire" and Nadab and Abihu felt the penalty for using it. This fire burned both night and day.

Vestiges of this are found in the mythology of the heathen. The Persian fire worshippers. The sacred fires of Brahma, and especially the fire of Vesta, so carefully tended by the Vestal Virgins. But our concern is not with heathenish ceremonies but with ourselves and the spiritual meaning of the text.

It is certain that literally it is nothing to us. We rear no altars. We cannot go back to types and shadows when substance is in our possession. We cannot talk as the Papists or Anglicans. We know nothing of material altars. Above all we cannot recognize the phrase "altar of Hymen." It is downright heathenism. Altars were never used for marriages. Nor for the Lord's Supper. Let Puseyites talk so foolishly, but we who are Christians know <u>the truth</u> and believe that Jesus is the only altar and sacrifice too. However, figuratively we may use the expression and apply the verse:

I.   TO THE ALTAR OF HEAVEN.

II. TO THE ALTAR OF THE SANCTUARY.

III. TO THE ALTAR OF THE FAMILY.

IV. TO THE ALTAR OF THE CLOSET.

V.   TO THE ALTAR OF THE HEART.

I.   <u>THE ALTAR IN HEAVEN</u>.

Our Great High Priest [Jesus] is ever before the throne offering the precious incense of his prevailing prayers. He will never suffer the fire to be extinguished. His love will never fail. It was not quenched by all the miseries, scorn, and trials he endured. It has not been destroyed by the backslidings and ingratitude of his children, and it shall never be quenched by height or depth or any other creature.

His activity will never tire. Even [the high priest's] Love, though mighty in purpose, wearies in practice. Not so our Jesus. He ever lives to intercede though millions have been borne on his breast, thousands of prayers offered, and myriads of petitions presented and wants relieved, yet he wearies not. Those who gave corn away in the famine in Ireland had to rest for sleep, and the most indefatigable member of parliament would tire if he had one thousandth part of the number of petitions to present, but [Jesus] is unwearied.

For Zion's sake he will not rest.
The fire shall never go out.

His merits shall never cease. [The man] who has the greatest influence with royalty may go too far in his requests. But Jesus never asks too much. He knows his own infinite merits and will not cease to prevail. No request has been denied.

His coffers are not exhausted. His arms need no staying up. No [statice] and myrrh are wanted, the fire is as everlasting as the throne before which it smokes. Oh, my Soul, rejoice in this glorious truth. Precious reflection of our great High Priest above. Lord fix it on my memory. R. 156.

It will apply

II. THE ALTAR OF THE SANCTUARY.

Though we have here no material altar, nor any altar of sacrifice, yet we have an altar of incense on which we present our united prayers, praises, groans, and thanks. The fire burning again starts. [The] altar of the sanctuary shall never go out. This may be understood:

[1. As a] promise. God will never leave us ~~you or without any witness~~ without his presence, without a minister. See in past times in the history of the church ~~men have always come when wanted~~ He has raised up a successor, ~~even~~ for the meeker men have been of forceful witness at the proper time. And though the fire has after burned dim, ~~yet~~ it has never been quite ~~dead~~ extinguished. So with yourselves, trust then for the future. And as to the future, we believe that the fire light shall yet burn brightly. Not in this village, yet in the wide world ~~shall blaze~~ on multitudinous altars throughout this wide world of dust.

[2.] As a command. We must not let it die out. We must keep it burning. You who ~~neglect~~ are absenting yourselves from the prayer meeting, or Sabbath School, or services on any account, do your best to quench the light.

Do not smother it by your contentions, nor ~~snuff out~~ extinguish it by your wrath, nor neglect it, [i.e.] starve it by indifference or parsimoniously withholding from it more than is right, but cherish this fire. ~~and never suffer it to go out~~

Your ancestors have kept it burning. ~~Your children will curse you if you lose it.~~ For your own sake, for your children's sake, for the world's sake, for Christ's sake, never suffer the fire upon the ~~altar of prayer~~ sanctuary altar to go out. ~~for ever~~

It will apply to . . .

III. THE ALTAR OF THE HOUSEHOLD.

Next to the altar of sanctuary stands the family altar. The tents pitched around the tabernacle should each be little temples. Most good men have officiated as priests at the altar. ~~preached it and I have heard of some who would not sleep in a house unconsecrated by family prayer.~~

How pleasant it is. It is [a] most delightful [scene] on earth to behold ~~to see a,~~ a humble family in the posture of devotion. Mean [is] the language, but noble the sound ~~sense~~ when the labourer prays. Oh scene most fair, a miniature of heaven's union.

How profitable it is. To the parents it prepares them for the day, or shuts out care at night. On the children the effect is most salutary. Children of praying families rarely turn out as others do. And the servants, how pleasant even to them.

Let not the fire go out.

If the sire be gone, let the son perpetuate it.
If the father be away, let the mother speak.
If you lack ability, better a form than none at all. But try in simplicity.

Let not the fire go out.

Do not let business put it aside.
Do not let worldly relations shame you.
Do not let sloth creep in or permit indevotion to blight the fruit.

If it be not burning, kindle it at once. Commence. Build the altar of earth or unhewn stone, but build I pray you.

IV. THE ALTAR OF THE CLOSET.

Some have no household, [but] all should have a closet. This is the very life of all the other fires save the first. The Sanctuary and Family borrow their fires [from] here. Therefore let this burn well. I would ply this subject more closely home than the others since this is the very hinge of our religion.

Burn here the fat of your sacrifices. Let your closet seasons be, if possible:

Regular in time and place.
Frequent, not less than twice a day.
Fervent. Effectual prayer availeth much.

Have you nothing to pray for? Let me suggest the Church, the Ministry, your own soul, your children, your relations, your neighbors, your country, and the cause of God and truth throughout the world. I pray God to give you something to pray about. But let us examine ourselves.

Do we engage cheerfully in it, or do the chariot wheels drag heavily[?] If so, let us begin again. Let us go with weeping. Let us set ~~Have~~ apart special seasons ~~A period especially~~ for extraordinary prayer: [for] fire should be smothered beneath the ashes. For if this continue to fail, or a worldly conformity, next you will go wrong ~~in the family~~, then in the church, and afterwards in the world. Therefore let us beware. Help oh God.

V. THE ALTAR OF THE HEART.

This is a golden altar indeed. The others are emptiness without this. Vile and deceitful as our hearts are, God loves to have them. Let us give God our heart and never let the fire go out.

It will not burn if the Lord does not keep it burning ~~for it is against its nature~~. Many foes will attempt to extinguish it, but if the oil behind the wall be put on, it will blaze higher and higher. But let us see to it that it is supplied. Put plenty of texts of Scripture on, for they are live coals; put sermons on, put prayers on, put [on] above all faith in Spirit.

How many neglect this altar, a vain shew is all. No heart work. How is it religion is a task[?] Not a privilege but a dull monotonous round[?] 'Tis because men are not real Christians. [They are] mere professors and not really regenerate. Come, let us trust in Jesus' one great altar, but at the same time, see after all these other altars of burnt sacrifice.

Lord assist me.

Amen.

Sermon No. 364

"GLORYING ALONE IN CHRIST"

Editor's Summary

Galatians 6:14 was an important passage for Charles. He would preach from this text at least three more times in his ministry: "Three Crosses" (*MTP* 24, Sermon 1447), "The Cross Our Glory" (*MTP* 31, Sermon 3482), and "Grand Glorying" (*MTP* 61, Sermon 1828). The later sermons share no notable similarities in structure or content with the one here. Also, we do not have a designated preaching occasion for this sermon, but it was likely composed during the transition from Waterbeach to London. Considering this timing, it's not surprising to find Charles reflecting on his past three years of ministry. He saw tremendous success during this time. And yet it would be a mistake to characterize the experience as "without trial." Along the way, there had been "trials of false brethren."

One of the most painful instances was the case of Mr. Charles. When Charles first met him, "he was the ringleader in all that was bad; a tall, fine, big fellow, and one who could, perhaps, drink more than any man for miles around him, — a man who would curse and swear, and never knew a thought of fear." However, under Charles's preaching, Mr. Charles professed conversion, and for a time, demonstrated great zeal for the church and for God. Yet as the months went on, Mr. Charles began to turn away from the faith and return to his drunken ways, much to his pastor's heartache, the shame of the church, and the gloating of her enemies. Eventually Charles feared "that there was no real work of grace in him." *Autobiography* 1:238 What made this case even more painful is that Mr. Charles was the first to profess conversion under Charles's ministry. *LS* 1, Sermon 54.

313

Perhaps even more disheartening than cases of church discipline were the ongoing challenges of false teaching. Charles admits here: "This must be to a gospel minister the sharpest trial of all, to see his labours marred by false teaching." Charles encountered many villagers throughout his ministry who held to a hyper-Calvinistic, Antinomian lifestyle that led to neglect of their families and their own morality. But even more concerning were the pastors and preachers who promoted such teachings.

> In those early days, I had sometimes to contend with the Antinominian preachers as well as with their people. I once found myself in the midst of a company of ministers and friends, who were disputing whether it was a sin in men that they did not believe the gospel. . . . I should not have imagined, if I had not myself heard them, that any persons would be so wicked as to venture to assert that "it is no sin for a sinner not to believe on Christ." *Autobiography* 1:260.

With the reality of sin within the church and false teaching without, Charles knew that Waterbeach was no "perfect church." But rather than glorying in successes or fixating on disappointments, he pointed his people to something greater to boast in, namely, "the glorious work of the Redeemer in our salvation." Whereas human accomplishments are always temporary, incomplete, and easily defeated, the cross is the ultimate display of divine love and wisdom, accomplishing the salvation of God's people and bringing Christ everlasting glory. As long as the church gloried in the cross alone, they would be safe in the years to come.

GLORYING ALONE IN CHRIST

Galatians 6:14

"But God forbid that I should glory, save in the cross of our Lord Jesus Christ, by whom the world is crucified unto me, and I unto the world."

The Minister who hopes to go through the world without trial will be mistaken. If he hopes to see a perfect Church he will be disappointed, for even Paul had his trials of false brethren. Surely this must be to a gospel minister the sharpest trial of all, to see his labours marred by false teaching. Paul, we see, yields not. He was no craven, but he manfully resists them. And how? Solely by the cross.

I.   A SOLEMN REPROBATION.

II. A BOLD CONFESSION.

III. A SINCERE ASSURANCE.

I.   <u>A SOLEMN REPROBATION</u>.

The Apostle rejects and reprobates every kind of glorying save one. The phrase "God forbid" may be understood either as a strong asseveration or a hearty prayer. [There are] instances of [the] first [and a] need of [the] second. Paul rejects boasting:

1. In his dignity. As [an] apostle. We must not boast of our talents or station.
2. In popularity. What is it[?]
3. In his usefulness. We must not glory.
4. In our denomination. Its ministers, numbers, doctors, converts, or increase.

5. In our peculiarities. Our orthodoxy and sound straight[-]lacedness.

6. In our experience and age.

7. In our vigour, wealth, [or] knowledge.

Let us cast them away as boastings.

II. A BOLD CONFESSION.

He says he did glory in one thing, and that was what his enemies despised, viz., the cross of Christ. By this he means the glorious work of the Redeemer in our salvation. In this he did right to glory. David and Isaiah did. The Cross is the marrow of Theology. He gloried:

1. In the <u>love</u> displayed on the cross.

2. In the <u>wisdom</u> in the atonement.

3. In the <u>security</u> of the work.

4. In the <u>completeness</u> of the work.

5. In the <u>results</u> of the cross.

6. In the <u>triumphs</u> of the cross.

7. In the <u>glory</u> God receives from it.

I might enlarge, but pray the good Spirit to enlarge it in your hearts.

III. A SINCERE ASSURANCE.

No Assurance like experimental assurance. Paul had this. He speaks of a double crucifixion.

1. A crucified world.

    A world rendered powerless to resist.
    A world rendered ghastly and unlovely.
    A world rendered to him a dying thing.

2. A crucified self.

    Self abhorred by the world.
    Self unable to join its evil pursuits.
    Self soon to be dead to it.

Here is the real reason why he could not glory in anything save Jesus. For on the one hand the world was made unworthy of his love, and [on the other] he was placed in such a position as not to be able to love it. And now brethren . . .

Here is:

A Joy. We may glory in Jesus.
A Test. Are we crucified[?]
A Prayer. "God forbid" etc.

Help oh King
Amen.

"JESUS SAVES FROM SIN"

Editor's Summary

Likely delivered in the afternoon service on April 23, 1854, this is the last sermon Charles preached as pastor of the congregation at Waterbeach Chapel. (See also Sermon 363, "The Perpetual Fire," which was preached in the morning.) Charles preached on this text in his first sermon in Waterbeach. *LS* 1, Sermon 33. He would also preach from it the following week at New Park Street Chapel (Sermon 365a, "Jesus the Savior from Sin") and at least one other time at the Metropolitan Tabernacle ("Jesus," *MTP* 24, Sermon 1434).

As can be seen in the introduction, Charles's intention in preaching from Matt 1:21 again, at the end of his Waterbeach ministry, was so that "Jesus may be Alpha and Omega with us." Yet beyond the same Scripture text, how do these two sermons compare? It's striking to see how much Charles grew over the span of 300 sermons and more than 600 preaching occasions. For one, he matured in his exposition of Scripture. In the first sermon, the fledgling preacher largely crafted a topical message, explaining the doctrines of justification and sanctification to the congregation. In "Jesus Saves from Sin," however, he follows the flow of the passage, first expounding on the name given by the angel, then explaining the salvation Jesus will bring, and finally describing the people Jesus will save. Charles allowed the structure of the passage to dictate the structure of his sermon.

Another area of growth was his use of typology. This is a skill that Charles continued to develop throughout his career. Here, he connects Jesus to Joshua son of Nun and Joshua the high priest, and shows how they point to the greater Joshua to come.

Finally, Charles progressed in his sermon application. In the first sermon, he provided solid theological teaching but made little personal application. Here, every point has some measure of personal reflection, and he concludes with six marks for his hearers to pursue in their day-to-day lives.

These differences are only homiletical. When it comes to the theology of his sermons, Charles remained unwavering in his commitment to Jesus Christ and the message of salvation. Earlier in his ministry, he preached:

> Pardon, — free, perfect, instantaneous, irreversible, bringing with it deliverance from the consequences of sin. . . . Imputation of righteousness, causing a man to be regarded as holy, sinless, worthy of commendation and reward.
>
> The salvation Jesus wrought is totally different from all others for it is salvation from sin. . . . So that we become innocent in the sight of God. Yea, and meritorious through the righteousness of Jesus.
>
> Sanctification, including deliverance from sin, and positive holiness . . . is gradual, imperfect, progressional. . . . This is the beauteous salvation Jesus gives . . . deliverance from the guilt, consequences, and effects of sin. *LS* 1:231.

At Waterbeach in 1854, Charles would teach: "A new nature, holy desire, and holy acts. This is a gradually progressive work. Now these three must go together. Thy God will not justify an unpardoned or unsanctified sinner at last." This is the unwavering message that the preacher would take with him to London.

JESUS SAVES FROM SIN

Matthew 1:21

*"And she shall bring forth a son, and thou shalt call his name
JESUS: for he shall save his people from their sins."*

As this was my first text in Waterbeach, so by the help of God it shall be the one with which I would close my stated ministry among you, in order that Jesus may be Alpha and Omega with us.

I.   LET US SPEAK OF [THE] GLORIOUS NAME.

II. OF THE WONDROUS SALVATION.

III. OF THE BLESSED PEOPLE.

I.   THE GLORIOUS NAME.

Jesus, or Joshua, "the Saviour." Two had borne this name before, Joshua the son of Nun and Joshua the son of Jozadak, who were both types of Christ.

Joshua the son of Nun:
>   Fought for Israel and overcame.
>   He led them through Jordan.
>   He divided their inheritance.
Joshua the son of Jozadak:
>   He restored the priesthood.
>   He rebuilt the temple.

But how much greater is "Joshua", or Jesus, the son of God. All [that] these did and more, he has done in his glorious day of salvation.

II. THE WONDROUS SALVATION.

The salvation Jesus wrought is totally different from all others, for it is salvation from sin.

1. From the result of sin. Anger of God. Death. Hell. Loss of heaven, Pardon.

2. From the guilt and charge of sin. So that we become innocent in the sight of God, yea, and meritorious through the righteousness of Jesus. Justification. This is instantaneous, perfect, unalterable, and brings with it all the rights which by nature only belong to perfection.

3. From the very being of sin. There is original depravity, and acquired habit, but these he plucketh out, and puts [in . . .] A new nature, holy desire, and holy acts. This is a gradually progressive work.

Now these three must go together. Thy God will not justify an unpardoned or unsanctified sinner at last. Oh, how glorious is this salvation. My soul, muse thereon often.

III. THE BLESSED PEOPLE.

Not known at first, but mingled with the [rest]. Some of all countries, ranks, and characters. Who shall be brought in[?] The marks are:

1. A sincere desire after heaven.
2. A devout seeking of God.
3. Diligent labour for it.
4. Great abhorrence of sin.
5. Sense of our own nothingness.
6. Humble reliance on Jesus.

And now my Father, make thy servant mighty at last to wrestle with sinners. Come oh Father to mine assistance by the ever blessed Spirit.

Amen
For <u>J.C.</u> sake.

"JESUS THE SAVIOR FROM SIN"

Editor's Summary

Charles received notice of the pastoral call from the New Park Street Chapel during the week of April 17, 1854. Knowing he would accept it, he preached his farewell sermons at Waterbeach chapel on Sunday, April 23. He had been living on 75 Dover Road in London since early March, so the logistics of moving were likely not too difficult.

Charles submitted his formal response to the church on April 28:

> I have received your unanimous invitation, as contained in a resolution passed by you on the 19th instant, desiring me to accept the pastorate among you. No lengthened reply is required; there is but one answer to so loving and cordial an invitation. I ACCEPT IT. *Autobiography* 1:352.

So now, on April 30, 1854, Charles preached his first sermon as the pastor of London's New Park Street Chapel.

Having moved from the countryside to the big city, would Charles adopt new methods? Would he adapt his preaching style and theology to better suit the citizens of London? No, what we see in "the first stone in [his] ministry . . . at Park Street" is that Charles would carry on with the ministry as he had before. This was the kind of preaching that God had blessed at Waterbeach, and Charles would proclaim the same gospel in London. And so, Charles preaches from the very same text that he used in his first and last sermon at Waterbeach Chapel.

This sermon shares the same themes and structure as that of the previous week, though the content is expanded. Many years later, Susannah Spurgeon would remark, "It is delightful to notice that JESUS was the keynote of his ministry both in

Waterbeach and in London, and that not one of his many thousands of Sermons was out of harmony with that opening note." *Autobiography* 1:229.

Interestingly, in this introduction, Charles does not promise that the name of Jesus will "be my loving theme as long as I am among you." He prays that the Holy Spirit will keep him from ever "forgetting that Christ is the gospel, and that preaching the gospel is preaching Christ." This is notable since Charles typically exuded great confidence as a preacher. But we must not forget that at this time, he is only nineteen years old and likely humbled and daunted by the prospect of pastoring this historic Baptist congregation. But what Charles would lack in age and experience, he would make up in faithfulness.

In the next seven years, a revival would break out under his preaching. In 1861, the church would finish constructing a magnificent new building, called the Metropolitan Tabernacle, which was large enough to seat the crowds flocking to hear him. In his inaugural sermon in that building, Charles would lay another "first stone" with these famous words:

> I would propose that the subject of the ministry of this house, as long as this platform shall stand, and as long as this house shall be frequented by worshippers, shall be the person of Jesus Christ. I am never ashamed to avow myself a Calvinist. . . . I do not hesitate to take the name of Baptist . . . but if I am asked to say what is my creed, I think I must reply—"It is Jesus Christ" . . . who is the sum and substance of the gospel; who is in himself all theology the incarnation of every precious truth, the all-glorious personal embodiment of the way, the truth, and the life. *MTP* 7:169.

JESUS THE SAVIOUR FROM SIN

Matthew 1:21

*"And she shall bring forth a son, and thou shalt call his name
JESUS: for he shall save his people from their sins."*

The Laying of the first stone ~~of~~ in a public ~~occ~~ building is usually looked upon as an interesting if not important occasion.

Such is the laying of the first stone in my ministry with you at Park Street. I may not be able to lay it with a silver trowel or in a masterly manner, but at any rate it shall have a good name engraven on it

I do not promise that this name shall be my loving theme as long as I am among you, but I hope it may, and I beseech the good Spirit to keep me ever from forgetting that Christ is the gospel, and that preaching the gospel is preaching Christ.

He ought to be Alpha and Omega, and now that he may be so, let us make him the theme of our first subject. Surely it will be a useful one:

I.   THE NAME.

II. THE PURPOSE.

III. THE PEOPLE.

I.   THE NAME. *"Jesus"*

A large volume, or even library of volumes, might be written on the famous titles of Christ, whethers it be the Seed of the woman, Shiloh, Angel, Prophet, Melchizedek, Redeemer, Holy One, etc. etc. But among them all there is none more sweet than this—Jesus.

Here we see it given at the annunciation. Again at the birth in the manger. To the shepherds, the blind men; nailed over his head. Ascension. This is therefore the sweetest of all. It means a Saviour. It had been borne by two persons before, each of whom were types of him. The first was Jesus or Joshua, the son of Nun, who was a glorious type of Jesus the Son of God.

> 1. He fought the enemies of Israel. He routed Amalek. He drove out the Canaanite. None could stand before him. So will Jesus fight our foes until they all be destroyed, and make sun and moon fight for us. Should the time be too short he will prolong the day, but this will not be, for he will finish his work.
>
> 2. He led them through the Jordan. Although at the time of harvest the river was high, yet it divided, and a dry passage was left for the people. So will it be when we pass the spiritual Jordan, all will be still until all are over.
>
> 3. He divided the inheritance. So has Jesus prepared our mansions and allotted to each his future portion.

The Second is Joshua the son of Jozadak, of whom little can be said as a type. In fact he is rarely mentioned as such, and as I find not the footstep of another I would tread the ground with caution.

> 1. For he builded the altar, restored the sacrifice, and continually [offered].
> 2. He rebuilt the temple.

But these are dim candles when compared with the splendours of Jesus the son of God. This is a name of condescension, love, sweetness, and every thing [that] please[s]. Let us sound it. It is like the music of the upper skies. Ah it is that music, for they have none other name to sing of there.

II. THE PURPOSE.

The Great design of [the] incarnation is Salvation from sin. Sin, like a tyrant, had usurped dominion over the world and no one could dethrone the monster. He would not resign, and no one had will or skill to dash him from his pedestal. But Jesus died and did it. He does it in three ways:

> 1. He saves from the punishment of sin. We were all condemned, but he was condemned for us and endured the death. For us now there is no wrath of

God, no angry glance, no second death, no fiery hell. The dungeons are broken open, the fetters are cast to the winds. None but Jesus could do this. Pardon is his exclusive gift. For he alone could satisfy justice, or as prince, sign the charter of forgiveness.

2. He saves from the guilt of sin. This is a godlike act. To remit the penalty is great, but to justify the offender, to make him innocent, nay even worthy, is a wonder of grace. But so it is. Jesus' righteousness is ours and we stand in the same position as unfallen ones, yea, even higher.

3. He saves from the power of sin. This is a part of the salvation which some do not like. But it is true, for it is <u>from</u> sin not <u>in</u> sin. Jesus drives out our sins by degree. Conversion begins a work which goes on in Sanctification and ends in Perfection in Glory. The two first are momentary, instantaneous, and complete works. This is gradual and progressive. What a work it is. It is the reversing of nature, making rivers run uphill and lions lie down with lambs. But how often it has been done.

III. THE PEOPLE

Who are they? Not all the world, for Christ does not save all.

Not the Jews. They perish still.
But <u>his</u> people. His with emphasis.

By choice, gift, purchase, and power. <u>His</u> people.

How can we tell them[?] There are marks and evidences. I will give you 7 marks, and to help your memory they shall all begin with "con." Conviction. Confession. Conversion. Consecration. Conflict. Consolation. But best of all <u>Con</u>fidence in Jesus. These are <u>the</u> people chosen and called. Let us be sure that we be among them. And now in summing up, I have given you:

1. Heavenly music in the name.
2. Heavenly intentions in the purpose.
3. Heavenly choice in the people.

Or Music, song, and songsters.
Jesus, salvation, his people.

Help me,
Oh God and King.

Sermon No. 366

"OPEN THOU MINE EYES"

Editor's Summary

Prayer meetings were a vital part of Charles's ministry in Waterbeach, and they would characterize his ministry in London from the very beginning. Reflecting on this many years later, he said:

> I rejoice that, ever since I have been with you, the spirit of prayer has never died out amongst us; and I earnestly entreat you never to let it do so. May our prayer meetings be sustained in fervor, and increased in number! Praying is, after all, the chief matter. Praying is the end of preaching. Preaching has its right use, and must never be neglected; but real heart devotion is worth more than anything else. Prayer is the power, which brings God's blessing down upon all our work. *MTP* 48:347.

Before being called to New Park Street Chapel, Charles was already participating in their prayer meetings. In his acceptance letter, he entreated the people to remember him in prayer and to pray that his youth and inexperience would not hinder his ministry. *Autobiography* 1:351–52. Now, as their pastor, he felt all the more urgency for the congregation to pray.

It appears that he organized a series of services devoted to prayer, and this sermon provided a meditation during that season. Preaching on a text he would not preach from again, Charles reminds his people of the humble dependence expressed by prayer and the rich knowledge of God that results from prayer.

It is also interesting that Charles's notes for this sermon are only an outline. In Waterbeach, he'd made it a regular practice to prepare his Sabbath afternoon sermons before the service and deliver them more extemporaneously. But his sermons in London tended to be manuscripts, which gave him more content in the pulpit and less

329

risk of running out of material. That is, until now. Charles would return to preaching extemporaneously, but he would do so at the Monday evening prayer service:

> Ever since I have been in London, in order to get into the habit of speaking extemporaneously, I have never studied or prepared anything for the Monday evening prayer-meeting. I have all along selected that occasion as the opportunity for off-hand exhortation; but I do not on such occasions select difficult expository topics, or abstruse themes, but restrict myself to simple, homely talk about the elements of our faith. When standing up, on such occasions, my mind makes a review, and inquires, "What subject has already occupied my thought during the day? What have I met with in my reading during the past week? What is most laid upon my heart at this hour? What is suggested by the hymns or the prayers?" *Autobiography* 1:365.

Besides allowing him to further develop his extemporaneous speaking skills, such a practice forced Charles to depend on God's guidance for his sermons. Perhaps this act of dependence prepared the preacher to lead his congregation in prayer. On this occasion, Charles could say, "The Lord be praised for help afforded in preaching this sermon."

366

OPEN THOU MINE EYES

Psalm 119:18

"Open thou mine eyes, that I may behold wondrous things out of thy law."

Here is a prayer extremely suitable to you and me at the commencement of the present services. I would use it myself and request you to put it up on my account and your own. We shall examine:

I.   THE DOCTRINE OF THE PRAYER.

II. THE SPIRIT OF THE PRAYER. WE WILL SPEAK OF THE ANSWER.

III. THE RESULT OF THE PRAYER.

I.   THE DOCTRINE OF THE PRAYER.

The doctrine of a man's prayer is often better than the doctrine of his sermons. The headrt knows more than the head.

1. The Doctrine of the imperfection of our nature.
2. The Doctrine of the necessity of supernatural assistance for the attainment of divine knowledge. These the psalmist must have believed or his prayer is nonsense.

II. THE SPIRIT OF THE PRAYER.

1. Intense longing after sacred knowledge.
2. Firm conviction that in the Bible alone could it be found.
3. Deep humility and sense of weakness.
4. Perfect Reliance on Divine teaching.

Oh that this Spirit would more thoroughly permeate my breast.

III. THE RESULT OF THE PRAYER.

1. Clear Knowledge.
2. Steadfast Knowledge.
3. [I]ncreased Knowledge.
4. Knowledge causing surprise and astonishment.

The Lord be praised for help afforded in preaching this sermon.

"THE MINISTERS"

Editor's Summary

With Charles's ministry in London begun, the customary step was now for the New Park Street Chapel to organize an ordination service for him. This was a meeting where other Baptist pastors were invited to come and examine Charles's theology, hear him preach, and affirm God's call on his life. In some cases, they might lay their hands on him, officially ordaining him to ministry not only in his church but among other Baptist churches. (From then on, he could also use the title "Reverend.") Such services were followed by a reception where the young pastor would hear speeches from his more experienced counterparts, receiving advice on all kinds of matters.

While Baptists did not require ordination for pastors, this practice became common because it encouraged greater connection among Baptist churches. Charles, however, was wary of any such practices. Writing to Deacon James Low the week after his first sermon, he stated,

> I have a decided objection to any public ordination or recognition. I have, scores of times, most warmly expressed from the pulpit my abhorrence of such things, and have been not a little notorious as the opponent of a custom which has become a kind of iron law in the country. *Autobiography* 1:356.

For him, these ceremonies seemed to have more in common with Rome than anything he found in Scripture. A true commission from heaven was worth more than "a thousand bulls from Rome . . . [and] all the graces of universities or appointments of bishops." If Deacon Low believed that such a meeting would benefit the church, Charles was willing to submit to it—but he would "endure it as *self-mortification*, in order that you may all be pleased." *Autobiography* 1:357, italics in the original. Not surprisingly, Charles was never formally ordained.

In his letter, he gave three reasons for his objections. First, he believed that the ministerial call comes only from God. Thus he was rejecting any idea that approximated the Roman Catholic teaching of apostolic succession. Second, as one who held to a congregational polity (as all Baptists did), Charles believed the only recognition that mattered was that of the local church.

> Every church has a right to choose its own minister; and if so, certainly it needs no assistance from others in appointing him to the office. You, yourselves, have chosen me; and what matters it if the whole world dislikes the choice? They cannot invalidate it; nor can they give it more force. *Autobiography* 1:357.

Third, he had little regard for extrabiblical traditions. Even less so if they undermined his work for the Lord.

Charles's ministry bore none of the typical marks of human approval. He'd never been to college; he had not been mentored by a London pastor—and yet God had blessed his preaching tremendously. So the last thing he wanted was to undergo a ceremony that implied something was lacking in his ministry. To underscore these convictions, Charles would preach this one-time sermon from Ezek 3:17–19 the following Sunday on the minister's true commission.

THE MINISTERS

Ezekiel 3:17—19

"Son of man, I have made thee a watchman unto the house of Israel: therefore hear the word at my mouth, and give them warning from me. When I say unto the wicked, Thou shalt surely die; and thou givest him not warning, nor speakest to warn the wicked from his wicked way, to save his life; the same wicked man shall die in his iniquity; but his blood will I require at thine hand. Yet if thou warn the wicked, and he turn not from his wickedness, nor from his wicked way, he shall die in his iniquity; but thou hast delivered thy soul."

The office of a gospel minister in some respects resembles that of the ancient prophets.

Though we cannot, like him of Horeb, raise the dead; nor like Isaiah pour forth eloquent predictions, or as Ezekiel foretel[l] certain coming and immediate judgments, yet like them we are commanded to teach, to warn, and to encourage. So much are we alike that the commission of Ezekiel will suit any gospel minister even of our day.

I. THE MINISTER'S COMMISSION.

II. THE MINISTER'S RESPONSIBILITY.

III. THE MINISTER'S COMFORT.

I. THE MINISTER'S COMMISSION.

Here is a scrap of ancient writing worthy of a place in the museum. It ought to be in every minister's study. It is the ultimatum of the King of Heaven to us in our doubts as to our calling. It is our Emperor's protocol to all his legions on.

It is the true ordination, a virtual installment worth as much as a thousand bulls from Rome with the mark of the fisherman's ring. Yea, worth all the graces of universities or appointments of Archbishops. Let us regard:

1. The wording of this ancient commission.
2. The office given thereby.

1. The wording of this ancient commission. It is of course worded in the court style of Heaven and each letter is divine.

Son of Man. Here is the title with which Ezekiel is addressed. Not "Right Reverend" or "the Very Venerable," but a humbling, graciously humbling title. "Son of Man." Daniel is once so called, but Ezekiel 90 times. This is the name Jesus called himself by when on earth, and therefore [it is] a glorious one.

The Gracious and all wise Father saw that so lofty an eminence might tempt Ezekiel to pride. He therefore styles him Son of Man. As much as to say:

Your visions, rank, talents, and office must not exalt you for you are [a] man. You must not lean on self for you are weakness, being only the Son of man. You must sympathize with your fellow creatures and deal with them not as a prince, a master, but as being like them, a Son of Man.

"I have made thee a watchman." Here we read on this ancient manuscript a true account of the making of a minister. God alone can do it. Two things are absolutely requisite to make a man a preacher, viz.:

1. Special gifts. Such as perception of truth, simplicity, aptness to impart, some degree of eloquence, and earnestness.

2. Special call. Let every man be moved thereto of the Holy Ghost. He must feel an irresistible desire to utter his soul in his master's cause.

No college, no Bishop, no ordination can make a man a minister. And he who can feel as Bunyan, Whitefield, Berridge, or Hill the strugglings of an earnest heart may hear in the air the voice "Son of Man, I have made thee a watchman."

"unto the house of Israel." Here was a limited commission, but ours is not; it is enlarged. The world is our parish. We are not ordered to cast the net alone in the pools of Heshbon, or the streams of Jordan, or the lake of Gennesaret, but we may cover all seas and rivers with the fishing boats, the navy of Jesus. Yet still it is for Israel's sake we go.

"therefore hear the word at my mouth." The ancient seers spoke not at random but spoke what they knew, being taught of God. Sometimes in dreams they heard heaven's message. Sometimes [from] a voice from on High but most commonly by vision. The Soul seems to leave the body and that narrow tube of vision called eyesight, and to see with its own eagle power, to pierce the thick cloud, to mount into the region of the tempest and find a home in the absolute remote which eye cannot see.

Thus did they hear, but now we have the written word only and this we must devoutly read. It becomes a minister diligently to search and study the blessed Scriptures, with all the assistance he can gain from holy men who have gone before, but chiefly from the most Excellent of all Instructors, the true Interpreter, the Holy Ghost.

"and give them warning from me." There are other parts of our duty but as this is the most arduous, it is mentioned.

Give the Christian warning if he is found backsliding or indulging in carnality. Give the Sinner warning of the demerit of his sin, of the strict justice of God, and of the fearful hell in which the ungodly shall suffer.

2. The Great office conferred by it. It is that of Watchman. Every Soldier of the Cross is bound to watch, but the minister [is bound] in a double sense. He is so called because:

    1. The ministry requires great vigilance. We cannot afford to sleep. We must take heed to false doctrine, false brethren, help the poor benighted ones, and give alarm of any danger around. He is to sit like the shepherd in the wilderness by night, like the untiring eagle, like the whisper-hearing sentinel.

    2. The ministry involves trouble. Few think of the watchman who tramples by their door. Hark, there is a scuffle. A fight, who is in it[?] The

watchman. How the wind blows, the snow is surely a foot deep. Pray, put list on the doors and stir the fire. Surely no one is out there [tonight]—except the watchman! His bare face meets the driving sleets, his fingers are numbed, his eyelids frozen. Well, well, never mind, that's his work. He is used to it.

So you come and sit and smile and enjoy the sermon, but there are some who criticize and find fault and slander and calumniate it. Well the minister must bear it. Ah, he is the watchman and need be a very tough veteran who has swallowed many nor-westers, or I know not where he will be in the midst of this rabble.

3. The ministry should be arousing. If there be a fire or a thief, or a door or shutter unfastened, he must not spare but cry aloud. We must cry aloud with all our might, not being afraid to disturb, or alarm, or hurt the feelings of the sleepers.

We may as well be asleep as the mumblers, or speak in such a way that none can really make out what we mean. Plain, blunt, honest truth.

Here then is the commission which every man who labours in word and doctrine should ponder over, [and] wear next [to] his heart and on his brow. It is to be feared that many are not alive to a sense of their real position. But having the next presentation to a living, or having purchased a benefice, they carelessly rush in where angels, if like them uncalled, would fear to venture.

II. THE MINISTER'S RESPONSIBILITY.

If the sentinel by sleep causes the death of a single person, he is a murderer. The watchman holds a responsible office. If the prisoner escapes, it shall be required at his hands.

So in the congregation and church. If the ungodly man is not warned he shall bear his own guilt, but my unfaithfulness will lie as a crime on me.

If the professing Christian falls, his fall is his own, but if I have not warned him I am guilty also.

If I do not utter the whole truth both of the threatenings, promises, and invitations of God, I shall be a sleeping sentinel, a careless captain, a negligent railway guard, and I shall be the slaughterer of my fellow creatures. Or if to the professor I give wine instead of medicine, a plaister instead of a lancet, or a stone for bread, I shall be a guilty wretch and God help me then, for nothing more requires help.

III. THE MINISTERS COMFORT.

1. The Lord's call to the office. "I have etc."
2. The Promises peculiar to that call, for every call hath its strength to perform it enclosed.
3. The blessed brow-hardening Spirit who makes us despise the fear or smile of man and thus keeps us from unfaithfulness.
4. The Fact that Success is not required of us, but faithfulness.

Now let us make some use of it.

1. Let us not think slightingly of preaching or hearing, for they are solemn.
2. Let the prayers of the saints rise up for their ministry.
3. Sinners, if you perish under a gospel ministry, your blood be on your own heads.

Oh my Father, set me free.

Amen.

Sermon No. 368

"DEAF CURED"

Editor's Summary

In this sermon on Mark 7:32–35 (Matt 7:32–35 was wrongly cited), Charles uses Jesus's healing of the deaf and mute man as an illustration of God's saving work in sinners. Here we see his conviction about God's "sovereign grace in a sinner's cure to conversion."

When Charles first began to supply the pulpit at the New Park Street Chapel, he wrote to his father describing the congregation's theology:

> The London people are rather higher in Calvinism than I am; but I have succeeded in bringing one church to my own views, and will trust, with Divine assistance, to do the same with another. I am a Calvinist; I love what someone called "glorious Calvinism," but "Hyperism" is too hot-spiced for my palate. *Autobiography* 1:342.

The influence of John Gill, a former pastor of the church, likely continued down through the decades, both in the congregation and generally among the Baptists in London. Gill's high Calvinism emphasized God's sovereignty to such an extent that it tended to minimize human effort and the use of means in salvation. Charles, on the other hand, stood in the stream of Andrew Fuller, who combined "glorious Calvinism" with a warm, evangelistic activism. In this sermon, we see Charles's attempt to bring the congregation over to his own views.

Against any who held to a more Arminian understanding of salvation, Charles makes clear that every sinner is spiritually dead apart from God's grace. No matter how loud the "thunder in Sinai" or how beautiful "the music of the cross," the sinner is deaf to it all and unable to respond. Likewise, no matter how long someone has attended church, if the person is unconverted, then he "can talk of religion fast enough but . . . not know the brogue of Canaan." The only solution is God's act of sovereign

341

mercy to open ears and loosen tongues. Only then, "the words of warning, counsel, love, rebuke, and doctrine are heard distinctly, and the sweet whisper of truth is now louder than the cataracts of eternal vengeance before."

For all who were tempted to place their confidence in human ability, Charles clearly proclaimed the necessity of God's sovereign work of regeneration before faith in the order of salvation. At the same time, Charles didn't deny the necessity of proclaiming the truth to those who are spiritually dead and the active process in which they engage in conversion. While he did believe that some sinners are "suddenly brought to know the truth without much preliminary conviction," he considered these instances of sovereign grace to be rare. High Calvinists would have emphasized such conversions more. Charles, however, presents a much more active engagement in the process of salvation, pictured in Jesus's approach with the deaf and mute man.

Rather than simply speaking a word of healing, Jesus used various means to bring the man along, and only at the end did he declare "the word of might which does it all." Likewise, in the conversion of a sinner, Christ uses the preaching of the Word to isolate that individual "as if all preaching was aimed at him"; to convict him of sin, to remove all other refuges, and to demonstrate sympathy until finally the Spirit brings about life through regeneration.

For the unconverted, their call is not to determine whether or not they are elect or to wait passively for conversion, but to hear the Word and respond by faith in the only Savior, the one who "sitteth in heaven and glories still in his power to save."

DEAF CURED

[Mark] 7:32–35

"And they bring unto him one that was deaf, and had an impediment in his speech; and they beseech him to put his hand upon him. And he took him aside from the multitude, and put his fingers into his ears, and he spit, and touched his tongue; And looking up to heaven, he sighed, and saith unto him, Ephphatha, that is, Be opened. And straightway his ears were opened, and the string of his tongue was loosed, and he spake plain."

No Book has been more honoured of God than the Pilgrim's Progress, and one reason is because it states plainly the road from the City of Destruction to Mount Zion. Now I believe that descriptions of the road are more useful than furious declamations urging us to run it. So do I think that God does often bless descriptions of the mode of sovereign grace in a sinner's cure to conversion as much or more than the most fiery exhortations. I think the case of this man will form an excellent outline of the usual mode adopted in the case of sinners, [the] spiritually diseased.

I.   THE MAN'S DISEASE A TYPE OF OURS.

II. CHRIST'S OPERATIONS A TYPE OF THE SAME SPIRITUALLY.

III. THE MAN'S CURE A TYPE OF OURS.

Good Spirit of all Grace, be pleased to make my sermon the means of spiritual cure to many of thine elect but yet diseased ones. Come Holy and Ever Active Spirit, exert thine omnipotence.

I. THIS MAN'S̶ [DISEASE] A PICTURE OF US.

<u>He was deaf</u>. He could not hear the voice of his friend, the whisper of his wife, or the prattle of his children. For him the streets had no music, the groves no warblings, the sea no murmur, the heavens no thunder, the h̶e̶a̶v̶e̶n̶'s̶ winds no sighings. Poor Man.

See the spiritually deaf. For him there is no thunder in Sinai, in vain the shrill blast of the trumpet or the terrible voice of the Eternal. Myriads of souls are shrieking in hell, "hollow groans, sullen moans, and cries of tortured ghosts" come upward, startling the convinced one, but this deaf man hears not. Then comes the music of the cross, the still small voice of Calvary, the melodious invitation of Jesus and, mingled therewith, the harping and harmonies of heaven. But all in vain.

Let the most charming hymns be sung to the most melodious notes. Let all the church belown̶g̶ join in the chorus, yea let the very Heavens, with the cherubim and perfect ones, resound the chant. Yet he hears not. Ah, though it be his sin, yet who can refuse to say "Poor Man."

"<u>He had an impediment in his speech</u>." When he attempted to tell a tale of woe he faltered and blushingly hid his head. He could not vocally join in the solemn prayer or swell the sacred song. He could hold little or no communication with his fellow man.

So with the spiritually dumb. The tongue is there, and so was the ear. No new organ is wanted but vitality and power put into the old. The man talks lustily enough in his shop or on change but he knows nothing of the language of Canaan. He does not pray. He will not sing. Give him a street song and he will go through it merrily, but set him down to a solemn Psalm and to be sure he has lost his tongue.

Some can talk of religion fast enough but they do not know the brogue of Canaan. If they speak the language, it is in such a broken way that you can see they are foreigners, however much they may dissemble the fact. Deaf and with faulty speech, here are but two ills of thousands which we feel. But though he could not hear or speak [h]is friends can, and therefore they bring him, and on his behalf beseech Jesus to heal him.

Do likewise.

II. CHRIST'S MODE OF CURE.

1. <u>He took him aside</u>. Here is the first act of sovereign mercy. He is isolated from the rest. So the Lord makes the man to feel as if all preaching was aimed at <u>him</u>. Each flash from Sinai points at <u>him</u>, each thunder seems to call for vengeance on him. Every doctrine, threatening, etc., like the waves of a sea, seems to roar and with ten thousand voices cry for him.

   No generalities now. All personalities. He becomes now a lonely, desponding being, it may be. He is often alone in his chamber, and why? Because the Lord hath taken him from the crowd.

2. <u>He put his fingers in his ears</u>. Christ could have opened the man's ears without this, but in the present case this was his plan. So many have been suddenly brought to know the truth without much preliminary conviction. But in most cases it is true that Christ puts his fingers into the ears.

   I was convinced of sin many times before I was converted. And so have many of you. You had the fingers of Jesus [put] in your ears.

3. <u>He spit</u>. To show the man that he must be healed in a humbling way, he spit. Some might have turned away and said "how disgusting." Like Naaman. But so it is, the gospel is very humbling. To the pride of life, to self righteousness and boasting. Sinner, he will humble you or else you must be lost.

4. <u>He touched his tongue</u>. He had just touched the tymphanum of his ear, and now the tongue is touched. The man essays to pray, but groans and sighs are all he utters. Have not you and I done the same[?] Tried to pray and said "I would but cannot pray"[?]

5. <u>Jesus looked up to heaven</u>. The man could not as yet hear, but this dumb language he could comprehend. From heaven all help comes. This is a lesson we must learn. All refuges of lies must be snatched away.

6. <u>Jesus sighed</u>. To show the man his sympathy, his grief for the ills of man. Next to a knowledge of the absolute need we have of divine aid comes a sense that Jesus really has pity on us, and when we believe, that there comes.

7. <u>Ephphatha</u>. The word of might which does it all. This is as much the fiat of omnipotence as "Let there be light." Sweet Jesus, speak the word and these deaf and dumb souls shall both hear and speak.

This is the Spirit's work.

III. <u>THE CURE</u>.

<u>His ears were opened</u>. What sounds gushed into his ears. The Gates were open and in flowed a host of glories. The flood gates are burst and a stream of nectar finds entrance. Anecdote of a woman who recovered hearing.

What a change now in the man. The mountains and hills sing, yea the trees clap their hands. Earth seems one orchestra. Now the words of warning counsel, love, rebuke, and doctrine are heard distinctly and the sweet whisper of truth is now louder than the cataracts of eternal vengeance before. And so strong now is his hearing that oft time he is enchanted with celestial melodies floating over Jordan's streams.

1. <u>He spoke plainly</u>. To speak at all is a wonder, but to speak plainly when not a sound had for years entered his ears was a miracle indeed. So the converted man speaks plainly on the grand points of the Gospel.

<u>Choked</u> as his utterance may be by tears and smothered in sighs, yet to God it is plain, and to us it should be.

And now we have ended this poem of a cure, this Aesculapian epic. Let us chant together a song of praise to the divine physician. He sitteth in heaven and glories still in his power to save. Do you long to praise him[?] Then trust him.

Lord give me words and unction.
Amen, Amen.

"CREATION OF MAN"

Editor's Summary

Charles lived during the time of Charles Darwin and the rising popularity of his work. Though *On the Origin of Species* would not be published until 1859, Darwin had begun to write on his theory of evolution in the mid-1840s in scientific journals and other publications. By 1854, the movement was gathering enough interest that Charles responded from the pulpit, early in his ministry at New Park Street: "The Creation of man is a subject which men have speculated on, and if we wish to see a mass of profound nonsense we must examine the various theories and answers having relation to man's creation." This sermon has no assigned Scripture text, but it is clear that he is referring to the events recorded in Genesis 1.

Charles would always reject the theory of evolution as incompatible with the Christian faith. A student once asked whether any Christian could justifiably hold to evolutionary theory. Charles's response centered on the incompatibility of Scripture with evolution: "Does Revelation teach us evolution? It never has struck me, and it does not strike now, that the theory of evolution can, by any process, of argument, be reconciled with the inspired record of the Creation." *Autobiography* 4:133.

Among his arguments was that Genesis 1 teaches that each creature was created "after [its] kind," and thus distinct from others. He also pointed out the lack of scientific evidence for any links between the animals. Yet in the end, Charles hesitated to rule out the impossibility of a Christian truly believing in both, though he was convinced that doing so is ultimately foolish. "I do not know, and I do not say, that a person cannot believe in Revelation and in evolution, too, for a man may believe that which is infinitely wise and also that which is only asinine." *Autobiography* 4:134.

From time to time, Charles would give weeknight lectures pertaining to secular subjects. On one such occasion in 1861, he titled his lesson, "The Gorilla and the Land He Inhabits." Though this wasn't a lecture on Darwinism specifically, Charles had to address the growing popularity of evolutionary theory. Speaking of the gorilla, he stated:

> Who can deny that there is a likeness between this animal and our own race? . . . There is, we must confess, a wonderful resemblance, — so near that it is humiliating to us, and therefore, I hope, beneficial. But while there is such a humiliating likeness, what a difference there is! If there should ever be discovered an animal even more like man than this gorilla is; in fact, if there should be found the exact facsimile of man, but destitute of the living soul, the immortal spirit, we must still say that the distance between them is immeasurable. *Autobiography* 3:54.

Charles believed that the uniqueness of man as a living soul and immortal spirit is what makes evolutionary theory impossible. This is what he highlights in this sermon. "Man was made in God's image not in the image of an inferior, or even superior, creature." And as beings uniquely made in his image, man is "the being God loveth best of all creation." Ultimately, however, Charles bore witness that the true pinnacle of creation is Christ, who will restore what Adam lost. Evolutionary theory cannot square with the evidence or the reality of the incarnation.

> What if this world was first created myriads of ages ago, as it probably was; yet in the succeeding epochs neither plant nor animal was created without respect to the divine ultimatum, which is redemption! Not a fossil lies in the rock which has not been moulded with a relation to the Lord Christ and his eternal redemption. Christ is the image of God, and all things bear traces of that image. *MTP* 35:154.

CREATION OF MAN

Amongst the wondrous things recorded in the word of God is the account of the pristine glory of man and his first origin. The Creation of man is a subject which men have speculated on, and if we wish to see a mass of profound nonsense, we must examine the various theories and answers having relation to man's creation.

We will not waste time by even glancing at the absurd theories of philosophers but come at once to the sublimely laconic Mosaic account. Here we find concerning man's creation:

I.   A SPECIAL TIME CHOSEN.

II. A SPECIAL COUNCIL HELD.

III. A SPECIAL MODEL SELECTED.

I.   A SPECIAL TIME CHOSEN.

The world had been redeemed from its inert chaotic state by the brooding wings of the sacred Dove. Light had been thrown from Heaven on the earth and darkness was divided therefrom. The blue firmament had been stretched on high and the green earth, clad in its new robe, sent up on high the forest tree and waving palm. The two bearers of light chased each other over the blue ethereal, while the stars looked sweetly on the as yet silent world.

Then were the waves divided by finny creatures, and the air was fanned by feathery wings. And to make all earth a dwelling place for living creatures, the hills and valleys teemed with creeping things, and cattle and beasts. Last of all the crowning labour forth came, "man," for whose comfort all these had been formed. Now we say that the time selected was a very appropriate one:

1. <u>It seems fitting that the best should be the last work</u>. We find a gradual progression in God's works of creation. From mere chaotic matter to ether[e]al substances such as light, then to vegetable life, and on through the lower grades of animals up to the highest degree of animal existence, putting on the apex of all the erect figure of man. It would not have seemed congruous that the loftiest creature should have been the first effect of Divine intelligence, and after that no progress, but rather a going back.

We admire in a sermon the man who gradually rises in ideas. Mankind love[s] a climax, and God has here given us one. A pyramid, the base of which is inert matter, and the summit the image of God. When the great drama of creation commenced it did not give its grandest act and then sink, but gradually rose in glory until the favourite of heaven and vicegerent on earth stepped forth upon the arena fresh from his Maker's hand.

2. <u>It seemed proper that the house should be built and furnished, so that the tenant might have an habitation</u>. It would not have been agreeable to the constant tenor of God's acts to make a creature like man and put him amid the shapeless masses of confusion which at first [God] made. No, man must have a place to stand upon, and it is found. Light made. But there is a ~~an~~ mixture of light and darkness midway between the two. Shall man be placed in darkness or twilight[?] "No," forthcometh day. Etc. Etc. Then when all is completed, out comes the king. All things are ready. A train of servants to do his bidding in all the elements: Food. Shade. Mossy seats. Music. All ready. This is the time to form man.

3. <u>God thus proves an undivided interest in creation</u>. Man did not assist his Maker to create or arrange, for he was not in existence. Let not man boast [of] himself, for flies were made before him and could have existed without him, but he could not without <u>them</u>. He did not help to form even an animalcule. See then how the honour belongeth unto God alone. There are other things which might be said upon the time, but we rather choose to leave it to you and turn next to the second point.

II. <u>A SPECIAL COUNCIL HELD</u>.

He who reads this without seeing in it plurality of persons in the Godhead is not a very wise man. It is certain that God took no council with any, for we are told in Isaiah that he took council with none. Ergo, not with angels. Nor is this pompous mode of speech used by monarchs, for this vain habit was not introduced until the end of [O]ld Testament Times. See the proclamations of Darius and Nebuchadnezzar.

It doth therefore undoubtedly respect the three persons of the Trinity, who are in council together. The Question then arises, why is this consultation? Certainly not because there was a lack of wisdom or skill, nor because the persons did not know the will of one another, for God is one and knows all things perfectly. But the figure is used to give us 3 ideas:

1. <u>The importance of the work</u>. When sun and moon and stars were formed there was no consultation; but of man there was. He is the pivot of the universe, a microcosm, a world in himself. The being God loveth best of all creation. God does not think slightly of man, let us not think so little of ourselves as to stoop to sin, nor of our brother as to despise him. Man is a great existence, for God said "let us make man."

2. <u>The wisdom displayed in the work</u>. All creation singeth of wisdom but man is leader of the band. Since the body of man is the dwelling of the Son, it was meet that it should have much wisdom expended on it and shall we ever know a tythe [tenth] of the mystery of man.

3. <u>The unanimity of the Godhead in it</u>. There is a tendency to think too little of one in comparison with the others. But they are one, and equal. In salvation. In this too. <u>Let us make man</u>.

III. <u>A SPECIAL MODEL SELECTED</u>.

Of nothing else, not of angels nor of the heavens, is this said but of man and man only. Man was made in <u>God's</u> image, not in the <u>image</u> of an inferior, or even superior, creature. Let us enquire wherein this image consists.

1. It may consist partly in the majesty and dignity which man possessed, making him the lord of all creatures. There may have been a lustre on his face like that on Moses, and doubtless he had a royalty now lost.

2. It may consist also in his being a really intelligent creature, a spirit, an intellect, like Deity.

3. It may also comprise that immortality which was the lot of Adam, for he could not die. His body, though capable of death, was preserved therefrom, perhaps by eating the fruit of the tree of life. But at any rate he could not die. But I rather prefer to follow the ancient words of our ancestors who wrote it as an article of their creed, that God created man in his own image in knowledge, righteousness, and true holiness.

In knowledge. Though he could not attain to such knowledge as his Creator possessed, yet he knew more than we do. Or at least he knew more certainly. His powers were not blunted. There was no vitiation or obliquity in his understanding, for he was as a creature perfect in this. How different the unregenerate.

In righteousness. He was entirely free from any inclination to evil. His will was free to either good or evil, but it had not any bias as ours has. This was justice in God.

In holiness. He was not only righteous in character but really holy in act. In him was no sin. He was a sun without spots.

Look on this passing picture and sigh over it, but still rejoice, for in Jesus we gain more than Adam lost.

Bless me, oh Lord.

"NO BONE BROKEN"

Editor's Summary

"No Bone Broken," built around a single verse from the account following the death of Christ in John's Gospel, gave Charles the opportunity to expound on the doctrine of providence. While he would not preach again on this text, he would return to this doctrine, offering words such as these in 1884:

> The infinite Lord appoints the date of every event; all times are in his hand. There are no loose threads in the providence of God, no stitches are dropped, no events are left to chance. The great clock of the universe keeps good time, and the whole machinery of providence moves with unerring punctuality. It was to be expected that the greatest of all events should be most accurately and wisely timed, and so it was God willed it to be when and where it was, and that will is to us the ultimate reason. *MTP* 30:687.

With the sermon here, Charles examines a text that he considered to be "so full of interest that the very angels look from windows of heaven" at the moment-by-moment fulfillment of prophecy in the last hours of Christ's life and the hours after his death. Like a lawyer making an argument, Charles presents several reasons why the legs of God's Son should have been broken—and yet providence intervened.

- The Roman soldiers would have obeyed a command to break his legs unless thwarted.
- The soldiers who beat Jesus did so with such brutality that they would have had no trouble breaking his legs as well unless thwarted.
- The Jews who demanded the death of Jesus would have wanted to see his body broken unless thwarted.

- Other legs were broken, as Jesus's would have been unless thwarted.

From this, Charles argues that the believer should look for providence everywhere.

He then explores why Jesus's legs were spared. First, to compel people to compare Jesus to the Passover lamb. Second, to show Christ's power over his own life and body. Third, to show how he bore our sins well; he did not break. Fourth, to show Jesus victorious over Satan. Finally, Charles relates the doctrine of providence to the doctrine of the church. Just as the bones of Jesus's body were not broken, the church may bruise but never break. It will not lose a member, lest the entire body remain incomplete. As Charles would say, "The word written of [Jesus's] body of flesh is equally true concerning his mystical body, which is his church. 'A bone of him shall not be broken.'" *MTP* 38:106.

NO BONE BROKEN

John 19:33

"But when they came to Jesus, and saw that he was dead already, they brake not his legs:"

Every circumstance in the life of Christ is important. Nothing is small which relates to him. From the manger to the cross, the very stones in his path are diamonds. His words are worthy of an angel audience. His acts deserve an eternity of wondering examination.

He is at a marriage, and marriage becomes a most honourable estate. He takes a child in his hands, and a child becomes a picture of Christian. The words "suffer etc." an evergreen motto for Sunday Schools.

But when he nears his end, his movements become so full of interest that the very angels look from the windows of heaven to watch his footsteps. Each hour fulfils a prophecy, each day flashes forth conviction that he is the true Messiah.

> Judas betrays him, "he that eateth etc."
> He holds his peace, "like a sheep, dumb etc."
> He is scourged, "by his stripes etc."
> He goes without the camp, "so did the heifer."
> He is nailed, "they pierce my hands etc."

So on all through his hours of agony. But now he dies—and surely all is over, for he said "it is finished." But no, there remains one type, nay more than one or two yet unfulfilled. His bones must not be broken, for the bones of the pascal lamb were all of them to remain entire. They are not broken. With devout wonder let us admire:

I. THE PROVIDENCE WHICH PRESERVED HIS BONES.

II. THE PURPOSE OF THIS PRESERVATION.

I. THE PROVIDENCE WHICH PRESERVED HIS BONES.

Good Flavel used to say that "he who observes providences shall never want a providence to notice." Similar was the expression of good Mr. Newton who said that "God had ordered which of the two streets he should go to St. Mary's by."

Precisely to the same import are the lines of Watts.

> "There's not a sparrow or a worm
> But's found in his decrees."

Now in this case we think we see very plainly; not the finger merely, but the very hand of God. He had ordained that the body of his son should not be broken as to its bones, and his decree is fulfilled although there seemed many things to prevent it. Pilate gave orders for the breaking of their legs and . . .

1. The Severity of Roman discipline stands in the way: for Roman soldiers are wont to obey even to the jot and the [tittle]. We know from what the centurion said that the R. soldiers obeyed at once: "do this," and without any consideration or thought "he doeth it." We read of Torquatus Manlius who ~~was~~ put to death his own son because he had fought a Gaul without permission.

    We think then that when the order was given, the soldiers would be likely to obey it at once, without question or debate. The command came from [headquarters]. It might mean that their legs should be broken if they were yet alive. But would soldiers think of this[?] Would they not be more likely blindly to obey[?] But God can turn the balance of probabilities, and if ~~he~~ Pilate or Caesar shall give an order contrary to his will, he will countermand it.

2. The Ferocious character of Roman Soldiers. War has a tendency to brutalize the mind, it cannot be thought that men familiar with blood will be the subjects of very tender emotions. War in ancient times was more savage than now, and the Roman soldiers must have been barbarous from what we read of them in Scripture. The men who could murder the innocents at Bethlehem imbrue [stain] their hands in the blood of Galileans engaged in sacrifice.

    [They who b]uffet, scourge, and spit on Jesus and then quietly sit down and raffle for his garments would not be likely to have much pity but would rather, after breaking with their iron bar the legs of the two wretches, take a savage delight in breaking the bones of one who called himself a God. But he who turneth rivers turned their fierce hearts. Lions once licked the feet of Daniel. Bears came out at the call of Elisha. And so shall men of cruel souls be turned by his power, for the hearts of all are in his hands.

3. The Savage Clamour of the Jews. When we consider that the Jews hated our Lord extremely, that they clamoured for his crucifixion, that they mocked him on the cross, were vexed that the title over his head should even seem to give respect to him, and that they requested that the legs might be broken—it excites our wonder that they should suffer the soldiers to leave our Saviour.

They would have been pleased to see his body mutilated. They had been eating the passover and would have been wise enough to see the type if only mentioned, and would have been taking precaution to prevent his resurrection. But it did not enter into their minds. Perhaps they were just wending their way homeward so as to be at home on Sabbath, which commenced that eventide. But so it was, they had gained a grant and then neglected to see the order fulfilled. Oh depth of providence. Wise men become fools and the subtle shallow. The learned Rabbi slumbereth, and the haughty Pharisee forgetteth when the Lord wills it.

4. The Circumstance of passing by Jesus. The Soldiers brake the legs of the first, perhaps the one who was penitent. His soul is so filled with rapture at the sweet promise of Jesus that when the cruel blow breaks his bones, and the marrow and blood fly out, although a scream comes forth, the melody of that blest sound sustains his heart: "today shalt thou be with me etc." Here was providence in the title over Jesus' head, for from it the thief learned the gospel, and providence in the blow which ended his existence and landed him in heaven.

Next they go to the miscreant on the other side and give his soul a swifter passage to the burning pit. But why pass by Jesus[?] But now they come, and a rough warrior lifts the iron bar; but see the man's head hangs down, the joints are motionless, he is dead. So they break not his legs, but at the same time [it is] manifest that it is not pity which restrains them, for one of them drives a spear into his side.

How the Infinite God wrought this we cannot understand, but let us believe in his wondrous Providence. Some will say "well I never noticed a providence there." Ah, but you should do so. Learn to notice the hand of God in the histories of his word and then in the histories of life.

Look for Providence, for it is everywhere, "for doubtless the sailing of a cloud hath a Providence for its Pilot, doubtless the root of an oak is gnarled for a special purpose. The foreknown station of a rush is as fixed as the station of a king, and chaff from the hand of a the winnower steered as the stars in their courses."

Look for Providence, for in so doing you will find comfort. The man who believes in providence believes himself to be as secure in a tempest as in a calm, as safe really in battle as in peace. He sees a bright spot in every cloud and believes them all to be "big with mercies.["]

Let me in leaving this part beg of you to look at the littles of providence as well as at the great. It is well said that "if Pestilence stalk through the land, ye say this is God's doing. Is it not also his doing when an aphis creepeth on a rosebud? If an avalanche roll from its Alp, ye tremble at the will of Providence. Is not that will concerned when the sear leaves fall from the poplar[?] etc." M. Tupper. 124.

All things are under the superintendence of the Most High and neither the littles nor the great are to be disregarded. May the blessed illumination of the Spirit shed a flood of light over the second part of our subject.

II. THE PURPOSE OF THIS PRESERVATION.

It does not seem probable that the great providence of God should have been exercised to preserve the body of Christ, and the evangelist John inspired to note the circumstance, if there were nothing in it.

And:

1. <u>It may be that the Holy Ghost thus designed to draw our attention to the pascal lamb as a type of Christ</u>. In 1 Cor. 5:7 we are told by Paul that the Lord Jesus is our passover, and this passage seems to run side by side with it as a "speaking act." We will only hint at a few points of manifest resemblance.

> This rite was instituted before the Law, either moral or ceremonial, had been given.
>
> So Jesus and his gospel are a something before, over, and superior to the law.

> The lamb without blemish, roasted with fire, eaten in haste, [and] with bitter herbs.
>
> Jesus in suffering, and is received with repentance.

> The lamb was the means of a double deliverance—from Egyptian bondage and divine vengeance.
>
> So doth Jesus work for us a twofold rescue from the double evils of our souls.

2. <u>This showed that his death was voluntary</u>. Jesus could not be forced to die. His first descent from glory was of his own will. He could save his life, as he did on one or two occasions. He made the men fall back. He said he could have twelve legions of angels. He told Pilate why he had power. His strength was in him, for he cried out just before death with a loud voice. So now he makes a reservation of his bones to show that he had power over his life and body, to take up or lay down. So men do with estates. So God with Job and Satan.

Now let us admire the death of Jesus from this point of view. See yon martyr; he dies and cannot avoid it. But see this man; a glance could slay his oppressors, a word would lay the whole host at his feet or blast them into hell. Let me love and sing and wonder.

3. <u>This showed how well he bore our sins</u>. No man knoweth how tremendous a burden hung on the shoulders of our Saviour at this most wondrous time. If the whole earth had endeavoured to sustain it, they would have perished a mangled heap of carcasses. Should the [whole] race of angels assay their strength, they too would soon totter and fall. But Jesus bore all and not a bone of him was broken.

Think of the sins of a lost world, the sufferings the elect would have suffered, the frown of his Father, the agonies of his soul. Oh 'tis a burden sinner, 'tis a burden too heavy for thee to bear, to carry thine own sins, much more the sin of myriads. Praise the Redeemer for his divine labours.

4. <u>This showed the victory of Jesus over Satan</u>. It had been foretold that the seed of the serpent should have an antagonist, and in [the] process of time the seed of the woman entered the lists. At first they fought in a wilderness, and there the Son of God was victor, but now came the struggle between man's enemy and man's friend.

Now they clasp each other and our champion falls, stained o'er with blood forced from him by the desperate tug of the foe. Like Xn in the valley he sighs, and to it again they fall. Still he suffers, and all his body is robed in gore—but now comes the last "conquer or die." Now champion, "Conquer and die" says he, and yields up the ghost.

Now see the two combatants. One has his head broken, he drags his broken frame with pain along, being just alive; but the other, how is he. He has scars, but not a bone is broken.

5. <u>This showed how his mystical body shall be</u>. I am glad to close with this since it is so rich in comfort to the saints of the Lord.

His people are his bones and flesh.
They may be bruised, but never broken.
Those who fall are hypocrite[s], shooting stars.
They never entered into vital union.
The head will never willingly lose a member, even if that member be sick.
The loss of one small member would render the body incomplete.

But shall there be an incomplete body of Christ in glory[?] No, for if so, there would be an incomplete heaven, and our Saviour would be inglorious. Nay, we are graven on his heart and written on the palms of his hands.

The mountains may depart etc.
<u>Hallelujah to free grace</u>.

"THE LORD REIGNETH"

Editor's Summary

From one verse in the shortest chapter in the Bible, Psalm 117, Charles develops a rich meditation on the sovereignty of God, returning to the refrain "The Lord reigneth" several times to underscore this truth. While Charles would not preach again on this text, he would affirm this doctrine many times. For example, he reminded his London congregation in 1877,

> After all the Lord reigneth, let the earth rejoice, let the multitudes of the isles be glad thereof. Still, despite all the hurly-burly of war, and all the wickedness of men in the dark places of the earth, and the detestable blasphemies of the heathen against the Most High, the Lord sitteth on a throne which never can be shaken. *MTP* 23:242.

Charles begins by emphasizing that the beauty of Scripture often lies in its simplicity. When words are crafted in this fashion, he notes, they are sublime. Thus, the simple notion that God reigns all the time, no matter the circumstances, makes for a fitting declaration and exhortation.

The Lord reigns in every place, exults Charles. Whether in heaven, on earth, in the army, or within crowded cities, the Lord reigns. Even in America, with its advocacy of slavery, the Lord reigns. This is as true throughout the nations of earth as it is in the depths of hell.

The Lord reigns, Charles says, in every age. From the creation of the world to the fall of Adam to the coming of Christ and the scattering of his disciples, the Lord reigns. In Charles's words, God's sovereign reign is the "key of the past," the "shield of the present," and "the banner of the future."

He goes on to exhort his hearers to believe and rejoice in this doctrinal truth, for it is rooted in the character of God. His people can trust that God will govern justly, wisely, and mercifully and will care for them as a Father.

Charles's mention of "the days of Bess" is likely an allusion to Queen Elizabeth I, who was known as "Good Queen Bess" by some Protestants. It is uncertain who, or what, the preacher is referring to by "the cards," though given the context, it could be the Catholic cardinals who were persecuting Protestant Christians during the reign of Queen Mary I. (Elizabeth I put an end to the persecution when she gained England's throne.)

The final exhortation here is, again, to rejoice in the sovereign reign of God. On another occasion, Charles would sum up every Christian's reason for rejoicing in this way:

> When the Lord shall make up his last account of his jewels in that great day, we shall be found in Christ, even as gems are found in a golden casket. In the Lord Jesus Christ all his elect, all his blood-bought, all his called, all his justified, all his believing people shall be found in that day. None of his redeemed shall be absent in the day when the sheep shall pass again under the hand of him that telleth them. All who were marked with the blood-mark here below shall be folded in the pastures of glory. *MTP* 32:429.

THE LORD REIGNETH

Psalm 117:1

"O praise the Lord, all ye nations: praise him all ye people."

What an advantageous position the Christian enjoys to look upon this world from. Other men are in the vale. He is on a hill and can see farther, but mists do gather even on hills, and the good man's eyes become beclouded. He becomes like David, foolish and envious, like a beast before God. But there remains one place where the atmosphere is clear, one place where we can discern. That place is sanctuary of the Lord. How sweet to come hither away from your toils and cares: may the Lord bless this means of grace.

The subject of my text is one peculiarly calculated to settle the mind that is in any way disturbed. The Lord reigneth:

I.   A GLORIOUS DECLARATION.

II. A FITTING EXHORTATION.

I.   A GLORIOUS DECLARATION.

How sublime are many of the sentences of Scripture. And if you seek the reason of their sublimity it lies in their simplicity. It is a mistake to suppose that high sounding words are sublime. Simplicity is the sire of sublimity, or rather, its only fitting robe. The Lord reigneth. I might launch forth into a thousand subjects, all of them profitable, but I choose rather to dwell on one point, and that is—

the Universality of this truth

. . . .

In Every Place. This is true. Carry me to heaven, up amid the wondrous hierarchy of angels, to the highest rank, the tallest of all the sons of the morning. Amid those ranks the truth is felt and delighted in **"The Lord reigneth."**

Descending to those gods below, kings and rulers, we enter the cabinet, we listen to the discussions of the divan and we hear not of the [M]ost [H]igh. He is forgotten, but even there **"The Lord reigneth."**

Go amid the army. See the warrior buckling on his ~~helm~~ armour and clasping his helmet. See the serried [closed] ranks. Hearken to the noise and tumult of the war, and as with sicken'd sight you turn away, yet remember **"The Lord reigneth."**

We turn to the more loving pursuits of peace and we survey the crowded city. The ~~blissful~~ bustling mart, the pleasant country. We launch on the sea [and] we pass over America. We see its slavery, its fanaticism and liberty. We see the cold northern regions of the Pole. We skim the Pacific and go to the new found regions of gold. Turn northward to busy China etc. etc. And when tired we rest, we can hardly understand the truth, but yet believe it, that in all those lands, fertile or sterile, barbarous or civilized, God reigneth. That on the highest mountain, on the stormiest billow, in the deepest chasm <u>God reigneth</u>.

Then fly we on to other worlds and close our great excursion by entering hell. And even here we see in burning characters **"The Lord reigneth."** He is the only Potentate, and his power extends so far that there is not room for another.

In every age. This is true. Monarchs have had their day and have passed into their graves, but this one never dies. When nothing save space existed. When Adam fell. When the world was full of sin. The flood. When Israel was in Egypt. When Canaan was in reprieve. When false gods were worshipped by Israel. When Nebuc[hadnezzar] led Israel captive. When the vessels were profaned. When the Jews were persecuted by Antiochus. When Jesus died. When his disciples were scattered. When Popery prevailed. When Smithfield smoked. When religion flagged. **"The Lord reigneth."**

So in every time of our experience. This fact is the key of the past, the silken clue of the labyrinth of providence. It is the shield and pavilion of the present, its helm and tiller. It is the star and banner of the future. The ultimatum. The top stone. The soul of all Eternity.

"The Lord Reigneth"

II. A FILLING EXHORTATION.

We are exhorted to rejoice in it.

1. We believe that he will govern most <u>justly</u>. Oppression, etc. will be punished and the right defended.
2. We believe etc. wisely. We can trust in his administrations.
3. We believe etc. <u>mercifully</u>, not allowing more suffering than is needful.

But the Christian can rejoice, for it is his Father who reigns, and will preserve him and all his own elect. The Church is safe. See the days of Bess. The cards. So, in future. Each member is safe, nothing can destroy if God reigns and looks on me.

And now to conclude, can we feel this a real source of joy to us, then we may believe that we are his. Then ought we to rejoice and lift up the voice. Rejoice, Rejoice.

"The Lord Reigneth"

"MERCY AND JUDGMENT"

Editor's Summary

Charles preaches from this psalm of David on the doctrine of hope in times of loneliness and temptation. While he would not preach again on this text, he would return to this doctrine. Preaching in 1892, Charles declared,

> If you want God, he is everywhere, he is here, he is nearer to you than your hands and feet, nearer to you than your eye or your nerve. He is within you, and round about you. You might ask, with the Psalmist, "Whither shall I flee from thy presence?" and find that task to be impossible; but if you really wish to find God, you may readily do so. *MTP* 38:425–26.

Charles begins here with a curious contrast between David's enthusiasm toward God's blessings and the joy-suppressing churchgoers of Charles's day who evidently preferred ministers who were "as cold as marble stones." His heart, however, reflected David's heart of zeal, and Charles would long advocate for a vibrant ministry and combat dullness at every turn.

The largest section of this sermon centers on God blessing the lonely with friendship and families, the pinnacles of which are found in God himself. The families that the Lord provides for the lonely include the universal, eternal family of God—known in part now, but fully one day when all the saints are united with Christ—and the visible family on earth, the church. While the doctrine of the church is not Charles's main purpose in the sermon, he does articulate believer's baptism and participation in the Lord's Supper as practices afforded to members of the church.

He also explores a second promise from this text: that God delivers prisoners from bondage. Noting that David is likely referencing the exodus of Israel from Egypt, Charles emphasizes other biblical examples of divine deliverance:

- God breaks the chains of sin.
- God breaks the chains of just punishment due to us by Jesus's payment of our debt.
- God breaks the chains of despair.

He then concludes this sermon with a plea to those still living in rebellion against God.

As he puts it, the rebellious are in a dry land fearing death, fearing what comes after death, and living with remorse. Using a rhetorical device for emphasis, Charles repeats the word "dry" three times just before pleading with God in prayer to "help" three times. It was his pastoral way of calling the rebels to come out of the dry land to the family of Christ.

This Christ-centered proclamation of the gospel is vintage Spurgeon and is something he proclaimed time and again:

> The Lord Jesus Christ has come to save his people from their sins, to break the chains of evil habit, to subdue sinful influences which now dominate us, and to put within us a new heart and a right spirit. *MTP* 32:243.

372

MERCY AND JUDGMENT

Psalm 68:6

*"God setteth the solitary in families: he bringeth out those which are
bound with chains: but the rebellious dwell in a dry land."*

How enthusiastic David was. In these cold times he would have been reproved for
over zeal, giving a loose to his imagination, and rising almost into frenzy.

Oh ye cold froglike Christians who want to have ministers as cold as marble statues,
look ye here and behold the rolling eye, and burning cheek, and high wrought extacy
of David while he sings. Sing unto God. Sing praises to his name. Extol him that
rideth on the heavens by his name Jah, and rejoice before him. Oh 'tis a blessed
frenzy. Religion without zeal, served up in a cold and formal manner, is most
tasteless and unprofitable. But to look at the verses of this rapt and burning poet,
here is one containing two blessings and a curse.

I.   BLESSING – THE SOLITARY IN FAMILIES.

This is literally true if we consider the case of Abraham, or of Ruth, or of
Hannah. It may also apply to Gentile believers who were indeed solitary, but
now are they as numerous as the stars of heaven. I shall however apply this
to the case of the man who sighs for help but still is found in darkness and
ignorance of Christ.

1.   Let us remark the sad state indicated by the word "solitary." Imagine a
foreigner suddenly set down in our country, having no friend, no money, no
knowledge of the language. He has never seen such strange costumes. He
does not see a face which he can recognize. He is a stranger and a foreigner,
no one gives him food. The night comes on and he sits down weary on the
door step, for he is "solitary."

369

So is the man whom conviction has wounded. He is a solitary man. He may live in society but he dislikes it. He cannot frequent the Ball Room or even sit in the family circle. Like the smitten deer he retires to die alone. Songs for a lodge in a vast wilderness, wishes like Adam to hide under the thick trees of the garden. Such is the solitary whom God setteth in families.

But this figure does not represent all the horrors of the word, and therefore we resort to another. See yon sailor. He has climbed a rock, his vessel is gone, his comrades are drowned. He looks and he is alone on the rock. He sees no vessel near, not even a screaming fowl is heard and is still. Only the stars look on him. He is Solitary.

So is the character I intend. His ship of false confidence is wrecked, he seems to himself to be the only one on the rock. No hope is near. He gives up all for lost and feels too much the meaning of the word solitary. Ah poor solitary one, there is hope even now. I see the sail in the distance.

But once more. A traveller has lost his way in the wilds of America. He is torn with the briars, he is weary, but still he tries to find his path. Impossible. And now he hears the loup [howls] of the wolf in the distance and he climbs a tree. Soon a score of them are at his feet, filling him with fear.

Suddenly the sun sets. Black night comes on. A storm is brewing. The wind rocks his tree to and fro, the thunder rolls, the lightnings make the sky bright around him, his hair stands almost upright. He calls for help but nature mocks him, the wolves continue their horrid howlings, and he fears he shall either be in their jaws or be killed by the lightning. Just as he ruminates on this, a shaft smites the next tree. Its trunk is severed, blasted by the flash.

Such is the solitary soul. He hears his sins like wolves upon him. His support is frail, death near, the anger of God above him, and he is in the most terrible state of trouble. Such is the man God will place in families.

2. Let us remark the great privilege expressed by the phrase "setteth in families." Solitary one, there is a friend near. The Psalmist points you to him, it is God. He mentions his name although he might have said "he," lest there should be any possibility of mistake. To be set in a family is to be made one of them and enjoy all the privileges. There are not two families but one, yet as they are separated they may be called <u>families</u>.

There is the family of <u>Christ mystical</u>. You poor sinner shall be by sovereign grace made a child, made a prince. "You are unworthy," say you. Ah, but the prodigal was not suffered to say that. You shall be fed with the fatted calf, wear the best robe and the golden ring, and then you shall be a joint heir with Christ.

There is the family of <u>Christ visible</u>, the visible Church. You ought to come into this if you are in the church of Christ. And if you do, you shall be one of the family. You shall be allowed to make an open profession of your faith by Baptism, sit at the supper of our Lord, join in our prayers, and in fact be one in a large family. I would I could promise you perfectly loving treatment, but I will hope that you will receive it.

But there is the family of <u>Christ perfected</u>, the church of the firstborn. Into this you shall be admitted, and have the full range of your Father's house and the glorious society of the saints in light. And now, poor solitary one, it may seem too good to be true, but it must be believed for the Lord hath said it. Even now, <u>He setteth the solitary in families</u>.

II. BLESSING – CHAINS BROKEN.

When we get one promise we mostly have another on the heels of it. God often pileth Pelion on Ossa, mountain on mountain. He is not sparing in his blessings. This promise too might be literally understood as relating to Israel from Egypt and many similar cases. But I chose rather to apply it to a spiritual loosening from chains. I shall speak of the works of God in breaking the chains of:

<u>Sin</u>. Men are chained by sin. Their evil habits are iron chains. Their evil passions drag them in willing captivity to evil. They are slaves to sin, but the Lord our God can, and will, break these chains.

<u>Justice</u> has put fetters on us and detains us until the hour of execution, but God breaks these, for Jesus has discharged the debt.

<u>Despair</u>. These are the firmest chains of all. For the man who wears them made the lock to them himself and has thrown the key away. And besides, like a lunatic, if we go near to help him he will strike therewith. But God rends the chains in sunder as if they had been tow and sets the soul free.

~~Poor~~ Despairing one, rejoice. Good Dr. Hawker and the man's not understanding. Oh the joy which release occasions when we are set free and put out of prison into the clear open air of Gospel grace and liberty.

III. CURSE – THE REBELLIOUS DWELL IN A DRY LAND.

A dry land in the east is necessarily a land of sterility and desolation. Such is the country of the rebellious. God's word ever represents the state of rebels as deplorable. There is little real joy to an ungodly man, for:

1. The fear of death terrifies, like the sword over the head at the feast.
2. The fear of what is after death terrifies—you are forging a chain to bind yourselves in for ever.
3. The remorse of conscience, which like an adder biteth at the heart.

To conclude, you dwell in a dry land. You know you do. How is it that when death comes you always seek another land to die in[?] You would turn Christian the~~m~~n. You know your principles are too hollow to bear the heavy foot of death. Ah young man, seek not to know the country of the rebellious. It is dry, dry, dry. But seek thou to be set in the family of Christ.

<u>Oh Lord help. help. help</u>

"EVERY CHRISTIAN A PRIEST"

Editor's Summary

While Charles would not preach again on this text, he indicates that the doctrine within it—that all true Christians are spiritual priests—is not isolated to Isa 61:6. In fact, in keeping with "the general tenor of inspiration," this idea and imagery can be found throughout the Bible. In 1897, he preached,

> Christ has made all of us, who believe in him, to be kings and priests unto God; there is no priesthood in the world that is of God save the high-priesthood of our Lord Jesus Christ, and, next to that, the priesthood which is common to all believers; and the idea of there being any priesthood on earth above and beyond the priesthood of all believers, is a false one, and there is no Scripture whatever to vindicate it, to justify it, or even to apologize for it, it is one of the lies of old Rome. *MTP* 43:366.

Intending to encourage the "meek and brokenhearted" with this doctrine of "Every Christian a Priest," Charles first wanted to clarify its meaning by tearing down the way it was practiced among the Greek Orthodox, the Roman Catholics, and the Church of England. At the core of what he calls the "error" of these traditions was their overemphasis on a distinction between clergy and laity that elevated the role of priest. As Charles would explain in a future message, "I blush to think that Englishmen should claim kinship with the Roman Antichrist, whose yoke our fathers tore from off their necks. The pedigree of every Anglican priest must of necessity have flowed through the Dead Sea of Popery." *MTP* 21:596.

Additionally, this sermon reveals yet another aspect of Charles's doctrine of the church: he believed in two biblical church offices, that of bishop and deacon. The Christian bishop is not at all like the Church of England's bishop, who is afforded elevated status and considered spiritually superior to other church members. Rather, a bishop in Charles's interpretation of Scripture was someone with the functional role of church leadership only. In terms of status, Charles, as church bishop, was no different than his congregants.

The remainder of the sermon extols the honor Christians share as members of a royal priesthood. Believer-priests are to carry out the duties of their office

- by self-sacrifice
- by solemn prayers, private and family
- by sacred praise

While much of this aspect is left for the reader to imagine due to the skeleton outline, Charles gave further context some years in the future:

> Suppose it is not the duty of forgiveness that is in question, but some other, such as that of holy self-sacrifice, how do you stand with regard to it? Have you made sacrifices for Christ? Have you given of your substance to his cause until you have pinched yourself in doing so? That is one of the sweetest things a Christian can ever do, and there is a great reward in doing that. Have you denied yourself some pleasure in order to spend your time in doing well to others? If so, I am sure it has proved to be one of the best things you have ever done. *MTP* 48:188.

EVERY CHRISTIAN A PRIEST

Isaiah 61:6

"But ye shall be named the Priests of the Lord: men shall call you the Ministers of our God: ye shall eat the riches of the Gentiles, and in their glory shall ye boast yourselves."

This verse is addressed to all meek and brokenhearted ones, to all mourners in Zion and all trees of the Lord's planting. It teaches the doctrine that all true Xn's are spiritual priests. This is not the only place where we find the same truth, the verse is not alone. We find originally that all heads of families were priests such as Noah, Abraham, Jacob, and Job.

Even under the Mosaic economy the same doctrine was held, for in Exod 19.6 God makes this a promise to Israel. In the N.T. we have it also in 1Pet. 2.5.9 and one of John's thanksgivings is this very fact. This also swells the song of the redeemed saints before the throne Rev.V.10. Thus we see that this is no isolated text but is consistent with the general tenor of inspiration.

I.   A DISTINCTION DESTROYED.

Under the Mosaic dispensation there were men chosen and specially appointed to act as priests. Now as we have seen that under the new system all are priests, the distinction ceases and the class becomes no longer needful. It is to be remarked that the pure religion of the Bible is the only one without priests on earth. The Greeks and Romans had their many sacerdotal ranks and various ranks of priestly men. The Druid, the Brahman, and the [blank] are varieties of the order. Popery could not be popery without rank and file, it would not be of the devil if it did not teach an unbloody sacrifice.

But Protestants ought to be free from the error. I would not have Catholic performers called priests, or if you must, then call them Popish or Romish

Priests. The Church of England is rotten in this point, for she too has her priests. This is one of our great points of dissent. We cannot allow that there is more than one priest of sacrifice, and we cannot lose our right to the priesthood in the gospel sense.

It is to be regretted that too much distinction exists between clergy and laity among certain mongrel dissenters. For my part, I see in the Bible two great offices of Bishop and deacon. As a Bishop I will not yield precedence to the Bishop of London, and as a Bishop I will not arrogate an atom of supremacy over the least one among you. We are brethren, all equal in the sight of God. Let no man rob you of your true dignity.

II. AN HONOUR CONFERRED.

All Christians become priests, members of a royal priesthood, and thus have an honour conferred. How great the honour, tongue cannot tell. We may perhaps see here and there a sparkle of the excellent glory while meditating on the way whereby this dignity becomes ours.

1. As being one with Christ.
2. As being chosen thereto, see Aaron not Moses. No provision made in case of failure of Aaron's family, for it could not happen.
3. Exod. XXIX.   By washing.
4.   By being arrayed.
5.   By being anointed.

This makes us priests for ever, never to die.

III. A SERVICE EXPECTED.

As Priests, we are bound to discharge an office and this [is] to be done:

1. By Self Sacrifice.
2. By Solemn Prayers, private [and] family.
3. By Sacred Praise.

Remember your high calling for ye are the priests of the Lord.

Bless me, Oh God.

"PENTECOST"

Editor's Summary

Charles's doctrine of the Holy Spirit is worth careful examination throughout all his sermons, and this one provides much rich material. He begins by acknowledging that God's ways and timing are not always our ways and timing. Usually, the activity of God in history is slow and measured. However, God can act with swiftness and power at any point, as he did at Pentecost.

Charles would preach this text again at least twice, under the same title (*MTP* 9, Sermon 511 and *MTP* 30, Sermon 1783). Sermon 511 resembles the message here, which means this one was preached at another congregation or he felt comfortable enough to deliver it again seven years later.

Using Acts 2:1–4 to explore the timing, cause, and effects of revival, he begins this sermon by noting God's sovereign control of Pentecost—when it took place, including its speed, that it occurred on a Sunday, and that it happened at a time when many Christians were gathered. He then observes that at the moment the Holy Spirit came, the disciples were assembled together and engaged in worship—unified worship.

In the next section, Charles describes the aspects of the manifestation of the Holy Spirit, citing patterns from the past in order to enable believers to recognize them in the future. Next, he explains the effects of the Spirit's arrival and articulates his view that the gifts of tongues and miracles have ceased for the present day, based on the strength and growth of the church. When the Holy Spirit comes in revival among God's people, states Charles, the effects include:

- the power to preach
- the guidance of the Spirit
- numerous conversions

As examples of authentic revival, Charles points to the ministries of George Whitefield and John Wesley, two of his heroes whom he would refer to many times, including in an 1859 sermon:

> To come down a little nearer to our own times, truly our fathers have told us the wondrous things which God did in the days of Wesley and of Whitefield. The churches were all asleep. Irreligion was the rule of the day. The very streets seemed to run with iniquity, and the gutters were filled full with the iniquity of sin. Up rose Whitefield and Wesley, men whose hearts the Lord had touched, and they dared to preach the gospel of the grace of God. Suddenly, as in a moment, there was heard the rush as of wings, and the church said, "Who are these that fly as a cloud, and as the doves to their windows?" They come! they come! numberless as the birds of heaven, with a rushing like mighty winds that are not to be withstood. Within a few years, from the preaching of these two men, England was permeated with evangelical truth. *NPSP* 5:307.

Charles concludes this message with the line "Attempt great things and expect great things," which is the title of a William Carey sermon at the Baptist Association meeting in 1792. Carey's words led to the formation of the Baptist Missionary Society and inspired Baptist churches to begin sending missionaries to the ends of the earth. Undoubtedly, Carey and his counterparts influenced Charles's passion for missions as well.

PENTECOST
Acts 2:1—4

"When the day of Pentecost was fully come, they were all with one accord in one place. And suddenly there came a sound from heaven as of a rushing mighty wind, and it filled all the house where they were sitting. And there appeared unto them cloven tongues like as of fire, and it sat upon each of them. And they were all filled with the Holy Ghost, and began to speak with other tongues, as the Spirit gave them utterance."

There usual method of progress in this world is by slow degrees. The world was seven days in making, the leading of Israel to Canaan and making them into a nation was a work of time. And so with the spread of truth. It is a blade and then an ear. Martyrs must bleed, missionaries must labour, and many ministers must preach ere a people will receive the blessed doctrines of our holy religion. It is a work of time as almost all good works seem of necessity to be.

Yet it is undoubtedly a fact that God could make a world in an instant, he could cause the glory of his name to burst at once like a sun on a beclouded planet, he could convert ten thousand as easily as one. This we believe, moreover, has been done. Multitudes have suddenly bestirred their slothful spirits and crowds have turned at once to the fear of God. In general we look with very just suspicions on revivals and regard them as the result of mere animal excitement, and alas we have seen too much to warrant us in our conclusions.

But let us not carry this conclusion too far. Let us not imagine that there cannot be large and overwhelming increases, for while God is omnipotent and prayer all prevailing, there is no limit to what may be. There are some authentic cases of revival who will dispute with Whit. and Wes. [Whitefield and Wesley] the honour of being the instruments of an immense impetus to vital godliness. Where is the man who disbelieves the soundness of the good effected by the Labours of the Haldanes, or Rowland Hill[?]

Here however we have an instance of a marvellous increase to the church. We shall do well to think of it looking at its time, its cause, and [its] effects.

I. THE TIME. WHEN PENTECOST WAS COME.

We might pass over this point with one single observation which shall be our first remark, viz. that it was:

1. A Set Time. Appointed by the Most High, and until that set time the Spirit came not. This fact should sober us in the midst of hopes, expectations, and struggles.

   God is a sovereign and although we pray and labour, we must ever feel a holy deference to his will. If it comes not when we wish, then let us still labour, believing that the day of Pentecost is not yet fully come. The oil of grace is stored in heaven, and in due time it will most assuredly descend upon us. But we remark again it was a . . .

2. A Sabbath day. It seems most probable that the day of Pentecost was on the first day of the week. In Lev. XXIII. 15 we are told that they were to complete 7 sabbaths, or 50 days, which would make the day of Pentecost fall on the first day.

   What an honour was thus put on the Xn Sabbath. Let us honour it too, and believe that if God ever bestows on us a day of Pentecost, it will most likely come not in the week days but on the blessed Sabbath, the pearl of days.

3. A Pentecost day. This day is said by the Rabbis of both ancient and modern Jews to have been the day of the giving of the law. 50 days after the coming out of Egypt. Now as the giving of the law on Sinai was a more clear manifestation of Mosaic law and polity, so also was the outpouring of the Holy Spirit a more perfect revelation to the disciples of the spiritual things of the new economy. The children of Israel knew but little of the Lord's will concerning them until they had been taught by Sinai's thunders and the children of the kingdom were but children until the rushing, mighty wind came and taught them.

But again the feast of ingathering was kept on this day. This was the harvest home day among the Jews, and so was it in this case a day of a great harvest of souls, and truly a harvest of souls is the true reward and harvest of a gospel minister.

4. A Suitable day. For on that day many souls out of all nations were in Jerusalem, for it would not have been of any use for the Spirit to be poured out when there were few people. But as many were gathered together, now was the time. These would tell to others, and the word would thus run round the wide earth and all people hear the sound thereof. We come now to consider . . .

II. THE POSITION – OF THE DISCIPLES.

They were engaged in obedient worship. Their master had bidden them stay in the city. They might have reasoned and questioned, but instead of it they obeyed and tarried. They were engaged in courageous worship. They did not fear the enemies who were thirsty for their blood, but boldly stood their ground. Oh, that we had more holy bravery, to fear nothing. *Cedo nulli* ["I yield to no one"] should be our motto. And when we see lionlike men in the church, then let us expect a Pentecost.

They were engaged in assembled worship. They were not at home but assembled, not forsaking the assembling of themselves together. One prayer is an arrow on high; when many join, it is a siege of the throne and it suffers violence. They were engaged in unanimous worship. Not one was absent. Some of [them] might be sick, some had business, but all were there. Thomas and all. How seldom can we see this. We rather often have to say "and David's seat was empty." They were engaged in loving worship. All of one accord. This is indispensable to the coming of the Spirit. The blessed dove flies not over troubled waters, but seeks the calm and quiet rivers of love.

One jar will spoil melody, one wrong note will destroy harmony, and one of evil eye may keep back the sacred influence. Like Pharaoh's lean kine, the disturbers will eat up the fat kine and be as hungry as ever. Diotrophes is a ruin to a church wherever he enters. Let us as a church walk in unity and be of one accord and of one mind. You cannot tell how important it is, but one thing we are sure of: if you would be in a posture to receive the Holy Spirit, ye must be all of one accord and often meet in one place.

III. MANIFESTATIONS OF THE SPIRIT.

These were miraculous and of course not to be expected now, but doubtless we can learn something therefrom. There were two manifestations: The Sound of Wind and the appearance of fire. The one an audible and the other a visible sign.

Wind and fire are usually the attendants of Divinity whenever manifested to mortals. Moses saw a burning bush, Sinai was altogether on a smoke. Fiery chariots and a whirlwind bore Elijah to heaven. 2 Kings 2.11. In Psalm. 18.8. Fire and wind are described in majestic language as the companions of God. In Isaiah XXX.30. We have a sound, tempest, and fire. In Ezek. I.4. Whirlwind and fire. In Nah. I.3.5. The Glorious presence of God is described in the same manner.

Now why have we detained you with these texts but to shew you that as the great Jehovah, and he alone is ever attended by this awful pomp, therefore the Holy Spirit is none other than God. A person in the Godhead, equal in majesty, honour, and divinity. We cannot find that any man who came from heaven was thus attended. Nor angel either. Angels. Moses and Elias. But now we come and look at these manifestations to learn something. We learn that this effusion of the Spirit was ~~unmistakeably from~~ and often is:

1. <u>Sudden</u>. All was still perhaps, or one of the brethren was engaged in vocal prayer, but all on a sudden to their great surprize it came. God often surprizes men by giving at singular times, and when his grace comes it often finds us unprepared to receive it.

2. From Heaven. The sound came from above, and true grace will come in the same way, so that no flesh shall glory in this presence.

3. <u>Mysterious</u>; like wind it cannot be known whence it cometh nor whither it goeth. So is the operation of the Spirit ever.

4. <u>Powerful</u>. A Rushing mighty wind. The power of wind is immense, but what is it to the mighty energy of the Spirit[?] Who can stay his work[?]

5. <u>Spreading</u>. It filled the house, the whole house. If we receive grace, others share therein. Other churches and the neighbourhood.

With regard to the symbol of the cloven tongues of fire, we may learn:

1. That the Holy Spirit enlightens all who receive his influence.
2. That he makes them candles to others, puts fire on them.
3. That where the Spirit truly comes, he abideth. It sat.
4. That he can in his plentitude give his power to as many as he pleases, for "he sat."

These are manifestations intended to teach us a lesson, and happy are we if we learn it. Let us hope that we may yet see signs equally clear, showing that the Lord is with us of a truth.

IV. EFFECTS OF THE SPIRIT.

There were several effects, some of them extraordinary and temporary, such as power to speak with tongues and to perform miracles. These have ceased simply because [they are] not needed. The church needed a cradle in its infancy, but now in its vigour and manhood it is an hirsute giant and can do without. But there were other effects which are equally needed in our day.

1. <u>The power to preach</u>. These men were unlearned and illiterate but they were the greatest preachers this world ever produced. And truly, some who now merely crawl would run, and those who preach the truth with little power would soon be mighty, if we had more unction from the Holy One. If you want a good minister, cry to God for his almighty Spirit.

2. <u>The Guidance of the Spirit</u>. These men were filled with the holy Ghost, which is the only infallible teacher. They were directed in all their movements by an inward adviser, a privy councillor; and so will the sons of God be, more and more as we hasten to the time of the consummation of all things.

3. <u>Numerous conversions</u>. The word from the lips of Peter and the others was very powerful, and produced an amazing effect. 3000 were born in a day by the simple communication of truth and the power of the Spirit therewith.

   And now brethren, cannot you and I sincerely long and pray for a baptism of the Holy Ghost like to this one[?] Have we not a right to expect it if we are of one accord and one mind[?] Do not our hearts leap when we hear of one conversion[?] How would we sing for joy if we saw a multitude. Attempt great things and expect great things, and surely you shall see great things.

Sermon No. 375

"GIDEON"

Editor's Summary

Charles delivered this short sermon on Judg 6:14 (a text he did not preach again) early in 1854, likely in January or February. When he arrived at New Park Street Chapel—a church once pastored by Baptist titans such as Benjamin Keach, John Gill, and John Rippon—he found only a "mere handful of people," and they were languishing in congregational decline. *Autobiography* 1:361.

Although Charles applies the words of this sermon to the people of God as a whole, his pastoral intent for his own people is also clear. When he remarks, "So does God find men in his church, for his church, to increase his church," his weary congregation would have understood the connection between the "Gideon" *out there* and the "Gideon" *in here*.

Through this sermon, Charles seeks to instill in his hearers an absolute assurance that God will raise up "Gideons" to advance the gospel. Indeed, the problem even then was not want of opportunity—after all, Jesus himself said, "Lift up your eyes, and look on the fields; for they are already white unto harvest" (John 4:35). Rather, the problem was finding courageous Christians who would labor in the pulpits, Sunday schools, and mission houses of England and the world. Charles later remarked that:

> God always finds men for his work. We sometimes see a lot of cowards run away, and we say to ourselves, "What will happen now?" Why, God will find better men than they are! And when there seems to be a paucity of really valiant men in Israel, God has them in training; and that awkward squad out there will yet become a band of brave men for the service of the house of God. *MTP* 38:528.

His conclusion contains the ground of this hope and assurance. He believed that God had provided a mighty, threefold "Panoply" to strengthen his servants. Indeed, every Christian could rest in "Providence," "Prayer," and the "Presence of God." Accordingly, Charles believed that every Christian, thus armed and equipped, should rush to the conflict and engage in the holy warfare of saving souls. In his view, the humble, obedient Christian was the useful Christian.

> He who is willing to teach infants, or to give away tracts, and so to begin at the beginning, is far more likely to be useful than the youth who is full of affectations, and sleeps with a white necktie, who is aspiring to the ministry, and is touching up certain superior manuscripts which he hopes ere long to read from the pastor's pulpit. . . . He who talks upon plain gospel themes in a farmer's kitchen, and is able to interest the carter's boy and the dairymaid, has more of the minister in him than the prim little man who keeps prating about being cultured. *Autobiography* 1:202.

GIDEON

Judges 6:14

"And the Lord *looked upon him, and said, Go in this thy might, and thou shalt save Israel from the hand of the Midianites: have not I sent thee?"*

It is a true saying that the Lord always finds men to do his work. Here was a nation to be delivered, and where could a man be found to do it[?] Does any one know? No.

But God does. He has a man threshing wheat in a winepress, little known and little cared about, but yet doing his duty and getting ready for his work.

So does God find men in his church, for his church, to [i]ncrease his church, to fight its foes or feed its sheep or build its palaces. We shall ever find that for the pulpit, the S. School, [and] the Mission, God is ever sending out Gideons.

I. LET US NOTICE WHO THE LORD'S GIDEONS OFTEN ARE.

1. They are men previously of mean estate. Such was Gideon, so Jephthah, and David, Amos. Our Saviour himself. His apostles. Luther, Bunyan, Carey, and many of our ministers. God often finds out the poorest, and the worst of the family. Perhaps some of you feel the same. Be not discouraged, for God chooseth the means.

2. They are men who have suffered the same calamity they are sent to rescue others from. Gideon was reduced to a small quantity of corn, for he threshed himself and not with oxen, or he did it for silence sake [lest] the oxen should low. We see he was in fear, for he threshed in the winepress. So we have suffered from the sins we wish to deliver others from.

3. They are at first unwilling to go.

4. They have but little faith and require many signs.

5. They are men who follow all God's directions.

II. LET US NOTICE THE ENEMIES THEY ARE CALLED TO CONTEND WITH.

1. Men of their own household. Joash etc.
2. Enemies in our own hearts.
3. Inbred corruption in the hearts of those we teach.
4. All the allurements of the wicked world and Satan. The draw shop, the brothel, the casino, the theatre, the infidel, the novel.

Evil men. Evil places. Evil Books.

III. LET US NOTICE WHEREIN OUR MIGHT CONSISTS.

Not in learning that is like Saul's armour, not in money or eloquence, but in:

1. Providence – which works for the overthrowing of our foes and our establishment in the truth and victory by it.
2. Prayer – of our own and that of the church. This is a mighty weapon to slay an enemy with. A Stone for Goliath's head. Here is our might.
3. Presence – of God, his smile, his arm, his word, his love, his Spirit.

Three Ps for our Panoply.

Now when this solace is thin
Go in this thy might.
When the children are unruly
Go in this thy might.

When you are [poor], sad, and depressed. When helpers fail and friends are few.

Still Go in this thy might.

Father <u>aid me</u>.

"THE NECESSITY OF FAITH"

Editor's Summary

For Charles, getting the gospel right was of the utmost importance. He expounds in this sermon on the "majestic and awful simplicity" of the doctrine of justification by faith and makes clear that "faith," including justification by faith, is *articula stantis vel cadentis ecclesiae,* or "the article by which the church stands or falls."

Like many before him, Charles was inspired in this by the convictions and example of Martin Luther:

> Luther used, in fact, to say — and we endorse it — that this matter of justification by faith is the article by which a church must stand or fall. That so-called church which does not hold this doctrine is not a church of Christ, and it is a church of Christ that does hold it, notwithstanding many mistakes into which it may have fallen. *MTP* 21:338.

Throughout his ministry, one of Charles's greatest concerns was the purity of the gospel, and specifically defending the doctrine of justification by faith. He admits here, "I would tremble lest I should lead you wrong and have you beware that you look to your steps lest you fail of the grace of God." He would deliver similar warnings to his flock in the years ahead: "Devils believe and tremble, and yet they are devils still. Put no confidence in the mere fact that you hold to an orthodox faith, for a dead orthodoxy soon corrupts. You must have faith in Christ." *MTP* 31:117–18. To this end, Charles's evangelistic urgency and zeal for clarity influenced the structure of this sermon.

Ever sensitive to the needs of his particular congregation, he begins with "An Explanation of Faith," making clear that faith is *not* bare intellectual assent or delight in sound doctrine. In his second point, he offers an "Exposition of the Doctrine" before turning to the third and fourth points: "Proof of the Doctrine" and "Application of the Text."

It appears that Charles preached on this text four more times: "Faith" (*NPSP* 3, Sermon 107); "Faith Essential to Pleasing God" (*MTP* 35, Sermon 2100); "How to Please God" (*MTP* 43, Sermon 2513); and "What Is Essential in Coming to God?" (*MTP* 47, Sermon 2740). While these later sermons share common thematic material, no significant overlap is apparent. However, one similarity is that the first Roman numeral of each deals with the nature and quality of "faith." (The first Roman numeral of "Faith" is the most similar.) This consistency reveals that teaching a proper understanding of faith was a defining characteristic of Charles's ministry.

As a pastor, indeed as a Christian, Charles longed that all people might be found pleasing in God's sight. And so he diligently proclaimed that "true religion is more than notion . . . it is believing *with the heart*." *MTP* 9:390, italics in the original. Meanwhile, he affirmed that "we are saved by faith, and not by works," although "faith is not only leaning on Christ, but obeying Christ." *MTP* 49:93. Charles warned with Augustine that "until you are personally acceptable to God through Jesus Christ everything that you do is displeasing, and even those things which you think to be virtues are only . . . 'splendid sins,' mere glittering dross." *MTP* 20:185.

376

THE NECESSITY OF FAITH

Hebrews 11:6

*"But without faith it is impossible to please him: for he that cometh to God must
believe that he is, and that he is a rewarder of them that diligently seek him."*

This is a very positive assertion. It is couched in the most unmistakable language. It
is "<u>impossible</u>" to please God. It is not explained away or guarded, but like a rugged
rock it stands in majestic and awful simplicity. We may be sure from the very fact
of the clear and unmistakeable language that it is a point upon which it is very
important that we should be right.

This is "*articula stantis vel cadentis ecclesiae*" [the article by which the church stands or
falls] – an error here is vital. I would therefore tremble lest I should lead you wrong
and have you beware that you look to your steps lest you fail of the grace of God.
This is the wicket gate, the only proper entrance into true religion. By the help of
God I shall attempt:

I.   AN EXPLANATION OF THE FAITH HERE MENTIONED.

II. AN EXPOSITION OF THE DOCTRINE OF THE TEXT.

III. A PROOF OF THE DOCTRINE OR A VINDICATION.

IV. AN APPLICATION OF THE TEXT.

I.   AN EXPLANATION OF THE FAITH HERE MENTIONED.

It certainly does not refer to the kind of faith called miraculous, referred to by
Paul. Nor can it mean:

1. A Bare Assent to the truth of the Bible. There are some who, if they do

not say so, yet seem to insinuate that to be a believer is simply not to be an infidel. This is the result of a flimsy divinity. But let me remind you that with many of us, to believe the Bible is as natural as to eat, for from early religious training we were led to do so.

Again some of us believe the Bible to be true in the same way as others believe that Milton wrote Paradise lost, viz. because we never saw any reason to the contrary. It is a mere act of the head. God has written other volumes in the same style and therefore this is his. But what can there be spiritual in this[?] For my part it seems to be as simple and natural an act as to believe that I am here.

But more—when we consider that devils believe, that the worst of men have this kind of faith, we are at once shut out from the idea of such a faith being at all saving. Nor is it even . . .

2. A Delight in Sound Doctrine. In these days doctrines are too much despised, but there is a certain party who exalt soundness of faith into the very throne of the Saviour. They suppose that if they love what is called savoury meat, they must therefore be children. But no. True religion is more than a smile at a bold assertion or triumphant proof.

Some of these people can come from the gin shop and then say "bless God for such food as this." This is not true faith, it is dead faith.

· ·

In order to the discovery of faith we may be allowed for a moment to look ~~its~~ at its constant antecedents, its shadow rather, which is conviction, the dark shadow of a bright object. Where this is not, there is no true faith. Be sure of this.

· ·

And we may well discern it by its consequents, or the things which follow, viz., good works. You tell the tree by its fruits, so must you judge faith by its effects. If a man says "I believe" and then lives in sin, write that man among the foolish virgins.

But what is faith, say you, after all[?] I answer that I conceive it to be such a belief in revealed truth as leads us to trust in Jesus for salvation, and to feel a hearty confidence in, and love to, God.

Faith toucheth the attributes of God. Thus:

> He is powerful. I will rely on his might.
> He is omniscient. I believe that he will keep me.
> He is just. His justice is what I trust to.
> Etc. Etc. Etc.

Faith toucheth Jesus Christ. Thus:

> He died. On his atonement I trust.
> He rose. I believe that I shall rise.
> Etc. Etc.

Faith toucheth the Holy Ghost. Thus in all his operations and influences. We believe that he will sanctify us.

> Faith is an eye, seeing the invisible.
> Faith is a hand, it grasps the Saviour.
> Faith is a foot, it walketh on the sea.
> Faith is a wing, it mounteth to heaven.

Confound it not with assurance. Assurance is the cream of faith. It is the corn from the blade of hope. You who can only just see Jesus and rely on him need not fear, for you are safe if you have only one finger in his hand.

II. AN EXPOSITION OF THE DOCTRINE OF THE TEXT.

And I cannot do better than pass in review many things which are considered as pleasing to God, and really are so if mixed with faith, but without it are not.

1. <u>Good works</u>. Obedience to the law of God is a duty of every man. Some imagine that they do render this perfectly, but it is for want of knowing better; they really do not. But without faith these are vain. These things are the ornaments, the cornices, the roof, but faith is the foundation. See Abel and Cain.

2. <u>Prayer</u>. This is an important part of religious worship, but without faith it is idle wind. It is like the Tartar windmill or the Catholic beads. Many make a form a reality, but too many keep the form a form merely. A form without sincerity is mockery.

3. <u>The Ordinances</u>. <u>Baptism</u> without faith is a farce. When performed on unthinking babes it is, to say the least, an absurdity. To say the worst, it is an awful crime against the Bible and God.

<u>The Lord's Supper</u> is a blessed feast of love, but if men without faith sit down, it is an effrontery offered to high heaven.

4. <u>Alms</u>. To Heathens, Societies, or the Poor. I love the patristic, the benevolent, the liberal, but more than this is required for your own safety. Heaven is worth more than you can give.

With all these it is impossible to please God if you have no faith.

III. A VINDICATION OF THE DOCTRINE.

[1.] Many men think it hard that they, if they are ever so good, will be lost and the greatest sinner saved if he repents and believes. It might serve to quiet this question a little if we remind them that God has a right to give as he pleases. You yourself claim a right to do what you will with your own.

If you should bid certain beggars knock at your door and you would relieve them, would it be hard if a man should bring an organ and play and expect you to come[?] No, say you, let him do as I please if he wants my charity. So does God.

2. It might also serve to put the objection out of countenance if I remind you of the reasonableness of the demand. God's attributes and character are well deserving of faith and confidence. But could any one alter it for the better[?] Say anything else and some are damned. Yea all are. Say "without good works," then we have none and we are all drowned in one sea.

3. But I must make a more crushing argument, and that is this: certain relations in life require faith. Husband and wife. Father and son. Master and servant. Friend and Friend. So as our Creator, Master, Father, [and] Friend, confidence is absolutely necessary.

4. But again, another argument. Motive is the essence of an action, and the man who has no faith in God cannot serve him from the motive which God loves. Fear, selfishness, love of merit, these are no true gospel motives, and actions wrought therefrom are *splendida peccata*, splendid sins.

However this is fact. You must believe or perish. It is not yours to choose but to yield, to stoop, to lie in the dust.

IV. AN APPLICATION OF THE TEXT.

<u>To Christians</u>. If faith pleases God, then the more of it the better. Doubt never pleases him, but rather dishonor[s] him. Be not afraid of assurance, fear not to climb the mountains as well as to descend the [valleys]. There is no reason why you should be so fond of unbelief. Get rid of him.

<u>To Unbelievers</u>. How sad your state is if viewed by the light of this text. Yours sins you confess cannot please God, but you thought that surely your good works did. But now it seems that you have never pleased God. What do you say, "you will not try"[?] No, No do not say so. That would be to ruin your own soul to gratify your pride. Nay, rather confess and seek mercy, and you shall find it.

Help. Help. Help.
Oh King.

"JESUS WORTH TEN THOUSAND"

Editor's Summary

The superlative excellence of Jesus Christ was an evergreen theme for Charles. While history bears witness that the true church has always adored her Savior, the particular focus given to the subject in the Anglo/American tradition was ignited by Jonathan Edwards's 1734 sermon "The Excellency of Christ," which argued, "There is an admirable conjunction of diverse excellencies in Jesus Christ." Jonathan Edwards, *Sermons and Discourses, 1734–1738,* WJE Online, Vol. 19, 566.

As a child of this tradition, Charles and his piety bore an Edwardsean stamp. Again and again throughout his ministry, Charles declared that "all the virtues of Christ [are] the best forms of virtue." He once challenged his hearers to "select any one trait in the Redeemer's character," and then promised, "you shall find in that respect he will surpass the greatest master of that virtue be he whomsoever he may." *MTP* 12:245.

To both Charles and Jonathan Edwards, Christ's glory was the pinnacle of perfection and therefore unutterable and unfathomable. In short, Christ is *so* glorious that Charles proclaimed:

> We must coin new words before we can describe the excellencies of Christ.
> In fact, we must have done with tongues, and go into that land where spirits
> utter their thoughts without the motion of lip or the expiration of breath, ere
> we shall be able to express the surpassing beauty, the unuttered excellency
> of the glorious character of Christ. *NPSP* 6:312.

In "Jesus Worth Ten Thousand," Charles seeks to express the all-surpassing worthiness of Christ Jesus, a passionate longing captured by the phrase "Give me Christ or I die." While Charles never preached on 2 Sam 18:3 again, he did previously refer to Ps 45:1, "My tongue is the pen of a ready writer," in the front matter of his fourth sermon notebook. *LS* 4:22–23. Here, his main divisions emphasize the quality and nature of true love for Christ, the resulting advantages of true love for Christ, and the compelling reasons for believing in Christ.

It is also noteworthy that at the beginning of the sermon, Charles digresses by saying, "The words of my text were originally addressed to David, but I shall apply them to David's Lord, for he is far more worthy thereof." This comment reflects a pattern of selective spiritualization. While Charles was careful to avoid excess, he nonetheless insisted to pastors-in-training, "Be not afraid to spiritualize, or to take singular texts. . . . But also draw from them meanings which may not lie upon their surface." *Lectures* 1:103. In fact, it appears that the impetus for Charles's spiritualization was pastoral concern.

In his introduction, he notes, "There are many opinions about our Saviour but we shall leave them. For if they are the ideas of ungodly men they are about as valuable as a blind man's treatise on colours." And so, Charles wanted to expound on the excellency of Christ in order to satisfy and inform the hearts and minds of his congregation. Indeed, as he says here, "Jesus is better than . . . all," and so the best thing for Charles to do was to preach Jesus Christ.

JESUS WORTH TEN THOUSAND

2 Samuel 18:3

"But the people answered, Thou shalt not go forth: for if we flee away, they will not care for us; neither if half of us die, will they care for us: but now thou art worth ten thousand of us: therefore now it is better that thou succour us out of the city."

We are now about to speak of things touching the king. May our tongue be as the pen of a ready writer. The words of my text were originally addressed to David, but I shall apply them to David's Lord, for he is far more worthy thereof.

I. I SHALL SPEAK OF A LOVING SOUL'S OPINION OF JESUS CHRIST.

There are many opinions about our Savior, but we shall leave them, for if they are the ideas of ungodly men they are about as valuable as a blind man's treatise on colours, or the musical grammar of a deaf man.

If the men are Laodicean Christians, their mouths are too much out of taste by swallowing lukewarm water and they have no power to judge. But the truly loving soul, he is the man, what does he say?

1. He loves Christ better than himself. True love is ever self[-]denying, it puts its object in the chief seat and setteth itself upon a footstool at the feet thereof.

   "I had better be slain than David," said these men, and so the true lover of Christ had rather suffer than that the cause of Christ should be injured. He fears lest others should insult his Lord, and he trembles lest he should do so himself.

If the cause prospers he will rejoice as much as in the increase of his own trade. If he must sacrifice all, he will do it. He will, like Curtius, leap into the chasm if he can fill it up. He will be bold for Christ. He will lose for his name.

2. He values Christ above a 1000 others. His relatives he loves, but not side by side with the Saviour. He sees great and good men, and thanks God for them, but he sets Jesus above them for Jesus is better than the[m] all. He being free from sin, and great not in some one virtue, but in every virtue. A mixture of the quintessence of all essences. A sun comprising all light, an ocean into which all rivers run. Nothing seems too good or great for him to do.

3. He values Christ when Christ is despised. He loveth a persecuted and footsore Christ. He can walk with his poor followers. He will defend him in all companies. He will bear scoff and scorn for his name's sake and love him amid scoffing and taunting.

II. I SHALL SPEAK OF THE ADVANTAGES A GOOD OPINION OF CHRIST CONFERS ON US.

1. It helpeth resignation. Trials must and will befall, and the true secret of life is to bend to the storm. But who will do it like the loving soul who values the Lord[?] Mr. Cecil's child and beads. Good man who saved his child from the fire. A full Christ lighteth up a dark and empty cupboard.

2. It quickeneth obedience. See Moses. See Mary in the garden. See the Martyrs. Loving obedience is the best obedience. A Mother and sick child. Love never tires.

3. It affordeth delight. The reason why we do not delight in Jesus more is because we do not love him more. Jonathan and David. Jacob and Rachel. That which we love, we long to see and to have in our presence. Be not afraid of prizing him too much.

4. It sharpeneth desire. The more we love, the more we long to see him and the more disconsolate shall we be at his absence. Give me Christ or else I die.

III. I SHALL SPEAK OF THE REASONS WHY THEY THUS THINK OF HIM.

1. Because they <u>believe</u> Christ prizes them. Jesus loves the smallest of his children. He prizes them as the apple of his eye, his jewels, his portion, his glory, his ornaments, his crown, his throne, his bride. He loves us better than heaven, or his Father's bosom, or his own life, for he died.

2. Because they <u>observe</u> his actions. They delight to muse on his deep descent, from heaven to earth. His labours and works of love. The many he has saved, the countless myriads he has sustained and piloted to glory.

3. Because they <u>commune</u> with his person. There is such a thing as communion with Jesus, and a sweet thing it is.

The soul talketh with its lover behind the door. It whispereth to him and he giveth the kisses of his love.

The more of this the better, for so much the more love.

Help oh Jesus.

"LOVE OF CHRIST TO US COMPARED WITH THE FATHER'S LOVE TO HIM"

Editor's Summary

As a young preacher, Charles was a man of his time, influenced by the resources for study available to him as he approached the biblical text. This sermon is unique among *The Lost Sermons*, as it is the only one where he made significant use of the same literary source—Simeon's *Helps to Composition*—across two sermons drawn from the same text. Charles specifically referenced the renowned preacher's 54th sermon skeleton, "A Comparison between the Father's Love to Christ, and Christ's to Us." Charles Simeon, *Helps to Composition; Or Six Hundred Skeletons of Sermons*, vol. 1, 3rd ed. (London: printed for T. Cadell and W. Davies, 1815, The Spurgeon Library). Hereafter, *Helps to Composition*.

In Charles's earlier sermon, "The Son's Love to Us Compared with God's Love to Him" (*LS* 1, Sermon 38), he followed Simeon's outline point for point. Intriguingly, when he revisits John 15:9, and Simeon's work, he largely follows his predecessor again, although Charles's main divisions show some development.

He begins by noting, "Force can never compel love. Love only can beget it," a comment that resonates with Simeon's own introduction:

> The law of God itself, with all its sanctions, could not change the heart. The gospel only can make sin odious, and holiness delightful. It effects this by revealing to us the love of Christ. Hence our Lord reminds us of his love in order to confirm our love to him. *Helps to Composition* 1:400–401.

Furthermore, Charles's main divisions correspond to Simeon's. Here, his "I. We have a comparison . . ." is like Simeon's "I. The nature and extent of Christ's love to us. The comparison in the text denotes not equality, but resemblance." Also, the first subdivision, "1. Without beginning," comes from Simeon. *Helps to Composition* 1:401. Similarly, Charles's "II. We have an exhortation . . ." is similar to Simeon's "II. The duty resulting from it. This part of the text requires application rather than discussion. It sets before us, not merely *our privilege* (which is, to continue in a sense of Christ's love to us) but *our duty*." *Helps to Composition* 1:402, italics in the original. However, Charles did include a third division as well: "III. We have a direction."

From what we know, Charles preached John 15:9 two other times, "Love at Its Utmost" (*MTP* 33:505–16) and "Cheering Words" (*MTP* 41:601–12). Due to the incomplete nature of "Love of Christ to Us Compared with the Father's Love to Him," it is difficult to determine if the later sermons shared significant overlapping content. Literary considerations aside, one point remains clear: Charles, even as a young pastor, was deeply concerned that his congregation burn with love for Jesus Christ. To that end, he heralded the magnificent love of Christ, who was "God's love incarnate among men." *MTP* 33:138.

LOVE OF CHRIST TO US COMPARED WITH THE FATHER'S LOVE TO HIM

John 15:9

"As the Father hath loved me, so have I loved you: continue ye in my love."

After last Thursday evening's sermon I assayed to prepare a subject for Sabbath day, but although many came I found none that I could settle upon for, like the harp of Anacreon, my soul would sound only love.

It would be an unspeakable mercy if we all could find it so evermore; and I am fully persuaded that the best way to inflame our souls toward him is to view his love toward us.

Force can never compel love. Love only can beget it. Love must be born not made. May it please the great Father of our Sspirits to give us more love to his son.

I. WE HAVE A COMPARISON.

II. WE HAVE AN EXHORTATION.

III. WE HAVE A DIRECTION.

I. WE HAVE A COMPARISON.

Fetched not from earth but from the highest heaven. I love existing between two existences having but one essence.

Between two persons of the adorable Godhead.

Well may we stand astonished upon the very threshold of our subject and lift up our hands with solemn wonder and surprise.

God is in himself essentially love. His love admits of degrees. One degree of it is **His love of benevolence** which extends to all his works and to all men whatever their character may be. All animals are made happy by him, and he sincerely desires to see all <u>men</u> happy. All providential blessings are the result of this love.

Far above this is his **discriminating love** towards some. This drowns the other. It is a Father's love; the other is only a Creator's love, an owner's benevolence. It is true God loves all, but it is just as true that he loves some more intensely.

But to us it seems that there is one degree of love which is apparently above even this, viz., **His love personal**. By which I mean that complacency and delight which the persons of the Godhead feel towards each other. It seems as if this love of God to God must be greater than the love of God to any Creature, however much delighted in.

Well this love personal is taken as the model of Christ's love to us.

It cannot be of the same degree, for the love of infinite to infinite cannot be for a moment to that of infinite to finite. Again we must remark that it is an <u>as</u> of Quality, not of <u>equality</u>. And here let us first remark that these two loves which are here compared are:

1. **Without beginning.** It is entirely out of our power to conceive of a time when the Father's love to the Son commenced.

[This page is followed by two blank pages in Charles's notebook.]

Sermon No. [379]

"INNER COURT WORSHIP"

Editor's Summary

Intriguingly, it appears that although Charles began composing this sermon on Ezek 43:5 (a text he did not preach on again), he decided not to move beyond his introductory comments. This sermon and the previous one, "Love of Christ to Us Compared with the Father's Love to Him," are the last ones in Notebook 8 that he left incomplete. The other two are "The Two Birds" (Sermon 352) and "Little Flock" (Sermon 361).

However, "Inner Court Worship" is distinct from the others in that Charles set aside two blank pages at the end of each of the others, while this is followed by ten blank pages. It likely indicates that Charles either intended to finish the previous three messages, or he finished them extemporaneously. The fact that he recorded a preaching occasion number (669) for "The Two Birds" also supports this view. Conversely, the numerous blank pages left after the introduction to "Inner Court Worship," along with its lack of a sermon number, imply that Charles moved on without ever finishing this message.

407

INNER COURT WORSHIP
Ezekiel 43:5

"So the spirit took me up, and brought me into the inner court;
and, behold, the glory of the LORD filled the house."

One of the greatest mercies we enjoy in England is the house of God, liberty to attend the same, and the number of the houses of prayer. What a pleasing thought that there are so many places dedicated to Jehovah. And what a mercy that so many attend. But we must never imagine that all who go there are real worshippers, for it is to be feared that only a minority are so. I pray God make his word a searching word tonight with you.

[This page is followed by ten blank pages in Charles's notebook.]

James. I. 17. The Father of Light   351

Some sciences and objects of study are to us inexhaustible. We might ever find fresh matter for instruction, wonder, & research. If we dive with the geologist, & bring up skeletons of extinct monsters, - signs of great convulsions, old & new format[ions] - or if we soar aloft, and with the astronomer measure heaven & count the stars, - we should ever be lost in the new discoveries we should make. The same may be said of all the natural sciences. Whatever the subject, it does not seem possible that man should say, "I have nothing to learn, I am master of it all."

But should it one day happen that our race should so progress, & become so increased in power as to leave nothing unknown, - should nature be stript of all her mystery, - the heavens, the sea, the earth, all perfectly understood, - there will yet remain one subject upon which the sons of men may meditate, dispute, & labour, but it shall still be Unknown ** That subject is, - God, + of whom, with humble reverence, = I am now to speak.

May it please the great Spirit of Wisdom to enlarge our minds, and guide our hearts into an understanding of the portion of truth concerning him made manifest in the text! We have, here, -

I. A majestic figure.

II. A glorious attribute.

III. A grateful acknowledgement.

I. A majestic figure. God is here called the Father of Lights, comparing him to the Sun.

It is most true that this lower world is the reflection of the upper. In it, once, the face of God might be seen as on some glassy lake; but sin has ruffled it & the portrait is broken, & presented only in pieces. Yet there are the pieces, the wrecks of the picture; we will not throw them aside. Let us lift up our eyes on high, and behold the only object worthy to be called an emblem of Deity.

We think we can see several ideas couched in the figure.

1. Independence or Self Existence. God is the only self-existent being; the sun is not really so, but he is far more independent than any other object we know of.

2. Sublimity is another idea suggested by the figure. The sun is one of the most magnificent of created existences when it should display the many & stars concealed, their blushing faces. Seen in my first of his course the sun is a grand object. When first he tinge the sky, when he sets on mid heaven, or retires in splendour, no grandeur is one of his attributes. He is too bright for me and apt to see, although we are at such infinite distance. So is God. Who shall describe him?

His servants are all glorified, the starry floor of the throne is glorious, what must for he be himself? Imagination almost starts in wonder dies away. Well my eyes veil their faces, for even their eyelid not endure his brightness, no man can see him, his train was all about stair. Borrow the eagle's eye and way, tow and read the glory overcomes you, you fall nothing to earth you do it again & again, & you will see that it is all man can see of him. Clouds and darkness are round about him, for he may not have it said of him. Dark with excessive light thy skirts appear.

All idea of nature is borrowed. Vegetables draw their nourishment from the soil, animals from there is one another, man from all, he is the greatest beggar in the universe. The moon lights his unfeebly set at the sun's lamp, the planets shine from her storehouse, Mother earth is dependant on the sun, it depends the pride of her children, what is the —a tiny globule dancing in the rays of that majestic orb? The sun gives but takes not. Destitute on all, retained from none, lend on none, but lives alone, in its own solemn loveliness.

Such is God, the I Am, who did or no borrowed throne, begs no leave to be, all things are of him, & by them, the need them not, at Here they all annihilated it would not infuse them. He could but had had all in himself. He had all in one. But we can scarce speak of him, who light himself in measured light, demanded dark dwells awfully retired from mortal eye or angels' piercing view. From single smile had from the first of time, & fill overflowing all the lamps of heaven; & that beam for ever through he boundless sky, should he hide his face, d'astonish'd own And all th'extinguish'd stars would looking veil, & hide from their spheres, and Chaos come again.

3. Power, again, seems a prominent idea. the Sun is as a giant coming out of his chamber, & like a strong man he rejoices to run a race. He drags the whole immense system along in his mighty course; nor dare any oppose him; [were it possible!] how mightily would he still move on. So is our God in this power; those known. this might, it is like himself, infinite: He speaketh & this word is power, he willeth & this will is omnipotence. Who can thwart his purposes? Shall nature? No. the hills melted like wax &c they skipped like rams. The floods divide. Fire, tempest, not. Beasts are tamed. He lifteth his finger & the floods arose; the droppeth it, they assuage. In vain could mountains, torrent, stars & elements war with him. who can conquer in battle with him? Shall man? No. He counteth them as the drop of the bucket. Counteth them as the drop of the bucket. He sitteth in heaven & hath them in derision. Shall hell withstand him? no. free love they fallen from the battlements of heaven! & in vain their loudest roar. Satan is chained & led as a conquered monarch in victor. He is God's slave & unwillingly doth his will: the beloved what a God is here! But this thought under they pillows; and when troubles rise, calmly sleeps on. His power protecteth.

4 But - Beneficence seems even more the leading idea. the Sun is the great Philanthropist: He is necessary to our being. no light, no heat, no life, no rain; nothing without him) the drew is necessary to our well-being; the drew is indeed a great Philanthropist; he visits to all every land, freely he gives & gives to all the prisoner he visits in his cell, the peasant in his cottage; freely & largely he bestows & curses him or blesses him; he is the same, he does not refuse his light even to the felon. Such is God. the good. the greatly good. Should he remove his face, the universe would not be heaven. All the universe would be a valley of bones, a perfect charnel-house. It does good is the side he confines not his mercies to a race. The Benthamites &c, are welcome, the evil receive his grace & lose their former natures. He gives to sinners & to the unthankful; & if men were not by nature blind, they would see by his light for the defect is in them & not in him. You the sun has shone in my cradle, it will beam on my deathbed & cast a gleam into my grave. So doth God the beneficent. the fields our path with sunshine, saith were a glowing vault without bars, with state throws it a light & opens the prospect of a more joyous.

II. A glorious attribute

The apostle having thus introduced the figure, finding that it did not bear the full resemblance of the invisible God, he was constrained to amend it by a remark that, unlike the Sun, our Father had no turning or variableness.

The sun has parallax; he rises at a different time each day; he sets at different hours. He moves into different parts of the heavens. He is clouded, eclipsed & even suffers a diminution of light from some mysterious decrease of the luminary's light which surrounds him. He has tropic, or turn, how he turns his chariot to the south, until at the solstice God bids him reverse his rein & he visits us once more. But God is here superior to all figures. He is inevitable; the sun changes, mountains crumble; the ocean shall dry, the stars shall wither from the vault of night, but He & He alone, remains the same.

Were we to enter into a full discourse on the subject of immutability, the time, even though multiplied by a high number, would fail us. But reminding you that there is no change in his power, justice, truth or truth, threatening or decree, I will

confine myself to the fact that this love to us knows no variation. How often it is called unchangeable, everlasting love. He loves me now as much as He did when first He inscribed my name in His Eternal book of election. He has not repented of His choice. He has not blotted me out; there are no erasures in that book; all who are written are safe. Nor does He love me less now than when He gave that grand proof of love; His fond Jesus; even now He loved me with the same intense, as when He poured out the vials of justice on His darling to save.

We have all had times which we consider times of special love, when this candle comes nearest to us & we basked in that smile; but let us not suppose that He really loved us more than now. Oh, no! He then discovered his contrivals are equally proofs of His love in light, in the valley of humiliation, in the valley of the shadow of death, in Vanity Fair, He will be the same love no matter more nor less than we say with seraphic voices the songs of heaven.

(Death sometimes, in the prospect, is

every trying to flesh & blood; but if they had well remembered, it would not be for we should know that He who helps Jacob to father up his feet, David to say although &c, & Stephen to fall asleep will be the same to [us] who trust in Him.

Throughout eternity there shall be no jars, not a breath of strife; but the same wonderful, blessed unity, that shall prevail for ever. loving us. Thanks be unto them for loving us.

III. A grateful acknowledgement

The apostle having introduced God as the Father of lights, & qualified the figure, now proceeds to ascribe all good gifts to Him alone. With indeed perfectly natural that at the rising it with day, is it not even welcome as that at the name of the greater Father of Lights we should lift up a song. Now what is said here is what Adam could have hymned in Paradise; it is what every Christian feels heartily willing to confess. Ever since the fall this verse has had an emphasis of meaning since in us by nature there dwells no good thing,

and our fall forfeited every right to any favour. So that our—

Natural gifts, as health, eloquence, health, life, happiness, come from him yet such graces we have nothing which we have not received. Earth one day shall make this song thrill through infinity heaven shall join the chorus, the region of chaos and old night shall shout aloud & even hell's unwilling voice shall swell out an acknowledgement of the fact. that every good gift, & every perfect gift & from above & cometh down from the father of lights with whom is no variableness neither shadow of turning — I have exceeded if with one you can day at the contemplation of Jehovah.

"Glory be unto the Father, & to the Son and to the Holy Ghost, as it was in the beginning, is now and ever shall be world without end Amen"

668.6/3

Lev. XV. XIV 4.5.6.7. The two birds.   352

It has been said "who that knows the worth
of prayer but wishes to be often there?" and
so it may be said of the Bible "who that
knows its worth but wishes to be often
reading it?"   If we consider its variety
it stands unrivalled for it contains deep
metaphysics, learned discourse on predestination
& other mysterious subjects, simple sermons,
lengthened history, parables, fables, poetry,
&c &c amongst its varied contents there
stands one subject worthy of study viz the
religion of that wonderful nation now
called Jews.   Volumes have been written
discussing the superstitions & ceremonies of
Mexicans, Mahometans, &c why should not
the Jewish religion be quite as worthy of
study? why? Men will not reply & yet
neglect it and we reply it is the perversity of
the human heart which neglects it simply
because it is revealed. If it had not been
it would have been an object of profound
research.   We however as Christians
feel a deep interest in all the affairs of
the peculiar nation since we believe that
they, & their rites were but types of our own
more clear and glorious religion.
Here is the ceremony performed upon

a leper after his healing. It was meet
that such a mercy should not pass unnoticed
It seems right to record our thanks for
which reason I most heartily approve of
thanksgivings after childbirth.
    Let us draw nigh with reverence & let
us not be offended if all that is visible
be two little sparrows. The insignificance
of the rite makes it a better sign of true
obedience since it is all the more humbling
to our pride.   But let us look & we see
I Christ typified in the bird which
died. There are two birds, one of which
must die. Christ or his people must die, the
one or the other. Christ dies for them.
1. Death was necessary. God said death
should be the forfeit of sin & so it must be
and in order that it might be certified
that it was really death.
    It was done publicly. So was Jesus publicly
executed. Crowds saw him die. Soldiers
left his legs unbroken. he was buried.
    It was done by shedding blood. Blood is a
vital thing & its shedding in ordinary if of
man a crime.   Murder was punished.
Things strangled were denied for food. &
blood was a sacred thing. yet was Jesus the
for without it there could be no remission.
His head, back, feet, hands & side ran
blood, his dying crimson made him a robe
    He died a bloody sacrifice.

2. The Blood was shed in an earthen vessel — Why? Unless it was that Jesus must become like one of us ere he could die or if he could die, it would not avail unless he died in human flesh. —

God had said man must die & every syllable must be kept, therefore a bird is chosen of the same nature as the other & to make it more vivid an earthen vessel is required. A Body hast thou prepared me. We do not sufficiently notice the condescension of Christ in becoming incarnate for it was great indeed. For a Spirit to be trammelled with matter, confined in his motion &c must be extremely disagreeable, yet this he did and became like unto us.

3. The running stream is suggestive of the spread of gospel blessings: for some drops would fall into the brook, hap on to the river & so by the ocean to every shore. Like Wickliffe's ashes borne away by Severn to all parts: so has the power of Jesus' blood been felt amid frozen ice or torrid heats. It has spread & will

Perhaps too it suggests the fact that like a stream christ ever runs, is inexhaustible and undiminishable — constant and free. — Wood, scarlet & hyssop all played their part in the crucifixion and mark Jesus as the appointed victim.

II. The Sinner.

353   II. Sam XII. 7 Thou art the man.

If we want heroes we must look for them
amongst the great cloud of witnesses.

It must be admitted that it requires more
real courage coolly to perform an action
than in the heat of passion or excitement
to venture upon it.   The one is mere
animal excitement, an all but invol-
-untary act, the first is the result
of true bravery based on solid convictin
& sincere love of right.   I call Noah
a hero for amid the taunt of an
ungodly world he continued his 120
years labours.   I call Elijah a hero who
ventured his all on his God when the
bullock was consumed.   I call the
glorious three a triumvirate of heroes
"be it known unto thee oh king we will
not worship thy Gods &c".   I defy the
annals of history to bring forth a more
noble mind that Daniels who prayed
not fearing the wrath of ~~Baba~~ Persia's
King.   Thus might I lead out a
vast host of mighties who feared not
the frown of any & courted the smile
of none.   But I chose at once to
introduce one of no mean order of

whom it is said
"And Nathan said unto David thou art
the man"
David had sinned awfully but being an
heir of mercy God will not let him
finally perish. Nathan shall be sent
to warn him, but what prudence it
required — & courage too. A parable is
put into Nathan's mouth he utters it,
any other man could have done that,
but see the King does not see that it is
meant for him, now here is the act
requiring boldness to drive the arrow
home. Nathan does it, we picture the
scene, how with solemn countenance
he extends his arm, points his finger &
firmly says "Thou art the man"
It brings to my mind Knox & Queen Mary
But the case teaches us how necessary
it is that every sermon should be
accompanied with a direct application.

I. Personal application of his subject — the
Minister's duty.

Our good old ancestors always wound
up their sermons with an Application.
No matter if there had been sixty
heads there would come at the end as
regular as clockwork, the improvement
or application; & I trust though we
are not in habit of concluding with

a formal "application" yet it is ever our
aim to send the truth home to the
heart. I shall attempt
1. To shew the necessity of direct preaching.
From analogy. The gospel is intended not
to gratify the taste but to save the soul,
to remedy a personal evil. Now in
such a case how should we naturally
act. — Look at the house in flames
a man is asleep how do we act!
Shall we talk of the effect of a combination
of gases to produce combustion & inform
him that burning is a painful death.
No we cry out, Fire, Fire, Man you
are in danger, your house is burning.
— The physician who talks of death &
alteratives, opiates, sudorifics, quinine,
&c may talk on — we want the man
who will say plainly "there that
is your disease & that your medecine.
The soldier at the head of
his troop will not descant on the
origin of nations, the quality of steel but
will cry aloud "on comrades on conquer
— or die" — Why then is the
minister to deal in generalities when
far more important matters are
concerned. If your house be burnt

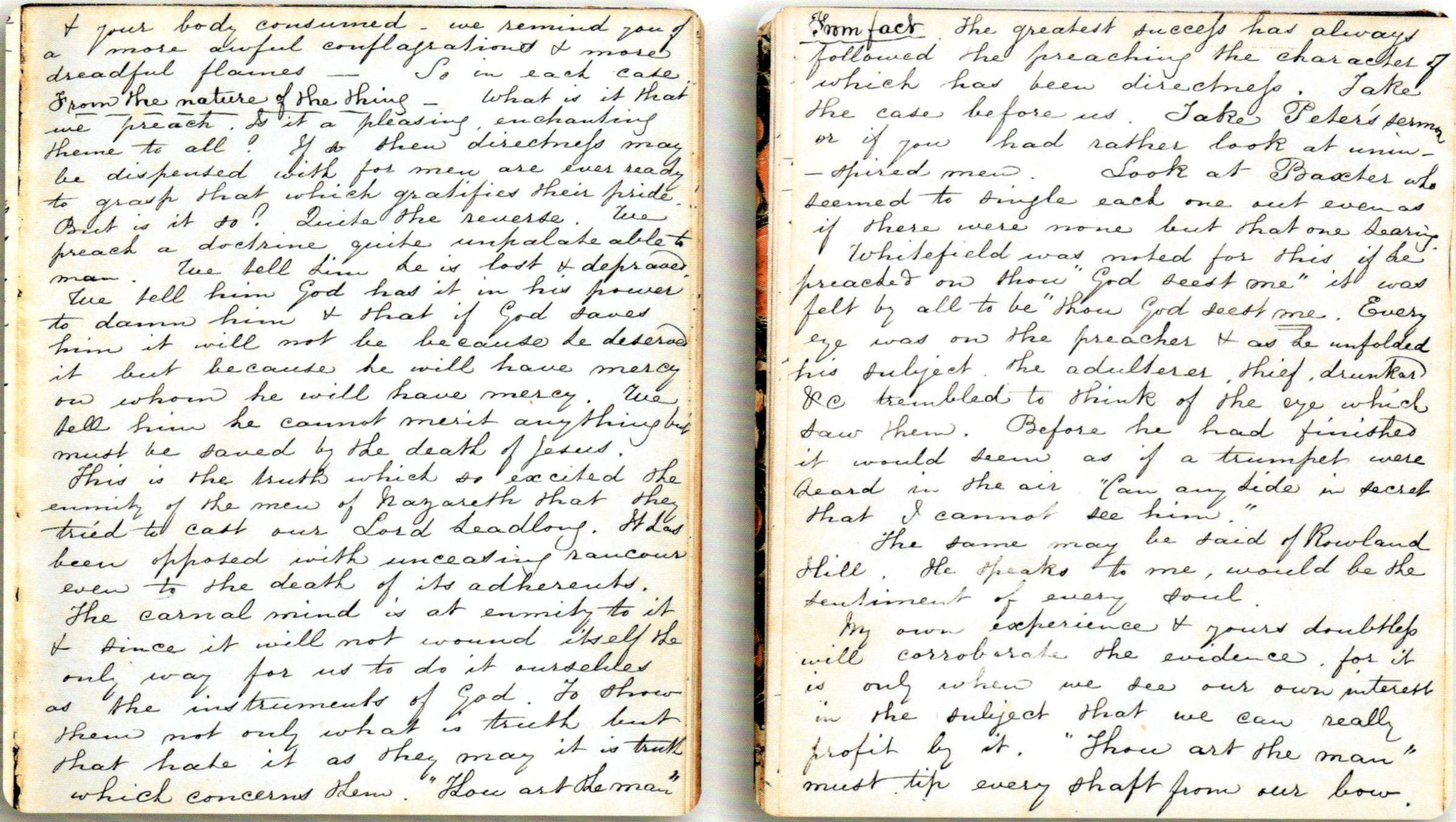

& your body consumed – we remind you of a more awful conflagration & more dreadful flames — So in each case From the nature of the thing — What is it that we preach. Is it a pleasing, enchanting theme to all? If so then directness may be dispensed with for men are ever ready to grasp that which gratifies their pride. But is it so? Quite the reverse. We preach a doctrine quite unpalatable to man. We tell him he is lost & depraved. We tell him God has it in his power to damn him & that if God saves him it will not be because he deserves it but because he will have mercy on whom he will have mercy. We tell him he cannot merit anything but must be saved by the death of Jesus.

This is the truth which so excited the enmity of the men of Nazareth that they tried to cast our Lord headlong. It has been opposed with unceasing rancour even to the death of its adherents.

The carnal mind is at enmity to it & since it will not wound itself the only way for us to do it ourselves as the instruments of God. To show them not only what is truth but that hate it as they may it is truth which concerns them. "Thou art the man"

In fact The greatest success has always followed the preaching the character of which has been directness. Take the case before us. Take Peter's sermon or if you had rather look at uninspired men. Look at Baxter who seemed to single each one out even as if there were none but that one hearing. Whitefield was noted for this, if he preached on "thou God seest me" it was felt by all to be "thou God seest me. Every eye was on the preacher & as he unfolded his subject the adulterer, thief, drunkard &c trembled to think of the eye which saw them. Before he had finished it would seem as if a trumpet were heard in the air "Can any hide in secret that I cannot see him."

The same may be said of Rowland Hill. He speaks to me, would be the sentiment of every soul.

My own experience & yours doubtless will corroborate the evidence, for it is only when we see our own interest in the subject that we can really profit by it. "Thou art the man" must tip every shaft from our bow.

2. To shew the nature of direct preaching.

1. It is not mentioning names or personality. This is much to be condemned for it never does any good or in extreme cases.

Our Saviour did it but then he was omniscient. he might say, ye generation of vipers — or Son thy sins are forgiven, we are uninspired & must know our position too well, to pretend to wield the thunder bolts of Jove. Occasions may however possibly occur when even personality is allowable such as Bourdaloue before Louis, when opening his eyes he said thou art the man, or Latimer to Henry, or Knox to Mary but few know how to do it, 99 out of a hundred miss their aim

It is imitating Christ. Let us look at his ministry. His sermon at Nazareth Luke IV. 25 was a bold declaration of divine sovereignty & applied though the effect was his expulsion. The Parable of the Vineyard Matt XX1. 45. The Scribes perceived that he spoke of them. How? No names were mentioned.

The woman of Samaria, the rich young man, the persons who charged the woman with adultery. Now this is the way, happy is the man who understands the blessed art.

3. To shew the reason why we have so little of it.

Mistaken notions of the office of the ministry Some think it is to instruct only & therefore are argumentative, historical & explanatory. Other think it is to interest. to refine &c these give us essays beautiful as marble statues or if not quite as cold. Some good men as Porteus have had some error or other, or perhaps were too delicate afraid of blood & broken bones. —

Want of piety, Those who have little concern for their own souls cannot be expected to have much for others. He who does not prize religion above gold will not care for others & therefore will not deal with them as one in earnest straight home into their consciences. Give us more piety & then more directness.

Want of courage. Some are deficient in this qualification — but if cowardice be indulged it becomes a sin. See Jonah. If evil seems to threaten one if I speak the truth, I must remember that there are far worse impending if I do not. I must speak. I am not able to refuse on peril of wrath. Why should we fear — let us speak truth & the ægis of Jehovah will cover us.

II. Personal application of the subject the
Hearer's duty

The Gospel is sent to men as individuals,
every thing in it is personal, it is valueless if
not applied. Christ himself avails not if
he be not heartily received within. No
one doctrine can edify or bless if not appropriated
If you would be saved you must seek for
salvation as a single individual.

You will be judged as individuals.
Men will not be judged by dozens or scores,
not by towns or countries but as single
persons. You are responsible for yourselves.
No proxies before the judgment seat. Say
what you will you must appear.

Men will be damned as individuals.
Each one shall have a hell to bear alone.
Depart shall be sounded in the ear of
each, cursed will be the name for every one.
No getting through heavens gate in a crowd.
Why then so foolish as not to apply the
truth to yourself. You will want to do
so when you come to die.

Sinner. It is your own concern not mine
let me entreat thee bethink thyself a
little. God says Man is lost
"Thou art the man". God says man
cannot restore himself "Thou art the man".

God says their heart is evil. Thou art the
man. He says Jesus died to save
Perhaps "thou art the man". Who can
tell you may be an elect one? Let me
see. (Dost thou repent. "Thou art the
man". Art thou desirous of Christ
dost thou now cry to him. "Thou art
the man". Saints are safe "Thou art
the man" Heaven is for believers.
"Thou art the man."

But do you sit hardened, then
prepare for judgment for "Thou art the man"
Hell gapes, "thou art the man" God
laughs at thy calamity "thou art the
man" I hear a shriek, I see a
damned soul "thou art the man.
O God give me thy might
amen. amen

681

Ezek. XVII. 22.23.24.   The Branch.   354

Short and weighty sayings always mark a
noble mind or at least Noble men have
often employed them. As Cæsar's Veni,
Vidi, Vici. &c —— but where are such
sublimely sententious phrases as in Scripture
He said "let there be light & there was light"
"Lazarus come forth" "It is finished"
and the one before us "I the Lord have
spoken and done it." — None other could
say so but he. His word is the same as
his deed & both are infallibly connected.
    Let us see the great work.

I. The Choice —
God having resolved to do a glorious work
namely salvation selects some one to have
the lead, management and labour of it
    This person — our Lord Jesus is here described
i. As a glorious person.
    In his divinity. He is truly the highest
branch of the high cedar. He was far above
principality &c equal with God, coeternal
with him, one with him
    In his humanity. He was as to his
descent of the tribe of Judah, the house of
David — of a royal race although a
Carpenter's Son. He had all the air
of a king about him. The features of David
were manifest in his face. He was fairer
than the sons of men — Being also

begotten of the Holy Ghost he was truly
a glorious personage & so fit for a
glorious business. But as he had
to do with fallen man he was required to come
As a humble person. a tender plant
a mere twig, despised & contemned
In his birth, education, estate, reputation,
character, food, lodging, death, & burial
he was a humble person. He was
just the person required glory veiled in
humility. Bone of our bone and yet
Lord over all, blessed for ever.

II. The Planting
God having chosen the Branch next
cuts it off & here is
Christ's descent from heaven, he was cut off
from the glories & worship of the higher
realms and tabernacled among men
Christ's death. He was cut off from the
land of the living — oh what a painful
cutting off was this. Admire the love
Christ's glory in his Church. Is set forth
by his being planted on a mountain.
for stability, visibility & loftiness the
Church is indeed a mountain & on this
the branch is planted. In the affections
of the bloodbought and bloodwashed throng.
He died as the wheat that he might not
be alone. Three times it is repeated perhaps
to show that the three persons are all

concerned. Here is the tree of life planted in the midst of the Church.

III. The fruit.

Christ is no barren plant, though the mountain of the church is naturally stony ground. Christ brings forth boughs and fruit.

The boughs are the great doctrines of grace, the great truths of our holy religion. As we seldom hear them mentioned a catalogue of them may be interesting. —

Election, personal, free, unconditional, eternal. Atonement, sufficient, efficacious, infallible. Justification. Effectual Calling by the Holy Ghost's irresistible power. Perseverance, certain, unfrustrable.

These are great arms from the root Jesus Christ and are loaded with fruit.

These fruits are the graces of Christians their comfort & support. These are faith, love, hope, joy, confidence, support &c.

Precious fruit I will live on thee for ever.

IV. The dwellers

All will not dwell there, but some of all sorts will.

All countries. Cold or hot, savage or civilized, east or west, Black or white.

All ranks. Some kings, nobles & lords, tradesman, farmer, sailor, soldier, beggar, the Soodra & Pariah.

All characters, if believers, the zealous, bold, fiery, the calm, deliberate, loving, gentle, serious, gay —

Old greyheaded sinners saved, & those called early in life.

All ages, the babe, the youth, the man the grey head, the old & decrepit Some of all sorts are under his boughs.

V. The Glory

We may be sure that the ultimate end of God's actions is his own glory. So will Salvation work & honour him.

High trees shall be levelled, green ones withered. Triumph awaits the banners of the cross. In a few more years Hallelujahs will rend the heavens and the crown come to him whose right it is. Even so. Amen.

See there believer the plant of renown, make thy boast in the Lord, and triumph in thy God.

680

1 John. III. 8. Christ destroying the works 355
of the devil.

This is the day (Xmas) when we feel constrained
to think of the birth of Jesus. Our neighbours
do so, and little as we, the sons of the
Puritans, are accustomed to regard days &
weeks, yet it does not seem to us sinful
or improper to remember the incarnation
of our Lord to-day.

No act of Deity is more worthy of
the attention of the universe than that
rightly called, the manifesting of the Son of
God. & Even creation the sight of which
made the morning stars sing together &
the sons of God shout for joy — did not
so much awake the admiration of
celestials as the scene of God veiling
himself in humanity. If we rightly
consider of it we shall feel the same
emotions. It is very right to read the book
of nature to see a present God in all
& make this earth the helper of our
devotion — but it is wrong to extol too
much the study of nature for to wise
men it will not have so much
attractions as the study of the mystery
"God manifest in the flesh."
I will not bear you to Bethlehem &

detain you with a view of the babe &
his mother. I will not even lead out
your mind to admire the love & the
condescension of the wondrous act,
although here would be a string of
topics profitable to us — but rather
I will keep to the text & consider
the purpose of this "manifestation".

The purpose mentioned in the text
is but one link in a chain of purposes
uniting the sinner saved & God glorified.
"To destroy the works of the devil".
Now we must understand all this in
a certain sense, viz. for his people,
for truly some of our race will feel
eternally the "works of Satan" & for
them these works are not destroyed.
But for believers Jesus came from
his high glories to destroy Satan's works.
And what are the works of our
great enemy. Come see believer the
ruin of his labours & sing upon
the desolations of his empire.
His works are like himself
abominable, evil & only evil.
Thanks be to God for their destruction

I. Sin.
II. Death.   } three works of Satan
III. Hell.   } destroyed by the Son of God.

I Sin. Is the work of Satan, there was no moral evil until he conceived it. He led astray the sons of the morning. He made war in heaven. He in the likeness of a serpent dropped the seed of sin into our mother's ear, from which has sprung a fearful harvest extensive as our earth. He laid the first black stone of the horrid palace which is now his dwelling, the chambers of sin.

But sin is destroyed by Jesus. It is driven from its haunts & as the result of the victory we see or shall see.
1. a rescued man
2. a rescued world

1. A rescued man. Man is full of sin it is in him by nature & oh how deeply by practise. He is fallen as to every shadow of good and utterly gone astray. Under the dominion of sin, & so captive to the devil. But Christ came to destroy sin for every believer & does actually accomplish the design.

His work for us. his agonies and death bought for us pardon, justification and acceptance with God. Our sins are put to death by his death. They were crucified on his cross and there expired. The devil by sin made me guilty but Christ by his righteousness makes me innocent. I am in God's sight as if I had never sinned. My sins are now annihilated, gone never to return.

Pardoned soul thou mayest fling the gauntlet at the world & say "Who is he that condemneth." Sinner great as thy sin is, be not in despair for for this purpose was he manifested, to take away sin. & thine shall be taken away entirely the moment thou believest.

His work in us. which he works by the Holy Spirit in our hearts is also most necessar to complete the destruction of sin — for even after pardon there still remains sin within us. Evil dispositions, desires, lusts are there but they must not reign there any longer. A stronger than he is come and the strong man armed must keep the house no longer.

Conversion bursts the door — it is the beginning of the great sanctifying process. And what a beginning it is, worthy of a God. It is a complete & reversion of the whole man. It is as if a river should reverse its course. The stormy sea become calm as a lake. and rock & adamant — like melted wax. Sin is dethroned & though it lurks in dens & caves its death knell is rung. It is a condemned outlaw. By the mighty work of the almighty Spirit, it groweth weaker and weaker until in glory the man becomes "without fault before the throne of God." There is the work of Satan demolished in two great ways by Christ. & we see lost man, perfect as at first ...

2. A rescued world. Man fell & the whole race fell in a mass. Let us look on the fallen world. made go by the craft of the devil. true is sickened at the first cursory view we see armies marching to shed each others blood deluded crowds bowing down to blocks cruel to one another, filthy, bestial,

Let us a moment — stay & review the sin of this world —

Idolatry, in its myriad forms, creed obscene, degrading, sickening, — the the masterpieces of the devil — Lust is shall be destroyed. Yea is to these now Bel boweth down & Nebo stoopeth, now shall the gods be cast to moles and bats & this blindness be removed.

War, which is murder on a large scale, shall one day cease. Vultures & wolves have been gorged with the flesh of men. But hell's bloodred flag shall be rent. The sword which is forged there shall be made a plough share & peace shall prevail.

slavery, that plague spot on the fair brow of America, that curse of curses shall be destroyed & the clank of the chain heard no more.

oppression of every kind shall cease no tyrant shall be found on earth.

robbery, dishonesty, lying, anger & bigotry all shall die. nor shall Antichrist be spared. Great Babylon shall fall, see, she reeleth to & fro her hour hasteth when she shall sit in the ground. The queen shall be made naked & her flesh shall be burned.

Then comes a renovated earth, for this purpose is the Son of God manifested, that he may destroy the works of the devil. Shout oh heavens for the Lord hath done it.

Sin is vanquish'd sin is slain
Christ hath broken the tyrants chain
Dash'd the idols from their seat
Made them dust beneath his feet
Hush'd the shout, & stayed the fight
Clear'd away the shades of night.
Shout the vict'ry once again
Sin is vanquish'd, sin is slain

IV Death. The second work of Satan is death. Adam & Eve would have lived on till now if they had not sinned. But sin has changed all nature. Now the skeleton form of death marches o'er the land & devours thousands at a meal. The world is a huge hospital, earth a grand cemetery for our race, its dust was much of it once alive, it is

an aceldema, or else a valley of dry bones. But death itself shall find a death. Death is destroyed.

By the rich support given to the saints Death ceases to be a punishment, in fact it is far more a blessing than a curse. Its triumphant shout drowns its feeble cry of pain. It is the gate of endless joy. Christian, death is destroyed.

By the resurrection. Death loses his prey. The body is released from his iron grasp. The old tyrant sat in a palace of skulls & bones, but it fled from him, bone came to its bone & lived. Oh that resurrection morn how will death weep to see its victims live. He shall disgorge his prey. His pall shall be rent into shreds, his coffin shall burst asunder, his grave rifled.

By Immortality. Death & Life have run a race & Death has won it hitherto. But Immortality is brought to light by the gospel & the bright discovery has chased away the spectres of the grave, lit up the vault with joy, & broken the scythe of the mower.

III. __Hell__. The chef'd'œuvre of Satan is hell, + this is not destroyed for the unbeliever but for the saint it is. Its numbers would have been infinitely greater if the elect had not been redeemed, but by Christ Hell has been despoiled + much depopulated. Its dungeons in which the saints should have been immured have been blasted with almighty thunder, the racks + fetters broken, its fires quench[ed] so far as the elect are concerned.

Satan is not King of hell or rather soon he will not be. He will be chained himself + become like one of the rest.

Now let us, like as the Roman looked on the ruins of Carthage with pride, look on these ruins with joy. Fallen towers, broken chains, opened dungeons, battlements battered down. Hallelujah. Jesus is our hero, see he comes. Sing oh ye angels he comes + at his chariot wheel drags three monsters Sin, Death + Hell all hail, all hail, King of Kings, thou hast bruised the dragon,

+ overcome his brood. See he smites off the head of each + holds their horrid heads aloft. The universe bends down in admiration, then claps its hands, + sings aloud, Glory, + praise + power + majesty + dominion + honour + might unto thee oh Son of God.

Christian join the anthem this morning, with all thy soul. "__He hath destroyed the works of the devil__"

689

Eccles. XI. 11. The words of the wise. 356.

We have no hesitation in referring these
words to the "words of the wise" contained
in the Scriptures. The words of other
wise men are excellent & worthy of remembrance but the infallible words
of inspired men are more to be reverenced

Here we may remark how many
more of these words are we possessed of
than Solomon was, he was wise, but
he that is least in the kingdom of
heaven is greater than he, i.e possesses
more light, more of "the words of the wise"

Here we have them collected in one volume
& not deficient in copies as in Josiah's time

Here we have --

I. Two figures setting forth the nature
    and effects of the Word. —

II. Two offices in relation to the
    going forth of the Word. —

I. Two figures setting forth the nature &
    effects of the word. —

Solomon was a wise man & put his
knowledge of nature into use in his
writings & preachings. There is scarce

an object in nature which he does not
make tributary to him — from the
ant, spider & coney, up to the eagle
horse & lion. Everything in pastoral
household or city life he mentions in
due place & in our text he went
to the herdsman & the carpenter &
borrowed, ideas from, the goad & nails.

The words of the wise are as goads.

A goad was an instrument used for
goading on cattle by pricking them.

To convince of sin. Men need something to
arouse them, to make them feel, to
penetrate into their hearts. Now the
word of the Lord is sharper than any
two edged sword. Heb. 4. 12. It pricked
the Jews to the heart. Acts. II. 37. It is
a sharp oxgoad penetrating the hide
& leather covering of the sinner, his
prejudice, his hardness, his contempt.

See it in Colonel Gardiner, Newton,
Bunyan & all sinners saved.

To urge in duty. Even the heirs of
heaven need urging on to their position.
They are apt to pitch their tents, to be
slothful, to sleep, to lay behind. our
God has many ways of urging us on

The words of the wise are as nails.

Fastened

Fastening. themselves the words
of God go deep & take firm hold on us.
Have we not forced it to. Had not some
warning text haunted us day by day?
Has not some comforting one heard
with us we knew not why? Many
texts have remained for years & have
not been rooted out but were of use.

Fastening. Nails are used to fasten
things together & the words of the wise
1. do fasten us to one another —
for when any disagreement would
occur, in comes a promise or a quietus
and binds us again into one body.
The more we study our Bibles the
more we shall love each other, the
words of men set apart, may sermons
are unsharable, may conversations
are schismatical; but the Bible
is a binding book & where 'tis ours
words are used & the creatures lovers
then we shall see Unity.
2. They fasten us to the truth
some are ever wavering, not knowing
anything rightly, ever changing, carried
away by every wind of doctrine,

by providential trials &c but the sweetest
method is by the goad of his word used
by the ministry. Every wise minister
will use a little of the goad & every nature
hearer will feel that he needs it. God's
ministers are not always to be mixing &
soothing & pedalines, they much d
also make the word a goading word. &
let their hearers be ever so much displeased
May God make it a goad to you & me.

To defeat enemies. When the ancient Is-
-raelites had neither sword nor spear, they
sharpened their ox goads & like Shamgar
did wonders therewith — so we also
learning the sword & spear of logic and
learning to Goliaths & Nimrods go out
with as weapons our carnal but might
for the pulling down of strong holds.
we attack infidelity in its Protean forms,
& rout it. we turn over our weapons
against Antichrist & the rocks on her
hills — we overturn idolatry. her
missionaries land our own island with
this goad in their hands; war ceases
old superstitions flee & the land is won
So empire can hold out, no enemy can
conquer it is destined to conquer;
the goad shall be the sceptre.

But the words of the wise fasten us so that we know what we believe. We may read controversial works & be unsettled but reading the Bible will never unsettle any one but confirm us in the faith. Here is solid ground for the sole of our foot. All doubts may be slain by these nails in the same way that Jael served Sisera.

3. They fasten us to Christ

When we might altogether forsake him, some warning nails us to him. When faith would fail & let go its hold on the Beloved, then comes a text and binds a silken cord around him and us. When Satan drags us away the nail holds us still it will not lose its hold it has pierced our heart & his heart & nails them eternally together & they cannot be rent asunder any more.

Let us see if we have had any of these nails driven into us. Has the goad touched us, if so here we can corroborate the evidence of the Preacher by our own experience.

Goads & nails fastened.

II. Two offices in relation to the going forth of the Word.

1. The Masters of Assemblies. No assembly can well be kept in order without a leader or master of assemblies. Such were the high priests, the prophets & afterwards the Sagans or rulers of the Synagogues. With us the minister who reads, expounds, offers prayer and preaches the word.

The masters of assemblies should be God-sent, God-taught, & God-loving men. May God give us many such.

Now the business of these men is to fasten the wise words.

By simplicity of speech. Explaining all dark passages, clearing up difficulties & taking care not to make it hard by using learned language. Let it be the gospel in deshabille, it is "most adorn'd when unadorn'd the most"

By illustration. This is a mighty means of fastening truth. All the prophets used it & our Saviour was very copious in it. No dry discourse but lively & interesting.

By earnestness. What a man does not feel himself, he cannot well make others feel. We want warmth; we want loving to souls & burning desire for their salvation & then the nails would fasten.

By the Spirit. but fastening will not avail if the great Spirit do not also come to our aid. But he can so deeply enfix it that the devil's irons can never wrench it out again.

Come friends have you ever had the nail thus fastened? Has it penetrated & lodged in your memory, judgment, conscience & heart?

2. The one Shepherd. There are many masters of assemblies but only one Shepherd. This is the common name of our Lord Jesus Christ & a very precious name. How sweetly doth it utter his nature and depict his worth. Shepherd.

There is but one, Ministers are only sheep with bells on to lead the others. He is the great Bishop of Souls.

Now it says that he gives the words the masters of assemblies only fasten them, he gives them the nails

Inspiration is the great work of the Spirit sent by our Lord. Every word of the Bible is inspired, not one letter (as originally given) can be confuted. It is from Jehovah as much as Creation itself.

Suggestion God gives his ministers texts by suggesting them to their minds. He does not inspire us but he leads our minds to subjects.

Assistance. when he aids, the text seems to break itself up. divisions & thoughts grow up — we speak our tongue runs on. thoughts flow apace. matter comes, & we rejoice to feel a happy liberty. now let us. Thank him for his words.

for a master of Assemblies but more for the one Shepherd.

Lam. II. 12. Unparalleled Sorrow 357

Jeremiah has well been called the weeping prophet. He is eloquent. The Eloquence of woe he had which is the most moving of all

There are innumerable touches of most unrivalled beauty. He wept o'er his beloved country, his temple & his nation. Oh had we right feelings we should weep over the church & over our fellow members. No troubles are really greater than church troubles

Here is the church complain. we shall note

I. The Complaint in the wrong mouth
II. The Complaint in the right mouth.

I. The Complaint in the wrong mouth.

When a believer takes it to himself & wants all the world to behold his sorrow and consider it as unique, solitary and unparalleled.

1. I will condemn the cry.
2. I will hush the cry.
3. I will supplant the cry.

1. I will condemn the cry. It is very wrong & foolish. It is false, it is sinful

It arises from ignorance. visit widows, asylums, unions, jails, dungeons, hospitals & they will tell you that you are not alone

It arises from impatience. It is proud nature kicking against its Maker.

2. I will hush the cry

You deserve it, therefore be still.
Your God does it resist not.
Your benefit is designed by it.
Your heaven will be brightened by it.

3. I will supplant the cry.

Consider how much better you are treated than some, you are a child of God, a reclaimed prodigal, a ransom'd slave — therefore be glad & say.

Was ever mercy so great
As that bestow'd on me

II. The Complaint in the right mouth.

Jesus could say it most truly & if we look at him we shall profit by it.

His life was singularly painful.

It was a life of Poverty, Persecution, Hatred, Ingratitude, Misrepresentation, Almost Loneliness — Besides his

358.

II Sam. XV.23. The King's passage of Kidron

There are many spots in the world of no great note geographically considered, but of immense interest as connected with actions or men. The pass of Thermopylæ, the rock of Plymouth. the village of Elstow, the church at Kidderminster — So in Palestine we have many a shrine Bethlehem, Jerusalem, Gethsemane & amongs a long list the little brook Kidron.

I. <u>Kings have troubles</u>. We sometimes murmur because we have brook Kidrons to cross. it is some slight consolation that others have to cross it too. Rank does not exempt from trouble.

Reason proves it. for we can all see that wealth & power have to do with body not with mind. Sceptres have no sway over pain & crowned heads are often aching heads.

History proves it. Sacred history accords a large amount of trial to King. Saul. David. Hezekiah. Josiah, &c — our own country tells us of many such case. William I Henry, I.II. Ed.II. Rich II &c &c — Albert

Now from this let us learn

Contentment with our lot

Resignation to trial

Thankfulness for any temporary release from trouble

sympathy for others and his keen feelings at the <u>sight of sin</u> & a dreary certainty of painful <u>death</u> in the end.

But his <u>death</u> was unparalleled in sorrow.

He deserved it not in the least.

He had no friend. Betrayed & forsaken.

No one ever had more ignominy

God forsook him.

Sin lay on him.

But the wonder lies here.

It was for others, his enemies.

Is it nothing to you, my hearers, did he not die for you, If he did not then weep over your ruin for you are inevitably lost. But if he did then fly to him, clasp his knees & be his servant for ever.

O God help me or I am undone. Amen

359.   Col. I. 27   Christ in you.

A religion without mystery would be no religion at all. The mysteries of Popery & Romanism & Puseyism are mysteries well calculated to exalt & enrich their mysteries & require much faith on the behalf of their votaries. They are mysteries of faith or rather lies. Our mystery is a mystery of experience & is here put in few words that although unknown by the natural uninitiated man, the spiritual may discern the secret of the Lord.

I. Christ — one feels humbled at the mere to name off in a stream of rhapsody in admiration of his nature glory, his creating work, his wondrous titles & his many crowns. But the Christ with whom our secret deals is Christ in incarnation, Christ incarnate, Christ the obedient servant, Christ the bleeding Redeemer, then the rising Conqueror, the constant intercessor. them the joy of the souls. Do we know the music of the name of our beloved? Do we feel that his glorious name is our strength? them we most likely know the rest of the mystery.

II. Christ in you. Christ crucified will save none of us unless he becomes Christ in us. This is the Holy Spirit's work. Christ in us is a comprehensive expression. How earnestly does the penitent desire Christ & long for them more

---

II The Story of Things had troubles.

He crossed the brook Kedron on that gloomy night. —

The brook he went over for us. The brook of our Kedron the Black Brook was the common sewer of the temple; all the filth ran there. All our sins have run into one stream & he had waded through the black tide. Let us muse awhile on Gethsemane.

The brook he goes over with us — our troubles, sorrows and griefs. He bore all as our Companion. Yea he is our companion now. every black stream we Having suffered he had

Atonement — he has gone over Kedron.
Companion — he had gone over Kedron.
Leadership — he first had gone over Kedron

I know assuredly that we would go over Kedron there is no other road to heaven had you not — he will help there.
Amen the thing.

360. See 345. S. Song II. 9. The Beloved in various postures.

Similitudes & allegories are beautifully adapted to fasten truth on our poor memories. Bunyan's Pilgrim makes us understand more of spiritual life than all other human works put together. & this Song tells us much of the love which subsists between Christ & his church in a manner likely to be remembered. It is to my well beloved touching my well beloved.

I. Christ in his approaches. He is like a roe, or young hart, swift, overleaping all difficulties & comely in his motions. So was Jesus when he came to earth. It was no unwilling descent but it was done with joyful alacrity when he went to die. No man took his life, he laid it down of himself & cheerfully gave up the ghost. When he comes to the penitent he rejoices to come. He is charmed at the sight of tears. When he comes to the afflicted No sooner do they call than he answers. Swiftly he comes to wipe our sorrows dry. He is never tardy but before we call he often answers.

II. Christ in concealment. He concealed his glory when on earth, or it would have caused a conflagration & death to mortals. Often he conceals himself from his people & the effect of that is searching, sorrow, repentance & groaning out after him. This is the reason why he is gone. Because we treated him with coldness. loved than they that watch for the morning. Do you? Christ believed in. the first act of the new man on coming out of darkness is faith in Jesus. It succeeds desire which is groping in the dark. Do we cast ourselves wholly on the merits of his agonies, & death if so we know the mystery & may go on to

Christ beloved. Love follows faith, it never precedes it. It is an embracing & pressing to the heart. It must be real, hearty, supreme, not effervescent but abiding. Have you this?

Christ rejoiced in. follows & ever is the fruit of desire, faith & love. This is Christ in you indeed when we can rejoice in trouble, yea in the article of death. Come let us see whether we understand this mystery. Christ in us.

III. Christ in you, the hope of glory. This is the finishing letter of the mystery, viz: to have a hope of glory. All men have a hope, but only a few have a hope of glory, but of that few how very few have a good hope of glory. Let us see if our hope is good. if it is Christ in us which gives us hope then it is right & good. Does our hope purify us, Does it abide in fiery trials. Dare you examine it, Is it built on the rock. If so — go on joyfully all the days of thy life for now thou knowest more than the wise men & the Ancient. You know a mystery, their philosophy knows not.

678. 686. 679

another two much, harboured sin, or neglected duty.   Remember if we have not the presence of the Lord Jesus Christ it is our own fault he hides behind our wall. The wall we built ourselves, he has built none, let us Knock it down. whatever it may be

III. Christ observing. Though we cannot see him, he can see us. He ever looks through the windows. Sometimes he looks

with grief to see our barrenness & death

with care & anxiety lest one little plant should die outright, or one spark be quenched.

with love. Lovers love to see each other so does our Saviour delight to behold us.

with joy when we do well, but ah how seldom is that. Remember beloved he is looking at us now — at our church, at our closet, at our life, at our heart.

IV. Christ manifesting himself. Sometimes we see him, he is not wholly hidden. But we see in part, it is not plainly & clearly but only through the lattices

we see by means, which are lattices. Prayer, Praise, the services of his house & especially the Lord's supper are golden lattices.

Mark he shews himself. we do not find him out by learning & research but he is his own discoverer.

He shows himself — not his works or words alone but himself.

Question & application.

360a   Job IV.17.18.19 Angels charged with folly.

Pride is natural to man. Every character & station has its peculiar pride, for pride has a thousand forms. It enters the cottage, the peasant sitting at his door sits as much a monarch as Cæsar.

The milkmaid tosses her head as proudly as the belle at court. He who digs the dark mine, or sweeps the crossing, or cleans my boots has a pride in him.

And as pride adapts itself to every rank so does it append itself to every thing.   There is the pride of dress, the pride of wealth. the pomp of power, the parade of learning & the wonder all men there is the pride of religion. This pride assumes a thousand shapes. with the Catholic or Mennonite it is the pride of good works & among ourselves it is too often the same — Righteous self is the hardest foe we have to contend with — Justifying ourselves before God. Eliphaz had once been convinced of the folly of this vice & labours to convince Job of it. We however will not look upon the words as those of Eliphaz but as they really are, the words of a being from the world of spirits. whom Eliphaz saw.

There is much talk at the present moment about spiritual manifestations, now instead of caring about these modern wonders let us listen to the words of a well authenticated apparition & learn therefrom our own littleness.

Some have imagined as the rich man did that spirits would be fit messengers to proclaim the will of heaven. But how thankful we ought to be that men are our ministers & not spirits for into what a state of dread was this good man thrown, we should not like to feel so terrified in God's house.

May God grant however that the echo of the sentences of this terrible being may have a humbling effect on us.

Three considerations to humble us.

I. The position of all God's servants.
II. The position of angels.
III. Our own position.

I trust that these three considerations may act as batteries against our pride & utterly abase its loftiness for this purpose I invoke divine assistance & now let us reflect on.

I. The position of all God's servants.

And at the mention of the word servants what a train of ideas arise. For all things are the servants of God the sun is but his footman, the moon a menial linkbearer of the darkness. Those wondrous orbs which roll in majestic circles, those erratic fires which burst upon us & then retreat, those lightnings which cleave the skies & the thunders which alarm the nations are but a portion of the brilliant retinue of servants who wait the behests of the omnipotent. Riding on the wings of the wind in his cloudy chariot he makes the clouds as the dust of his feet — All things obey him animate as well as inanimate.

There is behemoth who drinks a river at a draught & leviathan who makes the deep boil like a pot — but Eliphaz here refers only to intelligent beings who are the servants of God in a higher sense. But here too we find an innumerable host comprising it is said He put no trust in them.

1. He does not expect - or require any
<u>assistance from them.</u>

We talk of putting trust in men or princes
or of putting trust in God — & we mean
by that — expecting aid from them —
but God has need of none of his servants.
He does not want them as pillars to
his throne. Like the world he has
nothing to hang on. His own all
-sufficience bears the weight of his own
glories up. Turkey puts trust in
England & France to uphold it forever.
but God rests on none. All the Kings
of the earth lean on their nobles, or
their wealth, or their armies, but God
is the only Potentate. When he bares
his arm for war he does not depend
on legions of angels but he treads the
winepress alone. He could do as
well without us as we with us. Free
in his providence & grace he uses his
servants as instruments but they are nothing
more — he could work without them.
In conversion Saul. In Deliverance Egypt.
In conquest. Gideon. Invalidating all. In fact he puts
no reliance on our powers as auxiliary to his own

the glorious hierarchy of angels with their
varied ranks of principalities, powers &
dominions. Heat follow the countless armies
of the redeemed. Triumphing in a blood
- bought victory. & afterwards the
multitudes on earth ever faithful to their
King. In this one family we discern-
stars of the first magnitude. The undying
Enoch: the faithful Abraham: the
wrestling Israel: the meek Moses, the
beloved Samuel, the seraphic David:
perfect Job, bold Elijah, lamenting
Jeremiah now rejoicing &c together
with New Testament Saints & their
worthy successors the heroes of the Alps!
the confessors of Smithfield, the puritans,
& the long squadrons of noble mind
who yield not to the foe.
But of all these it must be said
<u>He put no trust in his servant</u>

This is not said of his servants on
earth alone but of those in heaven too.
Truly we can see why he should put
no trust in us for we cannot trust
ourselves, so changing are we, so frail,
so light that every wind blows us
about as it listeth — but of all his Saints

2. He does not entrust any part of his dominions to their government

The heathen supposed that one God could not superintend all the universe therefore their Zeus or Jove was represented as allotting different portions of his dominion to vicegerent Gods. Neptune shook his trident over the sea. Eolus ruled the winds Flora was queen of flowers. Pluto of hell &c — but our God has no lords to whom he has entrusted principalities & regencies. but he governs himself.

Earthly monarchs entrust their states to ministers & judges but he holds all authority & office in his own hands.

Worms & angels, sparrows & planets the hairs of our head & the stars of heaven are all under one lord.

God has not left me entrusted my soul to Gabriel — truly angels minister unto us but we are not entrusted to their guidance — nor is even a fly.

He overrules all mortal things, In him is all dignity vested. The shields of the earth are his. To him sceptres & crowns belong. We are all directly responsible to him & to him only.

Let us not seek after power in the church, for God does not intend us to be masters

3. He puts no trust in their wisdom he asks no council at their hands.

There are three who hold council in heaven & only three & those three are one — the one God. But God never asks the advice of his servants. In creation who instructed him. Is. XL. 12. In salvation, who devised the plan, who aided him in carrying it out. In providence, who tells him how to act. None. Not Gabriel ever ventures to intrude his advice. He has no cabinet ministers, no privy council.

What would the united wisdom, prudence & sagacity of all intelligences amount to — if compared with him. Were we all Solomons our learned lore would sound in his ear as the prattle of children. Our most prudent schemes would fail — He puts no trust in his servants. Let this humble us — let us think less of our own wisdom and more of his. Let us rejoice that infinite wisdom is engaged for us & no inferior powers for God would not trust the salvation of his tiniest child in the hands of the wisest Sanhedrim of angels

4. He does not entrust his ~~power~~ secret decrees to them nor make them his confidants.

He has purposes which he reveals by the mouth of his servants the prophets. He has secret purposes which neither mortal nor immortal knows of. The purposes of redemption were unknown to angels for they desired to look into those things. Most men make some one their confidant & entrust their secrets to a friend. but God's own bosom is the archive of his predestination. The day of judgment is unknown, it may come to day or tomorrow of that day & hour knoweth no man, nor the angels of God. Why should we seek foresight, why desire to pry into the future, it is concealed. let us learn humble deference, & cast away impudent inquisitive curiosity. — It is well for us that our own salvation is not entrusted to us, it is one of the decrees, but we are neither entrusted with the knowledge nor the fulfilling of the decrees of Jehovah. Newton's dream of the ring well sets out this idea. No man knows whose name is in the Lamb's book except by evidence & the getting of the elect to glory is not entrusted to God's servants

Here then in the position of all God's servants — in that he asks no aid from them, does not trust his empire to them, asks no council, & communicates no secrets — let us learn to humble ourselves before the mighty God of Jacob but here comes another thought.

II. The position of angels.

The wonderful apparition having delivered itself of one sentence pronounces another which at the first sound startles us exceedingly. As if not enough to trample on the pride of all the servants of God, angels themselves are made to bend. He charged his angels with folly. Now we are so often speaking of angels as glorious pure & without spot & the word folly is so frequently applied to sin. that we stand astonished to find seraphic hosts charged with folly. The word folly is applied in scripture to the grossest crimes. Shechem's rape of Dinah. Gen. XXXIV. 7. Deut. XXII. 21. Achan's theft. Joshua. VII. 15 — The violation of the concubine. Judg XX. 6 In Psal. 85. 8. Folly means sin. & in

2 Tim. 3.9. Jannes & Jambres have their revolt described as folly now if folly in this place means the same as in every other then we would have you notice the tense of the verb, he "charged" past, not "chargeth", present, If folly here implies sin then this refers to the fallen angels — & should teach us a lesson not to rely on our own power & free will for left to themselves even angels fell. Let us take heed that we rely on that mighty arm which held up & still holds up the elect angels, then are we safe.

But we think the "folly" here meant is not a sinful folly. For although all sin is folly all folly is not sin, True it is that to sin in any way shows folly or want of wisdom but every want of wisdom does not show sin.

Suppose that without learning Chinese I should go & preach the gospel to them in English — there would be no sin, but much folly.

Suppose I should venture alone on a rough sea, without any knowledge of oars it would not be sin if I went to save a drowning sailor but it would be folly now we think this is the folly intended in this place.

We generally impute folly to children & now & then in some conspicuous instances to mistaken men, now in this sense folly is used here.

In children there is a want of experience. Angels though longlived now are but as babes in God's sight ; only yesterday & there were none, they are only creatures of the last moment, ephemeral insects in his eyes — though to us they seem ancient.

In children there is a want of Knowledge. So angels know little of the past & Je. but little or nothing of the future. They are far wiser than we are but in comparison with Him they know nothing.

In children there is a want of prudence. Angels must be very sagacious & wise. but they are foolish when compared with that Mind which is God. They cannot see results & plan events in wisdom as he can they are charged with folly.

In children there is little lofty thought. Children do not think of empires, of astronomy, or geology but of trifles of mere trifles & though angels are lofty intelligences vastly superior to us, yet in the sight of the Lord of Hosts they are but children. their thoughts are not His thought as heaven is high &c

In angels & children there is a want of strength &c

Now if angels are so low where shall we lie, what are we, worms of the earth to be charged with — But here comes the third

<u>III. Our own position.</u>

This is as humiliating as anything, let us look at our —

<u>House</u> — our body, it is not of ivory but of clay — eastern houses made of clay can easily be broken into — they are not beautiful houses of ivory, not lasting mansions of marble but clay. Materialism is far from exalting, even when it is the most glorious that can be conceived; but there is a materialism to which I am bound which unites me with clay, not with pearls & gold but with dust & earth & mud. Then let me be humble

<u>Its foundation.</u> It rests on earth the bread which I borrow my existence from its surface. If bread supplies fail me I die. My heavenly dependance is on a firm rock: but all my earthly hopes & dependences are based on dust. I am mutable, changing, frail

<u>Its frailty.</u> I am crushed before the moth. & tiny insect may cause my death. or sooner than a moth, or like one may I be crushed or like one, as easily as I put it between my fingers can I be taken out of this life — let me then forego all pride.

My friends here are the three great inducements to humility. Let us allow them their proper weight. Let great thoughts of God give us low thoughts of ourselves. Let us seek to lie low at the feet of mercy. Humility exalts Christ & exalts us. Humility has all the promises, pride has none. Henceforth bend thy knee in reverence more profound & tremble lest thou a worm should even seem to usurp divinity. or justify thyself in his sight. Let the publican's prayer be ours ever & may we rejoice to feel ourselves less than the least of all saints.

— Father aid me by thy Spirit through the Son's merit

Luke XII. 31. 32. Little flock.   361

Right well has it been said that like
the stars on high & the sun & moon, the
words of God were written for all time
& not for our forefathers only. And as
we find the same light suits us, so
will the same promises if we are in
the same condition. I have taken
two verses that there may be something
for all —

The first verse has in it

I. Good advice.
II. Good promise.

I Good advice. Such as a mother
would give her son on leaving his home.
Some things we may not seek at all.
Some things we may seek in measure
one thing we should seek chiefly.

First. that is earliest
First. that is chiefly.
In taking a situation, in removing,
in settling, in emigrating, in all
seek first the Kingdom of God.
Seek it, to be a member of it.
Seek it, to spread its dominions
May the God who sought you, set
you seeking his Kingdom more & more.

362. Num. XVII. 8 Aaron's rod.

On so important a matter as the priesthood Moses is commanded to make an appeal to God — this by no means sanctions the use of lots, ordeals, pricking for text &c — for none of these are commanded nor are they for such important ends.

There are some things so deceptive & beyond our Knowledge that we often wish we could make an appeal to God & receive a verbal answer: this is however a foolish wish for the mode God told the Israelites of we may use as well as they. that is see what rod doth blossom.

T. Let us test various religions.

There are such a number that if we stand to analize & examine we shall be dead ere we decide. here however is an easy mode of decision. Which of them produces good fruit. Infidelity see its harvest reaped in the Reign of Terror. Boodhism. Brahmanism &c — produce cruelty, murder, infanticide, depradation, Catholicism with lust in priest & vice in people. Look at Mormonism.

But it is Protestantism, true & real not spurious like Puseyism, which bringeth forth fruit. Turn your eye to England, Scotland. America Australia & see there the liberty & holiness

363   Lev. VI. 13   Perpetual fire.

The fire (By the Rev. C. H. Spurgeon) *shall ever be burning upon the altar: it shall never go out.*

Altars are the first religious structures we read of. The date the origin in the most remote antiquity. It is probable that Cain & Abel offered their oblations upon altars. The first distinct mention of an altar is in Gen 8.20 where it is recorded that Noah builded an altar unto the Lord. — All along through the patriarchal period continual notice is taken of altars. Abraham never halted in his wanderings without building an altar. Doubtless Isaac of whom we know little, did the same & on several occasions Jacob anointed stones, set up pillars & erected altars.

When the Mosaic period arrived & a more complete revelation of the true God was given, in order that the unity of the people might be ensured a place was selected where all sacrifices should be usually offered viz - the tabernacle, the altars of the Lord of Hosts.

Amongst other altars in the sanctuary was one which was called the

II   Let us test characters.

All men in Great Britain call themselves Christians but they are not all so, some are dead & dry enough.

1. We cast out all persons obnoxious to civil law.
2. All dishonest, defrauding men.
3. All loose, lascivious characters.
4. All who swear profanely.
5. All who profane the Sabbath.
6. All neglect the Bible.
7. All prayerless persons.
8. All lovers of this world, covetous &c.
9. All who will not forgive.
10. All high doctrine & no practise men.
11. All self righteous persons.

One alone remains, the true, living soul

III.   Let us test ministers

All men are not called to this work. How can we tell whether they are or no.

1. They bud — they have talents, they preach true doctrine, they have acceptance.
2. They blossom - congregation affected. Some tears, some zeal, more prayer, many inquirers, hopeful signs
3. They bear fruit, Souls are saved. Some few at least turn to God with full purpose of heart ...

Ah how I long to bear fruit.

God grant it by Xt Jesus

Amen

altar of incense which it is said was
originally kindled by fire from heaven
& was never suffered to die out until
the Babylonian Captivity & perhaps not
even then. This was the fire which
was used for burning all the sacrifices
although no blood ever stained the
altar itself save on the day of atonement.
It was an incense altar not a sacrificial
one. All other fire saving this was
"strange fire" & Nadab & Abihu felt the
penalty for using it. This fire burned
both night & day.

Vestiges of this are found in the
mythology of the heathen. The Persian
fireworshippers. The sacred fires of
Brahma & especially the fire of
Vesta so carefully tended by the
Vestal Virgins. But our concern
is not with heathenish ceremonies but
with ourselves & the spiritual meaning
of the text. — It is certain that
literally it is nothing to us. we rear
no altars. We cannot go back to
types & shadows when substance is
in our possession. We cannot talk
as the Papists or Anglicans — we know
nothing of material altars — above all

we cannot recognize the phrase "altar
of Hymen". It is downright heathenism.
Altars were never used for marriages.
Nor for the Lord's Supper. Let Puseyites
talk so foolishly but we who are
Christians know the truth & believe
that Jesus is the only altar & sacrifice
too. However figuratively we may
use the expression & apply the verse

I. To the altar of Heaven.
II. To the altar of the Sanctuary.
III. To the altar of the Family
IV. To the altar of the Closet.
V. To the altar of the Heart.

I. The Altar in Heaven.
Our Great High Priest is ever before
the throne offering the precious incense
of his prevailing prayers. He will
never suffer the fire to be extinguished.
His Love will never fail. — It was
not quenched by all the miseries, scorn
& trials he endured. It has not been
destroyed by the backslidings & ingratitude
of his children, & it shall never be
quenched by height or depth or any other creature

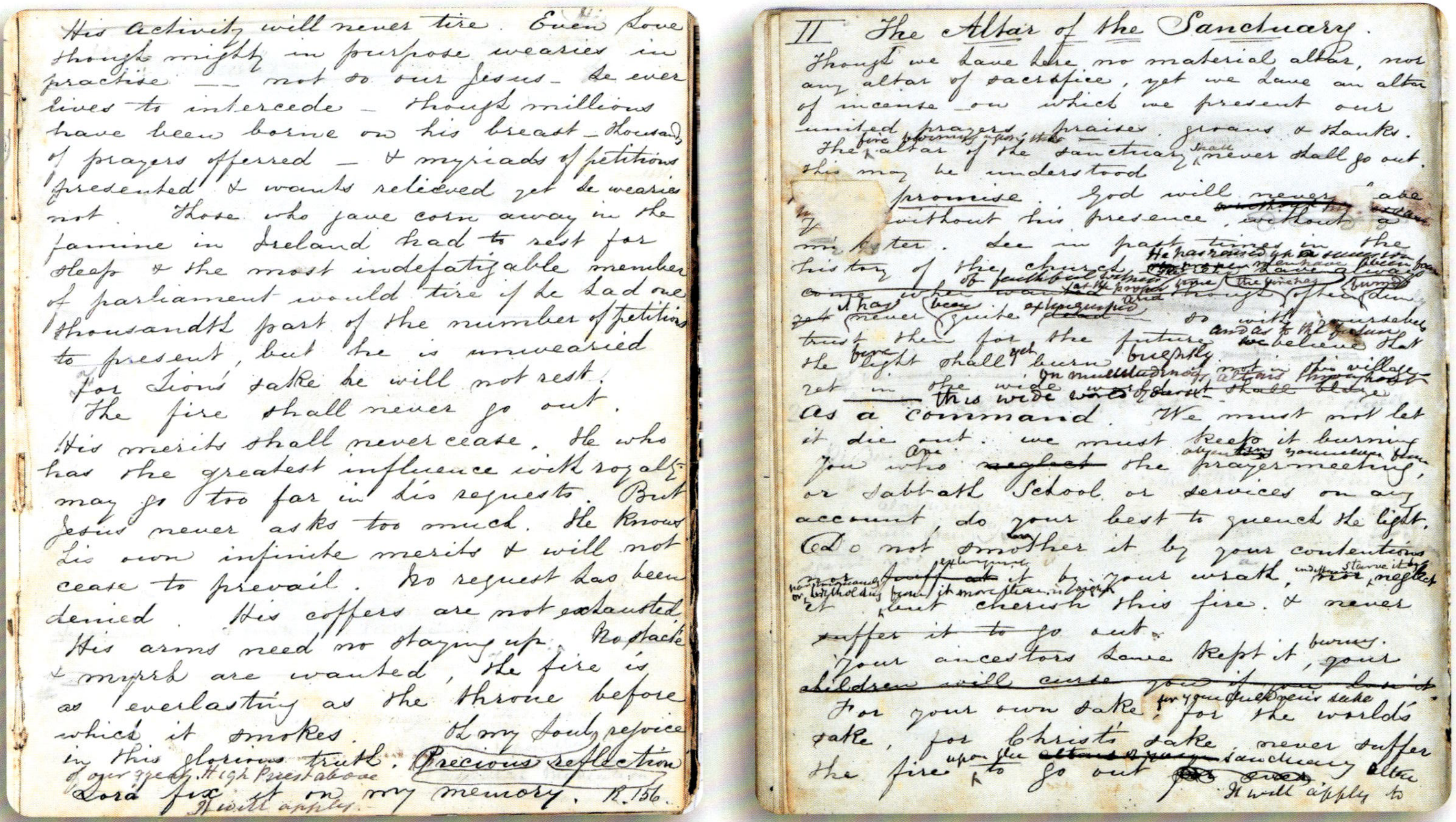

His activity will never tire. Even love
though mighty in purpose wearies in
practise — not so our Jesus— he ever
lives to intercede — though millions
have been borne on his breast—thousands
of prayers offered — & myriads of petitions
presented & wants relieved yet he wearies
not. Those who gave corn away in the
famine in Ireland had to rest for
sleep & the most indefatigable member
of parliament would tire if he had one
thousandth part of the number of petitions
to present, but he is unwearied
for Zion's sake he will not rest.
The fire shall never go out.
His merits shall never cease. He who
has the greatest influence with royalty
may go too far in his requests. But
Jesus never asks too much. He knows
his own infinite merits & will not
cease to prevail. No request has been
denied. His coffers are not exhausted.
His arms need no staying up. No stacte
& myrrh are wanted, the fire is
as everlasting as the throne before
which it smokes. O my soul rejoice
in this glorious truth. Precious reflection
of our great High Priest above
Lord fix it on my memory. R.156.
It will apply

II The Altar of the Sanctuary.
Though we have here no material altar, nor
any altar of sacrifice, yet we have an altar
of incense on which we present our
united prayers, praises, groans & thanks.
The fire burning upon the altar of the sanctuary shall never go out.
This may be understood
promise. God will never leave
without his presence, without a
minister. See in past times in the
history of the church. He has raised up a succession of faithful witnesses ... the fire has never quite expired. So with ourselves
and as to the future we believe that
the pure light shall yet burn brightly not in this village
yet in the wide world — in multitudes of altars throughout this wide world.
As a command. We must not let
it die out. We must keep it burning.
You who neglect the prayer-meeting,
or Sabbath School or services on any
account, do your best to quench the light.
Do not smother it by your contentions
nor extinguish it by your wrath, nor starve it by neglect
or withholding from it more than is right.
cherish this fire & never
suffer it to go out.
Your ancestors have kept it burning, your
children will curse you if you do not.
For your own sake, for your children's sake, for the world's
sake, for Christ's sake, never suffer
the fire upon the sanctuary altar to go out.
It will apply to

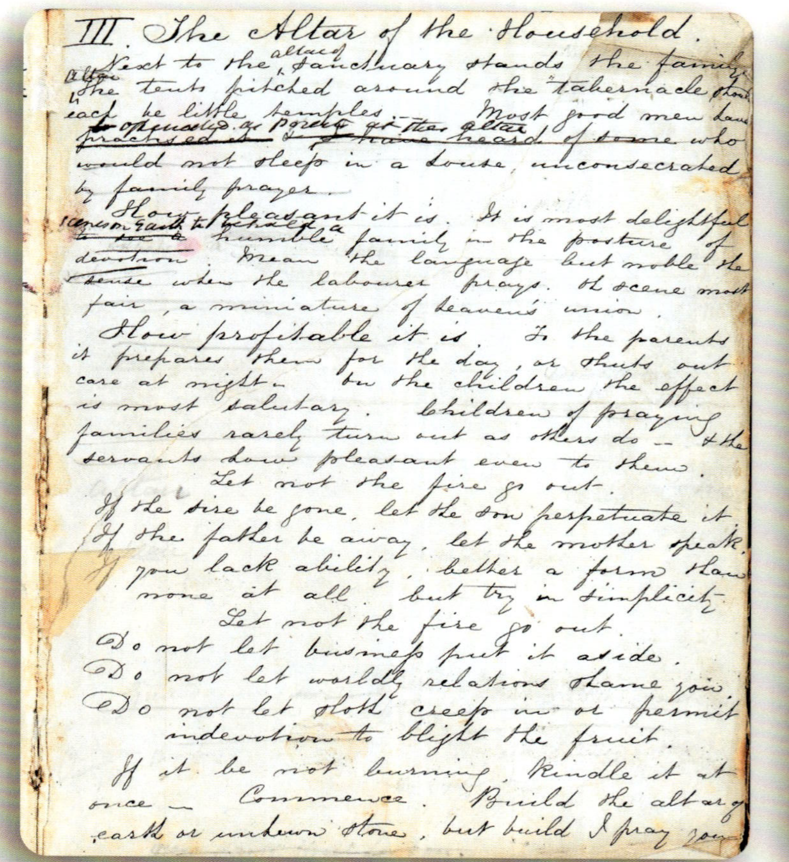

III. The Altar of the Household.

Next to the Sanctuary stands the family
the tents pitched around the tabernacle should
each be little temples. — Most good men have
practised it ... heard of ... who
would not sleep in a house, unconsecrated
by family prayer.

How pleasant it is. It is most delightful
... humble family in the posture of
devotion. Mean the language but noble the
sense when the labourer prays. A scene most
fair, a miniature of heaven's union.

How profitable it is. To the parents
it prepares them for the day, or shuts out
care at night. On the children the effect
is most salutary. Children of praying
families rarely turn out as others do — & the
servants how pleasant even to them.

Let not the fire go out.
If the sire be gone, let the son perpetuate it
If the father be away, let the mother speak.
If you lack ability, better a form than
none at all but try in simplicity—

Let not the fire go out.
Do not let business put it aside.
Do not let worldly relations shame you.
Do not let sloth creep in or permit
indevotion to blight the fruit.

If it be not burning, kindle it at
once — Commence. Build the altar of
earth or unhewn stone, but build I pray you

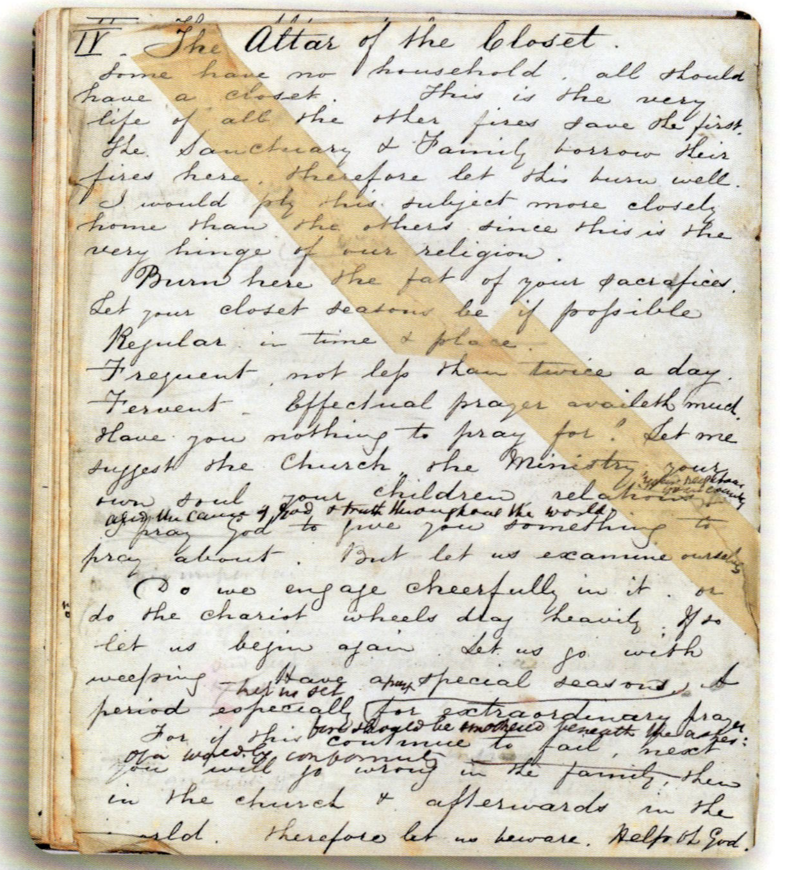

IV. The Altar of the Closet.

Some have no household, all should
have a closet. This is the very
life of all the other fires save the first.
The Sanctuary & Family borrow their
fires here, therefore let this burn well.
I would ply this subject more closely
home than the others since this is the
very hinge of our religion.

Burn here the fat of your sacrifices.
Let your closet seasons be if possible
Regular in time & place.
Frequent, not less than twice a day.
Fervent — Effectual prayer availeth much.
Have you nothing to pray for? Let me
suggest the Church, the Ministry, your
own soul, your children, relations ...
... pray God to give you something to
pray about. But let us examine ourselves.

Do we engage cheerfully in it, or
do the chariot wheels drag heavily. If so
let us begin again. Let us go with
weeping ... Have ... special seasons. A
period especially for extraordinary prayer.
For if this ... continue to fail, next
you will go wrong in the family, then
in the church & afterwards in the
world. therefore let us beware. Help O God.

364 Gal VI. 14. Glorying alone in Christ

The Minister who hopes to go through
the world without trial will be mista[ken]
If he hopes to see a perfect Church
he will be disappointed for even Paul
had his trials of false brethren.
Surely this must be to a gospel minister
the sharpest trial of all — to see his
labours marred by false teaching —
Paul we see yields not. He was no
craven. but he manfully resists them
& how? Solely by the cross.

I. A Solemn Reprobation.
II. A Bold Confession
III. A Sincere Assurance

I. A Solemn Reprobation.
The Apostle rejects & reprobates every
kind of glorying save one
The phrase "God forbid" may be underst[ood]
either as a strong asseveration or a
hearty prayer — Instances of first —
need of second. Paul rejects boasting
1. In his dignity — as apostle — we must
not boast of our talents or station
2. In popularity — what is it.
3. In his usefulness.

V The Altar of the Heart.
This is a golden altar indeed — The others
are emptiness without this. Vile & deceitful
as our hearts are, God loves to have them.
Let us give God our heart & never let the
fire go out —
It will not burn if the Lord does not keep
it burning for it is against its nature.
Many foes will attempt to extinguish
it, but if the oil behind the wall be
put on it will blaze higher & higher.
But let us see to it that it is supplied.
Put plenty of texts of Scripture on for they
are live coals, put sermons on, put
prayers on, put above all faith in the Spirit
How many neglect this altar, a
vain shew is all — no heart work. How
is it religion is a task — not a privilege
but a dull monotonous round.
'Tis because men are not real Christians
mere professors & not really regenerate.
Come let us trust in Jesus one
great altar, but at the same time
see after all these other altars
of burnt sacrifice.
  Lord assist me.
   Amen.

We must not glory

4. In our denomination — its ministers, members — doctors, converts or increase
5. In our peculiarities, our orthodoxy & sound straight-lacedness.
6. In our experience & age.
7. In our vigour, wealth, knowledge
   Let us cast them away as boastings

II. A Bold Confession.

He says he did glory in one thing & that was what his enemies despised — viz — the cross of Christ — by this he means the glorious work of the Redeemer in our salvation — in this he did right to glory. David & Isaiah did.
The Cross is the marrow of Theology.
He gloried —

1. In the love displayed on the cross.
2. In the wisdom in the atonement.
3. In the security of the work.
4. In the completeness of the work.
5. In the results of the cross.
6. In the triumphs of the cross
7. In the glory God receives from it
   I might enlarge but pray the good Spirit to enlarge it in your hearts.

III. A Sincere Assurance.

No Assurance like experimental assurance — Paul had this — he speaks of a double crucifixion.
1. A crucified world. —
   + world rendered powerless to resist.
   + world rendered ghastly & unlovely.
   + world rendered to him a dying thing.
2. A crucified self. —
   Self abhorred by the world.
   Self unable to join its evil pursuits.
   Self soon to be dead to it.
Here is the real reason why he could not glory in anything save Jesus. for on the one hand the world was made unworthy of his love & he was placed in such a position as not to be able to love it & now brethren.
Here is
+ Joy we may glory in Jesus.
+ Test, are we crucified
+ Prayer — God forbid &c.

Help oh King
Amen —

Matt. I. 21. Jesus saves from sin. 365

As this was my first text in Waterbeach & by the help of God it shall be the one with which I would close my stated ministry among you — in order that Jesus may be Alpha & Omega with us.

I. Let us speak of glorious name.
II. Of the wondrous salvation.
III. Of the blessed people.

I. The Glorious Name.

Jesus or Joshua "the Saviour"

Two had borne this name before.

Joshua the son of Nun & Joshua the son of Jozadak. who were both types of Christ

Joshua the son of Nun
Fought for Israel & overcame
He led them through Jordan
He divided their inheritance

Joshua the son of Jozadak
He restored the priesthood.
He rebuilt the temple

but how much greater is Joshua, or Jesus the son of God — all these did & more he has done in his glorious day of salvation.

II. The Wondrous Salvation.

The Salvation Jesus wrought is totally different from all others — for it is Salvation from sin.

1. From the result of sin — Anger of God— —death — hell — loss of heaven. Pardon

2. From the guilt & charge of sin so that we become innocent in the sight of God, yea & meritorious through the righteousness of Jesus. Justification.

This is instantaneous, perfect, unalterable & brings with it all the rights which by nature only belong to perfection

3. From the very being of sin

There is original depravity, & acquired habit but these he plucketh out — & puts.

A new nature, holy desire & holy acts this is a gradually progressive work.

Now these three must go together they God will not justify an unpardoned or unsanctified sinner at last.

Oh how glorious is this salvation My soul muse thereon often.

365 Matt. I. 21. Jesus the Saviour from Sin.

The Laying of the first stone of a public building is usually looked upon as an interesting if not important occasion. Such is the laying of the first stone in my ministry with you at Park Street.

I may not be able to lay it with a silver trowel or in a masterly manner but at any rate it shall have a good name engraven on it —

I do not promise that this name shall be my loving theme as long as I am among you, but I hope it may & I beseech the good Spirit to keep me ever from forgetting that Christ is the gospel, & that preaching the gospel is preaching Christ.

He ought to be Alpha & Omega & now that he may be so let us make him the theme of our first subject.

Surely it will be a useful one

I. The Name
II. The Purpose
III. The People.

III The Blessed People —
not known at first but mingled with the dust — some of all countries, ranks, & characters — who shall be brought in. The marks are —
1. A sincere desire after heaven.
2. A devout seeking of God.
3. Diligent labour for it.
4. Great abhorrence of sin.
5. Sense of our own nothingness.
6. Humble reliance on Jesus.

& now my Father make thy servant mighty at last to wrestle with sinners Come oh Father to mine assistance by the ever blessed Spirit
Amen
for J C s sake

I. The Name. "Jesus"

A large volume or even library of volumes might be written on the famous titles of Christ — whether it be, the Seed of the woman, Shiloh, Angel, Prophet, Melchizedek. Redeemer, Holy one, &c &c

but among them all there is none more sweet than this — Jesus. —

Here we see it given at the annunciation

Again at the birth in the manger — To the Shepherds, the blind men; nailed over his head, Ascension. —

This is therefore the sweetest of all It means a Saviour. —

It had been borne by two persons before each of whom were types of him — The first was Jesus or Joshua the son of Nun who was a glorious type of Jesus the son of God.

1. He fought the enemies of Israel He routed Amalek. He drove out the Canaanite. None could stand before him. So will Jesus fight our foes until they all be destroyed & make sun & moon fight for us Should the time be too short he will prolong the day — but this will not be for he will finish his work

2. He led them through the Jordan. Although at the time of harvest the river was high yet it divided & a dry passage was left for the people. So will it be when we pass the spiritual Jordan, all will be still until all are over.

3. He divided the inheritance. So has Jesus prepared our mansions & allotted to each his future portion

The Second is Joshua the son of Jozadak of whom little can be said as a type — in fact he is rarely mentioned as such & as I find not the footstep of another I would tread the ground with caution

1. For he builded the altar, restored the sacrifice & continually offered.

2. He rebuilt the temple. but these are dim candles when compared with the splendour of Jesus the son of God.

This is a name of condescension, love, sweetness, & every thing pleasant Let us sound it — it is like the music of the upper skies — ah it is that music for they have none other name to sing of there.

II. The Purpose.

The Great design of incarnation is Salvation from sin. Sin like a tyrant had usurped dominion over the world & no one could dethrone the monster. He would not resign & no one had will or skill to dash him from his pedestal. but Jesus died & did it. He does it in three ways.

1. He saves from the punishment of sin. We were all condemned but he was condemned for us & endured the death. For us now there is no wrath of God, no angry glance, no second death, no fiery hell. The dungeons are broken open, the fetters are cast to the winds. None but Jesus could do this. Pardon is his exclusive gift. For he alone could satisfy Justice or as prince sign the charter of forgiveness.

2. He saves from the guilt of sin. This is a godlike act — to remit the penalty is great but to justify the offender, to make him innocent, nay even worthy is a wonder of grace but so it is — Jesus righteousness is ours & we stand in the same position as unfallen ones, yea, even higher.

3. He saves from the power of sin. This is a part of the salvation which some do not like — but it is true for it is from sin not in sin. Jesus drives out our sins by degrees Conversion begins a work which goes on in Sanctification & ends in Perfection in Glory. The two first are momentary instantaneous & complete works — this is gradual & progressive. What a work it is. It is the reversing of nature making rivers run uphill & lions lie down with lambs. But how often it has been done.

III. The People

Who are they? Not all the world for Christ does not save all. Not the Jews — they perish still. But his people — His with emphasis, By choice, gift, purchase, & power. His people. How can we tell them there are marks & evidences. I will give you 7 marks & to help your memory they shall all begin with C.

Conviction — Confession — Conversion — consecration
— conflict — consolation
But best of all confidence in Jesus.
These are the people chosen & called.
Let us be sure that we be among them
And now in summing up I have given you.
1. Heavenly music in the name.
2. Heavenly intentions in the purpose.
3. Heavenly choice in the people.
or Music — song — & songsters.
Jesus — salvation — his people
Help me oh God & King.

366   Ps. CXIX. 18 Open thou mine eyes.
Here is a prayer extremely suitable
to you & me at the commencement of
the present services.   I would use
it myself & request you to put it up on
my account & your own.
We shall examine.
I. The Doctrine of the Prayer.
II. The Spirit of the Prayer.
we will speak of the answer
III The Result of the Prayer.

I. The Doctrine of the Prayer.
The doctrine of a man's prayer is often
better than the doctrine of his sermon
The heart knows more than the head.
1. The Doctrine of the imperfection of
    our nature.
2. The Doctrine of the necessity of
supernatural assistance for the
    attainment of divine knowledge.
These the psalmist must have
believed or his prayer is nonsense

II. The Spirit of the Prayer.
1. Intense longing after sacred Knowledge.
2. Firm conviction that in the Bible alone
    could it be found
3. Deep Humility & sense of weakness.
4. Perfect Reliance on Divine teaching
Oh that this spirit would more thoroughly
permeate my breast.
III The Result of the Prayer.
1. Clear Knowledge.
2. Steadfast Knowledge.
3. Encreased Knowledge
4. Knowledge causing surprise and
astonishment.
    The Lord be praised for help
afforded in preaching this sermon.

367.   Ezek. 3.17.18.19.   The minister.
The office of a gospel minister in some
respects resembles that of the ancient
prophets. Though we cannot like
him of Horeb raise the dead; nor like
Isaiah pour forth eloquent predictions
or as Ezekiel foretel certain coming
& immediate judgments yet like them
we are commanded to teach, to warn,
& to encourage. So much are we
alike that the commission of Ezekiel
will suit any gospel minister even
of our day.
I. The Minister's Commission
II. The Minister's responsibility.
III. The Minister's comfort.

I. The Minister's Commission.
Here is a scrap of ancient writing
worthy of a place in the museum.
It ought to be in every minister's study
It is the ultimatum of the King of
Heaven, to us in our doubts as to our
calling. It is our Emperors protocol to
all his legions ..   It is the
true ordination. a virtual instalment
worth as much as a thousand bulls
from Rome with the mark of the

fisherman's ring — yea worth all the graces of universities or appointments of Archbishops. Let us regard.

1. The wording of this ancient commission.
2. The office given thereby.

1. The wording of this ancient commission. It is of course worded in the court style of Heaven & each letter is divine. Son of Man. Here is the title with which Ezekiel is addressed — not Right Reverend or the Very Venerable — but a humbling, graciously humbling title. "Son of Man". Daniel is once so called but Ezekiel 90 times. This the the name Jesus called himself by, when on earth and therefore a glorious one. The Gracious & all-wise Father saw that so lofty an eminence might tempt Ezekiel to pride. He therefore styles him Son of Man. As much as to say. Your visions, rank, talents & office must not exalt you for you are man You must not lean on self for you are weakness being only the Son of man. You must sympathize with your fellow creatures & deal with them not as a prince, a master but as being like them a Son of Man.

"I have made thee a watchman" Here we read on this ancient manuscript a true account of the making of a minister. God alone can do it. Two things are absolutely requisite to make a man a preacher viz. 1 Special gifts — such as perception of truth, simplicity, aptness to impart, some degree of eloquence & earnestness. 2. Special call. Let every man be moved thereto of the Holy Ghost. He must feel an irresistible desire to utter his soul in his masters cause. No college, no Bishop, no ordination can make a man a minister & he who can feel as Bunyan, Whitfield, Berridge or Hill the strugglings of an earnest heart may hear in the air the voice Son of Man I have made thee a watchman "into the house of Israel" Here was a limited commission but ours is not, it is enlarged. The world is our parish. We are not ordered to cast the net alone in the pools of Heshbon, or the streams of Jordan or the lake of Gennesaret but we via cover all seas & rivers with the fishing boats, the navy of Jesus. Yet still it is for Israel's sake we go.

"therefore hear the word at my mouth" The
ancient seers spoke not at random but
spoke what they knew - being taught of
God - Sometimes in dreams they heard
heaven's message. Sometimes a voice from
on High but most commonly by vision.
The soul seems to leave the body & that
narrow tube of vision called eyesight - & to
see with its own eagle power - to pierce
the thick cloud, to mount into the region
of the tempest & find a home in the
absolute remote which eye cannot see.
Thus did they hear, but now we
have the written word only & this we
must devoutly read. It becomes a
minister diligently to search & study
the blessed Scriptures - with all the
assistance he can gain from holy men
who have gone before but chiefly from
the most Excellent of all Instructors, the
true Interpreter, the Holy Ghost.
"and give them warning from me."
There are other parts of our duty but as this
is the most arduous it is mentioned.
Give the Christian warning if he is
found backsliding, or indulging in carnality
Give the Sinner warning of the
demerit of his sin, of the strict justice
of God & of the fearful hell in which
the ungodly shall suffer. -

2. The Great office conferred by it.
It is that of Watchman! - Every
Soldier of the Cross is bound to watch
but the minister in a double sense.
He is so called because.
1. The ministry requires great vigilance
We cannot afford to sleep. we must
take heed to false doctrine, false brethren
help thee poor benighted ones & give
alarm of any dangers around
He is to sit like the shepherd in the
wilderness by night - like the untiring
eagle - like the whisper-hearing sentinel.
2. The ministry involves trouble.
few think of the watchman who tramps
by their door. Hark there is a scuffle
a fight who is in it - the watchman.
How the wind blows. the snow is
surely a foot deep - Pray put list on
the doors & stir the fire. Surely no
one is out there to night - except
the watchman! His bare face
meets the driving sleets his fingers are
numbed. his eyelids frozen. well
well never mind thats his work. he
is used to it — So you come &
sit & smile & enjoy the sermon but
there are some who criticise & find

fault & slander & calumniate it — well
the minister must bear it. Ah he's
the watchman & need be a very tough
veteran who has swallowed many
nor-westers or I know not where he
will be in the midst of this rabble.

3. The ministry should be arousing.
If there be a fire or a thief, or a
door or shutter unfastened he must
not spare but cry aloud. We must
cry aloud with all our might — not being
afraid to disturb or alarm or hurt the
feelings of the sleepers. We may as
well be asleep as be mumblers, or
speak in such a way that none can
really make out what we mean.
Plain, blunt, honest truth.
Here then is the commission which
every man who labours in word &
doctrine should ponder over, wear
next his heart & on his brow.
It is to be feared that many
are not alive to a sense of their
real position, but having the
next presentation to a living or
having purchased a benefice. They
carelessly rush in where angels if
like them uncalled would fear to venture

II. The Minister's Responsibility.
If the sentinel by sleep causes the death
of a single person he is a murderer.
The watchman holds a responsible
office — If the prisoner escapes it
shall be required at his hands.
So in the congregation & church.
If the ungodly man is not warned
he shall bear his own guilt but
my unfaithfulness will lie as a crimson
If the professing Christian falls, his
fall is his own but if I have not
warned him I am guilty also
If I do not utter the whole truth
both of the threatenings, promises,
and invitations of God — I shall
be a sleeping sentinel, a careless
captain, a negligent railway guard.
and I shall be the slaughterer
of my fellow-creatures.
or if to the professor I give wine
instead of medicine, a plaister
instead of a lancet or a stone
for bread. I shall be a guilty
wretch & God help me then for
nothing more requires help.

III. The Ministers Comfort.
1. The Lord's call to the office. "I have &c"
2. The Promises peculiar to that call for every call hath its strength to perf[orm] it enclosed.
3. The blessed brow-hardening Spirit who makes us despise the fear or smile of man & thus keeps us from unfaithfulness
4. The Fact that Success is not required of us, but faithfulness.

Now let us make some use of it.
1. Let us not think slightingly of preaching or hearing for they are solemn.
2. Let the prayers of the saints rise up for their ministry.
3. Sinners if you perish under a gospel ministry your blood be on your own heads.

Oh my Father set me free
Amen

368   Matt VII. 32.33.34.35. Deaf cured

No Book has been more honoured of God than the Pilgrim's Progress — & one reason is because it states plainly the road from the City of Destruction to Mount Zion. Now I believe that descriptions of the road are more useful than furious declamations urging us to run it. So do I think that God does often bless descriptions of the mode of sovereign grace in a sinners cure to conversion as much or more than the most fiery exhortations. I think the case of this man will form an excellent outline of the usual mode adopted in the case of sinners, spiritually diseased.

I. The Man's disease a type of ours
II. Christ's operations a type of the same
III. The Man's cure a type of ours. spiritually

Good Spirit of all Grace be pleased to make my Sermon the means of spiritual cure to many of thine elect but yet diseased ones.

Come Holy & Ever Active Spirit exert thine omnipotence

I. This man's diseased a picture of us.

He was deaf — He could not hear the voice of his friend, the whisper of his wife or the prattle of his children. For him the streets had no music, the groves no warblings, the sea no murmur, the heavens no thunders, the winds no sighings. Poor Man.

See the spiritually deaf. For him there is no thunder in Sinai, in vain the shrill blast of the trumpet, or the terrible voice of the Eternal. Myriads of souls are shrieking in hell "hollow groans, sullen moans & cries of tortured ghosts" come upward startling the convinced one but this deaf man hears not. Then comes the music of the cross, the still small voice of Calvary, the melodious invitation of Jesus & mingled therewith the harping harmonies of heaven — but all in vain. Let the most charming hymns be sung to most melodious notes, let all the church below join in the chorus, yea let the very Heavens with the cherubim & perfect ones resound the chant — yet he hears not. Ah though it be his sin yet who can refuse to say Poor Man.

"He had an impediment in his speech"

When he attempted to tell a tale of woe he faltered & blushingly hid his head. He could not vocally join in the solemn prayer or swell the sacred song. He could hold little or no communication with his fellow man.

So with the spiritually dumb, the tongue is there & so was the ear, no new organ is wanted but vitality & power put into the old. The man talks lustily enough in his shop or on change but he knows nothing of the language of Canaan, he does not pray, he will not sing.

Give him a street song & he will go through it merrily but set him down to a solemn psalm and to be sure he has lost his tongue.

Some can talk of religion fast enough but they do not know the brogue of Canaan, if they speak the language it is in such a broken way that you can see they are foreigners, however much they may dissemble the fact.

Deaf & with faulty speech here are but two ills of thousands which we feel.

But though he could not hear or speak
His friends can & therefore they bring him
& on his behalf beseech Jesus to heal him
                    Do likewise

II. Christs mode of cure

1. He took him aside. Here is the first
act of sovereign mercy he is isolated
from the rest. So the Lord makes the
man to feel as if all preaching was
aimed at him! Each flash from
Sinai points at him, each thunder
seems to call for vengeance on him.
Every doctrine, threatening &c like
the waves of a sea seems to roar &
with ten thousand voices cry for him.
      No generalities now - all personalities.
He becomes now a lonely, desponding
being it may be. He is often alone
in his chamber & why? because
the Lord hath taken him from the crowd

2. He put his fingers in his ears.
Christ could have opened the man's
ears without this but in the present
case this was his plan. So many
have been suddenly brought to
know the truth without much
preliminary conviction — But in most
cases it is true that Christ puts
his fingers into the ears.

I was convinced of sin many times
before I was converted. & so have
many of you. Put had the fingers of Jesus
in your ears.

3. He spit. To show the man that
he must be healed in a humbling
way, he spit. Some might have
turned away & said "how disgusting".
Like Naaman. But so it is the
gospel is very humbling. to the pride
of life, to selfrighteousness & boasting.
Sinner he will humble you or
else you must be lost

4. He touched his tongue. He had
just touched the typanum of
his ear & now the tongue is touched.
The man essays to pray, but groans
& sighs are all he utters. Have not
you & I done the same. Tried
to pray & said I would but cannot pray.

5. Jesus looked up to heaven. The
man could not as yet hear but
this dumb language he could comprehend
From heaven all help comes. His
is a lesson we must learn.
All refuges of lies must be snatched
away.

6. Jesus sighed. To show the man his sympathy. his grief for the ills of man. Next to a knowledge of the absolute need we have of divine aid comes a sense that Jesus really has pity on us & when we believe that there comes.

7. Ephphatha. The word of might which does it all. This is as much the fiat of omnipotence as "Let there be light". Sweet Jesus speak the word & these deaf & dumb souls shall both hear & speak.
This is the Spirits' work.

III The Cure
His ears were opened. What sounds gushed into his ears. The Gates were open & in flowed a host of glories. The flood gates are burst & a stream of nectar finds entrance. Anecdote of a woman who recovered hearing.
What a change now in the man. The mountain & hills sing, yea the trees clap their hands. Earth seems one orchestra — how the words of warning counsel, love, rebuke & doctrine are heard distinctly & the sweet whisper of truth is now louder than the cataracts of eternal vengeance before

& so strong now is his hearing that oft time he is enchanted with celestial melodies floating over Jordans streams.
2. He spoke plainly. To speak at all is a wonder but to speak plainly when not a sound had for years entered his ears was a miracle indeed
To the converted man speaks plainly on the grand points of the Gospel. Choked as his utterance may be by tears & smothered in sighs, yet to God it is plain & to us it should be.

& now we have ended this poem of a cure. this Esculapian epic let us chant together a song of praise to the divine physician
He sitteth in heaven & glories still in his power to save. Do you long to praise him then trust him.

Lord give me words & unction
Amen Amen

Creation of Man   369

Amongst the wondrous things recorded in
the word of God is the account of the
pristine glory of man & his first origin.
The Creation of man is a subject which
men have speculated on & if we wish
to see a mass of profound nonsense we
must examine the various theories & answers
having relation to man's creation
We will not waste time by even glancing
at the absurd theories of philosophers
but come at once to the sublimely
laconic Mosaic account.
Here we find concerning man's creation
I A Special time chosen.
II A Special council held
III A Special model selected.

I. A Special time chosen.
The world had been redeemed from
its inert chaotic state by the brooding
wings of the sacred Dove. Light
had been thrown from Heaven on
the earth & darkness was divided
therefrom — the blue firmament had
been stretched on high — & the green
earth clad in its new robe sent up
on high the forest tree & waving palm.
The two bearers of light chased each
other over the blue ethereal, while the
stars looked sweetly on the as yet
silent world. — Then were the waves
divided by finny creatures & the air
was fanned by feather wings. & to
make all earth a dwelling place for living
creatures, the hills, & vallies teemed
with creeping things, & cattle & beasts.
Last of all the crowning labour forth
came "man" — for whose comfort
all these had been formed.
Now we say that the time selected
was a very appropriate one
I. It seems fitting that he best should
be the last work.
We find a gradual progression in God's
works of creation. from mere chaotic
matter to etherial substances such
as light, then to vegetable life & on
through the lower grades of animal
up to the highest degree of animal
existence — putting on the apex of
all the erect figure of man.
It would not have seemed congruous
that the loftiest creature should have

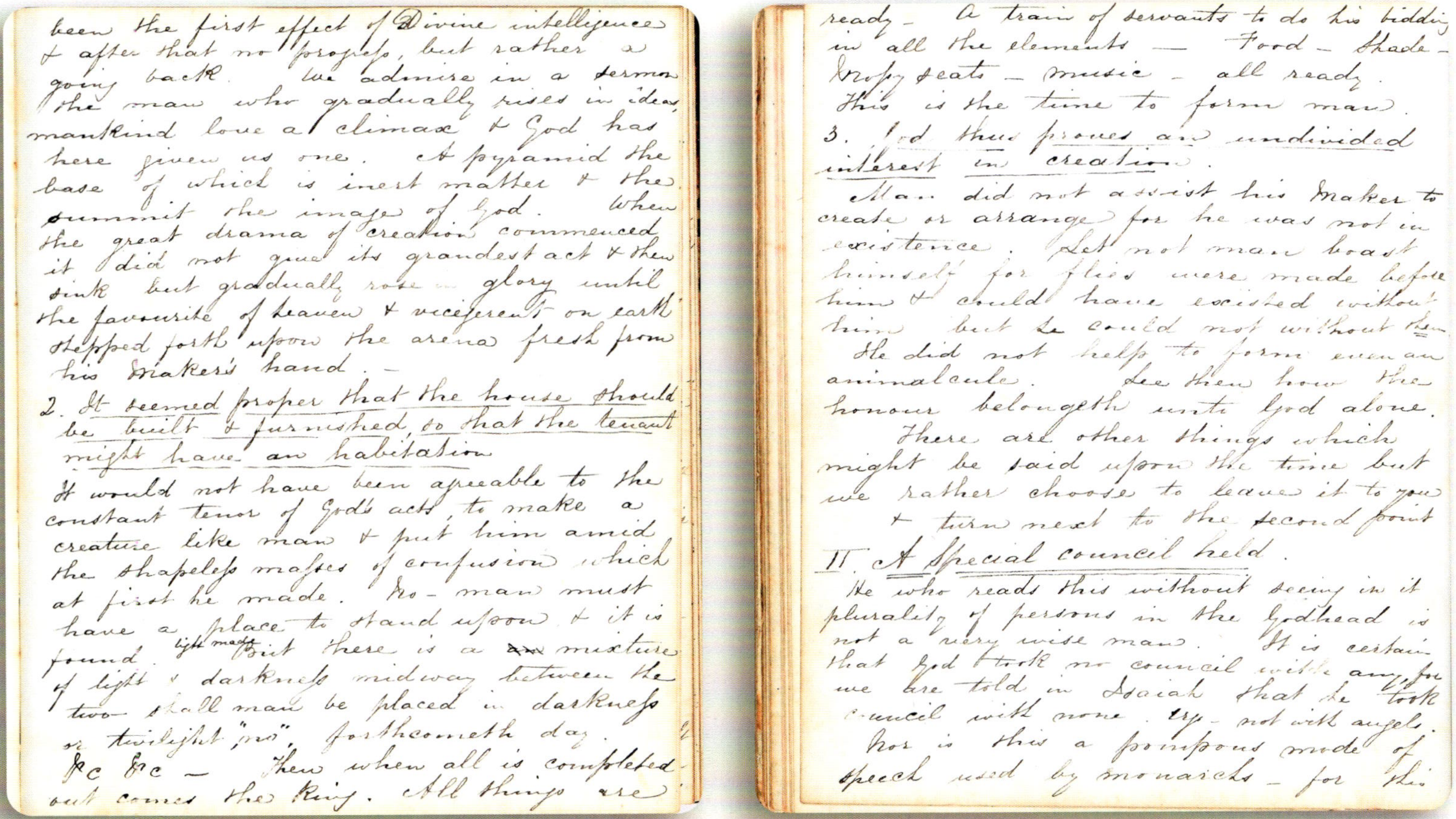

been the first effect of Divine intelligence
& after that no progress, but rather a
going back. We admire in a sermon
the man who gradually rises in ideas,
mankind love a climax & God has
here given us one. A pyramid the
base of which is inert matter & the
summit the image of God. When
the great drama of creation commenced
it did not give its grandest act & then
sink but gradually rose in glory until
the favourite of heaven & vicegerent on earth
stepped forth upon the arena fresh from
his Maker's hand. –
2. It seemed proper that the house should
be built & furnished, so that the tenant
might have an habitation
It would not have been agreeable to the
constant tenor of God's acts, to make a
creature like man & put him amid
the shapeless masses of confusion which
at first he made. No – man must
have a place to stand upon & it is
found. light made But there is a ~~an~~ mixture
of light & darkness midway between the
two shall man be placed in darkness
or twilight, "no", forthcometh day.
&c &c – Then when all is completed
out comes the King. All things are

ready – A train of servants to do his bidding
in all the elements – Food – Shade –
Mossy seats – music – all ready.
This is the time to form man.
3. God thus proves an undivided
interest in creation.
Man did not assist his Maker to
create or arrange for he was not in
existence. Let not man boast
himself for flies were made before
him & could have existed without
him but he could not without them
He did not help to form even an
animalcule. See then how the
honour belongeth unto God alone.
There are other things which
might be said upon the time but
we rather choose to leave it to you
& turn next to the second point
II. A Special council held.
He who reads this without seeing in it
plurality of persons in the Godhead is
not a very wise man. It is certain
that God took no council with any for
we are told in Isaiah that he took
council with none. Eg. – not with angels.
Nor is this a pompous mode of
speech used by monarchs – for this

vain habit was not introduced until the
end of old Testament Times. — See the pro-
-clamations of Darius & Nebuchadnezzar.

It doth therefore undoubtedly respect
the three persons of the Trinity who are
in council together. The Question then
arises why is this consultation? Certainly
not because there was a lack of wisdom
or skill, nor because the persons did not
know the will of one another — for God is
one & knows all things perfectly.

But the figure is used to give us 3 ideas
1. The Importance of the work. When sun
& moon & stars were formed there was
no consultation; but of man there was.

He is the pivot of the universe, a
microcosm a world in himself. The being
God loveth best of all creation. God does
not think slightly of man, let us not
think so little of ourselves as to stoop
to sin — nor of our brother as to despise
him. Man is a great existence for
God said "let us make man"

2. The wisdom displayed in the work
All creation singeth of wisdom but
man is leader of the band. Since
the body of man is the dwelling of the
Son — It was meet that it should
have much wisdom expended on it
and shall we ever know a tythe

of the mystery of man.
3. The unanimity of the Godhead in it.
There is a tendency to think too little
of one in comparison with the others.
But they are one, & equal. In Salvat—
So this too. Let us make man

III. A Special Model selected.
Of nothing else, not of angels nor of the
heavens is this said but of man &
man only —

Man was made in God's image not in
the image of an inferior or even superior
creature — Let us enquire wherein
this image consists. —

1. It may consist partly in the majesty
& dignity which man possessed, making
him the lord of all creatures. There
may have been a lustre on his
face like that on Moses & doubtless
he had a royalty now lost.

2. It may consist also in his being
a really intelligent creature, a spirit
an intellect like Deity.

3. It may also comprise that
immortality which was the lot
of Adam for he could not die.
His body though capable of death
was preserved therefrom perhaps
by eating the fruit of the tree

of life – but at any rate he could not die.
But I rather prefer to follow
the ancient words of our ancestors
who wrote it as an article of their
creed that God created man in his
own image in knowledge, righteousness
& true holiness.

In Knowledge Though he could not
attain to such knowledge as his Creator
possessed yet he knew more than we
do, or at least he knew more certainly.
His powers were not blunted. There
was no vitiation or obliquity in his
understanding for he was as a creature
perfect in this – How different the unregenerate
In righteousness. He was entirely free
from any inclination to evil. His will
was free to either good or evil but
it had not any bias as ours has. This
was justice in God
In holiness. He was not only righteous
in character but really holy in act.
In him was no sin. He was a sun
without spots.
Look on this passing picture & sigh
over it – but still rejoice for in Jesus
we gain more than Adam lost –
    Bless me the Lord.

370   John XIX. 33.   No bone broken.
Every circumstance in the life of Christ is
important.   Nothing is small which relates
to him. From the manger to the cross the
very stones in his path are diamonds.
His words are worthy of an angel audience.
His acts deserve an eternity of wondering
examination.   He is at a marriage &
marriage becomes a most honourable estate.
He takes a child in his hands, & a child
becomes a picture of a Christian. the words
"Suffer &c" an evergreen motto for Sunday Schools

But when he nears his end. his movements
become so full of interest that the very
angels look from the windows of heaven
to watch his footsteps.   Each hour
fulfils a prophecy, each day flashes forth
conviction that he is the true Messiah.
Judas betrays him, "he that eateth &c"
He holds his peace "like a sheep-dumb &c"
He is scourged " his stripes &c"
He goes without the camp "so did the deeper"
He is nailed "they pierce my hands &c
So on all through his hours of agony
but now he dies – & surely all is over
for he said "it is finished", but no
there remains one type. nay more than
one or two yet unfulfilled. His bones
must not be broken. for the bones of
the paschal lamb were all of them
to remain entire.   They are not broken

with devout wonder let us admire.
I. The Providence which preserved his bones.
II. The Purpose of this preservation.

I The Providence which preserved his bones.

Good Flavel used to say that "he who observes providences shall never want a providence to notice." Similar was the expression of good Mr Newton who said that God had ordered which of the two streets he should go to St Mary's by. Precisely to the same import are the lines of Watts.

"There's not a sparrow or a worm
"But's found in his decrees.

Now in this case we think we see very plainly, not the finger merely, but the very hand of God. He had ordained that the body of his son should not be broken as to its bones & his decree is fulfilled altho' there seemed many things to prevent it.

Pilate gave orders for the breaking of their legs &

1. The Severity of Roman discipline stands in the way: for Roman soldiers are wont to obey even to the jot & the titel. We know from what the centurion said, that the R soldiers obeyed at once "do this" & without any consideration or thought "he doeth it."

We read of Torquatus Manlius who was put to death his own son because he had fought a Gaul without permission. We think then that when the order was given the soldiers

would be likely to obey it at once, without question or debate. The command came from head quarters, it might mean that their legs should be broken if they were yet alive — but would soldiers think of this would they not be more likely blindly to obey. But God can turn the balance of probabilities & if he Pilate or Cæsar shall give an order contrary to his will he will countermand it.

2. The Ferocious character of Roman Soldiers.

War has a tendency to brutalize the mind, it cannot be thought that men familiar with blood will be the subjects of very tender emotions. War in ancient times was more savage than now & the Roman soldiers must have been barbarous from what we read of them in Scripture. The men who could murder the innocents at Bethlehem, imbrue their hands in the blood of Galileans engaged in sacrifice.

Buffet, scourge & spit on Jesus & then quietly sit down & raffle for his garments would not be likely to have much pity — but would rather after breaking with their iron bar the legs of the two wretches, take a savage delight in breaking the bones of one who called himself a God. But he who turneth rivers turned their fierce hearts. Lions once licked the feet of Daniel. Bears came out at the call of Elisha. & so shall men of cruel souls be turned by his power for the hearts of all are in his hands.

3. The Savage Clamour of the Jews.

When we consider that the Jews hated our Lord extremely, that they clamoured for his crucifixion, that they mocked him on the cross, were vexed that the title over his head should even seem to give respect to him & that they requested that the legs might be broken — it excites our wonder that they should suffer the soldiers to leave our Saviour.

They would have been pleased to see his body mutilated, they had been eating the passover & would have been wise enough to see the type if only mentioned, & would have been taking precaution to prevent his resurrection — but it did not enter into their minds. Perhaps they were just wending their way homeward so as to be at home on Sabbath which commenced that eventide. But so it was. they had gained a grant & then neglected to see the order fulfilled. Oh depth of providence

Wise men become fools & the subtle fallow. The learned Rabbi slumbereth, & the haughty Pharisee forgetteth when the Lord will it.

4. The Circumstance of passing by Jesus.

The Soldiers brake the legs of the first, perhaps the one who was penitent. His soul is so

filled with rapture at the sweet promise of Jesus, that when the cruel blow breaks his bones & the marrow & blood fly out, although a scream comes forth the melody of that blest sound sustains his heart. to day shalt thou be with me &c

Here was providence in the title over Jesus head for from it the thief learned the gospel & providence in the blow which ended his existence & landed him in heaven. Next they go to the miscreant on the other side & give his soul a swifter passage to the burning pit.

But why pass by Jesus — but now they come & a rough warrior lifts the iron bar — but see the man's head hangs down, the joints are motionless, he is dead — so they break not his legs, but at the same time manifest that it is not pity which restrains them for one of them drives a spear into his side.

How the Infinite God wrought this we cannot understand. but let us believe in his wondrous Providence.

Some will say "well I never noticed a providence there". Ah but you should do so. Learn to notice the hand of God in the histories of his

May the blessed illumination of the
Spirit shed a flood of light over the
second part of our subject.

II. The Purpose of this Preservation).
It does not seem probable that the great
providences of God should have been exercised
to preserve the body of Christ & the
evangelist John was inspired to note the circumstance
if there were nothing in it &

1.   It may be that the Holy Ghost thus
designed to draw our attention to the
Paschal lamb as a type of Christ.
In 1 Cor 5:7 we are told by Paul that the
Lord Jesus is our passover & this passage
seems to seem side by side with it as
a "speaking act" & we will not hint
at a few points of manifest resemblance.

{ this rite was instituted before the law either
moral or ceremonial had been given
& this seems to his gospel are a something
superior to the law over.

) the lamb without blemish roasted with fire,
eaten in haste, with bitter herbs &
is received with respect.
seems in suffering —

{ the lamb was the means of a double
deliverance — from Egyptian bondage &
divine vengeance.
So doth Jesus work for us a twofold
rescue from the double evils of our
souls. " & "

exted to them in the histories of life.
Look for Providence, for it is everywhere.
"for doubtless the sailing of a cloud hath a
"Providence for its Pilot. doubtless the root
"of an oak is marked for a special purpose,
"Fixed as the station of a wreath is as
"from the hand of & the wanderer stars
"as the stars in their courses.

Look for Providence & you will find comfort. The man who
believes in providence believes himself
to be as secure in a tempest as in a
calm, as safe, really in battle as in peace.
He sees a bright thought in every cloud
& believes them all to be "big with mercies"
& let me in having this past by of Providence

You to look at the littles of Providence
as well as at the great. We will not
that & Pestilence stalk through the
land, we say this is God's doing, it is
not also his doing when an apple caught
in a sudden & & an avalanche
rolls from its top. Ye. Ye tremble at the will
of Providence. Is not that will concerned
when the seas leaves fall from the poplar
&c &c. Luther. 124.

All things are under the superintendence
of the Most High & neither the littlest nor
the great are to be disregarded.

2. This showed that his death was vol-
-untary.

Jesus could not be forced to die. His first
descent from glory was of his own will. He
could save his life as he did on one or two
occasions. He made the men fall back.
He said he could have twelve legions of
angels. He told Pilate why he had power.
His strength was in him for he cried out
just before death with a loud voice.
So now he makes a reservation of his
bones to shew that he had power over his
life & body to take up or lay down. So
men do with estates. So God with Job & Satan.

Now let us admire the death of Jesus
from this point of view. See yon martyr,
he dies & cannot avoid it. But see this
man, a glance could slay his oppressors,
a word would lay the whole host breathless
at his feet or blast them into hell.
Let me love & sing & wonder.

3. This showed how well he bore
our sins.

No man knoweth how tremendous a
burden hung on the shoulders of our
Saviour at this most wondrous time.
If the whole earth had endeavoured
to sustain it they would have perished a
mangled heap of carcases. Should the
whole race of angels assay their strength

they too — would soon totter & fall.
But Jesus bore all & not a bone of
him was broken. Think of the sins
of a lost world, the sufferings the elect
would have suffered, the frown of his
Father, the agonies of his soul. Oh
'tis a burden sinner, 'tis a burden too
heavy for thee to bear, to carry thine
own sins, much more the sin of myriads.

Praise the Redeemer for his divine labour.

4. This showed the victory of Jesus
over Satan.

It had been foretold that the seed
of the serpent should have an
antagonist & in process of time the
seed of the woman entered the lists, at
first they fought in a wilderness &
there the Son of God was victor, but
now came the struggle between
man's enemy & man's friend.

Now they clasp each other & our champion
falls stained o'er with blood forced
from him by the desperate tug of
the foe. Like Xn in the valley he
sighs & to it again they fall. Still
he suffers & all his body is robed
in gore — but now comes the
last — "Conquer or die" now champion

371   Ps. CXVII. 1. The Lord Reigneth

What an advantageous position
the Christian enjoys to look upon
this world from. Other men are
in the vale, he is on a hill &
can see farther, but mists do gather
even on hills & the good man's eyes
become beclouded: he becomes like
David foolish & envious, like a beast
before God — But there remains
one place. where the atmosphere is
clear — one place where we can discern
that place is the sanctuary of the
Lord — how sweet to come hither
away from your toils & cares: may
the Lord bless this means of grace.

The subject of my text is one
peculiarly calculated to settle the
mind that is in any way disturbed.
The Lord reigneth —

I. A Glorious Declaration.
II A Fitting Exhortation.

I. A Glorious Declaration.
How sublime are many of the
sentences of Scripture & if you
seek the reason of their sublimity

"Conquer and die" says he. & yields up the
ghost —   Now see the two combatants
one has his head broken, he drags
his broken frame with pain along, being
just alive — but the other how is he —
he has scars — but not a bone is broken.

5. This showed how his mystical
body shall be.

I am glad to close with this since it is so
rich in comfort to the saints of the Lord.
His people are his bones & flesh.
They may be bruised, but never broken.
Those who fall are hypocrite, shooting stars.
They never entered into vital union.
The head will never willingly lose a
member even if that member be sick.
The loss of one small member would
render the body incomplete.

But shall there be an incomplete body
of Christ in glory — No — for if so there
would be an incomplete heaven. &
our Saviour would be inglorious.

Nay — we are graven on his heart
& written on the palms of his hands.
The mountains may depart &c
Hallelujah to free grace.

it lies in their simplicity. It is a
mistake to suppose that high sounding
words are sublime — simplicity is
the tire of sublimity — or rather its
only fitting robe —   The Lord reigneth.
I might launch forth into a thousand
subjects all of them profitable but
I chose rather to dwell on one
point & that is —
    the Universality of this truth
In Every Place. this is true. Carry me
to heaven, up amid the wondrous
hierarchy of angels, to the highest rank
the tallest of all the sons of the morning
Amid those ranks the truth is felt
& delighted in   "The Lord reigneth".
Descending to those gods below, Kings
& rulers — we enter the cabinet, we listen
to the discussions of the divan & we
hear not of the most high, he is
forgotten but even here "The Lord reigneth"
Go amid the army, see the warrior
buckling on his armour & clasp
his helmet. see the serried ranks
hearken to the noise & tumult of the
war & as with sicken'd sight you
turn away, yet remember
            "The Lord reigneth"

we turn to the more loving pursuits
of peace & we survey the crowded city,
the busy mart, the pleasant
country, we launch on the sea, we
pass over America, we see its slaves
its fanaticism & liberty, we see
the cold northern regions of the Pole,
we skim the Pacific & go to the
new found regions of gold, turn
northward to busy China &c &c
& when tired we rest we can
hardly understand the truth, but
yet believe it, that in all those
lands, fertile or sterile, barbarous
or civilized, God reigneth — that
on the highest mountain, on the
stormiest billow, in the deepest
chasm   God reigneth
    Then fly we on to other worlds
& close our great excursion by
entering hell & even here we
see in burning characters
    "the Lord reigneth"
He is the only Potentate & his
power extends so far that there
is not room for another.

In Every age. this is true. Monarchs have had their day & have passed into their graves but this one never dies

When nothing save space existed. — When Adam fell — when the world was full of sin — the flood — when Israel was in Egypt — when Canaan was in reprieve — when false gods were worshipped by Israel — when Nebu— led Israel captive — when the vessels were profaned — when the Jews were persecuted by Antiochus — when Jesus died — when his disciples were scattered — when Popery prevailed — when Smithfield smoked — when religion flagged —.

"the Lord reigneth"

So in every time of our experience —

This fact is the key of the past, the silken clue of the labyrinth of providence

It is the shield & pavilion of the present, its helm & tiller

It is the star & banner of the future — the ultimatum, the top stone, the soul of all Eternity

"The Lord Reigneth"

II. A Fitting Exhortation.

We are exhorted to rejoice in it.

1. We believe that he will govern most justly — oppression &c will be punished & the right defended.

2. We believe &c wisely — we can trust in his administrations.

3. We believe &c mercifully, not allowing more suffering than is needful

but the Christian can rejoice for it is his Father who reigns & will preserve him & all his own elect. ——

The Church is safe — see the days of Bess — the cards — so in future

Each member is safe — nothing can destroy if God reigns & looks on me

& now to conclude can we feel this a real source of joy to us, then we may believe that we are his.

then ought we to rejoice & lift up the voice — Rejoice, Rejoice

"The Lord Reigneth"

Ps. 68. 6   Mercy & Judgment.   372

How enthusiastic David was. In these cold times he would have been reproved for over zeal. giving a loose to his imagination and rising almost into frenzy. Oh ye cold prog-like Christians who want to have minister as cold as marble statues, look ye here & behold the rolling eye & burning cheek & high wrought extacy of David while he sings. – Sing unto God, sing praises to his name, extol him that rideth on the heavens by his name Jah. and rejoice before him.   Oh 'tis a blessed frenzy. Religion without zeal, served up in a cold & formal manner is most tasteless & unprofitable.

But to look at the verses of this rapt & burning poet – here is one containing two blessings & a curse.

I Blessing.   The Solitary in families.

This is literally true if we consider the case of Abraham, or of Ruth, or Hannah.

It may also apply to Gentile believers who were indeed solitary, but now are they as numerous as the stars of heaven.

I shall however apply this to the case of the man who sighs for help but still is found in darkness & ignorance of Christ

1. Let us remark the sad state indicated by the word "solitary".–

Imagine a foreigner suddenly set down in our country, having no friend, no money no knowledge of the language. He has never seen such strange costumes, he does not see a face which he can recognize. He is a stranger & a foreigner, no one gives him food, the night comes on & he sits down weary on the door step for he is "solitary". – So is the man whom conviction has wounded. he is a solitary man.   He may live in society but he dislikes it. He cannot frequent the Ball Room. or even sit in the family circle.   Like the smitten deer he retires to die alone. Longs for a lodge in a vast wilderness. wishes like Adam to hide under the thick trees of the garden.

Such is the solitary – whom God setteth in families.

But this figure does not represent all the horrors of the word & therefore we resort to another. .—

See yon sailor he has climbed a rock, his vessel is gone, his comrades are drowned: he looks & he is alone on the rock, he sees no vessel near not even a screaming fowl is heard & is still — only the stars look on him — he is solitary.

So is the character I intend. His ship of false confidence is wrecked

he seems to himself to be the only one
on the rock. No hope is near. He gives
up all for lost & feels too much the
meaning of the word solitary. Ah
poor solitary one - there is hope even
now. I see the sail in the distance

But once more - a traveller has
lost his way in the wilds of America
he is torn with the briars, he is weary
but still he tries to find his path

Impossible - and now he hears the
loup of the wolf in the distance & he
climbs a tree, soon a score of them
are at his feet filling him with fear.

Suddenly the sun sets, - black night
comes on - a storm is brewing, the
wind rocks his tree to & fro, the thunder
rolls, the lightnings make the sky
bright around him. his hair
stands almost upright. He calls for
help, but nature mocks him, the
wolves continue their horrid howling
& he fears he shall either be in
their jaws or be killed by the light.
just as he ruminates on this a
shaft smites the next tree its trunk
is severed, blasted by the flash -

Such is the solitary soul. he
hears his sins like wolves upon him
his support is frail, death near.

the anger of God above him & he is in
the most terrible state of trouble.
Such is the man God will place in
families

2. Let us remark the great privilege
expressed by the phrase "setteth in families"

Solitary one there is a friend near
the Psalmist points you to him, it is
God. He mentions his name although
he might have said "he", lest there
should be any possibility of mistake.

To be set in a family is to be made
one of them & enjoy all the privileges.
There are not two families but one -
yet as they are separated they may
be called families. -

There is the family of Christ <u>mystical</u>.
You poor sinner shall be by sovereign
grace made a child, made a prince.
"you are unworthy," say you. Ah but
the prodigal was not suffered to say
that - You shall be fed with the
fatted calf, wear the best robe &
the golden ring - & then you shall
be a joint heir with Christ.

There is the family of Christ <u>visible</u>
The visible Church, you ought to come
into this if you are in the church of

I shall speak of the works of God in breaking
the chains of —
Sin — men are chained by sin, their
evil habits are iron chains, their
evil passions drag them in willing
captivity to evil.   They are slaves to
sin but the Lord our God can &
will break these chains.
Justice, has put fetters on us &
detains us until the hour of execution
but God breaks these — for Jesus
has discharged the debt. —
Despair, these are the firmest
chains of all. For the man who
wears them made the lock to them
himself & has thrown the Key away.
& besides like a lunatic if we go
near to help him he will strike
therewith —   But God sends the
chains in sunder as if they had
been tow & sets the soul free. —
For despairing one rejoice. —
Good Dr Hawker & the man not understood
Oh the joy which release occasions
when we are set free & put out of
prison into the clear open air of
Gospel grace & liberty.

Christ & if you do — you shall be one of
the family. you shall be allowed to
make an open profession of your faith by
Baptism, sit at the supper of our Lord
join in our prayers & in fact be one
in a large family.   I would I could
promise you perfectly loving treatment
but I will hope that you will receive it.
But there is the family of Christ perfected
The church of the firstborn, Into this
you shall be admitted and have the
full range of your Father's house, &
the glorious society of the saints in
light. —   And now poor solitary
one, it may seem too good to be true
but it must be believed for the
Lord hath said it — even now
He setteth the solitary in families

II Blessing — Chains broken.
When we get one promise, we mostly
have another on the heels of it. God
often pileth Pelion on Ossa mountain
on mountain.   He is not sparing
in his blessings.
This promise too might be literally
understood as relating to Israel from
Egypt. & many similar cases.   But
I chose rather to apply it to a spiritual
loosening from chains. —

III. Curse. The Rebellious dwell in a
dry land

A dry land in the east is necessarily a land of sterility & desolation. Such is the country of the rebellious. God's word ever represents the state of rebels as deplorable. There is little real joy to an ungodly man. for.
1. The fear of death terrifies, like the sword over the head at the feast.
2. The fear of what is after death terrifies — you are forging a chain to bind yourselves in for ever.—
3. The remorse of conscience which like an adder biteth at the heart.
To conclude — You dwell in a dry land — you know you do —
How is it that when death comes you always seek another land to die in — you would turn Christian then — You know your principles are too hollow to bear the heavy foot of death — Oh young man seek not to know the country of the rebellious, it is dry, dry, dry.
But seek thou to be set in the family of Christ.
O Lord help. help. help

373 Isa. 61. 6. Every Christian a Priest

This verse is addressed to all meek, & brokenhearted ones. to all mourners in Zion & all trees of the Lord's planting. It teaches the doctrine that all true ones are spiritual priests — This is not the only place where we find the same truth the verse is not alone. We find originally that all heads of families were priests such as Noah, Abraham, Jacob & Job
Even under the Mosaic economy the same doctrine was held for in Exod. 19.6 God makes this a promise to Israel.
In the N.T. we have it also in 1 Pet. 2.5-9. & one of John's thanksgivings is this very fact. This also swells the song of the redeemed saints before the throne. Rev. V.10
Thus we see that this is no isolated text — but is consistent with the general tenor of inspiration

I. A Distinction destroyed

Under the Mosaic dispensation there were men chosen and specially appointed to act as priests. Now as we have seen that under the new system all are priests, the distinction ceases & the class becomes no longer needful. It is to be remarked that the pure religion of the Bible is the only one

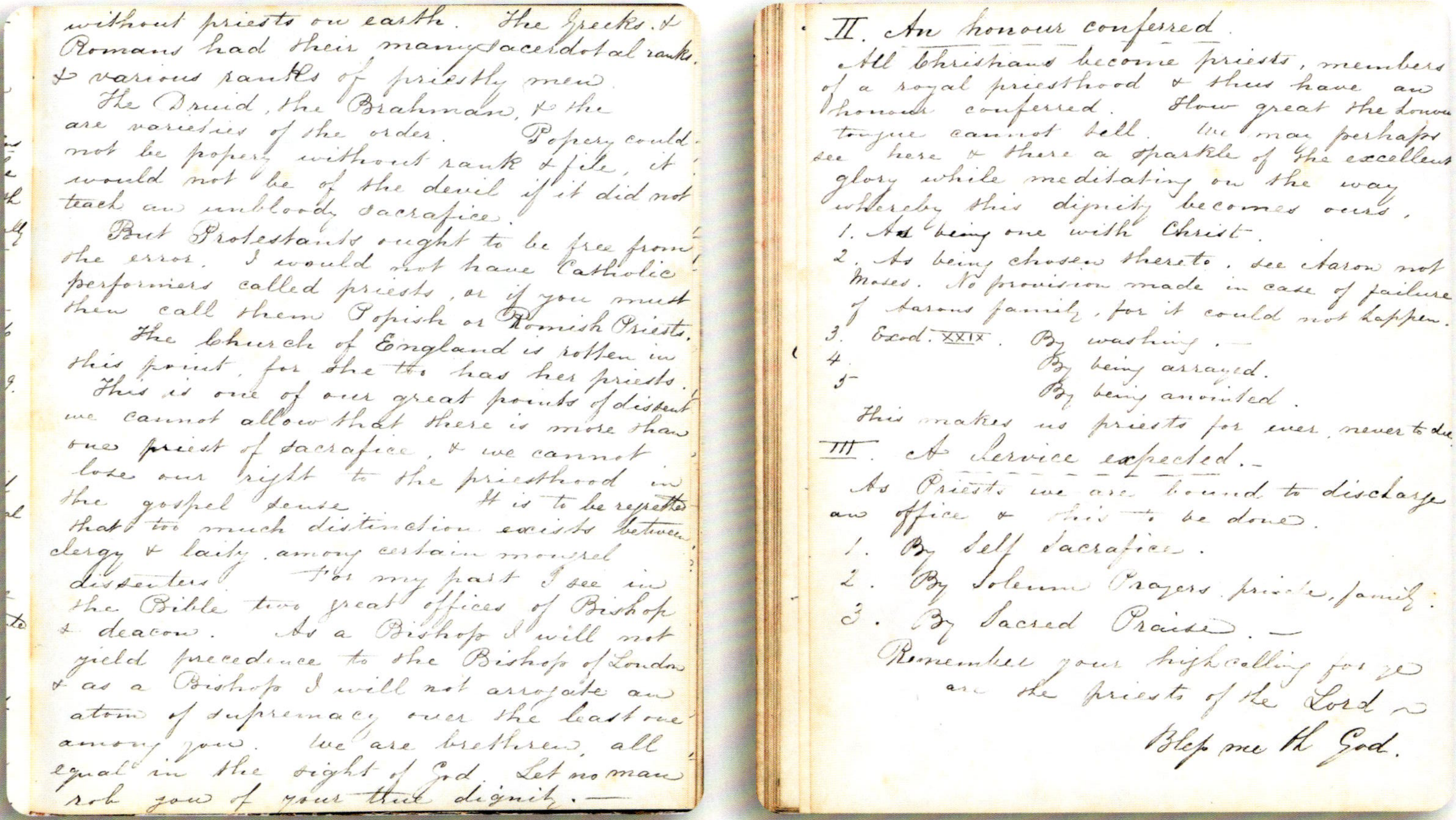
without priests on earth. The Greeks & Romans had their many sacerdotal ranks & various ranks of priestly men.

The Druid, the Brahman, & the are varieties of the order. Popery could not be popery without rank & file, it would not be of the devil if it did not teach an unbloody sacrafice.

But Protestants ought to be free from the error. I would not have Catholic performers called priests, or if you must then call them Popish or Romish Priests.

The Church of England is rotten in this point, for she too has her priests.

This is one of our great points of dissent we cannot allow that there is more than one priest of sacrafice, & we cannot lose our right to the priesthood in the gospel sense. It is to be regretted that too much distinction exists between clergy & laity among certain mongrel dissenters. For my part I see in the Bible two great offices of Bishop & deacon. As a Bishop I will not yield precedence to the Bishop of London & as a Bishop I will not arrogate an atom of supremacy over the least one among you. We are brethren, all equal in the sight of God. Let no man rob you of your true dignity.—

II. An honour conferred.

All Christians become priests, members of a royal priesthood & thus have an honour conferred. How great the honour tongue cannot tell. We may perhaps see here & there a sparkle of the excellent glory while meditating on the way whereby this dignity becomes ours.

1. As being one with Christ.
2. As being chosen thereto. see Aaron not Moses. No provision made in case of failure of Aarons family, for it could not happen.
3. Exod. XXIX. By washing.—
4. By being arrayed.
5. By being anointed.

This makes us priests for ever, never to die.

III. A service expected.—

As Priests we are bound to discharge an office & this is to be done.

1. By Self sacrafice.
2. By Solemn Prayers. private, family.
3. By Sacred Praise.—

Remember your high calling for ye are the priests of the Lord—

Bless me th God.

374

Acts. II. 1.2.3.4. Pentecost.

The usual method of progress in this world
is by slow degrees. The world was seven
days in making. the leading of Israel to
Canaan & making them into a nation was
a work of time. so with the spread
of truth. It is a blade & then an ear.
Martyrs must bleed. missionaries must
labour and many ministers must preach
ere a people will receive the blessed
doctrines of our holy religion. It is a
work of time as all good works seem
to be.
Yet it is undoubtedly a fact that
God could make a world in an instant.
He could cause the glory of his name
to burst at once like a sun on a
beclouded planet. he could convert
ten thousand as easily as one.
this we believe has been done;
multitudes have suddenly bestirred
their slothful spirits & crowds have
turned at once to the fear of God.
In general we look with very just
[ideas] on revivals. & regard them
the results of mere animal excitement
& also we have seen too much to
warrant us in our conclusions.

But let us not carry this conclusion too
far. let us not imagine that there
cannot be large & overwhelming
increase. for while God is omnipotent
& prayer all prevailing there is no
limit to what may be. — There are
some authentic cases of revival, which
will [?] with what the [?]
of being the instruments of awakening
men to vital godliness. where is the
man who disbelieves the good
effected by the Labours of the
Haldanes, or Rowland Hill. —
Here however we have an instance
of a marvellous increase to the church
we shall do well to think of it
bestirring at its time, its cause & effect.
I. The Time — When Pentecost was
we might pass over this point with our
single observation which shall be our
first remark — viz that it was.
1. At set Time appointed by the Most High
and until that set time the Spirit came
not. this fact should sober us in the
midst of hopes, expectations & struggles
God is a sovereign and although
we pray & labour we must ever feel

a holy deference to his will. If it comes
not when we wish, then let us still
labour — believing that the day of Pentecost
is not yet fully come. The oil of grace
is stored in heaven & in due time it
will most assuredly descend upon us.

But we remark again. it was a

2. A Sabbath day. It seems most probable
that the day of Pentecost was on the first
day of the week. In Lev. XXIII. 15 we are told
that they were to complete 7 sabbaths or
50 days which would make the day of
Pentecost fall on the first day.

What an honour was thus put on the
Sabbath — let us honour it too & believe
that if God ever bestows on us a day
of Pentecost it will most likely come
not in the week days but on the
blessed Sabbath, the pearl of days.

3. A Pentecost day. This day is said by
the Rabbis of both ancient & modern
Jews to have been the day of the
giving of the law. 50 days after the
coming out of Egypt. Now as the
giving of the law on Sinai was a.
more clear manifestation of Mosaic
law & polity, so also was the outpouring

of the Holy Spirit, a more perfect revelation
to the disciples of the spiritual things
of the new economy. The children
of Israel knew but little of the Lord's
will concerning them until they had
been taught by Sinai's thunders &
the children of the kingdom were but
children until the rushing, mighty
wind came & taught them.

But again the feast of ingathering
was kept on this day. This was the
harvest home day among the Jews, &
so was it in this case, a day of
a great harvest of souls & truly a
harvest of souls is the true reward
& harvest of a gospel minister

4. A Suitable day. For on that day
many souls out of all nations were
in Jerusalem, for it would not
have been of any use for the Spirit
to be poured out when there were
few people — but as many were
gathered together — now was the time.
These would tell to others, & the
word would thus run round the
wide earth & all people hear the
sound thereof.

We come now. to consider

II. The Position - of the disciples.

They were engaged in obedient worship. their master had bidden them stay in the city - they might have reasoned & questioned but instead of it they obeyed & tarried.

They were engaged in courageous worship. they did not fear the enemies who were thirsty for their blood, but boldly stood their ground. Oh that we had more holy bravery, to fear nothing, Cedo nulli, should be our motto. & when we see lionlike men in the church then let us expect a Pentecost.

They were engaged in assembled worship. they were not at home but assembled not forsaking the assembling of themselves together. One prayer is an arrow on high, when many join it is a siege of the throne & it suffers violence

They were engaged in unanimous worship. not one was absent. some of the might be sick, some had business, but all were there. Thomas and all. How seldom can we see this, we rather often have to say, & David's seat was empty.

They were engaged in loving worship. All of one accord. This is indispensable to the coming of the Spirit. The blessed dove flies not over troubled waters, but seeks the calm and quiet rivers of love.

One jar will spoil melody, one wrong note will destroy harmony, & one of evil eye may keep back the sacred influence. Like Pharoah's lean kine the disturbers will eat up the fat kine & be as hungry as ever. Diotrephes is a ruin to a church wherever he enters. Let us as a church walk in unity & be of one accord & of one mind. You cannot tell how important it is but one thing we are sure of - if you would be in a posture to receive the Holy Spirit, ye must be all of one accord & often meet in one place.

III. Manifestations of the Spirit.

These were miraculous & of course not to be expected now, but doubtless we can learn something therefrom.

There were two manifestations. The Sound of Wind & the appearance of fire. The one an audible & the other a visible sign. Wind and fire are usually the attendants of Divinity, whenever manifested to mortals. Moses saw a burning bush. Sinai was altogether a smoke, Fiery chariots & a whirlwind bore Elijah to heaven. 2 Kings 2. 11

In Psalm. 18.8 Fire & wind are described in majestic language as the companions of God.
In Isaiah XXX. 30. We have a sound, tempest & fire.
In Ezek. I. 4. Whirlwind & fire.
In Nah. I. 3. 5. The Glorious presence of God is described in the same manner.

Now why have we detained you with these texts but to shew you that as the great Jehovah & he alone is ever attended by this awful pomp – therefore the Holy Spirit is none other than God a person in the Godhead equal in majesty, honour & divinity. We cannot find that any man who came from heaven was thus attended – Nor angel either – Angels. Moses & Elias.

But now we come & look at these manifestations to learn something.

We learn that this effusion of the Spirit was ~~unmistakable for~~ & often is.

1. Sudden. All was still perhaps, or one of the brethren was engaged in vocal prayer – but all on a sudden to their great surprize it came. God often surprizes men by giving at singular times & when his grace comes it often finds us unprepared to receive it.

2. From Heaven. The sound came from above & true grace will come in the same way. So that no flesh shall glory in his presence

3. Mysterious, like wind it cannot be known whence it cometh nor whither it goeth So is the operation of the Spirit ever.

4. Powerful. A Rushing mighty wind. The power of wind is immense, but what is it to the mighty energy of the Spirit – who can stay his work

5. Spredding. It filled the house, the whole house. If we receive grace others share therein. other churches & the neighbourhood

With regard to the symbol of the cloven tongues of fire. We may learn.

1. That the Holy Spirit enlightens all who receive his influence

2. That he makes them candles to others, puts fire on them.

3. That where the Spirit truly comes he abideth. it sat –

4. That he can in his plenitude give his power to as many as he pleases for "he sat".

These are manifestations intended to teach us a lesson & happy are we if we learn it – let us hope that we may yet see signs equally clear, showing that the Lord is with us of a truth.

IV. Effects of the Spirit.

There were several effects, some of them extraordinary & temporary — such as power to speak with tongues & to perform miracles, these have ceased simply because not needed. The church needed a cradle in its infancy; but now in its vigour & manhood it is an astute giant & can do without.

But there were other effects which are equally needed in our day.

1. The power to preach — These men were unlearned & "illiterate" but they were the greatest preachers this world ever produced — & truly some who now merely crawl would run & those who preach the truth with little power would soon be mighty if we had more unction from the Holy One.

If you want a good minister, cry to God for his almighty Spirit.

2. The Guidance of the Spirit. These men were filled with the holy Ghost which is the only infallible teacher.

They were directed in all their movements by an inward adviser, a privy councillor & so will the sons of God be, more & more as we hasten to the time of the consummation of all things.

3. Numerous conversions. The word from the lips of Peter & the others was very powerful & produced an amazing effect.

3000 were born in a day, by the simple enunciation of truth & the power of the Spirit therewith.

And now brethren cannot you & I sincerely long & pray for a baptism of the Holy Ghost & like to this one.

Have we not a right to expect it if we are of one accord & one mind.

Do not our hearts leap when we hear of one conversion how would we sing for joy if we saw a multitude. Attempt great things & expect great things & surely you shall see great things

Judg. VI. 14 Gideon.

It is a true saying that the Lord always finds men to do his work. Here was a nation to be delivered and where could a man be found to do it. Does any one know? No. But God does. He has a man threshing wheat in a winepress, little known & little cared about, but yet doing his duty & getting ready for his work.

So does God find men in his church, for his church to encrease his church, to fight its foes, or feed its sheep, or build its palaces. We shall ever find that for the pulpit, the S. School, the Mission God is ever sending out Gideons.

I. Let us notice who the Lords Gideons often are.

1. They are men previously of mean estate. Such was Gideon, so Jephthah, & David, Amos. — Our Saviour himself. His apostles. Luther, Bunyan, Carey, & many of our ministers. God often finds out the poorest, & the worst of the family — Perhaps some of you feel the same, be not dis-couraged — for God chooseth the mean.

2. They are men who have suffered the same calamity they are sent to rescue others from. Gideon was reduced to a small

quantity of corn for he threshed himself & not with oxen, or he did it for silence sake least the oxen should low.—

We see he was in fear for he threshed in the winepress.—   So we have suffered from the sins we wish to deliver others from.

3. They are at first unwilling to go.

4. They have but little faith & require many signs.

5. They are men who follow all Gods directions.

II. Let us notice the enemies they are called to contend with.

1. Men of their own household. Joash &c

2. Enemies in our own hearts.

3. Imbred corruption in the hearts of those we teach.

4. All the allurements of the wicked world & Satan. The dram shop, the brothel, the casino, the theatre, the infidel, the novel. Evil men. Evil places, Evil Books.

III. Let us notice wherein our might consists.

Not in learning, that is like Sauls armour. not in money or eloquence but in

1. Providence — which works for

376.　Heb. XI, 6. The necessity of Faith.

This is a very positive assertion. It is couched in the most unmistakeable language. it is "impossible" to please God. It is not explained away or guarded but like a rugged rock it stands in majestic & awful simplicity. We may be sure from the very fact of the clear & unmistakeable language that it is a point upon which it is very important that we should be right.

This is "articula stantis vel cadentis ecclesiæ" — an error here is vital.

I would therefore tremble lest I should lead you wrong & have you beware that you look to your steps lest you fail of the grace of God.

This is the wicket-gate, the only proper entrance into true religion.

By the help of God I shall attempt

I. An Explanation of the faith here mentioned
II. An Exposition of the doctrine of the text
III. A Proof of the Doctrine or a Vindication
IV. An Application of the text.

---

the overthrowing of our foes and our establishment in the truth & victory by it.

2. Prayer — of our own & that of the church. this is a mighty weapon to slay an enemy with. A Stone for Goliah's head.

Here is our might

3. Presence — of God, his smile, his arm his word, his love, his Spirit.

Three P's for our Panoply.

now when this solace is thin
Go in this thy might.

When the children are unruly
Go in this thy might

When you are poorly, sad & depressed.
When helpers fail & friends are few.

Still Go in this thy might.

Father aid me

I. An Explanation of the faith here mentioned.
It certainly does not refer to the Kind of faith called miraculous — referred to by Paul.
Nor can it mean.
1. A Bare Assent to the truth of the Bible.
There are some who if they do not say so, yet seem to insinuate that to be a believer is simply not to be an infidel.
This is the result of a flimsy divinity. — But let me remind you that with many of us to believe the Bible is as natural as to eat, for from early religious training we were led to do so. —
Again some of us believe the Bible to be true in the same way as others believe that Milton wrote Paradise lost, viz — because we never saw any reason to the contrary — It is a mere act of the head.
God has written other volumes in the same style & therefore this is his. — But what can there be spiritual in this, for my part it seems to be as simple & natural an act as to believe that I am here.
But more — when we consider that devils believe, that the worst of men have this kind of faith — we are at once shut out from the idea of such a faith being at all saving.
Nor is it even

2. A Delight in Sound Doctrine.
In these days. doctrines are too much despised — but there is a certain party who exalt soundness of faith into the very throne of the Saviour.
They suppose that if they love what is called savoury meat they must therefore be children. but no. True religion is more than a smile at a bold assertion or triumphant proof.
Some of these people can come from the gin shop & then say bless God for such food as this.
This is not true faith, it is dead faith.
In order to the discovery of faith we may be allowed for a moment to look it at its constant antecedents its shadow rather which is conviction The dark shadow of a bright object
Where this is not, there is no true faith — be sure of this.
And we may well discern it by its consequents or the things which follow viz - good works. You tell the tree by its fruits, so must you judge faith by its effects. If a man says I believe & then lives in sin — write that man

among the foolish virgins —
But what is faith say you after all.
I answer that I conceive it to be such
a belief in revealed truth as leads us
to trust in Jesus for salvation & to feel
a hearty confidence in & love to God.
Faith toucheth the attributes of God — thus.
He is powerful. I will rely on his might
He is omniscient. I believe that he will keep me
He is just. His justice is what I trust to
&c &c &c
Faith toucheth Jesus Christ. thus.
He died — on his atonement I trust.
He rose — I believe that I shall rise
&c &c
Faith toucheth the Holy Ghost. thus.
In all his operations & influences.
we believe that he will sanctify us.
Faith is an eye seeing the invisible.
Faith is a hand it grasps the Saviour.
Faith is a foot it walketh on the sea.
Faith is a wing it mounteth to heaven.
Confound it not with assurance.
Assurance is the cream of faith, It is
the corn from the blade of hope.
You who can only just see Jesus
& rely on him need not fear, for you
are safe if you have only one finger
in his hand —

II An Exposition of the doctrine of the text.
And I cannot do better than pass —
review many things which are considered
as pleasing to God, and really are so
if mixed with faith, but without it
are not.
1. Good Works — Obedience to the
law of God is a duty of every man.
Some imagine that they do render
this perfectly — but it is for want of
knowing better — they really do not.
But without faith these are vain
These things are the ornaments, the
cornices, the roof — but faith is the
foundation — See Abel + Cain.
2. Prayer. This is an important part
of religious worship — but without
faith it is idle wind. It is like the
Tartar windmill, or the Catholic beads.
Many make a form a reality, but too
many keep the form a form merely —
A form without sincerity is mockery.
3. The Ordinances. Baptism without
faith is a farce. When performed on
unthinking babes it is to say the least
an absurdity, to say the worst it is

an awful crime against the Bible & God.
The Lord's Supper is a blessed feast of love
but if men without faith sit down it is
an effrontery offered to high heaven.

4. Alms. to Heathens, Societies, or the Poor?
I love the patriotic, the benevolent,
the liberal, but more than this is
required for your own safety. Heaven
is worth more than you can give.
With all these it is impossible to please
God if you have no faith. —

III A Vindication of the Doctrine. —
Many men think it hard that they
if they are ever so good will be lost &
the greatest sinner saved if he repents
& believes. It might serve to
quiet this question a little if we
remind them that God has a right
to give as he pleases. You yourself
claim a right to do what you will
with your own. If you should bid
certain beggars knock at your door
& you would relieve them, would it
be hard if a man should bring an organ
& play & expect you to come. No say
you let him do as I please if he
wants my charity — So does God.

2. It might also serve to put the objection
out of countenance if I remind you of
the reasonableness of the demand.
Gods attributes & character are well
deserving of faith & confidence. —
But could any one alter it for the
better — Say anything else — & some are
damned — yea all are. —
Say "without good works" then we have
none & we are all drowned in one sea.

3. But I must make a more crushing
argument & that is this, Certain relations
in life require faith — Husband & wife.
Father & son. Master & servant, Friend
& Friend. So as our Creator, Master
Father, Friend confidence is absolutely
necessary.

4. But again — another argument.
Motive is the essence of an action &
the man who has no faith in God
cannot serve him from the motive
which God loves. Fear, selfishness.
love of Merit these are no true gospel
motives & actions wrought therefrom
are splendida peccata, splendid sins.

377   II. Sam. XVIII. 3.   Jesus worth ten thousand

We are now about to speak of things touching the King may our tongue be as the pen of a ready writer.

The words of my text were originally addressed to David. but I shall apply them to David's Lord. for he is far more worthy thereof. —

I I shall speak of a loving soul's opinion of Jesus Christ. —

There are many opinions about our Saviour but we shall leave them. for if they are the ideas of ungodly men they are about as valuable as a blindman's treatise on colours. or the musical grammar of a deaf man.   If the men are Laodicean christians their mouths are too much out of taste by swallowing lukewarm water & they have no power to judge — But the truly loving soul. he is the man, what does he say. —

1. He loves Christ better than himself. True love is ever self denying. it puts its object in the chief seat & sitteth itself upon a footstool at the feet thereof.

I had better be slain than David

However this is fact. You must believe or perish. it is not yours to choose but to yield — to stoop, to lie in the dust.

II An application of the text. —

To Christians. —   If faith pleases God then the more of it the better. Doubt never please him but rather dishonour him.

Be not afraid of assurance, fear not to climb the mountains as well as to descend the vallies. There is no reason why you should be so fond of unbelief. Get rid of him

To Unbelievers How sad your state is if viewed by the light of this text.

Yours sins you confess cannot please God, but you thought that surely your good works did — But now it seems that you have never pleased God. What do you say "you will not try". No. No do not say so, that would be to ruin your own soul to gratify your pride.

Nay Rather confess & seek mercy & you shall find it —

Helps. Helps Helps
O King

said these men — & so the true lover of
Christ had rather suffer than that the
cause of Christ should be injured.
He fears lest others should insult his Lord.
& he trembles lest he should do so himself.

If the cause prospers he will rejoice
as much as in the increase of his own trade.

If he must sacrifice all, he will do it.
He will like Curtius leap into the chasm
if he can fill it up. He will be bold
for Christ. He will lose for his name.

2. He values Christ above a 1000 others.

His relatives he loves but not side by side
with the Saviour. He sees great & good
men & thanks God for them but he
sets Jesus above them. for Jesus is
better than they all. He being free from
sin — & great not in some one virtue
but in every virtue. A mixture of
the quintessence of all essences. A sun
comprising all light, an ocean into
which all rivers run. .— Nothing seems
too good or great for him to do.

3. He values Christ when Christ is despised.
He loveth a persecuted & footsore Christ
He can walk with his poor followers.
He will defend him in all companies
he will bear scoff & scorn for his name
sake & love him amid scoffing & taunting

II. I shall speak of the advantages a
good opinion of Christ confers on us.

1. It helpeth resignation. Trials must &
will befall. & the true secret of life is
to bend to the storm — but who will
do it like the loving soul who values
the Lord. Mr Cecil's child & beads
Good man who saved his child from the fire.
A full Christ lighteth up a dark &
empty cupboard.

2. It quickeneth obedience. See Moses.
See Mary in the garden. See the Martyrs.
Loving obedience is the best obedience.
A Mother & sick child. Love never tires.

3. It affordeth delight. The reason why
we do not delight in Jesus more is because
we do not love him more. Jonathan
& David. Jacob & Rachel. That which
we love we long to see & to have in
our presence. — Be not afraid of
prizing him too much.

4. It sharpeneth desire. The more we
love. the more we long to see him.
& the more disconsolate shall we be
at his absence — Give me Christ
or else I die.

III. I shall speak of the reasons why they
thus think of him.

1. Because they believe Christ prizes them.
Jesus loves the smallest of his children.
He prizes them as the apple of his eye, his jewels,
his portion, his glory, his ornaments, his
crown, his throne his bride.
He loves us better than heaven, or his
Father's bosom, or his own life for he died.

2. Because they observe his actions.
They delight to muse on his deep descent,
from heaven to earth. His labours &
works of love. The many he has
saved, the countless myriads he has
sustained & piloted to glory.

3. Because they commune with his person.
There is such a thing as communion
with Jesus and a sweet thing it is.
The soul talketh with its lover behind
the door. it whispereth to him. &
he giveth the kisses of his love.
The more of this the better.
for so much the more love
helps of Jesus.

378.   John. 15. 9   Love of Christ to us compared with
the Father's love to him

After last Thursday evening's sermon I
assayed to prepare a subject for Sabbath
day, but although many came I found
none that I could settle upon for like
the harp of Anacreon my soul would
sound only love. — It would be
an unspeakable mercy if we all could
find it so evermore; and I am fully
persuaded that the best way to inflame
our souls toward him is to view his
love toward us. Force can never
compel love. Love only can beget it.
Love must be born not made. May it
please the great Father of our spirits
to give us more love to his son.

I. We have a comparison.
II. We have an exhortation.
III. We have a Direction.

I. We have a Comparison
Fetched not from earth but from the
highest heaven. A love existing between
two existences having but one essence.
Between two persons of the adorable Godhead

Well may we stand astonished upon the
very threshold of our subject & lift up our
hands with solemn wonder & surprize.

God is in himself essentially love. —
His love admits of degrees. One degree of it
is His love of benevolence which extends to
all his works & to all men whatever their
character may be. All animals are made
happy by him & he sincerely desires to see
all men happy. All providential
blessings are the result of this love.

Far above this is his discriminating love
towards some — this drowns the other.
It is a Father's love, the other is only
a Creator's love, an owner's benevolence

It is true God loves all, but it is just
as true that he loves some more intensely.

But to us it seems that there is one
degree of love which is apparently above even
this viz — His love personal. By which
I mean that complacency & delight which
the persons of the Godhead feel towards
each other. It seems as if this love of God
to God must be greater than the love of
God to any creature however much delighted
in — Well this love personal is taken

as the model of Christ's love to us.
It cannot be of the same degree for the
love of infinite to infinite cannot be
for a moment to that of infinite to finite

Again we must remark that it is an
as of Quality not of equality.

& here let us first remark that these
two loves which are here compared are
1. Without beginning. It is entirely out
of our power to conceive of a time when
the Father's love to the Son commenced.

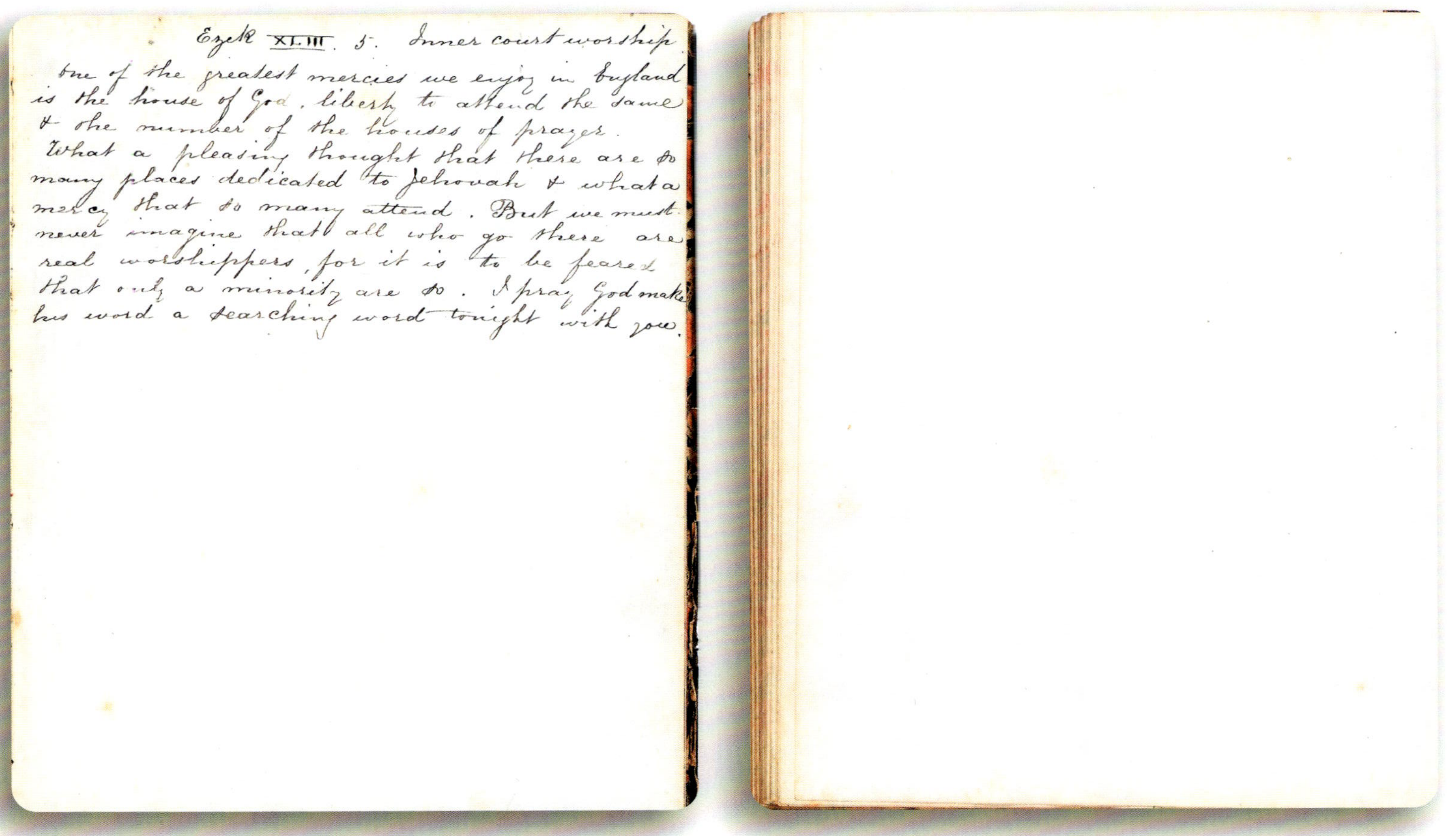

Ezek XLIII. 5. Inner court worship

One of the greatest mercies we enjoy in England
is the house of God. liberty to attend the same
& the number of the houses of prayer.
What a pleasing thought that there are so
many places dedicated to Jehovah & what a
mercy that so many attend. But we must
never imagine that all who go there are
real worshippers, for it is to be feared
that only a minority are so. I pray God make
his word a searching word tonight with you.

THE SERMONS

NOTEBOOK 9 (SERMONS 380–399)

Self Examination.
were the critics of ancien
ked the apostle Paul
the ship and doctrine —
his speech & said tha
powerful but his bodil
Paul has been at
dicate himself & now
away the sword, he
them — or rather
gain & bids them use
Examine your selves
uld it be for us if
at others, we were
k at home & mind
ard. Let me now
to a serious meditatio
t-ant subject and may
er of Hearts aid us with
t. —
lain the exhortation.
ow its reasonablene
ect you how to do it
hy. III. How. —

in the exhortation.
selves, &c. I will adher

VOL IX

Sermon No. 380

"SELF-EXAMINATION"

Editor's Summary

In late September through November of 1858, Charles found himself growing seriously ill and unable to preach. Though this was the first occasion of a debilitating sickness since arriving in London, it would not be his last. To this point, the church had been growing rapidly, with dozens of new members joining each month. They were also in the middle of a building project. Yet one indication of the seriousness of Charles's illness is the fact that, with him unable to chair meetings, the church had to cancel all congregational meetings for three months, despite the many matters of membership and business.

Even so, Charles did not want to disappoint the large crowds coming to hear him. So, on Sunday, October 10, 1858, a very weak preacher ascended the pulpit and opened the sermon with these words, "Owing to excruciating pain and continual sickness, I have been unable to gather my thoughts together, and therefore I feel constrained to address you on a subject which has often been upon my heart and not unfrequently upon my lips, and concerning which, I dare say, I have admonished a very large proportion of this audience before." *NPSP* 5:218. Charles then pulled out the notes that we have here.

The first time he preached this sermon would have been sometime in 1854. Now, four years later, due to his inability to prepare a new sermon, he decided to deliver this sermon again. As in previous cases, it's instructive to compare these sermons and trace Charles's development as a preacher and his use of notes in sermon delivery. However, what is perhaps more notable is the theme of self-examination.

We see in this sermon that his illness brought a measure of reflection and soul-searching. Even as Charles's sickness lingered week after week, he was reminded

505

of his mortality: "Now here is our soul, our own soul, an eternity, heaven, hell, all hanging on the answer to this question. Shall it be slighted? Shall we not rather be sure to examine thoroughly[?]"

Amid all the signs of outward success, here was a warning not to find his hope in his ministry. "Hearken to the groans of condemned ministers damned with crowds of their hearers." Charles's illness humbled him and reminded him of his dependence on God, and he sought to impart this to his congregation. It was not enough to be a part of the crowd, but what truly mattered was "the great touchstone, Is Jesus in you?" Sick and barely able to finish the sermon, Charles urged his "crowds of hearers" to examine themselves. In God's providence, this sickness would not be the end of his story.

On November 24, 1858, the church was finally able to hold a congregational meeting, and they affirmed the following entry unanimously, thanking God for their pastor's recovery.

> Whereupon it was resolved, that we desire as a church to record our devout and heartfelt thanks to our Heavenly Father for sustaining our Beloved Pastor during his indisposition and restoring him again to the Church in the enjoyment of health and we earnestly pray that his recovery may be marked by increasing success in the ingathering of souls to Christ and in building up his people in the knowledge and truths of the Gospel. "Church Meeting Minutes, November 24, 1858," *Church Meeting Minutes 1854–1861 New Park Street*, Metropolitan Tabernacle Archives, London.

SELF-EXAMINATION
2 Corinthians 13:5

"Examine yourselves, whether ye be in the faith; prove your own selves. Know ye not your own selves, how that Jesus Christ is in you, except ye be reprobates?"

The Corinthians were the critics of ancient times. They attacked the apostle Paul, distorted his Apostleship and doctrine, found fault with his speech, and said that his letters were powerful, but his bodily presence weak. Paul has been at great pains to vindicate himself, and now [that] he has wrested away the sword, he turns its point to them, or rather gives it back again, and bids them use it on themselves! <u>Examine yourselves</u>.

Ah, well would it be for us if instead of looking at others, we were sometimes to look at home and mind our own vineyard. Let me now lead your minds to a serious meditation on this important subject and may the great Searcher of Hearts aid us with his Holy Spirit.

I.   WE SHALL EXPLAIN THE EXHORTATION.

II. WE SHALL SHOW ITS REASONABLENESS.

III. WE SHALL DIRECT YOU HOW TO DO IT.

I   WHAT.   II. WHY.   III. HOW.

I.   WE SHALL EXPLAIN THE EXHORTATION.

Examine yourselves, etc. I will adhere to the words of the text.

<u>"Examine yourselves."</u> The words are simple and need no explaining: but to set them in a clearer light we will see how the word is used in ordinary life. One

part of the idea is <u>scholastic</u> and will be understood by every school boy or graduate. "Examine yourselves," catechize yourselves and see whether you could join in the song of the redeemed.

Another part of the idea is <u>military</u>. The soldier must be reviewed, the fortress or country to be attacked must be surveyed and examined. I find the original has in it the meaning of passing through, piercing through, traversing the heart. It implies therefore a thorough examination, and this we may call <u>the traveller's idea</u>.

But we are so continually in common life that it is quite unnecessary for us to suggest any further explanation. "<u>Whether ye be in the faith</u>." Not whether ye believe like so and so but whether ye be in "<u>the</u>" faith. Not of the faith but in it. Whether the faith holds you. Whether like the golden staves, you are in the golden rings. This is a vital point, it is the core of true searching, it includes all true spiritual experience.

"<u>Prove your own selves</u>." This is a stronger expression than the word examine. It implies a stricter and more testing enquiry. The goldsmith examines the coin, but to make assurance doubly sure, he proves the metal. So we ought to try ourselves. The axe is tried to see its temper, the ship is tried to see its sailing, the gun is tried to see its safety.

God tries us, and here we are exhorted to try ourselves. Now this cannot mean that we are to run into harm's way, or tempt the devil to tempt us. But we must see how we endure our necessary trials sent by God. Yet as the text is active, we believe that there are some right and just means which we may use for proving ourselves.

These are acts of <u>devotion</u>, let us see how our heart goes in prayer, meditation, and praise; and acts of <u>forgiveness</u>, let us try whether we can pardon our debtors; acts of <u>self-denial</u>, of leaving off evil habits; acts of <u>zeal</u>, let us try and see whether we can do the [unclear] works which others call imprudent. This "proving" is a very searching thing.

<u>Know ye not your own selves</u>? If not, then have you neglected your most proper study. We ought to be assured of our salvation, we ought to know whether Jesus be in us or no. We do not condemn doubters and we cannot approve doubts.

<u>Reprobates</u>. There is no reference here to the doctrine of reprobation. The word is never put in opposition to the word elect, but rather as in verse 7 it signifies the opposite of the word approved. It is much to be regretted that the doctrine of reprobation has always been considered as a necessary counterpart of election, but it really is not so. The word praeterition, or nonelection, would far better impress the idea. Many are elect who are at present without Christ in them. Here therefore the word simply expresses the sad state of all unconverted persons; they are reprobate silver, worthless.

"<u>Christ in you</u>" by hope, faith, and love. This is the grand text. This is the crown stamp; heaven's own image in us. Is Christ our joy, our delight, our all[?] Come let us examine and prove ourselves. Here it is clearly laid down as a duty and we are urged thereto.

II. WE SHALL ATTEMPT TO SHOW ITS REASONABLENESS.

1. It is too important a matter to take on guess. In daily life we examine only important things, and there we scrutinize narrowly. Meaner coins pass from hand to hand freely, but the sovereign must be examined and weighed. A Bank note for a very heavy sum will not be received in the dark.

   Now here is our soul, our own soul, an eternity, heaven, [and] hell all hanging on the answer to this question. Shall it be slighted? Shall we not rather be sure to examine thoroughly[?]

2. Mistakes cannot be rectified in the next world. If we leave our narrow box of time, no mistake can be altered. Now or never. Kill or cure. If you take poison there may be an antidote. If you hurl your purse into the sea it may be found again. But here once lost there is no recovery. "<u>Now or never</u>" let us repeat the sentence.

   Examine yourself. It will be of no use for you to cry "Lord I am mistaken," for he that is unjust shall be unjust still, and he that is filthy shall be filthy still. Examine therefore <u>now</u>.

3. Your heart is deceitful. It is hard to be impartial with one's self. The scales will turn on our side. When we have so false a witness in the box, we must not only examine but cross examine. He that trusteth to his own heart is a

fool. Our chameleon heart seems to have every colour of the rainbow and shifts and changes evermore.

4. The Devil will cheat you. Be assured that he does not want you to examine. He wants you to take all at hearsay and be lost. He will put false lights, he will blind your eyes, he will bid you not be so over precise. Be not ignorant of his devices.

5. Examine yourself because so many have been ruined. Many a tradesman has been ruined by not taking stock. Let the shipwrecks warn you of the rocks. Be not satisfied with being a professor [for] you may be lost with your profession as well as without it. Hearken to the groans of condemned ministers damned with crowds of their hearers. Would you shut your eyes as the ostrich and so think to avoid the hunter[?]

6. Examine yourselves for God will examine us. No base coin can deceive him. Tinsel and paint are not used in heaven. We must stand naked before God. Heaven is not such a masquerade as this world is. It is not a place for wolves in sheeps' clothing. Oh, what an eye God hath. It will read us through and through. May the thought of this ordeal lead you to stricter scrutiny, and now . . .

III. HOW TO DO IT.

1. Look for Experimental Evidences. Religion is not so much a matter of dogma and creed, as of inward experience. Some experience you need not wish for, but some is absolutely indispensable. Conviction, regeneration, answers to prayer, emptying of self, and filling with Jesus. Enjoyment of his smile. His help in trouble, his smile in distress. Sweet experience if this is truly ours.

2. Look for External Practical Evidence. Do you frequent the house of prayer and love it[?] Do you mingle with the saints in persecution[?] Do you forgive? Do you live honestly, soberly, and righteously[?] Do you long to be better and to let your light shine more brilliantly[?]

3. Look for Secret Practical Evidences.
   The Closet. How is it loved and attended to[?]
   The Bible. How is it valued, read[?]
   Meditation. Is it frequently on God, is it easy, is it your habit[?]
   Heart. Is that well kept[?]

4. Above all try yourself by the great touchstone. Is Jesus in you? Dost thou venture wholly on him[?] Is he precious[?] Is he thy advocate, friend[,] confidant, lover, all . . . [?]

Let me beseech you to examine and may God bless me,

Amen.

"BANQUETTING DAYS"

Editor's Summary

Charles preached on this text at least three more times in his ministry: "The Real Presence, the Great Want of the Church" (*MTP* 18, Sermon 1035), "Love's Vigilance Rewarded" (*MTP* 42, Sermon 2485), and "The Disconsolate Lover" (*MTP* 61, Sermon 3485). These later sermons don't appear to contain significant overlapping content or structural similarity, but as with all his messages on Solomon's Song, they focus on the church's intimacy with Christ, her Bridegroom.

This sermon addresses "banquetting days," the experience of unique seasons of joy in Christ. These rich experiences begin at conversion. Describing his own conversion experience, Charles recalled, "I can testify that the joy of that day was utterly indescribable. I could have leaped, I could have danced; there was no expression, however fanatical, which would have been out of keeping with the joy of my spirit at that hour." *Autobiography* 1:108. Sadly, such days do not last. Yet these experiences of intimacy are not forever gone. Charles believed that such experiences often come during times of trouble. Whether in affliction, or persecution, or spiritual warfare, Christ draws near to his people in joy.

> Our sick-beds are often as the doorstep of heaven; even when we are cast down, there is a sweet solace in our sorrow, and a profound joy about our apparent grief which we would not give away; God gave it to us and the world cannot destroy it. *MTP* 9:320.

In the coming years of his ministry, Charles would have ample opportunity to learn Christ's comfort in his sorrows. However, he explains here, "We need not go into the furnace to get a banquet, . . . for in ordinary means we may have it." This joy can be obtained through the ordinary means of grace: preaching, prayer, singing, Bible study, and the ordinance of baptism and the Lord's Supper; in other words, through the local church. Writing in 1868, Charles declared,

> To forsake the assembling of ourselves together would involve the loss of one of the dearest Christian privileges, for the worship of the church below is the vestibule of the adoration of heaven. If ever heaven comes down to earth it is in the communion of saints. Our Lord's table is oftentimes glory anticipated. The prayer meeting often seems to be held close to Jerusalem's city wall; it stands in a sort of border land between the celestial and the terrestrial; it is a house and yet a gate, fruition and expectation in one, the house of God and the very gate of heaven. Church fellowship is meant by our Lord Jesus to be the table upon which the daintiest meats of the banquet of grace are served up. *ST* August 1868:339–40.

The church was not just Charles's job; he loved the church. And he longed for his people to love the church also, because the church is the "banquetting house" where Christ meets with his people.

BANQUETTING DAYS
[Song of Solomon] 3:4

"It was but a little that I passed from them, but I found in him whom my soul loveth: I held him, and would not let him go, until I had brought him into my mother's house, and into the chamber of her who conceived me."

To appreciate poetry thoroughly one needs to be a poet, and it is true that to love this song we need to be in love with its object. He who could grasp the works of a certain orator, we are told, might rest assured that he was no mean orator himself, and truly he who can sing this canticle of rapture must be a member of the bride and a friend of the Bride-Groom.

This portion of the golden dialogue came from the mouth of the chosen bride. She recounts the experience of delight she had at the sight of him, the great refreshment of his shadow, and the sweetness of his fruit. Now she represents him as bringing her into the banquetting house with a banner waving over her head. Here is a double figure expressive of the idea of joy and feasting with triumph and victory.

The orientals thought much of banquets and made the banquetting room the best part of their mansion. The walls, floor, and furniture were of the most costly and elegant kind, and the feasts were generally most sumptuous and expensive. The other idea is as well understood in our country as in any other. The device upon it is, however, well worthy of notice for it is so to speak our coat of arms. The sacred banner of the Danes had a black raven, that of Constantine a cross, and ours has love on a Cross. This is the means of our conquest, the ornament of our strength.

And now from these words I deduce the doctrine that God's people have sometimes special days of feasting and joy. I shall, by the good help of God, attempt to notice these times, dwelling on each and attempting to show why on that occasion God thus manifested his love so peculiarly.

I. IMMEDIATELY AFTER CONVERSION.

Usually, but not always, the poor returning sinner receives after regeneration a season of joy and gladness such as he seldom knows afterwards. Our Lord has beautifully pictured this in the case of the prodigal, and I am sure many poor prodigals now find their reception the same. I know for my own part that I was brought into the banquetting house. Look at Pilgrim how he rejoiced when his burden was gone. And the biographies of many good men testify the same.

Now it may be that some souls here are mourning because the first glory seems to have departed, and although I cannot allow that our first <u>love</u> ought to flag, yet I may allow that our first joy usually does decline, and therefore let us look at this subject for our comfort.

1. Much of the first joy is the result of novelty; at least that contributes. The change is so great, the blessings so new, the sights so fresh that the soul thinks it can never have enough and could clap its hands in extacy of delight.

2. God gives more comfort because they are very weak. After being hunted by the devil, the soul is half dead and therefore wines and cordials are used.

3. Our enemies are then peculiarly full of rage. Satan will not willingly lose his subjects and brings fiery temptations to distress them. Therefore God doth sustain them the more.

4. God loveth to make this a notable time. It is our birthday, our marriage, our resurrection morning, and he would have it remembered. Therefore he giveth the day a coronal of glory. Truly we can say of the time of our espousals, ["]He brought me into his banquetting house.["]

II. IN SUFFERINGS FOR THE TRUTH'S SAKE.

Persecution, as it cannot destroy the children of God, so also it cannot destroy their peace. It is a miracle indeed that men should be able to rejoice in all the agonies of death aggravated by the torments of their foes, but so it has been. Witness Stephen, Paul, and Silas. Read the book of Martyrs and see what grace can do.

John Huss smiled at his iron chain and said it was not a greater burden than the cross to his Lord. Indeed so glorious has been the end of many that it has been imagined by some that they did not really suffer, but this is not true.

1. God sustained them to fulfill his promise. He has promised to be with us at all times, and this being one of the times, he thus fulfils his promise. The red names in the calendar are names which show the truth of God.

2. God sustained them as witnesses. For men could not help seeing that there was some truth in such a religion.

3. God sustained them as trophies to his glory. The good workm[a]n will let his work be tried and roughly used to test its real strength, so does our God.

If times of trial come again, let us trust that then we shall be brought into the banquetting house with the banner of love waving over us.

III. IN PERSONAL AFFLICTION.

No trouble seems joyous but grievous, but I believe that tried saints have the sweetest morsels and the most frequent banquets. And this arises partly from the fact:

1. That we are driven more from the creature to the creator. I lay tossing on my bed, and now I turn my face to the wall. The friend is dead, now I value the friend who sticketh closer than a brother.

2. Then we look more to the next world than when in health, and glimpses of glory are always good. Many a saint has blessed God for his sick bed and almost longed to return, and has sung:

> "Affliction may press me they cannot destroy,
> One glimpse of his love turns them all into joy.
> And the bitterest tears if he smile but on them,
> Like dew in the sunshine grows diamond and gem."

IV. IN THE USE OF MEANS.

We need not go into the furnace to get a banquet, and it would be idle to wish it, for in ordinary means we may have it. It is too frequently the case that we come to ordinances and go away unprofited, and that because we came not with hearty prayer thereunto or perhaps the minister was much to blame.

<u>Preaching</u> is a primary ordinance and many a sermon is like manna.

<u>Prayer</u> is another most important one, and if ever we get near God it is here, when we melt in love.

<u>Singing</u> too is not to be despised. It quickens the motions of the heart.

<u>Bible Study</u> and Meditation also—

But especially in the sacred ordinances of <u>Baptism</u> and the <u>Lord's supper</u>. The one is often a swim in a sea of rest. The other is a banquet of love.

God could bless without ordinances, but usually he does not, for he will honour his own ordinances and have us honour them too. Bless his name we have sometimes been at the banquetting house, and when we do not we will lie at the pool.

V. BEFORE, IN, AND AFTER ATTACKS OF SATAN.

<u>Before</u>. As good captains will look well to their men before battle so does our Leader. He puts us on the [D]electable Hills. He takes us to the house beautiful before we fight Satan. Jesus went from the Jordan covered with the Spirit straight into contest with Satan. Watch then.

<u>In</u>. None of us can tell how much grace it requires to withstand the devil. He that has had one fight with him will dread another. He groans all the fight through, and finds he has no strength to throw away but had need to use it all.

<u>After</u>. But it is after the fight that the triumph comes. Then the hand is seen with wine for cheering, fruit for feeding, and leaves for healing. The battle is over, the dragon is gone, and now the poor soul is ministered unto by angels. A triumph is awarded him and the King delighteth to honour him by inviting him to his banquet.

VI. IN THE ARTICLE OF DEATH.

God often keeps the best wine until the last. The last day is often the finest, and the door of the sepulchre hath golden nails in it. Could good men return, they would a tale rehearse of bliss in dying rich and rare.

Even what we see is worthy of all attention. We see the joyful eye, the uplifted hand, we hear the shout, and we can see that God is giving a banquet to the soul. Fear not to die, but fear to doubt, for he who doubts dies a hundred deaths in fearing one.

Oh God, help me.

"BRAND PLUCKED FROM THE FIRE"

Editor's Summary

This unfinished sermon likely hearkens back to an experience that Charles had during his time at Waterbeach. He tells the stor y in his autobiography of the day he could not come up with a sermon text as the afternoon service was approaching:

> Time was brief, the hour was striking, and in some alarm I told the honest farmer that I could not for the life of me recollect what I had intended to preach about. "Oh!" he said, "never mind; you will be sure to have a good word for us." Just at that moment, a blazing block of wood fell out of the fire upon the hearth at my feet, smoking into my eyes and nose at a great rate. "There," said the farmer, "there's a text for you, sir, — 'Is not this a brand plucked out of the fire?'" "No," I thought, "it was not plucked out, for it fell out of itself." Here, however, was a text, an illustration, and a leading thought as a nest-egg for more. Further light came, and the discourse was certainly not worse than my more prepared effusions; it was better in the best sense, for one or two came forward declaring themselves to have been aroused and converted through that afternoon's sermon. I have always considered that it was a happy circumstance that I had forgotten the text from which I had intended to preach. *Autobiography* 1:266.

"Brand Plucked from the Fire" is recorded in *The Lost Sermons*, Volume 5, Sermon 242 (*LS* 5:104). After the first preaching occasion, Charles preached the message at least six more times. He may have intended to revise this sermon for New Park Street, in order to preach it once more, but simply did not finish it. Another possibility is that, rather than rewriting the sermon, he decided to use his original notes and preach it more extemporaneously.

BRAND PLUCKED
FROM THE FIRE
Zechariah 3:2

"And the Lord *said unto Satan, The* Lord *rebuke thee, O Satan; even the* Lord *that hath chosen Jerusalem rebuke thee: is not this a brand plucked out of the fire?"*

How good God is to us as to teaching us. He has made the world his pulpit and nature his preacher. On high we see in Sun, moon, and stars—the Sun of Righteousness, the Star of Bethlehem, and the church, fair as the moon. On earth— the rose and lily, the cedar, sheep and lions, rivers, mountains, and fields give us sermons of sacred instruction.

So here we sit by our fire sides.

[This page is followed by five blank pages in Charles's notebook.]

"PROGRESS IN SACRED KNOWLEDGE"

Editor's Summary

For Charles, growth in "Doctrinal Knowledge" and in "Experimental Knowledge" was essential for the Christian life. He believed that "God has put in man a thirst after knowledge." Furthermore, he believed that "when God makes the man a new man, he does not destroy this desire but turns it to a new channel." For those in Christ, this "torrent of love of knowledge" is meant to run "over the golden sands of the Bible."

However, Charles notes one complication in this sermon, namely, that "the Creator alone knows all things intimately and perfectly." While man has been made to know God, it is "an inevitable part of our existence, that we should acquire knowledge by degrees." After all, "can we imagine that sacred wisdom is to be gained at once[?]"

Charles would later preach on Hos 6:3 two more times, "Constancy and Inconstancy—A Contrast" (*MTP* 15, Sermon 852) and "The Blessings of Following On" (*MTP* 21, Sermon 1246), the second of which shares some thematic content and structure with the sermon here. Charles organized this message into three main points: "I. A Great Truth. Knowledge of Divine Things Progressive"; "II. A Great Direction. Follow on to Know the Lord"; and "III. A Great Inducement. His Going Forth Etc." He directs most of his attention, however, to the second section, where he offers a brief catechism of sorts. His attention to detail and urgent tone are well explained when he warns, "It is utterly impossible to remain sound on other points if we forsake the doctrine of a three-[in]-one God, or in any way imbibe errors concerning the Godhead."

Consider some of his exhortations:

We must know a [T]rinity. If we do not, we shall always be making blunders. There is no doctrine upon which we can err more easily or fearfully.

We must know the Father. And if we make a mistake in underrating his power, his sovereignty, his love, his immutability, then [our] system will be a wreck.

We must know the Son. As the Eternal Son of God, really incarnate, but yet really God. To deny this is the unkindest stab of all, for Jesus is the heart of all true religion.

We must know the Spirit. For if we see him not in his true character we shall be wrong on the subject of regeneration, calling, preserving grace, sanctification, or in all and more.

However, Charles knew that growing in doctrinal and experiential knowledge was not for the faint of heart. Accordingly, he advised his congregation to remember the following in their quest to know the Lord:

1. Be not distressed because you know little.
2. Be not afraid of a doctrine because it is mysterious.
3. Keep to this "curriculum" and so matriculate for heaven. Above all, Love God much and so you will know him.

PROGRESS IN SACRED KNOWLEDGE

Hosea 6:3

*"Then shall we know, if we follow on to know the L*ORD*: his going forth is prepared as the morning; and he shall come unto us as the rain, as the latter and former rain unto the earth."*

God has put in man a thirst after knowledge. This thirst unquenchable impels men to make discoveries, to weary themselves by study, to intermeddle with all wisdom, and even to venture into the sea, the air, and the bowels of the earth. So insatiable is the soul of man that the sky must be measured, the stars numbered, the mountains weighed, and the very storms mapped in their course.

When God makes the man a new man, he does not destroy this desire but turns it in a new channel, and with the same force the impetuous torrent of love of knowledge runs over the golden sands of the Bible. It rejoices the soul when a new truth flashes on the mind. It grieves it when it finds itself still ignorant and a learner yet. So ye learners lately come to the school of sacred wisdom. Be not dismayed but listen to her words of comfort this morning.

I.   A GREAT TRUTH. KNOWLEDGE OF DIVINE THINGS IS PROGRESSIVE.

II. A GREAT DIRECTION. FOLLOW ON TO KNOW THE LORD.

III. A GREAT INDUCEMENT. HIS GOING FORTH ETC.

Wind up with a few words of advice to learners.

I. A GREAT FACT. SACRED KNOWLEDGE IS PROGRESSIVELY OBTAINED.

It is so, I am sure all will admit, and I suppose it is necessarily so. From our condition as creatures it seems to be an inevitable part of our existence, that we should acquire knowledge by degrees.

The Creator alone knows all things intimately and perfectly. But I suspect that all created intelligence is so formed that, like the plant, it has its blade and ear and various degrees of development ere it arrive[s] at maturity. So it is with us. I know in secular learning [that] at first it is the simple primer, the spelling book, the catechism, then the grammar, and elements of science, and so on till we can revel with delight in all the abstractions of mathematics or fairy regions of poetry.

And can we imagine that sacred wisdom is to be gained at once[?] Is a man to be a Christian sage in an instant, or a theologian in an hour[?] No, we begin with a slight tinge of light, and by degrees the sun arises.

True, there are some first principles which the babe knows as well as the hoary headed sire. There are certain Christian instincts, if I may so call them, which we have in the morning of Xn life. But still the main science of our Religion must be learned. We must wait patiently and expect it by degrees. See Ezekiel's river. Jesus' mustard seed.

This progress in Knowledge, I think is twofold – Doctrinal Knowledge
and Experiential Knowledge.

1. Turn we then to Doctrinal Knowledge. It is a fact that this is a gradual attainment.

   There are some mysteries in fact which are here below inexplicable altogether. Such as the Trinity, the Filiation of the Son, the Pr[o]cession of the Spirit, the origin of evil, the congruity of Sovereignty and responsibility, etc. etc.

   And other doctrines seem to be equally mysterious at first view. Such as <u>election</u>, of which the old divines said, "The doctrine of this high mystery of predestination is to be handled with special prudence and care." See Bapt. Confession. 10.

The young convert often objects to it. We begin Arminian but end Calvinistic. The enquirer had better make his <u>calling</u> sure, and then election must be right, but this is one of the things we shall learn by degrees.

[E]ffectual [C]alling, <u>Imputed Righteousness</u>, yea even Redemption itself must come under this category, <u>This shall ye know</u>. So also with many texts of Scripture, hard points, dark allusions, etc. They are classics you cannot read yet. The knowledge of these things is certainly important but not absolutely requisite, and no man needs to be in distress about them.

2. Experimental Knowledge from its very nature must be acquired and cannot be intuitive. Here too there are certain elements such as regeneration, conviction, [or] faith which every babe experiences, but there are heights and depths which none but advanced pilgrims know.

   The reading of biographies will give us much to talk of, but can never be a substitute for real experience. Just as the landsman may read of the sea but he cannot understand sea life

   Conflicts with Apollyon, [H]ills of [D]ifficulty, Doubting Castle, Delectable Mountains, and [L]ands of Beulah are to be read of and [are] far better known when seen ~~enjoyed~~. Providence has its mazes, its mysteries, but these we shall know more of. Our own hearts are as yet unexplored regions. The promises are not all tried. The banqueting house has not very often been entered.

   And now let me not be mistaken. I cannot desire for you that you may have all the experience some have. I do not want you to go over the stile, or after the Flatterer, or to slip when going down the hill. Seek the best experience and you will experience the best.

   One more caveat I must put in, viz., that while I believe it to be progressive, I would not have it interpreted that we all grow alike or grow at the same rate at all seasons. No. Some for wise ends are led into the secrets and learn much that they may be the more useful, and there are times when the same Xn grows far more rapidly than others. All children do not grow alike, plants do not always seem to increase. We sometimes learn as much in an hour as in a year at another season. God is as sovereign in this as well as other things. Let us seek to please him that we may increase in grace.

II. A GREAT DIRECTION. FOLLOW ON TO KNOW THE LORD.

There is no "if" in the original. We might supply "when" or "for," for it is not all conditional but is positive. Our good translators give us the "if" in italics so that we may not mistake [it], and certainly there are no "ifs" in our perseverance. The man who seeks to know the Lord is in the way to know every thing else.

1. If I seek to know God first, I may expect his aid in learning the rest.

2. If I know the Lord, I am in an advantageous situation. I can more easily go <u>down</u> from the Creator to his creatures, than <u>up</u> the hill from nature to its God. I have begun to build a house by laying the foundation. I have the keel of my ship. The root of all existence. I am repeating my alphabet with "a" first.

Let us expand the idea:

1. **We must know a [T]rinity.** If we do not, we shall always be making blunders. There is no doctrine upon which we can err more easily or more fearfully. If I look at the Son as the Father in flesh, or talk of the Spirit as an influence and not a person, I shall soon deny a number of other vital points. Away goes the atonement, election, etc. etc.

2. **We must know the Father.** And if we make a mistake in underrating his power, his sovereignty, his love, his immutability, then [our] system will soon be a wreck. Study God and then you must be of the truth. Some men are always looking on man and his position, which is very well. But to look on God as the Creator, absolutely God, would do them more good. Look on the sun and the light of the moon is there too. Look on God and the glory of all creatures is in him.

3. **We must know the Son.** As the Eternal Son of God, really incarnate, but yet really God. To deny this is the unkindest stab of all, for Jesus is the heart of all true religion. Know him in his offices, his love, his death, his resurrection, ascension, and second coming. He is the glass through which we discern all things aright. He is heaven rendered tangible.

4. **We must know the Spirit.** For if we see him not in his true character we shall be wrong on the subject of regeneration, calling, preserving grace, sanctification, or in all and more. It is utterly impossible to remain sound on other points if we forsake the doctrine of a three-[in]-one God, or in any way imbibe errors concerning the Godhead.

There are many ways of knowing and following on to know the Lord such as prayer, meditation, reading the Scriptures, experience etc., but by all means, let this be your main study: to know the Lord and to know him truly.

Here we shall only know in part but if we follow on to know, to the bed of death, the sepulchre, [and] the resurrection, we shall behold our all[-] glorious head and be for ever like him, and then shall we know even as we are known.

III. A GREAT INDUCEMENT.

1. We shall see glorious light if we go on, for his going forth is prepared as the morning. Gradual but certain. Casting a light on all, making darkness flee, and chasing our dreariness away. Here is joy indeed. In all learning there is profit, but in this the greatest of all. For joy and gladness shall be ours.

2. We shall be refreshed. By rain in the commencement and seasonable rain at all times. Our barren souls shall be revived. Our deserts made to bud.

We want the latter rain when we sow and the early rain when the seed is green. In fact we always want it. A Christian lives from hand to mouth, and a mercy it is to him that rain comes so constantly to refresh him.

Go on then to know the Lord and now let me advise you:

1. Be not distressed because you know little.
2. Be not afraid of a doctrine because it is mysterious.
3. Keep to this "curriculum" and so matriculate for heaven. Above all, Love God much and so will you know him.

Amen

"THE PIERCED SIDE"

Editor's Summary

It appears that Charles preached on this text three more times: "Jesus, the King of Truth" (*MTP* 18, Sermon 1086), "Second-Hand" (*MTP* 45, Sermon 2624), and "The King in Pilate's Hall" (*MTP* 49, Sermon 2826). However, none of these shares significant overlapping content or structural similarity with "The Pierced Side." This sermon, though, does seem to have been significantly influenced by John Gill's New Testament commentary.

Charles thought it best to "muse long" over the atoning death of Christ in order to prove two key points to his congregation:

1. That Christ's death was true, and necessary to his resurrection; and
2. That Christ's death secured both the blessings of justification and sanctification for the believer.

With respect to the first point, Charles asserts that "Jesus was proved to be really dead, for such a pierce was evidently enough to take away life even if not destroyed already." He further notes that "this is a very vital point, for if he died not then he did not rise. Redemption is not finished, and we are yet in our sins."

On this topic, Gill wrote:

with a spear pieced his side. . . . This the soldier did, partly out of spite to Christ, and partly to know whether he was really dead; and which was so ordered by divine providence, that it might beyond all doubt appear that he really died, and was not taken down alive from the cross; so that there might be no room to call in question the truth of his resurrection, when he should appear alive again. John Gill, *An Exposition of the New Testament* (London:

printed for the author, 1747, The Spurgeon Library), 2:109, emphasis in original. Hereafter, *An Exposition of the New Testament.*

Regarding the second key point, Charles sided with Gill against Albert Barnes, who claimed that "there is no meaning whatever in [the] double effusion" of bodily fluids that occurred when Christ's pericardium was ruptured by the soldier's spear. Gill's position was:

> *forthwith came there out blood and water.* . . . They signify the blessings of sanctification and justification, the grace of one being represented by water . . . and the other by blood, and both from Christ. *An Exposition of the New Testament* 2:109–10, emphasis added.

Charles did not simply regurgitate commentary material, however, but sifted it and amplified it devotionally. He speaks pleadingly of the blood, saying, "Our price, our ransom. The emblem of justification. Gushing from him. Oh poor sinner, here is pardoning mercy and forgiving love." As for the water, it is "our cleansing and purification. This is Sanctification which we all hope to experience."

THE PIERCED SIDE

John 19:34–37

"But one of the soldiers with a spear pierced his side, and forthwith came there out blood and water. And he that saw it bare record, and his record is true: and he knoweth that he saith true, that ye might believe. For these things were done, that the scripture should be fulfilled, A bone of him shall not be broken. And again another scripture saith, They shall look on him whom they pierced."

Last time we met before we partook of the Lord's supper we went to Calvary, and what went we there to see? A jewel rare and precious. A costly piece of workmanship. Yea! I say, and far more than this, the precious body of God's well beloved son, the casket which once contained his soul, the untenanted palace of the King of Angels. We may well be pardoned if we stay and muse long over the corpse of this murdered innocent, this King of Martyrs, this slaughtered priest, this injured friend.

And surely if the Holy Ghost was particular in recording, we may be particular in noticing each single event of this dread hour, each several action performed towards our Saviour. I can only bless God that he provided one biographer who should stand at the cross and make a careful note of all the proceedings upon mount Calvary. Come then again, let us go to Calvary and see this great sight. The body preserved from the breaking of its bones is yet to be maimed. And the hand which could not perform the one, most easily inflicts the other.

I.   THE IMPIOUS ACT.

II. THE WONDERFUL EFFUSION.

III. THE REMARKABLE PROPHECY.

May the Blessed Spirit aid me.

I.   THE IMPIOUS ACT.

Who is there amongst us who will not give the act this title[?] It was indeed an impious deed and each of us may bless God that we did not stand in that soldier's place, for:

1. The Dust of Saints is precious, and to put indignity upon their bones is an offence to heaven. Much more, then, to touch the body of the first elect. Truly the men who acquit Judas may set this man free as guiltless, but to me it seems a crime beyond the blackness of night.

2. This man knew or might have known that Christ was an innocent being, indeed a superior person, the Son of God. But though he knew, yet he hated the image of all virtue.

    Blair said that if Virtue should come down on earth all would love her, but alas for him, virtue did come, was incarnate, was hunted about the earth by the enmity of man, and now that she is gone, even the body she inhabited is pierced by a soldier.

    If we wanted proof of the depravity of our race here, we could find enough. An unfallen world would have hailed the Saviour, and if he had died they would have kissed the body and have pressed it to their bosoms. Ah what a stroke was there, all of us are criminals by unbelief etc., we pierced him, so says the prophecy. Oh fearful guilt, this is the epitome of sin. This stain must be on us unless we reap the benefit of the blood.

But while we weep over this, let us rejoice that:

   (1.) God's ends were answered. His Son was proved to be the Messiah of prophecy. See Zech. XII. 10. And what is more, [his Son] proved to be Jehovah, for the original passage reads it "<u>me</u>." Christ being really Jehovah.

   (2.) Jesus was proved to be really dead, for such a pierce was evidently enough to take away life even if not destroyed already, and this is a very vital point, for if he died not then he did not rise. Redemption is not finished, and we are yet in our sins.

The Jews never insinuated as the Gnostics did in later times, that he did not die in reality but only suffered syncope or protracted fainting. Here was proof positive of a real death. This thrust made the "It is finished" even more sure, and thus while grieving over the guilt, let us rejoice in the act, for by it faith doth live afresh.

Before we dismiss this point, let us look and admire our Saviour's body. See his side opened, and a passage made to his heart. Here is a window, one may read his heart through it. Here is a door, our wants and prayers find most ready access. Here is a treasure house for faith. Come thou unbelieving Thomas, reach hither thy hand and thrust it into his side and be not faithless but believing. Precious, precious Lord. I would long to lodge in this cleft, and seek to be bone of thy bone and flesh of thy flesh, and like as Eve was taken out of the first Adam's side, so would I in common with thy children rejoice in this thy side, believing that out of it were we formed.

II. THE WONDERFUL EFFUSION.

I had thought of saying, ["]the miraculous effusion,["] and I believe it was so, but almost all the writers on this point seem to think it was a natural effect of the spear thrust. The pericardium was pierced, and the small quantity of water contained therein flowed forth with the blood of the heart.

I should hardly imagine that naturally there would be a sufficient quantity of ~~blood~~ water in the pericardium to be noticed by John, and it seems the more improbable if he was stationed at any distance from him. If it was natural, might it not result from the separation by death of the red globules from the liquor sanguinis which constituted the water[?] I am however more inclined to regard it as being a miracle. Be it so or no, I am sure it has a meaning, and we will try and find it out.

Albert Barnes tells us that there is no meaning whatever in this double effusion, but with all deference to him, there was. Some will never allow anything but a literal meaning to the Bible, and in the height of critical learning laugh at the poor things who see more. But happy is the child who sees beauty in the fieldflower and hears the voice of God in the rolling thunder. Here however, we are not left in doubt, for in I John V.6 we find an evident allusion to this very circumstance. Not with water only—all the prophets came with water to purify and cleanse for the future—but they could not bring blood to atone for the past. This our Jesus did.

Blood. Our price, our ransom. The emblem of <u>Justification</u>. Gushing from him. Oh poor sinner, here is pardoning mercy and forgiving love. This is at once honouring to God and safe to man. Oh precious blood that fattens the soil of my heart. One drop might quench a flaming world. Blood was sacred by divine law but thy blood how sacred, how divine.

<u>Water</u>. Our cleansing and purifying. This is <u>Sanctification</u> which we all hope to experience. This is the true water of life. The Elixir of Immortal Life and Unsullied Purity.

These two are united, let none sunder them. Let us in preaching and life put them together. Now, oh double stream, flow o'er my head, give me a Baptism in thy floods and let me rise like sheep from the washing without spot or wrinkle or any such thing.

III. A REMARKABLE PROPHECY.

Not to dwell on what we have hinted at, viz., that the word "me" is used in the original. We would only observe that this may be regarded either as a promise or a threatening.

1. As a promise it was fulfilled in many of the Jews in Christ's day, and in both Gentile and Jew it shall be true: they shall look and be saved.

2. As a threat, when he comes in clouds of vengeance the sight will be awful indeed. Oh Lord help us to look <u>now</u> by <u>faith</u>, that we may not look <u>then</u> in terror.

Sermon No. 385

"PAUL'S COMMISSION"

Editor's Summary

"Paul's Commission" is one of four sermons in Notebook 9 that Charles left unfinished. The others are: "Brand Plucked from the Fire" (Sermon 382); "A Glad Congregation" (Sermon 386); and "[Untitled]" (Sermon 388).

Though he composed a strong start to this message, Charles did not complete all the main divisions and left essentially ten pages blank. Nevertheless, he preached on Eph 3:8 two more times in "The Unsearchable Riches of Christ" (*MTP* 13, Sermon 745) and "A Grateful Summary of Twenty Volumes" (*MTP* 20, Sermon 1209). Notably, only the first Roman numeral of "The Unsearchable Riches of Christ" has content and structure similar to "Paul's Commission."

Charles's introduction here helps to provide a tentative date for this partial manuscript:

> I this morning commence a new era in my history. Hitherto I have preached to you as a supply, but now as your minister, chosen by you without a dissenting voice. I feel that the work is great, and I am but ill qualified for it, and cannot better express the feelings of my soul than in the words of the text.

The phrase "chosen . . . without a dissenting voice" likely refers to the unanimous vote for his installment by the New Park Street Chapel congregation, which took place on Wednesday, April 19, 1854. *Autobiography* 1:352. Accordingly, Charles probably preached this sermon at New Park Street on April 30, following his last message as pastor of Waterbeach Chapel on April 23.

It appears that Charles was lightly influenced by John Gill's exposition of this passage:

This is an instance of the great humility of the Apostle; and indeed the greatest saints are, generally speaking, the most humble souls. . . . The reasons for their great humility are; because they have the largest discoveries of the love and grace of God and Christ, which are of a soul-humbling nature; they are most sensible of their own sinfulness, which keeps them low in their own sight. *An Exposition of the New Testament* 3:77.

Furthermore, Charles's reference to Placilla, Roman empress and wife of Theodosius I, indicates possible influence from the Thomas Brooks work, "The Unsearchable Riches of Christ." Thomas Brooks, *The Complete Works of Thomas Brooks* (Edinburgh: James Nichol; London: James Nisbet, 1826, The Spurgeon Library), 3:1–232. Although incomplete, what we do have here offers a unique reflection on Charles's understanding of his own call to ministry through a comparison to the apostle Paul.

PAUL'S COMMISSION
Ephesians 3:8

"Unto me, who am less than the least of all saints, is this grace given, that I should preach among the Gentiles the unsearchable riches of Christ."

I this morning commence a new era in my history. Hitherto I have preached to you as a supply, but now as your minister, chosen by you without a dissenting voice. I feel that the work is great, and I am but ill qualified for it, and cannot better express the feelings of my soul than in the words of the text. But leaving these thoughts, we will by divine assistance regard Paul's word with care. We notice:

I.   A PERSON CHOSEN.

II. A QUALIFICATION GIVEN.

III. A WORK ALLOTTED.

IV. A

I.   A PERSON CHOSEN.

In the eye of God, [Paul] was a most suitable person to perform his work. In our eye he seems to have been eminently adapted for his work, but in his own estimation he was altogether unworthy of so great an office. His humility was very great, although it is plain that he was no second[-]rate man, nor was he a man of mean spirit.

It was his humility which made him speak as he does in this place. And mark what his humility saith; it useth a double diminutive. Faith, love, and humility are such heavenly graces that there is no earthly language suitable to their lips, unless it can be loaded with hyperbole and improved by invention.

He puts himself at the foot of the lowest form of all, and adds his name to the list of the unworthy. How came Paul by this humility? We wish to know so that we too may procure it.

1. He remembered his former life. When he recollected how he had dragged men and women to prison, he could not but see his own unworthiness. Thus Jacob thought of the day when he passed over Jordan with a staff. David did not forget the meanness of his origin, but remembering it he cried "What am I etc."

    Those who have acquired riches should remember their former poverty. The healthy should visit the bed where they lay in sickness, and we all should remember the pit whence we were digged. Plasilla, the empress of Theodosius, used to say "Remember, O husband, what lately you were and what now you are; so shall you govern well the kingdom and give God his due praise for so great an advancement." Sir Thomas Gresham ever remembered the grasshopper which by its chirpings drew [someone] to see him when a foundling, and put the grasshopper in his coat of arms. We must not forget our former low estate, and when exalted by mercy, let us be humbled by our former poverty.

2. He understood his own depravity. [Paul] groaned under a body of sin and death. He was not a superficial searcher. He went deep into the recesses of his soul and saw his own vileness. He who knows his heart will humble his heart. It is said by old authors that the peacock, when it looks at its black feet, always lets fall its fine plumes, and surely it should be so with us.

3. He lived in communion with God. Of all humbling things, this is the most humbling. When I read the lives of pious and industrious divines I shrink into nothingness. How much more then if I contemplate the attributes and works of Christ my God[?] He who lived in the tropics will shiver in the cold. He who has been in king's palaces will know the meanness of his own house. The reason why we are proud is because we live far from God. Reflect on him and be abased. Hide thine eyes and fall prostrate; then shall the Lord visit us with mercy and give us all[-]sufficient grace.

II. A QUALIFICATION GIVEN.

[Blank]

[This page is followed by nine blank pages in Charles's notebook.]

"A GLAD CONGREGATION"

Editor's Summary

Yet again, Charles began composing a sermon—this one on Neh 8:17, a text he did not preach on again—but he did not complete it. This time, however, he left no pages blank. It's unclear why Charles did not complete the third main division: "III. What Should Make Us So?" In any case, "A Glad Congregation" is the third of four unfinished sermons in Notebook 9.

Here, Charles seeks to provoke God's people to great gladness. He opens his discourse by observing, "There are many ways of doing the same thing, and in religion the way of doing a thing is everything." His point *was not* that Christianity was the same as other religions, but rather, that Christianity has a unique motivation for holy living: gladness. In fact, Charles would later argue in "No Condemnation" (Sermon 399) that Christian gratitude is a unique response to God's grace in justification by faith. Said succinctly, "I am not restrained from sin by fear of law, but by love to the lawgiver." Accordingly, Charles believed that Christians ought to be a holy and happy people because of the great salvation bought and secured by Jesus Christ.

A GLAD CONGREGATION
Nehemiah 8:17

"And all the congregation of them that were come again out of the captivity made booths, and sat under the booths: for since the days of Jeshua the son of Nun unto that day had not the children of Israel done so. And there was very great gladness."

There are many ways of doing the same thing, and in religion the way of doing a thing is everything. Take for instance going up to the house of God: to some it is a burden, to others a delight. The best way to go to God's house is with shouts of joy, and when there, he is the true worshipper who rejoices in the service and is glad. God loveth a willing congregation who are glad at the remembrance of his holiness. Here we have a glad congregation.

I.   WHY WERE THEY GLAD?

II. WHY IT IS TO BE DESIRED THAT WE SHOULD BE GLAD?

III. WHAT SHOULD MAKE US SO?

I.   <u>WHY WERE THEY GLAD?</u>

When we see a large company all full of joy, we naturally enquire the reason. Is their corn and wine increased? Has victory crowned their nation? No, other reasons give gladness.

1. They are in their own Jerusalem.
2. They have heard the word of God and they understand its meaning.
3. They have once mourned over sin.
4. They have been sending portions to others.
5. They keep all the ordinances blameless.

Do not these things meet in some of us[?] If we have neglected one point, let us seek to amend our fault and be happy.

II. WHY SHOULD WE DESIRE TO BE GLAD?

1. For Comfort of ourselves and others.
2. For Unity in the church.
3. For Strength against temptation and in duty.
4. For Enlargement for others will join.

"COMING UP FROM THE WILDERNESS"

Editor's Summary

In this sermon, Charles takes a spiritualized approach to the Song of Songs, reading it as an allegory of Christ's relationship to the church. In the introduction, he laments that "it would be very difficult to see any connection between this verse and the context. In fact, I think there is none whatever." However, he found help by consulting John Gill's *An Exposition of the Old Testament* (4:640–41), and in particular Gill's *An Exposition of the Book of Solomon's Song*, which according to Charles was "the best thing Gill ever did." C. H. Spurgeon, *Commenting and Commentaries: Two Lectures Addressed to the Students of The Pastor's College, Metropolitan Tabernacle, Together with a Catalogue of Biblical Commentaries and Expositions* (London: Passmore & Alabaster, 1876), 113. Hereafter, *Commenting*.

Charles was an avid reader of Gill's commentaries and made use of them throughout his life—from his earliest days as an itinerant preacher to his final days at the Metropolitan Tabernacle. Notably, Charles would one day reserve some glowing comments for his co-laborer in ministry, saying:

> A very distinguished place is due to Dr. Gill. Beyond all controversy, Gill was one of the most able Hebraists of his day, and in other matters no mean proficient. . . . His great work on the Holy Scriptures is greatly prized at the present day by the best authorities. . . . For good, sound, massive, sober sense in commenting, who can excel Gill? *Commenting*, 8–9.

Charles was also impressed with his colleague's industry, remarking that "[Gill] was always at work; it is difficult to say when he slept, for he wrote 10,000 folio pages of theology." *Commenting*, 8–9. With Gill's prior ministry at New Park Street Chapel, it is likely that Charles was inspired by aspects of his life and service as well.

Turning to the text, Charles preached on Song 8:5 one more time in "Leaning on Our Beloved" (*MTP* 15, Sermon 877). That later sermon shares enough thematically and structurally that it was probably influenced by this earlier one.

Charles organized this message around three questions: "I. What Does the Questioner Say?"; "II. Who Asks the Question?"; and "III. Who Shall Answer It?" Demonstrating his pastoral care, he encourages his congregation by directing their attention to the struggle and suffering the church has endured while awaiting her final reward. Indeed, from the beginning, "when [the Church] was but in her cradle the kings stood up against [her], she has had to wade through seas of blood." Accordingly, Charles asks, "Do you wonder at troubles believer[?] Do you count fiery trial strange[?] You are in a wilderness and you must carry your joys into it, for they certainly do not grow there."

However, the church can endure hardship, struggle, or strife by "leaning on her beloved." Every moment of faithfulness, "every hour and minute as it flies," brings the Christian "nearer the verge of the wilderness," where at last he or she can enjoy full, uninterrupted communion with Jesus Christ.

COMING UP FROM THE WILDERNESS

Song of Solomon 8:5

*"Who is this that cometh up from the wilderness, leaning upon her
beloved? I raised thee up under the apple tree: there thy mother brought
thee forth: there she brought thee forth that bare thee."*

It would be very difficult to see any connection between this verse and the context.
In fact, I think there is none whatever. But let it be remembered that this is not a
grand poem of sublimity. It is not the measured march of a Paradise Lost, nor the
soaring grandeur of Ezekiel, or even the Hallelujah of David. But it is the Song of
Songs, which is Solomon's and might rightly be entitled "To the chief musician a
song of Loves."

Love has a language of its own, we do not expect it to speak as we speak. It sees
coherence and connection where the cold calculating mind sees none. It is like
an ancient prophetess upon the tripos; she is borne away with inward frenzy and
her words are hurried and impassioned. Like the Sibyl in the cave, she writes her
verses not in a book but on leaves which the winds seem to scatter here and there in
confusion. Yet are the fragments worthy of preservation, thrice happy is the man
who thinks so.

We note, then, that our text is a parenthesis in the song, an involuntary,
unconnected exclamation. Let us further remark that it is a question, but no answer
whatever is given. It is a question, but the interlocutor is so entranced by the
melting music of the song that he does not wish to interrupt it even to gratify his
curiosity by an answer to his question.

He sees before him a beautiful female, far surpassing all terrestrials in fairness. Her exquisite loveliness charms him and he stands astonished at the place of her birth, a wilderness, and yet he forgets this in the view of a second person upon whom she leans, who from his looks he concludes to be her beloved.

I.   WHAT DOES THE QUESTIONER SAY?

II. WHO ASKS THE QUESTION?

III. WHO SHALL ANSWER IT?

I.   WHAT DOES THE QUESTIONER SAY?

He says, "who is this[?]" and points to yon wilderness, and we see the sight. We will view:

1.   The Place, a wilderness. Well might the spectator be astonished to see beauty in a wilderness. The appropriate place of beauty seems to be 'mid myrtle groves and sparkling rills and flowery walks. We are astonished to see beauty in the wilderness. The wild rose astonishes us, the bloom of the heather draws our eyes to it. Could we have thought it that the king's daughter, the elect lady, the Bride, the Lamb's wife should have been in the wilderness[?] Yet there you must mostly look for her. Look not in the halls of Nineveh or the colossal palaces of ~~Nineveh~~ Babylon, but look in the plains of Canaan in the tent of Abraham.

Turn not to the palaces of the Pharaohs or the temples of Carnac, but search in the wilderness of Sin around the foot of thorny Sinai.

Go on to the days of Ahab and search out the children of the [M]ost [H]igh. Ye shall not see them crowned at Samaria and honoured in her streets, but there in the dark cave you see them, and on the mountain brow you see their leader wrapping his shaggy robes around him, fit garb for a prophet of the wilderness.

Let your minds rush on to more modern times. In the days of Pagan Rome, where is the church, where are her cathedrals and lofty spires[?] Ah expect them not. Down in the catacombs or in the ruins of some subterranean aqueduct you may mark a small assembly; that is the church, all glorious in the eyes of her beloved.

Hasten on to the times of Rome's Popery. Is that scarlet clad woman the bride[?] She lets herself be seen in robes of splendor. Is she the church[?] No. No. Look on the Alpine peaks or in the valleys of Piedmont. There she is, the church in the wilderness. And not to trace her further, I would remind you of the days when the Mayflower carried away the sons of God to the rocks of New England, when the covenanters met in their gloomy glens and the dissenters in their secret conventicles.

She is the church of the wilderness. There she has been and there she is. It is a wilderness, for it is <u>inhospitable</u>. She finds no one to entertain her, no friend to give her lodging. This is not her rest. There is no bed for her repose, no mansion for her dwelling. On the contrary her foes are many. When she was but in her cradle the kings stood up against [her], she has had to wade through seas of blood.

The ground is tracked with her gore. The stakes, the gloomy towers, the racks remain as gloomy waymarkers of her sore travail and labour. Smithfield is still witness to her pains. It has been to her a den of leopards. She has in the person of her children been sawn in sunder, or been made to wander in skin, etc. etc.

It is a wilderness, for it is <u>dangerous</u> and <u>full</u> of <u>troubles</u>. No one loves to journey through barren plains [or] over burning sands. There are thirst and hunger to be endured, toilsome march to accomplish, sinooms [hot desert gales] and winds to endure. The serpent lies in the path, the Amalekites come down from the mountain, the foot is blistered and the heart is faint.

Do you wonder at troubles, believer[?] Do you count the fiery trial strange[?] You are in a wilderness and you must carry your joys into it, for they certainly do not grow [there]. You will cry out in weariness, you will pant like the thirsty hart. Do not be astonished at it. "He told you no less, this is his will," therefore go on. It is a wilderness for <u>intricacy</u>.

The traveller often stands and wonders which way he ought to go. Wildernesses are pathless places. Shifting sands have no roads. We too in our daily life seem at times to be in a maze. We see straits too narrow for our sailings and rivers too boisterous to swim in. Have we not been like Israel before the Red Sea[?] And are not all the elect at times put at a nonplus to know the path of duty[?] Thanks be to God the stars are ever shining, the Star of Bethlehem points to the haven of peace. We follow it and are safe.

We come now to notice:

2. <u>The Direction</u>. They come up out of the wilderness. In this desert she has to journey not into it but out of it. She is leaving her troubles and her sins behind her, she is coming up. The saints do so:

1. Naturally, by <u>the lapse of time</u>. If I am one of the Lord's people, every hour and minute as it flies brings me nearer the verge of the wilderness. The worldling has his back to the sun and journeys on to deeper shades, but we are on our road to light, and each hour brings us nearer.

2. Spiritually, by <u>growth in grace</u>. The true sons of the Lord will daily increase their sanctification. Some do not believe in progressive sanctification, but such do err. We do not think that sin grows weaker, but we believe that the new man gathers strength on the road. So that it is ever a going <u>up</u> as well as <u>on</u>.

   There is a sense in which she may be said to have come up out of the wilderness in the <u>secret decree</u> of God when he chose her in her fallen and desolate state. And there is another yet to be accomplished when from the <u>graves</u> of the wilderness, all clad in white, leaning on the prince's arm, the church shall climb the mountain of Zion and never see the wilderness again. Surely at this sight angelic hosts shall shout, "Who is this ascending on high?"

3. We have a blessed <u>manner of march</u> to observe. She came up leaning on her beloved. We sometimes repeat it as leaning on "the arm" of her beloved, but it is not so. We lean on <u>him,</u> on his breast, his bosom, his person.

   The king's daughter is not to ride in a chariot, for wise purposes she walks the weary way, but oh the joy of a walk with such company. She leans on him and sometimes when the way is rough, he carries her. He presses her to his bosom and bears her on.

   Faith is the arm which leans on him, but it is not the strength of our arm but the strength of our beloved we trust to. For every thing we lean on him, in him all fullness dwells. This is the only place where the original word is used, and it is differently rendered. It signifies "<u>casting herself</u> on," which is stronger than leaning, a dropping into his arms, a falling upon him.

It means too "joining, associating with," and this shows the holy intimacy and constantly cleaving we should have with and to Christ. It has moreover, as Kimchi says, the idea of "rejoicing" or "delighting in." And surely we may put all these ideas together. She "leans," she "casts" herself on him to show her reliance. She leans to show her intimacy and her eyes bespeak her joy at his blessed company. Let us come to personal experience, do we lean there? In sickness, distress, doubts, and fears, is this our prop and pillar?

4. We must note the title given to Jesus. Not the Saviour, nor the priest, nor the king, but all these things in one. "Her beloved." "Beloved" he is by all the angels and saints on high, by his Father and the Spirit, but we must be able to say "my beloved." Compared with him nothing is lovely or to be desired, he is beyond all things "my beloved."

II. WHO ASKS THE QUESTION[?]

1. Sometimes the captious worldling says, "who is this coming out of the wilderness[?]" He hates the change which his companions experience. He does not believe in its reality, but taunts him with the past. As if past sin could destroy present grace.

2. Sometimes the admiring observer uses this expression. Beholding the holy conversation, the quiet demeanour, and submission of Christians. Often in the persecutions this cry was involuntarily uttered. "How can this be[?] How can men endure such tortures and agonies[?]"

3. Often the trembling [believer] puts the question fearing lest he is not of the body. "Shall I amongst them stand[?] Am I his beloved[?]" Yes, if thou canst but touch the hem of his garment thou shalt be made whole, and thou hast done it, and art his.

4. Even the firmest believer at times stands and wonders at the heights of grace as if they really were incredible. The grace seems too great for faith to hold in her hand, and really if we knew the value of heaven more, I fear we should less seldom read our title clear, for we should think it too good a place for us

and well exclaim, "who is this?" Thus favoured! Thus allowed to lean on the arm of Jesus.

III. WHO SHALL ANSWER IT?

Shall we ask the lookers on? Shall we consult bigots, or sectaries? Nor we will ask the bride and the brid[e]groom.

1. The <u>Bride</u> replies by confessing that she was once an infant deserted and left to perish. But her beloved bade her live. She doth not conceal her blackness by nature. She putteth her hands before her face, and though she be decked in jewels, she vaunteth not. She is undeserving and hell deserving, helpless without strength and destitute of goodness.

2. The Beloved replies. ["]She is mine elect, chosen before the foundation of the world. She is my purchased one redeemed with blood. She is my bethrothed, my pardoned, my justified, my soon to be perfected beloved. All fair in mine eyes, and without spot or blemish.["]

   1. If such her beauty now, what shall it be when she shall walk in white in glory, free from the breath of corruption or taint of guilt[?] Question of the future!

   2. Are we marching <u>up</u>, not down[?] Are we leaning, casting ourselves upon the beloved[?] Question of the present!

Sermon No. 388

"[UNTITLED]"

Editor's Summary

This is the last of four sermons in Notebook 9 that Charles left incomplete. Additionally, this is one of three sermons in the entire *Lost Sermons* series to which he did not assign a title. (The other two are Sermon 388 and Sermon 393.)

It does appear that Charles preached on this text two more times, in "A Sermon for the Time Present" (*MTP* 33, Sermon 1990) and "The Saviour Resting in His Love" (*MTP* 47, Sermon 2720). While the incomplete nature of this sermon renders comparison difficult, the two later sermons don't appear to share significant overlapping content or structure. The succession of incomplete sermons in this notebook (382, 385, 386, and 388) possibly indicates that Charles's blossoming ministry at New Park Street Chapel was redirecting some of his time away from message preparation.

[UNTITLED]

Zephaniah 3:16–17

"In that day it shall be said to Jerusalem, Fear thou not: and to Zion, Let not thine hands be slack. The Lord thy God in the midst of thee is mighty; he will save, he will rejoice over thee with joy; he will rest in his love, he will joy over thee with singing."

This day is this Scripture fulfilled in your ears. This day the ministers of the gospel utter these very words. This day I attempt to make mention of them, but it is God who only can effectually speak to the trembling heart.

I. TWO EVILS TO BE AVOIDED.

1. <u>Fear</u> which is hurtful and dishonourable. Not fear filial, but fear servile. Fear of man. Fear of our enemies. Fear of the Promises. This fear is injurious to us and to others, dishonouring to God and entirely unneeded.

2. <u>Slack Hands</u>. They were building a temple, let them not be slack. They had begun to serve God, let them not be idle. We have in the church some slack hands:

> careless and regardless of affairs.
> indolent and quarrelsome.
> fearful and backward.

Now be not fearful, be not slack.

II. REMEDIES FOR THESE EVILS.

[This page is followed by one blank page in Charles's notebook.]

"THE ONE MEDIATOR"

Editor's Summary

Charles Spurgeon loved Jesus Christ. For the Prince of Preachers, the theme of Christ's excellence was a fountain that could not run dry. Charles's statements in "Jesus Worth Ten Thousand" (Sermon 377) tell us much. He believed that "Jesus is better than . . . all" and that "all the virtues of Christ [are] the best forms of virtue." This is why he pined, "Give me Christ or else I die."

In this sermon on 1 Tim 2:5, a text he did not preach on again, Charles fixes his attention on Christ as the magnificent Mediator between God and man. Accordingly, he divided his sermon into three main sections: "I. The Necessity of a Mediator"; "II. The Glory of Christ as Mediator"; and "III. The Title He Assumes."

In the first segment, Charles notes that "because man was at war with God . . . a reconciliation must be made." The great distance separating God and man "necessitates a medium" even as justice itself "demands a day's man." In the second section, Charles focuses on the glory owed to Christ as mediator. Indeed, "[Christ] was himself offended as one person of the Godhead, yet he will become the reconciler." Furthermore, "discharging the office" required "many humiliations" including "Incarnation," "Service," and "Suffering." For Charles, Christ's willingness to accept suffering and humiliation in the plan of redemption heightened his glory. Finally, in the third section, Charles dwells on the title "The Man Christ Jesus," which he considers to be "the best of all [Jesus's] names." He loved Christ as "the quieter of noisy waves, the victor over evil demons and diseases," but he cherished the mediator "full of sympathy, of feeling, of love."

In terms of tone, this message is remarkably similar to Charles's later sermon, "The Man of Sorrows" (*MTP* 19, Sermon 1099), which would highlight Christ as the suffering Savior. Although the sermons do not share text, content, or structure, Charles's conclusion to the later sermon serves well as reflection for the present one:

> Let us admire the superlative love of Jesus. O love, love, what hast thou done! What hast thou done! Thou art omnipotent in suffering. Few of us can bear pain, perhaps, fewer still of us can bear misrepresentation, slander, and ingratitude. . . . Christ throughout life bore these and other sufferings. Let us love him, as we think of how much he must have loved us. . . . Brother, sister, what art thou doing for Jesus? I charge thee by the nail-prints of his hands, unless thou be a liar unto him, labour for him! I charge thee by his wounded feet run to his help! I charge thee by the scar in his side give him thy heart! . . . Lay not down thy harness, but work on as long as thou shalt live. Whilst thou livest let this be thy motto "All for Jesus, all for Jesus; all for the man of sorrows, all for the man of sorrows." . . . Live for him and be ready to die for him, and the Lord accept you for the "man of sorrows'" sake. Amen. *MTP* 19:131–32.

THE ONE MEDIATOR

1 Timothy 2:5

"For there is one God, and one mediator between God and men, the man Christ Jesus."

"<u>There is but one God.</u>" So far, we might gather from the book of nature. Unity of design bespeaks unity of authorship. Acute[-]minded heathens have discovered this and perhaps m one half of the population of the globe will join with us in the doctrine. But here we diverge. The Mahommedan puts in and Mahomet is his prophet, the Catholic puts in myriads of mediators, and only the orthodox truly say "<u>and one mediator between God and men.</u>" We shall by the help of the good Spirit attempt to speak of 3 things:

I.   THE NECESSITY OF A MEDIATOR.

We read of no mediator in Eden, but now one is wanted.

1. Because man was at war with God and a reconciliation must be made.
2. God, as judge, could not speak to a criminal not only found guilty, but actually condemned. Justice demands a day's man [arbiter].
3. The Distance now between a man and a God necessitates a medium. Heaven is too high to be climbed without a ladder.

II. THE GLORY OF CHRIST AS MEDIATOR.

This shines forth if we view him.

1. In Undertaking the office. He showed at once his condescension and his love. He was highly exalted above all creation. How wonderful that he should think of such a stoop. He was himself offended as one person of the Godhead, yet he will become the reconciler.

2. In discharging the office. It involved on him many humiliations, but chiefly:

    <u>Incarnation</u> – In the womb of Mary and in life.
    <u>Service</u> – In the fashion of a man he became obedient.
    <u>Suffering</u> – He endured the cross.

3. In the issue of his labour. His own exaltation, the reconciliation of men, and their glorification. Oh my soul be astonished at his glories.

III. <u>THE TITLE HE ASSUMES</u>.

"<u>The Man Christ Jesus</u>": Methinks this is the best of all his names. I love him as the quieter of noisy waves, the victor over evil demons and diseases. But oh I love thee most as "the man Christ Jesus." On Samaria's well, in Jerusalem's streets, in Gethsemane, yea in glory, I love him as the man Christ Jesus. Full of sympathy, of feeling, of love.

Oh ye who want a mediator, here he is. No mediator between us and Christ, but between God and man.

May God give us love to the mediator.

"THE ACCUSER OF THE BRETHREN"

Editor's Summary

This is the only time that Charles ever preached on Rev 12:10. He explains, though, that he did not intend for this sermon to focus on the background of the text, but rather, the meaning and characteristics of the phrase "accuser of the brethren."

The brief excursus that Charles provides up-front as to the timing of Satan's expulsion from heaven appears to follow Gill's view. *Exposition of the New Testament*, 3:731–32. But the bulk of this sermon centers on the accusing work of Satan, with particular focus on who he accuses.

First, as in the case of Job, Satan makes accusations before God. But where the Accuser brings charges, there is an Advocate to silence every claim. Charles notes that Jesus does this by "pleading the blood," a reference to Charles Wesley's hymn "Arise, My Soul Arise." Its third stanza reads: "Five bleeding wounds he bears, / received on Calvary; / they pour effectual prayers, / they strongly plead for me."

Next, Charles explains that Satan makes accusations against us, both to our enemies and our friends. To accuse us to our enemies has been Satan's practice throughout history, from the early church to the Anabaptists to George Whitefield and William Cowper. And so Charles directs believers to take comfort in this cloud of witnesses, but even more in the fact that Jesus endured the same.

Sowing discord among believers is another tactic of Satan. Charles would later say:

Perhaps we suspect others of not being all they ought to be; and, then, of course, our attitude towards them is not what it used to be. Then they begin to have hard thoughts concerning us, and in that way Satan has reason to rejoice because Christian people are weaned from each other, and very grievous sin is caused by the roots of bitterness that are thus planted in the soil of the church. *MTP* 53:213.

Charles then notes that the accusation Christians feel the most is the one that Satan makes to them personally. This manifests as evil thoughts, like the pilgrim Christian in John Bunyan's *Pilgrim's Progress*, who has blasphemous thoughts whispered in his ears. Satan further accuses God's people of committing the unpardonable sin or of not having repented enough.

Ultimately, Charles points believers to prayer and a return to the fountain filled with blood—a reference to William Cowper's hymn "There Is a Fountain Filled with Blood," and a reminder that "the passport to glory is the precious blood of Jesus. Access to God either on earth or in heaven is only by the blood of the Son of God." *MTP* 30:173.

THE ACCUSER OF THE BRETHREN

Revelation 12:10

*"And I heard a loud voice saying in heaven, Now is come salvation, and strength,
and the kingdom of our God, and the power of his Christ: for the accuser of our
brethren is cast down, which accused them before our God day and night."*

I shall not enter into an explanation of the context in full but would briefly remark
that the expulsion of Satan here spoken of is usually believed to refer, not to his first
expulsion from heaven, but to his typical fall at the time when persecution ceases
and the Roman emperors no longer listened to the foul accusation of the heathen,
but embraced Christianity for themselves. I am about to enter wholly and simply on
the subject of the agency of Satan as an Accuser of the Brethren.

This foul Spirit of Evil is not only the tempter of men to Sin, but he is likewise their
accuser. All things whereby he may ruin God's people come alike to him; he never
scruples at anything. The Accuser of the Brethren accuses them to three parties.

I.   HE ACCUSES BEFORE GOD.

II. HE ACCUSES US TO MEN.

III. HE ACCUSES US TO OURSELVES.

As the good Spirit may enable us, we shall notice each of these points, as he may
give us utterance and make some practical remarks as we proceed. May the Lord
give his servant wisdom in this thing.

I. HE ACCUSES US BEFORE GOD.

If the Scripture did not tell us this we might doubt it, for seeing the complete justification wrought out by Jesus, it would seem impossible that any should have the hardihood to lay anything to the charge of God's elect, and truly none can justly do so, for Satan did in the case of Job.

He accused Job of selfishness. He serves God for wages. Like Sir R. Walpole said, "every man has his price," and the devil insinuates that as long as Job could be rich by serving God, he would do so. We cannot at first conceive how it should come to pass that Satan should appear amongst the sons of God. But we must remember that it does not say he appeared in heaven, for there he could not go, but in the wide universe God holds his levée, and wherever Satan is, he may be said in human language to appear before God.

If Job then, that perfect man, was thus accused, can we hope to escape [Satan's] malicious accusations[?] See how he repeats his calumnies when he argues that Job is stolid unless the pain shall touch his own person. Oh what a thought, that Job should be slandered before high heaven. Do you imagine that we escape? Some men smile at this, but their sneer is not worthy of regard, for as an eminent commentator well observes, we never meet with a devil denier who is a good man; but on the other hand these men are usually the most impious of all, and acting like the [Jesuits] who denied the Pope for their Lord, yet know right well that he is so, and hope thereby to establish his dominion.

Let us now turn to Zech. III. There we see Satan standing before the angel of the Lord to resist Joshua, and we know not how many times he has been standing up to resist us in our prayers or songs of praises. But blessed be the name of God, we have an advocate, and as soon as an accusation is made he rises, and with matchless eloquence defeats the slanderer.

See what he pleads. He pleads electing love and effectual grace. Chosen and plucked from the fire. If we more fully entered into this subject, we should think more highly of Christ in his official character on high. Satan can easily bring a thousand charges against us. No need to watch long, and both day and night he does accuse us, but our advocate silences his clamour by "pleading the blood," as the old Wesleyan had it.

II. HE ACCUSES US TO MEN.

The Father of lies will lie everywhere. He thinks to destroy Christ's Church by slandering its member[s].

1. <u>He accuses us to our enemies</u>. From the earliest ages this was his practice. The Christians were accused of eating their infants at their supper, and of meeting by night for the vilest of all purposes.

   All fires were laid to their door, and even earthquakes and famines were said to be caused by their impiety. The same you find is true of the Vandois when persecuted by the Papists, and on the first outburst of the (so called) Anabaptists.

   The greatest preacher of these latter times, George Whit[e]field, was accused as Cowper has it of crimes that Sodom never knew. And scarcely ever does an eminent minister arise but Satan is sure to hatch some calumnies against him. It is part of our lot as minister to be maligned, and our missionary brethren do not escape.

   If then the champions of truth are assailed, should common Christians think this fiery trial "a strange thing[?]" **x** Just as I withdrew to dinner I found a letter giving me a sound thrashing for last Sabbath morning's sermon. **x** You and I must not expect to live without [accusation], and two things should embolden us to take up this cross most cheerfully:

   1. Our master had to endure it.
   2. It increases our reward in heaven.

2. <u>He accuses us to our Friends</u>. This is the most bitterly malignant bite of the old Serpent, and our Lord felt it when his heel was bruised. Judas, who had eaten [Christ's] bread, was enticed by Satan to betray him. Wounds in the house of one's friends are wounds indeed.

   1. Sometimes a calumny against a brother is received by the church as being a truth without due search being made to discover the truth of the charge. Now this is Satan's delight. To throw dust in the eyes of brethren. So that like the Trojans on the night of Troy's destruction they mistake friends for foes. Oh remember he is the accuser of the brethren.

   2. Sometimes one Brother imagines that another has treated him disrespectfully. He did not notice him in the street, or shake hands so

heartily, or invite him to his house. Now let us, if we find this in our hearts, at once remember that he is the Accuser of the Brethren and let us not believe him.

Paul once said of two women, "I <u>beseech</u> Euodias and I <u>beseech</u> <u>Syntyche</u> that they be of one mind." Two women had disagreed and Paul, to set them right, gives a beseech to each of them. It is Satan's work to plant roots of bitterness every where. Oh how sweet to know that the master will not cast us off even if all the disciples do so, and our Beloved will never be moved from his love by all the accusation of our enemy.

III. HE ACCUSES US TO OURSELVES.

I choose to mention this last because it is the one which, perhaps of the three, we feel most. And I pray my Master to give me one of his kind whispers that I may know how to speak a word in season.

1. <u>He accuses us of vile thoughts</u> which were none of ours. He injects blasphemies and then fathers them on us. Some know nothing of this matter, but I do. Swearing and oaths have rushed on my mind and would by no means depart, but they were none of mine. I hated them. If you hate them, they cannot be yours. Whip them and send them on to the right parish. He puts the cup in our sack and then charges us with the robbery. See Bunyan in Grace abounding to the chief of sinners. Poor Soul, tell the master about him.

2. <u>He accuses us of the unpardonable sin</u>. This is, I think, one of Satan's masterpieces. What God intended for good, Satan turns to evil. I confess, I know now what the unpardonable sin is. Some say it cannot be committed now, but I think it can.

However, I know it is something to do with the Holy Ghost, and I would have all men beware of dishonouring him. When a man has committed this, he is given over to final impenitence and unbelief, for where there is faith and repentance, in due time there shall be mercy bestowed. Despair is the greatest sin of all. To despise the power of the Spirit and say he cannot save you, would be to go very near that sin.

3. <u>He accuses us of not having repented enough</u>. Often does he hurl biographies at us. The lives of good men serve him for fiery darts, and right quickly does he let fly at us.

   But the shield of faith is the best defence here. We are not to be justified by our penitence, but by the blood of Jesus. Can we ever repent enough? Is not sin so horrible that no purgatories of fire could cleanse it, much less a purgatory of the water of our grief[?] I hang on Christ, and that is enough for me.

4. <u>He accuses us of our duties as being ill done</u>, and therefore unacceptable. Our sins he stirs up like sleeping spectres and bids them march before us in funereal procession while our duties, which he bids the Pharisee pride himself upon, he represents as being too stained with sin to be received.

   He takes our sermons, our prayers, and our works and calls them vanities at one time; at another [time] they are wonderful things. Our Faith he tells us is dead faith. Our spot is not the spot of God's children. He asks us whether the Lord's people are as we are. Now the way to settle this is to kneel in prayer, and searching our hearts, go once more to the fountain filled with [blood]. And now, beloved, once more I entreat you look to the Advocate and remember his peace-speaking blood. In all time[s] of trouble make this your shield, your refuge, and rock.

"NOWISE CAST OUT"

Editor's Summary

Charles returns to the theme of this sermon in several future sermons and preaches from this text six times: "The Certainty and Freeness of Divine Grace" (*MTP* 10, Sermon 599–600); "High Doctrine and Broad Doctrine" (*MTP* 30, Sermon 1762); "All Comers to Christ Welcomed" (*MTP* 40, Sermon 2349); "The Big Gates Wide Open" (*MTP* 51, Sermon 2954); "No. 3,000; Or, Come and Welcome" (*MTP* 52, Sermon 3000); and "The Last Message for the Year" (*MTP* 56, Sermon 3230).

Given Charles's preference for biblical terms over theological terms, it's easy to see why he states here, "I would to God that some theological terms had never been invented." This is not a rejection of theological method or a theological reading of Scripture, but rather, an insistence that following the Bible first often leads to clarity where otherwise there is theological confusion.

Charles would later explain his sermon divisions as "representing two sides of Christian doctrine. They enable us to see it from two stand-points — the Godward and the manward." *MTP* 30:49. The first division speaks of the secret will of God as a gift, a coming, a resolution, and a number. Charles's exposition of these terms show that "Providence and grace move on and produce God's great result" in salvation. As Charles underscored at another time, all kinds of people will come . . .

> Is there not a glorious width about my text. . . . A red man, or a black man, or a white man, or a yellow man, or a copper-coloured man, whatever he is, if he comes to Jesus, he shall in no wise be cast out. *MTP* 40:89.

The second division speaks of the revealed will of God. From the manward perspective of salvation, "one sinner has as much right to believe he is elect as any other in the same condition" because of the work of Christ, not the election of the sinner.

Here Charles appears to be quoting a line from John Stocker's hymn "Thy Mercy, My God, Is the Theme of My Song." The complete fourth stanza reads: "The door of thy mercy stands open all day / to the needy and poor, who knock by the way; / No sinner shall ever be empty sent back, / who comes seeking mercy for Jesus' dear sake."

Charles concludes with three words of comfort for all ministers, Christians, and poor sinners—directing them to the mercy of God, God's power to save, and the assurance God gives. As Charles would later say,

> From top to bottom salvation is all of grace, and all the gift of God by Jesus Christ. He did not come into the world, I say, to make us salvable, but to save us; nor to put us in the way of somehow or other meriting salvation; but he came himself to be the Saviour, and to save sinners. *MTP* 39:136.

NOWISE CAST OUT

John 6:37

*"All that the Father giveth me shall come to me; and him
that cometh to me I will in no wise cast out."*

Upon the first reading of this verse one feels inclined to break out with the angelic song, "Behold I bring you glad tidings of great joy etc." For truly here is great joy for all. The strongest in faith will find food for his soul in the first sentence, and the very weakest will find manna in the second.

I take it that if we could rightly grasp these two sayings of our Saviour we should never have debates in our mind about free will, predestination, and all the other lofty controversies of all time. I would to God that some theological terms had never been invented, and that men would confine themselves more to God's word, and less to bodies of divinity.

I.   THE ETERNAL "SHALL" – POSITIVE.

II.   THE ETERNAL "WILL" – NEGATIVE.

Oh Spirit of the living God, be thou my inspirer, that both theme and inspiration may come together.

I.   THE ETERNAL *"shall."* POSITIVE.

We have in these words four things at least spoken of: a <u>gift</u>, a <u>coming</u>, a <u>resolution</u>, a <u>number</u>.

1. "A GIFT," *"all that the Father giveth me"*

We are led to believe from various portions of God's word that the Father did present and give unto the Son a multitude as the reward of his labour. Two things require explanation: the word gift, and its tense. It may be asked how it can be a gift and yet a purchase, but I take it the word is purposely used to set forth the love of the Father and his part in the covenant. So that while the Son did really purchase it, [it] was not merely as a mercantile transaction, but the Father freely gave. David was to purchase the king's daughter, and yet he gave. Viewed as the Redeemer he purchased, as the Husband he received a gift.

Notice next the present tense, giveth. Not that it is done in time, but it notes the Godhead of Christ with whom everything is present, and again the [unchangeability] of the gift. The Father gives as much now as ever, he revokes not the decree.

We see then the Father giving to the Son an heritage. He had a right to give men for he made them, he is their sovereign. Oh what a gift, a host, a countless multitude. A motley herd of worms, but yet an army of immortals.

2. "A COMING."

How can we tell whether we were included in the gift[?] Why by this infallible sign, "coming to Christ." We come in grace and in glory.

In grace we come and 'tis a mournful march. When rousing from our sleep of death we retrace our steps to our Father. Sometimes we are months in coming. Tears wet the road and sighs rend our heart. We come spiritually when the heart desires Christ, and we are come when, by a sense of need, we cast ourselves upon him.

Come, not run. It is often a crawling, a creeping, but the text says they shall come. Not they shall run or even walk, but come, come anyhow—on the ground if no other way. You who are coming, take heart, and you who are longing to come, you are coming.

In glory we come to Christ, but oh how different a coming. Now they come with songs of everlasting joy. All creation joins in a tune of thanksgiving. Oh what a "coming" this. But we shall soon realize it when he shall say, "Come ye blessed of my Father." Oh my soul rejoice at the glad hope and count all present sorrows small.

3. "A RESOLUTION," *"shall"*

I look upon this shall as a great word, though some divines will not allow me so to do.

1. It is a prophecy of the Son. He is the prophet of his people and he here utters a prediction that they shall come. He in the future sees all his elect as if they were coming now. Can he be wrong[?]

2. It is an oath of the Son. He who speaks and his word is law. He who swears by immutable things now lifts his hand to heaven and vows that he will so accomplish his work that all shall come whom he has foreknown. Mark, it is the oath of one who has power to perform, and not power only, but all power.

3. It is a triumphant shout of the Son. He throws the gauntlet to the foe and bids them stay one of them. He foresaw his own agony and death, but further on he saw his resurrection and ascension and therefore could stand on the broken head of Satan and glory in the salvation of the chosen ones.

   The Jews must have felt this very galling to their pride to be told that though they came not, others would, and to the Pharisee [nowadays] it is the same. Providence and grace move on and produce God's great result.

4. "A NUMBER," *"all"*

It is a word which implies a knowledge of the number his Father had given him. Cyrus knew the name of every man in his army and so does Christ. He telleth the stars. In the dreary forest of the west there dwells an Indian who is one of the <u>all</u>. Up in the regions of the north some Laps and Fins and so on, but he knows <u>all</u>; not one is unknown.

And all shall come. They may be buried in heathen darkness, they may be bowing at the shrines of Popery, but they all shall come to grace. And if hidden under the waves of ocean or lying amidst a mingled mass of battle's slaughter, they all shall come in their own persons to glory. And what an all that will be. From Adam down to the last man, down to the millennium, all the way from Eden, what a multitude. But all the gift of God.

Certain modern Calvinists have started an idea that this refers not to persons but to things, but what are the things without the persons, and how could things come, and how would there be any connection between this verse and the discourse[?] I find neither Adam Clark nor Albert Barnes, who would both gladly say anything on the general side, have observed this, and therefore I think it a modern invention. So far we have been talking of the more secret will of God. Now we come to his revealed councils, and may the Lord enable me to speak well for his dear name.

II. THE BLESSED *"will"* NEGATIVE.

And let us remark:

1. <u>The Speaker</u>, "<u>unto me</u>," not to Father but the Son. The Father never gives audience to any who do not come through the Son's introduction. Like the Molossians we must take the prince in our arms if we go to the king. But first we must go to the Son, and who can refuse to go to one so loving[?]

2. <u>The Character</u>, "him." Mark how wide a field this pronoun gives. The rich and poor find welcome. As lady Huntington said, not <u>many</u> but the [<u>Methodists</u>] saved her. The wise may come and the fool. The half idiot, if he come, shall find welcome. I see not why any one should think himself excluded. As Crisp says, who is sound enough in all conscience, ["]one sinner has as much right to believe he is elect as any other in the same condition.["] But this is not the warrant. Our warrant is the death of Jesus, not election. Oh poor broken hearted one, why dost thou fear[?] Who has told thee thou art lost[?] The devil[?] But fear not.

3. <u>The Treatment</u>, ["]he will not cast out.["] Sometimes when a beggar comes to a rich man's door [the rich man] orders him away if he intends not to give him charity. And when the poor soul comes, it dreads lest it should be driven away without relief, but he will not cast out. "No sinner was ever empty sent back." None but hypocrites are driven away and these deserve it.

And if, when the soul first comes, he is not cast out, what is then the security of those who are in the door[?] Shall children be expelled[?] Shall loved ones be put into the cold midnight air[?] No, they shall never be cast out.

4. The powerful negative "nowise." The Greek is very strong. It is not, not, never, never, and the old Saxon word is, in itself, as powerful a word as can well be conceived. It puts to flight whole armies of objections. Great sin cannot hinder mercy. Old age and long delays hinder not. Going to other Saviours and relying on our works in past times will not cast us out now. A hard heart will not forbid our coming, for he can melt rocks and nether [mill stones].

Little faith shall not impede grace wholly. Our poor prayers shall not destroy us. And if all men cast out, Jesus will never do so. Oh what a blessed promise, what a sure foundation. He who comes, he who believes, is welcome and shall never, never lose the mercy he requests.

Here are to conclude three words of comfort:

1. One for me and all ministers. We shall not labour in vain. Christ shall see the travail of his soul, and although he does not save just whom and when we please, yet save he will and rejoice in his love.

2. One for all Christians. They may now rest secure in the covenant love of God. The devil cannot cast them out for he cannot enter into God's house, nor can the world, and God will not, so we are secure. Blessed Security.

3. One for poor sinners. Hear the word nowise over again. Let the experience of thousands and myself among them cheer thee on. Why doubt[?] He is able, he is willing. Doubt no more.

<u>Lord help me. Amen</u>

"THE BIBLE A CONQUEROR"

Editor's Summary

Charles appears to have preached on this text one other time, "The Bible Tried and Proved" (*MTP* 35, Sermon 2084), but it seems to have no overlapping content or structural similarity with "The Bible a Conqueror."

This sermon begins with a recognition that all books receive criticism—something that Charles often gave to other authors. On the front page of his personal copy of William Day's commentary on Isaiah, for example, he wrote, "This day sheds small light on the subject. Probably the writer had all the day in his name. The more often consulted, the less will it be esteemed. It was written for children, according to the preface and we pray the children do not have to read it."

The context here shows Charles's need to defend the veracity of Scripture against the critics of the day, which he variously classifies. First are those who kept the Bible "in an unknown tongue," as he later explains:

> The Romish Church for many years kept the sacred Scriptures in an unknown tongue, and resisted all attempts to translate the book of God into the vulgar language of the people. What a curse Rome has had resting on her head. To those who know the enormity of this wickedness in holding back the word of life, it is scarcely possible to think of Rome without invoking judgement upon her. What myriads of souls went down to the pit perishing through lack of knowledge during what were called the Dark Ages! *MTP* 11:424.

Second, the scoffers, those of "undraped atheism." Such a person is confirmation of "our conviction of the very truth which he denies," explained Charles. "The Holy Ghost told us, by the pen of Peter, that it would be so; and now we see how truly he wrote." *MTP* 43:421.

Third, among the false philosophers he lists geologists and ethnologists, whom he would eventually take a less friendly position toward as he got older. "We have seen the church attacked by weapons borrowed from geology, ethnology, and anatomy, and then from the schools of criticism fierce warriors have issued, but she survives all her antagonists." *MTP* 14:46.

Finally, the mythical interpreters of the Bible—those who redefine the resurrection and the atonement as fiction. In Charles's words, they were nothing more than "the subtlety of the old serpent." *MTP* 31:435.

Indeed, for Charles, the Bible lived on. As he would later say:

I do not think that our Bibles were given to us that we might merely employ them as telescopes to peer into the heavens. . . . Let us not so misuse the Word of God, but prize it as the bread upon which we are to live. *MTP* 44:319.

THE BIBLE A CONQUEROR
Psalm 12:6

"The words of the Lord *are pure words: as silver tried in
a furnace of earth, purified seven times."*

Good things will endure trial. The best of the good is its enduring the fire. So is
it with books. There is the fire of criticism which every book must pass through.
Do not imagine that any of you could write a book so immaculate that it will go
scatheless through the world. Write and rewrite, it shall still be criticised. The
friend and the foe will open their eyes upon it, and you will have the equivocal
pleasure of hearing your book abused where you hoped to have received applause.
Either it will be hissed out of existence, or it will have its ephemeral day, or it may
survive a century, and peradventure it may take a place among the constellation
of authors. But anyhow, it will be criticised, and many a furious onslaught it must
endure ere it stands on the mountaintop of acknowledged fame.

When God became an author, we might imagine that his volume would have been
received with respect and allowed to stand in the sanctum sanctorum far away from
common book life. Not so, it seemed as if the whole earth waited until the book was
born that they might crush and destroy it. It has passed through a series of conflicts
such as no other book ever endured. It has been purified seven times. Other works
have gained the pyramid of honour and are free from attacks, but our Bible has no
repose.

Homer, Horace, Virgil, Milton and the other poets wear their laurels and no
one attempts to snatch the laurel from their brow, but this great author is ever
being attacked. It is hatred of the Author which prompts the deed. It lives on.
It has increased in power and shall do [so] until the religion we profess shall

become universal and this God of Books shall be King over all. The Bible has had opponents of several classes. We will briefly mention them.

1. <u>Its physical force opponents</u>. The men who attacked it bodily minded not its contents but attacked it as a Bible. With these I class the men who aimed at keeping the Bible in an unknown tongue and were able to do so for a long time. Who gave it an illuminated border and confined it as a bird in a golden cage or a virgin in a palace prison.

   They resisted every attempt to translate it. They kept the key of knowledge and would neither enter in themselves nor suffer others to do so. But did they prevail[?] Did all the Bonifaces and the Innocents and Gregories and monks and friars manage to keep it in its tomb[?] No, out it came and multitudes beheld it.

   Once out they began to burn, but could they burn it up[?] No. Under the bed or in the box it lived and was read. Yea its very murderers helped to spread it. Tyndale lived on the sale of the books which his enemies bought for the fire.

   We have some of these brute force men now. Tale of a Soldier with tract. Priests of Rome. Our memories and the myriad copies forbid all fear from these. Alexandria's volumes may have been burned in the baths, but never shall the last Bible burn.

2. Its scoffers. Men of the Voltaire and Tom Paine school who tried to scoff it down and scout it without examination. Such men are usually uneducated nowadays. The French Revolution gave the world a disrelish for undraped atheism. Has the Bible been injured by one scoff[?] No. Its prophecy of the last days has been verified. Story of Wellington and the officer who found fault with the Bible. The Quaker upon G. Goliath.

3. Its false philosophers. Thousands of Quixotes have rushed against the windmill which grinds flour for the nations. Take a few of them: The Epicureans declared that certain concurring atoms by chance formed this world and fashioned all things therein. Buffon, with his great eternal pre-existent theory, breaking of the earth from the sun by contact with a comet. The Progressionists, with their ideas of the gradual formation of all creatures from certain molecules and their improvement into higher orders of life until man came. The Geologists who now stand side by side with Scripture, and we find no contradiction. Ethnology too is now on our side. New Philosophers are always rising, and sometimes nervous Christians fear for

their Bibles, but let them not fear, for in every thing the Bible will be borne out by science. Astronomy once seemed against us.

4. Its mythical Interpreters. These men tell us that all our histories and our revelation rise a mass of myths. That they ought to be preached but not believed by good philosophers. Are the ruined walls of Petra myths[?] Are the Jews myths? Are the Arabs myths[?] Are the stones in our Museum myths[?] I imagine the man's brains are myths, or certainly very small indeed.

It were well if it had not other opponents, but there are opponents in our hearts. Pride loving not to be a sinner or to own the truth. Free grace is never pleasing to the soul—we want to do. Fear not, the Bible will overcome these. Then will come the insinuations of Satan and the raillery of enemies, but fear them not, this book shall weather the storm.

Experience will try your faith in it, but fear not, the waves shall never dash upon this rock to move it one inch. That is the commentary which the heart makes when it can say tried and proved. I exhort you to try it for direction in difficulty

> comfort in trouble
> help against sin
> joy in death

"[UNTITLED]"

Editor's Summary

Charles begins this sermon (a text he would not preach again) with an excursus on astronomy. Seeing David as an astronomer is a clever way of depicting David's marveling relationship with the Creator and his creation, and Charles uses this to note that all true astronomers declare the heavens as the work of God. He then quotes the astronomer William Herschel, who claimed an "undevout astronomer is mad" for ignoring the influence of God's heavens on the minds and hearts of men.

This sermon is divided into two points, the first of which is a reflection on the significance of a God who honors insignificant humanity. Pointing to Christ, Charles recognizes how God stooped down to join humanity. To further support this image, the hymn-loving preacher cites verses from *Psalms, Hymns, and Spiritual Songs*, a collection of psalms written by Isaac Watts for singing.

Yet Charles never forgets that the glory of humanity is marred by sin. Even the best of men in their finest moments, such as William Wilberforce and his colleagues in their fight to abolish slavery, do not alleviate the damage done by sinful actions, wars, and bloodshed. Rather, all should look to Christ, "the director of Providence," for in Christ is humanity crowned with honor.

Charles concludes this section with a citation from another Isaac Watts hymn, "All Glory to the Dying Lamb." Its first two stanzas read:

All glory to the dying Lamb,
And never-ceasing praise,
While angels live to know thy name,
Or men to feel thy grace.

With this cold stony heart of mine,
Jesus, to thee I flee;
And to they grace my soul resign,
To be renew'd by Thee.

The second division examines the dominion given to humanity by God. The gift of creation bestowed on Adam was distorted by the fall; even so, God still reigns over creation in anticipation of the day that it meets its full restoration in Christ.

This already-and-not-yet perspective of the present and future rule of Christ is one Charles would return to throughout his ministry:

Let but the Church know her rights and claim them. . . . Let her, then, as Christ's queen, claim the earth as hers, and send her heralds forth from sea to sea to bid all men bow before him, and confess him to be their King. *MTP* 7:440.

[UNTITLED]

Psalm 8:5–6

"For thou hast made him a little lower than the angels, and hast crowned him with glory and honour. Thou madest him to have dominion over the works of thy hands; thou hast put all things under his feet."

This Psalm is the song of the Astronomer. David walked abroad at midnight and lifted his eyes on high. He saw the fair moon in her silver-axled car and her companions, stars, sailing along the sea of ether. He beheld the spangled army and broke forth with a song, "When I consider the heavens etc."

The Evil genius of Infidelity has wooed all the sciences, but they have all cast him off. He sought to dwell among the stars, but they shot their pure fire on him and said, "When he prepared the heavens I was there." He tried in turn every other science, but each cast him away, and foremost stands this science of astronomy so clearly declaring that the heavens are the work of God's fingers—that an "undevout astronomer is mad." I am not however about to make a lecture upon astronomy. I leave such things to Dr. Chalmers and other master minds. We proceed to notice the words of our text, and we see:

I. THE HONOUR BESTOWED ON MAN.

II. THE DOMINION BESTOWED ON HIM.

When David saw those mighty orbs he seemed to lessen and grow into a mere speck or atom dancing in the sun beam, and he could not but admire and wonder at the honour conferred on so insignificant a creature.

I. THE HONOUR BESTOWED ON MAN.

1. <u>The first sentence</u>, I take it, expresses that pristine honour which Adam had. He was a little lower than the angels. God has degrees of being. One of his creatures has the soaring wing, another creeps upon the earth. One is terrible in power, another insignificant in weakness. Man was made only a little second to the greatest of the creatures of God. Adam could almost make with Gabriel the strong and mighty, but alas he fell, and we became in sin lost, ruined, and broken.

Our crown is gone. Yet even now, wrecked and battered as we are, there remains in our race enough to show its original grandeur. The prince in rags has still the hair and gait of royalty. The slavery of sin and the sunburnings of transgression have not utterly defaced the nobility of man.

But if we want to understand how <u>fallen</u> man is, if you wish to see what being a "little lower than the angels" means now—you must see the Son of God, and son of man, in his incarnation, clossed with flesh, despised of men, spit upon, and mocked. Angels ministered to him in the wilderness. An angel strengthened him in the garden. He was a little lower than the angels. Pause my soul and weigh these words.

<u>"Lower than the angels"</u> The creator stoops beneath the created. For thee he did it all. Oh my soul, be filled with loving wonder. What means it[?] It means pain, and sorrow, and death. It means insult and scorn. How sweet to have a gospel translation of the Psalms and read the Saviour there.

> "Lord what is man or all his race
> Who dwell so far below
> That thou should'st visit him with grace
> And love his nature so[?]
> That thine Eternal son should bear
> To take a mortal form
> Made lower than his angels are
> To save a dying worm[?']"

But now we turn away from this first patent of man's nobility. It is too much blotted. The escutcheon is too defaced to leave us any room for glory; we look at the . . .

2. <u>The Second Sentence</u> sets forth the honours of our race under the second Adam. We are now crowned with glory and honour. Some men love to talk of the honours of war, the victory, the garment rolled in blood, the firm courage of battalions, and the heroism of generals. But oh when well considered, is there any honour to our race from war[?] Is not the glory a delusion[?] Should not the bloodstained drapery of war be hissed at instead of applauded[?]

Others of a better mould delight to dwell on the honour derived by our race from the names of sages and the deep penetrating researches of the wise, but I know a glory more lasting than that. Nor is the crown of our race made by the virtues of Howard, Clarkson, or Wilberforce, good and great as these are.

If we want to see the race honoured, look yonder. Look to the man who fills the middle throne. Look to the man who is girt about the paps with a golden girdle. Lo, on his head are many crowns, and in his hands [are] the sovereign keys of heaven, death, and hell. He is the director of Providence, the high priest of creation. He with his rainbow [wreath] and robes of storm shall soon come to be our judge. Oh the honours he has won for us. We are in in him equal to the angels, yea above them, for we can claim a nearer kindred to him than they. Oh my soul, care not for honour or grandeur, only dwell on this thought: thou art in him crowned with glory and honour

When thou art reviled and made the offscouring of all things by man, remember thy dignity, thy Brother, thy Husband sits on a throne, and thou in him art exalted far above all principality and power.

Oh what are all the trappings of men[?] Their lace and embroidery, their stars and ribbons, their crests, their coronets, their mitres, and their crowns compared with the glory of being allied to him who is crowned with glory and honour[?]

"All honour to the dying lamb etc."

II. THE DOMINION BESTOWED ON MAN.

1. <u>Here</u> again I take the first sentence to refer to the original grant of creation to Adam. He was God's vicegerent. King of this province of the empire of heaven. All creatures owned his dominion, they all came before him to receive their names.

The old pictures seem to catch the idea, where they represent Adam with a lion at his feet while all other beasts are sporting around him. This first grant has never been revoked entirely. Man is still lord of creation, but not as he used to be. It is true [that] he rules the thunder-maned horse and the strong sinewed ox. He tames the lion.

He overcomes the monsters of the deserts and the jungles, the mighty whale dies to yield him oil, and he levies a contribution on all things, but he is not as he used to be, the undisputed monarch of the earth. The locust and the canker worm laugh at his power, little though they be. The fierce lion rends him for his prey and the hungry wolf attacks him. Our blessed Saviour however had power over all creatures. The beasts in the desert hurt him not. The shoals come into the net at his bidding and the fish will turn tribute bearer for him.

Yet this sovereignty is marred. The large proportion of our race have no dominion, they fear as much as they are feared. Our crown remains but some of its jewels are gone.

2. <u>We look</u> with pleasure at the second sentence which shows us with our dominion restored in Christ.

All things are put under his feet. He is the universal sovereign. We have a right noble Captain. All things on earth obey him. The thunder utters not its voice without his leave. The ocean lifts not up its ~~voice~~ hands until he so ordaineth. The winds cannot so much as whisper, or the waves move, without him. Kings are in his hand. He manages their cabinet councils. The Imperious Autocrat unwittingly fulfills his decree. Both good and evil are his instruments.

<u>In Heaven</u>. Right willingly are his laws obeyed. The outstretched wings of seraph[s] quiver with delight if he doth but wish an errand to be performed. The ransomed adore his blest supremacy. And e'en in <u>hell</u>. He is the lord. In the deep recesses and dark caverns of the pit he is known terrible in the wrath of the Lamb. This <u>man</u> governs all. This <u>God[-]man</u> is the only potentate.

Now my soul behold thine own rank, for in him man is to be the lord of all things under God. Oh my soul, thou dost not know what thou shalt be. Ye ungodly ones, where is your hope and consolation[?] Oh my fellow Christian, rejoice in the Lord and [go] on to thy rest, thy glory.

Thy heaven, thy all.

Oh Lord, help.

"ELOQUENCE OF JESUS"

Editor's Summary

Charles preached on this text in "The Unrivalled Eloquence of Jesus" (*MTP* 16, Sermon 951). However, it doesn't appear to contain any overlapping content or structural similarity with this earlier sermon, in which Charles extols the virtue of eloquence as a gift and something of preeminent importance. Indeed, the Prince of Preachers placed a high value on eloquence, stating here that "the very acmé of my ambition is to have the eloquent tongue on fire with Christ's love, and by the blessing of the Spirit winning souls to Christ."

In a later sermon, Charles would say more:

Eloquence is difficult to acquire, but silence is far more hard to practise. A man may much sooner learn to speak well than learn not to speak at all. We are in such a hurry to vindicate our own cause that we damage it by rash speech: if we were calm, gentle, quiet, forbearing as the Saviour was, our pathway to victory would be much more easy. *MTP* 28:79.

Here, Charles explores the eloquence of Christ first in the manner in which he spoke and applies it to all preachers. The character of a man cannot help but come forth when he puts his thoughts to words. Further, whether or not one is trustworthy, like Christ, is discerned by hearing a person speak. The preacher's discretion, following the prudence displayed by the Savior, is also of importance. As Jesus's enemies sought to entrap him, his words confounded them. Clothed in love and humility, the eloquence of Christ revealed his perfection and absence of pride. Even more, Charles notes the value of the simplicity of Jesus's words. Children could understand him. The words of Christ also were serious yet cheerful, not marked by buffoonery. They were earnest, not staid. They were direct, and his hearers knew he spoke of them and to them.

The remainder of the sermon develops the matter spoken by Christ. His words were eloquent because they came from him and were about him. Charles observes, "Every syllable has its value, every sentiment is big with solemn meaning." To this central focus, Charles later added this word to all who would speak of Christ:

> When you take the *Bible* remember that Christ is the centre of the Scriptures. . . . Christ is the centre of the entire system of the gospel, and all will be seen to move with regularity when you perceive that he is the chief fixed point; you cannot be right in the rest unless you think rightly of him. He is the centre and King of all truth. *MTP* 17:634, italics in the original.

ELOQUENCE OF JESUS

John 7:46

"The officers answered, Never man spake like this man."

Eloquence is a wondrous gift. He who has it ever receives homage from man. It has a sovereignty in it which men willingly bow to. Like music it has charms to soothe, to conquer, to inspire, or to melt. Eloquence is the music of sense more than of sound, though both are combined in most orators.

He who has eloquence is more obeyed than the man of wealth or wisdom. When well applied it is the noblest gift man can be endowed with. I reckon the honour of a Christian orator to be the climax of earthly glory, and the very acmé of my ambition is to have the eloquent tongue on fire with Christ's love, and by the blessing of the Spirit winning souls to Christ.

The annals of the Bible are not barren of great men. Giants in every walk of life have their names engraven on the walls of this wondrous palace of revelation. Ask for a mighty warrior whose exploits rival Caesar? I show you Joshua, or David. Ask for a lawgiver and equal of Lycurgus? See there is Moses, the superior of every other.

Seekest thou wisdom? Ye have it in Solomon. Or heroism, ye beheld it in Daniel and the brave three who endured the furnace. And should ye enquire for poetry and eloquence, I bring you a cloud of silver tongued and golden mouthed orators. But foremost amongst them I mention the name of my Master, the Lord Jesus. He is the prince of preachers, the perfection of eloquence. The Grand Master of the brotherhood of orators.

The best tribute which can be borne to a man is that which his enemies are constrained to render. When Hatred giveth honour, it is honour molten in the furnace and free from the dross of flattery. The testimony to the eloquence of our

Saviour was given by officers who were sent to take him, by the Pharisees and chief priests. They came fully intent upon the execution of their warrant, but as the lion licked the feet of the spotless Una, so they listened to his words, were enchanted, and on returning empty handed could only exclaim,

"Never man spake like this man."

They could not touch him, his very looks unmanned them, their arm was nerveless, they were spell bound, entangled in a silken net, bound with invisible fetters of silver, riveted by the fascinating sound of the music of his voice. Our business this morning, by the help of the blessed Spirit, shall be to exhibit Christ as the "chief speaker." May you each hear his words and confess their power.

I. FOR MANNER AND II. FOR MATTER.
Christ excels all others.

I.   FOR MANNER.

A man may have much to say, but if he say it badly he has little power. The block of Parian marble is not so valuable as the statue cut from it. Truth needs to be incarnate in beauty, and thought should be solidified with elegance. Like apples of gold they are to be conveyed in baskets of silver, if we would attract beholders.

The wise man will value truth for its own sake. He loves her in dishabille, he rejoices in her however homely the words which are cast around her. But even he feels the magic of soft sounds, and loves the queen best in her state garments, while to the [passerby] the dress is all important if we would woo him to the love of goodness.

When we hear a speaker and simply regard his manner, two things are ever, though perhaps unconsciously, before us:
> The man's character
> and The man's style of speaking.

> The Man's Character will break out when he speaks, and much of a man may be learned from his sermons. Now in our Lord his hearers could not fail to observe a chain of virtues.

<u>Fidelity</u> was very prominent. Those who heard him could not but know that he was faithful to his trust. He never stifled a truth lest it should be unpleasant to his hearers. He stood, and like a crystal fountain, he allowed living waters to gush freely from his heart. He flattered not the rich, he told them it was hard for them to be saved. He crouched not to rulers, he defied the power of Herod the fox. He feared not frowns, for in the presence of Pharisees he cried "woe unto you scribes and Pharisees, hypocrites." All classes received their due. The lawyer who feared an indirect reproach, upon [Jesus's] order, received at once a home stroke. [Christ] courted no man's smile. The young man is bidden to sell his all. His followers are warned to count the cost. Like the moon he ~~feared~~ tarried not at the baying of the dog or the song of the admiring poet.

When you saw him on the mountain you saw "a man," a "freeman," a man unbound by the fetters of fashion, an athlete ready to wrestle with error of every kind. He had no temporizing in him. He went to Nazareth and what did he[?] He enters the synagogue, but he does not select a passage to please the people. He gives them election and sovereignty, and though they bite their tongues for wrath, he cares not. The truth must be spoken and he speaks it.

Laughing ridicule banters [at] him in vain. Harsh calumny puts him in her pillory, but he yields not to her. Flattery holds up her gewgaws [baubles], but he treads them under foot. Oh ye temporizing men who conceal your sentiments, look ye here and behold him whom ye call master, and blush at your vile cowardice. Oh may God help us to speak like Jesus, in measure. For in this respect "Never man spake like this man."

<u>Prudence</u>. But our Saviour's courage was not a rash imprudent daring. It was courage tempered with discretion. Hotheaded rashness has often spoiled the cause it intended to enrich. Truth has even now the scars of wounds which she received in the house of her friends.

Our Saviour never threw his pearls before swine. He expounded to his disciples the meaning of his parable, but the unthinking herd were satisfied with the husk. His favourites received the precious kernel, for the others would have trodden it under foot, and heaven's manna ought not to be wasted. The woman of Samaria asks him to solve the question in dispute betwixt her nation and the Jews. He talks to her of the water of life.

In vain his smooth-tongued enemies labour to entrap him. The Herodian retires, abashed by a few words upon a coin. The Sadducee sees his long tale of the woman and seven husbands scattered to the winds, and stands confounded when he hears that God is not God of the dead but of the living. The haughty Pharisee questioning [Christ's] authority bites his lip when fixed on the horns of a dilemma as to John's Baptism.

Nor could the whole phalanx of his foes entrap him in his speech. Alas my friends, we may soon be entrapped. The enemy may soon discover spots in our garments. The finest web of eloquence which mortal tongue hath ever woven has some false throws of the shuttle, some threads too slightly inter ~~woven~~ twisted. Oh that God would guard our lips and put an angel at our mouths to drive back every imperfect word, and only give a passage to those which are pure, lovely, and of good report. Oh faultless Jesus, inimitably infallible. Oh honey dripping lips of the fairest of the sons of men. Oh winged words of snowy whiteness, all honour and praise for ever I must yield and own that "never man spake like this man."

<u>Love</u>. But iron courage and cold discretion will not win the battle. Love is the mightiest as well as the fairest of the graces. A man who has love in his heart will soon find his way into other men's souls.

Surely my Master was all love. Never man was so full of love as he. Methinks I see him even now with big tears rolling down his cheeks, uttering his lament over Jerusalem. In all his discourses his eyes were rendered soft yet omnipotent by the power of love. His very threatenings, uttered in a tone of deep pity, sounded like the warnings of mercy and not the thund'rings of justice.

Oh those words on the cross, "Father forgive them." There is more real melody there than in the finest compositions of Handel. Surely the very demons must have been thrilled by its pathetic cadence. Oh what power love has over men. If we know that a man loves us, how readily do we drink in his words.

His eye sometimes floats in tears, his uplifted hand seems to beseech you to be reconciled to God, and his every movement seems to be baptized in love. Such and far more than I can describe was Jesus.

"Never man spake like this man."

Humility again was sweetly conspicuous. He was a man anointed above his fellows, but who could see any pride in him[?] The little child seemed to be his fit companion. The woman of Samaria could talk with him; vile as she was, he did not keep her at a distance. He was no lawn sleeved bishop. His hand was given to the poor. The common people heard him gladly. He was a <u>man</u>, not a man in his own caste, and a lord everywhere else. But he spoke like the servant of all.

I think humility [is] the rarest of all graces, and all the imitations of it I count as the offscouring of the earth. I long to be conformed to Christ, but pride's ear has been bored to the door post. But not Jesus.

"Never man spake like this man."

And now we note the style of Jesus, having long enough dwelt on his character, seeing that we can only give an outline of that mirror of all perfection.

The Style of Christ was <u>simple</u>. The Child could understand him. Some preachers, if they meet with a hard word in the week, must bring it out on Sabbath. But why should they do so[?] Hard words in a sermon are like stones in fruit. They may be almost unavoidable, but they are not ~~good~~ nourishing. Christ spoke the language of childhood. How exquisitely simple are his parables. How plain the meaning of the prodigal, the good Samaritan, or the house upon the sand.

Market Language Whit[e]field used, and after all what is better than good homely Saxon[?] May the Lord send us less philosophy and more simplicity, less of the college and more of common life preaching.

No one so simple as Jesus.

It was <u>serious</u>. There was no levity in Christ. He was deeply in solemn earnest and had no time for jokes. At the same time, I do not say as some do that Jesus never laughed. I think some old crabbed divine first said that when he had a fit of spleen. I am exhorted to rejoice, yea to leap for joy. Holy mirth well becomes a Christian, but the pulpit is not the place for buffoonery, for quips and fun. Smile we may, and eccentricity and oddity have been made useful. But remember it is eccentricity. A model preacher I would describe as serious yet cheerful, solemn yet joyful. I conceive that Jesus ~~was~~ would have been eminently so, though as a man of sorrows he could not be so joyful as we ought to be who are redeemed from all ills.

It was <u>earnest</u>. His words came from his heart. Some preachers seem to have a very low temperature to their hearts, somewhere below zero. Jesus did not stand motionless as a statue, as destitute of emotion as a picture and only moving his eyes as seldom as a Madonna. No, his was living eloquence. His lips had been touched not by the blue fringes of frost but by a live coal from off the altar. His very fingers would preach, his eye, aye, and all his body.

Should he not be serious who speaks of eternal things, who preaches sin's punishment and the only remedy[?] Should he prate on his usual time and turn the dry leaves of a manuscript[?] No, no, let his eye flash fire, let his bosom glow with real heat, let him plead with men as for his life, and wrestle as if <u>he</u> were the victim to be delivered.

It was <u>direct</u>. His hearers perceived that he spake of them. This was the secret of Rowland Hill's power. He gave home strokes. "Thou art the man" seemed to be the conclusion of all his sermons.

The self-condemned accusers left the woman in the temple alone. There was no mistaking him. His sermon had a hundred hands to grasp the hearers with. Nowadays this is called personality. And so, let it be. I accept it under this title and pray God to make all his ministers personal preachers.

Oh my friends, I tarry here. The lofty mountains out-top the power of language. Ask me to describe Cicero, or Demosthenes, and I can do it. But this man, the Lord Jesus, stands head and shoulders above them all. His strains are more than seraphic. If my tongue were to continue until it should be worn to a nothing, yea if the harps of glory should be worn away with constant playing, they could not sing the rapture of his voice, nor could I declare it.

II. FOR MATTER.

None has ever spoken as he has done. If the outward trappings of our Saviour's utterances are so excellent what must the body itself be[?] We do not profess to be able to unroll the garments and speak fully of the inhabitant; it needs another Christ to preach Christ fully. A man need speak as well as he to praise him fully. We will but briefly speak his praise.

Compare the truths he preached with those of the philosophers of remote or modern ages. They but amuse with pithy sayings, with half opened mysteries. They talk of time and the things there of. He speaks of eternity and its boundless cycles. Of death and what is beyond it. Of hell the pit prepared for the wicked, and of the mansions to receive the righteous. His message is from the One God. He tells of himself, the ransomer of captives, and [of] the Spirit, the Comforter of Mourners.

These are no trifles. These are not leaves from the wild forest trees. These are not broken shells from the deep ocean. They are pearls of price unbounded and gems of splendor unequalled. Every syllable has its value, every sentiment is big with solemn meaning.

Compare the truths he uttered with the testimony of all the prophets. Noah could preach righteousness but he could not declare the way, the truth, and the life. Moses could hold up the law and point to its rocky tablets, and each of the prophets in order had their errands, but [Jesus] is the marrow of them all. The fairest flowers from all the gardens of others make up that bundle of perfume called my beloved.

As some painters to make a landscape do ~~put~~ choose a tree from one place, a stream from another, and group them with a distant castle, so may you gather the beauties of all authors, the gems of all writers, the golden sentences of all orators, and the choice words of all divines. But could ye distil the quintessence from them all, and mingle them in one precious box of spikenard, sweet though it might be, sweeter than the breath of morn or the exhalations of flowers, ~~they~~ it could not equal the sweetness of my Lord's messages.

How know you this? says the scoffer. Know it[?] Why I have heard him speak and can bear testimony that no voice can be compared with his. This is after all the best way to understand the eloquence of Jesus. Have we not heard his voice in the still evening while walking in the garden of meditation? Did he not once sing outside my dungeon wall until I answered to his song and he delivered me? Ah, well can I say, as the voice of the turtle when winter is passed, so is the voice of my Beloved. So [as] the anthems of paradise, as the hymns of glory, as the hallelujahs of the ransomed, so is his speech to mine ear.

I add my name to the cloud of witnesses of this truth and doubt not that there are many here who most gladly say Amen. Oh that the deaf might hear the sound, and the dead be quickened by the strain. If the whole world could but hear, they would love him too. Sinner, let me tell thee one word of his musical language 'ere I close.

Come unto me all ye that labour and are heavy laden and I will give you rest.

Help. Oh, my King.

"FORGIVE US OUR DEBTS"

Editor's Summary

Prayer was a vital aspect of Charles's Christian life and ministry. He found it to be so personally necessary that he insisted, "Prayer has become as essential to me as the heaving of my lungs, and the beating of my pulse." *MTP* 49:476. As for his ministry, Charles sternly warned his congregation, saying, "Let me know the day when you give up praying for me, for then I must give up preaching." *Autobiography* 2:335.

In this sermon, Charles expounds upon the beauty of "The Lord's Prayer," and in particular Matt 6:12: "Forgive us our debts, as we forgive our debtors" (a text he did not preach on again). Interestingly, he begins his sermon with a lengthy introduction offering comment on the other verses of the prayer.

Charles opens his commentary by noting that the Lord's Prayer "is a most beautiful composition, among Christians there cannot be two opinions. It is the model prayer." However, his appreciation for the prayer was tempered by his desires to ward off the "formalism" that he associated with the Roman Catholic Church and the Church of England. Accordingly, he warns non-Christians, saying,

> None but Christian men ought to use it, for none but they can truly say "Our [F]ather which art in heaven." Every unconverted man who uses it, so far from worshipping God, actually insults him by calling him what he is not. How can he say "hallowed be thy name" when at another time he curses God[?]

In a similar vein, he also warns Christians against the dangers of dry repetition:

> I do not think that [the Lord's Prayer] was intended as a form to be ordinarily used in prayer by believers. I think it may be acceptable offered occasionally,

but I do not think our Saviour intended it as a prayer to be used on all occasions. I look upon it as a model, a beautiful model.

It also appears that Charles was lightly influenced in this sermon by John Gill's commentary on this passage (see *An Exposition on the New Testament* 1:51–54). On the "hallowing" of God, Gill wrote:

> [God] is sanctified by others, when they fear him, believe in him, call upon his name, use it reverently, submit to his will, acknowledge his mercies, regard his commands and ordinances, and live a holy life and conversation; all of which is earnestly desired by truly gracious folks. *An Exposition of the New Testament* 1:52.

Such "hallowing" honors God, and Charles's enduring aim was "ever to desire [God's] glory above all things." He believed it was man's duty to glorify God by humbly trusting in Jesus Christ. Only through faith in Christ can anyone be "forgiven once for all," and once forgiven, it becomes the Christian's "duty to forgive," a dim reflection of God's own glorious grace.

FORGIVE US OUR DEBTS

Matthew 6:12

"And forgive us our debts, as we forgive our debtors."

I would commence my discourse tonight by remarking on what is commonly called the Lord's Prayer. My views of it may sound strange but are by no means singular. It is a most beautiful composition; among Christians there cannot be two opinions. It is the model prayer. The difference of opinion will rest as to the use of it and here let me remark:

1. That none but Christian men ought to use it, for none but they can truly say, "Our Father which art in heaven." Every unconverted man who uses it, so far from worshipping God, actually insults him by calling him what he is not. How can he say "hallowed be thy name" when at another time he curses God[?]

2. I do not think that it was intended as a form to be ordinarily used in prayer by believers. I think it may be acceptably offered occasionally, but I do not think our Saviour intended it as a prayer to be used on all occasions. I look upon it as a model, a beautiful model. But I should no more think of using it as a prayer than I should think of getting inside the little model of our chapel which now stands in the vestry. It is a beautiful ground plan of a prayer, but we are left by God to build by it as our want may suggest or the Holy Ghost direct us. It is a most admirable pattern. It commences with a most endearing title, suggesting at once all that is tender and familiar coupled with authority and power.

Its first breathing is in solemn awe, an almost whisper, an ascription and a prayer at once. Then follows the glorious petition with which David closed his prayers, and coupled with it a desire so pure that none but Jesus could have conceived it. The most unselfish of petitions come first. So are we ever to desire his glory above all things.

But he forbids us not to ask for ourselves the needed benefits. "Give us this day our daily bread" is as sanctified an utterance as "thy kingdom come." He whose ever[-]opened hand supplies every want bids us ask, and well may we consent to do it, for his paths drop fatness. Bread in the threefold sense— the bread of natural food for this body, the animal part of me; bread of knowledge for my mind; and that best of all breads, the spiritual sustenance of my soul. There is a trinity in man, and the prayer is therefore triple.

And now a petition, the most humbling of all, appears in the centre, "Forgive us our debts" etc. The text includes:

I.   A PRAYER. *"forgive us our debts"*

II. AN ARGUMENT. *"as we forgive our debtors"*

III. A DUTY IS SUPPOSED VIZ FORGIVENESS.

I.   A PRAYER.

This prayer puts man in a very humiliating position. It calls him a debtor. And is he not so from the very nature of things[?] Are not all things debtors to their maker[?] Did he not turn them all on his mighty lathe? Are they not his handiwork? Save the Godhead, all beings are debtors. The glittering plumage of the angels was given them by him. The scorching furnaces of the sun are fed ~~by~~ with fuel by his hand, while this inferior clod is held together by his grasp.

Man, the wonder of all world, is much in debt. He has been fearfully and wonderfully made, the breath of his nostrils is not his own, nor the air he breathes. Ah, this is a debt man cannot pay, but this he never need ask to have forgiven. The word forgive supposes sin and points us to the real debt which we have contracted. Oh what a depth of meaning in those two words "our debts." Can any man in the world tell how great thy are? I trow not, until he has measured the ocean into drops and fathomed the abyss of interminable space. Our debts are of two kinds: Debts inherited and debts personal.

The <u>first</u> are by no means light. We are all members of one great corporation. Adam, as representative for us, failed and made himself and the whole race [bankrupt]. We are all as sharers liable. This is the worst kind of debt a man can have, for however much he may have he is still liable until the debts of the whole company are paid.

Some will say that they were no parties to the agreement. I answer that God has chosen the representative system as his mode of moral government, and it is better than any you or I could suggest. Adam stands or falls; on that one man hangs the whole race. How much better than to let every man stand or fall, for remember, if we fall representatively, we rise in the same manner. But if every man stood on his own footing we could never be sure thats any man would rise, yea no man could arise, and thus the race must perish.

Remember then, my brother, when thou askest for forgiveness, that thou hast an awful debt as one of a bankrupt society. A debt which like some bottomless chasm would require mountains to fill it up. A debt which like an horseleech cries evermore "give, give," and like behemoth drinks up rivers of merit at a draught. Truly when we meditate on this deep and mysterious subject we may well say "Forgive us our debts."

The <u>Second</u> kind of debts are those which most men will admit. Debts personal. Now let us set down and count our personal liabilities. I began to run into arrears very early. I did not reverence my parents, many youthful sins and crimes have disgraced my history. Wayward and giddy I ran headlong over the glassy sea of youth.

Some of you can remember black acts of lust which disgraced your ripening manhood. Sins against the world in running with its maxims. Sins against our companions in leading them astray. Sins against relatives. Sins against time, wasting its running sands. Sins against soul and body, against earth and heaven. Oh my poor soul, sins are as thick around thee as insects in the evening's sunshine.

How much owest thou to my Lord? Be calm oh ocean, let thy bosom be congealed into a continued sheet that I may write my debt upon it. Space fails. I will commence at one horizon and in broad lines write any sins on yonder firmament, but again I find the space too narrow. Ah Lord, I cannot tell how much I owe. It surpasseth my arithmetic. Dost thou still ask. Then I must ask those condemned spirits who have these four thousand years been drinking the brimstone of the boiling cauldron of the wrath of Almighty God. But they know not yet, nor can they know, till they have measured eternity and comprehended the infinite. To pay them were impossible, for I cannot reckon them. I only cry out ["]forgive me my debts.["]

Before we quit this prayer we must have three remarks which to help your memory we put in brief words: <u>To whom</u>, <u>by whom</u>, [and] <u>through whom</u>.

<u>To whom</u>, may we say, "forgive us our debts?" We need not question long. It is to our Father. None but he can forgive sins, for they are committed against him alone. How blasphemous is it for a Romish Priest to talk of forgiving sins, and not much less than that when the Clergyman of the Church of England kneels by the bed side of a dying man and reads "by authority committed unto me I absolve thee from all sin."

My friends I need not warn you against so dangerous an error as that of forgiveness of sins by man. It was presumption enough for Lucifer to desire to climb the throne of heaven. But where unto shall I liken the pride of that man who would act the God and pardon, in the Almighty's name, sins against the majesty of heaven[?] Oh vile potsherds of the dust, your arrogance is unbounded. Oh pitiful worms of the earth, wherefore ape omnipotence. Oh vile reprobates and blasphemers, how dare ye ascend the bench of judgment and acquit criminals, yourselves being doubly condemned.

<u>By whom</u> need this supplication to be offered? Surely this needs no reply. It suits alike the saint and the sinner. Manasseh may offer it in his dungeon, and Moses on the top of Pisgah. The bloody hands of Saul may be lifted up to heaven with it, but it will equally become the holy John. Jew and Gentile, rich and poor may well offer this common petition. Verily we are all debtors.

Yet it may be questioned how a child of God who is already pardoned can ask for pardon again. The reply is easy. I am forgiven once for all the moment I believe. Sin can never be laid to my charge, but then I may be chastised for sin, and I offer this prayer to turn away the rod from me, just as an erring child would to an offended father. I know [that] in one sense I am so forgiven that I need not ask for it anymore, but in ~~this~~ another sense I must make this my daily prayer, "Father Forgive." Again, by this may be intended ["]give me a sense of forgiveness,["] a fresh knowledge of it. Now where is the man who can say this day "I need not offer that prayer"[?] Save a few poor crazy perfectionists, I can find no such man on earth.

<u>Through whom?</u> The answer trembles on our lips. Already you guess the reply, Christ is the signature which renders our petition powerful. He is the ladder down which the mercies travel. Like Isis who came from heaven on a rainbow, all blessings come through the glories of his covenant. Show the Father the many coloured garment dipt in his vital blood. Strike this red gore upon your lintel. Preface and conclude with the all[-]potent name of Jesus.

In vain your tears, though you should weep like Niobe. Heaven cares not for thy sorrows unless thou dost mention the greater woes of Immanuel. Shoulds't thou rend heaven with thine outcries and wear the rocks with thy kneelings[?] It is all in vain until thou lookest to Calvary and beholdest the Surety who paid the debt that thou mightiest be forgiven. Ah, bleeding [S]ufferer, ever will I turn mine eyes to thee and mention nothing but thy name.

II. THE ARGUMENT. *"As we forgive etc."*

This does not at first look like a free grace argument, but it is. If it does not appear so, it is because we do not understand it. It does not mean that we are to ask forgiveness because we have forgiven others, but I take it to mean this. Lord I have many debts, but thy grace has looked upon me, and I have in consequence been led to forgive my debtors, therefore I plead this evidence. Surely thou wouldest not have showed me this favour if thou dids't intend to destroy me. No Lord. Thou hast taught me to forgive, now shew me another token for good by giving me an evidence of forgiveness.

It is the mark of a Christian to forgive injuries, and he is no Christian who has never learned to forgive. Oh foolish hypocrite, thou boastest that thy Lord has forgiven thee all thy debt, and yet there lies thy poor debtor in the jail who owes thee a pitiful hundred pence. Vile parasite of religion, thou art no genuine plant of the Lord. The Sons of God forgive till seventy times seven. This is one of the insignia of the free masonry of heaven. Good for evil is Godlike. To forgive is to be like God, to keep enmity is Satanic.

Oh when my enemy has spat upon me, has plucked my hair, and called me dog, is it not sweet to revenge my injury and trample him in the dust[?] No, it is sweet to a worldling's palate, but to the Christian there is a sweeter revenge than this: it is to waylay him with kindness, to feed him when he hungers, to pour wine into his parched lips, to set him by one's own fireside, to whisper peace to his troubled conscience, to tell him to forget the injury for it is all forgiven. There is mine enemy drowning. I will risk my life for him, this arm shall save him from the angry flood. I must forgive him for I am a child of Jehovah who passeth by transgression and sin. Thus you see this is an evidence of grace, not a plea of merit. Now:

III. THE DUTY.

It is plainly our duty to forgive, not debts of money (though in some cases these), but debts of trespass against us by our fellow creatures. A full forgiveness of all our fellows <u>Is necessary when we pray</u>. I bend my knee and ask forgiveness but there is enmity in my soul. My prayer is talking to the wind. I cannot offer my sacrifice, for enmity doth make a blemish in it. Be assured of this, all of you, there is no mercy for you until you have shown it to others.

What saith the Merciful God[?] Dost thou lift thine hands for mercy[?] Why, thou hast just now been griping thy brother's throat therewith. Vile creature, am I to blot out they crimes whilst thou art to be avenged[?] Justice spurns the miscreant from his throne. It matters not how the quarrel has arisen. It may be a family feud, an old hatred running in the blood, or it may be from some real injury. I charge you, forgive each other if you hope to be forgiven. If you meet each other on going out of the door, put forth the hand of pardon, or as long as heaven standeth, your unmercifulness shall be remembered.

Let me remind you <u>this is necessary at death</u>. You must soon gather up your feet in the bed. If you wish to die the death of the righteous, all enmities must leave your bosoms. Oh man, thy cherished hatred will hover over thee like an eagle preying on thy vitals. It will lay like a millstone on thy breast keeping down the breath of prayer. It will be a thistle in thy last bed. A demon scaring thine hours. I would not have thy deathbed for all the gold of Croesus. I would sooner die with a martyr at the stake than die with thee. But thou wilt <u>need it most</u> at <u>judgment</u>.

But a little while, oh mortals, and the great assize shall commence. The judge shall come with sound of trumpet. Then where will the unforgiving one appear[?] No difficulty to prophecy his doom. Go archangels, sever the goats from the sheep. They come, and this man stands first with Cain's mark on his brow. Drag up the miscreant. What hast thou to say[?] Wretch, dost thou plead for mercy[?] Does not the word choke thee[?]

Mercy, didst thou show any[?] Didst thou not pursue thy fellow like a bloodhound[?]

Mercy, because thou hast showed none, I will deal with thee as thou hast rewarded others.

Thine enmities shall be tied around thy neck like millstones for ever, while the iron whips of vengeance shall tear thee Eternally. May God give you grace to forgive, and evermore to pray "forgive us our debts as we forgive our debtors."

Amen.

"FAITH BEFORE BAPTISM"

Editor's Summary

Charles dedicated this sermon, preached at New Park Street Chapel, to the contentious issue of believer's baptism.

Historically, believer's baptism in England had proven to be a personal issue, a polity issue, and a political issue. Politically speaking, English laws such as the Corporation Act (1661) and the Test Acts (1673) prohibited Roman Catholics and Nonconformists from holding a wide-ranging number of public offices while also barring such students from universities like Oxford or Cambridge. Accordingly, until those laws were repealed, one's stance on the ordinances had significant implications.

On a personal level, Charles's baptism created a little friction within his own family, who were Independent Congregationalists. In the lead-up to his baptism by William Cantlow on May 3, 1850, Charles wrote to his father,

> I have come to a resolution that, by God's help, I will profess the name of Jesus as soon as possible if I may be admitted into His Church on earth. . . . I trust that I shall then feel that the bonds of the Lord are upon me, and have a more powerful sense of my duty to walk circumspectly. Conscience has convinced me that it is a duty to be buried with Christ in baptism, although I am sure it constitutes no part of salvation. *Autobiography* 1:119.

Ironically, it appears that a Church of England clergyman was in part responsible for Charles changing his view of baptism. In his autobiography, fourteen-year-old, unbelieving Charles recorded the following exchange at the Maidstone boarding school:

> Spurgeon — Oh, yes sir, I was; my grandfather baptized me in the little parlour, and he is a minister, so I know he did it right!

C[lergyman]—Ah, but you had neither faith nor repentance, and therefore ought not to have received baptism! *Autobiography* 1:49.

Having been bested in the argument, Charles wrote, "I resolved, from that moment that if ever Divine grace should work a change in me, I would be baptized." *Autobiography* 1:50. Indeed, praise be to God that he did!

Finally, it bears mention that the tone and argument of this sermon is similar to Charles's famous message, "Baptismal Regeneration" (*MTP* 10, Sermon 573), which sold the most individual copies of any of his sermons and elicited sharp responses from the Church of England (see A Layman, *The Church of England, and Baptismal Regeneration. A Review of the Sermon on Mark XVI.15, 16; Preached by the Rev. C. H. Spurgeon* [London: William Hunt, n.d., The Spurgeon Library]). Furthermore, it appears that this sermon, unusual for its lack of a sermon text, did not appear to influence the one he became known for. Charles's urgent and biting tone is captured well by his own words here: "You lead them to believe that there is efficacy in drops of water, we tell them they must be saved."

FAITH BEFORE BAPTISM

Then this is the only prerequisite before Baptism. I need not ask a candidate many questions as to his growth in grace, or degree of knowledge, if he sincerely and heartily believes. I am then quite satisfied and will baptize him. This is <u>the</u> question, and the only question. But on the other hand, this <u>one</u> thing is essentially necessary to the right reception or administration of the ordinance. This is the doctrine of the text, and I shall for a few moments speak upon:

I. DOCTRINE.

II. THE QUESTION WHICH NATURALLY ARISES.

I. THE DOCTRINE.

I think it superfluous to attempt a proof when the text declares as plainly as possible that Faith is necessary. I suppose there are none in my congregation so obtuse as to be unable to see this self-evident truth.

As to members of the [C]hurch of England, they will want no proof, for from their infancy they have been taught the doctrine and believe that repentance and faith are necessary before Baptism. Were I in argument with a Churchman I should not want a better book on my side than the Book of Common Prayer. With any really consistent believer in parts of the Book of Common Prayer, I am at no issue.

My combat is with those who say that others beside believers have a right to this ordinance. In their teeth I lift up my text and wonder how it is possible for them to escape. I have no doubt my brethren are desirous to be right and follow their judgments, and far be it from me to anathematize any man or pronounce curses on his head. I simply beg his ear a moment while I ask a question or two.

1. Brother why do you baptize infants? He replies, "because Abraham's seed were circumcised." Now this glorious reason reminds me very much of Tenterden Steeple and the Goodwin Sands. I can never see any connection here.

    But stay and hear our friend a moment or two. He says that Abraham's children were put into the Covenant by ~~Baptism~~ Circumcision and therefore ours ought to be put into it by Baptism. Oh my friend this is a poor argument, a mere cobweb which a child may sever.

    The first covenant was a covenant made with Abraham's seed according to the flesh. But now turn out the bondwoman and her sons. We who love the Lord are Abraham's seed. We are the circumcision but the covenant does not run in the blood. What an awful fallacy this covenant putting is. Surely Baptized children are no better than others. etc etc.

2. What barrier should there be? If our[s] be thrown down, what will you propose as a substitute[?] You have none. There is no halting place; next come horses and cows, ships and bells.

3. What evils [do] you bring on the people[?] You lead them to believe that there is efficacy in drops of water, we tell them they must be saved.

4. Why not open the Lord's table[?] Children ate the Passover, why not the Lord's supper[?] Every one is baptized, why not let them sit at the table[?]

Bid the world a welcome, turn the church and the world into one great common where sheep and goats feed together, and so shall you cause joy in the infernal regions, both hearty and lasting. How much better to obey God rather than man, and to ask this question only: dost thou believe[?]

II. THE QUESTION.

Is:

1. Why are not all believers baptized[?] Are they afraid of water? Do they fear to come out and put on the Lord Jesus publicly[?] Why lie in ambush, hidden in the stairs[?]

2. Are all who have been here baptized real and hearty believers? Oh this is a thing worthy of the serious personal inquiry of every professor here. How sad if the waters of baptism do testify against you.

3. Are the candidates real believers? If not, I charge you, stand back and venture not so vile an act as to be buried in hypocrisy. 'Tis a solemn thing. It is not to be rushed upon hastily. But if you believe, come on, there is no fear. Christ is all-sufficient. But beware for the future.

You pass the Rubicon; be careful.

"THE DAY OF VENGEANCE, THE YEAR OF ACCEPTANCE"

Editor's Summary

For Charles, the surety of the righteous vengeance of God was both a great comfort and high-octane fuel for evangelism. From the earliest days of his ministry as an itinerant preacher, Charles knew that heralding the gospel meant warning about hell, as seen in sermons such as "Future Judgment" (*LS* 1, Sermon 6); "Sinners Must Be Punished" (*LS* 1, Sermon 9); "The Day of God" (*LS* 2, Sermon 115); and "Set Thine House in Order" (*LS* 2, Sermon 134).

While the Victorian Age in which he lived saw unprecedented advances in science and medicine (such as the hypodermic syringe), death was an ever-present specter. Despite being born into an "era of progress," Charles's life expectancy at birth was only forty years. In an earlier sermon on Isa. 38:1, "Set thine house in order: for thou shalt die, and not live," he penned the following prayer at the head of his manuscript, "Gracious God, help me to write and preach this sermon just as if it were my last, if indeed it be not." *LS* 2:491.

This time, Charles both defends the righteous vengeance of God and urges his hearers to escape God's wrath through faith in Jesus Christ. Notably, the bulk of the manuscript is dedicated to his first main division, "A Day of Vengeance," with particular attention given to its secondary points: "1. Vengeance justified"; "2. Vengeance certified"; and "3. Vengeance magnified." It also appears that Charles preached on Isa 61:2 once more in "Proclamation of Acceptance and Vengeance" (*MTP* 23, Sermon 1369). However, this later sermon does not appear to contain any overlapping content or similar structure.

For Charles, it was key that God "proclaims a year of acceptance and a day of vengeance." His pastoral concern prompted him to confront the lie that the "God" of the Old Testament was a mean, spiteful, or harsh judge, while the "God" of the New Testament was kind, lenient, and forgiving. Rather, Charles upheld the biblical view that "it is not inconsistent with the highest benevolence for God to be a God of vengeance." In fact, he argues here that "vengeance in God is benevolence in another shape." Using the example of a judge, Charles asks, "Is the Judge malevolent because he condemns a criminal[?]," a question to which any party in search of justice would say "No." Accordingly, he argues that in the same way "there is as much benevolence on God's part in punishing as in pardoning."

While heralding the truth that "God will not spare the guilty" and that "he will have vengeance," Charles emphasized, "The day of vengeance has passed for every sinner who shall believe on the name of Jesus." Indeed, Charles marveled at the riches of God's grace as put forth in Jesus Christ, the righteous substitute for wicked sinners. He cherished that "strange union" where God made satisfaction for sinners by pouring out his wrath on his own beloved Son.

> Strange union. Vengeance and acceptance. Vengeance and love. Man could not have devised this. Sure this is the master work of God to unite such dissimilar materials and make redemption therewith.

THE DAY OF VENGEANCE, THE YEAR OF ACCEPTANCE

[Isaiah] 61:2

"To proclaim the acceptable year of the LORD, and the day of vengeance of our God; to comfort all that mourn."

We have no need to ask as the Eunuch did, "tell me, I pray thee, of whom speaketh the prophet this, of himself or of some other man?" for our Saviour ~~has~~ furnished us with the key to it when in the synagogue he took the book and said, "The Spirit of the Lord is upon me etc."

Our text represents our Saviour as making a proclamation in the name of God. He is the Logos, or Word of God, and by him God makes his proclamation to man. He had spoken once, yea twice, but man regarded it not. The Prophets had spoken in vain, but now the Prince, the Heir of all things, speaks. Listen oh Heavens and be attent oh earth. If Jeremiah could cry out "Oh earth, earth, earth, hear the word of the Lord," much more may we demand it now with emphasis, "Oh earth, earth, earth, hear the word of the Lord."

In the name of the Sacred Three he utters his voice [and] we will listen to the proclamation. It is double. He proclaims a year of acceptance and a day of vengeance. These demand our attention and shall receive ~~them~~ it. By your leave we will reverse the order of the sentences in the proclamation, and this gives us:

I.   A DAY OF VENGEANCE.

II. A YEAR OF ACCEPTANCE.

III. THE ORDINANCE OF THE LORD'S SUPPER CONTAINS A UNITED REMEMBRANCE OF BOTH.

I.   A DAY OF VENGEANCE.

Harshly these words sound in the midst of so many kind and tender commissions, but as they are here we would not wish to expunge them, believing that they are necessary ones.

In speaking from these words for a short time, we are called upon first of all to justify the use of the term vengeance as applied to God. Then we shall endeavor to certify the ungodly that vengeance will come, and again to show that the death of Christ was peculiarly a day of vengeance.

> Vengeance justified.
> Vengeance certified.
> Vengeance ~~satisfied~~ magnified.

1.   <u>Vengeance justified</u>. There would be little need for this were all men believers. The true believers never quarrels with the righteous vengeance of God, he knows it to be most just and admires it.

But there are some who will say that God is a God [of] all love and that he will not punish the guilty. How, say they, can the God of the universe be a God of vengeance[?] How can he delight in putting his creatures to misery[?] Oh ye creatures of yesterday, whence this arrogance? Shall the potsherds bring their maker to judgment? Will you charge him with cruelty? Stay. Remember, who art thou that repliest against God?

But if you wish to repeat your cry. Let me tell you that it is not inconsistent with the highest benevolence for God to be a God of vengeance. It is true that we are not to take vengeance on our fellow creatures, and it is benevolent on our part to forgive all injuries, but God as the judge of all must, if he be benevolent, punish sin. Suppose a magistrate to be a kind man. He signs a warrant for punishing an offender. Is he therefore unkind[?] Is the Judge malevolent because he condemns a criminal[?] Nay. There is as much benevolence on God's part in punishing as in pardoning.

Would it be good and tender of the great Ruler to leave us without laws to do as we please[?] Would any one desire to see universal anarchy[?] Do you wish for a reign of terror in which unbridled lust would riot[?] No, if there were no laws there would soon be an outcry of woe in the world. We should then ask to have some legislation, for the worst of all law is better than none at all.

Our prayer is answered, we receive a law, but how can there be a law without punishments[?] If any man may break law with impunity then law is nothing. Law without power is a laughing stock for sin. If then there must be punishments shall they be unexecuted[?] Shall the criminal be allowed to enjoy immunity? Oh were it so, ye would soon cry out that God were unkind. Even now while the wrath of God tarries we are apt to ask whether the God of heaven doth really behold the wrongs of his creatures. But if it were known that God would not punish the guilty, then the unbeliever might say that our God was not good or [else] he would come to the rescue of the injured and avenge the sufferings of the oppressed.

I say again that vengeance in God is benevolence in another shape. And much as I may startle some of you, I believe that hell itself is not a blot upon the love of God but that, rather, love to mankind constrained the God of justice there to banish the finally impenitent.

2. Vengeance certified. But if the ungodly man still rails upon the vengeance of God, let me assure him that he cannot prevent its truth. You may curse the lightning but that will not restrain it from shivering you. You may rail against the boiling ocean but it will not stay its roarings for you. So ye may blaspheme God but you cannot thereby save yourself from the awful fact of his punishing your sin.

There is in man a something called conscience which tells you all that you will be punished for sin; but should you have lulled conscience to sleep, come with me a moment. Do you see those plains covered with grass[?] Do you observe those men and women dancing in sinful pleasure[?]

Yes, those are the sons of God and the daughters of men. How happy they seem, but wait—they have a few more hours of respite. You will see soon that God punishes sin. Noah has entered his ark and a loud laugh goes up from the merry throng outside. But wait one moment—didst [you] hear that sound[?] Oh how awful. 'Twas the noise of the waters leaping from their hollow caverns. Didst [you] hear that other sound[?] 'Twas the voice of the waters above shouting back to their brethren beneath.

Haste away. The rain descends, the floods arise. The dancers are dismayed. The myriads of mankind are startled. They rush for the hills. How the tide thins their ranks. Higher. And but a few [remain] on the summit of the mountains, but they too are gone. We hear the last shriek of the strong swimmer in his agony. And now look at yon void, yon flood, covered with corpses of men, women, children, and cattle.

Will [God] break up the depths of the earth and rend the firmament to punish sin and shalt thou go unpunish'd[?] Is that not enough[?] Then I take thee to Sodom, to Egypt, to Korah's pit, to Jerusalem.

But why need this[?] You yourselves have seen sin punished in this life. You have seen the miserable wretch dragging his frame along and you have said, "see there the effect of sin." And you have beheld judgments on blasphemers by their sudden death or being overtaken with calamities unmistakably the result of no common providence but of the finger of God.

3. Vengeance magnified. God will not spare the guilty. He will have vengeance and he has done so. Of all days of vengeance, the death of Jesus was the day of vengeance of our God. Never did justice so awake its sword as on that day.

There was vengeance upon Sin in the person of Christ. He for a time stood in the place of his people. He was counted as a sinner and numbered with the transgressors. The sins of multitudes were laid upon him and he stood the master culprit of all, though in him personally there was no sin.

Oh who can picture the day of vengeance of our God. At the prospect of it he was exceeding sorrowful even unto death. Midnight has never before nor since been startled with such groans as those of Gethsemane. Never such sweat reddened a garden before. It were enough misery for a thousand lives, only with Jesus to contemplate the coming trial. But vengeance comes. She has been seeking a victim. Her sword is athirst for blood and winged to stay. She has long cried for vengeance and her hour is come.

She binds her prisoner and with knotted whips she flaggelates his shoulders and lacerates his body. Never such blows as hers. She makes them as heavy as her gigantic arm can enable her. He is betrayed, it is by a disciple. He is forsaken, and it is by Peter. He is accused, and of that worst of crimes, blasphemy. There was the essence of wormwood in all the drops he drank. He shall die, then let him be crucified. He must die, let it be with thieves. He must hang aloft before the crowd, then strip him naked. Scorch him with the Sun, then freeze him in the shade.

Lay on the strokes and spare not. Mark how rapidly the blows succeeded. He is dragged from tribunal to tribunal, scourged, mocked, spit upon, beaten again, hurried to crucifixion, and all in a brief space, as if vengeance was in haste to devour him at once and swallow him up quick. Oh day of vengeance thou art gone, but I would not forget thee. Oh my much injured Lord how can I ever repay thee[?] Suffer me to be dissolved in tears. Oh depths. Oh heights. Oh unutterables.

II. A YEAR OF ACCEPTANCE.

The day of vengeance has passed for every sinner who shall believe on the name of Jesus. And now not a day but a year of acceptance is come. The sorrows of Jesus were comparatively a day but his mercy is a year. The acceptable year is supposed by some to refer to the year of Jubilee, and truly we have a Jubilee through the death of our Saviour. This night I proclaim it. The Year of Jubilee is come. Bankrupt debtors, your debts are cancelled. Prisoners, ye are free. Slaves, this is the hour of liberty. Captives, ye are ransomed.

To as many as now hear my voice I cry aloud the year of Jubilee. Some of you careless ones will not hear it, but every sinner here [who] is sensible of his guilt will rejoice when I proclaim Jubilee. Young man, Jubilee, your sins are pardoned. Young woman drowned in tears, Jubilee. And thou Rahab the harlot, art thou here[?] Then Jubilee. To the vile, to the ungodly, to sinners, to outcasts, to reprobates, I proclaim aloud. The year of Jubilee is come.

The Acceptable Year. The year of acceptance of our <u>works</u>. Before this God could not hear prayer or praise. Sin spoiled all and barred all communion, but now the way is opened. By him our prayers accepted rise. Come sinner, this is the day of acceptance. If thou canst sigh he will accept it. On some days the easterns give presents and then even a flower is accepted. Come bring thy broken heart, thy sob, thy groan. This is the accepted day. And thou Xn, rejoice. Eat and drink for God accepts thee.

He accepts our <u>persons</u>. Defiled and full of sin they were, but now vengeance has washed them in blood, and being satisfied, has given us a robe of honour and we are accepted. We are all accepted in the beloved. Not only accepted members of the church below, but we shall be received into that above. In this our new Jubilee exceeds the old, for they could not proclaim acceptance with Jehovah. Oh Glory, Glory. Surely while I shudder at the rough blast of the day of vengeance I may exult in the calm sunshine of the year of acceptance.

III. THE TWO CONJOINED IN THE SUPPER.

Strange union. Vengeance and acceptance. Vengeance and love. Man could not have devised this. Sure this is the master work of God to unite such dissimilar materials and make redemption therewith. Let me muse awhile.

Vengeance has left the trace of its wrath. See the bread, emblem of a mangled body rent in sunder, left piecemeal as prey is torn by the lion. See again the cup. She has filled it with his blood, oh cruel vengeance, most just vengeance. I see thee at the table but I mark thy friend here too, whom thou hast lately kissed. I see acceptance there.

I sit at the table. Should I do that if unaccepted[?] I eat, I drink, and will he disown me[?] No. I am a child. Oh my master, give me that most excellent grace of love, that I dissolved in thankfulness may melt my soul into my sermon as the true vitality thereof.

<u>Help, Help, Help</u>

Sermon No. 398

"UNSAVOURY THINGS"

Editor's Summary

In this sermon, Charles demonstrates his willingness to spiritualize a text (within reason) when a homiletical or pastoral situation required it. Meanwhile, in his introduction, the young preacher addresses the danger of spiritualizing, saying:

> How foolish it is to take odd texts. To twist the word of God to a meaning never intended, and so startle the audience with one's learning and ingenuity. The ingenuity thus evinced is of the lowest order, and at the very best shows a wrong taste in the preacher who exhibits it, and a morbid appetite in the people who delight in it.

As quick as Charles was to "[enter] my protest against this mode of preaching," he also hoped that "I shall never fear to speak of a text because it sounds rather strange, for every word of God is good, and we, the public teachers of the people, ought not to leave a passage unexplained."

It appears that Charles further honed this conviction and skill of spiritualizing throughout his ministry. For him to have included the chapter "On Spiritualizing" in his *Lectures to My Students* is noteworthy. *Lectures* 1:102–16. In that chapter, Charles humbly deferred to the Christian allegorist John Bunyan, whom he called "the chief, and head, and lord of all allegorists." Indeed, such was Bunyan's skill that "[he] is not to be followed by us into the deep places of typical and symbolic utterance. He was a swimmer, we are but mere waders, and must not go beyond our depth." *Lectures* 1:114.

Although Charles would later preach on Job 6:6 in "A Cure for Unsavoury Meats; Or, Salt for the White of an Egg" (*MTP* 29, Sermon 1730), that sermon doesn't appear to contain any overlapping material. Rather, Charles focused in this sermon on six "unsavoury" things that could only be seasoned by God's grace: "1. Natural Infirmities";

625

"2. Reproof"; "3. Our Doctrines"; "4. Persecution"; "5. Afflictions"; and "6. Thoughts of Death." Consider the pastoral situations that must have prompted the following:

- [Persecution] is sometimes hard to bear. We often wonder how the holy martyrs could kiss their chains and walk so composedly to the stake, but we know that the grace of God was magnified, and they were carried above their trials.
- Afflictions are bitter draughts. . . . Yet as they must come, we must bear them. Not as the Stoic because we must, but as the Christian because God appoints them.

While the specific occasions that prompted these remarks will never be known, Charles's words bear witness to the earnest efforts of a young preacher seeking to encourage his congregation.

UNSAVOURY THINGS

Job 6:6

*"Can that which is unsavoury be eaten without salt? or is there
any taste in the white of an egg?"*

How foolish it is to take odd texts. To twist the word of God to a meaning never intended, and so startle the audience with one's learning and ingenuity. The ingenuity thus evinced is of the lowest order, and at the very best shows a wrong taste in the preacher who exhibits it and a morbid appetite in the people who delight in it.

I neither like the man who turns prophet and shuffles texts like cards to divine the fortunes of the world thereby, nor the minister who treats the Bible as a book to which he may attach any meaning in the world. But while entering my protest against this mode of preaching, I trust I shall never fear to speak of a text because it sounds rather strange, for every word of God is good, and we, the public teachers of the people, ought not to leave a passage unexplained.

Some expect that now they shall have an egg divided and subdivided so that their fancies may be tickled and amused. Such will be mistaken. I simply deduce from these words the general fact that there are some things so unsavoury in themselves that we cannot enjoy them without the addition of something else to make them savoury.

1. <u>Natural Infirmities</u> would be much less supportable were it not that some blessing is given by way of compensation. It is necessary that this world of sin should be partially a world of woe, but mark how good God is in alleviating sorrow. The blind boy who never saw light has often a great quickness of ear and sensibility of ~~feel~~ the fingers which repays his loss.

The Poor, if they lack the luxuries, often lack the diseases of the rich. God has scattered more equal portions than men imagine, and given in natural things a salt which renders them endurable.

2. <u>Reproof</u> is to no man pleasant. Some with stiff necks will not endure it, and to the most modest it is not sweet. Yet we know that reproof must be given by some one. Happy is the man who understands how to administer it aright.

We see our brethren sin and Christian love demands that we tell them of their error, but when we do it, let us do it kindly, for otherwise we cause pain. We lose our aim. We drive our friend further on still.

Let kindness and love be mingled with all. Beelzebub must not be cast out by Beelzebub. The wrath of man worketh not the righteousness of God. There is more power in the sunshine to remove the traveller's cloak than in all the howlings of the storm.

Especially in theological controversy let us remember that as Newton said, "Calvinists should be charitable," for they believe that a knowledge of the truth is the gift of God. Let us all learn to receive reproof with all thankfulness, but first let it be given in all tenderness.

3. <u>Our doctrines</u> never were nor ever can be pleasing to ungodly men. Some religions may be fashionable, but the gospel never is, especially those parts of it which are peculiar and discriminating. Now why is it they are unsavoury[?] We answer simply because the persons have no salt in their souls. Grace alone makes them savoury.

Again, if we wish to spread our religion, let us be careful to put therewith the salt of holy living of charitable behavior and lovely deportment. Naked bare religion will not do, we must have it covered with the garments of righteousness. We must mingle with our faith, holiness.

4. <u>Persecution</u>. This is sometimes hard to bear. We often wonder how the holy martyrs could kiss their chains and walk so composedly to the stake, but we know that the grace of God was magnified and they were carried above their trials.

Now we only feel the cruel mockings and jeers, but these are oftentimes too strong for us. But if we have grace with it, it will neutralize the sharpness and bitterness thereof. Remember for whom you bear reproach and what the future reward shall be.

5. <u>Afflictions</u> are bitter draughts, they are not joyous but grievous. Yet as they must come, we must bear them. Not as the Stoic because we must, but as the Christian because God appoints them.

The Vale of tears is pleasant if there be a well in it. If it be loss of property, a gain of grace [outbalances] the damage. If it be sickness, then spiritual health caused thereby exceeds the suffering. Poor Job complained that his troubles had no salt but surely none of us can thus complain while we feel that the hand is the hand of a living parent.

6. Thoughts of death, and death itself, are not agreeable. Yet some find it a pleasure to meditate on their dissolution and long for evening to undress that they may rest in God. See the ungodly man; if he is sensible of his awful danger he will die with shrieks and outcries. But make the Xn ever so sensible of his future and he will not fear; nay, rather, he will rejoice.

Religion is a charm against fear. It is the divining rod pointing to the wells beneath. God has given his children a ring, and death knows them by it and will not terrify them. Oh how seraphic some deathbeds have been. May mine be so. And do you each say, "may mine"? Then have salt in yourselves, and having divine grace, what or who can harm you[?]

Lord bless me,
For Jesus' Sake
Amen.

"NO CONDEMNATION"

Editor's Summary

"Marrow and fatness" are words of richness, an expression implying the kind of satisfaction that can only come from a savory meal. These are the words Charles uses here to describe the doctrine of justification by faith as expressed in Rom 8:1. While Charles only preached on this text one more time in his sermon "In Christ No Condemnation" (*MTP* 32, Sermon 1917), justification by faith alone was the bedrock of his pastoral ministry.

In this message, Charles endeavors to "explain as simply as I can, the way of justification through our Lord Jesus." His aim in preaching it was pastoral: "In these days of error and laxity of sentiment it well becomes us to contend earnestly for the faith once for all delivered to the saints." He knew that the "object" of his ministry was not "to impress but to instruct," and he did not want to leave his congregation an "untaught company."

Charles organized his sermon around three main divisions: "I. Concluding the Former Argument"; "II. The Succeeding Proposition"; and "III. A Personal Expression of Faith by All." In his first division, he claims that imputed righteousness has been proved with Christ's death making satisfaction for sin, thus freeing him from the law and subsequently establishing union with Christ. Here, Charles reminds all who will listen that "the broken law demanded a penalty," but notes, "Christ pays it all." Accordingly, the pastor assures his congregation that "we are saved by what Christ did and not by what we do."

In his second division, Charles develops the "succeeding proposition" of Romans 8, namely, that the believer—now free from the law—is indwelt by the Holy Spirit and adopted as a son of God on the basis of God's foreknowledge and election. As a result, no one can any longer bring a charge against the believer. However, freedom from the law does not imply loose living. Rather, Charles insists that "now, I am become a friend and lover of the law, but I am not its subject." He adds,

> I love to walk in its statutes, but when I err, greatly as I grieve at the folly, I do not dread punishment, for Christ has borne it for me. The terrors of the law of God with me can have nothing to do.

Some would slander justification by faith as "Antinomian" or "Antiscriptural," but this false charge could be disproven by the happy, holy living of God's people. While the "holiness" of some was due to "[having] the law hanging in terror over their heads," Charles found a superior motive: "I am not restrained from sin by a fear of law, but by love to the lawgiver."

Finally, Charles makes much of the resounding truth, "There is no condemnation." He reminds his congregation that for those in Christ, "there is not a particle of sin remaining, not a dram of woe"; they have only "perfect and unalterable pardon and free forgiveness."

NO CONDEMNATION
Romans 8:1

*"There is therefore now no condemnation to them which are in Christ
Jesus, who walk not after the flesh, but after the Spirit."*

Surely, beloved, you will not require any sermon after such a text, and should my
master be pleased to withhold his help from me, the text itself is marrow and
fatness.

It shall be my endeavor this morning to explain as simply as I can, the way of
justification through our Lord Jesus. I find there are many young persons and
fresh attendants here who, although they are really sincere in their love to Jesus
and [their] desires after him, yet are not sufficiently taught in the truths of the
Scriptures to be able to give a correct statement of this cardinal point. Remember,
it is not only the object of our ministry to impress but to instruct. I would have you
not an untaught company, but men and women with judgments informed and solid
in the truth. In these days of error and laxity of sentiment it well becomes us to
contend earnestly for the faith once delivered to the saints.

At the same time the most advanced Christian will be refreshed by hearing once
more the glorious truths which are at once his confidence and his glory, his delight
and his strength. The Doctrine of our text is that every believer is free from
condemnation and that simply because he is in Christ Jesus.

I find some persons saying "Oh, if I were able to live more free from sin, if I could
understand these matters as well as the minister, or if were I as able to pray as good
brother So and So, I should then believe that I was pardoned and accepted." The
doctrine of the text contradicts all this by declaring that if we are in Xt Jesus, if we
are now believers, however low our station or mean our attainments, we are free

from condemnation. I would be careful to have you all see plainly the sense of the words, viz., that every believer is free from punishments for his sins. And now:

I. I SHALL CONSIDER THESE WORDS AS THE GREAT CONCLUSION FROM THE FORMER ARGUMENT.

II. AS THE PROPOSITION OF THE SUCCEEDING CHAPTER.

III. AS A PERSONAL EXPRESSION OF FAITH BY ALL BELIEVERS.

I feel that I can do nothing without the Holy Spirit but I can do all things with it. Come therefore oh Holy One and supply thy people.

I. LET US LOOK AT THE WORDS AS THE CONCLUSION FROM THE FORMER ARGUMENT.

Paul in this sentence gathers up all his points, sums up all his logical discussion. He might have said with Solomon, "let us hear the conclusion of the whole matter," or with his own words on another occasion, "Now of the words which we have spoken, this is the sum." He has been moving the sword of his argument in the eair, and now he brings it down with all his might, uttering these words "There is therefore, now, no condemnation."

What had Paul been saying? Why does he say "therefore"[?] We will seek an answer.

1. He had proved <u>imputed righteousness</u>. Rom. IV. He declared that the righteousness which justified Abraham and David was not of works but imputed to them by faith.

   Do you not at once see how he could reply "<u>therefore</u> there is no condemnation." If the sins of God's people are not imputed to them and if all the good works which Jesus did are imputed to me[?] If I am regarded as having kept the law, then how can I be condemned[?]

   The law cries out "I demand a righteousness," and we give it at once the life of Christ. A garment is required at the wedding feast. I have put on my elder brother's royal robe. Shall I be expelled [from] the feast[?] My Jonathan has changed clothes with me, and dare any touch me now[?]

Adam in the garden was safe while he was sinless, but the righteousness of the second Adam is equally as spotless and far more glorious. Shall not that avail[?] I challenge justice to find a sin in me. I challenge the scrutiny of the last day. I can walk with God, yea, and before him in the land of the living.

"My beauty this my glorious dress,
 Jesus the Lord my righteousness."

Remember this then, that we are saved by what Christ did and not by what we do. The most [backsliding] saint will have the righteousness of Xt, and the most exemplary will have, can have, no more. Oh my soul when unbelief lays sin to thy charge, here is a never failing argument viz.

Imputed Righteousness.

2. He had spoken of the death of Christ as the satisfaction for sin. Rom. V. Christ's labour was not accomplished by his active life alone. There needed likewise a passive obedience—by way of atonement. Now as his works of holiness have furnished us with a robe of righteousness, so his sufferings have washed away our sins.

The broken law demanded a penalty. Christ pays it all. His sufferings were amply sufficient to vindicate the honour of insulted justice. Surely here is an argument against our condemnation.

I am sure that nothing but a bare reliance upon Jesus can ever give a substantial peace. The moment we mix any of our own [merit] with his merit we render the water impure. All the props we put around the rock do but weaken us instead of rendering us secure.

He who draws only from this well will never thirst, but the waters of self are brackish. If our eye be not single we shall be dark, but if we look alone to him, the Israelites have light in their dwellings.

If we consider the pains, groans, agonies, and throes of Calvary, Gethsemane, and Gabbatha, can we imagine that they are useless[?] Can we once suppose the failure of that work if in one case, then ad infinitum, "if one be lost, none are secure"[?] But blessed be the name of the Lord, he does not despise blood. Signed and sealed by that crucified hand, the covenant of love is secure.

3. <u>Oneness with Jesus</u> [which] the apostle mentions in Chapter VI. He declares that the ordinance of Baptism is designed to show our oneness with Jesus in his death and glorious resurrection. Christ and his people are as much one as husband and wife, as vine and branches, as members and body. No union can be conceived of, more near, more intimate, more exactly deserving to be described, as <u>absolute unity</u>.

Now the apostle might well say ["]Therefore there is no condemnation. If Xt and we are one, then if I am condemned Xt is condemned. Shall I be likely to put my own body to misery, yea, how can it be that one member of my body can be guilty if the head be not[?"] Oh my soul revel in this idea. I am married to Jesus and he has taken my debts upon him. I am lost in him. I have given up my own individuality. It is not I but Christ that dwelleth in me. Law, dost thou condemn, then thou shalt condemn my covenant head. My Ishi, my man, my husband.

> ["]Hail sacred union firm and strong
> How great the grace how sweet the song
> That worms of earth should ever be
> One with incarnate Deity.
> This sacred tie forbids our fears
> For all he is or has in theirs
> With him their head, they stand or fall,
> Their life, their surety, and their all.["]

4. Our death in Christ frees us from the law. If a man owes debts, the law cannot touch him after death. Now a Christian is dead to the law. He is a new man in Christ Jesus. He is not the same person.

Suppose the law sends its bailiff after me to arrest me. I say ["]Who do you want? Ah, I knew him once, but he is dead.["] I am quite another person. I am a newborn soul. There is a mistake in the indictment. I am a new man in Christ Jesus. True, here was one of my name some time ago, but he is dead, and I am not he, though alas I have to drag the dead body after me.

> Death makes a goal delivery to all captives.
> Death breaks iron chains in sunder.

Oh my soul, thine existence is a new existence. Thou hast been broken up and recast, regenerated. What a word, what an idea; re-, over again, generated. The change is so great that we are no longer the same, but <u>new</u> creatures in Xt Jesus.

Let us review the argument from these four points. 1. We are clothed in a perfect righteousness. 2. Christ has atoned for our sins. 3. We are one with Jesus. 4. We have died and are now new creatures. With a certainty there is now no condemnation.

II. LET US VIEW IT AS THE PROPOSITION OF THE SUCCEEDING CHAPTER.

This looks very much like a truth rising by way of guard from the last utterance of the apostle. He exclaims that he is bound to a body of sin and death, but lest any should think that therefore he is condemned, he cries out, ["]There is, however, no condemnation. Whatever conflict and contention there is within, there is no condemnation from God.["] For:

1. <u>He is free from the law</u>. The apostle affirms this most distinctly and other scriptures declare the same thing. Law can only affect those who are its subjects. Now, I am become a friend and lover of the law, but I am not its subject. I love to walk in its statutes, but when I err, greatly as I grieve at the folly, I do not dread punishment, for Christ has borne it for me.

   The terrors of law and of God with me can have nothing to do. Some men have the law hanging in terror over their heads, but I have not. I am not restrained from sin by a fear of law, but by love to the lawgiver. This is not Antinomian, at any rate it is not Antiscriptural. The first covenant, like Moses' tables, was broken in pieces. The new one is more glorious and more safe. The law in the ark, the law in Xt Jesus we love and long to obey more and more.

2. <u>He has an indwelling Spirit</u>. The heart of the believer is a mansion for the Holy Ghost. He dwells there, producing good works and bringing glory to God. Now if the Spirit in Jesus raised and glorified him, will the same Spirit allow us to be condemned[?]

   Would the Lord give his children the Spirit if he intended their destruction[?] Do we sweep the house we intend to pull down[?] Should we mend a garment if we intend to commit to the flames? Would the "holy one" transform our poor hearts into gorgeous palaces for his residence and then commission hell to desecrate it[?] God acts not thus. He wastes not his power and wisdom. If he renews, he does it completely. He finishes all his works. No, the presence of the Spirit in my soul is a pledge of my constant justification.

3. <u>We are adopted sons</u>. Adoption from its very nature precludes the idea of condemnation. Let a rebel be pardoned and surely a son may receive it for yet more numerous crimes, [both of them] having become the lawful joint heirs with Jesus of a heritage of blessedness. Condemnation is incompatible with the enjoyment of the eternal weight of glory made sure to all the seed. When faith has a vision of her dignity, when she goes to her casket of jewels and takes up a diamond with the word "Son" written on it, she fears not final condemnation. She sees her elder brother and shouts aloud.

> "Jesus my elder brother lives
> With him I too shall reign
> Nor sin, nor death while he survives
> Shall make the promise vain.
> In him my title stands secure
> And shall while endless years endure."

There are many more points of argument which I might dwell upon, but I choose rather to pass on to 28 etc.

4. <u>We are foreknown</u> etc. The apostle is waxing warm in his subject. He has been shooting arrow upon arrow at all idle fears, but now he seems to send a perfect shower of weapons. Like Milton's wars of the angels he hurls mountains on his foes. "For whom he did foreknow etc." He hardly stays to notice his foes, but as if indignant, he thunders on volley after volley. This is the grave of all doubts upon the subject of final perseverance. What? Condemn a foreknown one? What? Nullify the decree of predestination? What? Call a man to damnation? What justify and yet condemn? Give and then retract? No, his gifts are without repentance. He knows no variableness or shadow of a change.

5. There is no one to condemn. Our eloquent apostle had not yet exhausted himself. High as his wing had carried him, he still sweeps aloft. The Inspiration of God is on him, and like the horse whose neck is clothed with thunder, he laugheth at the spear and cries exultingly, "Aha, Aha."

Hark how he cries to the heaven of heavens and to the depths of hell. Methinks I hear that thundering voice echoing again and again through the caverns of hell[.] If God be for us who can be against us?

There lies that old serpent chained in his den and all his grim satellites. How they frown. While again the challenge rings through the horrid dens, they bite their chains, they roll their cursed eyes and gnash their teeth in agony, but they cannot answer. If God be for us who can be against us[?]

Oh I can picture faith having thus descended the shades beneath. Remounting to the earth, she spreads her wing and soon behold[s] the whole world and myriads of stars far beneath her. Now hear her voice again.

He that spared not his own son, but delivered him up for us all, how shall he not also with him freely give us all things?

She has soared where unaided power never yet could conduct the soul. Her eye grasps the infinite of space, eternity, and glory. She behold[s] worlds on worlds like golden grains of sand in the river of space. She sees cycles on cycles of time rolling on to eternity and aloft she sees the city of the blest, the streets of gold, the imperial palace of Deity, the splendors of the cloud[-]enshadowed throne. She claims all. She sees she one countless and unspeakable gift already given and counts all other things [as] far outdone by this, and with her outstretched arms she seems to become like her own Divine Author. Earth and heaven and eternity all lie within her circling grasp.

   All things are hers the gift of God,
   The purchase of a Saviour's blood.

And now she treads her own inheritance. She has entered the gates of pearls, her spotless feet stand firm upon the glittering pavement. Now hear her voice. As the terrors of hell had not daunted her, so the glories of heaven do not dazzle her. Hear her speak. Who shall lay any thing to the charge of God's elect[?] Ah, is not that too bold[?] Dost thou not fear lest from the dread mount of God some thunder bolt shall come to crush thine audacity? No, cries [F]aith and smiles. It is not presumption, my God loves this confidence again. She sounds her note. Who shall lay any thing to the charge of God's elect? And pointing to the throne she cries, "It is God that justifieth."

Once more hear her, for her eye burns with fire. Her tongue is like a trumpet blown by an archangel! ["]Who is he that condemneth?["] The voice rings through heaven, the glorified hear it and repeat it, "Who is he that condemneth?" And since none can answer, they take their harps in their hands and in one grand hallelujah they sing, "It is Christ that died, yea rather etc."

Yet still further inflated with the sound when the symphony has ceased, Faith once more comes to the church militant below. With songs of heaven vibrating in her ears she comes as a warrior in the Lord's hosts. She steps from amid the ranks, and in the Lord's name she challenges all foes. There is frowning tribulation draped in Black Armour, and lean distress like a wolf meagre and guant and grim. There is persecution stained in the face with the blood of men, with rack and fire and prison in his rear, and there is hungry famine, and shame faced nakedness, and there peril and the thirsty sword. She throws the gauntlet to them all. She bids them each defiance. She bids them separate one of the least of God's elect from Christ's love. Like the angel of victory, she cries to the hosts of God. On, on, on for in all these things we are more than conquerors, more than conquerors, more than conquerors. Fix your spears. Fear not, for I am persuaded etc. etc. Oh Giant faith. Oh wondrous faith. And now beloved in the third place.

III. THIS IS THE SHOUT OF FAITH UTTERED BY ALL BELIEVERS. THIS IS THEIR CONVICTION AND REAL EXPERIENCE. *"There is now no condemnation."*

Oh, can ye carry this in your hearts as a fact realized and manifested[?] Do you say to your own soul[?] ["]Soul there is <u>now</u> no condemnation.["] Already thy sin is all forgiven, all is gone, there is not a grain left. There is <u>no</u> condemnation, the last vestige of the curse is obliterated there is not a particle of sin remaining, not a dram of woe, not so much as the trail of the serpent. There is a perfect and unalterable pardon and free forgiveness.

Oh, my friends, I conjure you seek after the full assurance of faith. If ye have but little faith, neglect no means of increasing it, slight no ordinances. Walk in the midst of the road and be persuaded that strong confidence will be a foretaste of glory even on earth.

As for you who have no faith, do ye not envy our security[?] Do you not wish that you could be as confident as we are[?] Do you not think security is beyond all price, a jewel of the highest value[?] The Cross lays a fair and sure foundation, and if no others here can glory in it, I for one can sing.

"The arms of everlasting love
Around my soul he placed,
And on the rock of ages set
My slippery footsteps fast.
Satan may vent his sharpest spike,
And all his legions roar,
Almighty mercy guards my life,
And faith forbids my fear."

There is no Condemnation.

[This page is followed by eight blank pages in Charles's notebook.]

380

II Cor XIII. 5. Self Examination.

The Corinthians were the critics of ancient times. They attacked the apostle Paul disputed his Apostleship and doctrine — found fault with his speech & said that his letters were powerful but his bodily presence weak. Paul has been at great pains to vindicate himself & now he has wrested away the sword, he turns its point to them — or rather gives it back again & bids them use it on themselves! Examine yourselves.

Oh well would it be for us if instead of looking at others, we were sometimes to look at home & mind our own vineyard. Let me now lead your minds to a serious meditation on this important subject and may the great Searcher of Hearts aid us with his Holy Spirit. —

I. We shall explain the exhortation.
II. We shall show its reasonableness.
III. We shall direct you how to do it.

I What. II. Why. III. How. —

I. We shall explain the exhortation.
Examine yourselves &c. I will adhere
to the words of the text.
"Examine yourselves". The words are simple and need no explaining: but to set them in a clearer light we will see how the word is used in ordinary life.

One part of the idea is scholastic & will be understood by every school boy or graduate "examine yourselves": chatechize yourselves & see whether you could join in the song of the redeemed. — Another part of the idea is military. The soldier must be reviewed. The fortress or country to be attacked must be surveyed & examined. I find the original has in it the meaning of passing through, piercing through, traversing the heart. It implies therefore a thorough examination & this we may call - the traveller's idea

But we are so continually in common life that it is quite unnecessary for us to suggest any further explanation. "whether ye be in the faith". Not whether ye believe like so & so, but whether ye be in "the" faith. — not of the faith but in it — whether the faith holds you. Whether like the golden staves you are in the golden rings. This is a vital point, it is the core of true searching

it includes all true spiritual experience.
"prove your own selves". This is a stronger
expression than the word examine. It
implies a stricter & more testing enquiry.
The goldsmith examines the coin, but
to make assurance doubly sure he proves
the metal — So we ought to try ourselves.
The axe is tried to see its temper, the
ship is tried to see its sailing, the
gun is tried to see its safety. —
God tries us. & here we are exhorted
to try ourselves — how this cannot
mean that we are to run into harm's
way. or tempt the devil to tempt us.
But we must see how we endure our
necessary trials sent by God. —
Yet as the text is active, we believe
that there are some right & just means
which we may use for proving ourselves.
These are acts of devotion, let us see
how our heart goes in prayer. meditation.
& praise; acts of forgiveness, let us try
whether we can pardon our debtors,
acts of self denial, of leaving off evil
habits — acts of zeal, let us try & see
whether we can do the ~~[struck out]~~
works which others call imprudent.
This "proving" is a very searching thing

Know ye not your own selves? If not, then
have you neglected your most proper study.
We ought to be assured of our salvation
we ought to know whether Jesus be
in us or no. We do not condemn
doubters and we cannot approve doubts.
Reprobates. There is no reference here
to the doctrine of reprobation. The word
is never put in opposition to the word
elect, but rather as in verse 7 it
signifies the opposite of the word approved.
It is much to be regretted that
the doctrine of reprobation has always
been considered as a necessary counterpart
of election. but it really is not so.
The word praeterition or nonelection
would far better express the idea
Many are elect who are at present
without Christ in them. here therefore
the word simply expresses the sad
state of all unconverted persons, they
are reprobate silver — worthless. —
"Christ is in you" — by hope. faith. & love
this is the grand test — this is the
crown stamp — heavens own image — in us.
Is Christ our joy. our delight. our all.
Come let us examine & prove ourselves.
Here it is clearly laid down as a duty
and we are urged thereto. —

II. We shall attempt to show its reasonableness

1. It is too important a matter to take on guess. — In daily life we examine only important things & those we scrutinize narrowly.— Meaner coins pass from hand to hand freely, but the sovereign must be examined & weighed. A Bank note for a very heavy sum will not be received in the dark.—

Now Here is our Soul, our own soul, an eternity, heaven hell all hanging on the answer to this question. Shall it be slighted? Shall we not rather be sure to examine thoroughly.

2. Mistakes cannot be rectified in the next world. — If we leave our narrow box of time, no mistake can be altered. Now or never — Kill or cure. If you take poison there may be an antidote. if you hurl your purse into the sea it may be found again — but here once lost there is no recovery.

"Now or never" let us repeat the sentence. Examine yourself. — It will be of no use for you to cry Lord I am mistaken. for he that is unjust, shall be unjust still & he that is filthy shall be filthy still Examine therefore now

3. Your heart is deceitful. It is hard to be impartial with ones self. The scales will turn on our side. When we have so false a witness in the box, we must not only examine but cross-examine. He that trusteth to his own heart is a fool. Our chameleon heart seems to have every colour of the rainbow & shifts and changes evermore.

4. The Devil will cheat you. Be assured that he does not want you to examine. He wants you to take all at hearsay and be lost. He will put false lights, he will blind your eyes, he will bid you not be so over precise Be not ignorant of his devices.

5. Examine yourself because so many have been ruined. Many a tradesman has been ruined by not taking stock. Let the shipwrecks warn you of the rocks. Be not satisfied with being a professor you may be lost with your profession as well as without it. Hearken to the groans of condemned ministers damned with crowds of their hearers. Would you shut your eyes as the ostrich & so think to avoid the hunter

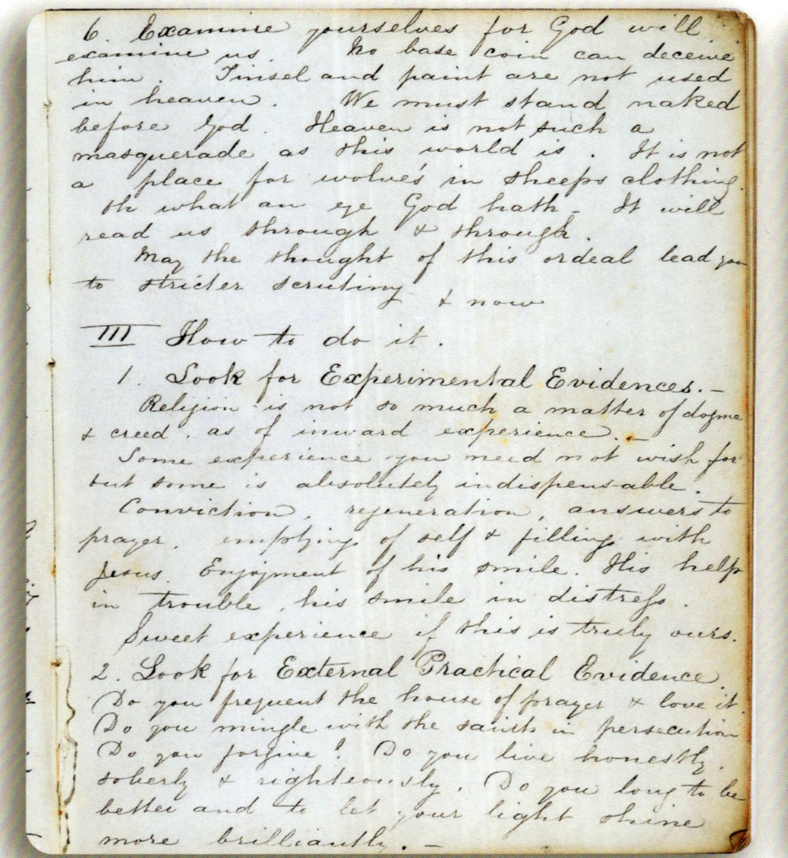

6. Examine yourselves for God will examine us. No base coin can deceive him. Tinsel and paint are not used in heaven. We must stand naked before God. Heaven is not such a masquerade as this world is. It is not a place for wolves in sheeps clothing. Oh what an eye God hath. It will read us through & through.

May the thought of this ordeal lead you to stricter scrutiny & now

III How to do it.

1. Look for Experimental Evidences.—
Religion is not so much a matter of dogma & creed. as of inward experience.—
Some experience you need not wish for but some is absolutely indispensable.
Conviction, regeneration, answers to prayer. emptying of self & filling with Jesus. Enjoyment of his smile. His help in trouble. his smile in distress.
Sweet experience if this is truly ours.

2. Look for External Practical Evidence
Do you frequent the house of prayer & love it. Do you mingle with the saints in persecution Do you forgive! Do you live honestly, soberly & righteously. Do you long to be better and to let your light shine more brilliantly.—

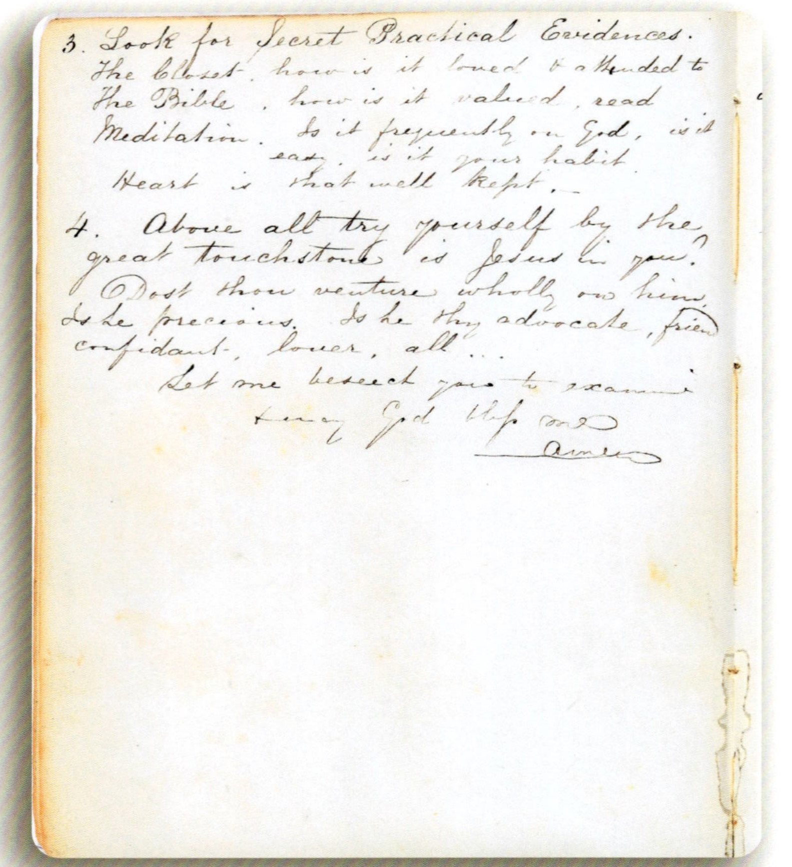

3. Look for Secret Practical Evidences.
The Closet. how is it loved & attended to
The Bible. how is it valued. read
Meditation. do it frequently on God, is it easy. is it your habit.
Heart is that well kept.—

4. Above all try yourself by the great touchstone. is Jesus in you?
Dost thou venture wholly on him. Is he precious. Is he thy advocate, friend confidant, lover, all...

Let me beseech you to examine
[...] God that soul
Amen

381 Cant. III. 4. Banquetting Days.

To appreciate poetry thoroughly one needs to be a poet, & it is true that to love this song we need to be in love with its object

He who could grasp the works of a certain orator we are told might rest assured that he was no mean orator himself & truly he who can sing this canticle of rapture must be a member of the bride & a friend of the Bride-Groom. —

This portion of the golden dialogue came from the mouth of the chosen bride

She recounts the experience of delight she had at the sight of him, the great refreshment of his shadow & the sweetness of his fruit. Now she represents him as bringing her into the banquetting house with a banner waving over her head.

Here is a double figure expressive of the idea of joy & feasting with triumph & victory.

The orientals thought much of banquets & made the banquetting room the best part of their mansion - the walls, floor & furniture were of the most costly & elegant kind — & the feasts were generally most sumptuous and expensive

The other idea is as well understood in our country as in any other. The device upon it is however well worthy of notice for it is so to speak our coat of arms. The sacred banner of the Danes had a black raven, that of Constantine a cross & ours has love on a Cross.

This is the means of our conquest, the ornament of our strength. —

And now from these words I deduce the doctrine that God's people have sometimes special days of feasting & joy. I shall by the good help of God attempt to notice these times dwelling on each and attempting to show why on that occasion God thus manifested his love so peculiarly.

I. Immediately after conversion.

Usually but not always the poor returning sinner receives after regeneration a season of joy & gladness such as he seldom knows afterwards. Our Lord has beautifully pictured this in the case of the prodigal — & I am sure many poor prodigals now find their reception the same. I know for my own part that

I was brought into the banquetting house. Look at Pilgrim how he rejoiced when his burden was gone. And the biographies of many good men testify the same.

Now it may be that some souls here are mourning because the first glory seems to have departed & although I cannot allow that our first love ought to flag, yet I may allow that our first joy usually does decline & therefore let us look at this subject for our comfort.

1. Much of the first joy is the result of novelty — at least that contributes. The change is so great, the blessings so new the sights so fresh that the soul thinks it can never have enough & could clap its hands in extacy of delight.

2. God gives more comfort because they are very weak. After being hunted by the devil, the soul is half dead & therefore wines & cordials are used

3. Our enemies are then peculiarly full of rage. Satan will not willingly lose his subjects, & brings fiery temptations to distress them. Therefore God doth sustain them the more.

4. God loveth to make this a notable time. It is our birthday, our marriage, our resurrection morning & he would have it remembered. Therefore he giveth the day a coronal of glory. —

Truly we can say of the time of our espousals. He brought me into his banquetting house.

<u>II</u>. In Sufferings for the truth sake.

Persecution as it cannot destroy the children of God so also it cannot destroy their peace. It is a miracle indeed that men should be able to rejoice in all the agonies of death aggravated by the torments of their foes, but so it has been. — witness Stephen, Paul & Silas. read the book of Martyrs & see what grace can do. John Huss smiled at his iron chain & said it was not a greater burden than the cross to his Lord. Indeed so glorious has been the end of many that it has been imagined by some that they did not really suffer — but this is not true.

1. God sustained them to fulfil his promise. He has promised to be with us at all times & this being one of the times, he thus fulfils his promise. The red names in the calendar are names which show the truth of God.

2 God sustained them as witnesses. For men could not help seeing that there was some truth in such a religion.

3. God sustained them as trophies to his glory. The good workmen will let his work be tried & roughly used to test its real strength, so does our God.

If times of trial come again let us trust that then we shall be brought into the banquetting house with the banner of love waving over us.

III. In Personal affliction.

No trouble seems joyous but grievous but I believe that tried Saints have the sweetest morsels, & the most frequent banquets. And this arises partly from the fact

1. That we are driven more from the creature to the creator. — I lay tossing on my bed & now I turn my face to the wall. The friend is dead, now I value the friend who sticketh closer than a brother

2. Then we look more to the next world than when in health & glimpses of glory are always good.

Many a saint has blessed God for his sick bed & almost longed to return. & has sung

" Affliction may prep me they cannot destroy
" One glimpse of his love turns them all into joy
" And the bitterest tears if he smile but on them
" Like dew in the sunshine grow diamond & gem

IV. In the use of means.

we need not go into the furnace to get a banquet. & it would be idle to wish it. for in ordinary means we may have it.

It is too frequently the case that we come to ordinances & go away unprofited & that because we came not with heart prayer thereunto or perhaps the minister was much to blame. —

Preaching is a primary ordinance & may a sermon is like manna.

Prayer is another most important one, & if ever we get near God it is here — when we melt in love

Singing too is not to be despised it quickens the motions of the heart.

Bible study & Meditation also —
But especially in the sacred ordinances
of Baptism and the Lord's Supper.
The one is often a throne in a sea of rest.
the other is a banquet of love.
God could bless without ordinances but
usually he does not for he will honour
his own ordinances & have us honour
them too —   Bless his name we have
sometimes been at the banqueting house
& when we do not we will lie at the pool

I. Before, in, & after attacks of Satan.
Before — As good captains will look
well to their men before battle so does our
Leader. He puts us in the delectable hill
he takes us to the house beautiful before
we fight Satan — Jesus went from the
Jordan covered with the Spirit straight
into conflict with Satan — watch then
In. None of us can tell how much grace
it requires to withstand the devil. He
that has had one fight with him will
dread another. He groans all the fight
through. & finds he has no strength to
throw away, but had need to use it all
After. But it is after the fight that the
triumph comes. Then the hand is

seen with wine for cheering, fruit for
feeding & leaves for healing. The battle
is over, the dragon is gone & now the
poor soul is ministered unto by angels.
& triumph is awarded him & the King
delighteth to honour him by enriching him
to this banquet.

VI. In the article of death.
God often keeps the best wine until the
last, the last day is often the finest. &
the door of the sepulchre hath golden nails in
it — Could good news return they would
a tale rehearse of bliss in dying rich & rare.
Even what we see is worthy of all
admiration — we see the joyful rise. The uplifted
hand — we hear the shout — & we can see
that God is giving a banquet to the soul.
Fear not to die, but fear to doubt — for he
who doubts dies a hundred deaths in
fearing me.   & God help me

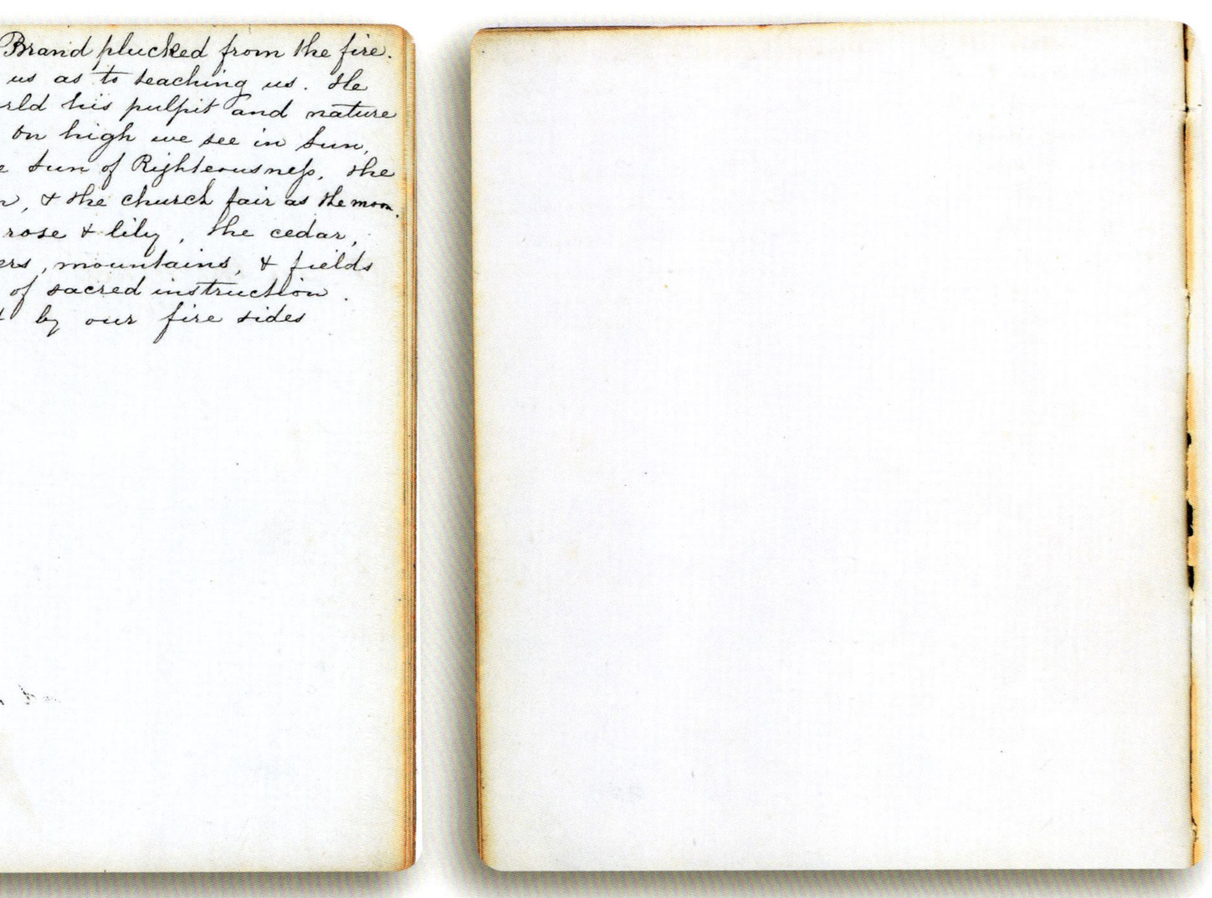

382   Zech. III. 2.   Brand plucked from the fire.
How good God is to us as to teaching us. He
has made the world his pulpit and nature
his preacher.   On high we see in Sun,
moon & stars — the Sun of Righteousness, the
star of Bethlehem, & the church fair as the moon
— on earth — the rose & lily, the cedar,
sheep & lions, rivers, mountains, & fields
give us sermons of sacred instruction.
So here we sit by our fire sides

383

Hos. II. 3. Progress in sacred Knowledge

God has put in man a thirst after Knowledge.
This thirst unquenchable impels men to
make discoveries, to weary themselves by study
to intermeddle with all wisdom & even to
venture into the sea, the air & the bowels of
the earth. So insatiable is the soul of
man that the sky must be measured,
the stars numbered, the mountains weighed
& the very storms mapped in their course.

When God makes the man a new man
he does not destroy this desire, but turns
it in a new channel. & with the same
force the impetuous torrent of love
to Knowledge runs over the golden
sands of the Bible. It rejoices the
soul when a new truth flashes on the
mind. it grieves it when it finds itself
still ignorant and a learner yet.

Ho ye learners lately come to the school
of sacred wisdom. be not dismayed but
listen to her words of comfort this morning.

I. A Great Truth.   Knowledge of divine things is progressive

II. A Great Direction.   Follow on to Know the Lord.

III. A Great Inducement.   his going forth &c

wind up with a few words of advice to learners

I. A great Fact.   Sacred Knowledge is
progressively obtained. —

It is so I am sure all will admit & I
suppose it is necessarily so. From our
condition as creatures it seems to be an
inevitable part of our existence, that we
should acquire knowledge by degrees.

The Creator alone knows all things
intuitively & perfectly — but I suspect
that all created intelligence is so formed
that like the plant it has its blade &
ear & various degrees of developement
ere it arrive at maturity. — So it is
with us I know in secular learning — at
first it is the simple primer, the spelling book
the catechism — then the grammar &
elements of science, & so on till we
can revel with delight in all the abstractions
of Mathematics or fairy regions of poetry.

And can we imagine that sacred
wisdom is to be gained at once — is a
man to be a Christian sage in an
instant — or a theologian in an hour
No — we begin with a slight tinge of
light & by degrees the sun arises.

True there are some first principles
which the babe knows as well as the

effectual calling, imputed Righteousness
yea even Redemption itself must come
under this category — This shall ye know

So also with many texts of scripture,
hard points, dark allusions &c they are
classics you cannot read not —
The knowledge of these things is certainly
important but not absolutely requisite
& no man needs to be in distress about them.

2. Experimental Knowledge from it is very
notice must be acquired & cannot but
inhere this too there are certain
elements such as regeneration. conversion.
faith which every babe experiences;
but there are heights & depths which
more but advanced pilgrims know.
the reaching of biographies will give
as much to talk of, but can never be
a substitute for real experience.
Just as the landsman may read of
the sea but do cannot understand
sea life. difficulty. Overlaying cattle
fields of difficulty. Overlaying cattle
delectable mountains, its bands of Beulah
are to be read of so far better when
seeing. — Providence has its mazes
its mysteries but these we shall know

---

hoary headed sire — these are certain Christian
instincts; if I may so call them, which we
have in the morning of our life — but
still the main science of our Religion
must be learned. we must wait patiently
& expect it by degrees. —
See Ezekiel's river — Jesus mustard seed
this progress in Knowledge I think is
twofold — Doctrinal Knowledge
& Experimental Knowledge.

1. Turn we then to Doctrinal Knowledge.
It is a fact that this is a gradual attainment
There are some mysteries in fact which
are there below inexplicable altogether —
such as the Trinity. The filiation of the Son.
the Procession of the Spirit. the virgin's genil.
the compass of Sovereignty & responsibility.
&c &c — And other doctrines seem
to be equally mysterious at first view
Such as election — of which the old divines
said. the doctrine of this high mystery of
predestination as to be handled with special
prudence & care — See Bapt Confession. 10. we
the young convert often objects to it. we
began Arminian. but end Calvinistic. the
enquirer had better make his calling sure
& these election must be right. but this
is one of the things we shall learn by degrees

more of. Our own hearts are as yet unexplored regions. The promises are not all tried — the banquetting house has not very often been entered.

And now let me not be mistaken I cannot desire for you that you may have all the experience some have. I do not want you to go over the stile or after the Flatterer, or to slip when going down the hill — seek the best experience & you will experience the best.

One more caveat I must put in, that while I believe it to be progressive I would not have it interpreted, that we all grow alike or grow at the same rate at all seasons. No. Some for wise ends are led into the secrets & learn much that they may be the more useful — & there are times when the same Xn grows far more rapidly than at others. All children do not grow alike, plants do not always seem to increase — we sometimes learn as much in an hour as in a year at another season. God is a sovereign in this as well as other things. Let us seek to please him that we may increase in grace. —

II. A Great Direction — Follow on to know the Lord. —

There is no "if" in the original we might supply "when" or "for" — for it is not at all conditional but is positive. Our good translators give us the if in italics so that we may not mistake & certainly there are no "ifs" in our perseverance.

The man who seeks to know the Lord is in the way to know every thing else
1. If I seek to know God first, I may expect his aid in learning the rest.
2. If I know the Lord I am in an advantageous situation. I can more easily go down from the Creator to his creatures, than up the hill from nature to its God. I have begun to build a house by laying the foundation. I have the Keel of my ship. The root of all existence. I am repeating my alphabet with "a" first.

Let us expand the idea.
1. We must know a trinity. If we do not we shall always be making blunders. There is no doctrine upon which we can err more easily or more fearfully.

If I look at the Son as the Father in flesh or talk of the Spirit as an influence and not a person I shall soon deny a number of other vital points. Away goes the atonement, election &c &c —

2. We must Know the Father. & if we make a mistake in underrating his power, his sovereignty, his love, his immutability then your system will soon be a wreck. Study God & then you must be of the truth. Some men are always looking on man & his position — which is very well. but to look on God as the Creator, absolutely God would do them more good. Look on the sun & the light of the moon is there too. Look on God & the glory of all creatures is in him

3. We must Know the Son. As the Eternal Son of God, really incarnate, but yet really God. To deny this is the unkindest stab of all. for Jesus is the heart of all true religion. Know him in his offices, his love, his death, his resurrection, ascension & second coming He is the glass through which we discern all things aright. He is heaven rendered Tangible

4. We must Know the Spirit. For if we see him not in his true character we shall be wrong on the subject of regeneration, calling, preserving grace, sanctification or in all & more. It is utterly impossible to remain sound on other points if we forsake the doctrine of a three one God, or in any way imbibe errors concerning the Godhead.

There are many ways of knowing & following on to Know the Lord such as prayer, meditation, reading the Scriptures, experience &c — but by all means let this be your main study — to Know the Lord & to Know him truly. —

Here we shall only know in part but if we follow on to Know, to the bed of death. the sepulchre, the resurrection we shall behold our all glorious head & be for ever like him & then shall we Know even as we are Known.

III. A Great Inducement.
1. We shall see glorious light if we go on
for his going forth is prepared as the
morning. Gradual but certain. Casting a
light on all, making darkness flee &
chasing our dreariness away. Here is
joy indeed. In all learning there is
profit but in this the greatest of all.
For joy & gladness shall be ours.
2. We shall be refreshed. By rain in
the commencement & seasonable rain at
all times — our barren souls shall be
revived — our deserts made to bud.
We want the latter rain when we
sow & the early rain when the seed
is green. In fact we always want it.
& Christian lives from hand to mouth
& a mercy it is to him that rain comes
so constantly to refresh him. —
Go on then to Know the Lord .
& now let me advise you. —
1. Be not distressed because you Know little.
2. Be not afraid of a doctrine because it is mysterious
3. Keep to this "curriculum" & so matriculate
for heaven — above all Love God much
& so will you Know him
Amen

John. XIX. 34. 37. The Pierced Side.
Last time we met before we partook
of the Lord's supper we went to Calvary
& what went we there to see? A jewel
rare & precious. A costly piece of workmanship.
Yea! I say & far more than this the precious
body of God's well-beloved son, the casket
which once contained his soul, the
untenanted palace of the King of Angels.
We may well be pardoned if we stay
& muse long over the corpse of this
murdered innocent, this King of Martyrs,
this slaughtered priest, this injured friend.
And surely if the Holy Ghost was
particular in recording we may be
particular in noticing each single event
of this dread hour, each several action
performed towards our Saviour.
I can only bless God that he provided
one biographer who should stand at
the cross and make a careful note of
all the proceedings upon mount Calvary.
Come then again let us go to Calvary
& see this great sight. —
The body preserved from the breaking
of its bones is yet to be maimed. &

the hand which could not perform the one, most easily inflicts the other.

I. The Impious Act. —

II. The wonderful effusion. —

III. The remarkable Prophecy. —

May the Blessed Spirit aid me. —

I. The impious Act.

Who is there amongst us who will not give the act this title. It was indeed an impious deed & each of us may bless God that we did not stand in that soldier's place — for.

1. The Dust of Saints is precious & to put indignity upon their bones is an offence to heaven. much more then to touch the body of the first elect. Truly the men who acquit Judas, may set this man free as guiltless, but to me it seems a crime beyond the blackness of night.

2. This man knew or might have known that Christ was an innocent being, indeed a superior person, the Son of God. But though he knew yet he hated the image of all virtue.

Blair said that if Virtue should come down on earth all would love her, but alas for him, virtue did come, was incarnate, was hunted about the earth by the enmity of man & now that she is gone, even the body she inhabited is pierced by a soldier.

If we wanted proof of the depravity of our race here we could find enough. An unfallen world would have hailed the Saviour & if he had died they would have kissed the body & have pressed it to their bosoms. — what a stroke was there, all of us are criminals we pierced him, so says the prophecy. Oh fearful guilt, this is the epitome of sin. This stain must be on us unless we reap the benefit of the blood.

But while we weep over this.

let us rejoice that

(1) Gods ends were answered. His son was proved to be the Messiah of prophecy. See Zech. XII.10 & what is more proved to be Jehovah for the original passage reads it me. Christ being really Jehovah.

(2) Jesus was proved to be really dead for such a pierce was evidently enough

to take away life even if not destroyed already & this is a very vital point for if he died not then he did not rise — redemption is not finished, & we are yet in our sins.

The Jews never insinuated as the Gnostics did in later times, that he did not die in reality but only suffered syncope or protracted fainting. Here was proof positive — of a real death. This thrust made the "It is finished" even more sure — & thus while grieving over the guilt let us rejoice in the act for by it faith doth live afresh.

Before we dismiss this point let us look and admire our Saviour's body see his side opened, & a passage made to his heart. Here is a window, one may read his heart through it. Here is a door our wants & prayers find most ready access. Here is a treasure house for faith. Come thou unbelieving Thomas reach hither thy hand & thrust it into his side & be not faithless but believing. Precious, precious Lord! I would long to lodge in this cleft, & seek to be bone of thy bone & flesh

of thy flesh & like as Eve was taken out of the first Adam's side, so would I in common with thy children rejoice in this thy side believing that out of it were we formed. —

<u>II</u>. The wonderful Effusion.

I had thought of saying, the miraculous effusion & I believe it was so — but almost all the writers on this point seem to think it was a natural effect of the spear thrust. — The pericardium was pierced & the small quantity of water contained therein flowed forth with the blood of the heart. I should hardly imagine that naturally there would be a sufficient quantity of ~~that~~ water in the pericardium to be noticed by John — & it seems the more improbable if he was stationed at any distance from him. — If it was natural, might it not result from the separation by death of the red globules from the liquor sanguinis which constituted the water. — I am however more inclined to regard it as being a miracle.

Be it so or no I am sure it has a meaning & we will try & find it out.

Water, our cleansing, & purifying. This is
the Sanctification which we all hope to
experience — This is the true water of
life. The Elixir of Immortal Life & Indwelling
Purity. These two are needed, let
no wonder them. let us in preaching
& life put them together. Now the
double stream flow o'er my head. gave
me a Baptism in thy floods & let me
rise like sheep from the washing
without spot or wrinkle or any such thing.

III. A Remarkable Prophecy
Not to dwell on what we have hinted
at viz. that the word "me" is used in
the original — we would only observe
that this may be regarded either as a
promise or a threatening.
1 As a promise it was fulfilled in
many of the Jews in Christ's day & in both
Gentile & Jew. It shall be true they shall
look & be saved.
2 As a threat — when he comes in
clouds of vengeance the sight will be
awful indeed. th Lord help us to
look now by faith — that we may not
look then in terror. —

Albert Barnes tells us that there is
no meaning whatever in this double
effusion — but with all deference to him
there was — Some will never allow
anything but a literal meaning to the
Bible & in the height of critical learning
laugh at the poor things who see more.
But happy is the child who sees
truth in the fieldflower & hears the voice
of God in the rolling thunder. Here
however we are not left in doubt for
in 1 John 5. 6 we find very
allusion to this very circumstance.
Not with water only — all the prophets
came with the water to purify & cleanse
for the future — but they could not bring
Blood to atone for the past. This our
Jesus did.
Blood — our price, our ransom. The
emblem of Justification. gushing from him
the poor sinner there is pardoning mercy
& forgiving love. This is at once th
cleansing to God & safe to man. th
precious blood that flatters the soul of
my heart. the drop might quench a flame
& world. Blood was sacred by divine law
but the blood how sacred, how divine

385

Eph. III. 8. Paul's commission. —

I this morning commence a new era in my history — hitherto I have preached to you as a supply, but now as your minister, chosen by you without a dissenting voice. I feel that the work is great & I am but ill qualified for it & cannot better express the feelings of my soul than in the words of the text — But leaving these thoughts we will by divine assistance regard Paul's words with care — we notice

I.   A Person Chosen.
II. A Qualification given.
III. A Work allotted.
IV. A

I. A Person Chosen.
In the eye of God he was a most suitable person to perform his work. In our eye he seems to have been eminently adapted for his work — but in his own estimation he was altogether unworthy of so great an office. His humility was very great, although it is plain that he was no second rate man, nor was he a man of mean spirit.

It was his humility which made him speak as he does in this place. And mark what his humility saith; it useth a double diminutive. Faith, love & humility are such heavenly graces that there is no earthly language suitable to their lips — unless it can be loaded with hyperbole, & improved by invention.

He puts himself at the foot of the lowest form of all, and adds his name to the list of the unworthy. How came he by this humility? We wish to know & that we too may procure it.

1. He remembered his former life.
When he recollected how he had dragged men and women to prison, he could not but see his own unworthiness. Thus Jacob thought of the day when he passed over Jordan with a staff. David did not forget the meanness of his origin but remembring it he cried "What am I &c — Those who have acquired riches should remember their former poverty. the healthy should visit the bed where they lay in sickness & we all should remember the pit whence

we were digged.   Plasilla the empress of Theodosius used to say "Remember O husband what lately you were & what now you are so shall you govern well the Kingdom & give God his due praise for so great an advancement."   Sir Thomas Gresham ever remembered the grasshopper which by its chirpings drew some one to see him when a foundling & put the grasshopper in his coat of arms.   We must not forget our former low estate and when exalted by mercy let us be humbled by our former poverty. —

2. He understood his own depravity.
He groaned under a body of sin & death. He was not a superficial searcher. He went deep into the recesses of his soul & saw his own vileness.   He who knows his heart will humble his heart.   It is said by old authors that the peacock when it looks at its black feet always lets fall its fine plumes. and surely it should be so with us.

3. He lived in communion with God.
Of all humbling things, this is the most humbling.   When I read the lives of pious and industrious divines I shrink into nothingness.   How much more then if I contemplate the attributes and works of Christ my God..   He who lived in the tropics will shiver in the cold.   He who has been in Kings palaces will know the meanness of his own houses.   The reason why we are proud is because we live far from God —   Reflect on him and be abased, hide thine eyes and fall prostrate then shall the Lord visit us with mercy and give us all sufficient grace.

II. A Qualification given.—

386

Nehemiah VIII. 17. A Glad Congregation.

There are many ways of doing the same thing & in religion the way of doing a thing is everything. Take for instance going up to the house of God, to some it is a burden, to others a delight. The best way to go to God's house is with shouts of joy, & when there he is the true worshipper who rejoices in the service & is glad. God loveth a willing congregation who are glad at the remembrance of his holiness. — Here we have a glad congregation. —

I. Why were they Glad?
II. Why it is to be desired that we should be glad?
III. What should make us so?

I. Why were they glad?
When we see a large company all full of joy we naturally enquire the reason. Is their corn & wine increased? Has victory crowned their nation? No — other reasons give gladness

1. They are in their own Jerusalem.
2. They have heard the word of God & they understand its meaning.
3. They have once mourned over sin.
4. They have been sending portions to others.
5. They keep all the ordinances blameless.

Do not these things meet in some of us. If we have neglected one point, let us seek to amend our fault & be happy.

II. Why should we desire to be glad?
1. For Comfort of ourselves & others.
2. For Unity in the church.
3. For Strength against temptation & in duty.
4. For Enlargement for others will join.

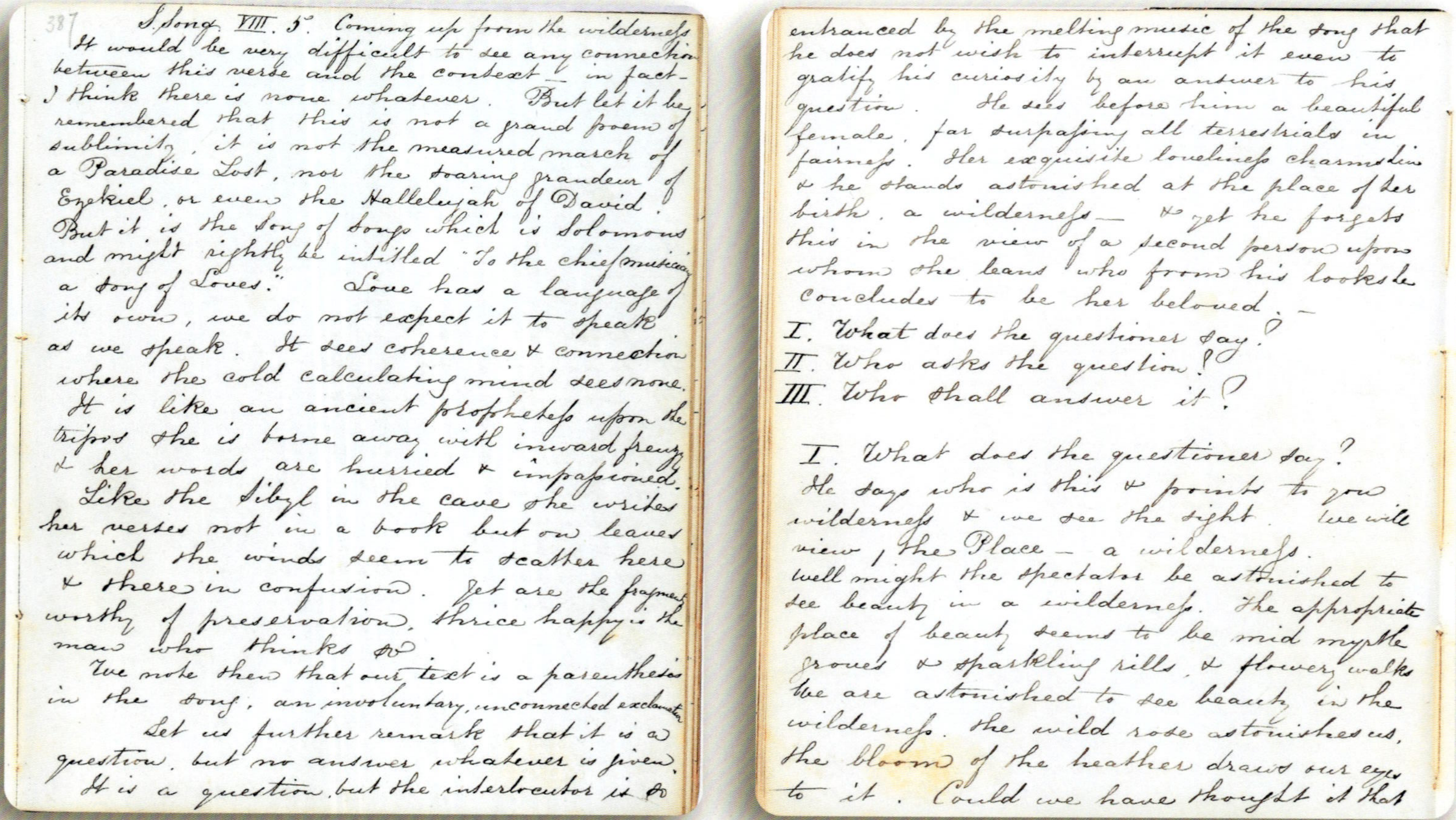

387

S. Song. VIII. 5. Coming up [from the wilderness]

It would be very difficult to see any connection between this verse and the context. in fact I think there is none whatever. But let it be remembered that this is not the [language of] sublimity. It is not the measured march of a Paradise Lost, nor the [soaring of] the Ezekiel. or even the Hallelujah of David. But it is the song of songs which and might rightly be entitled a song of songs. Love has [a language of its own] it now. we do not expect it to speak as we speak. It sees coherence & connection where the cold calculating mind sees none. It is like an ancient [Sibyl] — she is borne away with inward fire & her words are hurried & impassioned. Like the Sibyl. in the cave she [wrote] her verses not in a book which the winds deem to scatter here & there in confusion. [Yet worthy] of preservation. thrice happy. he man who thinks the man who thinks that our text is a parenthesis in the song. an involuntary, unconnected [remark]. let us further remark that it is a question. but no answer whatever is given. It is a question. but the [...]

enhanced by the melting music of the song that he does not wish to interrupt it even to gratify his curiosity by an answer to his question. He sees before him a beautiful female. far surpassing all terrestrials in fairness. Her exquisite loveliness charms him & he stands astonished at the place of her birth. a wilderness — yet he forgets this in the view of a second person whom whom she had who found his looked concludes to be her beloved. —

I. What does the questioner say.
II. Who asks the question?
III. Who shall answer it?

I. What does the questioner say? He says who is this & comes to you wilderness & we see the sight we will view! The Place — a wilderness. well might the spectator be astonished to see beauty in a wilderness. the appropriate place of beauty seems to be 'mid myrtle groves & sparkling rills. & flowery walks. the are astonished to see beauty in the wilderness. the wild rose astonished us, the bloom of the heather draws our eye to it. Could we have thought it that

the king daughter, the elect lady, the Bride the
Lamb's wife should have been in the wilderness
    Yet there you must mostly look for her.
Look not in the halls of Nineveh or the colossal
palaces of Babylon but look in the plains of
Canaan in the tent of Abraham.
    Turn not to the palaces of the Pharoahs,
or the temples of Carnac but search in
the wilderness of Sin around the foot
of thorny Sinai.   Go on to the days
of Ahab & search out the children of the
most high. Ye shall not see them crowned
at Samaria and honoured in her streets
but there in the dark cave you see them
& on the mountain brow you see their
leader wrapping his shaggy robes around
him, fit garb for a prophet of the wilderness.
    Let your minds rush on to more modern
times. In the days of Pagan Rome, where
is the church — Where are her cathedrals
& lofty spires — Ah expect them not.
Down in the catacombs or in the
ruins of some subterranean aqueduct,
may mark a small assembly; that is the
church, all glorious in the eyes of her beloved.
    Hasten on to the times of Romes Popery
is that scarlet clad woman the bride, the lets

herself be seen in robes of splendor. Is she the
church. No. No — Look on the Alpine peaks
or in the valleys of Piedmont there she is
the church in the wilderness. & not to
trace her further I would remind you of
the days when the Mayflower carried away
the sons of God to the rocks of New England,
when the covenanters met in their gloomy
glens & the dissenters in their secret conventicles
    She is the church of the wilderness.
There she has been & there she is.
It is a wilderness — for it is inhospitable
she finds no one to entertain her. no
friend to give her lodging. This is not
her rest. There is no bed for her repose.
no mansion for her dwelling. On the
contrary her foes are many — When she
was but in her cradle the kings stood
up against, she has had to wade through
seas of blood. The ground is tracked
with her gore. The stakes. the gloomy
towers, the racks remain as gloomy ways
of her sore travail & labour.
Smithfield is still a witness to her pains.
It has been to her a den of leopards. She
has in the person of her children been sawn
in sunder, or been made to wander in skin &c &c.

It is a wilderness — for it is dangerous & full of troubles. No one loves to journey through barren plains over burning sands. There are thirst & danger to be endured, toilsome marches to accomplish, simooms & winds to endure.

The serpent lies in the path. the Amalekites comes down from the mountain. the foot is blistered & the heart is faint.

Do you wonder at troubles believer, do you count the fiery trial strange. You are in a wilderness & you must carry your joys into it for they certainly do not grow there. You will cry out in weariness, you will pant like the thirsty hart. Do not be astonished at it. "he told you no less this is his will. therefore go on.

It is a wilderness for intricacy

The traveller often stands & wonders which way he ought to go. Wildernesses are pathless places. Shifting sands have no roads. we too in our daily life seem at times to be in a maze we see straits too narrow for our sailings & rivers too boisterous to swim in

Have we not been like Israel before the Red Sea. & are not all the elect at times put at a nonplus to know the path of duty.

Thanks be to God the stars are ever shining the Star of Bethlehem points to the haven of peace. we follow it & are safe

We come now to notice 2. the direction. they come up out of the wilderness. In this desert she has to journey, not into it but out of it. She is leaving her troubles & her sins behind her, she is coming up. The saints do so naturally by the lapse of time. If I am one of the Lord's people every hour & minute as it flies brings me nearer the verge of the wilderness. He worldling has his back to the sun & journeys on to deeper shades, but we are on our road to light and each hour brings us nearer.

Spiritually by growth in grace. the true sons of the Lord will daily increase their sanctificat Some do not believe in progressive sanct but such do err. We do not think that sin grows weaker but we believe that the new man gathers strength on the road. So that it is ever a going up as well as on

There is a sense in which she may be said to have come up out of the wilderness in the secret decree of God when he chose her in her fallen & desolate state. & there is another yet to be accomplished when from the graves of the wilderness all clad in white leaning on the prince's arm the church shall climb the mountain of Zion and never see the wilderness again Surely at this sight angelic hosts shall shout Who is this ascending on high!

3. We have a blessed manner of march to observe.
She came up leaning on her beloved. We
sometimes repeat it as leaning on "the arm" of
her beloved, but it is not so. We lean on
him, on his breast, his bosom, his person.

The King's daughter is not to ride in a
chariot, for wise purposes she walks the
weary way — but oh the joy of a walk with such
company.— She leans on him & sometimes
when the way is rough he carries her. He
presses her to his bosom & bears her on.

Faith is the arm which leans on him
but it is not the strength of our arm but the
strength of our beloved we trust to.

For every thing we lean on him, in him all
fulness dwells. This is the only place where the
original word is used & it is differently rendered.
It signifies "casting herself on" which is stronger
than leaning, a dropping into his arms, a
falling upon him. It means too "joing, associating
with", & this shews the holy intimacy &
constant cleaving we should have with & to Christ.

It has moreover as Kimchi says the idea of
"rejoicing" or "delighting in". And surely we may
put all these ideas together.—

She "leans", she "casts" herself on him to shew her reliance
she leans to show her intimacy & her eyes
bespeak her joy at his blessed company.

Let us come to personal experience, do
we lean there? In sickness, distress, doubts
& fears is this our prop & pillar.—

4. We must note the title given to Jesus.
Not the Saviour, nor the priest, nor the King
but all these things in one. "her beloved"
"Beloved" he is by all the angels & saints on
high, by his Father & the Spirit, but we must
be able to say "my beloved". Compared with
him nothing is lovely, or to be desired, he
is beyond all things "my beloved"

II. Who asks the Question.

1. Sometimes the captious worldling says who is this coming out of the wilderness. He hates the change which his companions experience. he does not believe in its reality, but taunts him with the past. As if past sin could destroy present grace.

2. Sometimes the admiring observer uses this expression. Beholding the holy conversation the quiet demeanour, and submission of Christians. Often in the persecutions this cry was involuntarily uttered. How can this be. How can men endure such tortures & agonies.

3. Often the trembling believer puts the question fearing lest he is not of the body. Shall I amongst them stand. Am I his beloved. Yes, if thou canst but touch the hem of his garment thou shalt be made whole & thou hast done it & art his.

4. Even the firmest believer at times stands & wonders at the heights of grace as if they really were incredible. The grace seems too great for faith to hold in her hand & really if we knew the value of heaven more I fear we should less seldom read our title clear for we should think it too good a place for us. & well exclaim who is this! thus favoured! thus allowed to lean on the arm of Jesus.

III. Who shall answer it?

Shall we ask the lookers on? Shall we consult bigots, or sectaries? Nor we will ask the bride & the

1. The Bride replies by confessing that she was once an infant deserted & left to perish. but her beloved bade her live. She doth not conceal her blackness by nature. She putteth her hands before her face, & though she be decked in jewels, she vaunteth not. She is undeserving & hell deserving, helpless without strength and destitute of goodness.

2. The Beloved replies. She is mine elect chosen before the foundation of the world. She is my purchased one redeemed with blood. She is my betrothed, my pardoned. my justified, my soon to be perfected beloved. All fair in mine eyes & without spot or blemish. —

1 If such her beauty now — what shall it be when she shall walk in white in glory. free from the breath of corruption or taint of guilt. Question of the future +

2. Are we marching up. not down, are we leaning, casting ourselves upon the beloved. Question of the present. +

388

Zeph. III. 16.17.

This day is this Scripture fulfilled in your ears.
This day the ministers of the gospel utter these
very words, this day I attempt to make
mention of them, but it is God who only can
effectually speak to the trembling heart.

I. Two evils to be avoided.

1, Fear which is hurtful & dishonourable.
Not Fear filial — but fear servile. Fear of man.
Fear of our enemies. Fear of the Promises.
This fear is injurious to us & to others
     dishonouring to God &
entirely unneeded —

2. Slack Hands. They were building a temple let
them not be slack. they had begun to serve God
let them not be idle. We have in the church
some Slack hands — careless & regardless of affairs
               indolent & quarrelsome.
               fearful & backward

now be not fearful, be not slack.

II. Remedies for these evils.

389

1. Tim II. 5. The One Mediator.
"There is but one God". So far we might gather
from the book of nature. Unity of design bespeaks
unity of authorship. Acute minded heathens
have discovered this and perhaps one half
of the population of the globe will join with
us in the doctrine. But here we diverge
the Mahommedan puts in & Mahomet is his
prophet — the Catholic puts in myriads of
mediators — & only the orthodox truly say
"and one Mediator between God & men"
we shall by the help of the good Spirit attempt
to speak of 3 things.—

I. The Necessity of a Mediator.
We read of no mediator in Eden, but now one is wanted
1. Because man was at war with God & a
reconciliation must be made.
2. God, as judge could not speak to a criminal
not only found guilty, but actually condemned
justice demands a days man.
3. The Distance now between a man & a
God necessitates a medium, Heaven is
too high to be climbed without a ladder.

II. The Glory of Christ as Mediator.
This shines forth if we view him.
1. In Undertaking the office. He showed at
once his condescension and his love. He
was highly exalted above all creation, how
wonderful that he should shrink of such a stoop.
He was himself offended as one person of the
Godhead, yet he will become the reconciler.
2. In discharging the office. It involved on
him many humiliations but chiefly.
Incarnation - In the womb of Mary & in life.
Service - in the fashion of a man he became obedient
Suffering - He endured the cross.
3. In the issue of his labour.— His own exaltation
the reconciliation of men — & their glorification
oh my soul be astonished at this glories.

III. The title he assumes
"The Man Christ Jesus": methinks this is the
best of all his names. I love him as the
quieter of noisy waves, the victor over evil
demons & diseases. but oh I love thee most
as "the man Christ Jesus." On Samaria's
well. in Jerusalem's streets. in Gethsemane
yea in glory I love him as the man
Christ Jesus. Full of sympathy, of feeling
of love.— Oh ye who want a mediator
here he is — No mediator between us & Christ
but between God & man —
May God give us love to the Mediator

390

Rev. XII. 10   The Accuser of the Brethren.

I shall not enter into an explanation of the
context in full but would briefly remark
that the expulsion of Satan here spoken of is
usually believed to refer, not to his first expulsion
from heaven but to his typical fall at the
time when persecution ceased & the Roman
emperors no longer listened to the foul accusation
of the heathen, but embraced Christianity for
themselves.   I am about to enter wholly
& simply on the subject of the agency of
Satan as an Accuser of the Brethren.
This foul Spirit of Evil is not only the
tempter of men to sin, but he is likewise
their accuser.   All things whereby he
may serve God's people come alike to
him, he never scruples at anything
the Accuser of the Brethren accuses
them to these parties

I. He accuses us before God.
II. He accuses us to men.
III. He accuses us to ourselves.

As the Lord Christ may enable us, we shall
notice each of these points as we may give
ed utterances to make some practical
remarks as we proceed. May the Lord
give his devout wisdom in this thing.

I. He accuses us before God

If the Scripture did not tell us this we
might doubt it, for seeing the complete
justification wrought out by Jesus, it
would seem unlikely that any one would
have the hardihood to lay anything to the
charge of God's elect & truly none can justly do
so. Yet Satan did in the case of Job. —
He accused Job of selfishness; He served
God for naught. dost Sir R Walpole said 'every
man has his price' & the devil insinuated
that as long as Job could be rich by
serving God he would do so.   We cannot
at first conceive how it should come to pass
that Satan should appear amongst the sons
of God, but we must remember that it does
not say he appeared in heaven, for here
he could not go — but in the wide universe
he holds his own livies and wherever when
God may be said in human language
to appear before God.   If God then that
perfect man was thus accused, can we
hope to escape his malicious accusations.
See how he repeats his calumnies when he
argued that Job is gold unless the pain
shall touch his own person. the what a height
that Job should be slandered before his done. Some
do you imagine that we escape? Some

men smile at this, but their sneer is not worthy of regard for as an eminent commentator well observes, we never meet with a devildenier who is a good man; but on the other hand these men are usually the most impious of all — & acting like the Jesuists who denied the Pope for their Lord — yet know right well that he is so & hope thereby to establish his dominion.

Let us now turn to Zech. III. there we see Satan standing before the angel of the Lord to resist Joshua. & we know not how many times he has been standing up to resist us in our prayers or songs of praises. But blessed be the name of God we have an advocate. & as soon as an accusation is made he rises & with matchless eloquence defeats the Slanderer. See what he pleads. He pleads electing love & effectual grace. Chosen & plucked from the fire. If we more fully entered into this subject, we should think more highly of Christ in his official character or Life.

Satan can easily bring a thousand charges against us. no need to watch long & both day & night he does accuse us, but our advocate silences his clamour by "pleading the blood" as the old Wesleyan had it.

II. He accuses us to men.

The Father of lies, will lie everywhere. He thinks to destroy Christ's Church by slandering its members.

1. He accuses us to our enemies. From the earliest ages this was his practise. The Christian were accused of eating their infants at their supper, & of meeting by night for the vilest of all purposes.

All fires were laid to their door & even earthquakes & famines were said to be caused by their impiety. The same you find is true of the Vaudois when persecuted by the Papists. & on the first outburst of the (so called) Anabaptists. The greatest preacher of these latter times George Whitfield was accused as Cowper has it of crimes that Sodom never knew & scarcely ever does an eminent minister arise but Satan is sure to hatch some calumnies against him. It is part of our lot as minister to be maligned & our missionary brethren do not escape.

If then the champions of truth are assailed should common Christians think this fiery trial "a strange thing" x just as I withdrew to dinner I found a letter giving me a sound thrashing for last sabbath morning's sermon x You & I must not expect to live without it & two things should embolden us to take up this cross most cheerfully. 1. our Master had to endure it .2. It encreases our reward in heaven.

2. <u>He accuses us to our Friends</u>. This is the most bitterly malignant bite of the old Serpent. and our Lord felt it when his heel was bruised Judas who had eaten his bread was enticed by Satan to betray him. Wounds in the house of ones friends are wounds indeed

1. Sometimes a calumny against a brother is received by the church as being a truth without due search being made to discover the truth of the charge. Now this is Satan's delight. To throw dust in the eyes of brethren. So that like the Trojans on the night of Troys destruction they mistake friends for foes. Oh remember he is the accuser of the brethren.

2. Sometimes one Brother imagines that another has treated him disrespectfully. He did not notice him in the street, or shake hands so heartily, or invite him to his house. Now let us if we find this in our hearts, at once remember that he is the Accuser of the Brethren and let us not believe him

Paul once said of two women I <u>beseech</u> Euodias & I <u>beseech</u> Syntyche that they be of one mind — Two women had disagreed & Paul to set them right gives a beseech to each of them. It is Satan's work to plant roots of bitterness everywhere. Oh how sweet to know that the Master will not cast us off even if all the disciples do so, and our Beloved will never be moved from his love by all the accusation of our enemy.

<u>III</u>. <u>He accuses us to ourselves</u>.
I choose to mention this last because it is the one which perhaps of the three we feel most. & I pray my Master to give me one of his kind whispers that I may know how to speak a word in season

1. <u>He accuses us of vile thoughts</u> which were none of ours. He injects blasphemies & then fathers them on us. Some know nothing of this matter but I do. Swearing & oaths have rushed on my mind & would by no means depart. but they were none of mine I hated them. If you hate them they cannot be yours. Whip them & send them on to the right parish. He puts the cup in our sack & then charges us with the robbery. See Bunyan in Grace abounding to the chief of sinners. Poor Soul tell the master about him.

2. <u>He accuses us of the unpardonable sin</u>. This is I think one of Satan's masterpieces. What God intended for good Satan turns to evil — I confess I know not what the unpardonable sin is, some say it cannot be committed now, but I think it can. However I know it is something to do with the Holy Ghost & I would have all men beware of dishonouring him. When a man has committed this he is given over to final impenitence & unbelief

for where there is faith & repentance, in due time there shall be mercy bestowed.

Despair is the greatest sin of all. to despise the power of the Spirit and say he cannot save you, would be to go very near that sin.

3. He accuses us of not having repented enough.

Often does he hurl biographies at us. The lives of good men serve him for fiery darts and right quickly does he let fly at us.

But the shield of faith is the best defence here. we are not to be justified by our penitence, but by the blood of Jesus. Can we ever repent enough? Is not sin so horrible that no purgatories of fire could cleanse it, much less a purgatory of the water of our grief. I lay on Christ & that is enough for me.

4. He accuses us of our duties as being ill done & therefore unacceptable. our sins he stirs up like sleeping spectres and bids them march before us in funereal procession while our duties, which he bids the Pharisee pride himself upon, he represents as being too stained with sin to be received.

He takes our sermons, our prayers & our works and calls them vanities at one time at another they are wonderful things. our Faith he tells us is dead faith, our spot is not the spot of Gods children. He asks us whether the Lord's people are as we are. Now the way to settle this is to kneel in prayer and searching our hearts so once more to the fountain filled with

And now, beloved, once more I entreat you look to the Advocate and remember his peace-speaking blood, In all time of trouble make this your shield, your refuge & rock.

39   John. VI. 37.   ...no wise cast out.

Upon the first reading of this verse one feels
inclined to break out with the angelic song
"Behold I bring you glad tidings of great joy":
For truly here is great joy for all. the strongest
in faith will find food for his soul in
the first sentence and the very weakest
will find manna in the second.
I take it that if we could rightly grasp
these two sayings of our Saviour we should
never have debated in our mind about
free will, predestination & all the other
hot controversies of all time.
I would to God that some theological terms
had never been invented & that men would
confine themselves more to God's word &
less to bodies of divinity. —

I. The Eternal "shall" — positive.
II. The Eternal "will" — negative.

th Spirit of the living God. be thou
my inspirer. that both theme & inspiration
may come together.

I. The Eternal "shall" positive.
we have in these words four things at least
a gift, a coming, a resolution,
a number

---

1 "a gift" - "all that the Father giveth me"
=/=/= we are led to believe from various portions
of God's word that the Father did present
& give unto the Son a multitude as the
reward of his labour.   Two things require
explanation — the word gift - & its tense
It may be asked how it can be a gift &
yet a purchase - but I take it the words
purposely used to set forth the love of the
Father and his part in the covenant
so that while the Son did really purchase
it was not merely as a mercantile transaction
that the Father freely gave.   David was
to purchase the King's daughter & yet he gave
viewed as the Redeemer he purchased, as
the Husband he received a gift.
notice next the present tense giveth
not that it is done in time: let it note
the Godhead of Christ with whom everything
is present to whom the unchangeable I
of the gift. the Father gives as much
now as ever. he revoked not the decree.
We see then the Father giving to the
Son an heritage. He had a right to give
men for he made them. he is their
sovereign. Oh what a gift, a host, a
countless multitude. A mother herd of worms
but yet an army of immortals...

2. "a coming" How can we tell whether we were included in the gift — why by this infallible sign — "coming to Christ."
we come in grace and in glory
In grace we come & 'tis a mournful march, when rousing from our sleep of death we retrace our steps to our Father.
Sometimes we are months in coming tears wet the road, & sighs rend our heart
we come spiritually when the heart desires Christ and we are come when by a sense of need we cast ourselves upon him.
Come, not run, it is often a crawling a creeping, but the text says they shall come not they shall run or even walk but come, come anyhow — on the ground if no other way. — You who are coming take heart & you who are longing to come you are coming
In glory we come to Christ, but oh how different a coming. Now they come with songs of everlasting joy, all creation joins in a tune of thanksgiving
oh what a "coming" this — but we shall soon realize it when he shall say "Come ye blessed of my Father". Oh my soul rejoice at the glad hope & count all present sorrows small.

3. "A resolution" "shall" I look upon this shall as a great word though some divines will not allow me so to do.
1. It is a prophecy of the Son. He is the prophet of his people & he here utters a prediction that they shall come. He in the future sees all his elect as if they were coming now. Can he be wrong.
2. It is an oath of the Son. He who speaks and his word is law. He who swears by immutable things now lifts his hand to heaven and vows that he will so accomplish his work that all shall come whom he has foreknown
Mark it is the oath of one who has power to perform & not power only but all power.
3. It is a triumphant shout of the Son. He throws the gauntlet to the foe & bids them slay one of them. He foresaw his own agony and death but further on he saw his resurrection & ascension & therefore could stand on the broken head of Satan and glory in the salvation of the chosen ones. The Jews must have felt this very galling to their pride to be told that though they came not others would & to the Pharisee now a days it is the same. Providence & grace move on & produce God's great result.

4" a number "all" It is a word which implies a knowledge of the number his Father had given him. Cyrus knew the name of every man in his army & so does Christ. he telleth the stars. In the dreary forest of the west there dwells an Indian who is one of the all. Up in the regions of the north some Laps & Fins & so on but he knows all not one is unknown.

And all shall come. they may be buried in heathen darkness, they may be bowing at the shrines of Popery. but they all shall come to grace. & if hidden under the waves of ocean or lying amidst a mingled map of battles slaughter they all shall come in their own persons to glory. And what an all that will be. From Adam down to the last man, down to the millenium all the way from Eden what a multitude. But all the gift of God.

Certain modern Calvinists have started an idea that this refers not to persons but to things, but what are the things without the persons & how could things come & how would there be any connection between this verse & the discourse. I find neither Adam Clark nor Albert Barnes who would both gladly say anything on the general side have observed this and therefore I think it a modern invention.

So far we have been talking of the more secret will of God, now we come to his revealed councils & may the Lord enable me to speak well for his dear name.

II. The Blessed "will" negative.

And let us remark.

1. The Speaker "unto me", not to Father but the Son. The Father never gives audience to any who do not come through the Son's introduction. Like the Molossians we must take the prince in our arms if we go to the king. But first we must go to the Son & who can refuse to go to one so loving.

2. The Character "him". Mark how wide a field this pronoun gives. The rich & poor find welcome. As lady Huntingdon said not many but she m saved her. The wise may come & the fool, the half idiot if he come shall find welcome. I see not why any one should think himself excluded as Crisp says who is sound enough in all conscience, one sinner has as much right to believe he is elect as any other in the same condition. but this is not the warrant our warrant is the death of Jesus, not election. Oh poor broken hearted one why dost thou fear. who has told thee thou art lost — the devil — but fear not.

3. The treatment, he will not cast out
Sometimes when a beggar comes to a rich
man's door he orders him away if he intends
not to give him charity — & when the poor
soul comes it dreads lest it should be driven
away without relief but he will not cast out.
No sinner was ever empty sent back.
None but hypocrites are driven away & these
deserve it — And if when the soul first
comes he is not cast out, what is then the
security of those who are in the door.
Shall children be expelled, shall loved
ones be put into the cold midnight air, no
"they shall never be cast out."
4. The powerful negative nowise
The Greek is very strong it is not, not, never, never
and the old Saxon word is in itself as powerful
a word as can well be conceived. It puts to
flight whole armies of objections.
Great sin cannot hinder mercy.
Old age and long delays hinder not
Going to other Saviours and relying on our
works in past times will not cast us out now
A hard heart will not forbid our coming
for he can melt rocks & nether millstones
Little faith shall not impede grace wholly,
our poor prayers shall not destroy us. And
if all men cast out, Jesus will never do so.
Oh what a blessed promise what a sure
foundation he who comes, he who believes
is welcome & shall never, never lose
the mercy he requests.

Here are to conclude three words of
comfort
1. one for me & all ministers. We shall
not labour in vain, Christ shall see the
travail of his soul & although he does
not save just whom & when we please
yet save he will & rejoice in his love.

2. one for all Christians. They may
now rest secure in the covenant love of
God. The devil cannot cast them out
for he cannot enter into God's house, nor
can the world & God will not so we are
secure. Blessed Security,

3. one for poor sinners. Hear the word
nowise over again. Let the experience of
thousands & myself among them cheer thee
on, why doubt, he is able, he is willing
doubt no more.

Lord help me Amen

392

Ps. XII. 6. The Bible a conqueror.
Good things will endure trial. The best of the
good is its enduring the fire. So is it with books
There is the fire of criticism which every book
must pass through. Do not imagine that any
of you could write a book so immaculate
that it will go scatheless through the world.
Write & rewrite it shall still be criticised
the friend & the foe will open their eyes
upon it — & you will have the equivocal
pleasure of hearing your book abused where
you hoped to have received applause.
Either it will be hissed out of existence,
or it will have its ephemeral day, or it
may survive a century — & peradventure
it may take a place among the constellation
of authors. But anyhow it will be
criticised & many a furious onslaught
it must endure ere it stands on the
mountain top of acknowledged fame.

When God became an author we
might imagine that his volume would
have been received with respect &
allowed to stand in the sanctum sanctorum
far away from common book life.
Not so it seemed as if the whole
earth waited until the book was born
that they might crush & destroy it.
It has passed through a series of conflicts

such as no other book ever endured.
It has been purified seven times.
other works have gained the pyramid
of honour & are free from attacks
but our Bible has no repose.
Homer. Horace. Virgil. Milton & the
other poets wear their laurels & no one
attempts to snatch the laurel from
their brow but this great author is
ever being attacked. It is hatred of the
author which prompts the deed.
It lives on. it has increased in power
& shall do until the religion we profess
shall become universal & this god
of Books shall be King over all.
The Bible has had opponents of several
classes — we will briefly mention
them
1. Its physical force opponents. The men
who attacked it bodily. Minded not its
contents but attacked it as a Bible.
With these I class the men, who aimed
at keeping the Bible in an unknown
tongue & were able to do so for a
long time. Who gave it an illuminated
border & confined it as a bird in a
golden cage or a virgin in a palace prison
They resisted every attempt to translate

it, they kept the key of Knowledge & would
neither enter in themselves nor suffer others
to do so. But did they prevail Did all the
Bonifaces & the Innocents & Gregories & monks
& friars manage to keep it in its tomb
no out it came & multitudes beheld it.
Once out they began to burn, but could
they burn it up. No. Under the bed,
or in the box it lived & was read.
Yea its very murderers helped to spread
it.. Tyndale lived on the sale of the books
which his enemies bought for the fire.
We have some of these brute force
men now — Tale of a Soldier with tract.
Priests of Rome. Our memories &
the myriad copies forbid all fear from
these. Alexandria's volumes may
have been burned in the baths, but
never shall the last Bible burn.

2. Its scoffers. Men of the Voltaire & Tom
Paine school. who tried to scoff it down
and scout it without examination.
Such men are usually uneducated
nowadays. The French revolution gave the
world a disrelish for undraped atheism.
Has the Bible been injured by one
scoff. No. Its prophecy of the last days
has been verified. Story of Wellington.
& the officer who found fault with
the Bible. The Quaker upon G. Goliath.

3. Its false philosophers.

Thousands of Quixotes have rushed against the windmill which grind flour for the nations —   Take a few of them.

The Epicureans — declared that certain concurring atoms by chance formed this world. & fashioned all things therein.

Buffon — with his great eternal pre-existent theory — breaking of the earth from the sun by contact with a comet.

The Progressionists, with their ideas of the gradual formation of all creatures from certain molecules & their improvement into higher orders of life until man came.

The Geologists. — who now stand side by side with Scripture & we find no contradiction.

Ethnology too is now on our side. New Philosophers are always rising & sometimes nervous Christians fear for their Bibles, but let them not fear for in every thing the Bible will be borne out by science.

Astronomy once seemed against us.

4. Its mythical Interpreters.

These men tell us that all our histories and our revelation are a mass of myths.

That they ought to be preached but not believed by good philosophers.

Are the ruined walls of Petra myths. Are the Jews myths? Are the Arabs myths. Are the stones in our Museum myths.

I imagine the mans brains are myths — or certainly very small indeed.

Ps. VIII. 5.6

393

This Psalm is the song of the Astronomers.
David walked abroad at midnight & lifted
his eyes on high. He saw the fair moon
in her silver-axled car. & her companions
stars sailing along the sea of ether. He
beheld the spangled army & broke forth
with a song "When I consider the heavens &c.

The Evil genius of Infidelity has wooed
all the sciences, but they have all cast him off

He sought to dwell among the stars but
they shot their pure fire on him & said
"When he prepared the heavens I was there"
He tried in turn every other science but
each cast him away & foremost stands
this science of astronomy so clearly declaring
that the heavens are the work of Gods
fingers — that an "undevout astronomer is mad

I am not however about to make a
lecture upon astronomy — I leave such
things to Dr Chalmers & other master minds

we proceed to notice the words of our
text — & we see

I. The honour bestowed on Man

II. The dominion bestowed on him.

When David saw those mighty orbs
he seemed to lessen and grow into a
mere speck or atom dancing in the
sun beam & he could not but

It were well if it had not other opponents
but there are opponents in our hearts.

Pride loving not to be a sinner or to
own the truth -- Free grace is never
pleasing to the soul - we want to do...

Fear not the Bible will overcome these.
Then will come the insinuations of
Satan & the raillery of enemies, but
fear them not this book shall weather
the storm.   Experience will try
your faith in it, but fear not the
waves shall never dash upon this rock
to move it one inch.   That is the
commentary which the heart makes when
it can say tried & proved. I exhort
you to try it   for direction in difficulty
comfort in trouble
help against sin.
joy   in death

admire & wonder at the honour conferred on so insignificant a creature.

I   The Honour bestowed on Man.

1 The first sentence I take it expresses that pristine honour which Adam had.

He was a little lower than the angels. God has degrees of being. one of his creatures has the soaring wing, another creeps upon the earth. one is terrible in power, another insignificant in weakness. Man was made only a little second to the greatest of the creatures of God. Adam could almost mate with Gabriel the strong & mighty but alas he fell & we became in sin lost, ruined & broken. our crown is gone. Yet even now wrecked & battered as we are there remains in our race enough to show its original grandeur.

The prince in rags has still the hair & gait of royalty. The slavery of sin & the sunburnings of transgression have not utterly defaced the nobility of man.

But if we want to understand how fallen man is, if you wish to see what being a 'little lower than the angels' means, now — You must see the Son of God, & son of man, in his incarnation, clogged with flesh, despised of men, spit upon & mocked

Angels ministered to him in the wilderness, an angel strengthened him in the garden. He was a little lower than the angels. Pause my soul & weigh these words. "Lower than the angels" The creator stoops beneath the created. For thee he did it all. oh my soul be filled with loving wonder. what means it — it means pain, & sorrow, & death. It means insult & scorn.

How sweet to have a gospel translation of the Psalm & read the Saviour there.

" Lord what is man or all his race
" Who dwell so far below
" That thou should'st visit him with grace
" And love his nature so.
" That thine Eternal Son should bear
" To take a mortal form
" Made lower than his angels are
" To save a dying worm

But now we turn away from this first patent of man's nobility. It is too much blotted. The escutcheon is too defaced to leave us any room for glory we look at the

2. The Second Sentence sets forth the honours of our race under the second Adam. We are now crowned with glory & honour. Some men love to talk of the honours of war, the victory the garment rolled in blood. the firm courage of battalions, & the heroism of

generals. But oh when well considered is there any honour to our race from war. Is not the glory a delusion. Should not the bloodstained drapery of war be hissed at instead of applauded. —

Others of a better mould delight to dwell on the honour derived by our race from the names of sages & the deep penetrating researches of the wise — but I know a glory more lasting than that.

Nor is the crown of our race made by the virtues of Howard, Clarkson or Wilberforce good and great as these are.

If we want to see the race honoured, look yonder. Look to the man who fills the middle throne. Look to the man who is girt about the paps with a golden girdle. Lo on his head are many crowns & in his hands the sovereign keys of heaven & death & hell. He is the director of Providence, the high priest of creation.

He with his rainbow wreathe & robes of storm shall soon come to be our judge. Oh the honours he has won for us. We are in him - equal to the angels, yea above them for we can claim a nearer kindred to him than they — Oh my soul care not for honour or grandeur — only dwell on this thought thou art in him crowned with glory & honour

When thou art reviled & made the offscouring of all things by man, remember thy dignity thy Brother, thy Husband sits on a throne & thou in him art exalted far above all principality & power. Oh what are all the trappings of men. Their lace & embroidery. Their stars & ribbons. Their crests, their coronets, their mitres & their crowns compared with the glory of being allied to him who is crowned with glory & honour.
. All honour to the dying Lamb &c

II. The Dominion bestowed on man.

Here again I take the first sentence to refer to the original grant of creation to Adam. He was God's vicegerent. King of this province of the empire of heaven.

All creatures owned his dominion, they all came before him to receive their names.

The old pictures seem to catch the idea, where they represent adam with a lion at his feet while all other beasts are sporting around him.

This first grant has never been revoked entirely, - man is still lord of creation but not as he used to be. It is true he rules the thundermaned horse & the strong sinewed ox - He tames the lion.

He overcomes the monsters of the deserts & the jungles — the mighty whale dies to yield him oil & he levies a contribution on all things — but he is not as he used to be, the undisputed monarch of the earth. The locust, & the cankerworm laugh at his power little though they be. The fierce lion sends him for his prey & the hungry wolf attacks him. Our blessed Saviour however had power over all creatures. The beasts in the desert hurt him not. The shoals come into the net at his bidding & the fish will turn tribute bearer for him.

Yet this sovereignty is marred, the large proportion of our race have no dominion, they fear as much as they are feared — our crown remains but some of its jewels are gone.

2. We look with pleasure at the Second sentence which shows us with our dominion restored in Christ. All things are put under his feet. He is the universal sovereign. We have a right noble Captain. All things, on earth obey him — the thunder utters not its voice without his leave — the ocean lifts not up its hands until he So ordaineth. The winds cannot so much as whisper. or the waves move without him. Kings are in his hand, he manages their cabinet councils. The Imperious Autocrat unwittingly fulfils his decree.

Both good & evil are his instruments. In heaven. Right willingly are his laws obeyed. the outstretched wings of seraph quiver with delight if he doth but wish an errand to be performed. the ransomed adore his blest supremacy.

And e'en in hell. He is the lord. In the deep recesses & dark caverns of the pit he is known terrible in the wrath of the Lamb. This man governs all. This Godman is the only potentate. Now my soul behold thine own rank for in him, man is to be the lord of all things under God —

Oh my soul. thou dost not know what thou shalt be. Ye ungodly ones. where is your hope & consolation. Oh my fellow Christian rejoice in the Lord & on, to thy rest. thy glory. thy heaven, they all

394   John. VII. 46. Eloquence of Jesus.

Eloquence is a wondrous gift. He who has it ever receives homage from man. It has a sovereignty in it which men willingly bow to. Like music it has charms to soothe to conquer, to inspire or to melt. Eloquence is the music of sense, more than of sound though both are combined in most orators.

He who has eloquence is more obeyed than the man of wealth or wisdom.

When well applied it is the noblest gift man can be endowed with. I reckon the honour of a Christian orator to be the climax of earthly glory & the very acmé of my ambition is to have the eloquent tongue on fire with Christ's love & by the blessing of the Spirit winning souls to Christ. —

The annals of the Bible are not barren of great men. Giants in every walk of life have their names engraven on the walls of this wondrous palace of revelation. Ask for a mighty warrior whose exploits rival Cæsar? I show you Joshua, or David. Ask for a lawgiver an equal of Lycurgus? See there is Moses the superior of every other. Seekest thou wisdom? Ye have it in Solomon. Or heroism, ye behold it in Daniel & the brave three who endured the furnace — And should ye

enquire for poetry & eloquence. I bring you a cloud of silver tongued & golden mouthed orators. — But foremost amongst them I mention the name of my Master, the Lord Jesus. He is the prince of preachers. The perfection of eloquence. The Grand Master of the brotherhood of orators.

The best tribute which can be borne to a man is that which his enemies are constrained to render. When Hatred giveth honour it is honour molten in the furnace & free from the dross of flattery. The testimony to the eloquence of our Saviour was given by officers who were sent to take him. by the Pharisees & chief priests. They came fully intent upon the execution of their warrant. but as the lion licked the feet of the spotless Una, so they listened to his words, were enchanted & on returning empty handed could only exclaim "Never man spake like this man" They could not touch him, his very looks unmanned them, their arm was nerveless they were spell bound, entangled in a silken net, bound with invisible fetters of silver, riveted by the fascinating sound of the music of his voice

Our business this morning by the help of the blessed Spirit, shall be to exhibit Christ as the "chief speaker", may you each hear his words & confess their power.

I For Manner & II For Matter.
Christ excells all others.

I. For Manner

A man may have much to say, but if he say it badly he has little power. The block of Parian marble is not so valuable as the statue cut from it. Truth needs to be incarnate in beauty & thought should be solidified with elegance. Like apples of gold they are to be conveyed in baskets of silver, if we would attract beholders.

The wise man will value truth for its own sake, he loves her in déshabille, he rejoices in her however homely the words which are cast around her — but even he feels the magic of soft sounds & loves the queen best in her state garments — while to the paper by the dress is all important if we would woo him to the love of goodness.

When we hear a speaker & simply regard his manner — two things are ever though perhaps unconsciously before us.
The Man's character
& The Man's style of speaking.

The Man's Character will break out when he speaks. & much of a man may be learned from his sermons. Now in our Lord his hearers could not fail to observe a chain of virtues.

Fidelity. was very prominent. Those who heard him could not but know that he was faithful to his trust. He never stifled a truth lest it should be unpleasant to his hearers. He stood and like a crystal fountain he allowed living waters to gush freely from his heart.

He flattered not the rich, he told them it was hard for them to be saved. He crouched not to rulers. he defied the power of Herod the fox. He feared not frowns for in the presence of Pharisees he cried "woe unto you scribes & Pharisees hypocrites." All classes received their due. the lawyer who feared an indirect reproach upon his order, received at once a home stroke. He courted no man's smile. The young man is bidden to sell his all. his followers are warned to count the cost. Like the moon he tarried not at the baying of the dog or the song of the admiring poet.

When you saw him on the mountain

You saw "a man" a freeman", a man unbound by the fetters of fashion, an athlete ready to wrestle with error of every kind.

He had no temporizing in him, he went to Nazareth & what did he. He enters the synagogue but he does not select a passage to please the people. He gives them election & sovereignty & though they bite their tongue for wrath he cares not.

The truth must be spoken & he speaks it. Laughing ridicule banters him in vain. Harsh calumny puts him in her pillory but he yields not to her. Flattery holds up her gewgaws but he treads them under foot. Oh ye temporizing men who conceal your sentiments look ye here & behold him whom ye call master & blush at your vile cowardice. Oh may God help us to speak like Jesus. in measure For in this respect "Never man spake like this man"

Prudence. But our Saviour's courage was not a rash imprudent daring. It was courage tempered with discretion. Hotheaded rashness has often spoiled the cause it intended to enrich. Truth has even now the scars of wounds which she received in the house of her friends.

Our Saviour never threw his pearls before swine. He expounded to his disciples the meaning of his parable, but the unthinking herd were satisfied with the husk, his favourites received the precious kernel. for the others would have trodden it under food & heaven's manna ought not to be wasted. — The woman of Samaria asks him to solve the question in dispute betwixt her nation & the Jews. He talks to her of the water of life.

In vain his smooth tongued enemies labour to entrap him. The Herodian retires abashed by a few words upon a coin. The Sadducee sees his long tale of the woman & seven husbands scattered to the winds & stands confounded when he hears that God is not God of the dead but of the living. The haughty Pharisee questioning his authority bites his lip when fixed on the horns of a dilemma as to Johns Baptism.

Nor could the whole phalanx of his foes entrap him in his speech.

Alas my friends we may soon be entrapped. The enemy may soon discover spots in our garments. The finest web of eloquence which mortal tongue hath ever woven. has some false throws of the shuttle, some threads too slightly interwoven. Oh that God would heard our lips & put an angel at our mouth to drive back every imperfect word & only give a passage to those which are pure, lovely & of good report. Oh faultless Jesus inimitably infallible — Oh honey dropping lips of the fairest of the sons of men, — Oh winged words of snowy whiteness — all honour, & praise for ever I must yield & own that "never man spake like this man".

<u>Love</u> — But iron courage & cold discretion will not win the battle. Love is the mightiest as well as the fairest of the graces. A man who has love in his heart will soon find his way into other men's souls.

Surely my Master was all love. Never man was so full of love as he. Methinks I see him even now with big tears rolling down his cheeks uttering his lament over Jerusalem. In all his discourses his eyes were rendered soft. Yet omnipotent by the power of love.

His very threatenings uttered in a tone of deep pity, sounded like the warnings of mercy & not the thunderings of justice.

Oh those words on the cross "Father forgive them" there is more real melody there than in the finest compositions of Handel. — Surely the very demons must have been thrilled by its pathetic cadence

Oh what power love has over men. If we know that a man loves us, how readily do we drink in his words.

His eye sometimes floats in tears, his uplifted hand seems to beseech you to be reconciled to God & his every moment seems to be baptized in love.

Such and far more than I can describe was Jesus.

"Never man spake like this man".

Humility — again was sweetly conspicuous. He was a man anointed above his fellows but who could see any pride in him. The little child seemed to be his fit companion — The woman of Samaria could talk with him, vile as she was he did not keep her at a distance.

He was no lawn sleeved bishop. His hand was given to the poor. The common people heard him gladly. He was a man, not a man in his own caste & a lord everywhere else. But he spoke like the servant of all. I think humility — the rarest of all graces & all the imitations of it I count as the offscouring of the earth. I long to be conformed to Christ, but pride's ear has been bored to the door post. but not Jesus. "Never man spake like this man".

And now we note the style of Jesus having long enough dwelt on his character.

Seeing that we can only give an outline of that mirror of all perfection.

The Style of Christ was simple. The child could understand him. Some preachers if they meet with a hard word in the week must bring it out on Sabbath. But why should they do so. Hard words in a sermon are like stones in fruit. They may be almost unavoidable but they are not good nourishing. — Christ spoke the language of childhood. How exquisitely simple are his parables. How plain the meaning of the prodigal, the good Samaritan or the house upon the sand.

Market language. Whitfield used & after all what is better than good homely Saxon.

May the Lord send us less philosophy, & more simplicity — less of the college & more of common life preaching

No one so simple as Jesus.

It was serious. There was no levity in Christ, he was deeply in solemn earnest & had no time for jokes. At the same time I do not say as some do that Jesus never laughed. I think some old crabbed divine first said that when he had a fit of spleen. I am exhorted to rejoice, yea to leap for joy. Holy mirth

well becomes a Christian, but the pulpit is not the place for buffoonery for quips & fun. Smile we may. & eccentricity & oddity have been made useful. But remember it is eccentricity

A model preacher I would describe as serious yet cheerful, solemn yet joyful.

I conceive that Jesus would have been eminently so. though as a man of sorrows. he could not be so joyful as we ought to be who are redeemed from all ills

It was earnest. His words came from his heart. Some preachers seem to have a very low temperature to their hearts — somewhere below zero —

Jesus did not stand motionless as a statue, as destitute of emotion as a picture & only moving his eyes as seldom as a Madonna

No, his was living eloquence. his lips had been touched not by the blue fingers of frost but by a live coal from off the altar. His very fingers would preach, his eye aye & all his body.

Should he not be serious who speaks of eternal things, who preaches sin's punishment & the only remedy. Should he prate on his usual time & turn the dry leaves of a manuscript — No. No. let his

II. For Matter. None had ever spoken as
he has done. If the outward trappings
of our favoured utterances are so excellent
what must the body itself be. We do
not profess to be able to unroll the garments
& speak fully of the inhabitant: it needs
another Christ to preach Christ fully.
no man need speak as well as he to
praise him fully. — we will but touch
speak his praise.

Compare the truths he preached with
those of the philosophers of remote or
modern ages. They but amuse with
frothy sayings with half viewed mysteries.
they talk of time & the things thereof
he speaks of eternity & its boundless cycles.
of death and what is beyond it of hell
the pit prepared for the wicked & of the
mansions to receive the righteous.
His message is from the true God. he tells
of himself the comforter of Mourners
& the Spirit the Comforter of Mourners.
these are no trifles. these are not
leaves from the wild forest tree — these
are not broken shells from the deep ocean
they are pearls I thrice unrivalled & gems
of splendour unequalled. Every syllable
had its value, every sentiment is big with

as flesh fire, let his bosom glow with
real heat, let him plead with men as for
his life. & wrestle as if he were the victim
to be delivered.

It was direct. His hearers perceived that
he spake to them. This was the secret of
Rowland Hill's power. He gave home
strokes. Thou art the man deemed to
be the conclusion of all this sermon
The self condemned accusers left the
woman in the temple alone. Thou
was no mistaking him. His sermon
had a hundred hands to grasp the
hearers with. nowadays this is
Called personality. And so let it be. I
accept it under this title & pray God
to make all his ministers personalpreachers.

Oh my friends I tarry here. The
lofty mountains outtop the power of language
& I can do it. But this brow, the
Sled Sea'd stands head & shoulders
above them all. His strains are more
than seraphic. If my tongue were to
condemn could it should be won to
a psaltery — sea of the harps of glory
should be won away with constant
glory, they could not sing the rapture it
the voice nor could I declare it

solemn meaning.

Compare the truths he uttered with the testimony of all the prophets. Noah could preach righteousness but he could not declare the way, the truth & the life. Moses could hold up the law & point to its rocky tablets — & each of the prophets in order had their errands but he is the marrow of them all. The fairest flowers from all the gardens of others make up that bundle of perfume called my beloved.

As some painters to make a landscape do choose a tree from one place, a stream from another, & group them with a distant castle — so may you gather the beauties of all authors, the gems of all writers, the golden sentences of all orators, & the choice words of all divines, but could ye distil the quintessence from them all & mingle them in one precious box of spikenard — sweet though it might be — sweeter than the breath of morn — or the exhalations of flowers — Hay it could not equal the sweetness of my Lord's messages.

How know you this! says the scoffer. Know it why I have heard him speak & can bear testimony that no voice can be compared with his. This is after all the best way to understand the eloquence of Jesus. Have we not heard his voice in the still evening while walking in the garden of meditation? Did he not once sing outside my dungeon wall until I answered to his song & he delivered me?

Ah. well can I say, as the voice of the turtle when winter is passed so is the voice of my Beloved. As the anthems of paradise, as the hymns of glory, as the hallelujahs of the ransomed so is his speech to mine ear. —

I add my name to the cloud of witness of this truth & doubt not that there are many here who most gladly say Amen. Oh that the deaf might hear the sound. & the dead be quickened by the strain. — If the whole world could but hear they would love him too. Sinner let me tell thee one word of his musical language 'ere I close.

Come unto me all ye that labour & are heavy laden & I will give you rest. — —   Help. oh. my King.

395

Matt VI. 12 Forgive us our debts.
I would commence my discourse tonight
by remarking on what is commonly called
the Lords Prayer. My views of it may
sound strange but are by no means of
singular. It is a most beautiful
composition. among Christians there cannot
be two opinions. It is the model prayer.
the difference of opinions will rest as to
the use of it & here let me remark.
1. That no real Christian men ought
to use it, for none but they can truly
say "Our Father which art in heaven";
every unconverted man who uses it, so
far from worshipping God, actually insults
him by calling him what he is not.
How can he say "hallowed be thy name"
when at another time he curses God.
2. I do not think that it was intended as
a form to be ordinarily used in prayer
by believers. I think it may be acceptably
offered occasionally — but I do not think
our Saviour intended it as a prayer to
be used on all occasions. I look upon
it as a model. a beautiful model. but
I should no more think of using it as a
prayer than I should think of getting
inside the little model of our chapel which
now stands in the vestry :— It is a

beautiful groundplan of a prayer but one
are left by God to build by it as our want
may suggest or the Holy Ghost directs. It
is a most admirable pattern. It
commences with a most endearing title
suggesting at once all that is tender &
familiar coupled with authority & power.
Its first breathing is in solemn awe.
an almost whisper. an ascription & a
prayer at once. then follows the
glorious petition with which David
closed his prayers & coupled with it a
desire to have—than none but Jesus
could have conceived it. the most
unselfish of petitions come first. so are
we ever to desire his glory above all
things. But he forbids us not to ask
for ourselves the needed benefits. "Give
us this day our daily bread" is as
sanctified an utterance as "thy kingdom
come." He whose ever-opened hand
supplies every want bids us ask & well
may we condescend to do it for his paths
drop fatness. Bread in the threefold
sense — the bread of natural food for
this body, the animal part of me, bread
of knowledge for my mind & that
best of all breads — the spiritual
sustenance of my soul. There is a

trinity in man & the prayer is therefore triple —. And now a petition the most humbling of all appears in the centre "Forgive us our debts "&c

The text includes

I   A Prayer "forgive us our debts"

II. An Argument. "as we forgive our debtors".

III. A duty is supposed in forgiveness. —

I. A Prayer —

This prayer puts man in a very humiliating position. It calls him a debtor. And is he not so from the very nature of things. Are not all things debtors to their maker. Did he not turn them all on his mighty lathe? are they not his handiwork? Save the Godhead all beings are debtors.   The glittering plumage of the angels was given them by him. The scorching furnaces of the sun are fed with fuel by his hand. while this inferior clod is held together by his grasp.   Man, the wonder of all would is much in debt — he has been fearfully & wonderfully made, the breath of his nostrils is not his own, nor the air he breathes. — Oh this is a debt man cannot pay — but this he never need

ask to have forgiven. The word forgive supposes sin & points us to the real debt which we have contracted. —

Oh what a depth of meaning in those two words "our debts"— can any man in the world tell how great they are? I trow not. Until he has measured the ocean into drops & fathomed the abyss of interminable space.

Our debts are of two kinds. Debts inherited & debts personal.

The first are by no means light. We are all members of one great corporation. Adam as representative for us failed & made himself & the whole race bankrupts.   We are all as sharers liable. — This is the worst kind of debt a man can have - for however much he may have he is still liable until the debts of the whole company are paid —   Some will say that they were no parties to the agreement. I answer that God has chosen the representative system as his mode of moral government & it is better than any you or I could suggest. Adam stands or falls; on that one man hangs the whole race. How much better than to let every man stand or fall — for remember if we fall representatively, we rise in the same manner — but if every man stood on his own footing we could never be sure that anyman would rise yea no man could arise & thus the race must perish. Remember then my brother when thou askest for forgiveness that thou hast an awful debt as one of a bankrupt society — a debt which like some bottomless chasm would require mountains to fill it up. A debt which like an horseleech cries evermore "give, give" & like behemoth drinks up rivers of merit at a draught. ——

Truly when we meditate on this deep & mysterious subject we may well say "Forgive us our debts."

The Second kind of debts are those which most men will admit. Debts personal. Now let us set down & count our personal liabilities. I began to run into arrears very early. I did not reverence my parents, many youthful sins & crimes have disgraced my history — wayward & giddy I ran headlong over the glassy sea of youth.

Some of you can remember black acts of lust which dis-graced your ripening manhood. Sins against the world in running with its maxims Sins against our companions in leading them astray. Sins against relatives. Sins against time. wasting its running sands — Sins against soul & body. against earth & heaven. Oh my poor soul — sins are as thick around thee as insects in the evenings sunshine. How much owest thou to my Lord? Be calm oh ocean, let thy bosom be congealed into a continued sheet that I may write my debt upon it — Space fails — I will commence at one horizon & in broad lines write my sins on yonder firmament but yet I find the space too narrow. Ah Lord I cannot tell how much I owe. It surpasseth my arithmetic. Dost thou still ask. Then I must ask those condemned spirits who have these four thousand years been drinking the brimstone of the boiling cauldron

of the wrath of Almighty God. But they
know not yet, nor can they know
till they have measured eternity &
comprehended the infinite. —

To pay them were impossible for I
cannot reckon them. I only cry out
forgive me my debts. —

Before we quit this prayer we must
have three remarks which to help your
memory we put in brief words.

To whom — by whom — through whom

To whom — may we say — forgive us our
debts? — we need not question long. It is
to our Father. None but he can
forgive sins - for they are committed
against him alone. How blasphemous
is it for a Romish Priest to talk of
forgiving sins — & not much less than
that when the Clergyman of the Church
of England kneels by the bed side of a
dying man & reads "by authority committed
unto one I absolve thee from all sin."

My friends I need not warn you
against so dangerous an error as that
of forgiveness of sins by man. It was
presumption enough for Lucifer to
desire to climb the throne of heaven

but where unto shall I liken the pride
of that man who would act the God
& pardon in the Almighty's name
sins against the majesty of heaven.
Oh vile potsherds of the dust - your
arrogance is unbounded. Oh pitiful
worms of the earth — wherefore ape
omnipotence. Oh vile reprobates &
blasphemers how dare ye ascend the
bench of judgment & acquit criminals
yourselves being doubly condemned.

By whom need this supplication to be
offered? Surely this needs no reply.
It suits alike the saint & the sinner.
Manasseh may offer it in his dungeon
& Moses on the top of Pisgah. The
bloody hands of Saul may lifted up to
heaven with it but it will & really
become the holy John. Jew & Gentile
rich & poor may well offer this common
petition. Verily we are all debtors.

Yet it may be questioned how a
child of God who is already pardoned
can ask for pardon again. The
reply is easy. I am forgiven once
for all, the moment I believe,

mention the greater owes of Immanuel.
thouldst thou read heaven with
thine outcries & wear the rocks with
thy kneelings — It is all in vain
until thou lookest to Calvary &
beholdest the Surety who paid the
debt that thou mightest be forgiven
th bleeding sufferer ever will I turn
mine eyes to thee & mention nothing
but thy name. —

II. The Argument: "as we forgive &c"—
This does not at first look like a
free grace argument but it is.
If It does not appear so, it is because we
do not understand it :— It does not
mean that we are to ask forgiveness
because we have forgiven others but
I take it to mean this. Lord I have
many debts, but thy grace has
looked upon me & I have in
consequence been led to forgive my
debtors— therefore— I plead this
evidence— thou wouldest not
have showed me this favour if thou
didst intend to destroy me. So Lord

his sin never be laid to my charge but then
I may be chastised for sin & I offer this
prayer to turn away the rod from one just
as an erring child would to an offended father.
I know in one sense I am to forgive
that I need not ask for it any more but in
another sense I must make this my daily
prayer "Father forgive": Again by the
may be intended give me a sense of
forgiveness — a fresh knowledge of it.
Now where is the man who can say
this day I need not offer that prayer.
Save a few poor crazy perfectionists
I can find no such man on earth.
Through whom? The answer trembles
on our lips. Already you press the reply
Christ is the signatures which renders our
petition powerful. He is the ladder down
which the mercies travel. Like I see
who came from heaven on a rainbow
all blessings comes through the glories
of his covenant. show the Father
the many coloured garment dipt in
his vital blood. Strike this red posts
upon your lintel. Preface & conclude
with the all protest name of Jesus
In vain you weep though you
should weep like Niobe. Heaven can
not for thy sorrows endless thou dost

Thou hast taught me to forgive, now shew me another token for good by giving me an evidence of forgiveness. —

It is the mark of a Christian to forgive injuries & he is no Christian who has never learned to forgive. Oh foolish hypocrite thou boastest that thy Lord has forgiven thee all thy debt & yet there lies thy poor debtor in the jail who owes thee a pitiful hundred pence. Vile parasite of religion — thou art no genuine plant of the Lord — The Sons of God forgive till seventy times seven.

This is one of the insignia of the free masonry of heaven. Good for evil is Godlike. — To forgive is to be like God - to keep enmity is Satanic.

Oh when my enemy has spat upon me, has plucked my hair & called me dog. is it not sweet to revenge my injury & trample him in the dust — No it is sweet to a worldlings palate — but to the Christian there is a sweeter revenge than this — it is to waylay him with kindness to feed him when he hungers, to pour wine into his parched lips, to set him by ones own fireside, to whisper peace to his troubled conscience, to tell

him to forget the injury for it is all forgiven. There is mine enemy drowning, I will risk my life for him, this arm shall save him from the angry flood. I must forgive him for I am a child of Jehovah who passeth by transgression & sin —

Thus you see this is an evidence of grace not a plea of merit. —

now
III The Duty. —

It is plainly our duty to forgive, not debts of money (though in some cases these) but debts of trespass against us by our fellow creatures. —

A full forgiveness of all our fellows Is necessary when we pray. I bend my knee & ask forgiveness but there is enmity in my soul. My prayer is talking to the wind. I cannot offer my Sacrifice for enmity doth make a blemish in it. —

Be assured of this all of you — there is no mercy for you until you have shown it to others. What saith the Merciful God. Dost thou lift thine hands for mercy. Why thou hast just now been griping thy brother's throat therewith — Vile creature — am I to blot out thy crimes — whilst thou art to be avenged — Justice spurns the miscreant from his throne.

It matters not how the quarrel has arisen, it may be a family feud, an old hatred running in the blood — or it may be from some real injury. I charge you forgive each other if you hope to be forgiven. If you meet each other on going out of the door — put forth the hand of pardon — or as long as heaven standeth — your unmercifulness shall be remembered. Let me remind you this is necessary at death. You must soon gather up your feet in the bed. if you wish to die the death of the righteous — all enmities must leave your bosoms. Oh man thy cherished hatred will hover over thee like an eagle preying on thy vitals.

It will lay like a milstone on thy breast keeping down the breath of prayer. — It will be a thistle in thy last bed — A demon scaring thine hours

I would not have thy deathbed for all the gold of Croesus. I would sooner die with a martyr at the stake than die with thee. — But thou wilt need it most at judgment.

But a little while oh mortals & the great assize shall commence. The judge shall come with sound of trumpet. Then where will the unforgiving one appear.

No difficulty to prophecy his doom. Go archangels sever the goats from the sheep — they come & this man stands first with Cain's mark on his brow. Pray up the miscreant. What last thou to say. Wretch dost thou plead for mercy. Does not the word choke thee. Mercy — didst thou show any. Didst thou not pursue thy fellow like a bloodhound.

Mercy — because thou hast showed none I will deal with thee as thou hast rewarded others. Thine enmities shall be tied around thy neck like millstones for ever. while the iron whips of vengeance shall tear thee Eternally. —

May God give you grace to forgive & evermore to pray "forgive us our debts as we forgive our debtors" — Amen.

396

Faith before Baptism

Then this is the only prerequisite before Baptism
I need not ask a candidate many questions
as to his growth in grace or degree of Knowledge
if he sincerely & heartily believes I am then
quite satisfied & will baptize him. This
is the question & the only question.

But on the other hand this one thing
is essentially necessary to the right reception
or administration of the ordinance.

This is the doctrine of the text & I shall
for a few moments speak upon

I. The Doctrine
II. The Question which naturally arises.

I. The Doctrine.

I think it superfluous to attempt a
proof when the text declares as plainly a
possible that Faith is necessary. I suppose
there are none in my congregation so obtuse
as to be unable to see this self-evident
truth. As to members of the church of
England they will want no proof for from
their infancy they have been taught the
doctrine & believe that repentance &
faith are necessary before Baptism.

Were I in argument with a Churchman
I should not want a better book on my
side than the Book of Common Prayer

with any really consistent believer in
parts of the Book of Common Prayer I am
at no issue. My combat is with those
who say that others beside believers have
a right to this ordinance. In their
teeth I lift up my text & wonder how
it is possible for them to escape.

I have no doubt my brethren are
desirous to be right & follow their judgment
& far be it from me to anathematize
any man or pronounce curses on his
head. I simply beg his ear a moment
while I ask a question or two. —

1. Brother why do you baptize infants?

He replies "because Abraham's seed were
circumcised". how this glorious reason
reminds me very much of Tenterden
Steeple & the Goodwin Sands. I can
never see any connection here. —

But stay & hear our friend a moment
or two he says that Abraham's children
were put into the covenant by
~~Baptism~~ Circumcision & therefore ours ought to
be put into it by Baptism. Oh my
friend this is a poor argument, a
mere cobweb which a child may sweep.

The first covenant was a covenant
made with Abraham's seed according

to the flesh. But now turn out the bondwoman & her son. We who love the Lord are Abrahams seed, we are the circumcision but the covenant does not run in the blood. What an awful fallacy this covenant youthing is.

Surely Baptized children are no better than others. &c &c.

2. What barrier should there be? if our be thrown down. what will you propose as a substitute — You have none. There is no halting place next come horses & cows, ships & bells.

3. What evils you bring on the people? You lead them to believe that there efficacy in drops of water — we tell them they must be saved —--

4. Why not open the Lords table. Children ate the passover why not the Lords supper. Every one is baptized why not let them sit at the table, Bid the world a welcome, turn the church & the world into one great common where sheep & goats feed together & so shall you cause joy in the infernal regions both hearty & lasting.

How much better to obey God rather than man & to ask this question only dost thou believe.—

II. The Question:—

1. Why are not all believers baptized. Are they afraid of water? Do they fear to come out & put on the Lord Jesus publicly why lie in ambush, hidden in the stairs.

2. Are all who have been here baptized real & hearty believers?

Oh this is a thing worthy of the serious personal enquiry of every professor here. How sad if the waters of baptism do testify against you.

3. Are the candidates real believers? If not I charge you, stand back & venture not so vile an act as to be buried in hypocrisy. 'Tis a solemn thing & is not to be rushed upon hastily!

But if you believe — come on - there is no fear. Christ is all-sufficient —

But beware for the future.

You pass the Rubicon, be careful.

397

LXI. 2.   The day of vengeance, the year of
acceptance. —
We have no need to ask as the Eunuch
did, "tell me I pray thee of whom speaketh the
prophet this, of himself or of some other
man?", for our Saviour ~~has~~ furnished
us with the key to it when in the
synagogue he took the book & said
The Spirit of the Lord is upon me &c.—

Our text represents our Saviour as
making a proclamation in the name
of God. He is the Logos, or Word of God
& by him God makes his proclamation
to man. He had spoken once yea
twice but man regarded it not. The
Prophets had spoken in vain, but now
the Prince, the Heir of all things speaks.
Listen oh Heavens & be attent oh earth.
If Jeremiah could cry out oh earth, earth
earth hear the word of the Lord, much
more may we demand it now with
emphasis oh earth, earth, earth hear the word
of the Lord.——
In the name of the Sacred Three
he utters his voice we will listen to
the proclamation. It is double.
He proclaims a year of acceptance &
a day of vengeance — these demand our
attention & shall receive ~~them~~ it.

By your leave we will reverse the
order of the sentences in the proclamat
& this gives us.
I. A Day of Vengeance.
II. A Year of Acceptance.
III. The Ordinance of the Lord's supp
contains a united remembrance of
both.——

I. A Day of Vengeance.
Harshly these words sound in the midst
of so many kind & tender commission
but as they are here we would not
wish to expunge them believing that
they are necessary ones.
In speaking from these words for a
short time, we are called upon first
of all to justify the use of the term
vengeance as applied to God. then
we shall endeavour to certify the
ungodly that vengeance will come
& again to show that the death of
Christ was peculiarly a day of vengeance
Vengeance justified.
Vengeance certified.
Vengeance ~~satisfied~~ magnified.

1. Vengeance justified.   There would be little
need for this were all men believers
The true believer never quarrels with the
righteous vengeance of God, he knows
it to be most just & admires it.
    But there are some who will say
that God is a God all love & that he
will not punish the guilty. How say
they can the God of the universe be a
God of vengeance. How can he delight
in putting his creatures to misery.
    Oh ye creatures of yesterday whence
this arrogance! shall the potsherds
bring their maker to judgment! Will
you charge him with cruelty! Stay
remember who art thou that repliest
against God!——   But if you wish
to repeat your cry. Let me tell you
that it is not inconsistent with the
highest benevolence for God to be a
God of vengeance.   It is true that
we are not to take vengeance on our
fellow creatures & it is benevolent
on our part to forgive all injuries,
but God as the judge of all must if
he be benevolent punish sin. Suppose
a magistrate to be a kind man,
he signs a warrant for punishing an
offender is he therefore unkind.

Is the Judge malevolent because he
condemns a criminal. Nay. There is
as much benevolence on God's part
in punishing as in pardoning.
    Would it be good & tender of the
great Ruler to leave us without law
to do as we please. Would any one
desire to see universal anarchy
Do you wish for a reign of terror, in
which unbridled lust would riot.
No. if there were no laws there
would soon be an outcry of woe in
the world. We should then look to
have some legislation — for the worst
of all law is better than none at all.
    Our prayer is answered, we receive a
law but how can there be a law
without punishments — if any man
may break law with impunity then
law is nothing. Law without power
is a laughing stock for sin. If then
there must be punishments shall
they be unexecuted. Shall the criminal
be allowed to enjoy immunity!
Oh were it so, ye would soon cry
out that God were unkind. Even
now while the wrath of God tarries

we are apt to ask whether the God of
heaven doth really behold the wrongs
of his creatures — but if it were known
that God would not punish the guilty
then the unbeliever might say that
our God was not good or he would
come to the rescue of the injured &
avenge the sufferings of the oppressed.

I say again that vengeance in
God is benevolence in another shape &
much as I may startle some of you
I believe that hell itself is not a
blot upon the love of God but that
rather, love to mankind constrains
the God of justice there to banish the
finally impenitent. —

2. Vengeance certified. — But if the
ungodly man still rails upon the
vengeance of God, let me assure him
that he cannot prevent its truth.
You may curse the lightning but
that will not restrain it from striking
you. You may rail against the
boiling ocean but it will not stay
its roarings for you. So ye may
blaspheme God but you cannot thereby
save yourself from the awful fact
of his punishing your sin.

There is in man a something called
conscience which tells you all that
you will be punished for sin. But
should you have lulled conscience
to sleep — come with me a moment
Do you see those plains covered
with grass, do you observe those men
& women dancing in sinful pleasure

Yes — those are the sons of God & the
daughters of men, how happy they
seem but wait — they have a few
more hours of respite — you will see
soon that God punishes sin. Noah
has entered his ark & a loud laugh
goes up from the merry throng outside

But wait one moment — didst hear
that sound — ah how awful — twas
the noise of the waters leaping
from their hollow caverns, didst
hear that other sound — twas the
voice of the waters above shouting
back to their brethren beneath.

Haste away, the rain descends
the floods arise — the dancers are
dismayed — the myriads of mankind
are startled — they rush for the

hills – how the tide thins their
ranks – higher – & but a few remain
on the summit of the mountains
but they too are gone. We hear the
last shriek of the strong swimmer in
his agony & now look at yon void
yon flood covered with corpses of
men, women, children & cattle –

Will he break up the depths of
the earth & rend the firmament to
punish sin & shalt thou go unpunished

Is that not enough – then I take
thee to Sodom, to Egypt, to Korahs
pit, to Jerusalem ––––

But why need this you yourselves
have seen sin punished in this
life – you have seen the miserable
wretch dragging his frame along &
you have said, see there the effect
of sin. And you have beheld
judgments on blasphemers by their
sudden death or being overtaken
with calamities unmistakeably the
result of no common providence but
of the finger of God. –

3. Vengeance magnified. God will not
spare the guilty, he will have vengeance
& he has done so –– Of all days of
vengeance, the death of Jesus was the
day of vengeance of our God. Never
did justice so awake its sword as
on that day. There was vengeance
upon sin in the person of Christ.

He for a time stood in the place
of his people, he was counted as a
sinner & numbered with the
transgressors. The sins of multitudes
were laid upon him & he stood
the master culprit of all, though in
him personally there was no sin.

Oh who can picture the day of vengeance
of our God. At the prospect of it he
was exceeding sorrowful even unto death.
Midnight has never before nor since
been startled with such groans as those
of Gethsemane. Never such sweat
reddened a garden before. It were
enough misery for a thousand lives
only with Jesus to contemplate the
coming trial.

But vengeance comes, she has been
seeking a victim, her sword is athirst

II. A Year of Acceptance.

The day of vengeance has passed for every sinner who shall believe on the name of Jesus. And now not a day but a Year of acceptance is come. The sins of Jesus were comparatively a day but his mercy is a year.

The acceptable year is supposed by some to refer to the year of Jubilee. So that we have a Jubilee through the death of our saviour. This might I proclaim it. The Year of Jubilee is come. Bankrupt! debtors your debts are cancelled. Prisoners ye are ransomed. Captives ye are ransomed. Slaves this is the hour of liberty.

To as many as now hear my voice I cry aloud the year of Jubilee. Some of you careless ones will not hear it but every sinner here. if his guilt will rejoice when I shout Jubilees — young man your sins are pardoned. Drunkard thou ... woman drowned in tears, young mad Jubilees. Rahab the harlot art thou here? New Jubilees — To the vile; to the unjust; to sinners,

for blood & wiped to slay, she had long cried for vengeance & her hour is come. She binds her prisoner & with knotted whips she flagellates his shoulders & lacerates his body. Never such blows as hers. She makes them as heavy as her gigantic arm can enable her. He is flogged. It is by a disciple. He is forsaken & it is by Peter. He is accused of that worst of crimes blasphemy. There was the essence of wormwood in all the drops he drank. He shall die. Then let him be crucified. He must die. Let it be with thieves. He must hang aloft before the crowd. Then strip him naked. Scorch him with the Sun. Then freeze him in the shade. Lay on the strokes & spare not. Mark how rapidly the blows proceeded he is dragged from tribunal to tribunal Everywhere mocked, spit upon, beaten, again. hurried to crucifixion. & all in a brief space. as if vengeance was in haste to devour him, at once to swallow him up quick. Oh day of vengeance thou art come, but I would not forget thee. It cry much injured Lord how can I ever repay thee. Suffer me to be developed ... the height, the unutterable ... depths. It heights. It unutterable ...

to outcasts, to reprobates, I proclaim aloud. The Year of Jubilee is come.

The Acceptable Year. — The Year of acceptance of our works. Before this God could not hear prayer or praise. Sin spoiled all & barred all communion, but now the way is opened. By him our prayers accepted rise. Come sinner this is the day of acceptance. If thou canst sigh he will accept it. On some day the easterns give presents & then even a flower is accepted. Come bring thy broken heart, thy sob, thy groan this is the accepted day. & thou X rejoice eat & drink for God accepts thee.

He accepts our persons. Defiled & full of sin they were. but now vengea[nce] has washed them in blood & bein[g] satisfied has given us a robe of honour & we are accepted. We are all accepted in the beloved. Not only accepted members of the church below but we shall be received into that above.

In this our new Jubilee exceeds the old, for they could not proclaim acceptance with Jehovah. Oh Glory Glory. Surely while I shudder at the rough blast of the day of vengeance I may exult in the calm sunshine of the year of accept[ance]

III. The two conjoined in the Supper.

Strange union. Vengeance & acceptance. Vengeance & love. Man could not have devised this. Sure this is the master work of God to unite such dissimilar materials & make redemption therewith.

Let me muse awhile.

Vengeance has left the trace of its wrath see the bread emblem of a mangled body rent in sunder — left piecemeal as prey is torn by the lion. See again the cup. She has filled it with his blood oh cruel vengeance, most just vengeance I see thee at the table. but I mark thy friend here too. whom thou hast lately kissed. I see acceptance there. I sit at the table. should I do that if unaccepted. I eat. I drink & will he disown me. No. I am a child. Oh my master give me that most excellent grace of love, that I dissolved in thankfulness may melt my soul into my sermon as the true vitalis thereof.

Help. Help. Help.

398

Job. VI. 6.   Unsavoury things. —

How foolish it is to take odd texts. To twist the word of God to a meaning never intended & so startle the audience with ones learning & ingenuity. The ingenuity thus evinced is of the lowest order & at the very best shews a wrong taste in the preacher who exhibits it & a morbid appetite in the people who delight in it. — I neither like the man who turns prophet & shuffles texts like cards to divine the fortunes of the world thereby, nor the minister who treats the Bible as a book to which he may attach any meaning in the world.

But while entering my protest against this mode of preaching, I trust I shall never fear to speak of a text because it sounds rather strange. for every word of God is good and we, the public teachers of the people ought not to leave a passage unexplained. —

Some expect that now they shall have an egg divided & subdivided so that their fancies may be tickled & amused — such will be mistaken.

I simply deduce from these words the general fact that there are some things so unsavoury in themselves that we cannot enjoy them without the addition of something else to make them savoury.

1. Natural Infirmities would be much less supportable were it not that some blessing is given by way of compensation. It is necessary that this world of sin should be partially a world of woe but mark how good God is in alleviating sorrow. The blind boy who never saw light has often a great quickness of ear & sensibility of the fingers which repays his loss. The Poor if they lack the luxuries often lack the diseases of the rich. God has scattered more equal portions than men imagine & given in natural things a salt which renders them endurable. —

2. Reproof — is to no man pleasant Some with stiff necks will not endure it & to the most modest it is not sweet. Yet we know that reproof must be given by some one, happy is the man who understands how to administer it aright. —

We see our brethren sin & Christian love demands that we tell them of their error but when we do it, let us do it kindly
for otherwise we cause pain
we lose our aim
we drive our friend further on still.
Let kindness & love be mingled with all.
Beelzebub must not be cast out by Beelzebub.

4. **Persecution**. This is sometimes hard to bear. We often wonder how the holy martyrs could keep their cheer & walk so composedly to the stake, but we know that the grace of God was magnified & they were carried above their trials. Now we only feel the cruel mockings & jeers but these are oftentimes too strong for us, but if we have grace with it; it will neutralize the sharpness & bitterness thereof. Remember for whom you bear reproach & what the future reward shall be

5. **Afflictions**. are bitter draughts they are not joyous but grievous yet as they must come we must bear them. Not as the stoic because we must but as the Christian because God appoints them. The vale of tears is pleasant if there be a well in it. If it be loss of property a gain of grace outbalances the damage. If it be sickness, then spiritual health caused thereby exceeds the suffering. Poor Job complained that his troubles had no salt but afterward now I as saw these complaints that the hand is the hand of a loving parent —

the wrath of man worketh not the righteousness of God. There is more power in the friendliness. It removes the travellers cloak shown in all the howling of the storm. Especially in the theological controversy let us remember that as Hewson said "Calvinists should be charitable for they believe that a foreknowledge of the truth is the gift of God. —

Let us all learn to receive reproof with all thankfulness but first let it be given in all tenderness. —

3. **Our doctrines**. never were nor ever can be pleasing to ungodly men, some religion may be fashionable, but the gospel never is. Especially those parts of it which are peculiar and discriminating. How why is it they are unsavoury. we answer, simply because the persons have not salt in their souls. Grace alone makes them savoury. — Again if we wish to spread our religion let us be careful to trust therewith the salt of holy living of charitable behaviour & lovely deportment. Naked bare religion will not do, we must have it covered with the garment of righteousness. We must mingle with our faith holiness.

6. Thoughts of death & death itself are not agreable! yet some find it a pleasure to meditate on their dissolution & long for evening to undress that they may rest in God.

See the ungodly man, if he is sensible of his awful danger he will die with shrieks & out-cries, but make the Xn ever so sensible of his future & he will not fear — nay rather he will rejoice

Religion is a charm against fear. It is the divining rod pointing to the wells beneath. God has given his children a sign & death knows them by it & will not terrify them: Oh how seraphic some deathbeds have been — may mine be so — & do you each day, may mine then have salt in yourselves & having divine grace what or who can harm you — Lord bless me —

For & Jesus sake
Amen

399   Rom. VIII. 1. No Condemnation.

Surely, beloved you will not require any sermon after such a text & should my Master be pleased to withold his help from me, the text itself is marrow & fatness.

It shall be my endeavour this morning to explain as simply as I can, the way of justification through our Lord Jesus. I find there are many young persons & fresh attendants here who although they are really sincere in their love to Jesus & desires after him, yet are not sufficiently taught in the truths of the Scriptures to be able to give a correct statement of this cardinal point. Remember it is not only the object of our ministry to impress but to instruct. I would have you not an untaught company but men & women with judgments informed & solid in the truth. In these days of error & laxity of sentiment it well becomes us to contend earnestly for the faith once delivered to the saints. At the same time the most advanced Christian will be refreshed by hearing once more the glorious truths which are at once his confidence & his glory, his delight & his strength.

The Doctrine of our text, is, that every believer is free from condemnation & that simply because he is in Christ Jesus.

I find some persons saying "oh if I were able to live more free from sin, if I could understand these matters as well as the minister, or if were I as able to pray as good brother So & So I should then believe that I was pardoned & accepted." The doctrine of the text contradicts all this by declaring that if we are in Xt Jesus, if we are now believers, however low our station or mean our attainments, we are free from condemnation.

I would be careful to have you all see plainly the sense of the words— viz— that every believer is free from punishment for his sins. & now.

I. I shall consider these words as the great conclusion from the former argument.

II. As the Proposition of the succeeding chapter.

III. As a personal expression of faith by all believers.

I feel that I can do nothing without the Holy Spirit but I can do all things with it. Come therefore oh Holy Ghost & supply thy people ——

I Let us look at the words as the conclusion from the former argument. Paul in this sentence gathers up all his points— sums up all his logical discussion. He might have said with Solomon "let us hear the conclusion of the whole matter" or with his own words on another occasion "now of the words which we have spoken this is the sum". He has been moving the sword of his argument in the pass & now he brings it down with all his might, uttering these words "There is therefore, now, no condemnation".

What had Paul been saying! why does he say therefore". we will seek an answer. —— Rom IV

1. He had proved imputed righteousness. He declared that the righteousness which justified Abraham & David was not of works but imputed to them by faith.

Do you not at once see how he could reply therefore there is no condemnation. If the sins of God's people are not imputed to them & if all the good works which Jesus did, are imputed to me. If I am regarded as having kept the law. then how can I be condemned — The law cries out I demand a righteousness & we give it

at once the life of Christ. A garment is
required at the wedding feast & I have put
on my elder brother's royal robe, shall I
be expelled the feast. My Jonathan has
changed clothes with me & dare any touch
me now. Adam in the garden was safe
while he was sinless, but the righteousness
of the second Adam is equally as spotless
& far more glorious, shall not that avail
I challenge justice to find a sin in
me. I challenge the scrutiny of the last
day. I can walk with God, yea & before
him in the land of the living.
My beauty this my glorious dress
Jesus the Lord my righteousness.
Remember this then — that we are saved
by what Christ did & not by what we do.
The most backsliding saint will have the
righteousness of Xt & the most exemplar
will have — can have — no more. Oh
my soul when unbelief lays sin to thy charge
here is a never failing argument viz
Imputed Righteousness.
2. He had spoken of the death of Christ as
the satisfaction for sin. Rom. V
Christ's labour was not accomplished by
his active life alone. there needed likewise
a passive obedience — by way of atonement
Now as his works of holiness has furnished

us with a robe of righteousness, so his
sufferings have washed away our sins.
The broken law demanded a penalty
Christ pays it all. His sufferings were amply
sufficient to vindicate the honour of
insulted justice — Surely here is an
argument against our condemnation.
I am sure that nothing but a bare
reliance upon Jesus can ever give a
substantial peace. the moment we mix
any of our own with his merit we render the
water impure. All the props we put
around the rock do but weaken us instead
of rendering us secure. He who draws
only from this well will never thirst
but the waters of self are brackish.
If our eye be not single we shall be dark
but if we look alone to him the Israelites
have light in their dwellings. — If we
consider the pains, groans, agonies &
throes of Calvary, Gethsemane & Gabbatha
can we imagine that they are useless.
Can we once suppose the failure of that
work — If in one case — then ad infinitum
if one be lost none are secure — but
blessed be the name of the Lord he does
not despise blood. Signed & sealed by that
crucified hand. the covenant of love
is secure.

4. Our death in Christ frees us from the law. ___ If a man owes debts, the law cannot touch him after death. How a Christian is dead to the law. He is a new man in Christ Jesus. He is not the same person. Suppose the law sends its bailiff after me to arrest me — Good day, who do you want? Oh I knew him once but he is dead. I am now another person. I am a new-born soul. There is a mistake in the indictment. I am a new man in Christ Jesus. True here was one of my name some time ago, but he's dead, & I am not he. Though alas I have to day the dead body after me. ___ Death makes a goal delivery to all captives. (Death breaks him chains in sunder). Oh my soul. Thine existence is a new — thou hast been broken up existence — regenerated — what a word — what idea — re — over again — generated ___ the change is so great, that we are no longer the same, but new creatures indeed. Let us review the argument from these few points. 1. We are clothed in a perfect righteousness. 2. Christ has atoned for our sins. 3. We are one with Jesus. 4. We have died and are now new creatures —: on which account there is now no Condemnation. ___

3. Oneness with Jesus the apostle mentions in Chapter VI ___ He declares that the ordinance of Baptism is designed to show our oneness with Jesus in his death & glorious resurrection). Christ & his people are as much one as husband & wife, as vines & branches, as members & body. No union can be conceived of — more near more intimate — more exactly deserving to be described as absolute unity. ___ how the apostle might well say thought there is no condemnation. If that & we are one that if I am condemned He is condemned Shall I the & he liable to put my own body to misery. Yea, how can it be that one member of my body can be guilty & the head be not. ___ Oh my soul. Level. this idea. I am married to Jesus & he had taken my debts upon him. I am lost in him. I have given up my own individuality. It is not I but Christ that dwelleth in me. Law, dost thou condemn, then thou shalt condemn my covenant head. My John, my own my husband. ___

Hail sacred union firm & strong
how great the grace how sweet the joy
That unions of wrist should ever be)
one with incarnate Deity.
Thy sacred ties forbids our fears
for all union or tie is theirs
with live, them head, they stand or fall
Their life, their surety & their all. ___

II. Let us view it as the proposition of the succeeding chapter.

This looks very much like a truth rising by way of guard from the last utterance of the apostle. He exclaims that he is bound to a body of sin & death — but lest any should think that therefore he is condemned, he cries out. There is however no condemnation whatever conflict, & contention these is within, there is no condemnation from God. For

1. He is free from the law. The apostle affirms this most distinctly & other Scriptures declare the same thing. Law can only affect those who are its subjects. Now, I am become a friend & lover of the law but I am not its subject. I love to walk in its Statutes, but when I err, greatly as I grieve at the folly, I do not dread punishment for Christ has borne it for me. The terrors of law & of God with me can have nothing to do. Some men have the law hanging in terrorem over their heads but I have not. I am not restrained from sin by a fear of law but by love to the lawgiver. This is not Antinomian. at at any rate it is not Antiscriptural. The first covenant like Moses tables was broken in pieces. The new one is more glorious & more safe. The law in the ark, the law in Xt Jesus we love & long to obey more & more —

2. He has an indwelling Spirit. The heart of the believer is a mansion for the Holy Ghost. he dwells there — producing good works & bringing glory to God. Now if the Spirit in Jesus raised & glorified him, will the same Spirit allow us to be condemned

Would the Lord give his children the Spirit if he intended their destruction. Do we sweep the house we intend to pull down. Should we mend a garment if we intend to commit to the flames? Would the "holy one" transform our poor hearts into gorgeous palaces, for his residence & then commission hell to desecrate it. God acts not thus. He wastes not his power & wisdom. If he renews, he does it completely, he finishes all his works.

No — the presence of the Spirit in my soul is a pledge of my constant justification

3. We are adopted sons. Adoption from its very nature precludes the idea of condemnation. Let a rebel be pardoned & surely a son may receive it for yet more numerous crimes — Having become the lawful jointheirs with Jesus of a heritage of blessedness. condemnation is incompatible with the enjoyment of the eternal weight of glory, made sure to all the seed. When faith has a vision

5. There is no one to condemn; the
eloquent apostle had not yet exhausted
himself. Flight as his wing had carried
him; he still sweeps aloft; he [illegible]
how; he knew & [illegible] the throne what
of God; on heaven & like the throne what
neck; clothed with thunder; he laughed
at the appear & cried exceedingly. Aha, aha.
Hark how he cries to the depths
of heaven; to the depths of hell.
Brethren, I hear that thundering now
echoing again & again through the
caverns of hell. O if God be for us who
can be against us. ¶ ¶ There lies that
old serpent chained in how dare &
all his power astablished — how the power
while again from the challenge rings through
[illegible] the air — they [illegible] their chains
the hurled down — they [illegible]
the roll their cursed eyes & prowl them

of her dignity, when she goes to her earthly
jewels & takes up a diamond with that
word "how" written on it the tears not
final condemnation. She heed her elder
brother & shouts aloud
  "Jesus my elder brother lives
  "With him I too shall reign
  "For in not death while he pleasures
  "shall make the promise vain
  "In him my title stands secure
  "And shall while endless years endure
There are many more forms of argument
which I might dwell upon but I choose
rather to pass on to 28 &c —
4. We are foreknown &c — the apostle
is [illegible] warm in his subject. He has
been shooting arrow after arrow at all
the fears. Shout now he seems to stand
the perfect shower of weapons. Like Milton
a [illegible] of the angels he hurls mountains
was to his foes. For whom he did forsake
on he thoroughly stays to notice his
He has foreknown; & then set apart
He has predestined [illegible] What? Condemn?
No foreknown, then justified? that is the
sadly after will; that is the subject
of final perseverance. What? O Condemn
a foreknown me? What? null it?
the decree of predestination? What? call
a man to damnation? What pretty
& yet condemn? Give & then retract
for his gifts are without repentance &c
Known no variableness, no shadow of a change

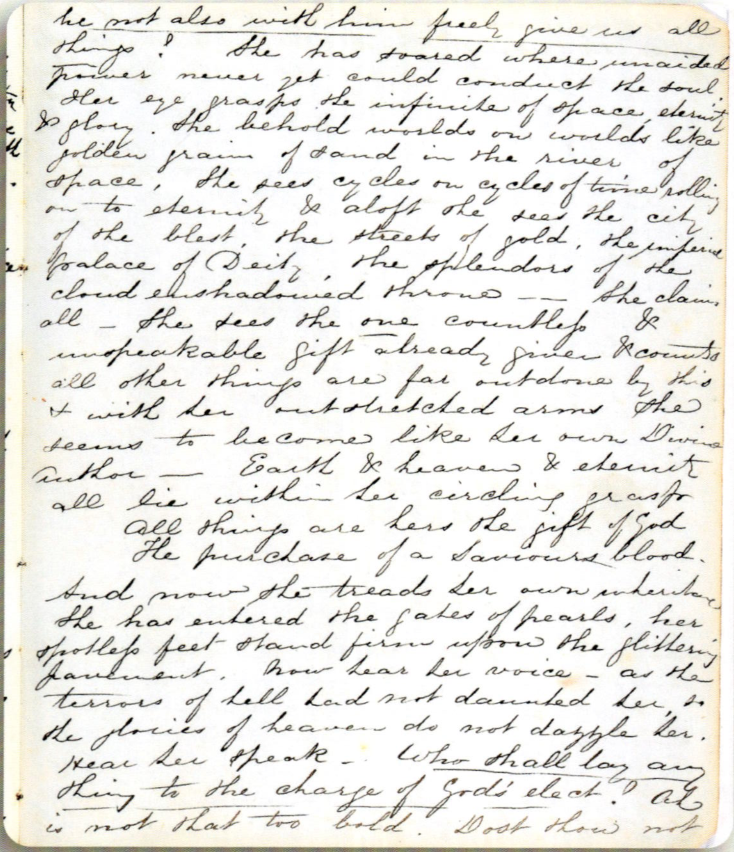

he not also with him freely give us all things! She has soared where unaided power never yet could conduct the soul. Her eye grasps the infinite of space, eternity & glory. She behold worlds on worlds like golden grain of sand in the river of space, she sees cycles on cycles of time rolling on to eternity & aloft she sees the city of the blest, the streets of gold, the imperial palace of Deity, the splendors of the cloud enshadowed throne — She claims all – she sees the one countless & unspeakable gift already given & counts all other things are far outdone by this & with her outstretched arms she seems to become like her own Divine author — Earth & heaven & eternity all lie within her circling grasp

All things are hers the gift of God
The purchase of a Saviours blood.

And now she treads her own inheritance. She has entered the gates of pearls, her spotless feet stand firm upon the glittering pavement. Now hear her voice – as the terrors of hell had not daunted her, so the glories of heaven do not dazzle her. Hear her speak – Who shall lay any thing to the charge of God's elect? Ah is not that too bold. Dost thou not

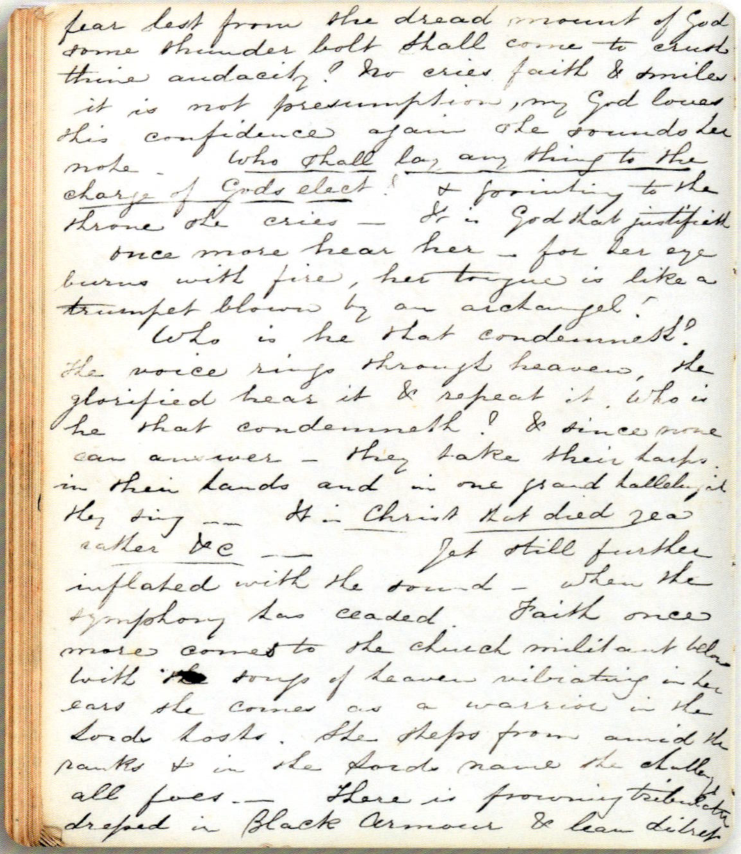

fear lest from the dread mount of God some thunder bolt shall come to crush thine audacity? No cries faith & smiles it is not presumption, my God loves this confidence again she sounds her note – Who shall lay any thing to the charge of Gods elect? & pointing to the throne she cries – It is God that justifieth once more hear her – for her eye burns with fire, her tongue is like a trumpet blown by an archangel!

Who is he that condemneth?

The voice rings through heaven, the glorified hear it & repeat it. Who is he that condemneth? & since none can answer – they take their harps in their hands and in one grand hallelujah they sing — It is Christ that died yea rather &c — Yet still further inflated with the sound – when the symphony has ceased. Faith once more comes to the church militant below with the songs of heaven vibrating in her ears she comes as a warrior in the Lords hosts. She steps from amid the ranks & in the Lords name she challenges all foes. — There is frowning tribulation dressed in Black Armour & lean dishef[…]

like a wolf meagre & gaunt & grim,
there is persecution stained in the face
with the blood of men with rack & fire
& prison in his rear, & there is hunger pain
& shame faced nakedness & there peril
& the thirsty sword — she throws the
gauntlet to them all — she bids them
each defiance — she bids them separate
one of the least of Gods elect from Christ
love. Like the angel of victory, she cries
to the hosts of God. on. on. on for
in all these things we are more than
conquerors — more than conquerors —
more than conquerors — fix your spears
fear not for I am persuaded &c&c

So Giant faith — oh wondrous faith.
and now beloved in the third place
III. This is the Shout of faith uttered by
all believers, this is their conviction
& real experience. —
"There is now no condemnation"
Oh can ye carry this in your hearts as a
fact realized & manifested. Dost you say
to your own soul. Soul there is now
no condemnation. Already thy sin
is all forgiven — all is gone — there is
not a grain left — there is no condemnation
the last vestige of the curse is obliterated

there is not a particle of sin remaining
not a drop of woe, not so much as the
trail of the Serpent. There is a perfect
& unalterable pardon & free forgiveness.

Oh my friends I conjure you seek after
the full assurance of faith. If ye have
but little faith — neglect no means of
increasing it, Slight no ordinances,
walk in the midst of the road & be
persuaded that strong confidence will
be a foretaste of glory even on earth.

As for you who have no faith, do ye
not envy our security, do you not wish
that you could be as confident as we
are. do you not think security is
beyond all price, a jewel of the highest
value — The Cross lays a fair &
sure foundation & if no others dare can
glory in it, I for one can sing.

The arms of everlasting love
Around my soul he placed
and on the rock of ages set
My slippery footsteps fast.
Satan may vent his sharpest spite
and all his legions too
almighty nearer guards my life
and faith forbids my fear —

Here is no Condemnation.

ABOUT THE PROJECT AT MIDWESTERN SEMINARY

In 1857, Charles Spurgeon—the most popular preacher in the Victorian world—promised his readers that he would publish his earliest sermons. For almost 160 years, these sermons were lost to history. With these volumes, these rediscovered sermons can finally be read, studied, and enjoyed by the millions around the world who admire Spurgeon's spiritual insights and literary grace.

This multivolume set includes full-color facsimiles of Spurgeon's original handwriting, transcriptions of his outlines and sermons, biographical introductions, and editorial commentary that further illuminate Spurgeon's work. Taken together, *The Lost Sermons of C. H. Spurgeon* add approximately 10 percent more material to Spurgeon's total body of literature, making it a must-have for pastors and scholars as well as the multitude of Spurgeon enthusiasts around the world

The Lost Sermons project was overseen by a team of scholars and researchers at Midwestern Baptist Theological Seminary in Kansas City, Missouri. Home of The Spurgeon Library, which houses nearly 6,000 volumes from Charles Spurgeon's personal library, and managers of spurgeon.org, Midwestern Seminary—under the leadership of President Jason K. Allen—is honored to be the steward of these early works of Spurgeon as it seeks to contribute to Spurgeon scholarship and research for the next generation.

SCRIPTURE INDEX

SUBJECT INDEX

O

Old Testament, *xiv–xv, 75–76, 113, 144, 157, 236, 351, 618*

Olney, Thomas (deacon at New Park Street Chapel, London), *242*

ordinances, *69–73*

Owen, Dr. John, *151*

P

Parker, Dr. Joseph, *280*

Passover, *354, 357–58, 614*

pastors, *xiii, xvii, 4–8, 34, 39, 69, 85, 90, 101, 105–6, 113, 129, 256, 264, 280, 305–6, 313–14, 319, 329, 333–34, 390, 398, 404*

    ministry, *29, 46, 71–72, 75*

Pastors' College, *xvii, 302*

Pentecost, *377, 379–81*

Pharisees, *53, 65, 143, 149, 357, 569, 594–96*

Pike, G. H.

    Charles Haddon Spurgeon, Preacher, Author Philanthropist, 105

Pontius Pilate, *356, 359*

Popery, *70, 72, 281, 364, 373, 375, 553, 575*

prayer, *8, 71, 85, 90, 92, 93, 128, 130, 133, 144, 149–51, 237, 268, 286, 295, 301, 304, 308–11, 315, 317, 329–32, 339, 344, 368, 371, 374, 376, 379, 381–82, 386, 388, 393, 408, 508, 510, 513, 518, 531, 537, 564, 566, 569, 577, 601–4, 606, 608, 617, 621, 623*

    Lord's Prayer, *601–3*

preachers, *xiii, 34, 45, 49–50, 105, 280, 302, 314, 320, 324, 362, 505, 591, 597–98, 617, 625, 627*

    Jesus, *53, 593*

    Pentecost, *383*

    sermon preparation, *3–4*

    Spurgeon, *xxiii, 6–8, 15–16, 69, 79–80, 96, 123, 242, 263, 283, 288, 330, 403, 549, 591*

pride, *xxi, 30, 42, 89, 92, 108, 147, 149, 238, 245, 261, 287–90, 293, 295, 336, 345, 395, 569, 575, 583, 591, 606*

prophecy, *16, 45, 249, 353, 355, 535–36, 538, 575, 582*

prophets, *xiv, 37, 43, 57, 75, 77, 81, 99, 107–8, 144,*

160, 268, 292, 335, 538, 599, 619

    Daniel, *81, 108, 145, 243, 336, 357, 593*

    Elijah, *7, 108, 243, 290, 382*

    Ezekiel, *55, 57, 249, 335–36, 528, 551*

    Isaiah, *81–82, 92, 316, 335, 350, 579*

    Jeremiah, *43, 155, 271, 273, 290, 619*

    Malachi, *43, 82*

    Nathan, *241, 243–44*

Protestantism, *303*

providence, *55–61, 121, 128, 154, 242, 272, 291–92, 306, 353–58, 364, 386, 388, 506, 529, 533, 571, 575, 585, 589, 622*

Puritans, *xvii, 8, 92, 151, 255, 257, 283, 291*

Puseyism, *70, 72, 281, 303, 308*

R

Rawlison, George, *235*

    Religions of the Ancient World, The, 235

regeneration, *342, 510, 516, 526, 529, 531*

religion, *xv, xxi, 17, 35, 51, 53, 70–71, 96, 108, 111, 117, 131, 144–45, 235–37, 246, 252, 281, 289, 301, 311, 341, 344, 364, 369, 375, 379, 390–91, 510, 517, 526, 528, 530, 545–46, 581, 607, 628–29*

repentance, *16, 49, 101, 103, 126, 286, 359, 568, 612–13, 638*

righteous, the, *44, 97, 133–34*

righteousness, *16, 19, 40, 44, 55, 82, 89, 92, 110, 159, 258, 320, 322, 327, 345, 352, 523, 599, 628, 637*

    imputed, *529, 631, 634–35*

Rippon, John, *5, 385*

Roman Catholicism, *289, 303, 334, 373, 601, 611*

Rome, *47, 51, 127, 333, 336, 373, 552, 579, 582*

Royal Surrey Gardens catastrophe, *119–20*

S

Sabbath, *25, 37, 40–41, 255, 271, 301, 304, 357, 380, 597*

Sacheverell, Henry

    Communication of Sin: A Sermon Preach'd at the Assizes Held at Derby, August 15th, 1709, The, 21